P9-CDX-300

HANDBOOK OF

ADDICTIVE DISORDERS

A PRACTICAL GUIDE TO DIAGNOSIS AND TREATMENT

Edited by Robert Holman Coombs

WILEY

John Wiley & Sons, Inc.

Copyright © 2004 by John Wiley & Sons, Inc. All rights reserved.

Published by John Wiley & Sons, Inc., Hoboken, New Jersey.
Published simultaneously in Canada.

Library of Congress Cataloging-in-Publication Data:

Handbook of addictive disorders : a practical guide to diagnosis and treatment / edited by
    Robert Holman Coombs.
        p. ; cm.
    Includes bibliographical references and index.
    ISBN 0-471-23502-4 (cloth : alk. paper)
    1. Substance abuse—Handbooks, manuals, etc. I. Coombs, Robert H.
    [DNLM: 1. Substance-Related Disorders—diagnosis. 2. Substance-Related
    Disorders—therapy. WM270 H2357 2004]
    RC564.15.H357 2004
    616.86—dc22

                                                                        2003063155

Printed in the United States of America.

10 9 8 7 6 5 4 3 2 1

For
Douglas Ray Coombs

Beloved Brother

Acknowledgments

I GRATEFULLY ACKNOWLEDGE five esteemed colleagues who added significantly to this book: Tracey Belmont, acquisition editor at John Wiley & Sons, for giving me the opportunity to develop and publish this book. Highly efficient and personable, she made the entire experience rewarding. Carla Cronkhite Vera, my invaluable assistant at UCLA, facilitated the book at every stage with her sterling efforts. She monitored myriad details, coordinated activities, suggested improvements, and, in her characteristic way, kept things running smoothly and punctually. Marie Gengler, who coauthored Chapter 16, offered critical suggestions for chapter drafts and Sandra Allen Brimhall compiled the indexes. Carol Jean Coombs, my life's partner, as always, provided valued insights and support.

R. H. C.

Contents

About the Editor

Robert H. Coombs, PhD, CAS, professor of biobehavioral sciences at the UCLA School of Medicine, is trained as a sociologist (doctorate), counseling psychologist (postdoctoral masters), family therapist (California licensed), certified addiction specialist and certified group psychotherapist. A Fellow of the American Association for the Advancement of Science, the American Psychological Society and the American Association of Applied and Preventive Psychology, he serves on the International Certification Advisory Committee of the American Academy of Healthcare Providers in the Addictive Disorders. Author or editor of 18 books and nearly 200 other manuscripts, his books include, *Drug-Impaired Professionals* (Harvard University Press), *Addiction Recovery Tools: A Practical Handbook* (Sage), *Addiction Counseling Review* (Houghton Mifflin/Lawrence Erlbaum Associates), *Handbook on Drug Abuse Prevention* (Allyn & Bacon), *Cool Parents, Drug-Free Kids: A Family Survival Guide* (Allyn & Bacon), *The Addiction Counselor's Desk Reference* (John Wiley & Sons), *The Family Context of Adolescent Drug Abuse* (Haworth), *Socialization in Drug Abuse* (Schenkman/Transaction Books), *Junkies and Straights* (D. C. Heath), and *Drug Testing* (Oxford University Press). He is coeditor (with William A. Howatt) of a *Book Series on Treating Addictions* (John Wiley & Sons). As a member of the California Commission for the Prevention of Drug Abuse, he developed the conceptual framework that guided the Commission's activities. A lecturer on addiction topics in the former Soviet Union and more than a dozen other countries, he is a recipient of the Award for Excellence in Education from the UCLA School of Medicine, the Distinguished Faculty Educator Award from the UCLA Neuropsychiatric Institute and Hospital, and was nominated for the Faculty Excellence Award from the UCLA Mortar Board Senior Honors Society.

Contributors

April Lane Benson, PhD
Center for the Study of Anorexia and
  Bulimia
Institute of Contemporary
  Psychotherapy
New York, New York

Steven Berglas, PhD
Marshall School of Business
Los Angeles, California

Arthur W. Blume, PhD
University of Texas at El Paso
El Paso, Texas

Gilbert J. Botvin, PhD
Weill Medical College
Cornell University
New York, New York

Patrick J. Carnes, PhD, CAS
Sexual Disorders Services
The Meadows
Wickenburg, Arizona

Linda Chamberlain, PsyD
University of South Florida
Tampa, Florida

Louis Charpentier, MS
Sexual Disorders Services
The Meadows
Wickenburg, Arizona

Helga Dittmar, DPhil
University of Sussex
United Kingdom

Claudia Flowers, PhD
University of North Carolina at
  Charlotte
Charlotte, North Carolina

David M. Garner, PhD
River Centre Clinic Eating Disorder
  Program
Bowling Green State University
University of Toledo
Sylvania, Ohio

Marie Gengler, BA
Columbia University
New York, New York

Anna Gerborg, MA
River Centre Foundation
Sylvania, Ohio

Kenneth W. Griffin, PhD, MPH
Weill Medical College
Cornell University
New York, New York

Beau Kilmer, MPP
John F. Kennedy School of Government
  at Harvard University
Cambridge, Massachusetts

Robert J. MacCoun, PhD
University of California at Berkeley
Berkeley, California

William G. McCown, PhD
University of Louisiana at Monroe and
  Center for the Research and
  Treatment of Personality Disorders
  and Addictions
Northeast Louisiana University
Monroe, Louisiana

Robert E. Murray, MD, PhD
Private Practice
Knoxville, Tennessee

Jeanne L. Obert, MFT, MSM
Matrix Institute on Addictions
Los Angeles, California

Jean Petrucelli, PhD, FPPR
Private Practice
New York, New York

Richard A. Rawson, PhD
UCLA Integrated Substance Abuse
  Programs
Los Angeles, California

Bryan E. Robinson, PhD
University of North Carolina at
  Charlotte
Charlotte, North Carolina

Jennifer P. Schneider, MD, PhD
Private Practice
Tucson, Arizona

Richard B. Seymour, MA
Haight Ashbury Free Clinics
San Francisco, California

David E. Smith, MD
Haight Ashbury Free Clinics
University of California Medical
  School
San Francisco, California

Janice Stimson, PsyD
Matrix Institute on Addictions
Costa Mesa, California

Ahndrea Weiner, MS, MFT
Matrix Institute on Addictions
Los Angeles, California

Robert Weiss, LCSW, CAS
The Sexual Recovery Institute
Los Angeles, California

Introduction

VARIOUS ADDICTIVE DISORDERS, the leading public health problem in America and other industrialized nations, undermine the health and well-being of countless individuals and families. Many clients seen by health professionals manifest addictive problems.

The term *addiction* usually conjures up images of alcoholics and other drug addicts who manifest physical and/or psychological need for chemical substances. Such individuals rely on substances to function or feel good (psychological dependence). When their bodies reach a state of biological adjustment to the chronic presence of a chemical substance (physical dependence), they require increasing amounts to achieve the desired effect (tolerance). When denied access to their chemical elixirs, their bodies experience adverse effects (withdrawal), typically the opposite bodily effects as those sought. Whereas opiates, for example, induce euphoria and pain relief, withdrawal symptoms include psychological distress and physical pain.

Researchers and clinicians traditionally limit addiction to alcohol and other drugs. Yet, *neuroadaptation,* the technical term for the biological processes of tolerance and withdrawal, also occurs when substance-free individuals become addicted to pathological gambling, pornography, eating, overwork, shopping, and other compulsive excesses.

Recent scientific advances over the past decade indicate that addiction is a brain disease that develops over time as a result of initially voluntary behavior. "The majority of the biomedical community now consider addiction, in its essence, to be a brain disease," said Alan Leschner, former Director of the National Institute on Drug Abuse (NIDA; 2001, p. 1), "a condition caused by persistent changes in brain structure and function." Most important, research on the brain's reward system indicates that, as far as the brain is concerned, "a reward is a reward, regardless of whether it comes from a chemical or an experience" (Shaeffer & Albanese, in press). For this reason, "more and more people have been thinking that, contrary to an earlier view, there is a commonality between substance addiction and other compulsions" (Alan I. Leshner, cited by Holden, 2001, p. 980).

In 1964, the World Health Organization concluded that since addiction had been "trivialized in popular usage" to refer to any kind of habitual behavior, such as gambling addiction, it was no longer an exact scientific term (World Health Organization [WHO], 1964). Since then, medically oriented clinicians have narrowly restricted this term in their diagnostic manuals to refer to chemical dependence.

Addiction is omitted from the latest diagnostic manual of the American Psychiatric Association, the *Diagnostic and Statistical Manual IV-text revision* (*DSM-IV-TR*; 2002). Instead, *DSM-IV-TR* lists these three forms of *chemical* abuse:

1. *Substance abuse disorders:* a maladaptive use of chemical substances leading to clinically significant outcomes or distress (recurrent legal problems and/or failure to perform at work, school, home, or physically hazardous behaviors, such as driving when impaired).
2. *Substance dependency disorders:* loss of control over how much a substance is used once begun, manifested by seven symptoms: tolerance, withdrawal, using more than was intended, unsuccessful efforts to control use, a great deal of time spent obtaining and using the substance, important life activities given up or reduced in order to use the substance, and continued use despite knowing that it causes problems.
3. *Substance induced disorders:* manifesting the same symptoms as depression and/or other mental health disorder, which symptoms, the direct result of using the substance, will cease shortly after discontinuing the substance.

By contrast, *DSM-IV-TR* classifies compulsive gambling as an "impulse control disorder" and groups it with fire setting.

Increasingly, research evidence shows that the neurobiology of nonchemical addictions approximates that of addiction to alcohol and other drugs. "Some chemicals or excessive experiences activate brain reward systems directly and dramatically," notes addictionologist William McCown (in press). "Essentially they provide too much reward for an individual's neurobiology to handle. For example, ingestion of certain chemicals is accompanied by massive mood elevations and other affective changes. These may lead to a reduction in other activities previously considered rewarding. Similarly, the ability of excessive behaviors to activate brain reward mechanisms alters normal functioning. This also results in a potentially addictive state." (McCown, in press).

Traditionalists may argue that the addictive disorders discussed in this book are really obsessive-compulsive disorders (OCDs). Though the OCD-afflicted individual may recognize that his obsessive thoughts lead to illogical and inappropriate behaviors, he still feels compelled to perform these actions and feels extremely anxious when resisting these ritualized behaviors. "There are no rewards associated with OCD behaviors," McCown points out, "except for the overwhelming reduction in anxiety." On the other hand, addictions are initially extremely pleasant experiences. This contrasts with OCD, which plagues people with intrusive, unwanted thoughts or obsessions, and is inherently distasteful (McCown, in press).

Where does one draw the line between an addiction and a passionately enjoyed activity? "Breathing is also addictive," noted the headlines of a *Newsweek* article (Levy, 1997, pp. 52–53). All addictions, whether chemical or nonchemical, share three common characteristics. Referred to as the three Cs (Smith & Seymour, 2001, pp. 18–19), they are:

1. *Compulsive use:* an irresistible impulse; repetitive ritualized acts and intrusive, ego-dystonic (i.e., ego alien) thoughts (e.g., voices in the head encouraging the addict to continue the addictive behavior).

2. *Loss of control:* the inability to limit or resist inner urges; once begun it is very difficult to quit, if not impossible, without outside help; the addict's willpower succumbs to the addictive power; though he or she may abstain for brief periods, he or she cannot stay stopped.
3. *Continued use despite adverse consequences:* escalating problems (embarrassment, shame, humiliation, loss of health, as well as mounting family, financial, and legal problems) do not dissuade the addict from the addictive behavior.

Regardless of addiction type, three needs initially motivate participants:

1. *Psychic rewards:* achieving a desired mood change; feeling euphoric "highs" and/or blocking out painful feelings; feeling good, pursuing such desired feelings, regardless of the cost, is the objective of all addiction.
2. *Recreational rewards:* having fun with other participants in these mutually enjoyable activities, especially during early stages, after which participants seek solitude with their "best friend," the addictive substance and/or activity.
3. *Instrumental (achievement) rewards:* performing better, and doing so with fewer worries, or gaining a competitive edge or advantage, and thereby, supposedly enhancing success and well-being.

In this regard, addictionologist Lynn Rambeck, a specialist in treating compulsive gamblers, broadly defines addiction as "a habitual substitute satisfaction for an essential unmet need." (personal communication, 2003).

I invited leading addition experts to contribute to this book. Each has a depth of academic and clinical experience and a proven record of significant publications on these topics. Two introductory chapters begin the book. The first, by David E. Smith and Richard B. Seymour, addresses the characteristics of addictive disorders. The second, by Patrick J. Carnes, Robert E. Murray, and Louis Charpentier, discusses the nature of interactive addictions, such as the cocaine addict who also experiences sexual compulsions.

Subsequent chapters focus on each addictive disorder, two chapters on each disorder: chemical dependence, compulsive gambling, sex addiction, eating disorders, workaholism, and compulsive buying. The first of these two address understanding and diagnosing the addictive disorder, and the second on treating it. Arthur W. Blume (Chapter 3) and Jeanne L. Obert, Ahndrea Weiner, Janice Stimson, and Richard A. Rawson (Chapter 4) discuss chemical dependence; Linda Chamberlain (Chapter 5) and William G. McCown (Chapter 6) explore compulsive gambling; Jennifer P. Schneider (Chapter 7) and Robert Weiss (Chapter 8) address sex addiction; David M. Garner and Anna Gerborg (Chapter 9) and Jean Petrucelli (Chapter 10) eating disorders; Bryan E. Robinson and Claudia Flowers (Chapter 11) and Steven Berglas (Chapter 12) workaholism; and Helga Dittmar (Chapter 13) and April Lane Benson and Marie Gengler (Chapter 14) compulsive buying.

Two additional chapters cover public policy and prevention. Beau Kilmer and Robert MacCoun discuss public policy issues related to addictive disorders (Chapter 15) and Kenneth W. Griffin and Gilbert J. Botvin review preventive tools and programs (Chapter 16).

Written to enlighten and assist helping professionals who deal with addicted clients, these practical chapters help shift the view of addiction from its tradition-based orthodoxy to a more enlightened and clinically useful model.

REFERENCES

American Psychiatric Association. (2000). *Diagnostic and statistical manual of mental disorders* (4th ed., text rev.). Washington, DC: Author.

Holden, C. (2001). Behavorial addictions: Do they exist? *Science, 294,* 980–982.

Leshner, A. I. (2001, Spring). Addiction is a brain disease. *Science and Technology Online.* Available from http://www.nap.edu/issues/17.3/leshner.htm.

Levy, S. (1996–1997, December 30–January 6). Breathing is also addictive. *Newsweek,* 52–53.

McCown, W. (in press). Non-pharmacological addictions. In R. H. Coombs (Ed.), *Family therapy review: Preparing for comprehensive and licensing exams.* Hoboken, NJ: Wiley.

Shaffer, H. J., & Albanese, M. (in press). Addiction's defining characteristics. In R. H. Coombs (Ed.), *Handbook of addictive disorders: A practical guide to diagnosis and treatment.* Hoboken, NJ: Wiley.

Smith, D. E., & Seymour, R. (2001). *Clinician's guide to substance abuse.* New York: McGraw-Hill.

World Health Organization. (1964). *Expert committee on drug dependence* [Tech. Rep. Service No. 273]. Geneva, Switzerland: Author.

PART I

DEFINING ADDICTION

CHAPTER 1

The Nature of Addiction

DAVID E. SMITH and RICHARD B. SEYMOUR

A Ghetto Addict: Cocaine Dealer Supporting His Habit by Dealing

He's getting too old for this and in moments of lucidity he knows it. It was all new and exciting when he started dealing at 11. By 14 he was still living with his grandmother in the projects. His mother was doing hard time in the state penitentiary. His father? Who knows? Then, the expensive sports shoes and his athletic jacket were his pride and joy. Both are now gone, gone into the pipe. It's a new century and the crack buyers who supported his habit have drifted away to other, more aggressive dealers and to other drugs. But for him, the pipe is everything and he is getting too old for this. Next week will be his 17th birthday.

**The Model Student: Sport Star
and Heroin Addict**

It started in his junior year of high school. Some older buddies took him along on a trip into the city. They knew a place where they could drink and the bartender didn't check IDs. He didn't drink very much or very often. After all, he was in training, a star athlete at the suburban high school he attended. His grade average wasn't spectacular, but it was good enough to get him into a college of his parents' choice. Going into the city was just a lark. After a few beers, one of the guys tossed a packet of white powder on the bar and said, "Let's go out back and have some real fun." When he snorted his first line of cocaine, he reports, the feeling was the same as when he had made a touchdown in the championship game and everyone in the stands was standing up and shouting his name. What a great feeling! When the cocaine got to be too much for him, he was introduced to heroin. The opiate that he snorted took the edge off the cocaine stimulant jangles and made it all bearable again, but he kept needing more.

3

A Housewife: Alcoholic and Chain Smoker

She lit yet another cigarette off the spent one, crushed the butt in the ashtray that was already overflowing onto the kitchen table and refilled the glass of sherry. Outside her kitchen window, the sun shone and birds sang in the backyard trees. The children had left for school hours ago, but she was still in her bathrobe, the breakfast dishes were still on the table. There was plenty of time to clean the house and think about dinner. In the meantime, just one more glass of sherry and another cigarette.

An Aggressive Executive: Cocaine Addict

He had smoked pot and, yes, dropped a little acid back in the Summer of Love, but he'd never really been a hippy and all that was way behind him as he built a highly competitive consulting business. He was a moderate drinker, a couple of martinis at a business lunch, wine with dinner, maybe a cocktail. One evening when he was 35, a business associate working with him on a grueling assignment gave him a prescription stimulant to help him keep going. He soon realized that stimulants gave him a competitive edge. Soon thereafter, he discovered that cocaine was even better than amphetamines. By the time he entered treatment, his consulting business and his personal life were in shambles.

A Retired Executive with Late-Onset Alcohol Addiction

Alcohol was part of his climb up the corporate ladder and he did like his drinks. While he was working and empire building, however, there really wasn't time to waste. Drinking was an adjunct to business activities. Those occasions when he did go over the line, he had assistants to take care of things and to make sure that no unpleasantness developed. Then he retired to afternoons at the Club and evenings that went on forever and no assistants to help when he passed out during dinner. His doctor called it late-onset alcohol addiction, but it had been there all along. Throughout his working life, Mr. Big had an entire staff of enablers to feed his denial and help him through. In retirement, he had the leisure to indulge his addiction to alcohol and he found his family actually made lousy enablers. They hired an interventionist who orchestrated an intervention and for the first time in his life, Mr. Big had to face his addiction. The family stood by him and remained involved in family therapy. He and they survived, but many do not.

As you can see from these examples, there is no addict profile. Movies such as *Traffic* and *The Twenty-Fifth Hour* have brought the breadth and depth of addiction to popular culture and awareness in the United States. Addicts come in all ages, sizes, and economic circumstances. One thing has become clear to those of us who are working in the field of addiction medicine: Addiction is not limited to those who are the stereotypical dregs of humanity. Many addicts are highly capable and successful individuals. Addiction is a democratic disease and an equal opportunity illness. Who is susceptible? Anyone. Although sons and daughters and grandsons and granddaughters of people who have had problems with alcohol and other drugs are thought to be more susceptible to the disease, anyone can become addicted.

WHAT IS ADDICTION?

Addiction is a disease in and of itself, characterized by compulsion, loss of control, and continued use in spite of adverse consequences (Coombs, 1997; Smith & Seymour, 2001) (see Box 1.1). The primary elements of addictive disease are:

- *Compulsion:* In alcohol and other drug addiction, this can be the regular or episodic use of the substance. The person cannot start the day without a cigarette and/or a cup of coffee. Evening means a ritual martini, or two, or three. In and of itself, however, compulsive use doesn't automatically mean addiction.
- *Loss of control:* The pivotal point in addiction is loss of control. The individual swears that there will be no more episodes, that he or she will go to the party and have two beers. Instead, the person drinks until he or she experiences a blackout and swears the next morning, "Never again!" only to repeat the behavior the following night. The individual may be able to stop for a period of time, or control use for a period of time, but will always return to compulsive, out-of-control use.
- *Continued use in spite of adverse consequences:* Use of the substance continues in spite of increasing problems that may include declining health, such as the onset of emphysema or even lung cancer in the chronic smoker, liver impairment in the alcohol addict; embarrassment, humiliation, shame; or increasing family, financial, and legal problems.

While compulsion, loss of control, and continued use in spite of adverse consequences are the primary characteristics of addictive disease, there are a host of other qualities of addiction.

ADDICTION IS CHRONIC AND SUBJECT TO RELAPSE

Many people equate addiction with simply using drugs and therefore expect that addiction should be cured quickly, and if it is not, the treatment is a failure. In reality, because addiction is a chronic disorder, the ultimate goal of long-term abstinence often requires sustained and repeated treatment episodes. Nearly all addicted individuals believe in the beginning that they can stop using drugs on

---

BOX 1.1
Qualities of Addiction

Addiction is a brain disease characterized by:

- Compulsive use,
- Loss of control, and
- Continued use despite adverse consequences.

Genetics + Environment = Addiction (Maybe)

AD = G + E

Addictive Disease = Genetics + Environment

their own, and most try to stop without treatment. However, most of these attempts result in failure to achieve long-term abstinence. Research shows that long-term drug use significantly changes brain function and these changes persist long after the individual stops using drugs. These drug-induced changes in brain function may have many behavioral consequences, including the compulsion to use drugs despite adverse consequences—the defining characteristic of addiction (Leshner, 1999).

ADDICTION IS PROGRESSIVE

The disease becomes worse over time. As the disease progresses, craving emanating from the old or primitive brain's reward system creates compulsion despite knowledge that resides in the new brain's prefrontal cortex that compulsive use leads to adverse consequences. Once the cycle of addiction is started by the first fix, pill, or drink, the reward system, fueled by a mid-brain system involving the dopaminergic system of the nucleus acumbens, is activated. A new paradigm for addiction can be described as a *drug-induced reward system dysfunction.* Addiction then becomes a disease of the brain just as diabetes is a disease of the pancreas. The brain, being a much more complicated organ, becomes involved in a complex neurochemical cascade in which the old brain sends out strong craving signals that the new brain attempts to control via the will. Denial is learned and recovery is learned, but there is a biological basis to addictive disease residing in the primitive brain.

Experience shows us that the disease worsens during active use and also during periods of abstinence and sobriety as well. We would expect the disease to get worse during active use but its growth in abstinence may come as a surprise. Individuals who resume use of alcohol or other psychoactive drugs after periods of abstinence progress to full addiction more rapidly with each period of returned use. As Chuck Brissett illustrated in his concept of the sleeping tiger, like an animal in hibernation, the disease continues to grow while in remission and if reawakened will be a full-grown beast (Seymour & Smith, 1987).

DENIAL—VICTIMS ARE INCAPABLE OF SEEING THAT THEY HAVE A PROBLEM

At Alcoholics Anonymous meetings and addiction conferences, the line: "Denial isn't just a river in Egypt," continues to get a laugh. Denial may be learned but it too has a nonconscious foundation. The addict is incapable of seeing the insanity of his or her behavior, but is capable of manipulating family, friends, and coworkers into enabling behavior. Wives will call the place of employment and make excuses for the addict. Coworkers will cover for them. Family and friends will act as though there is nothing wrong with passing out at the dinner table or under the Christmas tree. Often a process of intervention is the only means of bringing the addict into treatment.

THE DISEASE IS POTENTIALLY FATAL

Given the progressive nature of addiction, the disease only becomes worse over time (see Box 1.2). The good news is that most of the primary effects of addiction

---

BOX 1.2
Often but Not Always a Factor in Addiction

Tolerance + Withdrawal = Physical Dependence

---

are reversible and will eventually disappear with treatment, abstinence, and recovery. The bad news is that within the practice of alcohol and other drug addictive behavior the primary effects are toxically cumulative and result in death if the disease is not treated.

THE DISEASE IS INCURABLE

In the recovering community it is said that, "When a cucumber becomes a pickle, it cannot go back to being a cucumber." Once an individual has crossed the line into addiction, there is no going back. Any attempt at returning to noncompulsive, in-control use is doomed to failure and rapid descent back into full addictive behavior. All too often, individuals in long-term recovery who have experienced remission from the worst effects of their active disease will decide that they are cured and attempt to drink or use in a controlled way. Use may start with a glass of wine at a wedding or some other significant social function. For a short period, the addict may see no adverse effects and conclude that over time a cure has taken place. The sleeping tiger has been prodded and all too soon comes fully awake and the addict finds him or herself once more in the grips of the disease. Not all drug abuse is addiction, but the rapidity of relapse is clear proof of the disease.

THE DISEASE CAN BE BROUGHT INTO REMISSION

Although addiction is incurable in the sense that addicts cannot return to nonaddicted use, the disease can be brought into remission through a program of abstinence and supported recovery (see Box 1.3). Not using removes the cog that drives the addiction. The disease may progress in abstinence, but so long as there is no

---

BOX 1.3
Substance Abuse in the United States

There are an estimated 12 to 15 million alcohol abusers/alcoholics in the United States (SAMHSA).

Among full-time workers, 6.3 million are illicit drug users and 6.2 million are heavy alcohol users (SAMHSA).

About 70% of alcoholics are employed (NY State Office of Alcoholism and Substance Abuse Services).

Direct and Indirect costs of alcohol and drug abuse consume 3.7% of the U.S. Gross National Product.

---

use, there is no active addiction. However, mere abstinence is not enough. Will power is no match for this disease, and while you may be able to remain abstinent for a period of time without help, the maintenance of that abstinence can involve a tremendous and often losing effort. In the recovering community, this is called "white knuckle sobriety." You are gripping sobriety so hard that your knuckles are drained of blood in the process. The best hope for many is in the support of other recovering addicts in one or more of a variety of self-help fellowships.

Note: Not all substance abuse is addiction. Opponents of the disease or medical models of addiction often try to paint their proponents as rigid doctrinarians who maintain that any individual who drinks or uses drugs is an addict in need of treatment, membership in alcoholics anonymous, and lifelong abstinence (Marlatt, Blume, & Parks, 2001). In reality, diagnosis utilizing the disease concept of addiction is based on specific, evidence-based criteria, and if anything, rules out substance abuse problems that do not fit the criteria for addiction.

ADDICTION AS A CHANGING PARADIGM

As is true with most concepts concerning the nature of human behavior, the disease concept is not an immutable law but rather the most recent paradigm in an evolution of conceptualizations, each in its turn an attempt to meld observed phenomena with prevailing opinions to create an acceptable synthesis. Rarely will one paradigm be universally adopted. The disease paradigm, in fact, has several different wordings although the general concepts tend to be congruent within the addiction treatment field. It is generally understood to be an expansion based on the disease concept of alcoholism, first developed by Elfrin M. Jellinek (1960):

Addiction affects the:

- Cerebral cortex,
- Midbrain, and
- Old brain.

ADDICTION AS PHYSICAL DEPENDENCE

When we were first writing articles and teaching classes on addiction, the emphasis was on the drug itself. Addiction was seen as synonymous with physical dependence characterized by increasing drug tolerance and onset of physical withdrawal symptoms. It was generally believed in the treatment community that the drugs, by their action, created addiction. As a result, the primary goal of treatment was detoxification, clearing the system of the toxic substance or substances and treating withdrawal in the belief that once the perceived cause of continued use, that is, the pain of withdrawal, was eliminated, the addict could return to a nonaddicted life (Inaba & Cohen, 2000).

This paradigm worked to some extent in a world where addiction appeared to be limited to opiate and opioid pain killers and sedative-hypnotic substances, including alcohol, with which there was a pronounced development of tolerance, or the need for more drug in order to meet desired effects and rapid onset of physical withdrawal symptoms.

Even here, however, the frequency of relapse among detoxified opioid addicts made it clear that tolerance and withdrawal were not the only components of addiction. Something lured addicts back to active use and no amount of socioeconomic aid, vocational rehabilitation, jail time, or remembrance of the pain of withdrawal was sufficient in many cases to keep addicts away from the drugs.

In 1972, David Smith, MD, founder of the Haight Ashbury Free Clinics and George R. Gay, MD, director of the Clinics' Heroin Detoxification, Rehabilitation, and Aftercare Program, edited a book of articles on the background, social and psychological perspectives, and treatment of heroin addiction titled *It's So Good Don't Even Try It Once*. The title was a quotation, the words of a young middle-class addict. We speculated at the time that these words "catch some of the essential ambiguity in the young heroin user's position. He has gone beyond the counterculture, or around it, to arrive at what seems like simple self-destruction. But is that how he sees it? And is heroin really a universal evil that we can all feel safe in condemning, or could it be that our social-political system is the true culprit? What is heroin, what does it do to you, how 'good' is it and where (if anywhere) is the new drug scene leading us?" (Smith & Gay, 1972)

At that time, treatment for addiction at the Haight Ashbury Free Clinics consisted of detoxification with the help of nonnarcotic, symptom-targeted medication given on a daily basis along with counseling. A team of physicians, counselors, and pharmacists worked together to ascertain the patient's symptoms each day during the detoxification process. Aftercare consisted of a period of individual and group counseling aimed at rehabilitating the clean addict to a normal life pattern, including employment. Vocational rehabilitation was offered through a crafts shop and retail store on Haight Street until federal funding ran out and rehabilitation was reabsorbed into the general treatment facility.

The primary treatment alternatives were methadone and therapeutic communities. At that time, however, most of the Clinics' patients were young, new addicts whose use of low-potency heroin precluded the utilization of methadone as either a substitution and eventual withdrawal protocol or within a maintenance program, preferring to detoxify with medications that were not serious physical dependence producers and which had low street value, precluding patients from trading their medication on the street for heroin and other drugs.

In 1974, the Clinics attempted to start an aftercare program as a therapeutic community based in rural Mendocino County, an idyllic location about 3 hours north of San Francisco. A federal grant specified that the project needed to have demonstrated acceptance and approval from the local neighbors, however, and this was not forthcoming. The Rural Rehabilitation Center would have provided long-term residential treatment for selected drug patients, but by 1974, the specter of drug-induced violence—spurred by sensationalist reports based on the behavior of methamphetamine addicts suffering from paranoia with ideas of reference (sometimes with good reason in an era of armed and territorial young drug dealers)—had given rise to a climate of fear, even in rural areas and the rise of what came to be termed "nimbyism," that is, we would love to see these people helped, but not in my backyard.

With the spread of heroin use by young members of the counterculture in the late 1960s and the return of addicted veterans from Vietnam in the early 1970s, the shortcomings of the physical dependence paradigm became increasingly obvious. Detoxification wasn't the whole answer. As the 1970s progressed, increasing problems with drugs outside the opioid and sedative-hypnotic/alcohol categories, such as methamphetamine, cocaine, phencyclidine, and even marijuana, led to the development of a two-tiered system in which the drugs that produce obvious physical dependence and those that produce what was termed *psychological dependence* came to be seen as hard drugs and soft drugs with differing treatment approaches.

PHYSICAL DEPENDENCE AS A CULTURAL ICON

Otto Preminger's 1955 film *The Man with the Golden Arm* is a near perfect exemplar of the "Addiction as Physical Dependence" paradigm that shaped public attitudes about drug dependence for a generation. Frank Sinatra's performance as the heroin-addicted gambler, in and out of treatment, subject to relapse and ever-increasing tolerance, seared our consciousness, while Preminger's depiction of both criminal justice-sponsored "treatment" consisting of "cold turkey" withdrawal and the addict's world graphically portrayed the moral degeneracy that was seen as a key component of addiction at that time.

THE MORAL DEGENERACY/WILLFUL DISOBEDIENCE MODEL

Outside the treatment community, addiction is all too often considered to be the result of low morality or actual criminal behavior. Such attitudes are largely responsible for the development of stereotypes depicting addicts as criminals and moral degenerates. Until recently, the Universal Code of Military Justice characterized alcoholism and other forms of addiction as "willful disobedience."

At the turn of the nineteenth-century, addiction within the middle class was generally treated in physicians' offices and private drug clinics and often by opiate maintenance. All of that began to change after the 1914 passage of the Harrison Narcotic Act and a series of subsequent court decisions that stripped the medical profession of its rights to treat opioid addicts. At the same time, treatment passed into the hands of the criminal justice system and was concentrated in prison hospitals such as the one in Lexington, Kentucky (Musto, 1987).

In the 1940s and 1950s, the prevailing concept of "treatment" was guided by the moral degeneracy/willful disobedience model and limited to federal prison facilities wherein addicts were detoxified without benefit of what today is considered minimal treatment. When these individuals were released and usually relapsed within a short period of time, the criminal justice attitude that addicts were untreatable was reinforced and spread into the general population through news articles and films such as *The Man with the Golden Arm*. Until recently, recovering military veterans were blocked from receiving education and other benefits that had elapsed while they were in active addiction because the government maintained a policy that stated their addiction was "willful disobedience" and not a disability (NCA News, 1988; Seessel, 1988).

A SYMPTOM OF UNDERLYING PSYCHOPATHOLOGY VERSUS DUAL-DIAGNOSIS

Within the mental health treatment community, addiction was often considered a symptom of underlying psychopathology. The problem with this paradigm is that it can lead the practitioner to attempt treatment of mental health problems without addressing primary addiction. Darryl Inaba, the long-time director of Haight Ashbury Free Clinics' Drug Treatment Project and now the Clinics' chief executive officer, has always cautioned that psychiatric diagnoses of practicing addicts should be written in disappearing ink. Often, psychotic symptoms are

---

BOX 1.4
Comorbidity

Among full time workers, 1.6 million are both heavy alcohol and illicit drug users (SAMHSA).

80% to 90% of alcoholics are heavy smokers (Drug Strategies).

There are 6.5 million persons with co-morbid substance abuse and mental illness disorder.

50% to 75% of general psychiatric treatment populations have alcohol or drug disorders (Miller & Gold, 1995).

20% of liver transplants are received by alcoholics.

---

drug induced and disappear in the course of detoxification and aftercare. This is not always the case, however. Many addicts have a dual diagnosis of addiction and mental illness. Roughly 40% of the patients seen at Haight Ashbury's Substance Abuse Treatment Services (SATS) are dually diagnosed. We also learned that treating mental problems while the patient is still practicing active addiction is a waste of time, counterproductive, and potentially dangerous. A team approach that addresses both diagnoses is the most practical and productive way to treat patients with both addictive disease and mental health problems. (See Box 1.4.)

A DISEASE CONCEPT OF ALCOHOLISM

The disease concept of alcoholism didn't begin with Jellinek (1960). In 1785, a Philadelphia physician named Benjamin Rush published a temperance tract entitled "An Inquiry into the Effects of Ardent Spirits upon the Human Mind and Body," in which he wrote that alcoholism is a disease. In 1804, an Edinburgh physician named Thomas Trotter stated his belief that habitual drunkenness was a disease. Milam and Ketcham, in their groundbreaking book on alcoholism *Under the Influence* (1981) point out that Trotter's statement caused a storm of protest, particularly from the church and the medical profession. Not only did Trotter raise "depravity" to the status of a "disease," thereby confusing the line between good and evil, he proclaimed that "the drinker cannot be held responsible for his own actions and is thus protected from moral condemnation and judgment." The medical professional, whose involvement with the drunkard had been limited to treating physical complications, performing autopsies, and signing death certificates, was equally outraged. The alcoholic was a subject of fear and disgust that physicians wanted as little to do with as possible.

The idea that alcoholism is a disease gained credence in the 1930s and 1940s with the founding of Alcoholics Anonymous (AA) by two "drunkards" and the movement's undeniable success. According to Milam and Ketcham (1981), "AA demonstrated for the first time that alcoholics in significant numbers could recover and return to productive, useful lives. Most importantly, it proved that alcoholics, when they stayed sober, were decent, normal human beings and not hopeless degenerates." At that point, all it took was a respected scientist of the caliber of E. M. Jellineck to proclaim in acceptable medical terms that alcoholism is indeed a disease (Box 1.5).

BOX 1.5
Alcoholism: A "Closet" Disease

NIAAA estimates that 7% of the U.S. population—14 million adults, suffer from alcohol abuse or dependence.

An estimated 25% of adults either report drinking patterns that put them at risk or have alcohol-related problems.

40% suffer from co-morbidity however, more than 20% of those treated remain abstinent 12 months after treatment.

A DISEASE CONCEPT OF ADDICTION IN GENERAL

Although the disease concept of alcoholism came to be tacitly accepted, even the mainstream of recovering alcoholics continued to view addiction to any other drug as some combination of moral degeneracy, willful disobedience, and/or physical dependence intentionally entered into by the addict. Health professionals in general tended to share this opinion, while those involved in the treatment of addiction continued to view physical detoxification as the beginning and end of addiction treatment. With the exception of a few visionaries such as Chuck Brissett, who spoke of addiction as a "Three-headed Dragon," composed of physical, mental, and spiritual components, most who studied or practiced addiction treatment saw the problem as one of physical dependence.

The physical dependence paradigm remained viable as long as the principle drugs involved in addiction were seen as opiates and sedative-hypnotics. Both of these classes of drugs produced tolerance and physical withdrawal symptoms that usually frustrated any attempts at abstinence that were not reinforced. With the appearance of hallucinogens, the widening use of marijuana and the spread of stimulant drugs, such as methamphetamine and cocaine, none of which produced the classic tolerance and withdrawal symptoms that fit the model for addictive drugs, something had to change. First, there came attempts to reconfigure the existing paradigm. Opioids and the more powerful sedative drugs were labeled "hard" drugs, while LSD, marijuana, cocaine, and other stimulants became "soft" drugs. The result was general confusion that became particularly acute with the appearance of "crack" cocaine, quickly recognized as extremely potent in causing loss of control and continued addictive use. The solution was to adopt a modified version of the disease concept of alcoholism, after all, alcohol is not unique but one of a family of addictive drugs.

ADDICTION AS A BRAIN DISEASE

In 1999, on the basis of extensive research undertaken by the National Institute on Drug Abuse (NIDA) and other corroborative research, NIDA Director Alan I. Leshner declared addiction "a brain disease." In his introduction to *Principles of Drug Addiction Treatment: A Research-Based Guide*, Leshner (1999) says:

> Drug addiction is a complex illness. It is characterized by compulsive, at times uncontrollable drug craving, seeking, and use that persist(s) even in the face of

extremely negative consequences. For many people, drug addiction becomes chronic, with relapses possible even after long periods of abstinence.

The path to drug addiction begins with the act of taking drugs. Over time, a person's ability to choose not to take drugs can be compromised. Drug seeking becomes compulsive, in large part as a result of the effects of prolonged drug use on brain functioning and, thus, on behavior.

The compulsion to use drugs can take over the individual's life. Addiction often involves not only compulsive drug taking but also a wide range of dysfunctional behaviors that can interfere with normal functioning in the family, the workplace, and the broader community. Addiction also can place people at increased risk for a wide variety of other illnesses. These illnesses can be brought on by behaviors, such as poor living and health habits, that often accompany life as an addict, or because of toxic effects of the drugs themselves.

ARE WE THERE YET?

We have learned more about the human brain in the last few decades than was known through all of human history. We know much more today about the nature of addiction than was known 10 years ago, and in an accelerated research climate, more is being learned. Any paradigm is a working model, subject to reevaluation and revision, if not outright rejection. As teachers of addiction medicine who have seen major changes in our curriculum, we feel safe in saying that the understanding of addiction will continue to change as more is revealed through scientific research in the laboratory and through field experience in the treatment of addictive disease. Are we there yet? Hardly. However, evidence-based treatment of addiction and many addicts' experience of long-term sobriety through a combination of treatment and supported recovery indicate that we are probably at least on the right road.

It would be comforting to believe that we have reached the summit in our understanding of addiction. Unfortunately, the more apt simile is that we are all laboring in the labyrinthine passages of a doctrinal Tower of Babel, where various paradigms and numerous by-paradigms have their champions and apologists. The nature of the disease and even the question of whether addiction is a disease are as hotly contested as ever. Each new discovery about brain chemistry leads to a counterdiscovery and yet more controversy, while proponents of an addiction as criminal behavior successfully lobby legislators to build prisons instead of supporting treatment. Clearly, there exists a need for policy research and education that shows addiction is a public health rather than a criminal justice issue.

ORGANIZING AND SPREADING THE WORD

Acceptance of alcoholism as a disease by the mainstream occurred first in good part because of the efforts of Alcoholics Anonymous and the *Big Book of AA*. Bill Wilson, cofounder of Alcoholics Anonymous had Doctor Silkworth, a physician, write an introductory chapter to the *Big Book,* which described the disease of alcoholism as an allergy of the body and a compulsion of the mind. Even though Dr. Bob Smith, the other cofounder of AA was cross-addicted to both alcohol and barbiturates, most of the early leaders of AA were pure alcoholics and wanted drug addiction considered an outside issue. This thinking led Marty Mann to form the National Council on Alcoholism, which served as the platform for the New York

Society on Alcoholism and eventually the American Society of Alcoholism, which motivated the American Medical Association to declare that alcoholism was a disease in 1956 and to reaffirm that declaration in 1966.

However, the 1960s generation of alcoholics and addicts were mostly cross-addicted. In recognition of this fact, the Haight Ashbury Free Clinics, founded in 1967, extended its philosophy of "Health care is a right, not a privilege" to include "Addiction is a disease and addicts have the right to treatment." That philosophy contributed to the formation of the California Society of Alcoholism and Other Drug Dependencies (CSAODD), later consolidated to the California Society of Addiction Medicine (CSAM), in 1972 by Jess Bromley, MD, and Gail Jara of the California Medical Association (CMA). Here, the strategy was to get the backing of organized medicine for doctors in addiction medicine so that the disaster of the 1920s, when the American Medical Association (AMA) came out against physicians treating addicts in New York and Louisiana and thus contributed to these doctors' arrest by law enforcement. At the national level, Dr. Doug Talbott's, American Academy of Addictionology in Georgia collaborated with the New York Society on alcoholism to form the American Society of Alcoholism and Other Drug Dependencies (AMSAODD), now the American Society of Addiction Medicine (ASAM), with recognition of addiction medicine as a medical specialty and acceptance that all addictions including alcoholism are diseases.

Dr. Talbott was instrumental in developing diversion and treatment programs for addicted health professionals in the 1970s and worked with a national coalition of physicians including Dr. David Smith in providing treatment and reentry for physicians who successfully completed a rigorous diversion and treatment program. This coalition provided a core that contributed to the founding of ASAM. Both Talbott and Smith were among the ASAM founders; both are now past presidents of ASAM and continue to be highly active in promoting the Society's national priorities.

THE HAIGHT ASHBURY FREE CLINICS:
AN EVOLUTIONARY MODEL

In its origins and development, the Haight Ashbury Free Clinics and our role in that development can be seen as an evolutionary model of the changing paradigm of addiction. Picture if you will the mid-1960s: We are a nation at war within and without. Many young people are going off to fight in Vietnam; many others here at home are rebelling against what they see as a stifling establishment, trying new life relationships, developing a fascination with psychoactive drugs, especially marijuana and lysergic acid diethylamide (LSD). Established attitudes and the national drug prevention efforts have been locked in the criminal justice centered "willful disobedience/moral degeneracy" model since the 1920s. Addiction treatment is available only through prison hospitals such as the one in Lexington, Kentucky. Addicts are criminals, jazz musicians, and other moral degenerates who quickly relapse when released from these facilities.

Led on by the books of Jack Kerouac, the poems of Allen Ginsberg and the works of other writers and artists of the "Beat Generation," America's young people have begun experimenting with marijuana and discovering that the dire warnings of immediate catastrophe are untrue. The ambiguity of marijuana and its long-term dangers can be seen and appreciated in a brief vignette:

A young college student was introduced to marijuana by an older man, a jazz musician, who often held court in a bohemian bar in San Francisco's North Beach. Although he did not seem to suffer any immediate consequences, the student was well aware of all the negative things he had been told about this drug. After ruminating for several days, he went to the bar and asked the man if he thought there was anything to the rumors of marijuana being addictive. The older man looked at the boy in disgust and answered: "Son, I've been smoking reefer every day for the last 15 years and I haven't seen any sign of addiction yet."

Encouraged by the perception that they had been lied to about marijuana, many young people extended their experimentation to the psychedelic drugs, primarily LSD. By the winter of 1966, a distinct youth culture had developed around two antipodes, the peace and civil rights movements and the use of psychoactive drugs. On January 14, 1967, a gathering of over 50,000 people came together in San Francisco's Golden Gate Park. This gathering, called both the Gathering of the Tribes and the Human Be-In, featured presentations by Timothy Leary, PhD, self-styled LSD guru, poetry readings by Allen Ginsberg and other transitional Beat poets, and music from such newly emerging "acid" rock bands as the Grateful Dead, Big Brother and the Holding Company, Jefferson Airplane, and the Sopwith Camel. Hell's Angels motorcycle club members watched over lost children and a prominent underground chemist parachuted into the proceedings, showering the crowd with 5,000 doses of his own highly potent LSD. The story of this gathering spread through the national media and it soon became common knowledge that, come June, thousands of young people would be heading for San Francisco to join in the fun.

At that time, David Smith was a postdoctoral toxicology student at the University of California at San Francisco medical center, doing research on the effects of psychoactive drugs on animals. Smith had also been selected to head up the Alcohol and Drug Abuse Screening Unit at San Francisco General Hospital. Living in the Haight Ashbury, Smith soon realized that what they were trying to study in the lab was being replicated in the neighborhood all around them. Smith began observing the growing youth culture community and learned from it of the coming influx of an estimated 100,000 counterculture youth. When the city government reacted with hostility and the health department with indifference, several colleagues joined Smith in planning a health center within the Haight Ashbury. At a time when the medical establishment was becoming increasingly bureaucratized and centralized in large hospital units that were often inaccessible, increasingly judgmental, and often hostile to members of the youth culture, a new approach to community medicine was badly needed (Sturges, 1993).

What emerged from these plans was the Haight Ashbury Free Medical Clinics. The core philosophy of the Clinics was that health care is a right, not a privilege, and should be free at the point of delivery, demystified, nonjudgmental, and humane. When it opened on June 7, 1967, staffed by volunteer health professionals and community activists, the Clinics operated around the clock providing services on a first-come, first-serve basis. The initial concern of the planning group was that the influx of young people would create a massive street population with little knowledge of hygiene and minimal available health care, a situation primed for contagious disease outbreaks of every variety.

Smith soon found that along with a rich spectrum of general problems, they were encountering an increasing number and variety of problems involving drug use. Initially, these were primarily acute toxicity episodes with LSD and other psychedelics. The medical establishment treated these "bad trips" as psychotic breaks and employed treatment responses that often exacerbated the problems. Clinics' staff learned talk-down techniques from community groups that had been dealing with bad trips for several years and had much better results.

As more young people crowded into the Haight Ashbury and demands exceeded supplies of psychedelics, other drug problems emerged. Perhaps the most critical of these was the spread of methamphetamine "street speed" from San Francisco's Tenderloin District into the youth culture. High-dose methamphetamine use alternated with high-dose barbiturates to produce an "upper/downer" syndrome, often characterized by drug-induced paranoia with ideas of reference that made the streets a dangerous place to be (Smith & Luce, 1971).

One client who was taking phencyclidine (PCP) on a daily basis became convinced that he was Jesus Christ. Complicating the case was the fact that over a dozen other people living in the same house commune and in the immediate neighborhood were also convinced that the man was Jesus and had signed on as his disciples. A counselor suggested that if the man wanted to prove that he was a reincarnated messiah, he should stop taking PCP for a week. The man did and, after a week, he admitted that he had "made a terrible mistake while under the influence of a powerful drug."

A Shifting Paradigm and the Free Clinics Movement

By 1969, cracks were beginning to show in the addiction paradigm that labeled all addicts criminal degenerates. Soldiers were returning from South East Asia addicted to heroin and heroin use was spreading to the children of privileged Americans, including those of lawmakers. The next few years saw the development of the president's Special Action Office for Drug Abuse Prevention (SAODAP) and the National Institute on Drug Abuse (NIDA). While the emphasis of both was on the development of methadone treatment and maintenance programs for entrenched heroin addicts, they also were aware of the potential of the growing number of free and community clinics for providing drug treatment for younger addicts and preaddicts.

The concept pioneered by the Haight Ashbury Clinics was being replicated throughout the United States and overseas. The Berkeley Free Clinic quickly followed Haight Ashbury. Five more free clinics opened before the end of 1967. The movement spread to Seattle, Detroit, Vancouver, and Toronto (two). Twenty-eight more opened in 1968, spreading the movement to Los Angeles, Atlanta, Boston, St. Louis, Chapel Hill, Durham, Chicago, Washington, DC, Las Vegas, Portland, Denver, Philadelphia, Minneapolis, Bellevue, Champaign, Montreal, and Winnipeg. By 1970, there were over 70 free clinics in North America.

A National Free Clinic Council

In October of 1968, Smith met with several colleagues, including several Berkeley Free Clinic founders to plan a national organization with the following six objectives:

1. To collect and disseminate information on youth problems, in particular drug abuse.
2. To organize communities to investigate specific health needs and to suggest educational and treatment programs to alleviate these needs.
3. To dissolve the credibility gap surrounding the entire drug issue and create a more honest and humanitarian approach.
4. To act as a clearinghouse for information.
5. To provide educational material.
6. To provide a speakers bureau.

The group planned a National Free Clinic Council symposium for January 1970 that was attended by over 300 free clinic workers representing most of the 62 clinics then in operation and published proceedings the following year (Smith, Bentel, & Schwartz, 1971).

The federal government was now taking notice of the movement and people within the National Institute of Mental Health (NIMH) and saw the free clinics as a means to disseminate drug treatment to new populations outside the criminal justice system. At a meeting that coincided with the second National Free Clinic Council Symposium, which took place at the Shorham Hotel in Washington, DC, in January 1972, NIMH announced that it was interested in forming a task force with NFCC to determine their position on funding free clinics. The resulting firestorm could be predicted, given the zeitgeist of that time, the pervading suspicion of government, and the spectrum of political philosophies at the various free clinics. The outcome, however, was funding for drug treatment and treatment training, the establishment of a funded national office for NFCC in San Francisco with its own national newsletter and five years of communication and interaction within the free clinic community.

The free clinics had grown out of the community as a means of providing direct relief from the medical problems found in the community. They could see that the best way of accomplishing this was to remain free from the Lilliputian bondage that forced patients and clinicians to conform to preset rules and regulations that were detrimental to the pursuit of health. As Smith often said, the "free" in free clinics means much, much more than just free of charge. Maintenance of a philosophy based on "Health care is a right, not a privilege," nonjudgmental, demystified and humane required administration, but it needed to be "organic" administration. In time, they codified procedures while continuing to respond to community needs and working together to create an organic structure with built-in resiliency and flexibility that allowed the Haight Ashbury Free Clinics to survive numerous crises and to, in the blessing of Star Trek's Spock and current CEO Darryl Inaba, "Live long and prosper."

THE CLINICS AS AN EVOLVING ENTITY

The Haight Ashbury Free Medical Clinics evolved from the temporary unit set up during the Summer of Love in 1967, as much a University of California at San Francisco research project as a treatment center. It developed and received the first federal grant for treating heroin abuse without methadone. Besides the original site, its facilities included a whole building devoted to drug treatment, a psychological services unit, a growing women's needs clinic, a commune health outreach program bringing hygiene and preventive medicine to the urban and rural communes of Northern California, and a federally funded vocational rehabilitation program called "Crackerjack." The Clinics' corporate entity, Youth Projects, Inc., also provided fiscal management for the National Free Clinics Council.

ADDICTION MEDICINE DEVELOPS

It was during Richard Seymour's tenure as the Haight Ashbury Free Clinics' chief executive officer, from 1973 to 1978, that his education in addiction medicine really began. The Clinics were going through the growing pains of early youth, as was the whole field of addiction treatment. Treatment and recovery had not yet come together. The nature of addiction was not well understood. It was generally believed that the goal of treatment was detoxification and hopefully some work on reentry. In fact, the Clinics' drug treatment unit was called the Heroin Detoxification and Aftercare Program.

There were very few scientific experts in the field, especially at the free and community clinic level. The people who knew most about drug abuse were the drug abusers themselves. Consequently, the individuals who successfully completed detoxification were frequently hired as "peer" counselors and to do other jobs around the clinics. Today, with a clearer understanding of the chronic nature of addiction, most treatment centers have a time ruling on hiring. The Haight Ashbury Free Clinics' is two years clean and sober. But in 1973 if one wanted to have a staff, there was little choice. We often hired within weeks of users completing treatment—and suffered the consequences. Seymour soon found that, next to chronic fiscal anemia, staff recidivism and subsequent turnover was the Clinics greatest problem.

DUAL DIAGNOSIS: TAD AND BIPOLAR DISEASE

In those days, little was known about dual diagnoses, or the combination of drug and mental health problems. Seymour's first encounter with dual diagnosis was through a young man we will call Tad.

There were individuals who were not in good enough shape to qualify as staff but were tolerated to hang around the Clinics offices to run errands and do odd jobs. Tad was one of these, a small and wiry man of indeterminate age who had close to zero affect. Rumor had it that he was from a wealthy family, had hung with some of the top psychedelic gurus, and had burned out on LSD. Nobody knew for sure, and nobody knew what his real name was. He spent his days being tolerated at the Clinics offices and Seymour had heard that he would go weeks without actually communicating with anyone.

Seymour started giving Tad errands and no-brainer things to do around the office and talking to him. After several weeks of this, he came to the office one day and asked if Seymour could give him some more challenging things to do. It dawned on Seymour that his unofficial therapy was working. He was responding. Seymour gave him more work: collating papers, then some simple filing. Yes! He was showing affect, smiling, even joking on occasion. Seymour gave him more to do and soon he was racing around the offices.

On a Saturday a few weeks later, Seymour got a phone call from David Smith. He had just seen Tad arrive at the Clinics offices in a limo. Tad had told David as he rushed inside that he had to make an important phone call to his friend the Maharaja of Ranjipur. Minutes later, Seymour received a call from the grants and contracts administrator. Seymour could hear shouting in the background. Tad was marching up and down the hall and shouting orders to invisible people. We got him admitted to the San Francisco General Psychiatric Ward for the maximum time we could, which was about 72 hours. After that, the whole manic progression reversed itself until Tad was as he had been when Seymour first came to the Clinics. About that time, he dropped out of sight. On his next manic swing, he died from a barbiturate overdose while trying to self-medicate. His body was found a few days later in his room. In those days, the links between bipolar disease and addiction were little known or understood. There were no effective means at hand for recognizing Tad's multiple problems. Then, there was nothing to be done. Today, we can do much more.

WRITING IT DOWN: TRAINING AND EDUCATION

Not all of Seymour's education was as extreme as this first exposure to bipolar disease. Seymour evolved from CEO to director of training and education, finding that although there was much innovative work being done at the Clinics, few of the clinicians had time to write about what they were doing. With his background in writing and journalism, Seymour was able to step in and do service as the "midwife" bringing the Clinicians' experience into published daylight. In the process, Seymour received the best education in addiction, psychopharmacology, and treatment available at that time.

Drug treatment was a new field, rarely represented at colleges, universities, or even medical schools. David Smith points out that when he was pursuing his doctoral and postdoctoral studies at UC San Francisco, he had only one course in addiction. This was an elective taught on a Saturday by Dr. Earle M., author of the "Physician, Heal Thyself" article in the *AA Big Book* (Alcoholics Anonymous, 1976). Everything else had to be learned through experience.

As drug problems increased through the 1970s and treatment expanded to meet them, the need for effective treatment staff multiplied throughout the country. Education and some form of certification became a primary concern and Robert DuPont, MD, then the director of both SAODAP and NIDA, convened a number of meetings in the Washington, DC, area to that end. While national efforts remained cumbersome, counselor groups were organized in various states and provided an impetus to develop their own credentialing systems, generally based on a combination of supervised work at treatment centers and school-based education in various aspects of addiction and treatment. Working with one of the state counselor associations in California, Seymour helped to develop a program of course work at Sonoma State University that became a model for counselor training. While many of the students were in recovery themselves, academic training provided a background and support for their own experience, making them more effective counselors and a buffer against relapse as their confidence and expertise increased through learning.

PRESCRIPTION DRUG ABUSE IN THE MIDDLE CLASS

It was in the early 1970s that the Haight Ashbury Free Clinics was instrumental in a dramatic expansion in the nature and demographics of drug abuse. Although alcoholism had been accepted as a widespread disease, other drug abuse and addiction was still seen within a context of criminal, jazz, and artistically bohemian circles that had expanded to include the youth counterculture and returning veterans.

By 1971, however, Dr. Donald R. Wesson and Smith were testifying at Senate subcommittee hearings on the abuse of amphetamines and barbiturates. Their activities resulted in a "theme" issue of the *Journal of Psychedelic Drugs* titled "The Politics of Uppers and Downers" (1972). Smith and Wesson characterized this new population as:

> Individuals involved are generally in the 30 to 50 years age group and obtain their supply of barbiturates from physicians rather than from the black market. Most are of middle or upper socioeconomic class and have no identification with the young drug taking subculture. Their general pattern of obtaining intoxicating doses of barbiturates is to sequentially visit several physicians with complaints of sleeping difficulty or nervousness. Also, because of their conventional middle class appearance, pharmacists are more likely to refill their prescriptions without notifying the physicians.

Move over Aquarius, this was the dawning of the age of middle class polydrug abuse! Once identified, this polydrug abuse posed a number of new problems for enforcement. For one, these were not illegal drugs being clandestinely manufactured or smuggled into the country. For another, most of the abusers were getting their supplies with legitimate prescriptions. Who then, if anyone, was breaking the law. Further, these abusers maintained a very low profile, did not share their abuse with others, and were firmly convinced that they were not drug abusers in any way, shape, or form.

The National Institute on Drug Abuse (NIDA) had a potential solution to these problems. That was to work with Smith, Wesson, and their colleagues to develop polydrug research protocols, entice middle class clients into treatment, and then figure out ways to treat them. The result was the NIDA-funded West Coast Polydrug Project with Smith and Wesson as its principal investigators.

Realizing that the clients they were targeting wouldn't come to a drug treatment center in Haight Ashbury, they leased a nondescript building in the heart of a middle class neighborhood just downhill from the University of California Medical Center. No signs were posted or anything else that would distinguish the stucco duplex from similar dwellings. The treatment staff wore jackets and ties. Women on the staff wore dresses and tailored suits. Only the frequency of respectable looking individuals arriving and departing throughout the day would indicate anything out of the ordinary.

In its own way, the Polydrug Project was very much part of the Clinics. It carried the concept of *Free* forward into new areas of research and treatment. All treatment there was also free. The staff was able to approach developing substance abuse problems without being bound by traditional medical models. As a consequence, much of what was developed and written about is still considered new approaches to treatment and used by chemical dependency units and other middle class oriented treatment programs. Among these procedures is the pheno-barbital substitution method for sedative-hypnotic withdrawal, a procedure that greatly decreases the chance of life-threatening seizures during withdrawal.

As middle class patients were diagnosed and studied at the center, it became clear that they were not using drugs for the same reasons that the drug subcultures were. In most cases, they were self-medicating for a wide variety of disorders, including chronic pain and long-term emotional disorders. If you merely detoxified them from the chemical dependency, you were still left with a rebound of the underlying problems. New approaches included helping these patients deal with the reasons they were using and providing alternative means of both physical and emotional pain control. By 1976, the government decided that it had all the data it needed on polydrug abuse and treatment and terminated funding for the Project. For us, this was a repeat of 1967, when an academic mentor told Smith the Summer of Love was over and it was time to close the Clinics and get back to work at the UC Medical Center. As far as Smith and Wesson were concerned, the Polydrug Project had a life and a mission that had to be fulfilled. No matter what the government thought, there was still research to be done. There were clients in the midst of treatment who couldn't be abandoned. Our work continued, patients were taken into the overall practice and activities were merged into other programs in the Clinics. Our work with the West Coast Polydrug Project introduced the concepts of the 12-Step AA recovery into drug treatment and developed a greater understanding of both the causes and consequences of addiction (Seymour & Smith, 1987).

THE MARRIAGE OF TREATMENT AND RECOVERY

In the 1980s with the advancement of the disease concept of addiction, the drug treatment field began to incorporate the concept of recovery into its goals and objectives. While detoxification and some form of aftercare were the watchwords of treatment centers that were not engaged in maintenance in the 1970s, it became increasingly clear that what we had seen as the goal of treatment—detoxification—was really the beginning. Much of the impetus toward incorporation of the recovery concept in treatment came from a coterie of recovering physicians and other health professionals who promoted the values of supported recovery, primarily through adherence to the 12-Step program of Alcoholics Anonymous and Narcotics Anonymous, in their own lives and those of their patients. The *Minnesota model* exemplified by Hazelden had been in practice for several decades, but the spread of recovery into the medical treatment area was accelerated by several national figures coming forward, not only to talk about their own recovery but to directly support treatment efforts as well. One of the most notable was Betty Ford, wife of President Gerald Ford, who had established the Betty Ford Center in southern California. Recovering physicians from the center pioneered the marriage of recovery and treatment in their inpatient facility while the Haight Ashbury Free Clinics collaborated with the Merrit Peralta Chemical Dependency Hospital in Oakland, California, in presenting an annual series of recovery-centered conferences to benefit Plaza House as a residence program for recovering health professionals.

By the late 1980s, it had become clear to many that treatment as we knew and practiced it was primarily a bridge between active addiction and active recovery.

Robert DuPont, past director of the NIDA and SAODAP and president of the Institute for Behavior and Health, Inc., and John McGovern, Clinical Professor of Medicine at the University of Texas Medical School at Houston, Texas, held a series of meetings that brought together key experts from all facets of prevention, treatment, human services, and mutual aid programs to map out the ways in which the health professions and other service organizations could incorporate recovery into their work. The resulting book, *A Bridge to Recovery: An Introduction to 12-Step Programs* (DuPont & McGovern, 1994), provides a blueprint for understanding recovery and utilizing organized referral into self-help fellowships.

THE HAIGHT ASHBURY FREE CLINICS TODAY

Today, the Haight Ashbury Free Clinics include 22 treatment sites throughout the San Francisco Bay Area. Its Substance Abuse Treatment Services continue to provide free treatment for a wide demographic of patients, the majority of whom are among the homeless, destitute, working poor, and the increasing ranks of those with no health insurance and who would be unable to gain treatment on their own. Treatment availability at the Clinics represent a ray of hope for the increasing numbers of medically disenfranchised people in today's precarious economy and convoluted medical delivery system. The Clinics represent a key link in the treatment chain that has seen the development of the California Society of Addiction Medicine, the American Society of Addiction Medicine, and now the International Society of Addiction Medicine. The Clinics have maintained and expanded their impact on training, research, and policy development. David Smith is the medical director for the State of California Alcohol and Drug Programs (ADP). He and Richard Seymour are the medical director and coordinator, respectively, of the California Collaborative Center for Substance Abuse Policy Research (CCCSAPR), a partnership of the Haight Ashbury Free Clinics and drug research entities at the nine campuses of the University of California. Seymour is the education and training manager for the clinics, coordinating their continuing education (CME) programs and the annual conference, held each year by HAFC and CCCSAPR at the University of California at San Francisco Laurel Heights Conference Center. He is also the director of Haight Ashbury Publications, founded by Smith, which began publishing the *Journal of Psychedelic Drugs,* now the *Journal of Psychoactive Drugs,* in 1967, the *International Addictions Infoline,* and in partnership with Drug Abuse Sciences, Inc., AlcoholMD.com. Seymour is also on the board of the recently formed International Society of Addiction Journal Editors (ISAJE).

A number of other Clinics staff members have become key movers in the addiction field, including Darryl Inaba, John Newmeyer, Sarah Calhoun, Diana Amodia, and Ben Eiland, as well as individuals who have taken what they learned at the Clinics to other treatment and policy positions throughout the United States.

VULNERABILITY TO THE DISEASE OF ADDICTION

Currently more and more researchers in the field of addictionology believe that the reason for drug addiction is indeed a combination of the three factors of heredity, environment and the use of psychoactive drugs (DuPont, 1997; Leshner, 1999):

Heredity + Environment = Addiction (Maybe)

Because individual personalities, physiology, and lifestyles vary, each person's resistance or susceptibility to excessive drug use also varies (Inaba & Cohen, 2000). Genetics appear to have a major role on how the brain responds to and processes psychoactive substances (Smith & Seymour, 2001) (see Tables 1.1 and 1.2).

While heredity does seem to be a major factor in vulnerability to addiction, it is not the only factor. Studies show that twin children living in foster homes tend to share abuse or abstinence patterns similar to their biologic parents' (Goodwin, 1976), and there is evidence that if both biological parents are alcoholic, the child is about 400% more likely to be alcoholic (Inaba & Cohen, 2000). Many alcoholics and other addicts do not follow a parental pattern. There are many sons and daughters of alcoholics and other addicts who never abuse or become addicted to alcohol or other drugs. Heredity plays a major role, but not a decisive one. Anyone can become an addict, especially if they work at it.

However, the genetic revolution will impact on all brain diseases including addiction since the root of addiction lies in the old or primitive brain and is fundamentally an irrational process. This is why intelligent people such as doctors will drink and drug themselves to death even though intellectually they understand the horrors of addictive disease. Addiction lies in the nucleus accumbens-dopamine system described as the reward pathway of the midbrain. This primitive part of the brain provides the neurochemical instinct to survive. Neuroscientists are now describing addiction as a drug-induced dysfunction in this reward pathway as it sends out the neurochemical message that if you don't continue to use you will die, even though the new brain learns that continued use will lead to external environmental destruction and death (Addictive Disease=Genetics+Enviroment). Dante described this in *the Inferno,* saying, "The lowest rings of Hell are for those who yearn for what they fear." James Watson and Francis Crick, the discoverers of DNA in 1953, predicted that the new genetic frontier is the brain, including the genetics of instinct. This will help us understand the genetics of addiction and compulsion so that we may intervene earlier on high-risk individuals as we do with diabetics.

Environment, including accessibility to alcohol and other drugs, is an equally necessary component of the equation. According to Inaba and Cohen (2000):

> The environmental influences that help determine the level at which a person uses drugs can be positive or negative and as varied as stress, love, violence, sexual abuse,

Table 1.1
Issues in Diagnosis

1. Tolerance,
2. Withdrawal,
3. Withdrawal avoidance,
4. Socially dysfunctional use,
5. Use despite problems,
6. Cannot stop,
7. Salience,
8. Preoccupation, and
9. Cannot limit use.

Table 1.2
Conditions Attributable to Substance Abuse

Disease Category	Substances	Risk Percentage
AIDS (adults)	IV drug use	32
Asthma	Passive smoke and smoking	27
Bladder cancer (male)	Smoking	53
Breast cancer	Alcohol	13
Cheek and gum cancer	Smokeless tobacco	87
Endocarditis	IV drug use	75
Esophageal cancer	Alcohol and smoking	80
Low birth weight	Smoking	42
Pancreatitis, chronic	Alcohol	72
Pregnancy (placenta previa)	Smoking	43
Seizures	Alcohol	41
Stroke	Smoking and cocaine	65
Trauma	Alcohol and other drugs	40

nutrition, living conditions, family relationships, nutritional balance, health care, neighborhood safety, school quality, peer pressure and television. The pressures and influences of environment, particularly home environment, actually shape and connect the nerve cells and neurochemistry a person is born with, thereby helping to determine how that person will use psychoactive drugs. Even one's diet affects brain chemistry.

ADDICTION, PSYCHOACTIVE SUBSTANCES, AND THE MID-BRAIN

How do psychoactive substances produce addiction, even among creative and intelligent individuals? The overall process involves two different areas in the human brain. Denial and recovery take place in the cerebral cortex, and addiction and craving take place in the more primitive mid-brain (see Box 1.6). Psychosocial treatment (counseling and the development of a program of supported recovery, such as that found in 12-Step fellowships) can combat denial and engender recovery, but is frequently sabotaged by the powerful fundaments of addiction, including craving, that lie inaccessible to reason within the mid-brain. Drug treatment medication, including anti-craving agents, become important adjuncts to treatment, making it possible for psychosocial treatment to take place.

Medical interventions in drug abuse treatment are based on a variety of goals (see Box 1.7). In acute withdrawal and detoxification, medication goals may include withdrawal symptom suppression through symptomatic medication or drug replacement. Replacement and taper strategies are particularly important in detoxification from sedative-hypnotic drugs, such as alcohol and benzodiazepines, which present a danger of potentially fatal seizure during withdrawal.

Other medications, such as amino acid combinations, may work as neurotransmitter precursor loads. These are particularly helpful in the treatment for cocaine abuse, because cocaine exhausts several neurotransmitters in the brain. As these neurotransmitters are replenished, however, craving for cocaine becomes stronger. Anti-craving agents are usually used once acute withdrawal is over and detoxification has been successfully completed. Essentially, the brain is like a chemical

---

BOX 1.6
Alcoholism Neurochemical Profile

Alcohol preferring versus nonpreferring rat profile:

- Fewer serotonin neurons in the hypothalamus.
- Higher levels of enkephalin in the hypothalamus.
- Higher levels of GABA neurons in the nucleus accumbens (NA).
- Reduced dopamine supply in the NA.
- Reduced densities of dopamine D2 receptors in the mesolimbic areas.

---

symphony of inhibitory and stimulatory neurotransmitters. Addiction disrupts this symphony. Recovery rebalances the brain and medications help in rebalancing.

Anti-craving agents work in a variety of ways to reduce mid-brain craving. Craving is not a result of a lack of will power, therefore the exercise of will is not a viable means of eliminating craving. Many individuals need help to avoid the overpowering urge to use drugs so that they can participate in psychosocial treatment used in postdetoxification aftercare.

There is a high dropout rate of patients early in drug abuse treatment, often shortly after detoxification. Patients rarely come into treatment to become fully abstinent. They come in because their lives are a mess and their use is totally out of control. As soon as things start coming together for them, the craving for their drug of choice returns and, if unchecked, will propel them out of treatment and back into active addiction. Anti-craving agents bolster whatever desire they may have to stay in treatment, providing an extended window of opportunity for the treatment to be reinforced and hopefully take effect in leading them beyond their "need" for the drug.

BOX 1.7
Alcohol Treatment Medications

Medications approved in the United States for alcohol treatment:

- Antabuse (disulfiram)
- Naltrexone

Medications studied for use in alcohol rehabilitation:

- Antabuse (disulfiram)
- Lithium
- Serotonin reuptake blockers (fluoxetine, citalopram)
- Acamprosate
- Opiate antagonists (naltrexone)

SUBSTANCE ADDICTION AND PROCESS ADDICTION

The disease concept of addiction has moved our thinking into seeing addiction as a behavioral disease with specific behavioral characteristics. Physical dependence on certain substances can still be a factor in addiction, but it is no longer our sole definition of addiction. Suppose 10 patients are hospitalized for surgery. All 10 receive opioid medication for postoperative pain management. In the course of their pain management, they all develop physical dependency and are tapered from the medication in the process of their treatment. Nine of the 10 were happy to have the medication, but didn't really care for the effects and were glad to be done with it. The tenth reacted by thinking, "Where has this been all my life! It's the answer to all my problems." What has happened is the awakening of a compulsion, probably involving genetic predisposition. In this case, the compulsion involves the use of a drug, seeing that substance as a desired panacea, or at least a means to providing something that has been perceived as missing in the person's life. Other forms of addiction may include other compulsive behavior syndromes that have their being in the old brain.

Both substance and process addiction may respond to:

- Medications such as SSRIs.
- Psychosocial counseling.
- 12-Step recovery groups.

Do the same rules apply to other compulsive behaviors? Shifting to a behavioral paradigm of drug addiction that pivots on the loss of control over compulsion opens the door to comparisons with other compulsive behaviors. This volume is called *Addictive Disorders: A Practical Handbook.* Because it contains chapters on what the editor must consider a variety of addictive behaviors, it infers that there are basic similarities between drug addiction and a variety of other behaviors.

Neither of us is by any means expert in diagnosing or treating these behaviors, nor do we know at this writing what the authors of the following chapters will say about them. We have been asked by the editor of this book, however, to evaluate whether each of the following falls within the definition of addictive disease as we have presented it. We therefore present our opinion on each of these categories, asking you, the reader, and you, the authors of the following chapters, to bear with us in this attempt:

COMPULSIVE GAMBLING

Gamblers Anonymous (GA) defines gambling as "any betting or wagering for self or others, whether for money or not, no matter how slight or insignificant, where the outcome is uncertain or depends upon chance or skill" (GA, 1998). Inaba and Cohen (2000) report that there are four categories of gamblers. These are: (1) recreational social gamblers who are able to separate gambling from the rest of their lives; (2) professional gamblers for whom gambling is a business at which they are able to make a living; (3) antisocial gamblers who will steal to gamble and have no conscience; and (4) pathological gamblers who are obsessed with gambling, getting the money to gamble, and figuring out ways to stay in action. Pathological gambling seems to be a pathological disorder requiring more episodes and larger amounts of money bet to relieve anxiety and tension.

According to Inaba and Cohen's adaptation of the *Diagnostic and Statistical Manual of Mental Disorders* (*DSM-IV*; APA, 1994) the symptoms of persistent recurrent pathological gambling are five or more of the following:

1. Preoccupation with gambling.
2. Gambling with increased amounts of money.
3. Repeated unsuccessful efforts to control, cut back, or stop gambling.
4. Restlessness and irritability when attempting to control, cut back, or stop.
5. Gambling as an escape.
6. Attempts to recoup previous losses.
7. Lying to others to conceal gambling.
8. Illegal acts to finance gambling.
9. Jeopardization or loss of job, relationship, or educational or career opportunity.
10. Reliance on others to bail gambler out of pressing debts.

These symptoms would appear to fit into the pattern of compulsion, loss of control, and continued activity in spite of adverse consequences that are our primary characterization of addictive disease. Although there is not a drug involved, the activity of gambling, in and of itself, could be seen to correspond to a substance.

SEX ADDICTION

What has been called sexual addiction is characterized by sexual behavior over which the addict has no control, no choice. Here again we see the pivotal loss of control as the key to aberrant behavior that can include masturbation, pornography, serial affairs, phone sex, as well as compulsive visits to topless bars and strip shows. Inaba and Cohen (2001) point out that some sexual addiction activities can result in legal difficulties, such as prostitution, sexual harassment, sexual abuse, voyeurism, exhibitionism, child molestation, rape, and incest. Several sexual disorders are listed in the *DSM-IV*, but these do not involve compulsivity. A basic behavioral pattern involving compulsion, loss of control, and the potential for continued socially or personally damaging sexual activities would seem to mimic the pattern seen in drug addiction. In fact, Sexaholics Anonymous (SA) and other affiliated groups see compulsive sex as a progressive disease that can be treated.

EATING DISORDERS

There are a variety of eating disorders, including anorexia (which has been defined as an addiction to weight loss, fasting, and control of body size), bulimia (a process of bingeing and then purging with the aid of vomiting, laxatives, or fasting) and compulsive overeating. All three of these disorders have been referred to as addictive disorders. In all three cases, the elements of process addiction are present. All three exhibit compulsive behavior that is out of control. Victims of anorexia and bulimia have developed a distorted body image of themselves as overweight, no matter how dangerously underweight they have become. This can be seen as a form of denial. Compulsive eaters continue to eat to health and life-threatening extremes. All three fill the criteria of continuing out-of-control compulsive behavior in spite of adverse consequences that can be life threatening in all cases. It should be noted that food, in and of itself is psychoactive, providing many of the feelings that are prized in drug addiction. The absence of food, the faster's high, also produces psychoactive effects.

WORKAHOLISM

It has been argued that the present day American working culture, with its emphasis on long hours, multitasking, constant communication via cell phones, e-mails, faxes, and so on has produced an environment in which virtually everyone is a workaholic. It is even postulated that you have to be a workaholic to survive in the working world. Paradoxically, workaholism is not productive. Genuine workaholism by definition involves the repeating of nonproductive activity. Workaholism can be seen in the individual who spends long hours writing unnecessary memos when a few words communicated correctly would suffice. The program coordinator who maintains a dozen parallel tracking systems is most likely a workaholic. Generally, it is a compulsive and repetitive exercise of counterproductive efforts that in time will damage the individual and his or her coworkers, bringing down real productivity. We suppose that in extreme cases the out-of-control workaholic could work him or herself to death, but the most usual consequence is exhaustion and unemployment. The truly productive worker learns the quickest and most direct way to get the job done. To the best of our knowledge, very few people on their deathbeds ever say, "Gee. I should have spent more time at the office."

COMPULSIVE BUYING

The *DSM-IV* (APA, 1994) places compulsive shopping within Impulse Control Disorders Not Otherwise Specified. Inaba and Cohen (2001) see the roots of compulsive buying as similar to those of compulsive gambling, a means of developing a sense of self worth and feeling good. With the proliferation of credit cards and other means of easy buying and the ubiquitous nature of advertising, compulsive buying is a process addiction with a legion of enablers.

COMPULSIVE BEHAVIOR IN GENERAL

All of these behaviors appear to be related to drug addiction in terms of compulsivity, loss of control, and continued activity in spite of adverse consequences. Do they fall within the scope of addictive disease? We think so. Perhaps the following chapters will fill in their story.

Is there a root cause to all addiction? Is it a question of brain chemistry? It has been postulated that such behaviors such as compulsive gambling have to do with the activity's affect on neurotransmitters, particularly those that are stimulated by such substances as cocaine and the amphetamines. We have often heard the term *adrenaline junkies* applied to individuals who indulge in thrill-seeking behavior. Interviews with compulsive gamblers suggest that rather than elevation of self-worth or the desire to win, the motivating factor is an internal rush. Perhaps we could make a case for these compulsive behaviors being primarily a means of activating the psychoactive substances that exist in our brains, thus accomplishing a form of gratification similar to what is experienced by alcohol and other drug addicts. The process addictions appear to be the use of compulsive behavior to fuel the dysfunctional reward system in the primitive brain and in many cases are treated successfully with techniques similar to those utilized in drug addictions, including medications such as the SSRIs and active participation in a 12-Step recovery group.

SUMMARY AND CONCLUSION: ADDICTION IS A PARADIGM IN PROGRESS

Drug addiction is a brain disease. It is a disease entity that is characterized by compulsion, loss of control, and continued use in spite of adverse consequences. Like diabetes, it is a chronic disease that at best is controlled rather than cured. Its victims are subject to periodic relapse, but these lapses can be learning experiences, properly handled they can bring the victim closer to long-term sobriety. While the disease is incurable, it can be brought into remission through a program of abstinence from all psychoactive substances and active supported recovery.

Is this the final word on addiction? Probably not. The disease concept of addiction is a paradigm in progress. Although much has been learned about the brain and human behavior in recent years, there is still much, much more to learn. With addiction, we are dealing with a highly complex mix of physical, spiritual, and psychological factors. We are attempting to understand a dynamic that does not exist in a vacuum. There is much yet to learn, for example, about the relation between drug addiction and other compulsive behaviors, such as those described in this book.

For the moment, the disease concept enables us to recognize addiction as a treatable affliction rather than a criminal behavior and places these issues where we believe they belong, in a public health and medical context. What is needed now is expansion of the base of knowledge, demystifying of addiction, destigmatizing of the addict, mainstreaming of addiction treatment, and developing policy to support the treatment environment.

Unfortunately, societal views of addiction are often not based on science, but rather perceptions of who the addict is. The Haight Ashbury Free Clinics early financial support came from rock concert benefits organized by Bill Graham of the Fillmore Auditorium in San Francisco. Federal aid didn't arrive for national treatment until the Vietnam War era of the 1970s. The president's Special Action Office for Drug Abuse Policy (SAODAP) was first headed by Jerome Jaffee, MD. The guiding principle was that no addict should have to commit a crime because he or she can't get treatment and we can't put our troops in jail for getting strung out in a foreign and unpopular war. Two-thirds of the money allocated for drugs in the federal budget went for treatment during the 1970s, but tragically when the perception of the addict shifted to lower socioeconomic nonwhite people, the government's approach became one of criminalization rather than medicalization. As a result, 80% of the people incarcerated by criminal justice have drug problems but only 5% receive treatment. A counter-revolution, fueled by Proposition 36 in California, which remanded adults charged with possession and other drug-only crimes to treatment instead of incarceration, has hopefully signaled the beginning of a shift forward into the new medical model.

RECOMMENDED READINGS

Inaba, D. S., & Cohen, W. (2000). *Uppers, downers, all arounders* (4th ed.). Ashland, OR: CNS Publications. This book, now going into its fifth edition is the quintessential text on all aspects of drug and process addiction. Useful as a college text, it is highly readable and contains a wealth of information and insights.

Milam, J. R., & Ketchem, K. (1981). *Under the influence: A guide to the myths and realities of alcoholism.* Seattle, WA: Madrona. This book remains the prime source on all aspects of alcoholism.

Smith, D. E., & Seymour, R. B. (2001). *Clinician's guide to substance abuse.* New York: McGraw-Hill. This book is strongly recommended for any health professional who is not an addiction medicine specialist. It was written and published in the hopes of bringing addiction treatment into the medical mainstream and contains the essence of all aspects of addiction diagnosis, treatment, and referral.

REFERENCES

Alcoholics Anonymous. (1976). *Alcoholics Anonymous: The story of how many thousands of men and women have recovered from alcoholism* (3rd ed.). New York: Author.

American Psychiatric Association. (1994). *Diagnostic and statistical manual of mental disorders* (4th ed.). Washington, DC: Author.

Coombs, R. H. (1997). *Drug-impaired professionals.* Cambridge, MA: Harvard University Press.

DuPont, R. L. (1997). *The selfish brain: Learning from addiction.* Washington, DC: American Psychiatric Press.

DuPont, R. L., & McGovern, J. P. (1994). *A bridge to recovery: An introduction to 12-step programs.* Washington, DC: American Psychiatric Press.

Gamblers Anonymous. (1998). *Gamblers Anonymous combo book.* Los Angeles: Author.

Goodwin, D. W. (1976). *Is alcoholism hereditary?* New York: Oxford University Press.

Inaba, D. S., & Cohen, W. E. (2000). *Uppers, downers, all arounders* (4th ed.). Ashland, OR: CNS Publications.

Jellinek, E. M. (1960). *The disease concept of alcoholism.* New Haven, CT: Hillhouse Press.

Leshner, A. (1999). *Principles of drug addiction treatment: A research-based guide.* Bethesda, MD: National Institute on Drug Abuse.

Marlatt, G. A., Blume, A. W., & Parks, G. A. (2001). Integrating harm reduction therapy and traditional substance abuse treatment. *Journal of Psychoactive Drugs, 33*(1), 13–21.

Milam, J. R., & Ketcham, K. (1981). *Under the influence: A guide to the myths and realities of alcoholism.* Seattle, WA: Madrona.

Miller, N. S., & Gold, M. S. (1995). The role of the psychiatrist in treatment or relapse in addictive disorders. *Psychiatric Annals, 25,* 673–678.

Musto, D. F. (1987). *The American disease: Origins of narcotic control* (Rev. ed.). New York: Oxford University Press.

NCA News. (1988, October 21). Congress eliminates willful misconduct from VAQ definition of alcoholism. *NCA News.*

Seessel, T. V. (1988). Beyond the Supreme Court ruling on alcoholism as willful misconduct: It is up to Congress to act. *Journal of the American Medical Association, 260,* 248.

Seymour, R. B., & Smith, D. E. (1986). *The Haight Ashbury free medical clinics: Still free after all these years 1967–1987.* San Francisco: Partisan Press.

Smith, D. E., Bentel, D. J., & Schwartz, J. L. (1971). *The free clinic: A community approach to health care and drug abuse.* Beloit, WI: Stash Press.

Smith, D. E., & Gay, G. R. (1972). *It's so good, don't even try it once.* Englewood Cliffs, NJ: Prentice-Hall.

Smith, D. E., & Luce, J. (1971). *Love needs care: A history of San Francisco's Haight-Ashbury free medical clinic and its pioneer role in treating drug-abuse problems.* Boston: Little, Brown.

Smith, D. E., & Seymour, R. B. (2001). *Clinician's guide to substance abuse.* New York: McGraw-Hill.

Smith, D. E., & Wesson, D. R. (1972). The politics of uppers and downers: Editors' introduction. *Journal of Psychedelic Drugs, 5*(2), 101–104.

Sturges, C. S. (1993). *Dr. Dave: A profile of David E. Smith, MD, Founder of the Haight Ashbury Free Clinics.* Walnut Creek, CA: Devil Mountain Books.

CHAPTER 2

Addiction Interaction Disorder

PATRICK J. CARNES, ROBERT E. MURRAY, and LOUIS CHARPENTIER

IN THE EARLY 1990s, I (Carnes) had been researching sex addiction for almost two decades. This included a 5-year, in-depth study of 1,000 recovering sex addicts and their partners. In the study, relatively few addicts (less than 13%) indicated they had only one addiction. We learned from these participants that one of the most striking factors in successful sustained recovery was effectively addressing all the addictions present. More importantly, we learned that addictions did not simply coexist but interacted with one another. In 1994, on the basis of this study and clinical experience, I proposed a model of addiction interaction. In teaching and clinical practice, the model underwent revision and refinement. This chapter summarizes the model we used to make sense of this complex interweaving of addictions and deprivations.

In 1998, we used the model of addiction interaction as a form of psychoeducational intervention in our dual diagnosis inpatient setting that addressed multiple addictions. The goal was to test whether the model was useful to patients in understanding their own dynamics. This chapter reports on our clinical experience, which leads us to looking at comorbidity in a new and useful fashion. We were also able to gather data that supported the overall concept. This effort took us closer to understanding the realities our patients faced. What emerged in the extensive research of those I originally followed is formalized here. They opened the door to understanding the biggest factors in relapse: multiple addictions, their deprivation partners, and the interactions among them.

In another 10 years, we will become more familiar with how the brain affects addiction. However, many clinicians who are not trained in biology have trouble understanding brain functions. Without a biological background, the vocabulary of the brain's anatomy and circuitry seems incomprehensible and complex. We recommend that you, in order to understand how the neuropathways of the brain facilitate addiction interaction, read *Craving Ecstacy: The Chemistry and Consciousness of Escape* (Milkman & Sunderwirth, 1987). It is designed for therapists who are not familiar with neurobiology. This chapter is focused on clinical practice, but we encourage you to explore the brain chemistry of addictions as well.

THE CASE FOR MULTIPLE ADDICTIONS

Clinically we have a rich history of people who have approached the problem of multiple addictions. The most obvious argument is that addictions have similar structure. Many have argued at length about the parallels and commonalities across addictive disorders. A good example of this genre is Jim Orford's classic work *Excessive Appetites: A Psychological View of Addictions* (Orford, 1985). His book is a methodical, systematic critique of addiction theory. Orford offers one of the best discussions of the problems of social context, normal versus excessive, and the similarities across addictions. He makes the distinction between biology and psychology in addiction, which in light of modern brain research would be considered an artificial and outmoded distinction. Yet his comparison of the dynamics of excessive appetites is one of the most thorough expositions of multiple addictions. He writes:

> The way in which "alcoholism" became a specialty, divorced from the general study of behavior, was perhaps inevitable but regrettable. When it has been linked with other kinds of behavior at all, it has usually been placed alongside "drug addiction," a marriage which has emphasized the pharmacological basis of behavior. . . . Equally, if not more useful, parallels are to be drawn between drinking, gambling, and sexual behavior. . . . The triad of drink, sex and gambling share many features (including) each has given rise to fascinating and similar logical and semantic problems . . . (Orford, 1985, p. 6)

Part of the resolution of logical and semantic issues comes from the science of the brain. Howard Shaffer's work on the cognitive chaos in addictionology recognizes achievements in neuroscience. He points to breakthroughs in our understanding of the brain as underlining the artificiality of such propositions as there being a distinction between physical and psychological dependence and the premise that addiction must involve a chemical external to the body. He points out for example that, "pathological gamblers experience addiction, including tolerance and withdrawal, often in the absence of any drug use" (Shaffer, 1997, p. 1573). Milkman and Sunderwirth made the case that all addictions accessed certain neuropathways and that those "rivers in the mind" in fact were more important to understand than the multitude of ways addicts accessed them (Milkman & Sunderwirth, 1987). Perhaps Alan Leshner, the former director of the National Institute for Drug Abuse, put it best when he summarized this position of addiction as a "hijacking" of the brain. He defines addiction as a "brain disease that manifests as compulsive behavior" (Leshner, 2001).

An intriguing perspective on the brain and addictions is provided by another classic, H. Huebner's *Eating Disorders, Endorphins, and Other Addictive Behaviors*. He documents the similarities of the various addictions including compulsive overeating. But he extends the argument from a neuroscience point of view to include deprivation. He sees the architecture of addictions as sharing common features with various forms of compulsive avoidance such as anorexia nervosa or sexual aversion. This is an important observation echoed by others including Carnes. Patients experience excessive behavior at both ends of the spectrum, but with the same endorphin reward (or dopamine). This chapter argues that deprivations are also part of the "dance" of addiction interaction.

One of the most powerful arguments for understanding addiction as a large co-hesive whole is made by Mihaly Csikszentmihalyi in his book *Flow: The Psychology of Optimal Experience* (1990). Yet, its conclusions have been largely ignored by addiction professionals. *Flow* is based on over 180 studies from all over the world about the composition of optimal experience. Basically, he presents the anatomy of when people are at their very best describing that state as "flow." What is often overlooked is the phantom optimum, addiction, which has the same structure as optimum performance. Csikszentmihalyi argues powerfully that addiction is a problem of attention and consciousness. The perversion of flow can happen with any activity that requires focus. He writes, "Almost any activity can become addictive in the sense that instead of being a conscious choice, it becomes a necessity that interferes with other activities . . . (we become) captive of a certain kind of order" (p. 62). Thus, he echoes Milkman and Sunderwirth and other above-mentioned authors who speak of violence, crime, and other high-risk activities becoming compulsive behaviors.

One way to validate the science of this paradigm is to note the vast numbers of clinical studies that have documented the coexistence of excessive behaviors. Box 2.1 contains quotes from a selection of studies that have underlined the connections between coexisting disorders. The intent is not to be exhaustive since the sheer amount of evidence extends far beyond the purposes of this chapter. We need to conceptualize these disorders in a way that fits the realities of our patients—and is consistent with our literature if we look for the patterns.

Discussions of etiology support that addictions occur in constellations. From a genetics perspective, there are those who have argued that DNA configurations are similar for those with eating disorders, alcoholism, drug addiction, and other compulsive behaviors (Nestler, 2001). Trauma specialists have emphasized the role of Post Traumatic Stress Disorder in the genesis of addictive disorders. Bessel van der Kolk's recent arguments for "complex" PTSD, is virtually foundational for looking at excessive behaviors as part of traumatic reactivity and alteration in the brain (van der Kolk, 2001). Family therapists have noted that addictions become systemic in the family. For example, mother's obesity interacts with father's substance abuse and compulsive infidelity. Even in examining the role of the Internet in addictive behaviors, note clinicians' language about the computer as a catalyst. Examples would be referring to machine video poker as the crack cocaine of gambling (Panasitti & Schull, 1992) and describing Internet sex as the crack cocaine of sexual compulsivity (Cooper, Putnam, Planchon, & Boies, 1999). Even from the perspective of how addictions come to be, clinicians note common causes and even use common language.

The proliferation of patients attending more than one type of recovery group or groups that address the needs of those with multiple addictions treatment also support the concept of multiple addictions. Twelve-Step fellowships serve people who have problems with every excessive behavior. The viability of the principles of Alcoholics Anonymous has manifested in such diverse groups as Sex Addicts Anonymous, Overeaters Anonymous, Gamblers Anonymous, and Debtors Anonymous. Perhaps one of the best examples of the evolution of understanding of multiple addictions from a patient perspective is the advent and success of Recovering Couples Anonymous. This fellowship welcomes addicts of all types because the commonalities of couples dynamics is common to all forms of addictive behavior. In fact, Carnes found that one of the key factors in a successful outcome was

---

BOX 2.1
Examples of Addiction Co-Morbidity

"For the contemporary drug addict, multiple drug use and addiction that includes alcohol, is the rule. The monodrug user and addict is a vanishing species in American culture" (Miller, Belkin, & Gold, 1990, p. 597).

"As many as 84% of cocaine addicts, 37% of cannabis addicts, 75% of amphetamine addicts, and 50% of opiate addicts were also alcoholic. Other studies have shown that 80% to 90% of cocaine addicts, 50% to 75% of opiate addicts, and 50% of benzodiazepine/sedative-hypnotic addicts were alcoholics" (Miller & Gold, 1995, p. 122).

". . . clinical studies suggest a high comorbidity between eating and alcohol use disorders . . ." (Stewart, Angelopoulos, Baker, & Boland, 2000, p. 77).

". . . Lesieur and Blume (1993) noted that 47% to 52% of pathological gamblers also exhibit symptoms of abuse or dependency for alcohol or other drugs" (Winters, Bengston, Dorr, & Stinchfield, 1998, p. 186).

"The alcoholic under the age of 30 is addicted to at least one other drug—most commonly cannabis, followed . . . by cocaine, and then benzodiazepines" (Miller & Gold, 1995, p. 122).

"Therapists working with individuals abusing alcohol, tobacco, and other drugs should be aware of the comorbidity of gambling in this population" (Sweeting & Weinberg, 2000, p. 46).

"Similarly, in female alcoholics, comorbid eating disorder rates far exceed prevalence estimates for eating disorders in the general female population" (Stewart, Angelopoulos, Baker, & Boland, 2000, p. 77).

"The results of our co-twin control analyses indicated that early initiation of cannabis use was associated with significantly increased risks for other drug use and abuse/dependence and were consistent with early cannabis use having a causal role as a risk factor for other drug use and for any drug use or dependence" (Lynsky et al., 2003).

"In conclusion, identification of multiple drug addiction is critical in the diagnosis and treatment of today's alcoholics and drug addicts. Unless contemporary treatment methods are adapted to fit changing patient characteristics, attempts at rehabilitation may be futile" (Miller & Gold, 1990, p. 596).

---

attendance in a couples 12-Step format. Similarly, in every clinical genre of excessive behavior, there exist articles on the importance of cognitive behavioral intervention, trauma treatment, and family system intervention.

Howard Shaffer describes the addiction field as experiencing the classic stages of an emerging field of science (Shaffer, 1997). There is, almost always, a stage of conceptual confusion and "blurring" of issues. What is clearly emerging is an understanding of excessive behavior as addictive disorders that share similar features, causes, and even cures. As part of that clarification, we are proposing a model that integrates the addictions and propose that the addictions have metapatterns that are important and discernable clinically. We call this *addiction interaction disorder.* What this means is that the addictions do more than coexist. They, in fact, interact, reinforce, and become part of one another. They in effect become packages. These packages can be unbundled and each addiction approached separately, which is the current level of practice. Yet equally important is that they can be approached as a whole. The criteria we propose as examples of addiction interaction are discussed next.

ADDICTION INTERACTION DIMENSIONS

We identified 11 dimensions in which addictions impacted or in some way related to one another. These dimensions include:

1. *Cross tolerance* in which there is a simultaneous increase in addictive behavior in two or more addictions or in which there is a transfer of a high level of addictive activity to a new addiction with little or no developmental sequence. Sometimes this transfer can be gradual then mutually exclusive.
2. *Withdrawal mediation* in which one addiction serves to moderate, provide relieve from, or avoid physical withdrawal from another.
3. *Replacement* in which one addiction replaces another with a majority of the emotional and behavioral features of the first.
4. *Alternating addiction cycles* in which addictions cycle back and forth in a patterned systemic way.
5. *Masking* in which an addict uses one addiction to cover up for another, perhaps more substantive addiction.
6. *Ritualizing* in which addictive rituals or behavior of one addiction serves as a ritual pattern to engage another addiction or addictive behavior.
7. *Intensification* in which one addiction is used to accelerate, augment, or refine the other addiction through simultaneous use.
8. *Numbing* in which an addiction is used to medicate (soothe) shame or pain caused by other addiction or addictive bingeing.
9. *Disinhibiting* in which one addiction is used frequently to chronically lower inhibitions for other forms of addictive acting out.
10. *Combining* in which addictive behaviors are used to achieve certain effects that can only be achieved in combination.
11. *Inhibiting* in which one addiction is used to substitute or deter the use of another addiction that is thought to be more destructive or socially unacceptable.

The idea that addictions affect one another is not new. Nineteenth-century medical texts, for example, would refer to such interaction using the global term of *intemperance.* The underlying concept was that the use of alcohol and tobacco would lead to excessive eating, sexual behavior, and other misdeeds. If a person was intemperate in one area, they would be intemperate in others creating "false appetites" (Overton, 1987). Another phrase frequently used was *morbid appetites,* which were codified as suffering from some sort of "mania" such as nymphomania, dipsomania, narcotomania, kleptomania, or pyromania. The German translation of mania extends this concept to words like *Geltungssucht* (power or status mania) and *Arbeitssucht* (work mania). These "diseases of the will" coexisted and would lead to one another.

Yet the insight that chronic, excessive, or problematic use of behavior affects other chronic, excessive, or problematic behaviors is commonplace in contemporary clinical literature. We use a term like *co-morbid* to indicate coexistence. Other terms are also used including *multiple addictions* (Carnes, 2001; Miller & Gold, 1995), *coexisting addictions* (Wines, 1997), *coexisting pathologies* (Amico, 1997), *dual addictions* (Griffin-Shelley, Sandler, & Lees, 1992), *cross addiction* (Johnson, 1999), *multiple misdrug use* (Campbell, 1996), *multiple substances* and *polysubstance dependence* (*DSM-IV-TR*, 2000). The fact of coexistence causing issues is neither new nor currently unnoticed.

The implications, however, are significant. First of all, such a model assumes that addictions have many forms. There are those that argue that addictions can evolve in the form of gambling, food, sex, work, and certain financial behaviors as well as the traditional categories of alcohol and drugs. Such conceptualization also argues that addictions tap into similar processes and etiologies. The logical next step is that these addictive processes weave together in some patterned ways that would be recognizable. If that were true, the implications would be more than significant.

First, the argument is made that a major factor in relapse in addictive disorders is failure to recognize and treat companion addictions that were part of the addictive process. Consider the patient who almost always uses drugs while gambling. By insisting on a chemical or gambling focus alone, we recreate the problem we used to have by insisting that alcohol and drug dependence had to be addressed separately. The patient realities were that they used them concurrently. It would be more functional to treat the issues together. The result could be that treatment of one could lead to escalation in another to make up the deficit of stopping the treated addiction. The use of the untreated addiction could cause relapse in the treated addiction. In chemical dependency centers, patients are often told that if they stop drinking and using drugs their other problems will straighten out. More likely the scenario will be that when they gamble (the untreated addiction), they will return to drugs (the treated addiction). Another consideration is that as part of relapse prevention, clinicians could prepare patients for the possibility that they would replace one addiction for another.

Perhaps one of the classic examples of all of these dynamics is the story of Bill W., the cofounder of Alcoholics Anonymous, whose compulsive sexual behavior escalated dramatically after he achieved alcohol sobriety. His behavior was a significant issue in the governance of AA in its early days. A portion of the royalties on books he wrote for AA still go to the heirs of his last mistress. Professionals knowledgeable about financial disorders also notice chronic money problems throughout his life. Bill W. had numerous opportunities to make great sums of money but sabotaged each of them. He and his wife Lois, in fact, moved 54 times in their marriage. His story is straight out of Debtors Anonymous.

Knowing about his sexual and financial issues helps to explain his depression in the early 1950s. In part, his dark days stand in stark contrast to the "promises" about which he so beautifully wrote and that have inspired so many. While a giant in the field of recovery, he did not have the benefit of insights we now understand about the course of multiple addictions. By focusing on only one issue, the addiction process can reemerge and still define a person's life (Hartigan, 2000; Robertson, 1988).

If treatment planners look at multiple addictions simultaneously, they could dramatically impact the technologies used in treatment itself. To make that concept concrete, consider a first step done on cocaine alone when compulsive sex was always present. Many addiction therapists fail to ask how patients acquired their cocaine. Routine inquiry quickly reveals that sex is for many patients the key variable in cocaine acquisition. Thus a first step on cocaine alone would mean that there was a sense of reality about one issue while the distortions of the other remain unchallenged (Washton, 1989). Relapse probability is high under those circumstances. Further, and perhaps more importantly, if they are of the same family of illnesses, they have common etiologies. Responsible treatment would mean that treatment providers must address the underlying issues. In other words, staying sober would not be enough to sustain recovery. The patient must be able to address the common factors driving both the cocaine and the sexual excess. Without changing the programming, you will get the same result—relapse.

If true, logic would also require reorganization of our diagnostic codes. Gambling, sexual issues, eating, and chemicals would virtually require their own axis to be systematic. Further, we would need some "meta" model to integrate the addictions in terms of their impact on each other. This model would have to have verifiable criteria with an empirical base so prevalence could be established. Hopefully it would be simple to use, reflect the realities of patients' lives, and be comprehensible to the patients. To consider such an "umbrella" concept is mind boggling. Just considering the professional issues for such a convergence alone is overwhelming. It is the classic issue of a paradigm shift in which a new paradigm proves more adequate than conventional models. Seldom does that happen without controversy.

In family therapy, the problem of overarching concepts was confronted early because of the challenge of multiple mental health issues existing in one family. This challenged pioneer therapist Minuchin to observe:

> Therapists, like other human beings are a product of their society. They are . . . members of a guild who are trained by the same method, read the same books, and transmit similar ideas . . . the idea that the patient contains her own pathology retains its grip on modern therapists who defend their interventions eloquently. In the field of helping people, beliefs speak with a clearer, sharper voice than results. (Minuchin, Rosman, & Baker, 1978, p. 76)

Could it be that multiple internal issues relating to one another within a person also escape the notice of our diagnostic categories? In the field of scientific inquiry, Gregory Bateson, one of the grandfathers of systemic thinking, commented on the importance of looking for "metapatterns":

> The pattern which connects is a "metapattern," a pattern of patterns. More often than not, we fail to see it. With the exception of music, we have been trained to think of patterns as fixed affairs. It's easier and lazier that way, but, of course, all nonsense. The truth is that the right way to begin to think about the pattern which connects is to think of it as a dance of interacting parts, secondarily pegged down by various sorts of physical limits and by the limits which organisms impose by habit, and by the naming states and component entities. (Bateson, 1978, p. 47)

In addressing this issue, we need to remember that addiction is a field in which we debated for decades about treating alcohol and drug dependence together. When we fold in eating disorders, sexual disorders, pathological gambling, and other forms of compulsion and addiction, we escalate professional divergences dramatically. Yet we need to remember Bateson's dance and ask, "What are the realities of our patients?" Said in another way, do we continue to look at this from the perspective of our clinical training or from the perspective of the patient who has the problem? We approach the problem by using what patients say about themselves and integrating that perspective with emerging science. A closer look at each of the dimensions of addiction interaction follows.

CROSS TOLERANCE

Cross tolerance occurs in three ways. First, we notice cross tolerance when there is a simultaneous increase in addictive behavior in two or more addictions. This would indicate a connection between them wherein the activity level in both addictions increases. For example, consider the patient in which drinking and machine poker (gambling) get worse at the same time. It is the parallel leap in activity that should catch the clinician's attention.

For another patient who struggled with compulsive working (workaholism) and sex addiction, 110-hour weeks were not uncommon. Having affairs with people he worked with was also not uncommon. The sexual complications at work included employees, vendors, and a key board member who was also an investor. He told his spouse that he had to keep up the pace because they would be ruined if he stopped and if he was successful they would never have to worry about money. However, these short-term situations stretched out to years. He clearly recognized that both the amount of sexual activity and the risks he took escalated. Similarly, the amount of his work continued to grow as did the business risks.

In treatment, he made a drawing that creates a metaphor for how his addictions were escalating in similar ways. There are two pillars (representing his two addictions). They are like barriers within which reality had no sway. Reality is clearly outside of these "goal posts" to indicate how risk-taking was part of the problem. To further emphasize the point, he used the metaphor of dropping a feather (his workaholism) and a rock (his sexually compulsive behavior). He notes at the bottom that the two "fall at the same rate in a vacuum" which shows how cross tolerance affected him. To further emphasize his understanding of the concept, the rock and feather were headed for a black pile labeled "death" to underline the gravity of his addictive behaviors.

The other way to know that cross tolerance is present is when there is a sudden shift in addictive practice. A good clinical illustration of this situation is the story of a 38-year-old anesthesiologist who began treatment for cocaine addiction. In completing his history, we found that he had a long history of sexual acting out in a wide variety of circumstances. He was taking risks to the point that he had breached sexual boundaries with patients. Then he discovered cocaine. He ceased all sexual behavior immediately and within two weeks was using cocaine daily. Moreover, he was using cocaine at a level that usually takes years for a cocaine addict to tolerate. Clearly, the principle is that an addict can swap addictions including a level of tolerance for the new activity that was impacted by the previous one. To make an analogy, it would be like switching majors in college with the majority of the credits transferring.

Another clinical example involves work and sex. Our patient reported running a car wash business in which he was very successful. He worked very long hours and was hardly ever available for his family. He eventually sold his company for a great deal of money. Within days, he was spending almost the same amount of time in strip shows and gentlemen's clubs. During treatment, it became very clear to him that he swapped one fairly well-developed addiction for another. Usually sex addicts report that the development of their addiction has episodic use until it becomes continuous and escalating. This patient reported immediate continuous use that was escalating. He drew a picture of working in the car wash and then a calendar to represent how brief the transition was to sex becoming a problematic part of his life.

A third pattern we recognize is when there is a transition in which one addiction blends into another. Eventually the first addiction subsides and the second one is in full force. There is no cessation of addiction use, but more of a phase in/phase out process that occurs. A frequent example that occurs clinically is sexual behavior being replaced by amphetamine use. There is no abrupt switch, but rather continuous shading. Nor is there any break in usage of either addiction. Clearly, the goal is to maintain an altered state at a certain level even though a transition is taking place.

Withdrawal Mediation

Withdrawal mediation occurs when one addiction serves to moderate, relieve, or avoid physical withdrawal from another addiction. A classic example would be nicotine use at an Alcoholics Anonymous meeting. Twelve-Step meetings are known for strong coffee, cigarettes, and sweets. But the "smoke-filled room" is the greatest irony. Cigarettes cause more physical problems than alcohol does. Yet people in recovery use cigarettes to alter mood as they would alcohol. And it has significant consequences. This brings up the issue of "giving up too many addictions at once," which is debated in professional as well as recovery circles. The reality remains that nicotine use "cushions" the pain of early recovery by reducing anxiety. Many treatment facilities have gone smoke-free precisely because of this issue.

Addicts will often string together a number of addictive behaviors in a sequential pattern. Consider a patient who uses cigarettes and chewing tobacco to start his ritualized addictive process. He goes online and binges on pornography. He smokes and chews while surfing sexual sites. He will go on doing this for 10 to 12 hours. At the conclusion of the sexual binge, he feels terrible about what he has been doing, the risks he took, and the time he wasted. He vows never to do it again. Then he binges on pizza and other food for days. The food becomes soothing to him after his sexual behavior. Thus, the withdrawal mediation can be episodic as well as continuous as in the AA example.

Replacement

Replacement occurs when one addiction replaces another with the majority of emotional and compulsive features. As we noted with the story of Bill W., one addiction can emerge after another has been addressed. For this reason, addiction professionals may do harm when they tell their substance abuse patients that everything gets better if people stop using drugs and drinking alcohol. Patients need to understand that other addictions may emerge with time if they are not aware of the potential problem. Unlike cross tolerance, or withdrawal mediation, this is when a period of time has elapsed (at least six months to a year is common) between the cessation of an addictive behavior and onset of new behavior.

> A stockbroker named Lennie came from a wealthy family that hit hard times when Lennie was 13. He responded to the family financial crisis by going out and getting jobs. By age 15, he had three jobs in addition to school. Even more remarkable was that he managed to get a small bank loan on a business he had started. After college, he became a stockbroker and married into a very wealthy family. He became the manager of his wife's trusts. He found his work on the trading floor to be extremely stressful. By his mid-twenties, he was using marijuana daily as a way to cope with the intensity of the brokerage business. His wife expressed concerns that he dismissed because the business demanded that he perform well and marijuana did that for him.
>
> When he was 31, his wife Phyllis went to get some money from one of her accounts without mentioning it to Lennie. She was horrified to discover that she could access no funds. All of her funds were leveraged on margin purchases of speculative stocks. She was furious and convened an intervention on his marijuana use. In her mind, it was pot that caused such a serious breach in Lennie's judgment. Lennie went to treatment for substance abuse and Phyllis attended family week. During family week, they were assured that if the marijuana use stopped all the other problems would go away.
>
> Lennie refrained from using marijuana and after a few months Phyllis returned her accounts to him for management. Lennie started to leverage the accounts again even though he was drug free. About 6 months after treatment, he was in a significant cash flow bind. In a desperate gesture, he placed some bets and won. This windfall not only saved the day financially, but encouraged him to bet further. He won again, which confirmed to him that he had a "system." Now he was regularly betting using his wife's funds. In pathological gambling, it is the early wins that hook the addict.
>
> At the end of his first year of recovery, Lennie still had not used marijuana. His wife considered his treatment a success. Yet Lennie was in bad shape. His betting and use of margin accounts was creating extraordinary stress. His main fear was that his wife would find out about his leveraging her funds again. A colleague suggested he might go to a "massage parlor" nestled in one of the office buildings in this exclusive financial district. He found that sex relaxed him in the way marijuana did. His visits to prostitutes became daily and sometimes twice a day. The costs of his sexual behavior added to the cash flow problems. His wife finally discovered a business card from an escort service and his house of cards came down.

Notice the following: First, the treatment staff never identified compulsive debting as a problem nor had they seen the use of the margin accounts as a form of gambling behavior. Essentially, this set of problems waited and actually blossomed into clear pathological gambling. The sex addiction problem emerged almost a full year after treatment. When Phyllis came to treatment for family week the next time, she was an angry woman. She distrusted professionals because the ones she saw the first time told her their problems were over if Lennie stopped using marijuana. By that standard, Lennie was still sober. From our perspective, not all the problems were addressed and Lennie had found new, destructive ways to replace his old strategies to combat stress.

ALTERNATING ADDICTION CYCLES

Addicts notice that their addictions have patterns in which the addiction focus shifts. The addiction cycles weave back and forth in a patterned systemic way. Catherine was a classic example.

> Catherine was physically and sexually abused as a child. Her mother was a prostitute with a compulsive gambling problem (very common in the sex industry). In high school, she was promiscuous and anorexic with food. As an adult, her sexual behavior was out of control and she maintained her self-starvation in order to be attractive. Her "cure" was to get married. Like many abuse victims, she could be sexual even with anonymous people, but if someone really mattered she became sexually aversive or *sexually anorexic*. While married, she was compulsively nonsexual but she started to compulsively overeat and gained over a hundred pounds. She admitted that the weight was a defense against sexual overtures.
>
> She divorced, lost the weight, and went back into food starvation. Anonymous sex and sex with high-risk men became the order of the day. She got married again and repeated the pattern of sexual aversion and compulsive overeating. She married four times and each time put on a hundred pounds. The sexual extremes and the food extremes became literally interchangeable modules depending on whether she was married or not. In two separate drawings, she presented the two patterns of her life: thin and sexually out of control, and obese and sexually aversive.

Catherine's pattern is quite common in our experience and raises a significant theoretical issue. If eating extremes and sexual extremes become interchangeable, it suggests common etiology as well as interaction. Also notice that deprivation and addiction are both part of the exchanges. This would support Huebner's proposition that deprivation and addiction share similar psychological "architecture" to be able to serve similar functions. Clearly the two illnesses are interactive.

> Betty also noticed a set of rhythms. She would have a period of serious sexual bingeing with many partners. Then she would have a very intense, dramatic relationship that would break up. This would be followed by serious alcohol and drug use that would last quite some time. Then there would be another period of sexual bingeing followed by another all-consuming relationship followed by an extended time of drug and alcohol abuse characterized by its isolation and despair. In the time line she presented in treatment, she realized that she had repeated the same cycle 11 times. Further, she recognized that each phase of the cycle was getting longer. The numbers of partners and the risks she took in the sexual phase was growing. The "love" relationship progressively was more violent. The drugs became more dangerous including heroin in the later cycles. There emerged a predictable pattern and a progressively deteriorating situation.

Obviously these different periods of compulsive behavior have some relationship with one another. Predictable sequencing implies an order to the behaviors. The progressive nature of each becoming longer and more risky suggests that each phase is worsening in some collective metapattern of progression. Both Catherine and Betty had prior treatment experience. Both made significant progress when they could see the larger patterns of the weave of their sexual behaviors.

MASKING

Often in treatment we hear the phrase "I did it because I was drinking." What are clearly problematic behavior patterns are dismissed by the patient as the result of being under the influence (of alcohol). For example, it is less shameful to be an alcoholic than a sex addict. Yet, under closer scrutiny it becomes clear that while the patient is under the influence, that patient's sexual behavior becomes compulsive. The patient saw it as totally an alcohol problem. Yet, this type of patient will admit with time that they are always sexual in unwanted ways when they drink. In these cases, we often find that when sober they would be sexually aversive.

These situations also fit other addiction interaction criteria. They fit the alternating cycles patterns as well as what we will come to call *fusion.* Fusion occurs when the addictions are always present together. Masking occurs in these situations because the patient perceives the problem as the less shameful addiction. In fact using one addiction to cover up for another, perhaps more destructive addiction is a clinical sign that the addictions are tied together. Most patients, when they understand that masking was an essential part of their denial system, go on to discover how many ways the behaviors related.

RITUALIZING

Rituals have long been recognized as part of addictive behavior. Rituals are used to induce trance and to prep for special experiences. When part of addictions, they are usually part of a sequence leading to significantly altered mood. The drug addict has very specific preparations as part of getting high. The gambler has formulaic rituals as part of insuring the windfall. The sex addict uses extensive rituals to enhance sexual pleasure. Food preparation rituals are frequently part of compulsive overeating. Interaction among addictions occurs when the rituals for one addiction are the same rituals or significantly overlap for another. Many counselors miss significant data when they fail to ask how their patients acquired cocaine, which is often sexually. They may buy it from their prostitutes or use cocaine as part of highly ritualized behavior such as extended periods of masturbation.

One of the classic examples of the merging of rituals occurs in the movie *Looking for Mr. Goodbar.* It is the story of a young woman who is a sex addict, drug addict, and alcoholic. In the movie, she dies ultimately from her drug use. Yet the story line is about her unremitting search for sexual conquest. She has the typical elaborate dressing and cruising rituals that precede picking up men in bars. In one scene, she asks the bartender to join her in a drink. He refuses telling her that he never takes the first drink because after having one he cannot say no. As he walks away, she mutters to herself, "I know, I have the same problem with men."

The movie illustrates how her rituals of preparation to find men involve going to bars, drinking, and using drugs. They are in fact the same behaviors. The rituals then link the various compulsive behaviors before they start or one behavior enhances or is ritualistic to the other behavior. One of our patients was compulsive sexually on the Internet and gambled pathologically on the Internet as well. He had elaborate rituals around bringing his computer online. The rituals of starting his machine and accessing his modem would initiate both sexual fantasies and windfall fantasies. Part of his recovery was to recognize that he could not access a computer without getting into trouble.

INTENSIFICATION

Addictions intensify each other. In its most complete form, addiction makes fully potent other addictive behavior. We call this *total fusion*. Neither addiction separately is sufficient: Only simultaneous use is sufficient. Think of the cocaine addict who has certain compulsive sexual behaviors and only acts out on cocaine. He does not act out sexually separate from the cocaine nor will he do cocaine without the sexual behavior. The addictions have become fused or inseparable. We have patients who hyperventilate tobacco smoke and compulsively masturbate. These patients find confined spaces to concentrate smoke such as a closet or bathroom and masturbate while hyperventilating the smoke. They describe unique highs that result ultimately in never smoking without masturbation or masturbating without smoking in the confined area. The two addictions are joined neurochemically, and only reproducible in this fashion.

Some patients exhibit *partial fusion:* Addicts combine addictions in such a fashion to be more potent than each addiction separately. Some of the behavior is independent part of the time. In the sex addiction field, one of the better known examples is compulsive prostitution. Over two-thirds of men who use prostitutes compulsively have significant financial disorders as well, such as compulsive debting or spending. The eroticization of money becomes so complete that they can tell you the dollar amount of credit or cash that becomes sexualized. Diligent therapists are very thorough about following the money trail to disrupt the compulsive behavior. Most often we find that spending/debting problems extend to other parts of the addict's life as well. In other words, the addictions are not exact overlays of one another. They act out the addictions together, but also separately.

Many patients describe *multiple binge behavior.* The alcoholic, sexually addicted, compulsive gambler goes to the topless casino for one-stop shopping. Often addicts will binge in additive fashion to enhance mood alteration. Yet, they will pursue the behaviors independently. Many patients who fit the criteria of fusion dependence report that they started with multiple binges. They progressed then to partial fusion, and then full fusion. Figure 2.1 creates a graphic representation of the phases of addictive fusion.

Another way of understanding intensification from a fusion perspective is referred to as *inclusion.* In this situation, there is one addiction that subsumes all the rest. Thus a sex addict may also be addicted to marijuana, cocaine, alcohol, gambling, and caffeine. Sex if not totally fused is partially fused with the others. Figure 2.2 shows how such a constellation of mutual intensification might look in a patient.

NUMBING

In trauma literature, van der Kolk and others talk about how trauma survivors will engage in addictive behaviors that are highly stimulating followed by a collection of behaviors that are calming or soothing (van der Kolk, 1988). High arousal is followed by numbing. One of the trademarks of posttraumatic stress disorder is seeking high-risk repetitions of earlier victimization. Then numbing behavior is designed to calm the system down as a way to help regulate affect. An example would be spending the evening in the streets doing risky, dangerous sexual behavior then coming home and using alcohol, compulsive masturbation, and compulsive

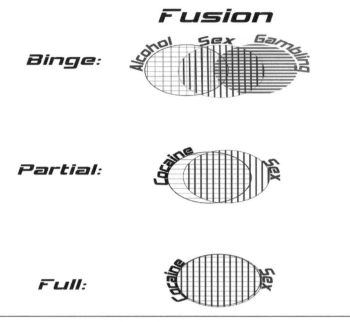

Figure 2.1   Fusion

eating to soothe. We have had patients include in the soothing such mundane things as television and such self-destructive behaviors as cutting (self-harm) to bring a sense of calm. Clinically, what most stands out is how compulsive behavior is used to soothe or "numb" out. These behaviors are then inextricably tied to the original arousal behaviors.

Figure 2.2   Inclusion

DISINHIBITING

Another form of interaction that is clinically obvious is use of one addiction to lower inhibitions for another addiction. One patient summarized it in this way, "I would think of what I wanted to do sexually, but I would have to get drunk to do it." Historically, we may have diagnosed such a patient as an alcoholic. Yet clearly, his starting point and end goal is sexual. His drinking then enables the other compulsive behavior. We have two addictions tied together in a fundamental way. Neither behavior is necessary without the other.

COMBINING

All addiction professionals are familiar with the practice of combining uppers and downers. Yet many addicts take the practice of mixing addictive behaviors far beyond tailoring drug interactions. Usually the goal is to preserve a specific high by prolonging the feeling in whatever ways possible. An analogy would be like surfing an ocean wave. The idea is to get on the edge of the wave and then make adjustments to stay there until it crashes. The addict will create a wave and try to stay on it for weeks until the body gives out. Then the addict will rest, recover, and gather strength for another run.

This phenomenon is common enough to appear in popular literature. Novelist John Sanford writes of the adventures of Lucas Davenport, detective and police chief. Consistently in his stories, there is an antagonist who is pharmacologically savvy. He is a physician, a pharmacist, or a scientist who understands drugs and their impact on the brain. Usually this character is up to no good with high-risk, illegal, often sexual activities. Sanford manages to capture in his characters this "riding the wave" phenomenon where sex, high-risk activities, and various drugs are used to stay on the edge of the wave. Patients who combine to prolong or adjust highs are literally surfing on the interactions of their addictions.

INHIBITING

One addiction is used to substitute or defer the use of another that is thought to be more destructive or socially unacceptable. Some examples would be:

- Cocaine addict who uses marijuana so he will not use cocaine.
- Woman who used alcohol to restrict her compulsive overeating.
- Sex addict who used heroin to avoid anonymous sex.
- Compulsive overeater who used nicotine to limit food intake and caffeine use.
- Compulsive gambler who would gamble on the Internet to avoid high-risk (child pornography) Internet sex.

ADDICTION AND DEPRIVATION: MIRRORS OF INTERACTION

To fully comprehend comorbidity and addiction interaction, another meta-level must be explored. So far we have shown how there are patterns of excessive behavior that interweave and reinforce one another. For a picture that truly reflects the world of our clients, we must also note how deprivations interact with each other and with the excessive behavior patterns we call addictions. Deprivations are more than simply avoidance. They are driven by preoccupation and obsession. They have serious life consequences. They are the mirrors of excessive behavior, often being the reciprocals of addictions. Wherever you have addictions, you have the shadow of the deprivations. Wherever you have compulsive deprivation as the problem, addiction most often is compensating somewhere.

In each of the addictive illnesses discussed in this book, there is some corresponding deprivation. Eating disorders are the most obvious. Some people take care of their anxiety by overeating compulsively. Others react to their fear by self-starvation or food anorexia. Some do both. They binge with food and then they purge. We call this bulimia. Bulimics will eat a meal and then be repulsed by what they have done. They will induce vomiting, use diuretics, or go without food for the rest of the day. Sometimes, the obese overeater will go into dieting mode and be anorexic for a period of years. The pattern is still one of binge and purge only measured in a longer period of time. Another example is the person who compulsively eats but controls weight through compulsive athleticism. People with this pattern spend endless hours working out to attain a goal of 8% body fat. The problem remains the same. One extreme behavior is matched by another.

The patterns of extreme living can be seen across the addiction spectrum. In sex addiction, we have sexual compulsivity and sexual aversion (sometimes called sexual anorexia). Seventy-two percent of sex addicts report a binge-and-purge pattern in their behavior. Often there is a period of sexual acting out followed by an extended period of sexual abstinence. About a third of sex addicts also fit the criteria for being sexually aversive. This can occur, as in eating, with extended periods of being sexually anorexic or sexually acting out. Another variation on a theme is when sex addicts act out with people they do not like or even know but are compulsively nonsexual with their intimate partner. This pattern most commonly emerges in sexual abuse victims who find it too risky to be sexual and loving with the same person.

In finance and work, we also see people living in the extremes. We have compulsive spenders who buy things to relieve anxiety and distress. Also there are hoarders who are obsessed with preserving what they have. Some people binge and purge in this area. Consider the woman who buys expensive clothes because she needs them as a professional woman in the workplace. When she takes the clothes home she is ravaged by doubts about her choices and feelings of unworthiness for such clothes, so she returns them. Her life becomes a series of overlapping cycles of buy and return. Consider the compulsive debtor who makes a significant income, yet incurs so much debt that he is chronically impoverished trying to make payments. Attitudes toward money also reflect excess and deprivation. In wealth obsession, a person becomes fixated with the accumulation of money. Reflect on the physician who checks his Schwab accounts between every patient. There are people of means or of poverty who refuse to take responsibility for their check book. They avoid anything to do with money.

To call those who spend endless hours working, workaholics, misses the point. For some, work is living on the edge, taking great risks for great gains; yet everything else is neglected. Some people cannot bring themselves to work. Procrastination and work avoidance becomes compulsive out of fear of success. For others, work is mind numbing and avoidant. Debtors Anonymous first introduced the common phenomenon of compulsive underearning. An example would be the woman with two PhDs selling perfume at Macy's. Another form of underearning is sabotaging work success of which Bill W., the cofounder of AA, was a master. He and his wife Lois moved 54 times in their lives due to financial chaos. He had completed law school and passed the bar exam but refused to go through the graduation ceremony, so he was never able to practice law. He invented corporate profiling thereby creating three different opportunities to make a fortune. He sabotaged all three. It was not until he worked with an organization in which he pledged never to receive a salary that his genius was allowed to show.

Thus, a model emerges of excess and deprivation about work and money. Bill W. lived on the anorexic side of work and money and on the compulsive side of sex and alcohol. In the complex mosaic of multiple addictions and deprivations, the interactions are exponential. To see those connections, we must first focus on the anatomy of the deprivations and what they have in common.

DEPRIVATIONS

Deprivation is an abhorrence of a need as a way to defend against anxiety and/or terror. Like addictions, deprivations are often triggered by trauma, in which case having a need is dangerous. If a child is sexually abused and terrified, they may become sexually aversive. In two studies of Catholic orders of women, over 80% of those women were sexually assaulted as children. Thus, the choice of a lifestyle of celibacy may be more about safety than a spiritual calling. In some families, needs are problematic, so the growing child learns how to pretend not to have needs. Usually ignoring fundamental needs is accompanied by some self-deprecation or self-abuse. Being needless in a certain area is reflective of core beliefs of unworthiness or self-punishment.

A compulsive deprivation is often accompanied by secondary gain or compensating entitlement. Consider the physician who works over a hundred hours a week sacrificing everything to help others and then feels very sexually entitled. Parallel that concept with attorneys or clergy. Reflect on the number of clergy who have preached against promiscuity but who have problems themselves. In their public life they are purging, and in private they are bingeing.

These extremes can even be seen as part of cultural and social dynamics. The following examples illustrate this point:

- A clinical report that suggests the reason for an unusually high frequency of sexual aversion in black women is because of the unacknowledged sexual atrocities of slavery. Hearing the stories while the dominant culture refuses to talk about what happened has a dramatic impact.
- An entire cult commits suicide to enable the members to move to the next level. We discover that all the male members were castrated. Further, we learn that the cult leader had been arrested 15 years earlier as a sex offender.
- A report in the *Journal of the American Medical Association* describes posttraumatic stress disorder in third-generation descendents of holocaust survivors. One of the clear signs of PTSD is traumatic abstinence or compulsively going without.
- In Bell's classic *Holy Anorexia,* he describes the impact of the Black Plague in medieval Europe. After each round of illness, people would go into extreme

ascetic pilgrimages with little food, no sex, and whipping (self-flagellation). He notes that today if a patient is not eating, sexually aversive, and cutting him or herself, we would hospitalize him (Bell, 1985).

Similar rhythms are seen in families. A longitudinal study of families in which both parents were alcoholic revealed that their offspring were not only teetotalers but they tended to marry other teetotalers. They had children who grew up in the early 1970s who were alcoholics and drug addicts. In sex addiction, clinicians frequently observe that as one spouse progressively becomes more out of control sexually, the other spouse shuts down and becomes sexually aversive. In early therapy, the sex addict is asked to commit to a 12-week celibacy contract. Upon learning this, it is not uncommon for the aversive spouse to be overwhelmingly attracted. This phenomenon occurs despite being very angry after learning of all the betrayals by the addict.

Clinically, deprivation appears in many forms. Food anorexia, sexual anorexia, compulsive debting, hoarding, saving, compulsive underearning, and compulsive athleticism are examples of depletion, extraordinary denial of needs, and disciplined avoidance. The following criteria form a profile of deprivation:

- *Excessive control:* Rigid, judgmental attitudes drive extreme efforts to limit, curb, or avoid needs.
- *Compulsive behavior:* Pattern of avoidance behaviors occur over time.
- *Efforts to initiate:* Steps are taken to get out of "diet," survivor, or phobic attitudes but they fail.
- *Obsession:* Preoccupation with perceived risk or danger exaggerates concerns.
- *Loss of time:* Obsession causes loss of time and missed opportunities.
- *Affects obligations:* Extreme measures often interfere with work, relationships, and responsibilities.
- *Continuation despite consequences:* Problems because of aversion or avoidance create real and obvious problems but does not stop behavior.
- *Despair:* Hopelessness emerges over chronic nature of problems.
- *Shame:* Feelings of defectiveness because of having a need or because of struggle with deprived state.
- *Escalation:* Increasing intensity evidenced by less and less.
- *Distress:* Anxiety, restlessness, and irritability at the prospect of being forced out of the deprivation mode.
- *Losses:* Deprivation brings losses over time as opportunities fade.
- *False safety:* Ignoring needs brings feelings of safety and even superiority for not giving in to needs.
- *Anxiety reduction:* Apprehension and worries decline because avoidance allows relief and engenders altered state.

In many ways, deprivations have the same structure and features as addictive behavior, are often interactive with the addictions, and are part of the compulsive cycles. In effect, they are part of the same family of illnesses. Table 2.1 is a comparison of addiction characteristics and deprivation characteristics. Table 2.2 is a profile of sexual anorexics and sexual addicts. Note that their histories are parallel and they share common features.

One of the classic expositions of this position is Heubner's *Eating Disorders, Endorphins, and Other Addictive Behaviors* (1993). He makes the argument that in

Table 2.1
Addiction and Deprivation Characteristics

Addiction	Deprivation
Compulsive behavior.	$\rightarrow$ Compulsive behavior.
Loss of control.	Excessive control.
Efforts to stop (out of control—chaos).	Efforts to initiate (supercontrol repression).
Preoccupation obscures risk.	Obsession exaggerates risk.
Loss of time affects obligations.	Loss of time affects obligations.
Continuation despite obvious consequences. Despair. Shameless.	Continuation despite obvious consequences. Despair Shameful.
Escalation: More is better.	Escalation: Less is better.
Distress: Anxiety, restlessness, irritability.	Distress: Anxiety, restlessness, irritability.
Losses.	Losses.
False empowerment.	False safety.
Reduces anxiety.	Reduces anxiety.

effect a deprivation such as anorexia nervosa shares the same psychological architecture and internal dynamics as compulsive overeating. In part that is why a patient is capable of switching from one deprivation to the other so easily. The beliefs, histories, obsession, and even elements of the neurochemistry are shared. This also helps to understand the binge-and-purge phenomenon. Heubner further argues that deprivations and addictions in a number of categories also cross back and forth in part because they serve the same functions. The case of Catherine on page 41 illustrates this modularity.

Clinically, a patient like Catherine illustrates the almost modular characteristics of addictive and deprivation behavior. If the therapist meets her in her married state she would say, "I used to be promiscuous, but look at me. I am a blimp." The therapist might respond by focusing on her eating disorder. However, that would probably result in her losing weight, acting out sexually, and feeling too

Table 2.2
Sex Addict and Anorexic Profiles

Profile Dimension	Anorexics (%)	Addicts (%)
Meet criteria for depression	56	52
History of sexual abuse	67	50
History of physical abuse	41	43
History of emotional abuse	86	77
Other addictions/compulsions	67	71
Other addicts in family	65	59
Rigid family	60	60
Disengaged family	67	59

shameful to tell her therapist. She will drop out of therapy because her therapist missed the larger pattern and did not see the underlying issues which are core to the interactive nature of addiction and deprivation.

> Frank is another example of the extremes forming a balance. He had a severe problem with cocaine and anonymous sex. The two almost always went together. When he arrived in treatment, he was living out of the trunk of his 1988 Pontiac. He had to give up his apartment because his money was spent on sex and cocaine. He existed by going to soup lines and homeless shelters. In treatment, his therapist learned he had a trust fund of over three million dollars. Frank did not really know the amount because he had not looked at his check book in over two years.

> Martha came to treatment for posttraumatic stress disorder. She was sexually abused by her father from age five until she ran away to live in the street. She survived by prostitution and panhandling. She was married and had two children. When she came into treatment, she was diagnosed with alcoholism, sexual aversion, and bulimia. She and her husband had to take out a second mortgage to pay for treatment. During her therapy, it was revealed that she had a secret bank account with almost a million dollars in it. She started it when she was living in the street. She would deposit the money she made by prostitution rather than spending it on herself.

These cases illustrate the dynamics of deprivation and addiction. They also represent living in extremes which is a typical reaction to trauma. Another conceptual model of how these work together was proposed by Fossum and Mason whose book *Facing Shame* is one of the pioneering classics of family therapy (Fossum & Mason, 1986). They proposed a shame cycle that starts with perceived standards that are beyond normal such as a "diet." When the dieter no longer can tolerate the discipline, there is a binge that results in feeling shameful. The dieter recommits to the unrealistic standard. The bingeing is called *acting out* and the dieting is called *acting in*. Figure 2.3 is a graphic of Fossum and Mason's model of the cycle of shame. They formulated how deprivations and addictions could be used as parts of an affective kaleidoscope of binge and purge.

From the point of view of addiction interaction, it is important to summarize the logic of the modularity of addiction and deprivation. We notice the following characteristics about addictions and deprivations:

- Same characteristics.
- Similar histories.
- Usually found together.
- Predictable patterns of substitution and interchangeability.
- Interact with one another on a number of levels in a systemic fashion.

The logic of this profile would indicate the same family of illnesses. Now it is important to be able to discern the ways in which the interaction can be noted by the clinician.

ADDICTION INTERACTION IN CLINICAL PRACTICE

The obvious implications of addiction interaction as a metamodel concept start with screening and assessment. The model provides a framework for not only

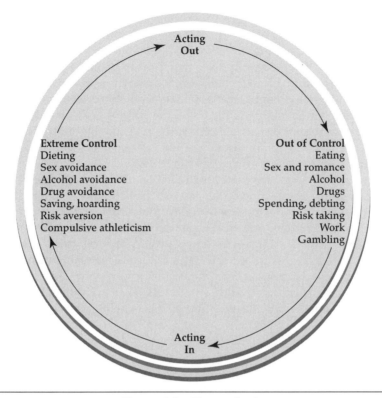

Figure 2.3 Shame Cycle

accessing all the addictions involved, but also how they affect one another and the patient's functioning. More importantly, it provides a more useful tool to understand addictions as a "package" and not coexisting pathologies to be approached individually and perhaps sequentially. One of the initial challenges is which addiction to approach first or whether you can approach them simultaneously. Our position is that they can be addressed simultaneously and sequentially.

A hierarchy exists in approaching multiple addictions. Violence is the first clinical issue. Violence toward others and violence to self must be contained. Then an assessment of all the issues involved must take place. Often the outlines of all the addictions do not appear at once. The clinician starts with the ones that are apparent with full confidence that "more will be revealed." Yet the clinician's best efforts should be to initiate a withdrawal process. Clearly, if substance abuse is present, ceasing chemical use is mandatory otherwise therapy is fruitless.

Yet if they are chemically dependent and sexually addicted at the same time, focusing only on the chemicals also becomes self-defeating. Clear boundaries around sexual behavior would be the minimum. Most treatment facilities ask for an abstinence agreement for a minimum amount of time. This contract is an opportunity to facilitate the withdrawal process from sexual acting out. Untenable situations arise within the treatment milieu if this is not done. For example, a sex addict who has no guidelines or awareness of multiple issues may focus on seducing other patients. "Cosmic relationships" can blossom in a withdrawal context. Multiple-addicted patients require a residential stay or intensive outpatient supervision to accomplish a comprehensive withdrawal process. To focus on one addiction at a time allowing other addictive behaviors to persist is self-defeating.

Once engaged in the treatment process, patients must explore each addiction in depth. If chemically dependent, there is much to learn about pharmacology, the culture of drugs, and the impact on behavior. If sexually addicted, there is much to learn about sexual development, the arousal template, and issues specific to relapse prevention. If problem gambling is the issue, the patient needs to learn about risk and the brain, the role of the windfall fantasy, and money obsession. Each area presents the challenge of information, specific strategies critical to recovery, and personal understanding of the etiology of the illness.

There must also be a way for patients to see how their compulsive behaviors fit together. Combining depth of experience with the breadth of interaction is the chief challenge of addiction treatment today. We must develop curriculum and treatment designs that allow patients to get what they need to address each addiction and also integrate them in a substantive way. We believe this to be the central factor in the limited success in our efforts to reduce recidivism rates in addiction treatment. Three examples of clinical strategies follow that could be used in a more comprehensive approach to addictive illness. They are the multiple addiction time line, the neuropathic interview, and the addiction interaction self-assessment workshop.

MULTIPLE ADDICTION TIME LINE

We ask patients to construct a time line of major events in their life. They then stratify the time line by creating a line for each addiction in which they determine the onset, worst moments, examples of powerlessness and unmanageability, and key events (for example, DUIs or arrests). This allows the patient to notice how the addictions relate to one another. Phases become quite clear when one addiction becomes prominent and then switches with another in some patterned way. Or the patient will notice periods in which all addictions were escalating simultaneously.

The time lines also allow the patient and therapist to notice what events triggered addictive behavior. Specific family issues might appear, for example. The therapist has the opportunity to notice how losses, grieving, and trauma are woven into addictive bingeing. The more comprehensive picture sets the stage for exploring the underlying issues that drive the addictive process. At this early point, the issues of long-term treatment start to emerge. Patients report this process is a relief because they understand the mechanisms of their use. They begin to see that they are not hopeless degenerates but responding to wounds that when addressed will allow them to live a very different life. The multiple-addiction time line also facilitates acceptance of the "package" their combined illness presents. While it is important to see each one, taken together there is new appreciation of the pressures of their lives.

THE NEUROPATHIC INTERVIEW

Another strategy is the neuropathic interview. Patients receive a brief lecture on addiction neuropathways of the brain. We have found the model of arousal, satiation, and fantasy developed by Milkman and Sunderwirth a useful way to talk to patients about how their brain uses different behavior to achieve different results. We also include deprivation as another strategy the brain uses to cope with stress. Of primary importance for the patient is to grasp that a full under-standing of addiction requires knowing how compulsive behavior is used to achieve various ends. Knowing the end results opens up a discussion on how to prevent relapse.

Then the counselor uses a large piece of newsprint to "interview" patients on the typical scenarios that emerge in their lives as addicts. Usually this is done in a group context so that all can benefit from one another in understanding how com-plex weaving of compulsive behaviors works. Each patient tells their typical pat-terns and the counselor then draws the sequence of events on the newsprint. As the counselor interviews the patient, care is taken to draw out whether the behavior was about arousal, efforts to relax, or to escape and the role of deprivation. As each patient presents, there is often excitement as the patients start to get their arms around this complex concept. There is literally a bandwagon effect in seeing how much they have in common.

Important realizations emerge out of the process. Patients are able to discern that their addiction is not the same all the time. Consider the male patient who de-scribed acting out in a men's room. Often it was exhilarating and he feared no consequences. But at other times, he felt very fearful but he wanted to find some-one so he could have sex in order to get to sleep. Two distinct patterns emerge with very different affective sets, although the same compulsive behavior was part of each pattern.

The other discovery has to do with how ritualized and woven together the com-pulsive behaviors are. Consider the following examples: A woman patient de-scribed a very predictable cycle in her life. She used LSD, Ecstasy, and cocaine prior to sex. She would feel bad about her sexual behavior and use marijuana to calm her-self followed by binge eating. After sleeping, she would use Ecstasy to get up in the morning so she could send her kids to school. Once patients experience the neuro-pathic interview, they are able to make the patterns explicit, label the affect and purpose of each compulsive phase, and name the triggers for the behavior.

Figure 2.4 was developed from a neuropathic interview with a thirty-seven-year-old professional man. It starts in the middle with his awareness that his trig-ger was being alone, with unstructured time, and noticing an attractive woman. He was aware that as it started his body would tremble and shake—the result of a com-bination of fear, arousal, and anticipation. He then would find hard liquor, drink, and smoke. He then would get in the car and head for the adult bookstore. On the way, he would take caffeine tablets and ibuprofen knowing from experience that loading up on these would help with the headache that would ensue. At the adult bookstore, he would buy inhalants (poppers) which heighten viewing pornogra-phy. The inhalants made him into what he termed a "lust monster." He would spend the next three to four hours masturbating and watching pornography.

The next stage was to initiate sex with others in the bookstore. To do that, he would drink more liquor. Before he would have an orgasm, he would smoke. After the orgasm, he would leave the store taking additional doses of ibuprofen. When he would get home, he would "crash" and sleep it off. It would take him days to recover. This pattern was highly ritualized with each step having to be in place to work. He was combining compulsive behaviors to create an architecture embedded in his brain's cravings. To label him an alcoholic would be beyond sim-plification. To call him a sex addict trivialized the gravity of what he put his body

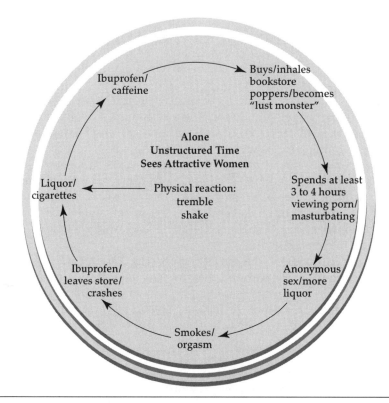

Figure 2.4 Neuropathic Interview

through. By assisting in the delineation of the pattern, therapy can trace back to how it emerged and the functions it performed for the brain.

ADDICTION INTERACTION
SELF-ASSESSMENT WORKSHOP

Our patients attend an addiction interaction workshop designed to help them assess and understand patterns in the interaction of their compulsive behaviors. We provide a standardized list of criteria of all addictions and talk about how various addictions might fit the criteria. Patients then rate each of their addictions using a standard Likert Scale and total up their ratings for each addiction. Figure 2.5 is a sample of the worksheet they use in the workshop. This phase of the experience teaches them the common characteristics of addictions. The net impact is that the patient's own self-assessment puts in perspective the power of their addictions in their lives. It is routine to hear patients make comments like "I used to think my problems were about chemicals. What I realized is that sex addiction was my most serious problem."

The second phase of the workshop continues with a lecture on addiction interaction disorder. The addiction interaction criteria described earlier in this chapter are presented followed by a discussion of each characteristic. Patients are given worksheets in which they record various ways they fit the patterns. They are asked to think through the relapse prevention implications of the patterns

Rate each criteria in each addiction separately. Use the following scale to rate each addiction:

1 = Never a problem; 2 = Occasionally a problem; 3 = Sometimes a problem; 4 = Often a problem; 5 = Consistently a problem

Criteria	Example: Two Drug Addiction	—	—	—	—	—	Row Totals
1. Loss of control	4						
2. Compulsive behavior	4						
3. Efforts to stop	2						
4. Loss of time	3						
5. Preoccupation	5						
6. Inability to fulfill obligations	2						
7. Continuation despite consequences	3						
8. Escalation	3						
9. Losses	5						
10. Withdrawal	1						
Totals							

Figure 2.5   Assessment Criteria Worksheet

they recognized. The key question, how addictions interact to make them more vulnerable to relapse, is then discussed. The patients bring this information back to their groups and into the treatment process.

The original patterns of addiction interaction evolved out of discussions with patients and clinical observation. While clinically useful, we were concerned whether patients themselves were able to identify and use the concepts. We believe that for a concept to be useful it needs to be understood by patients as relevant to their experience. We started to gather data in the form of patient worksheets. In all, 650 patients participated in the addiction interaction workshop between June of 1999 and January of 2003. In this data gathering effort, the first ten patterns were used. Through content analysis we were able to pinpoint when patients thought particular dimensions fit their addiction patterns. Table 2.3 summarizes the patient's ability to recognize the patterns in their own lives.

Only 6.5% (42 out of 650) of the participants found none of the concepts relevant. At the other extreme, 4.4% felt they could identify with all 10 criteria. Table 2.4 summarizes patient recognition by criteria. The criteria recognized the very least was alternating addiction cycles (41.5%) and the most identified was fusion (61.5%). One of the most interesting outcomes was a write-in category. A number of patients added inhibiting. They explain that they used one addiction to inhibit the use of another. This "lesser of two evils" option emerged spontaneously in 6.8% of the sample. Thus, we have added an eleventh pattern to the model of addiction interaction.

This research was conducted to see if the concepts were recognizable to patients and therefore reliable validation of the concepts. From a methods perspective, the data reflects the teaching of the workshop as well as the influence of the groups. Further content analysis is subject to error and rater evaluation. Yet, the strong results are suggestive of the viability of addiction interaction disorder as a viable concept that is useful to patients. Further validation comes from this "hypothesis seeking" approach since a new category also emerged out of patient experience.

Table 2.3
Patient Recognition of Addiction Interactions (AI)

Number of AIs/Person	Valid Percent	Frequency
0	6.5	42
1	5.8	38
2	7.1	46
3	12.0	78
4	12.2	79
5	11.4	74
6	12.5	81
7	11.2	73
8	9.7	63
9	7.2	47
10	4.4	29
Total	100.0	650

Table 2.4
Patient Recognition of Specific Addiction Interaction Dynamics

Addiction Interactions	Valid Percent	Frequency
1. Cross tolerance	60.8	395
2. Withdrawal mediation	55.8	362
3. Replacement	42.8	278
4. Alternating cycles	41.5	269
5. Masking	45.3	294
6. Ritualizing	41.5	267
7. Fusion	61.4	399
8. Numbing	53.8	350
9. Disinhibiting	41.7	271
10. Combining	46.1	299
As a mostly spontaneous write-in by patients:		
11. Inhibiting	6.8	44
Total		650

The next step is to construct a dichotomous questionnaire and interview protocol that will be tested for reliability and validity. Once developed, these assessments will be used with large samples to research prevalence in a more systematic, empirical fashion. Once established, the most important question could be answered: Do programs that use multiple addiction approaches and use addiction interaction disorder as a concept have better outcomes? We believe that would be the case.

IMPLICATIONS AND DISCUSSION

Addiction interaction disorder as a concept cuts to the core of much of the controversy about addictive disorders. If addictions interact at some primary levels they share etiology and structure. Moreover, we treat each issue separately with specialists in each area who are largely disconnected from other specialists in other areas. The result is a piecemeal approach with often scattered results. We vastly underestimate what we are up against and keep searching for the silver bullet that will increase our recovery rates. Further, addiction is fighting for political strength, not to be subsumed by a pharmacologically driven mental health community that has an anti-addiction bias.

It is bad enough there are still parts of psychiatry that do not accept alcoholism. It is much worse when we see the stigma against addiction as a will power problem that is really about character. The very worst is that addiction professionals have not banded together across various specialties to martial political support, funding, and research so success for our patients is more achievable.

If addiction interaction proves a viable, validated concept, it will clear up much of the conceptual chaos Howard Shaffer and others have so patiently documented as existing among addiction researchers. Further, the diagnostic frameworks of the *DSM* can more systematically be shaped to fit our patient realities rather than schools of thought and professional training. The biggest challenge will come to us as addiction professionals. If each patient is to receive the depth of treatment in each addiction and the breadth of treatment necessary across issues, the 28-day program loses its legitimacy. We envision a three- to five-year process involving many specialties and formats. What we do will change. Consider how understanding addiction interaction will change the breadth of a "first step." Think about the person who has a number of addictions and how they handle going to 12-Step meetings. If they attend every meeting for which they qualify, they would not have a life. That statement is not to negate the value of 12-Steps; rather it is to point out the level at which things will have to change.

Addiction is our number one health issue. Of the top 10 health goals the United States government has specified, 5 of them fit within an addiction framework: obesity, substance abuse, sexual promiscuity, nicotine, and violence. Addiction is our number one social problem. Most crimes are committed under the influence. Addiction is our number one problem in schools, our number one source of child abuse, and our number one source of violence in our culture. To create different outcomes and to confront the issue for what it is will require a massive paradigm shift. To succeed in that level of understanding, we must start with the realities of our patients. They have multiple addictions and those addictions become intricately involved with one another.

RECOMMENDED READINGS

Carnes, P. J. (1991). *Don't call it love.* New York: Bantam Books. This long-term study of one thousand addicts and their families is the work out of which addiction was originally formulated; addictionresearch.com. Researchers and clinicians will find extensive bibliographies on multiple addictions on this dedicated web site. It is sponsored by the American Foundation for Addiction Research (AFAR), a public charity with the mission to support research in all addictive behaviors.

Leshner, A. (2001, Spring). "Addition Is a Brain Disease." National Academy of Sciences: Issues in *Science and Technology Online.* A recent formulation of Leshner's position on addiction as a "brain disease" manifesting as compulsive behavior supports the concept of addiction interaction.

Milkman, H., & Sunderwirth, S. (1987). *Craving for ecstasy: How our passions become addictions and what we can do about them.* San Francisco: Jossey-Bass. This fine work is an older, but still one of the best introductions to the neurochemistry of multiple addictions for those who do not have a chemistry or biology background.

REFERENCES

American Psychiatric Association. (2000). *Diagnostic and statistical manual of mental disorders* (4th ed., text rev.). Washington, DC: Author.

Amico, J. (1997). Assessing sexual compulsivity/addiction in chemically dependent gay men. *Sexual Addiction & Compulsivity: Journal of Treatment and Prevention, 4,* 291–297.

Bateson, G. (1978). Breaking out of the double bind. *Psychology Today, 12*(3), 43–51.

Bell, R. M. (1985). *Holy anorexia.* Chicago: University of Chicago Press.

Campbell, R. J. (1996). *Psychiatric dictionary* (7th ed.). New York: Oxford University Press.

Cooper, A. C., Putnam, D. A., Planchon, L. A., & Boies, S. C. (1999). Online sexual compulsivity: Getting tangled in the net. *Sexual Addiction & Compulsivity: Journal of Treatment and Prevention, 6*(2), 79–104.

Csikszentmihalyi, M. (1990). *Flow.* New York: Harper & Row.

Fossum, M. A., & Mason, M. (1986). *Facing shame: Families in recovery* (pp. 105–122). New York: Norton.

Griffin-Shelley, E., Sandler, K. R., & Lees, C. (1992). Multiple addictions among dually diagnosed adolescents. *Journal of Adolescent Chemical Dependency, 2,* 35–44.

Hartigan, F. (2000). *Bill W.* New York: St Martin's Press.

Heubner, H. (1993). *Endorphins: Eating disorders and other addictive behaviors.* New York: Norton.

Johnson, M. (1999). *Cross-addiction: The hidden risk of multiple addictions.* New York: Rosen Publishing Group.

Leshner, A. (1999). Science-based views of drug addiction and its treatment. *Journal of the American Medical Association, 282*(14), 1314–1316.

Leshner, A. (2001, Spring). Addition is a brain disease: National Academy of Sciences. *Science and Technology Online.*

Lynsky, M. T., Heath, A. C., Bucholz, K. K., Slutske, W. S., Madden, P. A., Nelson, E. C., et al. (2003). Escalation of drug use in early onset cannabis users versus co-twin controls. *Journal of the American Medical Association, 289,* 427–433.

Milkman, H., & Sunderwirth, S. (1987). *Craving for ecstasy: How our passions become addictions and what we can do about them.* San Francisco: Jossey-Bass.

Miller, N. S., Belkin, B. M., & Gold, M. S. (1990). Multiple addictions: Co-synchronous use of alcohol and drugs. *New York State Journal of Medicine, 90,* 596–600.

Miller, N. S., & Gold, M. S. (1995). The role of the psychiatrist in treatment or relapse in addictive disorders. *Psychiatric Annuals, 25,* 673–678.

Minuchin, S., Rosman, B., & Baker, L. (1978). *Psychomatic families.* Boston: Harvard University Press.

Nestler, E. (2001). Psychogenomics: Opportunities for understanding addiction. *Journal of Neuroscience, 21*(21), 8324–8327.

Orford, J. (1985). *Excessive appetites: A psychological view of addictions.* New York: Wiley.

Overton, F. (1987). *Applied physiology including the effects of alcohol and narcotics.* New York: American Book.

Panasitti, M., & Schull, N. (1992). A discipline of leisure: Engineering the Las Vegas casino. H195A-H195B: GN4 .3; 127 Anth.

Robertson, N. (1988). *Getting better.* New York: Morrow.

Shaffer, H. J. (1997). The most important unresolved issue in the addictions: Conceptual chaos. *Substance Use and Misuse, 32*(11), 1573–1580.

Stewart, S. H., Angelopoulos, M., Baker, J. M., & Boland, F. J. (2000). Relations between dietary restraint and patterns of alcohol use in young adult women. *Psychology of Addictive Behaviors, 14,* 77–82.

Sweeting, P. D., & Weinberg, J. L. (2000). Gambling: The secret invisible addiction. *Counselor: The Magazine for Addiction Professionals, 1,* 46–50.

van der Kolk, B. (1988). The trauma spectrum: The interaction of biological and social events in the genesis of the trauma response. *Journal of Traumatic Stress, 1*(3), 273–290.

van der Kolk, B. (2001). The assessment and treatment of complex PTSD: Traumatic Stress. In R. Yehuda (Ed.), *Traumatic stress.* Washington, DC: American Psychiatric Press.

Washton, A. M. (1989). Cocaine may trigger sexual compulsivity. *U.S. Journal of Drug and Alcohol Dependency, 13*(6), 8.

Wines, D. (1997). Exploring the applicability of criteria for substance dependence to sexual addiction. *Sexual Addiction & Compulsivity: Journal of Treatment and Prevention, 4,* 195–215.

Winters, K. C., Bengston, P., Dorr, D., & Stinchfield, R. (1998). Prevalence and risk factors of problem gambling among college students. *Psychology of Addictive Behaviors, 12,* 127–135.

PART II

CHEMICAL DEPENDENCE

CHAPTER 3

Understanding and Diagnosing Substance Use Disorders

ARTHUR W. BLUME

CHEMICAL DEPENDENCE IS perhaps the most prevalent of the addictions, and often co-occurs with others, such as compulsive gambling (Part III), sex addiction (Part IV), and eating disorders (Part V). My first exposure to diagnosing and assessing chemical dependence came as a summer intern over 20 years ago at a publicly funded detoxification and inpatient treatment center for the indigent. I had no intention of doing such work professionally prior to this experience, but the internship changed my vocational direction. Not long afterward, I became a counselor in a hospital-based treatment center, later to become a certified substance abuse counselor.

My clinical work predated my interest in research, and I have conducted therapy with hundreds of people with chemical dependence and their families, and several hundred of those patients had both severe psychiatric disorders and chemical dependence. There have been many different types of patients along the way, from millionaires to street people, children to the retirees, including a variety of different cultures. What has always interested me about chemical dependence is that the abuse of substances can present itself in so many different ways and affect people from such diverse backgrounds. Many patients went on to be highly active in Alcoholics Anonymous or Rational Recovery and did well, while others did nothing at all and also did well. However, some did not do well, which shows that our field has much work to do to help those who seek our help. The incredible complexity of chemical dependence is what ultimately led me to be a researcher as well as a clinician.

The content of this chapter represents not only my experience as a clinician but also the incredible breadth of research being conducted in this area to improve our care of all chemically dependent people. Being a clinician and a researcher in the complex field of chemical dependence is quite challenging but also is quite rewarding. I hope that it will be for you as well.

CHARACTERISTICS OF CHEMICAL DEPENDENCE

Chemical dependence is a major health problem in the United States and, because of numerous negative health and widespread financial consequences, affects all citizens in some way. When chemical dependence is a part of your family, the consequences seem obvious, but chemical dependence affects us all through higher insurance premiums for medical care; increased tax dollars to support law enforcement, prisons, and disability; and the risk of injury from intoxicated drivers or armed criminal action, to name a few societal consequences. Addictions, including chemical dependence, are often typified by what has been called the *three-Cs* (compulsive use, loss of control, and continued use despite adverse consequences).

COMPULSIVE USE

Chemically dependent people use alcohol and/or other drugs in a compulsive fashion. Compulsive use has been described to me by my patients in this way: "One is never enough, and more than one is too much." The sentiment related in such a statement highlights the ambivalence present in a person who feels addicted to a substance: The patient is aware of his or her reliance on substances while at the same time understanding that this reliance has taken on a life of its own. Compulsive substance use means that the habit of using has taken on a life of its own.

There seem to be three important aspects related to compulsive substance use. First, compulsive use is governed by reinforcement principles. Addictive substances tend to stimulate the pleasure centers of the brain (e.g., the nucleus accumbens) in such a way that makes the person seek such an experience again and again. This stimulation of the pleasure center produces the highs or euphoric experiences that tend to positively reinforce the act of using the substance. But as tolerance develops and the highs become more difficult to come by, the person may find that the pleasurable rewards come only intermittently and without any predictable pattern. Researchers, beginning with B. F. Skinner, found that intermittent reinforcement is a particularly powerful way to keep a person hooked into a behavior (discussed in greater details later in this chapter). An example of the power of intermittent reinforcement is illustrated by a pigeon in a cage that will keep pecking away at a lever or bar to get seed, even if the seed falls into the cage only once every so often. And just like the pigeon, a person can get hooked into compulsive drug use by expecting the next time to be good even if the last 20 were not so good.

However, not all reinforcement is related to pleasure. Sometimes drug use is reinforcing because it ameliorates bad feelings or symptoms. Because of the body's tendency toward homeostasis, or neurochemical balance, the body experiences rebound lows after the end of drug induced highs. Sometimes this rebound is referred to as *withdrawal*. These rebounds are uncomfortable, and may motivate the person to try and minimize or avoid the lows by using substances again. The process of avoiding or taking away the aversive consequences of withdrawal symptoms is called *negative reinforcement* (see greater details later). Substance abuse also can be negatively reinforced when the person uses substances to reduce other mental or physical health symptoms, such as anxiety, depression, or chronic pain (see details later in this chapter).

Second, compulsive substance use seems to be influenced by cravings for substances. Cravings have been described to me as powerful and sometimes sudden urges to use substances. Physical cravings seem to occur as a direct result of withdrawal symptoms. When the drug is not being administered, the body is out of balance, and aversive symptoms can occur, ranging from a hangover to a seizure. Cravings may be triggered to avoid physical withdrawal symptoms.

Furthermore, there is evidence that chronic and/or heavy substance use may permanently alter a user's neurochemistry, which in turn may cause the person to experience aversive symptoms such as anxiety or depression. It is unclear whether these alterations are irreversible, but such neurochemical changes may persist over a period of months or even years. I have had patients tell me that they were experiencing physical cravings, some after months of recovery, only to discover from a behavioral analysis (discussed later in this chapter) that the cravings were being cued by discomfort related to anxiety or depression. Some pharmacological agents can be useful to treating physical withdrawals, or in controlling depressive or anxiety symptoms that may trigger cravings for substances. (See Box 3.1.)

Another type of craving a person may experience is a psychological craving, which is related to experiences associated with substance use rather than to chemical effects. One example of psychological craving I have often heard concerns missing social experiences associated with substance use, such as wanting to play pool at a favorite watering hole or missing socialization with using friends. The person will initially perceive a craving that seems physical, but when you investigate further, the craving is not physical at all but related to missing a drinking or using experience. Psychological cravings are extremely powerful, though, and can lead a person to relapse. Treatment of these types of cravings focuses on exposure to emotional triggers and changing behavioral responses and beliefs related to expectancies about substance use.

Psychological cravings are frequently tied to expectancies or beliefs about expected results of substance use. Some of my colleagues have referred to positive expectancies about substance use as *euphoric recall* of substance use experiences. Positive expectancies tend to glamorize the use of substances and often link substance use with a particularly pleasant event. Advertisers for tobacco and alcohol

---

BOX 3.1

Compulsive use may be dictated by:

1. Reinforcement principles.
2. Cravings.
3. Habitual behavior.

REINFORCEMENT TERMS CAN BE CONFUSING

Often, people don't understand differences of positive and negative reinforcement and confuse negative reinforcement and punishment. Positive reinforcement involves pleasurable consequences related to substance use for the user. Negative reinforcement occurs when a person is rewarded by the dissipation or withdrawal of an aversive consequence, such as a substance reducing withdrawal or psychiatric symptoms. Both positive and negative reinforcement play a part in establishing the addictive process.

products try to capitalize on these positive expectancies to sell their products. Expectancies will be discussed in greater detail later in this chapter.

Third, compulsive use also is related to the habitual behavior of using the substance. Behavioral scientists often say that "the best predictor of future behavior is past behavior," and with good reason. Habits are deeply rooted in our cognitive processes and are often outside of our normal awareness of what we are doing, which is why habits are difficult to break. Habitual memory is part of implicit memory, which is the type of memory related to things like driving a car or riding a bike. Can you imagine unlearning how to ride a bike? But in a sense, that is what a person with chemical dependence must do to break a compulsion which may have lasted for years or decades.

Habitual memory also tends to be automatic. A good example of the automatic processes of habitual memory occurs when a person is driving to work on autopilot, and then suddenly realizes that he or she does not remember driving the past 10 blocks along the way. It is the same for compulsive drug or alcohol use: The person may find her- or himself using or drinking without any memory of reaching for the substance, lighting up, or uncorking the bottle. Habit can place the person on cruise control when he or she needs to be applying the brakes.

LOSS OF CONTROL

Loss of control is observed in many people who are chemically dependent, and many people who are chemically dependent describe their substance use as sometimes out of control. Loss of control has been attributed by some professionals as a user's inability to predict when or how much of a substance he or she will use. It also has been described as powerlessness over use of the substance.

The research has not clearly identified what mechanisms may be involved with loss of control, although we certainly have some clues. From alcohol research, we know that as a person consumes more alcohol, the resulting intoxication causes alcohol myopia, a loss of perceptual abilities related to the increasing impairment caused by the chemical effects of alcohol. Basically, alcohol (or drug) myopia limits awareness of surroundings at the same time behavior is becoming more disinhibited. Substances often impair higher cognitive functions associated with awareness, planning, and judgment. As the brain becomes more intoxicated, higher cognitive functions tend to shut down, causing perceptual difficulties and problems with judgment. With both awareness and judgment impaired, it becomes more likely that a person will overdrink or overuse drugs since consumption cannot be adequately monitored. Loss of control may be related to this process of diminished awareness. Myopia also can adversely affect interpersonal relationships since the intoxicated person may misperceive social cues and become aggressive. In a sense, myopia is like wearing blinders while driving a bike with no brakes downhill.

Sometimes patients report that cravings lead to loss of control. However, it is unclear whether cravings are directly responsible for loss of control or whether cravings are simply a first step. In the relapse prevention research, cravings have been linked to slips or lapses, but usually a full-blown relapse is related to guilt or shame caused by the slip (or an abstinence violation effect). Research on relapse suggests that negative emotions may be the ultimate trigger for loss of control rather than the physical cravings themselves (Marlatt, 1985; also see section on emotional factors later in this chapter).

Loss of control also has been linked in some research to expectations. Self-fulfilling prophecies have been studied to some extent. In a famous study, alcohol-dependent subjects were studied to see whether they lost control because of tasting alcohol or because they believed drinking alcohol would cause loss of control. At the time of the study, it was thought that loss of control in alcohol dependent people was triggered by ingesting alcohol. However, in this study people who were alcohol dependent and drinking alcohol (but thought they were drinking tonic water) did not lose control, but people who were alcohol dependent and not drinking alcohol (but were told they were) did report loss of control (Marlatt, Demming, & Reid, 1973). Beliefs must play a part in loss of control if alcohol dependent people are fooled by a placebo drink. Other studies have found that people who expect to lose control of their substance use will, and those who don't expect to lose control usually will not. For instance, low confidence in the ability to control using behavior in certain situations has predicted loss of control in those situations. So, for some chemically dependent people in certain situations, loss of control seems to be related to beliefs rather than biological processes. (See Box 3.2.)

Regardless of the reason it occurs, losing control is frequently reported by people who are chemically dependent and has to be taken seriously. Assessing those situations in which people report a loss of control may provide clues to whether the experience is related to overdrinking, to cravings, or to a person's belief system. Interventions to prevent loss of control must then focus on the specific triggers that may cause the perception of loss of control in the patient.

Continued Use in Spite of Consequences

Finally, chemical dependence is defined by its results. The use of chemicals can cause aversive consequences with the potential to cause harm to the user and the people around the user. However, many times, perhaps because of myopia or perhaps because the consequences are not identified as important or associated with substance use, a person who is chemically dependent may not be aware of the need

---

BOX 3.2
Loss of Control

Loss of control may be related to:

1. Substance-induced myopia.
2. Cravings.
3. Expectations that loss of control is inevitable.

What's the Buzz on Substance-Induced Myopia?

- With increased intoxication, awareness of the world is reduced.
- Intoxication often causes impairment in higher cognitive functions related to perception, interpretation, judgment, and decision making.
- Interpersonal relationships can be adversely affected by myopia, since interpersonal behavior can be misinterpreted.
- Since behavior also is disinhibited, myopia can lead to aggressive behavior.

to change using behavior. Awareness of negative consequences of addiction also is complicated by simultaneous positive experiences for the user (such as the high, escape, and socialization) that may minimize the aversive consequences to the user.

Researchers have attempted to determine what kinds of consequences are necessary to catch the attention of people who are chemically dependent. My research has found that substance-related consequences may increase motivation to change *if* they can be directly linked to substance use by the user and *if* they are important consequences to the user (Blume & Marlatt, 2000). However, there seems to be great variability for what kinds of consequences may cause the person who is chemically dependent to decide to change. Furthermore, research suggests that the impact of aversive consequences have to outweigh the pleasurable experiences of the substance to convince a person that change is desirable.

The impact of consequences on the course of chemical dependence among youth and young adults is more complicated than for older adults. Young users often do not have the obvious health consequences and sometimes are spared from consequences by the safety nets of family or other systems that try to protect them. Adolescence also is a time of natural novelty seeking related to maturation, and novelty seeking leads to risk taking and sometimes contributes to an underestimation of the risks of certain behaviors. Awareness of consequences may be diminished in part in youth because there is less recognition of potential risks. Given these factors, it should come as no surprise to discover that among young adults consequences do not seem to be as important for influencing substance use behavior as they may be among older adults.

DEPENDENCE VERSUS ABUSE

The *Diagnostic and Statistical Manual of Mental Disorders,* 4th edition (*DSM-IV-TR;* American Psychiatric Association [APA], 2000) specifies that the symptoms of substance related disorders may include tolerance; withdrawal; loss of control; unsuccessful efforts to cut down or quit; increased time committed to finding, using, or recovering from substance use; impairment in specific areas of one's life; and continued to use in spite of consequences. To meet criteria for abuse, a person must experience negative consequences of substance abuse to such a degree that it impairs at least one area of life function. To meet criteria for dependence, a person must have three or more of the symptoms stated above.

Theoretically, substance abuse does not usually involve any evidence of physical dependence, although we know that even social users can experience tolerance and withdrawal. More typically, substance abuse involves aversive consequences related to substance abuse in a particular area of a person's life, such as impairment in a relationship or problems at school or work. Dependence, on the other hand, often involves physical dependence (but it does not need to by *DSM-IV* definition) and/or impairment in multiple areas of one's life.

However, the odd thing about *DSM-IV* criteria is that a person can meet dependence criteria without any physical addiction symptoms, and since the diagnosis can be made by meeting criteria for three out of seven possible symptoms, two people can be diagnosed as dependent on the same substance without sharing a single symptom. Furthermore, I have worked with people who do not meet dependence criteria but exhibit signs of being physically dependent on a substance.

Another interesting twist is that because of *DSM-IV* diagnoses there can be movement from abuse to dependence but not vice versa, reflecting a linear model of progression hypothesized after a very small study was conducted decades ago. One criterion for a diagnosis of substance abuse is that a person has never met a diagnosis for dependence on that substance. This definition suggests one-way linear progression: A person can get worse (that is, dependent), but once dependent a person is always dependent. However, as you'll see later in this chapter, research on the natural course and history of substance abuse and dependence finds that people routinely move back and forth between experiencing multiple symptoms to having few or no problems even while still using substances. The research challenges the assumptions that chemical dependence is a life sentence for all people. The more typical abuse pattern is fluid and cyclical rather than linear. There are problems and inconsistencies with how we currently diagnose abuse and dependence. However, what may be most important is to identify who is at high-risk for continued difficulties rather than to be concerned about the nuances of present diagnosis. Later in this chapter is a discussion of predictors, and how to assess these predictors, which will help clinicians to identify and step up care for those patients who may be at great risk for worsening problems.

PSYCHOLOGICAL VERSUS PHYSICAL DEPENDENCE

Perhaps a more meaningful distinction than the one made between abuse and dependence is the distinction made between psychological and physical dependence. Psychological dependence occurs when a person believes they need the substance in order to cope, whereas physical dependence results from actual physical changes that cause tolerance and withdrawal symptoms. However, as previously mentioned, tolerance and withdrawal are natural processes that even social drinkers can experience, so it is important to be careful when using these symptoms as markers for problems.

The distinction between psychological and physical dependence acknowledges that chemical dependence can be both behavioral and biological. Some researchers assert that certain substances may not have physically addictive properties (such as cocaine) but that the substances may be psychologically addictive since they may be highly reinforcing to the user. However, I think that it is sometimes difficult to determine the differences between psychological and physical addictive processes, since in my experience both processes seem interrelated. Combining psychological and medical care addresses both types of dependence concurrently.

PREVALENCE OF CHEMICAL DEPENDENCE

Epidemiological research has determined that the prevalence of chemical dependence in the United States may be 6% to 9% of the population, and an additional 5% to 10% may meet criteria for substance abuse (Substance Abuse and Mental Health Services Administrations [SAMHSA], 2002). The most widely abused substances in the United States are alcohol and tobacco, but the typical pattern is for a person to abuse more that one substance at a time. So, for instance, many of my patients who have been alcohol dependent also have abused another substance, usually marijuana and/or tobacco.

Substance abuse cost American society approximately $140 billion in 1998 (Office of National Drug Control Policy, 2001). Chemical dependence has been linked to a variety of health problems including accidental deaths, suicides, homicides, hepatitis and other liver diseases, heart and kidney diseases, cancers, and

---

BOX 3.3
Costs to American Society Related to Chemical Dependence

Between 11% and 19% of Americans may abuse substances.

$140 billion in costs to our society in 1998.

Associated with heart disease, cancers, strokes, COPD, and unintentional accidents: the five leading causes of death in 2000.

Over 1 million people are incarcerated in American prisons on drug-related offenses.

HIV. Many of these health problems are in the top 10 causes of death in the United States for different age and ethnic groups. For instance, liver diseases associated with substance abuse were the tenth leading cause of death for adults aged 25 to 34 in the year 2000, the sixth leading cause of death for adults aged 35 to 44, the fourth leading cause of death among adults aged 45 to 54, and the seventh leading cause of death for adults 55 to 64 years of age. HIV, which is highly associated with chemical dependence, was the tenth leading cause of death for adults aged 15 to 24, sixth for aged 25 to 34, fifth for aged 35 to 44, and eighth for adults aged 45 to 54, during the year 2000. Finally, the top five killers in the United States for all age groups during 2000, heart disease, cancer, strokes, chronic obstructive pulmonary disease, and unintentional injuries, have been found to have some direct or indirect association with substance abuse (National Center for Injury Prevention and Control [NCIPC], 2002). In addition, chemical dependence has been identified as a cause of traumatic brain and spinal cord injuries, cognitive impairment, hypertension, malnutrition, severe burns, and drownings. (See Box 3.3.)

American Indians and Alaska Natives have the highest chemical dependence rates of any group (13.9%; SAMHSA, 2002) followed by those who reported being biracial or multiracial in ethnicity. Asian Americans have the lowest rates (3.6%) of any ethnic group. However, gender differences within certain ethnic groups are not captured by these overall statistics. For example, substance dependence is much higher for Hispanic/Latino men than women. Some groups that have high dependence rates, like some American Indian communities, also have very high abstinence rates, much higher than majority culture.

People with co-occurring psychiatric disorders are high risk for chemical dependence, regardless of ethnicity or gender. Some of the most commonly co-occurring psychiatric disorders with chemical dependency are depressive, anxiety (e.g., posttraumatic stress disorder and social phobia), antisocial and borderline personality, and bipolar disorders; and schizophrenia. Chronic pain also has been associated with some types of chemical dependence. The research suggests that abuse of substances by some chronic pain patients may begin because they are undermedicated for their pain, tempting the person to seek more medications. However, many people with chronic pain abused substances prior to the injury that caused the pain, and sometimes the substance abuse actually contributed to that injury.

Many prevention specialists use these statistics to develop profiles of who may be at risk for chemical dependence. However, treatment services are not being utilized by members of these diverse, minority populations in numbers that reflect their dependence rates. The discrepancy between the statistics on dependence in certain high-risk groups and the numbers that have sought and successfully completed treatment are disturbing, suggesting that many of these high-risk groups may be underserved. It is unclear what factors are preventing treatment seeking by these high-risk groups, but research is being encouraged by the National Institute on Health to examine potential roadblocks to services.

THE COURSE OF CHEMICAL DEPENDENCE

There are different models describing the development of chemical dependence. Beginning in the 1940s, Jellinek developed a disease trajectory based on observational and self-report data from severely alcohol dependent patients. The trajectory showed a steady to steep slide from prodromal or early stages of addiction to chronic late stage addiction, which either ended with the death, imprisonment, or recovery of the person. For years, many treatment professionals believed that this trajectory was the typical course for addictions, with a highly prescribed progression of symptoms and consequences. However, Jellinek later revised his model by proposing that there were five different types of trajectories for alcoholics, and three of these trajectories were not considered by Jellinek to be chronic, progressive, or even related to disease (Jellinek, 1960).

More recently, researchers have been interested in the naturalistic studies of untreated alcoholics to determine whether the disease trajectory was indeed sufficient to explain the course of addictions. The findings of these studies have been quite interesting and tend to challenge the view that all chemical dependence is chronic and progressive. These studies found that many untreated people with chemical dependence have a more cyclical course in their addictions, rather than a linear and progressive course. Many people with chemical dependence successfully abstain without treatment even after a period of severe dependence. The research found that some chemically dependent people move through cycles of severe abuse followed by periods of control, and sometimes followed by relapse, so that the trajectory may be cyclical rather than strictly linear. If anything, the natural course of addictions research suggests that there are individual differences among people who are chemically dependent and that not everyone follows the traditional disease trajectory of progression of symptoms. These results led many leading researchers to suggest that "One size *does not* necessarily fit all" when it comes to predicting or treating chemical dependence (or any other mental disorder, for that matter).

Predicting the course of substance abuse is not easy. Some of my patients have told me they are addicted from the very first drink or line. However, we know that other people manage to abstain, sometimes without the aid of therapy or treatment, after a period of severe dependence. It seems important to understand why some people with chemical dependence can change on their own whereas others cannot.

Clearly some patients have extreme difficulties reaching and maintaining their treatment goals and tend to have multiple relapses. Because of the pattern of multiple relapses, these patients become discouraged about hopes for recovery. I have found that these patients often remain keenly aware of the need to change using behavior, and often are motivated to change, but seem to be unable to sustain behavior change over the long term. It may have been this type of patient that Jellinek studied when he developed his chronic progression trajectory, and many of us have worked with patients like these. Frequently, these patients have other problems that complicate recovery prospects, such as a co-occurring psychiatric disorder. One of the principal concerns with these patients is their low self-efficacy, which will be discussed later in this chapter in the section about cognitive predictors influencing substance use. However, not every patient with chemical dependence falls into the multiple-relapsing-and-discouraged category.

Other alcohol research has identified different patterns of abuse, such as a chronic, maintenance type pattern (a person who uses about the same every day) versus a binge type pattern. Another distinction is between late onset versus early onset of alcohol dependence. It is unclear whether the distinctions made in alcohol research are useful as applied to drug dependence. However, for alcohol dependence, the research found that binge abuse patterns can cause as many life problems as regular drinking patterns and that earlier onset of dependence likely results in a poorer prognosis than does a late onset of dependence.

FINAL NOTE ABOUT CHEMICAL DEPENDENCE AS DISEASE

In 1956, the American Medical Association (AMA) defined alcoholism as a chronic and progressive disease with a specific course and symptomology. The AMA was responding in part to preliminary research by Jellinek. This declaration led to increased compassion in the care of people who were chemically dependent. The declaration by the AMA also allowed for third-party reimbursement for treatment, since addiction was defined as a treatable disease.

However, research since that declaration has not identified a single specific course related to the chronic progression of alcohol abuse and dependence, let alone a specific course for other drug addictions. In fact, the Institute of Medicine (1990) reported that people tend to move in and out of addictive problems, that progression is not always present, and that the trajectory for addictive symptoms is not necessarily well-defined or linear. Although the declaration by the AMA resulted in some very positive events in the treatment of addictions, it is unclear from the research how helpful it is to speak of an addictive process as a medical disease, especially since some patients do not follow a progressive symptom trajectory or experience chronic problems.

I have worked with many patients who have benefited from believing that they had a disease and they were powerless and then found substantial help in support groups such as Alcoholics Anonymous or Narcotics Anonymous. However, I also have worked with many other patients who found no value in believing they had a disease, nor in believing they were powerless, and they got better, too. Indeed, since the research suggests that many people get better without accepting powerlessness or a disease model, it is probably more important to work with the patient's understanding of their addictions rather than attempting to use your own understanding and coercing your patient into using it, too.

PREDICTORS OF CHEMICAL DEPENDENCE

BIOLOGICAL PREDICTORS

One of the more potent predictors of whether a person will be at risk for chemical dependence is a family history of addictions. The risk seems to increase if chemical dependence is present in the nuclear family. Many have suggested that chemical dependence runs in families and that it may be transmitted across generations. How much of the familial transmission of chemical dependence is genetic versus behavioral is unclear. Although twin studies suggest that a genetic transmission of chemical dependence is possible, more than a decade of work has been unable to identify the genes responsible for chemical dependence. In fact, even if a gene pattern were identified for alcohol dependence (as an example), there is no guarantee that the gene pattern for alcohol dependence would be the same for another drug dependence. Furthermore, familial transmission can also be explained by behavioral factors, such as modeling by parents or siblings of drinking and using drugs to escape, avoid, or cope with stress or problems. Familial transmission is likely a combination of a genetic predisposition, possibly related to emotional vulnerability or sensitivity, and of modeling by family members who may be using to cope with life, albeit in a dysfunctional way.

The evidence suggests that the greatest biological risk factor for chemical dependence is having another psychiatric disorder. As mentioned previously, the statistics about co-occurrence of psychiatric disorders with substance abuse are quite high, with estimates ranging from one-third to two-thirds of all chemically dependent people having one or more comorbid psychiatric disorders. Evidence exists for the intergenerational transmission of certain mood and anxiety disorders, as well as schizophrenia and antisocial personality, so a genetic link of intergenerational substance abuse may be imbedded in the intergenerational transmission of other psychiatric conditions. Many of my patients with co-occurring disorders have told me that their chemical addiction began as an attempt to self-medicate psychiatric symptoms (self-medication will be discussed in greater detail subsequently). However, with some patients, it is difficult to know which came first: the psychiatric symptoms or the substance abuse.

BEHAVIORAL PREDICTORS

Trying to determine a specific behavior pattern that predicts whether a person will become addicted has proved difficult. For instance, researchers have attempted for decades to determine a psychological profile for people who are chemically addicted but have not found a single addictive personality, in spite of commonly held beliefs by many people that there is such a personality. As mentioned, there are certain psychological disorders with specific clusters of symptoms that have a high co-occurrence with substance abuse and dependence (e.g., depressive, borderline, or antisocial disorders), but there is no single personality type for people with addictive behaviors.

Behavioral principles do go a long ways toward explaining the addictive processes, even though chemically dependent people have varying personalities. For instance, *positive reinforcement,* something pleasurable happening after a behavior occurs that makes repeating a behavior more likely, can happen when people get high or when they feel relaxed and joyful while using substances. This may not happen every time that a person uses. A reinforcement that doesn't occur regularly is often referred to as being on a *variable* or *intermittent* (random or unpredictable) schedule. Behavioral researchers have determined that a variable reinforcement schedule produces behavior patterns more difficult to change than behavior patterns reinforced on a regular basis. This occurs because a person cannot predict

---

BOX 3.4
Reinforcement Schedules and Using Substances

Continuous reinforcement means that it occurs regularly after every use, which becomes less likely as tolerance develops.

Intermittent or variable reinforcement is more likely after tolerance develops, which occurs in a random and unpredictable fashion that keeps the person coming back for more.

Chemically dependent people likely are experiencing both intermittent positive and negative reinforcement, since the substance sometimes makes them high, takes away withdrawal, and self-medicates (but not always).

---

which use will be rewarded, so, just like gambling, a person keeps using in hopes this will be the time he or she will hit the euphoric jackpot. (See Box 3.4.)

In the same way, using substances can be negatively reinforcing for a person. *Negative reinforcement* occurs when an activity removes an aversive event or consequence, therefore making it more likely that the behavior will be repeated (just like positive reinforcement). Sometimes this involves lifting a punishment and other times it might involve removing nasty physical symptoms, such as drinking to beat a hangover or using to avoid the chills. Negative reinforcement also can occur on a variable or intermittent schedule, meaning that sometimes the use alleviates the nasty symptoms, but not always. Addiction can develop as a result of these powerful behavior patterns (desiring pleasure and avoiding discomfort) reinforced in a random and unpredictable way. The compulsion to use may arise as a conscious choice to seek highs and avoid lows, but eventually, the behavior takes on a life of its own as reinforcement becomes less predictable.

Self-medication also can be thought as negative reinforcement. The person may use the substance to relieve aversive psychiatric or physical symptoms, such as depression, anxiety, or chronic pain. More often than not, the substance use may actually make the symptoms worsen over the long term. However, since using had been negatively reinforced at times by relieving symptoms, the patient may continue the use of substances to self-medicate, even if the substances make the symptoms worse.

Some of the most interesting behavioral research concerning addictions is related to a person's ability to cope with other people or with environmental stress. Clinicians often discover that people who abuse substances often have problems with skills in interpersonal situations, during drinking and using events, in daily living, and in solving problems. When working with a patient who is having trouble coping without substances, I assume it is a problem with skills. However, the next step is to determine whether the problem is that the person never learned the skill at all or is not using appropriately the skill he or she knows. The inability to effectively use skills in drinking or using situations, or in a situation that might trigger a desire to drink or use, is highly predictive of worsening problems of substance abuse. The therapist who suspects a problem with using skills in high-risk situations will have to assess whether the skill has ever been learned or has been learned and is not being used in the appropriate way or time.

COGNITIVE PREDICTORS

Addiction researchers also find that addictive processes are influenced by patient beliefs. Behavioral researchers have looked at what many people call *the self-fulfilling prophecy,* and have found that a person's beliefs about outcomes are often related to future behavior. With regard to chemical dependence, what a patient believes about the outcomes of using, their ability to cope in certain situations, or their ability to change their behavior may be a critical factor in what really does happen next.

Beliefs about what may happen when a person uses or drinks, called *expectancies,* seem to predict future drinking and using behavior. Expectancies can involve beliefs about the positive *or* negative effects of using the substance. Expectancies have been found by researchers to be extremely difficult to modify; and, in some cases, positive expectancies remain potent even when a person has been clean and sober for some time. Most of the research has focused on the power of positive expectancies to perpetuate the using habit. Indeed, positive expectancies make it hard for a person to want to change their using behavior because of the belief that good things, like getting high or avoiding worry or improving mood, will occur after using substances.

Other important beliefs concern a person's ability to control behavior in certain situations to meet his or her goals. Self-efficacy (first researched by Albert Bandura), or the perception of control and mastery in a particular situation, is predictive of using behavior among people with chemical dependence. Self-efficacy research has focused primarily on the competence and confidence people feel about coping successfully (without losing control or without using) in high-risk situations. With chemical dependence, self-efficacy means both confidence and skill in negotiating high-risk drinking or drug using situations. The research has found that people with low self-efficacy often do poorly in certain high-risk situations. For instance, low self-efficacy has predicted greater loss of control of substance use in particular situations. As a therapist, I want to know what those high-risk situations are for my patient and then assess how confident the patient feels in coping successfully (without losing control). If self-efficacy is low, then skills may need to be taught or confidence needs to be developed by succeeding at small steps toward the ultimate goal.

Some people become discouraged, as mentioned earlier, possibly because of multiple relapses. Hopelessness related to discouragement also can influence future behavior. In this instance, hope must be generated in the patient to improve outcomes. Furthermore, some research has suggested that the beliefs of therapists about their patient's chances for recovery may influence how well the patients actually do. Both patient and therapist beliefs could become self-fulfilling prophecies in the course of the addiction, so it is important to assess whether those beliefs may hinder the patient's chances at changing his or her substance-use behavior.

COGNITIVE PROBLEMS RELATED TO SUBSTANCE ABUSE

Finally, neuropsychological deficits have been associated with chronic and long-term chemical dependence. We know that chemical abuse increases the risk of neurocognitive insult from several different sources, including neurotoxicity, malnutrition, liver dysfunction, and sleep disturbances such as apnea. Neurotoxicity often occurs from an overstimulation of various receptor cells in a process called *excitotoxicity.* If this excessive firing continues chronically, there is a risk of cell death, which affects other cells (National Institute on Alcohol Abuse and Alcoholism [NIAAA], 1997). Malnutrition can occur because of lack of self-care and because substance abuse depletes specific vitamins and minerals from the body that are necessary for proper brain function. For example, heavy alcohol consumption, associated with thiamine deficiency, has been identified as a cause of the Wernicke-Korsakoff syndrome.

Liver dysfunction and lowered immune function related to heavy chronic substance use can be an indirect cause of brain insults via increased risk of infections. Hepatitis B and C, for example, are known to contribute to potential neurological damage, and cirrhosis can cause high ammonia levels within the brain that can lead to mental confusion. Heavy substance abuse has been linked to sleep apnea and has the capacity to lower blood oxygen levels in the brain to harmful levels. This reduction of blood oxygen levels is associated with a wide-variety of brain insults, including executive cognitive function deficits such as impaired memory, visuospatial performance, planning, and organizing abilities (Lezak, 1995).

Memory problems among people who are chemically dependent are common, including significant short-term memory deficits. These memory deficits seem more pronounced when the person is under stress or when confronted with a complex learning task or problem solving. Strangely, long-term memory seems to remain more intact than short-term memory. This may be a mixed blessing, since longer term memory also may be the repository of positive expectancies related to substance use, and short-term memory seems important for new learning and awareness (in this case, of recent consequences and the need to change).

Problems with abstraction, long-term memory, and visuospatial abilities have been known to occur for months and even years after a person has abstained, so even recovery does not mean the person is out of the cognitive woods. People who have difficulties with chronic relapse may be experiencing cognitive problems that are hard to detect. Furthermore, substance-induced depression can contribute to mental sluggishness, but depression can be treated and cognitive deficits related to depression seem reversible.

Long-term substance abuse also has been associated with executive function problems. Executive cognitive function includes working memory functions, problem-solving skills, impulse control, abstraction abilities, attentiveness, planning, initiation and cessation of behavior, and organizational skills. Obviously, these are important skills needed to control behavior, make well-reasoned choices, and determine the need to change. Indeed, research has found much poorer treatment outcomes among people with executive function deficits. That is the bad news, but the worse news is that it may not take long-term abuse to experience such deficits. Slight but noticeable memory and executive function deficits have been found in some early adolescent youth who abuse substances.

However, it is unknown whether the deficits are due only to chemical toxicity of substance abuse or whether some of the neuropsychological problems may predate substance use. There is evidence that substance abuse may be associated with antisocial behavior and impulse control problems, and these difficulties have been linked to potential neuropsychological deficits and problems. Also, attention-deficit and hyperactivity problems seem to frequently co-occur with substance abuse, but it is unclear whether the substance abuse caused the attention problems or whether the deficits preceded the substance abuse. We simply do not know whether cognitive vulnerabilities may contribute to later substance abuse, but we have our suspicions.

Furthermore, it is possible that some of the problems, such as antisocial behavior, impulse control problems, and attention deficits and hyperactivity may be symptoms of prenatal substance exposure that may have escaped detection. Research has found that these symptoms are associated with known prenatal toxicity. Fetal alcohol effects and other substance exposure are much more difficult to detect if there are not obvious physical signs or mental retardation. In these instances, the symptoms are more likely to be behavioral and attributed to causes other than prenatal toxic exposure.

The good news is that longitudinal research has found that some of the cognitive deficits may be reversible. There seem to be two different phases of cognitive recovery. The first phase occurs more rapidly and is associated with the detoxification process of abstaining from substances. In this phase, mental confusion and some acute cognitive problems show noticeable clearing and recovery with abstinence. Many clinicians refer to this process colloquially as, "the patient is clearing from his or her mental fog."

However, other cognitive problems, some more subtle, may persist for several months or years, as mentioned, but eventually some of these are reversible. In this second phase of cognitive recovery, it seems that the brain is healing itself over time. This process of healing seems related to other factors, such as the duration and severity of chemical abuse (less, of course is better), the age of the patient when abstaining (younger is better), the age of onset of chemical dependence in the patient (older is better in this case), and the length of abstinence (and longer, of course, is more helpful).

Because there is some evidence that cognitive processes may be able to regenerate over time, some therapists have introduced cognitive rehabilitation strategies into treatment. The goal and focus of cognitive rehabilitation is to exercise specific brain functions to stimulate regeneration, which recalls the analogy that is often used with physical exercise and flexibility: "If you don't use it you lose it." Cognitive rehabilitation strategies have been used with good results among patients with brain injuries associated with strokes, traumatic accidents, or anoxia, so there is great hope that these strategies will work well with patients who have abused substances.

And What about Denial?

I have intentionally avoided talk about denial until this point of the chapter for several reasons. The original meaning of denial comes from a model of addictions that includes the use of defense mechanisms to perpetuate addictive processes. However, using this original definition, researchers have found little evidence of defense mechanisms associated with addictions, including a specific defense mechanism of denial.

In more recent times, clinicians and laypeople have used the word *denial* to describe a cluster of behaviors that appear on the surface to include a very dishonest assessment of one's current conditions and circumstances. More often than not, the label of *being in denial* is not complimentary, and I for one have seen it used as a weapon against noncomplaint patients by therapists in an effort to get the patient to accept the truth about their current life circumstances. However, as a researcher, I also know that therapist confrontation is linked to poorer outcomes when used with chemically dependent patients. I personally do not see the value in confronting denial since research suggests that confrontation might slow recovery rather than accelerate it. Using Motivational Interviewing (Miller & Rollnick, 2002) to avoid such confrontation has been found to be effective with many patients.

Besides, there are many reasons a person may not have awareness, some which may not be related to dishonesty at all. For one, cognitive dysfunction often means that the patient has problems with awareness and with processing new information and could make the person look like they are in denial when they are simply impaired. Furthermore, not everyone experiences severe consequences when using substances. Adolescents have completely buffaloed many therapists trained in an adult model of addiction, often because adolescents do not respond to, or even have the same types or numbers of, consequences that adults do. Finally, what may be important consequences to you or I may not necessarily be important to our clients. As a clinician and researcher, using the word denial is not very helpful. It is an emotionally laden term that may not even accurately describe the nature of the problem behavior.

EMOTIONAL PREDICTORS

Many researchers investigating the relationship of emotions and chemical dependence have found interesting associations. First, many researchers have found that a substantial number of people who are chemically dependent have difficulties identifying and expressing emotions in socially acceptable ways.

BOX 3.5
Cognitive Factors and Emotions Predicting
Changes in Substance Use

Cognitions include:

- Expectancies.
- Self-efficacy.
- Awareness of consequences.
- Level of motivation to change.
- Neurocognitive problems.

Common emotions associated with addictive processes include:

- Anger.
- Sadness and grief.
- Shame and guilt.
- Regret and rumination.
- Happiness.

Many chemically dependent patients have difficulties identifying and regulating their emotions, much to their detriment.

Many treatment centers have their patients talk openly and deliberately about their emotions in group therapy or try to encourage patients to monitor their emotions on diary cards or on self-monitoring forms. This is done to encourage patients to practice identifying what they are feeling at this moment. Many patients I worked with often could not express what they were feeling, confused thoughts with feelings, or confused certain feelings with others. (See Box 3.5.)

Having difficulties with identifying emotions makes perfect sense when considering that substance abuse tends to blunt emotions. Many of my patients told me they often used substances to escape certain emotions. So, it should not come as a great surprise that a chemically dependent patient would have difficulty expressing what she or he is feeling at this particular moment, since feeling may have been avoided for many years. So, it is not uncommon for chemically dependent patients to underexpress or overexpress their emotions or to confuse one emotion with another emotion.

Some researchers have suggested that people with chemical dependence often have problems with emotion dysregulation, which simply means they are not very skilled at controlling or expressing emotions. It is quite possible that the lack of emotion regulation skills may have predated substance use, and the lack of these skills may have left the person particularly vulnerable to the rawness of emotions. Some researchers are interested in how some people may be more naturally vulnerable to the experience of emotions, often referred to as *hypersensitivity* or *wearing his or her heart* (or emotions) *on his or her sleeve.* Certainly a fair number of my patients told me, "I think I feel things more strongly than others do," or "I feel like I wear my heart on my sleeve and others have crushed it." There seems to be empirical support for the assertion that some people may be more sensitive to the sensation or expression of emotions than the average person, just like similar evidence exists that people with anxiety disorders tend to be more sensitive to changes in their bodies than the average person.

People who feel emotionally vulnerable may be naturally attracted to the emotionally altering properties of drugs and alcohol, as well as to the escapes that substance use may provide. Furthermore, it is conceivable that many substance users were reared in homes where emotions were inappropriately expressed. Without appropriate role models for emotional expression, some chemically dependent patients never learned how to express emotions in socially appropriate ways. This would certainly be the case in homes where one or more members abused substances or where parents were abusive or neglectful. For instance, if emotional expression was punished in the home, then a person reared in that home might be at risk to avoid their expression, whereas if emotional volatility was the norm in the home, then a person reared in that home would be at risk to become emotionally volatile as well.

As mentioned, many chemically dependent patients have a tendency to confuse an emotion with thoughts or with other emotions. Sometimes this confusion is because he or she has not learned to identify his or her feelings, and other times the confusion is because the emotion is misidentified. In my experience, patients who were raised in families where emotions were taboo or underexpressed often have problems with confusing emotions with thoughts. To give an example, one of my patients had a hard time understanding when he was angry. When asked what he was feeling, he would often respond with thoughts like "I didn't think that was fair," or "Well, it wasn't very nice what they did to me," or "I didn't appreciate them doing that." It would take several explanations on my part about the differences between the interpretations (thoughts) that he was expressing about particular situations and the feelings that underlay the thoughts, before the patient could identify his emotions.

Many patients can express one emotion, but they often confuse many other emotions for the one they are good at expressing. An example is the patient who has no problem identifying anger but often feels anger to the exclusion of other emotions. Many of my chemically dependent patients have expressed anger when in fact they were embarrassed, ashamed, hurt, sad, or feel they are losing control of a particular situation. Anger comes more easily since it has some protective qualities about it: Anger can push away more painful feelings and threatening people or situations.

Inappropriate expression of emotions often has other consequences than merely avoiding true feelings or painful situations. Inappropriate expression of emotions can contribute to experiencing other negative interpersonal consequences. For example, expressing emotions in socially inappropriate ways can cause other people to avoid contact with the person. Inappropriate emotional response can contribute to increased social isolation, which then can further contribute to the interpretation that many substance using patients have of being social misfits (see following section). Sadly, the inappropriate expression of emotions may cause less exposure to people who might be able to model more socially appropriate ways to feel and express emotions. Furthermore, when alcohol and other drugs enter into the equation, with their disinhibiting effects, emotional dysregulation is often exacerbated.

Several specific emotions have strong associations with the course of chemical dependence. For instance, the expression of anger is very commonly associated with chemical dependence. There may be several reasons for this. First, anger is an emotion that has been associated with conduct disorder and antisocial personality disorder, behavior disorders that frequently co-occur with chemical dependence. Chemically dependent people with antisocial symptoms have been found to be at high risk for worsening substance abuse over time and for poor prognosis in treatment. Second, anger and aggression are strongly correlated as well; and, frequently, aggression and substance abuse go hand in hand. The prognosis for people who commit aggressive acts while using substances is quite poor, since aggression frequently leads to averse consequences such as legal complications, academic failure and vocational difficulties, and relationship problems.

Even for those chemically dependent patients not necessarily clinically antisocial, anger is often a part of their difficulties. The anger may have developed because of abuse, neglect, or being mistreated by others, or it may be related to frustration that has developed over time, often because of inadequate coping skills. My experience has been that people who have problems with chemical dependence have to learn how to manage their anger to succeed at recovery.

Sadness and grief are commonly experienced emotions by patients with chemical dependence, but these emotions are generally buried behind a barrier of anger. Many of the events that contribute to the experience of the sadness and grief may have occurred prior to the onset of substance abuse. In those instances, sadness and grief may be related to abuse, neglect, losses, or sometimes depression.

But events causing sadness and grief also can accumulate after the onset of substance abuse. People who abuse substances are at high risk to experience a variety of negative consequences, including life changes and losses. Some of the most frequently experienced life changes and losses include events such as losing a job; experiencing family and relationship problems, separations, and divorces; losing money or possessions and having financial problems; being exposed to violence and possibly unnatural death of friends or family; homelessness; and loss of self-esteem, respect, friends, health, important values, or spiritual meaning and purpose. Most of the chemically dependent patients I worked with had experienced at least one meaningful loss in their lives, although it may or may not be attributable to their substance use. Even if the loss is not directly attributable to substance abuse, the patient may be using substances to avoid thinking about the loss.

However, research shows that for many people major life changes are not as frustrating as what have been called *daily hassles*. This same research shows that people can often rise up to meet the major life challenges but may get beaten down over time by trying to cope with the little hassles that occur day to day. These hassles are often perceived as annoying and frustrating and often without solutions. Many of these daily hassles cause psychological stress, which has been identified as related to substance abuse. (The relationship of psychological stress and chemical dependence is discussed in greater detail in the next section on environmental factors.)

Another potentially toxic emotion linked to substance abuse is shame. Among people who are chemically dependent, shame that predates the onset of substance abuse is often related to abuse, although in some cases I have seen shame linked to a sense of personal failure unrelated to victimization. It is difficult to know with precision how many people with chemical dependence were abused as children, but the number must be sizeable. Of all people who are chemically dependent, 10% to 50% were abused as children, depending on the definition of abuse and the population being studied. The association of abuse with onset of chemical dependence is significant enough to warrant investigation. However, therapists must be very cautious when investigating such issues, since there is a substantial body of research suggesting that therapists can actually introduce false memories of abuse into a patient's belief system, sometimes unwittingly. Furthermore, new research suggests that focusing on abuse early in treatment may be harmful to some patients.

In addition to the high occurrence of abuse premorbid to substance use, people who are chemically dependent are generally more vulnerable when impaired, so they are at risk for further victimization. It is common for victims of adult abuse to be under the influence or intoxicated at the time of attacks, and their attackers are often impaired as well. Many times the abuse is done by an acquaintance—a person who may have been using with the victim at the time. Shame also can develop after onset of chemical dependence, related to perceived personal failings, which are more likely to occur when a person is impaired. Many treatment programs emphasize work on shame, but it may be more important to empower the person in treatment rather than to discuss past failings and traumas (i.e., focus on the present rather than the past).

Another principle emotion associated with substance abuse is guilt, which is often associated with violating rules, trust, or personal principals. To begin with, many treatment programs act as if all patients experience guilt related to their behavior while drinking or using drugs, but unfortunately that may not be true. Since some people who are chemically dependent also have a comorbid antisocial

personality disorder, it is unlikely that those patients will experience guilt or remorse as you or I. The concern for people with antisocial personalities is not violating rules or principles but rather concern about getting caught. With this being said,
some patients with chemical dependence will not experience or respond to guilt.

However, the majority of people with chemical dependence do experience
guilt, often related to something done while intoxicated. Patients may have hurt
other people, conned other people, violated their own belief systems, or violated
the trust of others. Behaviorally speaking, the best way to combat guilt is to use
correction or overcorrection. An example of correction is having a child spell a
word correctly after he or she misspells a word in school. Using the same example, overcorrection would include having the child spell the word correctly but to
do so 10 or 20 or even 50 times. The goal of overcorrection is not to punish but
rather to have the person do it right until he or she makes doing it right a habit.

Alcoholics Anonymous developed one way to correct behavior by making
amends to other people (when it won't harm them). Other ways include exaggerated restitutions, doing the same behavior repeatedly until it becomes habit, or
simply committing to change behavior for good. The danger inherent in guilt is
that it often leads the person to believe that he or she is trapped, without an opportunity to change. This feeling of being trapped or stuck has led some patients
to say, "Oh, what the heck, it is too late anyway" and then continue down the same
behavioral path.

Relapse research has identified guilt and shame as extremely toxic to a recovering person. When a person slips back into old behavior, he or she often experiences
guilt and shame that eventually may lead to hopelessness. What the patient (and
therapist) does with the patient's guilt and shame will predict whether the person
returns to maintenance or continues to slip into old behavior (Marlatt, 1985).

In addition, both regret and rumination (when thought processes are stuck and
cycle through the same things repeatedly, which stops forward progress) have
been linked to chemical dependence. There are two very obvious reasons why this
is the case. First, chemical dependence often causes poor judgment in behavior
that leads to interpersonal problems and/or interferes with personal goals. In the
case of interpersonal problems, regret may arise from lost opportunities or violations of trust with significant others, friends, families, and children. Regret also
may arise from not being able to achieve goals for self or not being able to meet
personal expectations for one's life. In a very real sense, a life of impairment is a
set-up for the experience of regret. However, my own research has found that regret, though painful, might motivate people to change their substance use (Blume
& Schmaling, 1998).

The second reason that regret and rumination are related to substance abuse is
the high co-occurrence of chemical dependence with depressive disorders. Depressive disorders are typified by ruminative thinking and response styles, as well as
regret. Rumination is akin to a squirrel running on a round treadmill. When ruminating, a person spins around and around with obsessive thinking that paralyzes
the ability to solve the problem and move forward with solutions. Although in
many instances it remains unclear what comes first, the depression or the chemical
abuse, it is clear that depressive thought and behavioral processes, such as regret
and rumination, are quite common among people who abuse substances.

Finally, how could I forget happiness and joy? Yes, patients with chemical dependence seem to have a problem with experiencing a wide variety of emotions,

even positive ones. In chemical dependence, emotional dysregulation can occur with all types of emotions. Regardless of whether the emotions are positive or negative, some people do not know how to respond appropriately to emotions. For some of my patients, joy felt awkward and foreign, even causing some discomfort (like they were not supposed to feel joy), and for others it is cause for a substance-related celebration that inevitably leads to emotional lows.

Some clinicians have suggested that chemical dependence could be considered a disorder of emotions. Emotions are inextricably linked to the process of addiction in very obvious and also in more subtle ways. Emotions also tend to interact with cognitions to create very complicated beliefs related to substance use. When treating addictive behaviors, the emotional content of the addictive behavior chain must always be thoroughly assessed and ultimately intervened on to promote lasting behavior change.

ENVIRONMENTAL PREDICTORS

Chemical dependence also has been associated with environmental factors. For instance, we know that chemical dependence is associated with poverty. Stress also seems to be related to substance abuse, and many of my patients reported drinking or using for relaxation or stress reduction. There are many different types of psychological stress that may contribute to substance abuse, including job stress, unemployment, familial stress, economic stress, daily hassles, or major life changes or crises. Some researchers have speculated that environmentally crowded conditions, often associated with increased psychological stress, may be linked to increased substance use, although crowding usually co-occurs with poverty. Other environmental stressors linked to chemical dependence include abuse, traumatic events, and oppression.

There is a growing body of literature on the power of expressed emotion in families to influence the course of psychiatric disorders, including chemical dependence. Expressed emotion is just what it sounds like: emotions that are expressed verbally and even nonverbally by significant others toward the patient. Anecdotally, I have worked with many patients who talked about drinking or using substances after a family member expressed a negative emotion toward them, and I have had a few family members tell me they expressed the emotion to punish or push the patient away. Clearly, being in an emotionally supportive environment can improve the prognosis of someone who is chemically dependent.

One researcher, Dr. Marsha Linehan (1993), has talked about how a poor fit with the environment (namely, not fitting into the family, school life, or other important social network) may cause psychiatric problems if the poorness of fit causes the person to feel like an outsider or constantly invalidated or put down. Many of my chemically dependent patients discussed with me how they felt out of step with their families, or even with society, and that this may have led to certain choices that eventually led to drug and alcohol use. Certainly abusive and neglectful situations would fall under the heading of an invalidating environment.

Many patients from ethnic-minority groups feel similarly, since the majority culture often has much different values and expectations than the ethnic-minority communities. Since substance abuse can be rampant in some of these communities, researchers have been interested in the relationship of cultural competence with chemical dependence. The results of this research have suggested that the ability to function competently in both cultures (in the home culture and in the culture of the larger society), may be associated with lower substance abuse and with better outcomes among those who do abuse substances. Successfully coping without substances in ethnic-minority communities may involve being skilled in two or more cultures, so you may wish to encourage participation in traditional practices at the same time you teach computer skills, which is exactly what we did in a program with American Indians and Native Alaskans.

There also are major cultural differences in the way that substance use is viewed within our country. As an American Indian, I am familiar with attitudes about substance use in Native cultures, which can be quite different than the attitudes in majority culture. For one, some forms of substance use are sanctioned and done in conjunction with traditional religious practices, whereas other forms of substance use are viewed as extremely detrimental to communities and sometimes lead to individual users being subtly excluded from the community for the sake of the community.

Cross-cultural differences like these, which are not peculiar to Native cultures, may cause problems for White therapists and researchers working with minority clients. For instance, since many ethnic-minority communities have highly communalistic values and have relational worldviews, viable solutions to chemical dependence often involve communal rather than individualistic solutions. This may cause a clash of worldviews between ethnic-minority patient and a White therapist or researcher. One example of this clash occurs when the patient uses traditional healing practices in conjunction with more traditional treatment practices, often without the traditional therapist's knowledge.

Furthermore, many of the ethnic-minority patients with chemical dependence I worked with report feeling varying degrees of prejudice and cultural isolation after they leave their home communities. Many also report some degree of culture shock and problems with adjustment to majority culture. Some of these patients told me that substance use provides some escape and relief from the environmental stress related to feeling different than the majority, whereas others see their substance use as rebellion against the oppressive majority society. Understanding the function of the substance abuse within its cultural context is extremely important to provide the culturally appropriate treatment intervention.

Cultural values and mores also seem to be associated with the prevalence of chemical dependence in certain societies. Many leading researchers believe that early exposure to adults who model safe substance use practices and responsible substance use in society may promote more moderate substance use in those societies. Examples cited include France, which has widespread and early exposure to alcohol, yet has much lower cirrhosis rates than the United States, or the Netherlands, which legalized marijuana in coffee shops two decades ago, but has lower marijuana abuse rates than the United States.

The history of dealing with substance abuse in the United States is different than many other Western countries. One major difference is that the United States had a period of prohibition, a history not shared by other Western nations. The United States also experiences great tensions between the desire to solve drug abuse problems by law and regulation and the desire to solve drug abuse problems through public health methods, such as providing treatment options for those who want to quit using substances.

Some Western nations have resolved the conflict by relying more heavily on a public health model rather than the court system and have decriminalized or

"However, before intervention can occur, we must know where to intervene. This requires that we conduct thorough assessments of our patients to understand what things we cannot change, what things we can change with the help of our patients, and the wisdom to know the difference. Assessments provide that wisdom."

reduced penalties for substance use. In other societies, some legal restrictions we take for granted in the United States, such as legal drinking ages, have never been in place or enforced. It is unclear what direction U.S. public policy on substance abuse will move in the future. However, the effects of tensions between treating drug abuse as a moral problem versus treating it as a health problem are evident in the United States since more than one million people are incarcerated on drug charges and since limited treatment options have left a large number of patients on waiting lists for treatment centers.

Researchers also looked at the effects of marketing practices in the United States, which have been linked to positive alcohol and smoking expectancies. Advertisement does work. In the United States, certain industries, such as gambling and other forms of entertainment, collaborate and are tied into chemical use, which places additional pressures on the public to engage in potentially addictive behaviors. Also, the United States is a society of fast food, Internet shopping, and satellite television: Our society places great value on satisfying impulses quickly. It is unclear how the societal modeling of instant gratification affects chemical dependence, but difficulties with impulse control have been linked to problems with substance abuse.

In summary, there are many internal and external factors that seem to influence the development of chemical dependence. Some, such as genetic factors or familial history, may be beyond our clinical manipulation or control at this time, but they do serve to flag certain high risk groups that should be targeted for prevention interventions. However, other factors that are cognitive, behavioral, emotional, and environmental can be changed, even after chemical dependence has been diagnosed. This is good news for those of us who work with chemically dependent patients.

However, before intervention can occur, we must know where to intervene. This requires that we conduct thorough assessments of our patients to understand what things we cannot change, what things we can change with the help of our patients, and the wisdom to know the difference. Assessments often provide that wisdom.

ASSESSMENT OF CHEMICAL DEPENDENCE

ASSESSING HISTORY AND DIAGNOSIS

Therapists working with chemically dependent clients want to know several important facts about the client's substance use. We want to know what they are using, how much, and when. We want to know what kinds of consequences they are experiencing related to their substance use and whether there are other major life changes that may have occurred recently. Other details that we may wish to understand include the client's expectations related to substance use, his or her self-efficacy about not losing control in different situations and level of motivation to change substance use, and whether he or she has the skills necessary to change.

It is important to determine the function of the substance use in the client's life. To ascertain the function, I conduct a function analysis of a person's typical substance use during a typical day or week. First, I ask the patient to describe in great detail what a typical day is like for her or him and how substance use is a part of that day. Next, I ask the person to tell me his or her goals of substance use at different points of the day. In conjunction, I ask the client to talk about the consequences of the substance use, both positive and negative. I may ask the person to go backwards in time from the moment of first substance use, and tell me all the steps that led to the actual moment of using the substance. This kind of function analysis is also referred to as a *behavior chain analysis.*

This kind of function analysis is extremely helpful to determine behavior chains—those series of events or steps that immediately lead up to the use of substances. Identifying these links in the chain are useful because you get valuable information about steps or triggers leading up to substance use, and it also allows you to determine different places in the behavior chain that you may wish to intervene to stop the behavior. A function analysis allows you to determine potential antecedents and consequences to using and helps you formulate potential strategies to help the person.

This kind of analysis can be helpful in another way. If you are working with patients who do not believe they have a problem, sometimes using a function analysis can help you break the ice. When working with people who may not be aware of their problems, you can ask them about the typical day and how using substances fits into that day. Then, in the midst of this discussion, you may also wish to ask, "So, what are the good things that happen to you immediately after using?" And after the person has responded, you can ask, "So, what are the not so good things about using?" Notice how the way the questions are asked makes it less likely that a person may get defensive, since you are asking about the good things first, and you are not using the word *bad* in the second question, which I have found raises resistance with patients. These questions were inspired by Motivational Interviewing (MI; Miller & Rollnick, 2002) which is a highly skilled way to work with chemically dependent patients, but using the MI style is a skillful way to conduct an assessment, too.

Function analyses can be conducted during standard biopsychosocial interviews. Biopsychosocial interviews are conducted with the goal of determining the physical, personal, and social history of a patient, with particular attention to how that history is related to substance use and misuse (in the case of a patient with chemical dependence). Such interviews are standard of care for all mental and physical health services, so I will not go into great detail here. However, besides assessing potential problem areas that need to be targeted in therapy, these interviews also provide an opportunity to discover the strengths a person brings into therapy, as well as uncover what kinds of social support the person may have to encourage their efforts in therapy.

Diagnostic assessments are often conducted in conjunction with functional assessments. Since diagnostic assessment generally means, "Does he or she meet *DSM-IV* criteria?" the best instrument to use is the Structured Clinical Interview for *DSM-IV*, or SCID. The SCID is a structured interview that asks specifically about *DSM-IV* criteria. Conducting the full SCID can take a significant period of time but will provide both substance related and other mental health diagnoses. However, you may wish to opt for administering the substance use disorders section only if time is of concern. Conducting the SCID manually requires some training, and since it is a structured interview, trainees should be checked for adherence by a seasoned administrator. There are computerized versions of the SCID that can be administered more rapidly with some that can be self-administered by the patient, and these will automatically provide accurate patient diagnoses for you.

Diagnostic assessment can be very powerful, since it often leads to labeling a patient. How therapists use a label can have some potentially important consequences. Past research has found that labels can be helpful if they provide the patient with useful information, such as what treatment will help with a given condition. However, labels also can be harmful if the label tends to stigmatize the patient and leave the patient feeling isolated or without hope. Therapists have to be careful with what they do with diagnostic information and how they may present that information to patients to ensure that the diagnosis does no harm. I tend to avoid sharing diagnoses with a patient. If asked about a diagnosis by the patient, I usually tell her or him that it is really irrelevant whether I think they are chemically dependent, but it is more relevant what she or he thinks about him- or herself (Alcoholics Anonymous, 1976).

The other concern that I have as a researcher and therapist is the use of colloquial terms such as *alcoholism* or *alcoholic*, or *addict*. These terms, although potentially helpful to some recovering people who find help in self-help programs, are not useful for all people. In fact, some people have reported that such terms are stigmatizing and, therefore, potentially harmful. Besides, such terms are not diagnostic (those terms are not defined in the *DSM-IV*) and are usually emotionally laden and not complimentary terms in our society. I do not use these terms with my patients. If they want to define themselves that way, it is fine with me as long as the label doesn't lead to helplessness, but I do not think it is helpful to use an unscientific term devoid of diagnostic meaning to describe a patient with chemical dependence.

Physical health assessments also are important, if you have the resources to do so. Panels that determine whether liver enzymes are elevated or whether other physical changes have occurred not only provide useful information in treating a person with chemical dependency, but also the information sometimes can be used to motivate the client to change. I recommend to new patients that they get a thorough physical examination to err on the side of caution concerning their well-being. Furthermore, medical assessments sometimes can grab the attention of someone who is otherwise unaware of negative substance-related consequences. However, for some patients, health concerns are not as important as we would hope they would be. I have witnessed reactions of hopelessness in some of my patients when they received unexpected bad news about their health. For instance, when told they are HIV positive or positive for Hepatitis C, some people have a tendency to give up. In those cases, it is important to provide hope for future cures and treatment and make clear that taking care of one's self physically buys time for medical breakthroughs.

There are several brief measures that ask about particular symptoms of chemical dependence that are often used in lieu of the SCID in medical or other clinical settings where assessment time is limited. These brief measures are not diagnostic, but responses that exceed established cut scores can suggest a high likelihood of chemical dependence. Some of the most well-known instruments include the Michigan Alcoholism Screening Test (MAST), which includes a long and short version; and its cousin, the Drug Abuse Screening Test; the four-item CAGE questionnaire; and the 10-item Alcohol Use Disorders Identification Test, which was developed by the World Health Organization. There also is the CRAFFT, which is a more recent brief measure developed specifically to detect potential chemical dependence in adolescents and youth. The CAGE and the CRAFFT names reflect acronyms from the questions asked on those tests.

These screening measures have the advantage of providing rapid assessment with some accuracy, but they are not without flaws and cannot provide you with a definitive diagnosis. I have used these instruments as a first step toward identifying possible substance abuse, but recommend a full or partial SCID when a person has entered treatment.

ASSESSING SUBSTANCE USE PATTERNS AND CONSEQUENCES

Diagnostic measures do not assess substance use patterns or consequences in a very meaningful way. However, there are a wide variety of measures that do that are often easily obtainable. The most common assessments are structured interviews such as the Addiction Severity Index (ASI) family of instruments originally developed in the Veterans Administration system. The ASI, as well as the Adolescent Drug Abuse Diagnosis and the Comprehensive Adolescent Severity Inventory, and Teen Addiction Severity Inventory (which are designed to be administered to youth), assess substance abuse lifetime and recent consumption patterns for multiple substances, as well as assessing several life domains where negative substance-related consequences may have been experienced, such as vocational and health. These interviews can take some time to administer, and you need to be trained by an expert administrator, but these interviews provide a wealth of information about the patient. The ASI also can be administered by computer.

However, since instruments like the ASI ask for a breadth of information, sometimes the details are not fully assessed. For consumption patterns, there are instruments specifically designed to assess recent substance use patterns, such as the Steady Pattern Chart and Other Drug Use Questionnaire from the Form 90, as well as the Time Line Follow-Back Interview. The Comprehensive Drinker Profile (CDP) and its shorter version, the Brief Drinker Profile (BDP) are similar to the ASI family of instruments because they include assessment of problem areas related to alcohol use, but they also include the Steady Pattern to determine consumption as well as the MAST for screening purposes. The CDP and BDP are much shorter, therefore, take less time to administer, but do not assess some life domains as thoroughly as the ASI family of instruments.

With the assessment of consequences, there are several interesting instruments that can be used. The Drinker Inventory of Consequences (DrInC) and Inventory of Drug Using Consequences (InDuC) family of instrument assess both the lifetime and recent frequency of substance-related consequences in a variety of life areas. Each of these instruments has scale scores for particular life domains, such as interpersonal or physical consequences. There are other more specific instruments available such as the LOSS-QR which assesses frequency and

---

BOX 3.6
What to Assess?

The function of the substance use in the person's life across different situations.

The consequences of substance use, including current physical health.

Diagnosis and patterns of use.

Psychosocial factors influencing behavior, such as expectancies, self-efficacy, motivation, and knowledge of skills.

Neuropsychological function, especially with memory and executive function.

---

importance of particular losses related to substance use. The Problem Oriented Screening Instrument for Teenagers and the Rutgers Alcohol Problem Index are brief assessments of consequences that are more typically experienced by adolescents and youth. The Personal Experiences Inventory (PEI) also assesses consequences experienced by youthful substance users and is longer and similar to the CDP and BDP since the PEI also assesses consumption patterns.

There also are a variety of assessments to determine those psychosocial factors discussed previously that seem to predict the future course of substance use, such as expectancies, self-efficacy, motivation to change, and the ability to problem solve and use coping skills (including distress tolerance, interpersonal, and emotion regulation skills). Many of these assessments provide useful information about the extent of substance use problems in a patient, as well as some predictability of prognosis. (See Box 3.6.)

Assessing expectancies can be illuminating since it can tell you whether the person has an unusually high number of positive expectancies about substance use. Typically, these expectancies perpetuate substance use. Furthermore, high numbers of positive expectancies about a substance may suggest that the person will have a difficult time changing his or her behavior, and knowing what the expectancies are provides you with information about the direction of therapy. There are many useful measures of expectancies available, including measures that assess positive and negative expectancies, expectancies associated with different types of substances, and measures that assess expectancies for adults and youth.

Assessing self-efficacy can be useful for determining chemical dependence. To begin with, assessing self-efficacy can determine those situations where the client believes that he or she does not have control of his or her substance use. Furthermore, assessing self-efficacy can help with treatment planning, since it highlights areas in a client's life where the person may not feel competent in negotiating without substance use. The Alcohol Abstinence Self-Efficacy Scale and the Situational Confidence and Drug-Taking Confidence Questionnaires are probably the most well-known instruments to assess self-efficacy to avoid drinking or using in various high risk situations.

In addition, assessing motivation is critical. Many substance abuse therapists are now using the Transtheoretical Stages of Change Model (Prochaska, DiClemente, & Norcross, 1992) to conceptualize where a patient may be on the road to change. By establishing at what stage of change a person may be, the therapists also can determine what might be the best therapeutic strategies to use with the patient. Assessing the person's motivation to change also can provide you information about the person's awareness of the desire to change substance use. There are many useful assessments of stages of change, including the University of Rhode Island Change Assessment (URICA), Stages of Change Readiness and Treatment Eagerness Scale (SOCRATES), and the Brief Readiness to Change Questionnaire. Sometimes using such a questionnaire allows the patient to reflect on the consequences of substance use, while providing you with useful information about the patient.

Finally, skill deficits or inappropriate use of skills can be predictive of continued problems with chemical dependence. Assessing skills can be quite useful in determining the course of therapy. To assess the ability to solve problems and use coping skills effectively, the Situational Competence Test (SCT) can be quite useful. In the SCT, the therapist describes a problem or stressful situation and then asks what the patient would do under those conditions to solve the problem. How the patient solves these problems can provide information to the therapist about whether the patient has the ability to skillfully cope with certain high-risk situations without losing control.

Another good way to determine whether the person is capable of effectively solving problems and coping with stress is to observe how the patient interacts with other people in your clinic, in a group, or even in session with you. Finally, I like to include role play in session to observe the patient in action or to actually observing the patient interact with other people in real-world situations. Assessing these interactions can provide information about why certain consequences are occurring and may provide tips on where potentially useful interventions can occur in therapy.

There also are instruments that can assess mood and emotions, which can be helpful to use. A couple of well-known instruments include the Profile of Mood States or the Multiple Affect Adjective Check List, which ask about various moods and emotions that the patient is experiencing at the present. Furthermore, using interpersonal interactions in session or in group settings related to emotional issues can identify problems with expressing emotions appropriately, and whether those problems may be related to a skills deficit. If it is related to a problem with skills, then teaching some form of emotion regulation becomes the next course of action.

If you are interested in learning more about assessment of chemical dependence, there are several helpful sources listed in Recommended Readings at the end of this chapter. However, some assessment tools can be found on the Internet including the National Institute on Alcohol Abuse and Alcoholism (NIAAA, www.niaaa.nih.gov), National Institute on Drug Abuse (NIDA, www.drugabuse .gov), or the Substance Abuse Mental Health Services Administration (SAMHSA, www.samhsa.gov).

ASSESSING NEUROCOGNITIVE FUNCTION

The neurotoxicity of substances can cause cognitive changes that may complicate the course of chemical dependence. Chronic substance abuse has been associated with cognitive changes, such as motor and memory problems and executive function deficits that can cause problems with remembering new information, judgment, planning, abstraction abilities and problem solving, awareness, and self-regulating and controlling behavior. There are many good standardized neuropsychological tests for memory, including verbal and visual, recall and recognition, and even working memory that have norms and also often have manuals discussing specific deficits than are seen among special populations, such as people abusing substances. To assess attention, concentration, and executive functions, there also are many interesting and specific standardized tests with manuals and population norms. Some neuropsychological tests can be self-administered either manually or on a computer, but many tests must be administered by a trained therapist.

Assessment of neuropsychological deficits or problems may not always be clinically evident. For instance, I have worked with many patients who appear quite normal in session but act bizarrely and disinhibited out of session. Frequently, executive function problems are not readily available, and patients can appear fairly normal in superficial interpersonal interactions but are unable to carry on in life situations without major problems and difficulties. Such is the nature of executive function problems. This is why I would highly recommend that chemically dependent patients get a thorough neuropsychological work-up to see whether there may be subtle cognitive changes not readily apparent even to trained therapists. I generally suspect such difficulties if a patient motivated to change is having problems controlling his or her behavior or remembering what to do to achieve his or her goals for recovery.

Many clinicians may not have the resources to conduct full neuropsychological evaluations, and there are brief assessments available that can be administered relatively quickly. The most commonly used assessment is the Mini Mental Status Examination (MMSE). The MMSE can often determine if a person is having difficulties with orientation and memory. The MMSE was designed to be a screening tool (not diagnostic), so it may not be able to identify the specific cognitive problem. Furthermore, the MMSE is not particularly sensitive to identifying the more subtle executive function problems.

ASSESSMENT AS PART OF THERAPY

Assessment is a crucial part of the therapeutic process. Conducting thorough assessments in the areas discussed will help identify problem areas that need to be addressed for a successful outcome, identify what strengths and supports the person may have to encourage his or her efforts, and help identify what kinds of treatment modalities and strategies may be most helpful (and best match) for the patient. In addition, assessment throughout treatment is truly the only way to document progress toward treatment goals. Finally, research suggests that assessment can act as an intervention, prompting some people to change their behavior. Assessment, as knowledge, is a powerful tool to promote change.

FINAL THOUGHTS

One thing we do know about chemical dependence is that diagnosing and assessing it can be quite complicated. Chemical dependence involves biological, psychological (including behavioral principles, cognitions, and emotions) and environmental factors that influence its onset, course, and treatment. Because of the interactions of biological, psychological, and environmental factors there can be great differences between the presentations of chemical dependence in different patients. However, research has made many advances in the past few years, and there have been some promising treatments developed for people who are chemically dependent. For those of you in the field or thinking about entering the field, I hope that you found this chapter interesting and helpful. Most important, keep up your good work.

RECOMMENDED READING

ETIOLOGY OF CHEMICAL DEPENDENCE

Marlatt, G. A., & VandenBos, G. R. (Eds.). (1997). *Addictive behaviors: Readings on etiology, prevention, and treatment.* Washington, DC: American Psychological Association.

McCrady, B. S., & Epstein, E. E. (1999). *Addictions: A comprehensive guidebook.* New York: Oxford Press. These books are highly recommended because they cover a breadth of areas related to the etiology and assessment of addictions. The Marlatt and Vanden-Bos book is a collection of arguably some of the most important articles written in all the major areas of addiction research, whereas the McCrady and Epstein book has very recent and specific information about addictive processes in a variety of population groups, as well as specific information about treating chemically dependent patients.

ASSESSMENT OF CHEMICAL DEPENDENCE

Donovan, D. M., & Marlatt, G. A. (Eds.). (1988). *Assessment of addictive behaviors.* New York: Guilford Press. This is arguably the most comprehensive book written on assessing chemical dependence over a variety of substances and among a variety of populations. A newly revised edition of this book will be released in the near future.

Miller, W. R. (1996). *Form 90: A structured assessment interview for drinking and related behaviors.* Project MATCH Monograph Series, Vol. 5. Rockville, MD: NIAAA. This monograph also can be obtained from NIAAA and includes a variety of measures to assess the consumption patterns of chemical dependence.

Miller, W. R., Tonigan, J. S., & Longabaugh, R. (1995). *The Drinker Inventory of Consequences (DrInC): An instrument for assessing adverse consequences of alcohol abuse.* Project MATCH Monograph Series, Vol. 4. Rockville, MD: NIAAA. This monograph can be obtained from NIAAA and includes a variety of measures to assess the consequences of chemical dependence.

NIAAA. (1995). *Assessing alcohol problems: A guide for clinicians and researchers.* NIAAA Treatment Handbook Series, 4. Bethesda, MD: Author. This handbook can be ordered from NIAAA and has a number of good instruments for assessing the psychological factors predicting alcohol dependence.

NIDA. (1994). *Assessing drug abuse among adolescents and adults: Standardized instruments.* Rockville, MD: Author. This handbook can be obtained from NIDA and has a wide variety of measures assessing psychological predictors of drug use other than alcohol for both adults and teens.

SAMSHA. (1993). *Screening and assessment of alcohol- and other drug-abusing adolescents.* Treatment Improvement Protocol Series, 3. Rockville, MD: Author. This handbook can be obtained from SAMSHA and it specifically covers assessing chemical dependence among youth.

SAMSHA. (1995). *Alcohol and other drug screening of hospitalized trauma patients.* Treatment Improvement Protocol Series, 16. Rockville, MD: Author. This SAMSHA manual provides ways to assess chemical dependence among patients hospitalized for traumatic accidents. Furthermore, each of these federally produced manuals (2 through 7 above) is relatively inexpensive or free.

REFERENCES

Alcoholics Anonymous. (1976). *Alcoholics Anonymous: The story of how many thousands of men and women have recovered from alcoholism* (3rd ed.). New York: Author.

American Psychiatric Association. (2000). *Diagnostic and statistical manual of mental disorders* (4th ed., text rev.). Washington, DC: Author.

Blume, A. W., & Marlatt, G. A. (2000). Recent important losses predict readiness to change scores in people with co-occurring psychiatric disorders. *Addictive Behaviors, 25,* 461–464.

Blume, A. W., & Schmaling, K. B. (1998). Regret, substance abuse, and readiness to change in a dually diagnosed sample. *Addictive Behaviors, 23,* 693–697.

Institute of Medicine. (1990). *Broadening the base of treatment for alcohol problems.* Washington, DC: National Academy Press.

Jellinek, E. M. (1960). *The disease concept of alcoholism.* New Haven, CT: College and University Press.

Lezak, M. D. (1995). *Neuropsychological assessment* (3rd ed.). New York: Oxford University Press.

Linehan, M. M. (1993). *Cognitive-behavioral treatment of borderline personality disorder.* New York: Guilford Press.

Marlatt, G. A. (1985). Relapse prevention: Theoretical rationale and overview of the model. In G. A. Marlatt & J. R. Gordon (Eds.), *Relapse prevention: Maintenance strategies in the treatment of addictive behaviors* (pp. 3–70). New York: Guilford Press.

Marlatt, G. A., Demming, B., & Reid, J. B. (1973). Loss of control drinking in alcoholics: An experimental analogue. *Journal of Abnormal Psychology, 81,* 233–241.

Miller, W. R., & Rollnick, S. (2002). *Motivational interviewing: Preparing people for change* (2nd ed.). New York: Guilford Press.

National Center for Injury Prevention and Control. (2002). *Ten leading causes of death, United States, 2000.* Available from http://webapp.cdc.gov/cgi-bin/broker.exe.

National Institute on Alcohol Abuse and Alcoholism. (1997). *Ninth special report to congress on alcohol and health.* Rockville, MD: Author.

Office of National Drug Control Policy. (2001). *The economic costs of drug abuse in the United States, 1992–1998* (Publication No. NCJ-190636). Washington, DC: Executive Office of the President.

Prochaska, J. O., DiClemente, C. C., & Norcross, J. C. (1992). In search of how people change: Applications to addictive behaviors. *American Psychologist, 47,* 1102–1114.

Substance Abuse and Mental Health Services Administration. (2002). *2001 national household survey on drug abuse* (NHSDA). Available from http://www.samhsa.gov/oas/nhsda/.

CHAPTER 4

Treating Substance Use Disorders

JEANNE L. OBERT, AHNDREA WEINER, JANICE STIMSON, and
RICHARD A. RAWSON

IMAGINE THAT A visitor from another planet walked into your office one day and sat down and said, "Please explain to me what substance abuse treatment is and more specifically, what substance abuse counselors do." First, you would have to explain to him or her about addiction and alcoholism, the peculiar disorders (diseases?) that consist of behaviors that defy common sense. Your visitor might wonder why people don't "Just say no" when, for some individuals, the excessive use of drugs and alcohol produces negative or possibly even life-threatening consequences? You would have to explain that although treatment-seeking individuals want to stop drugs and/or alcohol and become productive citizens, they are unable to stop, and your job is to help them. Now comes the hard part—explaining exactly what treatment is and how it works. Some parts of the treatment, such as giving medication to relieve withdrawal systems would be easy enough, but the really tough part is explaining how words, conversations, discussions, and therapy give addicts and alcoholics some new ability to discontinue their potentially fatal habit. You would probably explain that your job requires you to be a teacher, case manager, therapist, sponsor, supportive person, and to perform other helping tasks. However, the interview with the alien visitor could easily end without your being able to clearly and specifically describe what you do and why you do it in the process of delivering treatment to a substance dependent individual.

During the 1960s, 1970s, and the early part of the 1980s, when most substance abuse treatment was done in an inpatient hospital or other residential setting, your role would have been fairly uncomplicated. You would probably have been in recovery and your job would have primarily consisted of being a role model and mentor to other individuals and to encourage their getting involved in the 12-Step program of Alcoholics Anonymous.

Sometime during the late 1980s and 1990s your role would have probably shifted from working as a residential counselor to working in an outpatient setting. Recent data from the federal government reported that by 2001, over 80% of the individuals treated for alcoholism and addiction were treated in outpatient settings. Furthermore, this number does not include the large numbers of individuals who receive outpatient assistance from individual psychotherapists and doctors in private practice setting that are not categorized as outpatient substance abuse treatment programs. This shift occurred mainly because of managed-care cost containment strategies and has resulted in many more substance abuse treatment professionals delivering treatment using outpatient interventions and techniques. So you would likely need to be able to describe services that could be used in an outpatient setting.

The purpose of this chapter is to provide you with a twenty-first century definition and explanation of substance abuse treatment as it currently exists in the United States. We will look at how our present service delivery system has evolved and what characterizes treatment today. The latter half of the chapter will focus on both the skills that you can effectively use to help someone stop using drugs or alcohol and on how you can most effectively teach those skills to patients in a manner that will engage and retain them in the outpatient treatment process.

THE EMERGENCE OF THE SUBSTANCE ABUSE COUNSELOR AS A HEALTH CARE PROFESSIONAL

The field of substance abuse treatment has significantly changed in the past 20 years. As recently as the early 1980s most of the clinical staff delivering treatment to people with drug and alcohol problems were recovering users who wanted to share with others the sobriety they had earned. Some of them were health care professionals (i.e., physicians, psychotherapists, and social workers), but most were not formally trained in delivering professional health care services. Instead, they were individuals who achieved sobriety via 12-Step, self-help programs who were willing and able to offer their own strength, hope, and courage and to share their own experiences in seeking sobriety with others needing help.

For the most part, the professional health care community was more than willing to abdicate care of those with significant drug and alcohol problems to the recovering paraprofessional community. Individuals with drug and alcohol problems are difficult to treat and make challenging patients/clients. They don't always tell the truth, they often misuse the medications given to them, and they often abuse the people who try to help them. Their lives are out of control; they are unpredictable, fail to keep appointments, and don't follow treatment recommendations.

In the early 1980s, few professionals had any training about the nature of effective substance abuse treatment (there was little available literature, even if there had been a desire to train professionals). As a result, of repeated unfulfilling experiences in treating drug and alcohol users, many in the professional treatment community developed a negative attitude toward treating addicts and alcoholics. For those addicts and alcoholics who sought help, many found professional help of little value and, in many cases, the response by the treatment professional was to blame the patient for not being good. As a result, drug and alcohol abusers developed distrust and dislike for professional caregivers, and these feelings were mutual. The mutual skepticism grew into a deep, gaping chasm with bidirectional animosity.

Today, despite advances in knowledge and the science of drug and alcohol treatment, the gap between the recovering community and professional treatment providers still remains. Evidence of this gap is demonstrated when a person seeking treatment asks you, the professional provider, "Are you recovering?" or "Have you ever abused drugs or alcohol yourself?" The question reflects a perception, reinforced by some recovering individuals, that only a person who has personally experienced a substance abuse problem and enters recovery can truly be helpful to addicts and alcoholics. This belief is a peculiarity unique to the substance abuse treatment field. The same individual seeking care for a broken leg or toothache would be unlikely to care whether his or her doctor or dentist had personal experience with the ailment in question. Even within the mental health community, it would be unusual for a patient to assume that a therapist's personal mental health history was a necessary credential to demonstrate appropriate qualifications.

In the past two decades, the fields of psychiatry, psychology, social work, and the counseling professions have attempted to improve their expertise in the treatment of alcoholism and drug addiction. Substantial efforts have been made to increase our understanding about the science of addiction and about effective ways to treat people with drug and alcohol problems. All members of your treatment team (as well as those determining payments for treatment) are being encouraged to base treatment plans on interventions with proven effectiveness rather than on personal beliefs and personal experiences.

Therapists trained in effective modalities for working with general mental health problems need to consider how to integrate interventions that are known to be helpful in working with drug and alcohol abusers into their therapeutic repertoires. As an example, the use of insight-oriented therapies that focus on presumed psychodynamic problems with a patient who is in the very early stages of drug/alcohol recovery is not only of little value, but can be counterproductive. For many individuals in the early stages of recovery, exploration of long-term psychodynamically charged issues can be anxiety provoking; drug and alcohol users frequently respond to increased anxiety by using drugs and alcohol; hence, raising the patient's anxiety level is likely to increase the chance of relapse. The recommended course of treatment is to first concentrate on helping the patient learn some basic skills to stop alcohol and drug use. Once that is accomplished and the patient has experienced a substantial period of sobriety, it may be perfectly safe and even advisable to do the more psychodynamically oriented work.

Counselors who are successful in the substance abuse and dependence treatment programs of the future will have to be able to work as part of a multidisciplinary team. As more effective medications are developed for use with drug and alcohol abusers, physicians will need to be included as part of the treatment team. You will often be asked, and should be trained to offer, to monitor the patient's medication-taking while you are also doing your own counseling and psychosocial treatment. Some patients will need social services. Part of your job will be to identify those needs and be able to direct patients to places where they can get assistance with obtaining food, health care, housing, and jobs. Ideally all members of your team will be housed at the same location and will regularly meet together to integrate the care plan for patients. Currently, this is frequently not the situation. In the current world of substance abuse treatment you and the other members of the treatment team are likely to be separated geographically and to be paid from different sources. While you are probably the most appropriate person to coordinate the care of each patient, it is frequently very difficult to perform this function.

This time consuming case management responsibility is not always appreciated by other members of the treatment team and is often not reimbursed, so it is a thankless task. However, it is clear that this coordination function, if successfully carried out, will ultimately result in a synchronized, effective treatment episode.

It is becoming increasingly clear that counselors have to be comfortable working with patients who are not necessarily ready to begin treatment when they first walk in the door. For a variety of reasons, individuals who are exceedingly ambivalent about the need for treatment are being pushed into treatment settings with increasing frequency. There are many factors that are contributing to this trend. Workplace drug testing identifies people who are abusing drugs but may not yet perceive the use as problematic. Family members and significant others who are exposed to drug and alcohol abuse information may bring in reluctant participants. Schools are beginning to test students whose behavior is suspect and refer them for treatment, hoping to address the problem before serious clinical problems emerge. Probably the biggest source of individuals who are pushed into treatment is the criminal justice system, where the choice is between treatment and incarceration. The research literature around the use of motivational techniques has documented that it is possible to make a positive impact on a substance abuser, even if they are not sure they want help or are ready to stop drinking or using drugs.

DRUG ABUSE TREATMENT

THERAPEUTIC COMMUNITIES

Organized treatment of individuals dependent on illicit drugs (heroin, cocaine, amphetamines, and barbiturates) in the United States began in Santa Monica, California, in the 1950s. It began with a self-help organization consisting of recovering individuals who provided housing and peer therapy for males who were abusing or dependent on drugs. Charles Deiderick, the leader of Synanon, created a community of addicts who lived together under a common roof and followed a strict set of rules and organizational principles. Other similar programs then began to appear, including Phoenix House and Daytop Village. The goal of these programs was to change the participants' way of life and to teach them how to live life according to an entirely new set of principles. "The game" was a group therapy developed for the purpose of promoting attitude and behavior change. It involved marathon group sessions in which fellow drug users confronted each other about current and previous behavior that was seen to be the essence of the addicted lifestyle and psyche. Therapeutic Communities (TCs) were rapidly created in large metropolitan areas throughout the Unites States, providing a template for the treatment of many illicit drug users well into the 1960s and 1970s.

Many of the TCs operating today look quite different from those initially established. A large percentage of them have integrated medical and psychiatric services and have adapted their treatments in response to research evaluation efforts. Staff training and credentialing is constantly being improved. Despite the evolution of TCs over the several decades into a more mainstream treatment service, the TC still exists today as a major component of the U.S. addiction treatment system.

The concept that peer counselors who have firsthand experience of addiction and recovery make the most desirable treatment providers grew out of the TC approach. Considerable resistance to changing this attitude still remains in our treatment system. In addition, the use of the aggressive, confrontational strategies employed in the TC group therapies has legitimized some approaches that have little or no evidence of being effective and, in some cases, may be counter therapeutic and damaging. Finally, there are those who wonder: If addiction is a disease and not willful misbehavior, why do some TCs appear to have more in common with boot camps than with health care facilities?

PHARMACOLOGIC APPROACHES

The early chasm that developed between the medical community and the drug abuse treatment system has perpetuated reluctance on the part of many treatment programs to use medications in the treatment of drug and alcohol abuse. This attitude is slowly disappearing as the need to use pharmaceutical aids increases with the rising popularity of utilizing integrated approaches. Presently, as well as historically, there has been a scarcity of medications designed specifically to aid patients in recovery. Professionals treating opiate dependence have had the lion's share of such options partly because of the popularity of substitution therapy with this class of drugs.

Vincent Dole, MD, an endocrinologist and Marie Nyswander, MD, a psychiatrist, initiated the first large-scale, explicitly medical approach to the treatment of opioid abuse and dependence in New York City when they began using methadone as a treatment agent. They viewed the use of methadone to help opiate addicts reduce withdrawal symptoms and eliminate drug craving and consequent drug-seeking behavior to be as rational a medical approach as the use of insulin for the treatment of diabetes. Their treatment approach also recognized and addressed the social, psychological, and behavioral needs of patients, and their treatment plans included much more than medication alone. Treatment with methadone rapidly gained favor as a modality, bringing medical personnel clearly into a prominent role with this treatment approach.

The debate surrounding methadone as a treatment tool continues even today. Advocates echo Dr. Dole in pointing out that, for a long-term opiate dependent individual, the expectation of living a drug-free life is probably unrealistic. Addiction, particularly to opiates, is a chronic, relapsing condition. Long-term methadone treatment, when combined with adequate counseling, behavioral therapies, and other support services, can eliminate the use of illicit drugs and return the individual to a productive, relatively healthy lifestyle. Methadone has been used and studied for over 30 years. It is not intoxicating or sedating when it is properly prescribed and one dose lasts 4 to 6 times as long as a dose of heroin. It relieves craving, suppresses withdrawal and is medically safe, even when used 10 years or more. In attending clinics to obtain their dose, patients have ready access to health care services they might otherwise not access. Beside the benefit to the patient, treating diseases commonly associated with intravenous drug abuse, that is, HIV/AIDS, Hepatitis B and C, and so on, is a significant benefit to the public, reducing the spread of these public health threats. Methadone advocates also cite the fact that the rate of mortality among opiate dependent patients in methadone treatment is far lower than for individuals who have not been in methadone maintenance treatment.

Those opposed to methadone treatment resist the idea that anyone should be expected to take a medication indeterminately or that one opiate-based medication should be substituted for another. The idea that methadone treatment for heroin addiction is analogous to insulin for a diabetic has not yet received popular acceptance. It is not particularly popular with other addiction treatment providers who are schooled to focus on abstinence as the ultimate goal. Further, it has not been well understood nor accepted by either mainstream medicine or psychiatry.

Partly as a result of its political unpopularity, the methadone clinic treatment network has been chronically underfunded and severely stigmatized. While the establishment of the methadone treatment system was a very important benchmark in the evolution of the U.S. treatment system, many of the aforementioned problems have reduced its acceptance as a treatment option and have led to its suboptimal impact as a treatment modality.

While methadone is the most widely studied and empirically proven medication treatment for opioid dependence, three other medications have recently been made available. Levo-alpha-acetyl-methadol (LAAM) is, like methadone, a long acting opioid. It was approved in 1993 for use as a substitution therapy for heroin addiction. Its main advantage over methadone is that it has a longer duration of action and can be taken as infrequently as 3 times per week. While LAAM has some advantages over methadone, it has not been widely used and there still are some outstanding safety concerns that have not been fully resolved.

Naltrexone and naloxone differ from the substitution therapies. These medications block the effects of morphine, heroin, and other opiates. They can be used on an acute basis as antidotes for heroin overdose (naloxone) because of their antagonist qualities, or they can be used on a chronic basis to prevent relapse (naltrexone) since they block the pleasurable effects of heroin. Naltexone can be particularly useful for recovering physicians and nurses who need to work in situations that expose them to opiates. As with methadone, studies show that all of these agents are most effective when combined with behavioral therapies.

The final medicine for treatment of opiate dependence, buprenorphine, was approved by the U.S. Food and Drug Administration in October of 2002. Buprenorphine is a particularly attractive treatment because its addiction potential is significantly milder than methadone or LAAM and it creates weaker opiate effects, thereby limiting overdose potential. The use of these types of medications, however, has historically been limited to highly regulated narcotic treatment programs (i.e., methadone clinics).

The passage of the Drug Addiction Treatment Act of 2000, combined with the buprenorphine legislation, has the potential of significantly altering the landscape of treatment options for people dependent on opioids. The Drug Addiction Treatment Act sets standards for physicians who choose to get trained and offer these treatments in their offices. Buprenorphine is now available for the treatment of patients who have developed dependence on prescription painkillers, such as OxyContin, in addition to those addicted to heroin. This signals a return to the practice of treating people with addictions in the private offices of physicians and, hopefully, will lessen the stigma of this disease in the United States. The Act stipulates that patients treated by physicians with buprenorphine should be referred to or somehow connected with a counselor who can deliver the psychosocial portion of the treatment. This mandate creates another opportunity for you to become part of a professional partnership, working with physicians to maximize this treatment modality.

ALCOHOLISM TREATMENT

SOCIAL MODEL/MINNESOTA MODEL

The treatment system for alcohol abuse and dependence in the United States evolved from the Alcoholics Anonymous (AA) movement that began in the 1930s. The 12-Steps and Traditions of AA originated as a social movement to promote behavior and attitude change in response to the teachings and examples described in the Big Book. The 12-Step program itself is not formally a treatment program. It is described by members as a fellowship, which is a more apt description because people at the meetings do not conduct assessments, arrive at diagnoses, dispense medications, write treatment plans, provide case management, or do group or individual therapy. In an extensive overview of the theory of 12-Step oriented treatment (Wallace, 1996), the author states, "[B]oth the history of AA and modern thinking reveal implicit and explicit concern with multidimensional models of addiction." This approach of self-help and peer support following the tenets of AA to help people stop drinking alcohol was the earliest organized attempt to provide assistance to people abusing alcohol.

In many communities, loosely organized temporary housing facilities were established by AA program members to provide newly sober alcoholics with places to find support for their recovery attempts. These facilities (sometimes called *Oxford houses*) were not licensed or staffed by medical or mental health professionals. They offered food and housing and required involvement in AA activities. These programs were referred to as *social model* programs, as they offered a range of basic support services for these alcoholic residents, along with the support of the AA fellowship. This approach is the predominant service model that has been (and still is) used by homeless shelters and organizations, such as some of the Salvation Army programs.

During the 1950s and 1960s, much of the treatment for alcohol dependence consisted of detoxification in drunk tanks and dry out hospital units with no follow-up services. A number of recovering physicians who had successfully entered recovery began to organize physicians' groups with the goal of providing ongoing alcoholism recovery services to patients, some of whom had completed inpatient programs. These services included necessary medical care for safe treatment of withdrawal symptoms delivered in conjunction with the introduction and promotion of long-term AA participation as the road to recovery. Without formal addiction training, the medical and counseling services were typically provided by physicians and peer counselors whose expertise was primarily predicated on their personal involvement in alcoholism and subsequently AA. The most well-known of the programs that pioneered this AA-within-a-medical-setting approach were the Long Beach Naval Hospital in Southern California and several treatment centers in Minnesota. The acceptance and application of this approach expanded most rapidly in Minnesota and, thereafter, became known as the Minnesota Model.

In the 1960s and into the 1970s, the Minnesota Model evolved into a 28-day program that provided an immersion experience in the philosophy and practice of AA. While the types and varieties of ancillary services differed at different treatment centers, the main thrust of promotion of AA as the exclusive road to recovery became quite dogmatic and inflexible and proponents had little interest or openness to alternative approaches. The institutional acceptance of the Minnesota Model as the predominant medical treatment approach for the treatment of alcoholism was promoted by the National Council on Alcoholism and the legislative efforts of Senator Harold Hughes (D-Iowa) who promoted health insurance coverage for this service.

Inpatient hospital treatment programs began to use the 12-Step-based programs and the 28-day Minnesota Model program gained widespread utilization during the 1970s and 1980s. Minnesota Model programs generally operate as an organized service delivered by medical and nursing professionals providing 24-hour, medically supervised evaluation and withdrawal management in a permanent facility with inpatient beds. Services are delivered under a defined set of physician-approved policies and physician-monitored procedures or clinical protocols. Twenty-four hour observation, monitoring, and treatment are available. The treatment philosophy makes extensive use of 12-Step program participation and posttreatment support.

In the 1980s, the programs were broadened to provide treatment for drug users during the cocaine epidemic when many middle-class stimulant abusers were trying to find help for their cocaine abuse. The significant financial success of these programs contributed greatly to the rise in health care costs in the United States during this period. The 28-day length of stay evolved from agreements between the insurance companies and the hospital administrators rather than from any empirical findings relative to clinical appropriateness. As the economic picture changed in the 1990s, managed care companies began to challenge the need for longer term programs. This whittling down effect on payments for inpatient care has continued until, at the change of the millennium, 28-day programs for the treatment of substance abuse are the exception and not the rule. The majority of residential care programs have a more diversified set of treatment plans and services. There is tremendous geographic variation in the availability of these treatment service units, however.

As of this writing, some parts of the United States still have 28-day inpatient programs widely available; and, in other areas, they are almost nonexistent. The popularity of AA programs to assist drug and alcohol abusers, however, continues. These self-help programs are free of charge, numerous, and readily available and are still considered to be a widely utilized source of help for drug and alcohol abusers in the United States today.

OUTPATIENT TREATMENT

The aggressive, boot camp-like therapeutic communities of the 1950s and 1960s utilized treatment groups that generally consisted of painful confessions; dramatic confrontations; and tearful, emotionally cathartic insights. These were joined in the 1970s and 1980s by the emotion-eliciting, spiritually oriented, 12-Step-based group approaches that were widely utilized in the 28-day Minnesota Model treatment facilities. The former type of group therapy was generally employed in the treatment of drug abusers while the latter was more often used in programs treating primarily alcoholics. Both types of substance abuse treatment modalities are highly emotional and dramatic. They are favored by the media when portraying drug and alcohol recovery programs—partly because of their inherent drama and partly because they were, for so long, representative of the standard treatments offered.

The earliest actual outpatient programs began as store-front outreach centers that offered a collection of informal counseling and referral services. While these facilities were seen as resources established to help addicts and alcoholics, they were generally not viewed as facilities that delivered organized treatment. The programs that delivered methadone to heroin users and the 12-Step programs were the two recognized forms of service delivery on an outpatient basis. These treatments were for specific populations, but they contained the seeds of what would become the principles of effective outpatient treatment.

This combination of informal and specialized outpatient treatment, together with the residential and inpatient treatments described earlier, provided the basis for the development of outpatient treatment for all classes of drug and alcohol abusers as well as middle-class drug users when the cocaine epidemic, the emergence of HIV, and the reduced spending for treatment converged on the scene in the early 1980s.

The most widely utilized form of treatment today is outpatient treatment. It has gained in popularity since the 1990s for several reasons. To contain costs, treatment providers began to investigate effective ways to shorten or eliminate inpatient stays and to provide effective, structured outpatient programs. In addition, many of the stimulant abusers who were treated in protected inpatient environments relapsed within weeks of being released from residential treatment. They were not getting the skills and information, or the opportunity to practice using them, in the residential programs. More often than not, they returned to drug use soon after going back to their homes and jobs. Outpatient treatment provided an opportunity for them to experience a learn-as-you-go approach to recovery with the treatment program providing structure and support as they resumed their daily living.

The organized treatment delivery system did not convert easily to this new form of treatment. The transition was fraught with problems, some of which continue today. Many of the staff who had been involved in designing and providing residential and inpatient services shifted their focus to outpatient treatment. As a rule, the programs they created and operated utilized the same philosophy and treatment approaches as their previous residential programs. There was little recognition that outpatient treatment required a new paradigm; the philosophy of outpatient treatment and the content of the programming had to change significantly to be successful. An inpatient program in which patients go home to sleep at night is not synonymous with an effective outpatient program. In outpatient settings, the application of emotionally based, insight-oriented therapy techniques does not address the immediate needs of the newly abstinent substance abuser who is struggling to maintain sobriety. It is likely that these traditional substance abuse group methods may be counterproductive in the early weeks or months of recovery. Traditional inpatient and residential treatment providers are frequently not able to be experts at both inpatient and outpatient service delivery.

Despite these obstacles, outpatient approaches had become widely employed as the first treatment of choice for substance abuse patients by the end of the 1990s. Outpatient treatment, however, encompasses an almost unlimited collection of activities from psychotherapy to case management and referral services to self-help groups. Then, how did the cognitive-behavioral approaches that were first developed in the 1980s come to be viewed as the treatment of choice for professional outpatient programs?

In the book, *Treating Substance Abuse: Theory and Technique* (Rotgers, Keller, & Morgenstern, 1996), Frederick Rotgers notes that the behaviorally based approaches to treatment of psychoactive substance use disorders (PSUDs), along with the motivational and pharmacotherapeutic approaches, are the most closely linked with existing scientific knowledge. He emphasizes that these approaches are not only open to scientific scrutiny, they insist on it (p. 193). He continues to outline, in detail, seven advantages of using behavioral therapies in the treatment of PSUD:

1. They are amenable to being flexed to meet specific client needs.
2. They are readily accepted by clients because the persons being treated are highly involved in planning their own treatment and choosing their own goals.
3. The philosophy and interventions are soundly grounded in established psychological theory.
4. There is a high degree of linkage between scientific knowledge and treatment practices.
5. Treatment progress can be easily assessed with clear guidelines.
6. Clients are empowered to make their own behavior changes.
7. There is strong empirical and scientific evidence of efficacy.

With the increased emphasis on using treatments with empirical foundations and conceptualizing substance use disorders as chronic relapsing conditions, these behavioral treatments have gained in popularity. Alan Marlatt contributed to the field a systematic way of examining the process of relapse (Marlatt & Gordon, 1985). He focused on differentiating internal and external stimuli associated with relapse and was able to articulate the process of relapse in a clear and rational way. When the principles of behavioral therapy were paired with the understanding of relapse prevention, the stage was set for the development of organized, structured outpatient treatment systems that used cognitive and behavioral interventions to address the process of recovery.

You may be more familiar with relapse prevention as it was presented by Terrance Gorski (Gorski, 1986, 2000). While Marlatt's work was developed within an academic research context, Gorski, working contemporaneously and independently from Marlatt, developed a model of relapse and intervention with more widespread acceptance in the clinical arena. The collection of techniques developed from the work of both Marlatt and Gorski have become known as relapse prevention (RP) strategies. Gorski presented many of the RP concepts in terms of a disease or medical model of alcoholism from the perspective of a recovering counselor. These concepts have provided an organizing principle around which many outpatient treatment programs have been designed since these techniques offer practical, relevant approaches for addressing client needs (Donovan, 2002; Rawson et al., 1993). While some of the evaluation research on RP methods have employed individual counseling models, the use of groups has been the primary paradigm used for applying RP techniques.

Relapse prevention skills are more easily utilized by counselors when they are organized into manuals. A number of treatment manuals containing RP protocols have been published by the National Institute on Drug Abuse (NIDA;

www.nida.nih.gov). The NIDA manuals include a good deal of theoretical explanation for the approach being described. Results of controlled evaluations are included along with comprehensive goals for the therapist and specific strategies designed to assist the therapist in meeting those goals. The guidelines are very detailed and are written for a fairly well educated population. These manuals are excellent resources for sophisticated clinicians and research people who wish to study a given element of the overall treatment process. They often require very skilled supervision and/or teaching when they are used at the community clinic level. They generally do not outline an entire program or purport to define an all-inclusive treatment program.

Integrated Outpatient Models   At about the same time as the NIDA manuals were being developed, several groups began to develop formal intensive outpatient programs that utilized manualized treatment protocols specifically designed to produce standardized treatment episodes that could be systematically replicated and evaluated (McAuliffe, 1990; Rawson, Obert, McCann, Smith, & Scheffey, 1989; Zackon, McAuliffe, & Chien, 1993). These manuals include structured, easy-to-follow outlines for entire treatment programs using research-based methods and cognitive-behavioral, RP techniques for clients and their families.

McAuliffe and associates developed a treatment program that includes the use of RP strategies combined with self-help concepts. The Recovery Training and Self-Help Model (RTSH) has been evaluated in the treatment of opioids addiction and compared to standard treatment. Originally, it was developed as an outpatient group aftercare modality for opiate dependent patients in New England and Hong Kong. It proved to help reduce the possibility of relapse to opiates and also helped patients find work. The idea is to do systematic RP work when the patients are in treatment (Recovery Training) while, at the same time, providing motivation and support for continued abstinence and social reintegration (Self-Help). This model has been expanded into a program called the Cocaine Recovery System. In this integrated model, the program designers postulate that recovery from cocaine addiction be divided into three stages. In the first stage, the clients are taught to avoid triggers and supplies; second, they are integrated into a community of recovering people until their addiction extinguishes; and, finally they are taught to move into conventional society and gradually begin to function more fully beyond the recovering community (McAuliffe, 1991).

Programs delivering services based on protocols began to gain recognition for offering clinically viable programming with demonstrated efficacy that could be readily learned by front-line clinical staff in community-based programs. The standardized protocols have the added advantage of being easily evaluated and simply revised to include the most recent research findings. The remainder of this chapter will describe the principles, elements, and interventions of one such treatment protocol, the Matrix Model of Intensive Outpatient Treatment (Obert et al., 2000; Rawson et al., 1995). Included will be helpful hints given by the clinical staff who have been using this model with patients for more than 10 years.

The Matrix Model of Intensive Outpatient Treatment   The Matrix Model was developed in response to the cocaine and methamphetamine epidemics of the 1980s and 1990s. The treatment system at that time offered no relevant and appropriate option to stimulant users who generally did not need inpatient treatment and could not relate to alcohol-targeted treatments. The Matrix Model incorporated empirically supported treatment elements, including relapse prevention, education, and family involvement into a manualized, nonconfrontational, structured, cognitive/behavioral program. The treatment components are relapse prevention groups, individual counseling sessions, family education groups, and urine and breath alcohol testing. Group meetings are guided by written topics and focus on current issues and activities. The Model was broadened to treat stimulant abusers in groups with clients who are also dependent on alcohol and opioids. The concepts that were originally developed specifically to address the issues of stimulant users are most often used in clinics where client groups consist of people using, abusing, and dependent on a variety of substances. The Matrix outpatient treatment protocol, as well as other primarily outpatient programs, has a number of elements that are key to making treatment on an outpatient basis successful. The elements are:

1. Creating explicit structure and expectations.
2. Establishing a positive and collaborative relationship with the client.
3. Teaching information and cognitive-behavioral concepts.
4. Positively reinforcing desired behavioral change.
5. Providing corrective feedback when necessary using a motivational interaction style.
6. Educating family members on the expected course of recovery.
7. Monitoring drug use through urine and breath alcohol testing.
8. Introducing and encouraging self-help participation.

Programs without these key elements are not as likely to be effective in the delivery of outpatient treatment. The following section of this chapter focuses on how to incorporate these key elements into an outpatient program.

CREATING EXPLICIT STRUCTURE AND EXPECTATIONS   Structure is a critical element in any effective outpatient program. In your groups and individual outpatient therapy settings with substance abusers it is essential to provide treatment within a structured format. The idea is to create a protective shell for the client within which recovery can occur. Inpatient programs have brick-and-mortar structures. In outpatient treatment, the structure has to be created with clearly defined and predetermined activities. Structure decreases stress and provides consistency and predictability, which are all counter to an addictive lifestyle. Structure also establishes a group norm and atmosphere that promotes the learning of new skills, such as identifying triggers and cravings. Topic-focused groups foster a safe environment for self-discovery and experimentation with new thoughts and behaviors.

Having your clients keep a schedule for each day's activities will help them establish a new, safer lifestyle. Scheduling time serves several functions. One of the primary advantages of scheduling is the creation of an activity plan. The act of creating a predetermined set of activities requires clients to use their minds to think through future activities. Mastering the skill of learning to purposely determine behaviors prior to acting on them is an important step toward creating a sober lifestyle.

It is important to point out here that the term *scheduling* can be misleading. Many of us think of an appointment book when we hear this term. The purpose of this exercise is *not* to have people list one appointment after another. Not only would that be grueling and exhausting, it would be impossible to maintain such a pace. When we talk about making a schedule, the intent is more like planning your time. A realistic time plan would probably include watching television, reading the paper, taking naps, and so on. It is important to schedule recreational activities and things that are normally part of someone's routine but are not dangerous events.

Some of the possible scheduling pitfalls are:

1. Clients may forget to include leisure activities, time to rest or relax, and so on. One helpful way to make sure your client is creating a schedule that is realistic is to review the events of typical drug-free days and see what a normal routine is for that person. If the schedule created is too different from normal habits, it will be difficult for the client to incorporate it into his or her regular routine.
2. Clients may have difficulty making an hour-by-hour schedule. If this is the case, it is perfectly alright to simplify the process. One way to do that is to use a small, pocket-sized card with the day divided into four sections— morning, midday, afternoon, and evening. To begin scheduling is easier if the client can just plan activities for those four times of day. Some clients may have trouble learning this skill at all. If this is the case with your client, try having them talk about what they did for the past day or two and then guess at what they are likely to do in the next 24 hours. You can write his or her schedule as they talk about it.
3. Some families want to help determine what the recovering person should be doing. Spouses and parents, especially, have many ideas for things that have been neglected or that they would like to have the client do with them. Many clients are still filled with guilt and shame and can be easily convinced that they should do whatever family members want rather than what they need to do for themselves. If someone else's wishes and desires are often the basis for the schedule, sooner or later the recovering person will get resentful and will not find the scheduling useful or helpful.

Beside providing a way to identify upcoming high-risk situations, scheduling is also useful for developing alternative plans to avoid risky circumstances. An added benefit is the opportunity this exercise gives the therapist to review the client's daily living in detail and help identify the potential problem areas. We do not get to be with our clients 24 hours a day, and it is unusual for the counselor to have a clear understanding of what the client's life is actually like. Reviewing the schedule is a good way to strengthen your awareness of your client's lifestyle.

A side benefit of the scheduling is that it keeps clients accountable for their time, thereby avoiding having free time to acquire and use mind-altering substances. The scheduling of time encourages the creation of a more balanced lifestyle for your clients, which includes but is not limited to work, family, leisure, and recovery activities. This helpful tool will reduce feelings of being overwhelmed in early recovery and/or of neglecting oneself in an attempt to immediately resolve problems created by the addiction. Box 4.1 shows a handout that can be used to guide your clients in scheduling. Table 4.1 is a sample of a blank schedule.

If the client creates a safe schedule and proceeds to follow the schedule, relapses will be avoided. Make certain you keep a copy of the schedule and review it at the beginning of the next session to see whether the process is working

---

BOX 4.1
Scheduling: Is It Important?

Scheduling is a difficult and tedious thing to begin doing if you're not used to it. It is, however, an important part of the recovery process. People addicted to drugs or alcohol do not schedule their time. People who schedule their time are not actively addicted individuals:

- *Why is it necessary?* If you begin your recovery in a hospital, you have the structure of the program and the building to help you stop using. As an outpatient, you have to build that structure around yourself as you continue functioning in the world. Your schedule is your structure.
- *Do I need to write it down?* Absolutely. Schedules that are in your head are easily revised by your addicted brain. If you write it down while your rational brain is in control and then follow it, you will be doing what you *think* you should be doing (rational brain) instead of what you *feel like* doing (addicted brain).
- *Who decides what I schedule?* You do! You may consider suggestions made by your counselor or family members, but the final decision is yours. Just be sure you *do* what you wrote down. Changes should be limited as much as possible.

Most people can schedule a 24-hour period and follow it. If you can, you are on your way to gaining control of your life. If you cannot, you may need to consider a higher level of care as a start.

---

for your client. Let the client know that schedules can be changed, but they must be physically erased or crossed out when the new activity is inserted. This process allows the client time to think through the feasibility and safely of the desired change.

Prior to entering a recovery group, it is important for you to meet with your client in an individual session. This provides the opportunity for the two of you to clearly articulate expectations. Learning about your client's positive and negative expectations on treatment can present an occasion for rapport building and education regarding treatment issues. Some examples of expectations to discuss might include what your client expects from the program and/or sessions, the group process, and of you. Many times clients are also concerned about what will happen should a relapse occur. Likewise, you might convey information about the program, thus avoiding uncertainty about the program and its rules. Some examples of your expectations may include consistent attendance, adherence to group rules, and how better to cope with relapse if it occurs. This mutual review of expectations will help to engage your client in a collaborative venture as the therapeutic process begins. Finally, it is imperative that you utilize the initial meetings to impart your belief that the client can achieve a satisfying, sober lifestyle. Keep in mind that whether the initial sessions are group, individual, or family meetings the basic principles just discussed will apply, with each session ending on a positive supportive note.

Table 4.1
Daily/Hourly Schedule

8:00	_____	8:00	_____	8:00	_____
9:00	_____	9:00	_____	9:00	_____
10:00	_____	10:00	_____	10:00	_____
11:00	_____	11:00	_____	11:00	_____
12:00	_____	12:00	_____	12:00	_____
1:00	_____	1:00	_____	1:00	_____
2:00	_____	2:00	_____	2:00	_____
3:00	_____	3:00	_____	3:00	_____
4:00	_____	4:00	_____	4:00	_____
5:00	_____	5:00	_____	5:00	_____
6:00	_____	6:00	_____	6:00	_____
7:00	_____	7:00	_____	7:00	_____
8:00	_____	8:00	_____	8:00	_____
9:00	_____	9:00	_____	9:00	_____
10:00	_____	10:00	_____	10:00	_____
11:00	_____	11:00	_____	11:00	_____

Notes: _____

Another helpful tool in creating structure is to use focused topics in your recovery groups. The Matrix program has a protocol that includes topics for each session. These topics can provide a focus for each session and keep the structure in place. As an example, the topic might be "Taking Care of Yourself." By having a handout that explains the concept and includes questions that can be used by clients to personalize the discussion, it will be easier for you to keep the group focused, and clients will have concrete information to take with them at the end of the session. Box 4.2 is an example of a topic that could be used in a recovery group.

Potential Problems

- You may find that you have difficulty delivering the topic material and paying attention to the group dynamics simultaneously. For example, you may be reviewing a topic where one client is discussing a high-risk situation they were in, while another client is becoming agitated and triggered as a result of the discussion. This is not an uncommon occurrence in the therapy group. Instruct your clients not to use graphic stories during group discussions. Avoiding triggering conversation will allow the person speaking to be better heard while, at the same time, other group members will feel safe and contained.
- A cognitive-behavioral orientation can be very engaging and a nonjudgmental stance communicates positive regard for the client. However, you may feel that adhering to one kind of theoretical orientation is too dry. Your first impulse might be to deliver treatment by doing what feels good thus becoming a process group. The down side to this is, while everyone may feel good at the end of the group or session, your clients may have failed to learn new

BOX 4.2
Taking Care of Yourself

People with an addiction do not take care of themselves. There may not be enough time or energy to attend to health and grooming when you are using. How you look becomes unimportant. Health is secondary to drug and alcohol use. Not caring for oneself is a major factor in addicted people losing self-esteem. To *esteem* something means you value it. You acknowledge its importance.

Recovering people need to recognize their own value. In recovery, your own health and appearance become more important as you care more for yourself. This importance is part of starting to like and even respect yourself.

Attending to the following will strengthen your self-image as a healthy, drug and alcohol-free recovering person:

1. Have you seen a doctor for a thorough check-up?
2. When is the last time you went to the dentist?
3. Have you considered getting a new look next time you cut your hair?
4. Are you paying attention to what you are eating? (i.e., too much, too little, or inadequate nutritional value?)
5. Do you still wear the same clothes you wore during your using episodes?
6. Do you need to have your vision or hearing checked?
7. What exercise do you do regularly?
8. Is your caffeine or nicotine intake out of control?

If doing all these things at once is too overwhelming, work on one or two items each week. Decide which are the most important and do them first. As you look and feel better, you will increase both the strength and the pleasure of your recovery.

The first thing I need to do to take care of myself is:

_____

_____

behavioral skills necessary to stabilize them in their recovery. The cognitive-behavioral interventions, coupled with a client-centered philosophy, have proven to be the most effective modality in working with clients who are trying to achieve initial abstinence. More emotional approaches, which are often used in residential treatment programs, do not have the same degree of empirical validity in outpatient treatment settings.

• When you are running a recovery group, you may find that pacing, staying on topic, and time management prove challenging. At times, group members may be disruptive and interrupt the group with crosstalk or impulsive behaviors. Speaking calmly and redirecting clients is an effective way to keep the group focused and on task. (With methamphetamine use there maybe some cognitive impairment, which should not be confused with *resistance* or *noncompliance*.)

- Conflict can sometimes occur between third-party pressure and where the client is in terms of the stage of recovery. Third-party pressure can come from law enforcement, third-party payers, family, or work. For example, a third-party payer may insist on discharging a patient for failure to be compliant to the case manager's expectations versus the treatment facility's treatment plan. It is important that the counselor attempt to mediate these conflicting viewpoints without adopting a you-better-do-this-or-else stance.
- Mandated clients who have not decided they need or want treatment may present a problem within the group dynamic. These clients have not yet recognized a need to change their behavior and are therefore not ready to hear suggestions on becoming drug free. Scheduling an individual session or two with these clients and working with them to help move them to a place these clients can consider change can be very effective. Often the cohesiveness and positive momentum of the group can also move them in this direction.
- It is not unusual for an intoxicated patient to show up for group. If another counselor is available on site, he or she can work with the client to ensure safe transportation home. Any discussion on the matter of drug or alcohol use should be avoided until the next appointment. If possible, an individual session should be scheduled to address the particular issues surrounding the relapse. The effect of such an event on other group members should not be ignored. They may need to discuss their reactions, and possible triggering, resulting from being in such close proximity to a relapsing colleague.

ESTABLISHING A POSITIVE AND COLLABORATIVE RELATIONSHIP WITH THE CLIENT

Most important to successful treatment is the relationship between you and your client. For effective treatment to occur, two things must take place: (1) the client must be engaged in the process and (2) the client must return for the next session. It is your responsibility to create an environment safe enough for both of these to occur utilizing a client-centered therapeutic stance. That is, offering accurate empathy, positive regard, warmth, and genuineness. It means treating your client with dignity, respect, and listening attentively and reflectively to his or her unique experience without imposing judgment. By doing this, you communicate a feeling of empathy that will separate your client from his or her behavior; while staying problem-focused on how mind-altering substances are impacting his or her life.

A collaborative relationship will develop when you accurately hear your client's concerns and opinions. For example, when your client identifies problems that exist between him and his probation officer, he begins to articulate a treatment goal, and together you can define clearer objectives. Moreover, this motivates your client to look at how drugs or alcohol can affect relationships. Conversely, when you are confrontational and impose treatment goals and demands, your client will likely view you as an authoritative or adversarial figure, further complicating the problem. Setting mutually agreed on goals engages your client as an active participant. In addition, it validates and acknowledges the client's expertise and experiences, thereby reinforcing the therapeutic alliance. This collaborative climate increases the client's readiness to learn new skills and practice more adaptive coping strategies and establishes an environment where the successes and failures of using these new strategies can be shared.

Potential Problems

- Research has shown that your attitude as a counselor strongly influences how well your client does in treatment. The people that you believe will do better in treatment are influenced by your expectations. However, sometimes clients are unable to do as well as the counselor might like, resulting in the counselor feeling frustrated and annoyed. When the client seems unable to meet his or her goals, it may be time to have an individual session to reconsider what treatment goals might be attainable. The procedure that is most effective is to continue to move your expectations down to create goals that are possible for your client to achieve. Once the client experiences success, you can begin slowing moving in the other direction.

- In early recovery, or as a result of stimulant use, clients may have some cognitive difficulties or memory problems. Just because someone has been successfully detoxified from a mind-altering substance, do not assume that his or her brain is fully healed. Research has shown that the healing process from stimulant abuse can take a year or more. Even more surprising is the finding that these problems get worse before they get better. For instance, the recovering person's memory at 60 days without drug use is likely to seem more impaired than at 30 days. Cognitive impairment can be misconstrued as resistance or deliberate noncompliance.

- During different stages of recovery, clients may experience mood problems. For example, in the later stages a client may experience an irritated depression, coupled with lethargy and apathy. These symptoms are signals for you to educate or remind him or her that this is a predictable stage of recovery, that it is a temporary condition, and that it will eventually end. If the recovering person thinks this is the way it feels to be sober, and this is what they will be experiencing from now on, the tendency is to relapse.

- All clients come for chemical dependency treatment with some degree of ambivalence. Some may have been coerced into treatment by the justice system, family, or work and do not yet view themselves as having a problem. Rather than deal with *how* the recovery process should go, clients in this early stage of readiness for treatment need to be talking about *whether* they should even be in such a process. Starting immediately to talk about the steps someone needs to take to stop using before they have made a decision about whether they want to enter the process will inevitably result in the client being hostile and the therapist being frustrated.

TEACHING INFORMATION AND COGNITIVE-BEHAVIORAL CONCEPTS   A key component of many of the cognitive-behavioral outpatient treatment programs, including the Matrix model, is to educate your client about the disorder. Clients need to be provided information about the etiology of chemical dependency and the prognosis for recovery. This helps them gain an understanding of predictable changes that will occur in their thinking, mood, and relationships over the course of several months. This education process identifies and normalizes symptoms, thereby empowering them to draw on resources and techniques to help manage the symptoms.

While cognitive-behavioral outpatient therapy is structured and focused on relapse prevention, it is individualized using the client's unique experiences, thoughts, and behaviors. Educating clients about the concepts and eliciting their reactions helps build the relationship and engages the client in the treatment process. To avoid clients taking a black-and-white approach to their recovery, it is important to explain that the cognitive-behavioral approach is compatible with other treatment adjuncts, such as pharmacology, alternative medicine, and support groups, and that it can also be modified to include specific cultural rituals.

The educational process teaches clients to self-monitor and utilize the information gained in preventing relapse. The goal of self-monitoring is to bring into awareness any annoying or uncomfortable symptoms, thoughts, warning signs, high-risk situations, and subtle precipitating events. The client is given skill training to identify triggers, develop coping skills, and manage immediate problems. Encourage him or her to practice and experiment with new behaviors outside the clinic setting. In the group, ask them to report back what worked and what didn't work, what obstacles were encountered, and what changes need to be made to make the interventions successful in the future. Through this process, clients become the experts on their own individual recovery processes.

Providing education about relapses and how to prevent a slip or lapse from turning into a full-blown relapse is empowering your client to recover. Help him or her to view relapse as an opportunity to reassess the treatment plan. What worked? What didn't work? What needs to change? Your clients are in training to be experts on their own diseases of addiction and recovery. They need to be able to articulate what specific triggers and thoughts lead to cravings. They must also be able to explain what skills and interventions work well for them. As the counselor you must make special effort to ensure that they take ownership and credit for changes that they worked to achieve.

This process of teaching clients something new each session and using the group time to process how the information fits for each client in his or her particular situation and recovery circumstances is a very different process than the usual therapy group that is conducted around feeling states or a residential group that is focused on breaking through defenses. Tables 4.2 and 4.3 compare a typical cognitive-behavioral group to both a therapy group and groups conducted in a residential setting. These styles of conducting groups are very different and some counselors have difficulty adjusting their personal group leader style accordingly.

If you are conducting the cognitive-behavioral groups properly, you will notice that the interaction is more likely to be therapist to client than client to client. This

Table 4.2
Cognitive-Behavioral Outpatient Therapy
Is Different from General Therapy

1. Focus is on abstinence.
2. Focus on behavior versus feelings.
3. Visit frequency results in strong transference.
4. Transference is encouraged.
5. Transference is utilized.
6. Goal is stability (versus emotional catharsis).
7. Bottom line is always continued abstinence.
8. Frequently pursues less motivated clients.
9. The behavior is more important than the reason behind it.

Table 4.3
Cognitive-Behavioral Outpatient Therapy
Is Different from Residential Therapy

1. Less confrontational.
2. Progresses more slowly.
3. Focus is on present.
4. Core issues not immediately addressed.
5. Allegiance is to therapist (versus group).
6. Nonjudgmental attitude is basis of client-therapist bond.
7. Change recommendations based on scientific data.
8. Changes incorporated immediately into lifestyle.

is the teaching model that works best with this style of group facilitation. While clients are not forbidden to interact, they are asked to only do so when they want to share an understanding or speak from their own experience. They are discouraged from probing, questioning, or confronting other group members. If these guidelines are followed, the group remains a safe place for everyone involved and all the group members leave the group feeling prepared to reenter their environment. Goals such as breaking through someone's defenses or getting someone in touch with his or her feelings are not appropriate for outpatient groups with people in the early stages of recovery. Clients who leave a group feeling uncomfortable are at higher risk of relapsing. They need to develop coping skills to use when they feel emotionally vulnerable before they can safely address sensitive, underlying areas of therapy.

Potential Problems

- When therapists do not utilize a client-centered approach and lapse into lecturing or preaching, the information may become too didactic and boring for the client. Sometimes clients will wander off topic. When this happens gently redirect them back to the topic and focus on what it means to them in their specific situation.
- Therapists insufficiently trained in delivering cognitive-behavioral therapies may have difficulty adhering to a treatment protocol and maintaining structure in the group. It may feel like the lack of focus on feelings is missing the mark and ignoring important issues. The concept is that strongly probing- and feeling-oriented therapy is more appropriately done after the client has 6 months to 1 year of sobriety. By that time, they will have learned the skills for avoiding drug and alcohol use and, hopefully, will have gained coping skills that can be used to help deal with powerful underlying issues. Raising these issues too soon puts the client at high risk of using in response to overpowering emotional triggers.
- Without specific education regarding the neurochemical changes that we now know accompany recovery from stimulants, clients' inability to think clearly, remember accurately, and focus may be misconstrued as resistance or deliberate noncompliance. Rather than requiring cognitive performance that is unrealistic and impossible, you remind the recovering user that the recovery process takes much longer than imagined, that feeling worse before

you feel better is progress, and that the goal is to get through this stage without relapsing so that the client can emerge with an intact, strong recovery.

POSITIVELY REINFORCING DESIRED BEHAVIORAL CHANGE   Rigorous research and empirical evidence support positive outcomes when contingency management (positive reinforcement) is added to cognitive-behavioral therapy. Simple ways of administering positive reinforcement include verbal praise for attendance, using newly learned skills, giving clean urine tests, and active participation in group. The positive verbal reinforcement helps clients feel supported and models supportive behavior. Encouragement and praise decreases negative attitudes and expectations about therapy. In general, the feedback helps clients modify their behavior.

Research has shown that clients who receive reinforcement for clean urines can often stop drug use long enough to engage in the treatment process and gain new skills. Another reinforcing technique is the recording of sober days on a calendar. This technique is implemented in the Matrix Model at the beginning of each group session using a simple reinforcement exercise. To implement this exercise, clients are asked, when they enter the group room, to place dots on a calendar for each sober day. The session opens with each one of your clients saying his or her first name, drug of choice, and number of days sober. This public recording of data provides a means for analyzing the patterns of your clients' problems and successes in treatment, serves as a reminder of what stage of recovery the client is in, and also serves as a powerful reinforcement for gaining drug-free days. Box 4.3 outlines a typical relapse prevention group format giving an approximate time frame for each group element.

PROVIDING CORRECTION FEEDBACK WHEN NECESSARY USING A MOTIVATIONAL INTERACTION STYLE   AA is considered by many to be the only way to get clean and sober. Because it has been around since the 1930s, it is familiar to most of the public and is frequently an available resource. Because of the very nature of its anonymity, there is little data conclusively showing how many people have gone in and out of the 12-Step meetings, but it is fair to say that millions of people worldwide have attended at least one 12-Step meeting since its inception. It is important to recognize that not everyone responds favorably to the concepts of the 12-Steps or to the groups themselves. Despite the fact that there are many self-help groups to aid and support the recovering community, it is sometimes difficult to find self-help groups that are not AA meetings. It is with this in mind that you need to recognize that your clients will not always be ready to embrace the idea of attending 12-Step meetings. Miller and Rollnick (2002) report that clients who complete an abstinence-based treatment program followed by AA have a 65% chance of staying drug and alcohol free for 1 year. He compares that to the 80% rate of abstinence at 1 year if they simultaneously attend AA and an outpatient treatment program. This supports our findings at Matrix. In our experience, Matrix Model clients who combine a cognitive-behavioral approach with attendance at self-help groups tend to do better in treatment and to have an easier time sustaining long-term recovery. It is helpful to let clients know these statistics and hear the experiences of senior group members who have used the 12-Step programs. It is incumbent on you to find ways to educate clients who are resistant, disinterested, lazy, or uneducated about getting involved in the 12-Step community, about the potential benefits, and do all that you can to encourage them to add the spiritual, fellowship component to their program.

BOX 4.3
Relapse Prevention Group Therapy Format: 90-Minute Group

First 15 minutes:

- Enter dots on individual calendars to indicate days drug free since last meeting.
- Introduction of new group members.
- Check in with name, number of days sober, and any triggers or cravings since the last group (solutions to those triggers and cravings).

Next 45 Minutes:

- Introduction of topic.
- Clients discuss topic and relate it to specific life circumstances.
- Summarize topic and important issues relative to it.

Next 25 minutes:

- Client concerns, problems, or other matters are brought up (opportunity for input and encouragement from other group members).
- Review client schedules and address any expected high-risk situations.

Last 5 minutes:

- End group on a positive note and with a pledge to confidentiality and the choice of sobriety.

After group meet with any patients who appear troubled, angry, depressed, or who are experiencing cravings.

When working with recovering people, it is important to keep reminding them that structure is one of the most important components of recovery. Adding self-help groups as part of the treatment plan to help create structure is highly recommended. For those clients who enjoy the meetings, this will be easy to accomplish. The question then becomes how do you motivate those who do not want to go to meetings? Some counselors and third-party payers attempt to force compliance by using ultimatums but that does not help empower clients to create a positive lifestyle choice for themselves. Resistance to 12-Step or other spiritual involvement is a significant issue. It is important to recognize that clients have many different religious and spiritual beliefs. It is important to acknowledge these differences and to respect the barriers they create in choosing whether or not to be involved in these groups. You will need to normalize the discomfort but, at the same time, encourage them to sample different types of meetings. The goal is to validate their fears and or indifference while at the same time educating them on the importance of this aspect of the recovery process and how it can contribute to long-term success in recovery (see Box 4.4).

BOX 4.4
Tips for 12-Step Resistant Clients

Research shows that continued participation in support groups helps maintain ongoing sobriety. Instruct your clients on this fact. Education may lower resistance.

Suggest going for the fellowship rather than for getting sober.

Explain to them that they can try different drug-of-choice meetings instead of one that focuses only on their drug of choice.

Teach them about all the varied meetings. For instance, in the 12-Step meetings, there are participation meetings, speaker meetings, "big book" meetings, and candlelight meetings.

Encourage them to find other friends or family members to go with them.

Have group members or individual clients research other types of meetings in the vicinity and then share information with each other.

Use the Internet to get support in recovery from online meetings.

If you happen to be a counselor who is also in recovery, one of the challenges you may encounter is separating your own recovery from that of your client. Remember that how you achieved sobriety is not necessarily the same as how others might attain it. It is important that you do not set an agenda for your clients. Otherwise their recovery becomes what you want them to do and not necessarily what is therapeutically appropriate. Recovering counselors (and sometimes those who aren't) might not be aware of their own prejudices for making recovery happen in a preconceived way. Seeking supervision on your own issues is imperative to avoid countertransference issues that might surface in your delivery of treatment.

EDUCATING FAMILY MEMBERS ON THE EXPECTED COURSE OF RECOVERY   When your client is going through recovery, it is important to take into account not only the individual but also his entire family system as well. Your family system includes all those people who are part of your everyday existence and are close to you. So, not only will it include those born into your family but also partners, close friends, associates, and people who are part of your extended family. In some facet or another, all these people will be affected by and will affect the recovery process. The first step in understanding what happens to the family as the addiction develops is to understand the nature of addiction.

Family members need to be involved in treatment whenever possible. Studies show that treatment works better when at least one supportive family member is engaged in the treatment process. One of the reasons it is important for significant others to be involved is to help them be better prepared for changes that may happen during the recovery process. This will allow them to have a better understanding of what is normal for the recovering person and some of the difficulties they may encounter.

It is normal for the client to not want family members involved, especially those who may be overbearing or critical. However, it is to the client's advantage to realize that other people involved in his or her life have some responsibilities of their own in the recovery process. Family members who have been interacting with the client during the progression of the disease have been affected by the process and need to make some changes of their own.

In the initial stages of treatment, family members need to decide whether they are willing to be part of the recovery process. It is very important that the invitation to be included should come from the program or the therapist directly, as opposed to being sent through the client, in which case it is rarely delivered without an editorial.

Family and friends have an easier time being involved if the *addiction* is viewed as the problem rather than the using person being the problem. Additionally, when the family recognizes addiction as a chronic medical condition as opposed to believing the addicted person is crazy, bad, or stupid, they are more willing to help support the recovery process. Information on the process of addiction is just as important for family members as it is for the recovering person.

Not all family members will want to be a part of the recovery process, despite urging by you or the client. There are many valid reasons for this. Family members may feel they cannot put themselves through any more of the emotional turmoil. These people usually still care very deeply for their affected family member but cannot stand to keep watching them destroy his or her life. Usually they have been through this process several times and are exhausted—emotionally and financially—from multiple unsuccessful attempts at recovery.

Another reason that family members are unwilling to participate may be that they are very angry. They may be tired of all the family resources being expended fruitlessly on battling the addiction. Many family members say they doubt they could ever trust the person with the addiction again. Others say they are just tired of all the lies and they want out. Still others are willing to believe that the person might get better but do not want to invest the time and energy to be part of the process. These family members might say something like, "This is your problem not mine. Go get fixed and when you are all better we can continue our lives together."

Despite all these scenarios, it is often possible to find at least one family member who is willing to participate. Note that the degree to which a family member is willing to get involved is strictly up to them. The helping professional needs to be ready to accept that some people can't immediately choose to join the recovery process. Often, if the person with the addiction is willing to start into the program and shows some progress, family members can then be approached again and asked to assist the recovery. Just because a family member does not choose to be actively involved at the outset of treatment, it should not be assumed they are forever unwilling to participate. The counselor should, with the consent of the client, continue to report progress and issue open invitations for involvement to family members. Boxes 4.5 and 4.6 present guidelines for helping family members help themselves and their loved ones in treatment.

URINE AND BREATH ALCOHOL TESTING   The most accurate means of monitoring clients for drug and alcohol use during treatment is through the use of urine and breath alcohol testing. The variety of testing options available today makes it much easier for programs to regularly administer the tests than in the past. Tests can be analyzed on site or sent out to laboratories. Specimens can be obtained observed or unobserved (Table 4.4). Whatever procedure you use, the goals are the same—to monitor your client's use and provide structure for him or her. The attitude of the

---

BOX 4.5
Benefits of Family Involvement

Family involvement is associated with better treatment compliance and outcome.

Family members have clearer understanding of the road map for recovery.

Patients and family members understand their respective goals and roles in recovery.

Family members and patients get support in the recovery process.

---

person presenting the testing policy will often determine how resistant the client will be to being tested. Clients often say things like, "You don't need to test me. Why would I come in here and lie about using? I will tell you if I use." It's important to let new participants know that the testing procedure is a standard part of the program, that sometimes it is difficult for people to talk about a relapse, and that many clients end up appreciating that they can't get away with using and not talking about it.

One important point to take into consideration is that urine testing should not be presented primarily as a monitoring measure. Instead of being used as a policing

---

BOX 4.6
Goals for Family Member(s)

BEGINNING STAGE (1–6 WEEKS)

Make commitment to treatment.

Recognize addiction as a medical condition.

Support discontinuation of drug and alcohol use.

Learn to recognize and discontinue triggering interactions.

MIDDLE STAGE (6–20 WEEKS)

Decide whether to recommit to the relationship (leave or trust).

Learn to be supportive instead of coaddicted.

Begin finding ways to enrich your own life.

Practice healthy communication skills.

ADVANCED STAGE (20+ WEEKS)

Learn to accept the limitations of living with an addiction.

Develop an individual, healthy, balanced lifestyle.

Monitor self for relapses.

Be patient with the process of recovery.

Table 4.4
Problems Encountered in Observing Specimens

Following are some reasons why a counselor may have problems when trying to obtain a urine specimen from a client:

Problem	Solution
Client is afraid he may get kicked out of the program.	Educate the client on the recovery process and let him know that relapse does not mean failure in treatment and does not disqualify him from continuing in your practice or program.
Client may think the group or therapist would think less of him.	Teach the client that recovery is a process and that each client's recovery process is different. Reinforce that others understand and have been in his or her shoes.
Client may believe that use of medication prescribed by a doctor or dentist is not the same as a real relapse.	Educate your client about other medications that can trigger a relapse to his or her drug of choice. Advise your client to tell you about all medications prescribed during the course of treatment and initiate communication with the prescribing physician.
Client is unable to urinate.	Let the client know at the beginning of a session that her or she has to test that day. Supply water. Let the client know you are not in a hurry and you will wait.

device, testing should be seen as a way to help a person discontinue drug use. Urine testing helps you and the client keep his or her behavior in line with the recovery process. Urine and breath alcohol testing that is done in a clinical setting is different from urine testing that is done for legal monitoring. Clinical tests are not tracked as closely as those that are destined for use in a courtroom. Referral sources and others who want to use the testing for the latter purpose should be advised to do their own, more closely supervised collection. It puts a clinician in a difficult position to try to be both the client advocate and the monitor.

It is not uncommon to receive the results of a drug test and find drug use that was not previously admitted. This situation can be seen as a useful therapeutic opportunity for you and might lead to some insight into your client's behavior. Perhaps he or she was embarrassed to talk about the use in group, or maybe you were out of town and the client did not want to disclose the information with the counselor replacing you. An unexpected positive test is an extremely significant event in treatment. It may mean that there was a single occasion of use, or it might indicate a return to chronic use. Clients will frequently say, "That is impossible. My urine test can't be positive. There must have been a mistake." It is preferable not to allow an argument to ensue in this situation. It is highly unlikely that any given client will be able to use regularly when a positive urine test is the only indicator that treatment is not working. One way to handle such a situation and not damage your rapport with the client is to say, "It is possible there was a mistake. It is highly unlikely that two mistakes would happen concurrently. If we don't get another dirty test, there may not be a problem. Why don't we concentrate on some other aspects of your treatment for now." By letting go of the argument, you allow your client to maintain dignity and to choose when and where to talk to you about what is really going on. Box 4.7 lists some other tips for dealing with positive urine tests.

Some clients will admit to their drug use. This honesty needs to be acknowledged and reinforced. Sharing about their relapse instead of waiting for a positive test to emerge is a sign that recovery is working but that certain areas in their treatment need strengthening. When your client makes a partial confession of use, it may be as open as he or she is able to be about admitting the relapse. Do not attempt to extract the entire confession but assume that there was drug use and move on to other issues.

INTRODUCING AND ENCOURAGING SELF-HELP PARTICIPATION   Matrix Model cognitive-behavioral groups are traditionally run by a professional counselor and a recovering person who assists the group leader and who serves as a role model for other members of the group. The co-leaders are selected by the group leader from among those clients who finish treatment and are doing well in their continuing recovery. The stipulation is that they are attending 12-Step meetings and going to the Social Support group or doing some form of therapy. This frees them from needing to use the group as a participant and allows them to be there for the other group members.

Having a co-leader in the group helps you, as a therapist, in several ways. It allows you to illustrate points you are trying to make by asking the co-leader to relate his or her personal experience with the issue. This makes the material relevant and understandable for people earlier in the recovery process. You can also teach the co-leader to be gently confrontational by personally relating his or her own view of situations being discussed. For instance, a co-leader can say, "I, personally, can't drink alcohol—not even socially—because I know that if I do I will eventually relapse again to using the first cousin of alcohol—cocaine. So, it may be different for you, but I know that drinking would put my recovery in jeopardy." These words, coming from someone who is not a counselor but is another

---

BOX 4.7
Tips for Working with Dirty Tests

- Reassess the period of time surrounding the test. Perhaps there were other indications of a problem, such as missed appointments, statements made in group or individual counseling of strange or out of the ordinary behavior.
- It is best not to confront your client. Instead, give him or her the opportunity to explain the result. For example, "I received your urine result the other day and it came back positive for cocaine. Did anything happen in your recovery that you forgot to tell me about?"
- Do not get into a power struggle about the legitimacy of the test results. Listen to what your client has to say and work him to find ways of keeping his environment safe.

Regardless of what the client tells you, trust that there was at least one instance of use. Many times increasing the frequency of testing helps to determine the extent of the drug use.

recovering person, much like the client, are much more powerful than anything you could say.

If you are a recovering person and a counselor, allowing someone else to take on the role of "Do like I did" helps keep the boundaries between your professional self and your recovering self much clearer and allows you to relate closely to a wider group of clientele rather than just to those whose patterns of use and recovery mimic your own. Finally, in our experience, people who are in the first year or two of recovery are better able to relate to clients who are in early recovery than people who have been drug and alcohol free for years. For all these reasons, having a co-leader is very helpful to the group leader and aspiring to be a co-leader is very motivating to group members who are becoming eligible as they work toward having a successful treatment episode.

Case Study

When Mitch came into my office he was afraid and ashamed. He said he had achieved over 6 years of recovery in the past and he couldn't believe that he was here, 9 years later, in the same situation. Mitch reported using cocaine off and on for the past 3 years. His wife had filed for divorce, his law practice was suffering and his partner was threatening to buy him out, his health had deteriorated and his teenage children had stopped speaking to him. He was frustrated and frightened that he was unable to obtain the sobriety he once held so dear. He appeared to be tired, and he was saying he was ready to do whatever it took to regain his sobriety but, from my experience, I knew his ambivalence was just beneath the surface. The desire not to use again, by itself, would not be enough to create a recovery state. His hope was to be able to work on resurrecting his law practice at the same time he was regaining his sobriety. He asked if I thought outpatient treatment was a viable option. After assessing his drug use history, mental status, and overall health, I decided he was a good candidate for intensive outpatient treatment.

He reiterated that he was uncomfortable in his last program because he always felt that he wasn't getting sober "their way." He managed to obtain abstinence for a period of 6 years after leaving treatment. However, he never went to 12-Step meetings or worked on his recovery with like-minded people once he left the program. He stated that his 6 years of abstinence was by sheer will and determination and that he was not interested in going to a program if it was going to be like the last one. He didn't want counselors yelling at him or attempting to use guilt to convince him to change his life. He asked if treatment was still like that. I assured him that he and his recovery choices would be respected and that we would be giving him some tools to enable him to succeed in treatment. Here is Mitch's treatment experience:

> What I appreciated most of all from my time in this treatment program was that even though at times I felt resistant to changing I was never confronted or made to feel like I was a bad client. This was such a different approach than my last time in treatment. When my counselor told me that I would not have to get a sponsor and work the 12-Steps in order to succeed in treatment, I was so relieved. Although she emphasized the importance of a recovery support system, it was not required as a condition for being in the program. Later, when other clients encouraged me to

consider attending 12-Step groups to help me in my recovery, I was able to decide to go on my own. Not only did I attend them, I actually started enjoying them. My prior program had never believed me when I said that I didn't feel that the AA approach was right for me. It was a nice change to hear that I wasn't going to fail treatment if I didn't go to AA. What I liked about this approach to treatment was that I felt I had choices. I was being given information that I could choose to use to direct my own recovery. I appreciated being told that I could use the 12-Step meetings for fellowship and not for therapy. If I chose to go, it was because I had made the decision to do so not because that was the way my counselor had done it and insisted I do it the same way.

I grew to appreciate the structure of my outpatient program. I knew that I needed some serious accountability (sometimes I felt I needed to be locked up). I liked the fact that we didn't always talk about feelings in group. I found the educational part of my program very beneficial. In my previous treatment, group members would talk in graphic detail about the drugs they used. I frequently left group feeling like using drugs. The meetings were very triggering. What I liked about these groups was the structure. There was a treatment manual that we worked out of with a different topic for each group. The group meetings were very predictable. We left every group with scientifically validated information. It was as predictable as a class in recovery but with an instructor who listened to me instead of lecturing. Some of the group topics were practical, such as learning to schedule our time or stopping our using thoughts. Others explained brain chemistry changes in very easy-to-understand terms. Still other topics talked about why using other drugs and alcohol is a bad idea. I looked forward to putting dots on the calendar for the drug-free days I had prior to group. I felt like I could talk about the problems I was having without feeling judged.

One time I tested positive for cocaine. I was very surprised when my counselor asked to talk to me in an individual session. She asked if there was something I forgot to tell her. She said she was concerned because I had a positive drug test and wondered if there was something more she could do to help me help myself. I was stunned. I didn't tell her about my drug use because I did not want to hear that I was not serious enough about my recovery or be lectured in front of the group. When she talked with me about the relapse, I felt so liberated. Wow, I am not a pariah. I am not a bad person. From that point forward, I felt more comfortable talking about my struggles.

One member of our relapse prevention group was someone who had graduated from the program 1½ years ago. He had relapsed while he was in treatment and had figured out how to make the program work for him. In the beginning, I felt he wasn't like me. I thought my problems were much more severe than those he had experienced; but as he talked about the problems he had during treatment, I found myself wanting to be able to do what he had done. His presence in the group and his very frank input inspired me when I was feeling hopeless and gave me a way to relate very personally to the things we were being taught. I felt that if he could get sober and create a new life for himself, I could do the same.

When I entered treatment, my wife was angry with me and said that she was not willing to participate in the program. She told my counselor that I had created this problem and I was the one who needed to do the work to correct the situation. She got a letter from the program inviting her to Family Group and wouldn't go. She called my counselor to make sure she knew about all the times I had lied and cheated during my last using period.

My counselor asked her to try to view this disease like any other chronic, relapsing condition. She said my wife could learn more at the educational lectures about how the disease affects a person. She asked my wife whether she would be willing to come to a conjoint session with the counselor if I was able to have one month of sobriety. My wife reluctantly agreed to that. Knowing that I had to demonstrate that I could do this to get her to begin to trust me and to agree to be involved in the process served as a motivation for me. Although I did have a small slip once during that month, my wife's anger gradually subsided and she came to a session with the counselor. Since then, she has attended the family groups and is planning to continue the series, even after I graduated from the intensive phase of the program. I do think that if she had been *required* to attend things might not have gone the same way.

I realize now that the lessons I learned during my first attempts at recovery served as building blocks for a process that is still ongoing. Some of the things I most appreciated about this last formal treatment episode were learning some of the scientific things about this addiction process, including what is happening to my brain; being given small steps to accomplish along the way that eventually led to where I am now; and, finally, being assured all along that I have choices, getting support in examining the consequences of those choices and feeling, and, in the end, that I was able to learn about the tools and make the choices to get to where I am now.

I am now in an aftercare group that I attend without fail on a weekly basis. I have become a co-leader in the same group I used to attend as a client, and I have a recovery support system that was not in place the first time I got sober. I believe that the approach used in this last treatment episode helped me appreciate the importance of being respected, of respecting myself, and of having the freedom to make the choices I made that resulted in my ongoing recovery.

Evaluating the Approach

Evaluations of the Matrix Model have not definitively established its efficacy, but a review of these studies justifies support for this approach. Cocaine and methamphetamine users benefit from the Matrix Model treatment. They respond positively during treatment and appear, in at least some cases, to sustain gains for periods of more than 2 years. The current multisite trial of the Model may provide more information on its efficacy in general and with specific patient populations (Native Americans, Hawaiians, women, and drug court patients). As more becomes known about methamphetamine-related cognitive impairment, treatment materials might be modified to accommodate the intellectual and perceptual levels of these patients. For example, there is some evidence that methamphetamine use may result in cognitive impairment that is more pronounced for verbal versus pictorial comprehension. As a result, treatment materials might be more beneficial if they included pictures with the text. Finally, the complement of psychosocial treatment along with some yet-to-be-determined medication may result in reduced craving, mood elevation, or better cognitive functioning, and, therefore, improved retention and better response to the Matrix Model.

SUMMARY

It is easy to forget that we have been treating individuals with substance use disorders in an organized service delivery system for less than 50 years. We have been systematically applying science to the study of substance use disorders on a large scale for just over 25 years. Outpatient treatment has only been an organized form of care for just over a decade. As we enter the twenty-first century, we are just now using scientific information to guide the evolution and delivery of substance abuse care. Much of what is currently delivered as treatment is based on our current best guess of how to combine some science-based (e.g., cognitive-behavioral therapy and pharmacotherapies) and some self-help (12-Step programs) approaches into optimal treatment protocols. We are at the beginning stages of determining how this should best be done to produce optimal patient outcomes with an effective outlay of health care dollars.

At the present time, there are techniques and tools that provide individuals with useful assistance and knowledge on how to stop using and refrain from returning to drugs and alcohol. It is no longer acceptable to simply do what feels right to the counselor. Organizations and professionals who specialize in treating substance use disorders are an accepted part of the U.S. health care delivery system. As in all other areas of health care, there is a rapidly increasing dependence on the use of scientific information to shape and improve the future of the field. Within the past decade, MDs, psychologists, social workers, family therapists, nurses, and allied health professionals have all incorporated knowledge about the identification and treatment of substance use disorders into categories for licensure and certification requirements.

The tools and techniques presented in this chapter that are available for the treatment of individuals with substance use disorders comes from the perspective of authors who have been delivering this form of treatment for the past two decades. We are optimistic that as the blending of science and practice efforts increasingly influence the services delivered, we will get new tools and new information to improve the treatment field. It is the ethical responsibility of the clinical practitioner in the substance abuse field, as in other fields (i.e., cancer and heart disease), to stay informed about new and more effective clinical procedures. The field of substance abuse treatment is becoming increasingly professional and those of us who are part of the system need to continue to stay abreast of the new developments so that we can encourage and sustain this trend. The use of new knowledge and new treatment techniques and tools can make the difference in promoting a successful recovery experience for some of the individuals who currently are unsuccessful with existing treatments. As these new approaches with sound scientific support emerge, we will revise our methods and add new treatment options. We have begun to define some clearly effective treatment elements, but there is much to learn and much room for improvement.

RECOMMENDED READING

Obert, J. L., McCann, M. J., Marinelli-Casey, P., Weiner, A., Minsky, S., Brethen, P., et al. (2000). The Matrix Model of outpatient stimulant abuse treatment, history, and description. *Journal of Psychoactive Drugs, 32*(2), 157–164. A detailed description of the Matrix Model and its evolution, its article also includes summaries of research on this topic.

Rawson, R. A. (1998). *Treatment of stimulant abuse* CSAT: TIP #33 (Chair, CSAT Consensus panel). Rockville, MD: DHHS. A free resource in easily readable form, this government publication includes all research-based approaches to stimulant abuse treatment.

Rawson, R. A., and Obert, J. L. (2002). Relapse prevention groups. In D. W. Brook & H. I. Spitz (Eds.), *Group psychotherapy of substance abuse*. Washington, DC: APA Press. A description of the Matrix Model in general relapse prevention terms, one of many types of group therapies.

REFERENCES

Donovan, D. M. (2002). Relapse prevention in substance abuse treatment. In J. L. Sorensen, R. A. Rawson, J. Guydish, & J. E. Zweben (Eds.), *Drug abuse treatment through collaboration: Practice and research partnerships that work.* Washington, DC: American Psychological Association.

Gorski, T. T. (1986). Relapse prevention planning: A new recovery tool. *Alcohol Health and Research World, 11,* 6–11, 63.

Gorski, T. T. (2000). CENAPS model of relapse prevention therapy (CMRPT). In J. J. Boren, L. S. Onken, & K. M. Carroll (Eds.), *Approaches to drug abuse counseling* (pp. 21–34). Bethesda, MD: National Institute on Drug Abuse.

Marlatt, G. A., & Gordon, J. R. (Eds.). (1985). *Relapse prevention: Maintenance strategies in the treatment of addictive behaviors.* New York: Guilford Press.

McAuliffe, W. E. (1990). A randomized controlled trial of recovery training and self-help for opioid addicts in New England and Hong Kong. *Journal of Psychoactive Drugs, 22*(2), 197–209.

McAuliffe, W. E., Albert, J., Cordill-London, G., & McGarraghy, T. K. (1991, August 25). Contributions to a social conditioning model of cocaine recovery. *International Journal of Addictions* (9A–10A), 1141–1177.

Miller, W. R., & Rollnick, S. (2002). *Motivational interviewing: Preparing people for change* (2nd ed.). New York: Guilford Press.

Obert, J. L., McCann, M. J., Marinelli-Casey, P., Weiner, A., Minsky, S., Brethen, P., et al. (2000). The Matrix Model of outpatient stimulant abuse treatment: History and description. *Journal of Psychoactive Drugs, 32*(2), 157–164.

Rawson, R. A., Obert, J. L., McCann, M. J., & Marinelli-Casey, P. (1993). Use of relapse prevention strategies in the treatment of substance abuse disorders. *Psychotherapy, 30*(2), 284–298.

Rawson, R. A., Obert, J. L., McCann, M. J., Smith, D. P., & Scheffey, E. H. (1989). *The neurobehavioral treatment manual.* Beverly Hills, CA: Matrix Center.

Rawson, R. A., Shoptaw, S. J., Obert, J. L., McCann, M. J., Hasson, A. L., Marinelli-Casey, P. J., et al. (1995). An intensive outpatient approach for cocaine abuse treatment: The Matrix model. *Journal of Substance Abuse Treatment, 12,* 117–127.

Rotgers, F. (1996). Behavioral theory of substance abuse treatment, bringing science to bear on practice. In F. Rotgers, D. S. Keller, & J. Morgenstern (Eds.), *Treating substance abuse, theory and technique* (pp. 193–194). New York: Guilford Press.

Wallace, J. (1996). Theory of 12-Step-oriented treatment. In F. Rotgers, D. S. Keller, & J. Morgenstern (Eds.), *Treating substance abuse, theory and technique* (p. 14). New York: Guilford Press.

Zackon, F., McAuliffe, W. E., & Chien, J. M. (1993). *Addict aftercare: A manual of training and self-help.* Rockville MD: National Institute on Drug Abuse.

PART III

COMPULSIVE GAMBLING

CHAPTER 5

Understanding and Diagnosing Compulsive Gambling

LINDA CHAMBERLAIN

The world had nothing in it except the thought of gambling or that act. Even when I was on my way to gamble I didn't want to go, yet I could not stop my car and turn around. I had a sense of dread and yet a giddiness at the same time.

—Gayla, a compulsive gambler

WHAT IS COMPULSIVE GAMBLING?

GAMBLING IS ONE of the most ancient and universal aspects of human behavior. Games of chance have been with us throughout human civilization and in virtually every culture. Gambling may have evolved from a desire to predict the future and control the outcome of fate. Artifacts and other records indicate that the Chinese, Babylonian, and Etruscan civilizations engaged in gambling earlier than 3000 B.C. The American Revolution was financed, in part, through lottery proceeds (Pavalko, 1999). The desire to win wealth, prestige, and freedom through taking chances is a force that is entrenched in the human condition.

The most basic definition of gambling is "to play games of chance for money or other rewards" (Cambridge International Dictionary, 1996). Any activity that has an uncertain outcome and involves risking something of value with the hope of increasing one's wealth, status, or security can be described as *a gamble.* The goal of all forms of gambling is to win more than you lose. The reality is that all popular forms of gambling are based on the *absolute certainty* that, ultimately, the gambler will lose more, over time, than they will win. So the paradox of gambling begins. Most gamblers know that the "odds are in favor of the house" but also believe that they can "beat the odds."

The National Council on Problem Gambling (NCPG) defines problem gambling as "gambling behavior that causes disruptions in any major area of a persons life" (NCPG, 2000). In this chapter, I will explore what that broad definition of problem gambling really means and how people's lives are not only disrupted but also devastated when they lose control of the impulse to gamble. Like an addiction to psychoactive substances, compulsive gambling is a disorder that generally begins as an enjoyable pastime, makes life more exciting and fun, and brings the possibility of financial success and freedom from worry. There is, however, another aspect of gambling that "belies its enjoyment and exposes its potential for ruination" (Galski, 1987, p. xiii).

As is true with alcohol and many drugs, the majority of those who indulge do so on a limited, managed basis and experience few, if any, serious or long-lasting consequences. Like other addictions, the compulsion to gamble progressively takes over an increasing amount of their time, money, and energy. What was once an exciting afternoon going to the casino with friends becomes an obsession that takes over one's thoughts and dreams. Most social or recreational gamblers continue to enjoy the occasional trip to the racetrack, casino, or bingo hall. Estimates are that between 60% and 80% of the adult and adolescent population of the United States has engaged in some form of gambling. For approximately 5% to 7% of those who play these games of chance, gambling will become a detour from their plans and goals—a detour that will lead them to unimagined losses, devastated relationships, financial ruin, and possibly death.

Those who become addicted to gambling find themselves caught in a serious behavioral disorder that is associated with job loss and unemployment, depression, anxiety, substance abuse, theft, dishonesty, family disruption, and suicide. From prevalence studies conducted in the United States (Volberg, 1996), problem and pathological gamblers in the general population were significantly more likely than nongamblers to be male, under age 30, non-Caucasian, and unmarried. They reported starting to gamble at a much earlier age (preteen or early teenage years for male gamblers) and were at higher risk for committing criminal offenses to finance their gambling or cover their loses.

One trend appears clear: The prevalence of compulsive gambling is increasing. Along with the increase in gambling problems, the nature of compulsive gambling may be changing. New forms of gambling and increased access to a variety of gambling venues means that those who may be likely to develop a problem probably will. Internet gambling, the spread of casinos, government supported lotteries, and other forms of gambling are now available to anyone. While Las Vegas and Atlantic City remain Meccas devoted to the dream of instant wealth, gambling has become integrated into daily life. The taboos or prohibitions that once defined gambling are now extinct. "Judged by dollars spent, gambling is now more popular in America than baseball, the movies, and Disneyland—*combined*" (O'Brien, 1998, p. 4).

Until the past decade, problem gambling was almost exclusively a territory populated by adult males. Several trends are becoming clear in studies of gambling and problem gamblers. First, the percentage of women who are experiencing problems related to gambling is increasing. Welte, Barnes, Wieczorek, Tidwell, and Parker (2002) notes that a "1975 national survey found male participation (in all forms of gambling) to be 13% higher than female participation, the current study (2002) shows a gap of only 4%" (p. 335). The Welte study also indicates that gambling participation particularly has grown among the elderly and lower socioeconomic groups. The authors conclude that the "growth of gambling opportunities throughout the society has been associated with the profile of the gambling population shifting to become more female, older, and less white" (p. 337).

The other trend that is emerging is the rapid increase in gambling among the young. A prevalence study that reviewed data from 7,500 adolescents, aged 13 to 20 years, indicated that between 9.9% and 14.2% of adolescents were already experiencing or at risk for developing serious gambling problems (Shaffer & Hall, 1996). If you have visited a casino in the past decade, it is easy to observe a significant change in the nature of the games that are available. Video versions of popular casino games, such as poker, blackjack, roulette, and keno, fill the majority of the casino floor. Space devoted to the more traditional table variety of these games is shrinking. Adolescents and younger adults have been raised on video games and the Internet. The ease of transition from nongambling video games to video gambling is an expectation in the gaming industry—an expectation that is certain to be fulfilled. Many researchers suspect that early involvement in gambling may be a risk factor for developing a gambling problem later in life (National Center for Responsible Gaming, 1999).

Research into pathological gambling has also revealed that individuals undergoing treatment for drug or alcohol disorders, prison populations, and persons suffering from other psychiatric problems such as depression, bipolar disorder, antisocial personality disorder, and attention-deficit/hyperactivity disorders also have a higher rate of gambling problems (National Center for Responsible Gaming, 1999). Comings (1998) notes that as with most addictions, the common perception is that people should be able to control their involvement and those who overindulge have only themselves to blame. While it is important for individuals to take responsibility for their own behavior, it is equally clear that biological and genetic factors can play a role in increasing the risk of becoming a pathological gambler. Certainly, compulsive gambling, like other addictions, tends to run in families.

As we begin to look more closely at patterns and symptoms of pathological gambling, it may be helpful to explore the dynamics of an addiction that is not based on psychoactive substance use. What are the similarities and what are the differences? Can we really call a behaviorally-based problem and addiction?

IS COMPULSIVE GAMBLING AN ADDICTION?

When defining *addiction,* are you correct to include problematic patterns of behavior such as compulsive gambling? Should the term addiction be limited to disorders caused by the ingestion of psychoactive substances or can the definition be broadened to include what are often referred to as *process addictions?* How do we define the repetitive, highly problematic patterns of behavior that can occur with such activities as eating, spending, sexual activity, and gambling? Is the term addiction a suitable term to apply to behaviors that are certainly routine and pleasurable for the majority of the population but can become overwhelmingly destructive forces for some people?

The argument concerning whether gambling is an addiction is unnecessarily controversial (Kusyszyn, 1980). Some professionals assert that gambling could not possibly be addictive and that compulsive behavioral patterns such as problem gambling or excessive sexual behavior are manifestations of other psychological dilemmas. To many clinicians working with gamblers, this is an outmoded yet still popular view. The *Diagnostic and Statistical Manual of Mental Disorders-IV,* fourth edition, text revision (*DSM-IV-TR;* American Psychiatric Association [APA], 2000) lends some support to this view. Pathological gambling is classified as a "Disorder of Impulse Control" (*DSM-IV-TR*, pp. 671–674) and placed in the same category as hair pulling (Trichotillomania), fire setting (Pyromania), and shop-lifting (Kleptomania). This pseudodistinction between chemical ingestion and problem behaviors not directly caused by chemical ingestion, as a criterion for addiction, conflicts with current definitions of the concept of addiction (McCown & Chamberlain, 2000). Is it helpful for researchers or clinicians to draw a distinction between disorders that are chemically based and those that are not? Many professionals working with the issue of addiction believe it is not useful. Addiction has common features whether or not use of a psychoactive substance is involved. Throughout this chapter, the terms *compulsive gambling, pathological gambling,* and *problem gambling* are used to describe similar patterns of gambling activity. In the research and literature, it is common for these terms to be used somewhat interchangeably to describe the patterns of addiction to all varieties of games of chance.

Researchers and clinicians have proposed definitions of addiction that would include compulsive gambling and other behavioral or process-based disorders. The general theory of addictions proposed by Jacobs (1986, 1988) offers the concept of an altered state of identity. His theory views the continuous use of the addictive substance or activity as a method through which addicts detach psychologically from daily reality and become so engrossed in the changed psychological state brought about by the substance or activity that their identity is altered. Herscovitch (1999) asserts, "all addicts, regardless of the nature of their addiction, maintain their addictive behavior despite obvious harmful consequences" (p. 33). Peele (1979) proposed "an addiction exists when a person's attachment to a sensation, an object, or another person is such as to lessen his appreciation and ability to deal with other things in his environment or in himself so that he has become increasingly dependent on that experience as his only source of gratification" (p. 56). Shaffer (1989) claims that compulsive gambling may be an example of a *pure addiction*—an addiction uncomplicated conceptually by matters of physical dependence and biochemistry (p. 7). Shaffer (2002) further asserts that "experience is the currency of addiction" (p. 4) and that "a reward is a reward, regardless of whether it comes from ingesting a psychoactive drug or having an exhilarating experience . . . where there is a reward, there is the risk of addiction" (p. 5).

Much current thinking in the addiction field focuses not on a particular substance or activity but on the neurological and behavioral changes that occur over time as the basis for defining addiction. Essentially, addiction truly is in the brain of the beholder. Addiction, regardless of the object, is the result of "self-induced changes in neurotransmissions that result in behavior problems" (Milkman & Sunderwirth, 1987, p. 6). Advances in the scientific understanding of brain and neurotransmitter function in addiction have led to a departure from the outdated moralistic models of addiction.

When you compare the commonalties between psychoactive, substance-based addictions and gambling, the similarities (see Table 5.1) are clear and compelling.

Given the strong similarities between the two patterns, it is clear that compulsive gambling more closely fits the *DSM-IV-TR* definition of a substance-related disorder than that of an impulse-control disorder. Thus far, however, those who compile the categories and definitions of disorders in the *DSM* have not adopted the term addiction as a diagnostic category. For many working with alcoholics, drug addicts, compulsive gamblers, and others who repeat these compulsive

Table 5.1

Commonalities between Pharmacological Addictions and Gambling

Symptoms or Behavior	Alcohol and Other Drugs	Compulsive Gambling
Cravings	Yes	Yes
Denial of problem's severity or existence	Yes	Yes
Disruption of families	Yes	Yes
Effects on specific neurotransmitters	Yes	Unknown
High relapse rate	Yes	Yes
Loss of control	Yes	Yes
Lying to support use or activity	Yes	Yes
Preoccupation with use or activity	Yes	Yes
Progressive disorder	Yes	Yes
Tolerance developed	Yes	Yes
Used as a means of escaping problems	Yes	Yes
Withdrawal symptoms common	Yes	Yes

Source: From *Best Possible Odds: Contemporary Treatment Strategies for Gambling Disorders* (p. 17), by W. McCown and L. Chamberlain, 2000, New York: Wiley.

patterns, it seems more sensible to explore the different manifestations of this type of problem behavior under the umbrella of addiction.

So If Gambling Is an Addiction, What Is It an Addiction To?

> How do you make a small fortune gambling? Start with a large fortune.
>
> —Popular joke in Las Vegas

At first glance, the answer to the question, "What is gambling an addiction to?" seems obvious: Gambling is an addiction to money. Since the goal of gambling is to win money through skill and/or luck, then those who become compulsive gamblers must have an overwhelming desire to win lots of money. It is certainly true that winning money is what initially attracts people to gambling. Everyone who gambles counts on good fortune or skill at playing a game to help him or her beat the odds. Many compulsive gamblers experience a significant win early in their gambling and describe that experience as a turning point in the development of the compulsion to gamble.

I would argue, however, that money is not the focus of the addiction for gamblers. If compulsive gamblers were truly addicted to money, then the enormous losses that inevitably occur would stop them from continuing. Instead, money is simply the equivalent of the delivery system for the addiction to gambling, just as a syringe is the delivery system for an addiction to heroin. Money allows gamblers to pursue their addiction, but it is not the source of the addiction.

Addictive gambling is about experiences much more basic to our human nature. Milkman and Sunderwirth (1987) categorize addictions according to the nature of the experience. He describes three primary types of addiction: addiction to stimulation, addiction to sedation, and addiction to fantasy. Unlike drugs, which are largely either stimulants or depressants (with the notable exception of hallucinogens), gambling fulfills all of Milkman's categories of addiction. Most notably, gambling is about fantasy. When you buy a lottery ticket, what you buy is a certain number of hours to fantasize about what it would be like to win, the houses or cars you would buy, the places you would travel, or how you would be free of financial worries. Gambling is primarily a fantasy-based activity. Even more, it is an extension of our culture—a culture that values someone who takes chances and makes good or someone who defies the odds and comes out ahead. As I explore later in the chapter, gamblers also seek either the stimulation or sedation that gambling supplies.

THE THREE Cs AND COMPULSIVE GAMBLING

The three Cs that define addictive behavior can help explain compulsive gambling. We'll apply the three Cs—compulsive activity, loss of control, and continued use despite adverse consequences to the dynamics of gambling—and help you compare the patterns to those outlined in other chapters that focus on substances as the basis of the addiction. You will see that many of the symptom patterns that are observed in alcohol and drug addiction are mirrored in patterns of compulsive gambling.

The common elements of preoccupation, tolerance, denial, progression, withdrawal, and relapse are as evident in the histories of pathological gamblers as they are in the histories of alcoholics. Both chemical addicts and compulsive gamblers exhibit uncontrolled or unmoderated behavior in relation to their activity or drug. The life problems and consequences that accompany substance-based addictions are mirrored in the experience of compulsive gamblers. Family conflicts and domestic violence, financial problems, periods of extreme depression and anxiety, suicidal thoughts and attempts, and numerous other effects of an addiction are evident regardless of the object of the addiction.

COMPULSIVE ACTIVITY

> I was driving home from work—my usual route—and wasn't thinking about anything in particular. It had been more than 2 months since I had gone to the casinos and I was still sorting out how I would pay back all that I owed my family. I looked over at a billboard on the side of the highway and all it said was "Ka-ching" and the name of a casino. Thirty minutes later, I was sitting in front of a slot machine. Four hours later, I had spent my entire paycheck for that month and written several bad checks. I don't even understand what happened.
>
> —Judy, a 47-year-old retail clerk

The first C, compulsive use or activity, is easily observed in problem gamblers. Stein, Hollander, and Liebowitz (1993) defines compulsive gambling as "a conflict between a gambler's stated intention, such as to not gamble, or to not gamble more than X amount, and the actual behavior, which violates the intention." Similar to the pattern you see with alcohol or drug addicts, problem gamblers almost always approach gambling with good intentions and a commitment to control their behavior. The alcoholic's pledge that, "I'll only have two beers on the way home" is translated into, "I'll only gamble $20.00 and go home" with compulsive gamblers.

Inevitably, the stories that problem gamblers tell provide vivid descriptions of the compulsion to engage in gambling. Many relate feeling overcome by irresistible urges and impulses and they experience strong discomfort if they don't find a way to act on the urges. Frequently, problem gamblers will tell stories describing a fugue-like state during which they find themselves engaging in unplanned, spontaneous gambling activity. When they find that they are out of money and unable to continue, pathological gamblers may beg, borrow, or steal to return to the activity.

The impulse to gamble can be triggered by a wide variety of stimuli, both internal and external. Living in a culture that not only endorses but also actively encourages gambling means that problem gamblers will be continuously confronted with messages that may activate the impulse to gamble. Gamblers have described everything from a trip to a fast-food restaurant that hands out scratch tickets to grocery shopping and purchasing items that have Instant-Winner promotions as experiences that have awakened the impulse to gamble. Watching films depicting gambling, hearing someone talk about winning at a casino, or being invited to join the office sports betting pool are examples of events that have triggered clients in recovery. Once the compulsive gambler is triggered, they frequently begin acting as if in a trance—a trance that is broken only when the gambling experience comes to an end.

If you visit a casino and want to see the compulsion to gamble in action, watch people playing slot machines: Particularly watch for those playing several machines simultaneously. Eventually, a player is likely to hit a jackpot large enough that they are forced to stop playing until a casino employee can check the machine and make the payoff. Compulsive slot gamblers will not be able to stop long enough to wait for the attendant and will continue without interruption to play other machines if possible. One slot gambler described feeling "really annoyed when I would win . . . I was glad to have more money to gamble with but hated to have to wait for them to reset the machine, especially if other people were playing the machines next to me and I had to stop altogether."

LOSS OF CONTROL

I knew that I had to stop. I had been awake for almost 3 days with only a few hours sleep. I hadn't called in to work to say I was ill, I didn't eat or bathe or even get dressed. I spent almost 72 hours watching the stock reports on CNN and racing to my computer to try and salvage my losses. I had gambled in the market and played the margins for almost a year. Now all of it, all $600,000 that I didn't really have, was being swept away. Even during those 3 days, I still was trying to finance more "investment" any way I could, even threatening family and friends. I could not face the losses. Even worse, I couldn't face stopping.

—Stan, a 52-year-old CEO

Without money, he couldn't live, he couldn't gamble. Without the gambling, he had nothing. He was nothing. He couldn't imagine not gambling at this point, couldn't imagine giving up the rush, the feelings of power and importance that didn't seem to come from anything else.

—Don in *Compulsive* (Nelson, 1998)

In his book, *The Chase* (1984), Lesieur vividly describes the downward spiral that is created when individuals lose control of the urge to gamble. The loss of control of the impulse to gamble is often set in motion by the *chase*. The chase is the solution that exacerbates the problem. In the history of most compulsive gamblers, they describe repeated experiences in which they lost more money than they intended to and continued to gamble to try and reclaim some of their losses. The more they lose, the more they gamble. The chase means that gamblers are gambling to try and win back money they lost gambling.

As Milkman and Sunderwirth (1987) describe, "In some patterns of behavioral excess, a person may continue an experience that is no longer pleasurable because of a growing aversion to the sensations brought about through stopping it" (p. 108). Gamblers describe the end of a gambling binge in similar terms to alcoholics describing waking from a blackout. They have lost a sense of time and often are unaware of how much money they have lost. Gamblers frequently feel strongly disoriented and exhausted when they finally run out of resources to stay involved in the game. When the reality begins to become apparent—that they have written bad checks, missed important family or work obligations, compromised their ability to meet financial obligations—the overwhelming sense of despair or depression is unavoidable.

One strategy that several gamblers have related as a way to win back losses is to *double down*. They double each bet they make following a loss with the intention of winning a bet that will eliminate their losses. The problem is that for most gamblers money is a finite resource and this strategy can only go so far. When the money is gone after the last bet is placed, the gambler often experiences an overwhelming sense of guilt, remorse, and anger that they were cheated out of their money.

The experience of being overpowered by the impulse to gamble is embedded in the stories of compulsive gamblers. Loss of control doesn't imply that the gambler bets on everything all the time. What most addicts experience is a loss of predictability—an increasing struggle to establish and maintain limits to their behavior with the repeated experience of exceeding those limits in an unpredictable, intermittent manner. Like those addicted to substances, gamblers will enter a betting situation with the intent of staying for a limited time and playing with a predetermined amount of money. On some occasions, that is exactly what they do. Increasingly, however, they find they cannot adhere to the limits and regularly break promises to themselves about how they will manage their gambling. Loss of control is characterized by a loss of predictability.

Loss of control also encompasses the experience of gambling becoming increasingly pervasive in a person's life. What generally begins as an occasional trip to a casino or racetrack becomes more and more a part of the individual's life. The same progression that one finds with other addictions is replicated with gambling. Entertainment becomes entrapment. Other types of entertainment are abandoned to devote more time to gambling (e.g., financial resources that may have been committed to vacations or other special purposes are funneled into gambling).

CONTINUED USE DESPITE ADVERSE CONSEQUENCES

> I remember one day several months ago sitting at the slot machine and thinking "there goes my house."
>
> —Betty, a 65-year-old investment counselor

After I lost the last bet that day, I had a fuzzy awareness that my children would not be going to college after all, that my bank would be hit in a day or so with a stack of fraudulent checks, and that there was no way I could go home and face my wife. I planned to drive my car off the road on the way back home. At least they would get the life insurance.

—Robert, a 33-year-old computer programmer

All addictions have the power to rob people of their health, mental well-being, financial security, and, ultimately, their life. None, however, seem to have the same level of destructive potential, for both the addict and their family, as compulsive gambling. After working for almost 2 decades with substance abuse and dependence, the opportunity to work with gamblers initially seemed like a tremendous relief. No more being mistaken for the ex-wife when an alcoholic was going through DTs, no danger of an intoxicated adolescent throwing up in the office, no fear of a stimulant addict suddenly going into cardiac arrest. Gambling appeared to be a clean addiction—one that could certainly create financial havoc but didn't come with the messiness that was a part of working with substance abuse.

Naive clinicians, even those with many years of experience in working with other addictions, are often unprepared for the extreme damage that compulsive gambling can inflict on the addict and his or her family, friends, and careers. The expected financial disasters are certainly evident in the careers of most compulsive gamblers. The damage that may not be so easily recognized is the toll on the gambler's relationships, sense of self, emotional well-being, and capacity for hope. Severe depression and suicidal ideation or intent is synonymous with the crash that compulsive gamblers experience. The risk for self-destructive behavior is higher than in any other addiction.

With all addictions, the longer addicts are able to hide their behavior, the more debilitated they become. Compulsive gamblers become masters at hiding their activity. Unlike substance abusers, there are not the obvious signs of intoxication. You can't smell a bad poker hand on someone's breath; gamblers don't stumble around because their horse didn't come in; a person doesn't pass out when they have overdosed on a slot machine. Consequently, problem gamblers can hide their problems for longer periods and become more severely disabled by their addiction.

As the relationship with gambling grows, other aspects of the gambler's life diminish or disappear. Lesieur (1993) describes the abandonment that family members feel and notes a study of wives of compulsive gamblers that found they were 4 times more likely to attempt suicide than the general population. A common fear of spouses of compulsive gamblers is that the gambler is involved in a romantic affair. They are not where they are supposed to be, miss family commitments, and lose time from work. There is money missing that is unexplained and the gambler is on an emotional roller-coaster that often includes irritability, defensiveness, and threats or incidents of domestic violence. It is not unusual for the spouse of a compulsive gambler to describe an initial reaction of relief when learning that his or her partner is gambling—a relief that is quickly replaced by anger and despair when the impact of the gambling becomes apparent.

The mystery that confronts gamblers in the final stages of their gambling is how they could have allowed themselves to dig such a deep hole. Along with financial losses, their lying and deception, loss of discipline and control, feelings of shame and embarrassment, and tremendous fear of the consequences that will result from their gambling create an overpowering sense of dread and depression. As noted, suicidal thoughts are common for compulsive gamblers in the final stage of their addiction. For some, it is a last attempt to leave behind some money to help the family handle the debt they would leave behind. At least the family would have the money from life insurance if the death appears to be an accident. As Don in *Compulsive* muses, ". . . but one of the few things left from the fiasco of the previous year was several hundred thousand dollars worth of life insurance" (Nelson, 1998, p. vi). It is not unusual for addicted gamblers to seek help first when they are in the throes of a suicidal depression.

Unlike substance addictions, compulsive gambling has a peculiar twist that significantly impacts the extent of the consequences that gamblers experience. With alcoholics, when they begin to experience the more serious medical and situational problems associated with alcohol abuse, they do not believe that more drinking will improve the problems. With gamblers, however, it is typical that they experience times during their gambling when they are at bottom and have a substantial win. Substance addiction is more linear in it's downward progression. Gambling is nonlinear. Problem gamblers will be playing out the last $10 from a series of bad checks they wrote to the casino and will hit a jackpot that covers their losses. They will hit a bet on the last football game of the day and be able to get the money back in the office before their theft is discovered. Gambling is both the problem and the solution. All compulsive gamblers know that the next bet may be the one that gets them out of the hell that gambling has put them in.

PATTERNS OF COMPULSIVE GAMBLING

Problem gamblers tend to develop a pathological relationship with gambling in one of two ways: gambling becomes either a trance-like escape or a powerful stimulant. Just as some substance abusers prefer the effect of central nervous system depressant drugs and the anesthesia they provide, other drug users prefer the rush and animated high of amphetamines or cocaine. Gamblers also pursue different emotional experiences through their gambling activity. The patterns of Escape gambling and Action gambling follow somewhat different courses but lead to the same inevitable conclusion.

ACTION GAMBLERS

> I was on a high, a rush that was better than cocaine, better than sex, better than being there when my son was born. I didn't really care about whether or how much I won or lost, I just wanted to stay at the table.
>
> —Bill, a 38-year-old truck driver

> You know the only thing worse than losing big the first time you go into a casino? Winning big.
>
> —Dan Savage in *Skipping Towards Gomorrah* (2002, p. 55)

In the case of action gambling, the compulsion often begins when someone who has been a recreational gambler has a big win. Action gamblers are predominantly males who generally view gambling as a skill to be learned and as a desirable way to make a living without the drudgery of employment. Action gamblers describe their experience as an unequaled rush of sensation—an ecstatic state in which they feel powerful and special. When gamblers play their game of choice, or are in action, they experience a sensation similar to a strong adrenaline rush. The sensation is heightened when there is a big win or lucky streak, but the emotional experience continues as long as they are playing. "I was wrong. It's not about money; it's about risk and danger and purchasing a little of the action . . ." (Savage, 2002, p. 64).

Action gamblers tend to play games that involve some level of skill, such as poker or blackjack, craps, or handicapping sporting events or races. Part of the stimulation is from playing the game well enough to beat the odds. Action gamblers enjoy the recognition and status that comes from being a good player. They often describe some system they have learned or developed that will give them an advantage in the games they play. They tend to be much more competitive personalities who indulge in the notoriety of being a high roller. Winning the respect of others, being perceived as talented and skilled, and feeling the excitement of overcoming the odds is the target experiences for action gamblers. Many action gamblers feel most stimulated when they are in a position of coming from behind during a period of intense gambling. Some action gamblers have even described as purposely taking irrational risks to provide themselves with the stimulation of digging out of the hole.

The etiology of the emergence of a gambling problem follows different paths for action and escape gamblers. Box 5.1 outlines the common dynamics described by pathological action gamblers.

This group is largely composed of males who fit the traditional picture of a problem gambler. They start at a younger age, often through involvement with other men in the family. Involvement in family card games or making friendly bets on sporting events is a typical introduction to gambling. As noted in Table 5.2, there is a progression of involvement with gambling that typically increases after a significant win or winning streak. The progression from recreational gambling to pathological gambling, when it occurs, may take years or even decades.

Until the past 2 decades, the majority of compulsive gamblers would have fit the description of an action gambler. A trip to a casino in the 1980s would have presented a picture of an overwhelmingly male population clustered around card tables, roulette wheels, sports books, and craps tables with a smaller population of women on the periphery at slot machines. More recently, however, there is a rapidly growing group of gamblers who take another approach and gamble for very different reasons.

Escape Gamblers

I was sitting playing a particular slot machine that I liked when it hit a jackpot. I remember begin so annoyed that I couldn't go back to playing until someone came to pay out the jackpot and reset the machine. The winning didn't matter so much, I just wanted to keep playing.

—Stacy, a 72-year-old retiree

So I sat down and put my money in a machine. It wasn't money though; it was a chance to be alone and back into a fantasy world. I left that machine when my

BOX 5.1
Etiology of Action Gamblers

Predisposing Factors

Family of origin.
Personality.

Introduction to Gambling

Introduced by friends of family.
Begins betting at an early age.
Occasional gambling.
Experimenting with new types of gambling.
Developing a relationship with gambling.
Deviant behavior.
Precipitating or traumatic event.
Experiences a big win.

Winning Phase

Frequent winning.
Fantasizes about winning.
Increases amount of money bet and time spent gambling.
Lies about gambling.
Brags about winning.

Losing Phase

Chases losses.
Loses time from work or school.
Cannot stop gambling.
Begins to accumulate debts.
Relationship with family and friends impacted.
Frequently borrows money.
Drops nongambling activities.
Becomes irritable, restless, depressed.

Desperation Phase

Unable to pay debts.
Sells possessions or family valuables.
Increases drug or alcohol use.
Thoughts of committing crimes to finance gambling.
Loss of job or drops out of school.
Withdraws from family and friends.
Blames others.
Shame, guilt, despair.
Thoughts of or attempts at suicide.
Emotional, physical, financial breakdown.

money was taken too fast because I knew at that rate I wouldn't get to stay in the "no thinking fantasy world" for very long.

—Gayla, a 38-year-old homemaker

Escape gamblers seek the emotional numbing and trance-like state that they experience through gambling. They are seeking sedation and anonymity. They generally play games that allow them to remain more anonymous such as video poker, slot machines, and lotteries. The majority of this type of gambler are women. Escape gamblers are more likely to gamble alone and seek out the sensation of escaping from daily problems or concerns that they experience when gambling. It is common for women gamblers to describe themselves in a relationship with the casino staff and the favorite machines that they play. It's *my machine* at *my casino* with *my person* that brings drinks or change. Box 5.2 outlines the common dynamics described by pathological escape gamblers.

Escape gamblers often begin gambling much later in life, after children have left home, when they are retired, or when their work life is less demanding. Many women who are escape gamblers are single, widowed, or divorced. If married, they are likely to be in unhappy marriages with men who have substance abuse problems or are emotionally unavailable or less intelligent (Lesieur, 1993). Many describe being in relationships that are emotionally dead or distant and relate patterns of involvement with their spouses in which they are unassertive and distant. Gambling begins as a temporary way to escape life or problems.

Boughton (2002) interviewed women to research their reasons for gambling, which they described as "for fun" (80%), "for excitement" (77%), and "for entertainment" (72%). In her sample, 40% to 60% related they gambled to "cheer myself up" (61%), "deal with boredom" (52%), "relieve stress" (53%), and "be free to do what I want" (56%). A pattern of gambling to manage depression or boredom was common to the majority of women gamblers. Women who have gambled recreationally only a few times a year are more likely to develop a pattern of compulsive gambling later in life when they are free of child-rearing responsibilities and settled into jobs or marriages that are not satisfying or stimulating.

Unlike action gamblers, escape gamblers tend to engage in games that are more likely to be based solely on chance and involve little or no skill. Since escape and emotional numbing is the desired effect, games that involve minimal contact with others who might evaluate their play is preferred. Escape gamblers don't want a dealer looking at them disapprovingly if they decide to split a pair of 10s in blackjack. They prefer the video version of the game. Casinos are increasingly dedicating space to video versions of poker, blackjack, slots, and keno. In addition to attracting more women gamblers, it is highly likely that these types of games will appeal to younger gamblers who are already primed by a childhood of video arcade games.

In therapy with escape gamblers, the clinician is often challenged by the rapid progression of problems and the strong attachment to gambling that these individuals describe. The progression from recreational gambling to compulsive gambling can occur in as little as several weeks or months. There is not the same likelihood that the problem begins to spiral following a big win. Frequently, there has not been a significant win in their gambling history. It's not the excitement; it's the relief of losing themselves in the activity. As one 70-year-old woman described, "The casino is one of the few places I can go and feel safe and welcome. The other is the

BOX 5.2
Etiology of Escape Gamblers

PREDISPOSING FACTORS

Physical, emotional, or sexual abuse.
Poor relationships.
Losses.

VALUES

Denial of gambling as a problem.
Maintain family trust is important.

GAMBLING HABITS

Onset later in life.
Faster progression of compulsive behavior.
Seeking to escape from loneliness or boredom.
Begins as social activity and entertainment.
Participates mainly in games of chance.
Fewer big-win experiences.

EMOTIONAL CONSEQUENCES RELATED TO GAMBLING

Becomes emotionally dependent on gambling.
Preoccupied with gambling.
Depression.
Secretive about excess gambling.
Guilt about both financial losses and failure to meet standards of behavior.
Guilt over lost time with family.
Shame related to dishonesty.
Fears of being revealed and disgraced.

FINANCIAL CONSEQUENCES RELATED TO GAMBLING

Loss of household money.
Credit card problems.
Use of money from family savings or accounts.
Sale of valued family possessions.

RECOVERY ISSUES

Denial that gambling is a problem.
Frequently does not want to stop gambling.
Partner may not intervene.
Family less supportive in getting help.
Child care.
Male dominated treatment and recovery services.

shopping mall." In some sense, women who are gambling to escape are often re-peating a pattern of dedication to a relationship that has become destructive. They are sure that the odds will change, and they will be secure and happy once again. Action gamblers are aware that they are engaging in a game of chance; escape gam-blers are immersed in a relationship.

DIAGNOSTIC CRITERIA

For more than a year, I thought (he) was having an affair. Money was unaccounted for from our accounts, he wasn't at work some afternoons when he was supposed to be, he had these wild mood swings and would threaten to hit me if I didn't back off asking him about where he would be on nights he came in late. When he first admitted he had a gambling problem, I was relieved. Then I was unbelievably pissed.

—Sheila, 36-year-old wife of a problem gambler

Unlike substance-based addictions, there are generally no physical or medical signs or symptoms available to aid in the diagnosis of gambling problems. The cri-teria is behaviorally based and largely obtained from either first-party or collat-eral interviews. As with other addictions, subject credibility is a concern. With gambling problems, this issue is often magnified since gamblers are so adept at hiding their dilemmas. Spouses or partners, business associates, physicians or mental health professionals may be aware that something is wrong but have no ev-idence that gambling is a factor. Problem gamblers are more likely to give the ap-pearance of having a mood disorder (particularly bipolar disorder) a form of depression or anxiety disorder, or a personality disorder such as narcissistic or an-tisocial personality disorder.

McGurrin (1992) describes the following common characteristics found among action-oriented pathological gamblers:

- Pathological gamblers often vacillate between periods when they express extreme confidence in their ability to succeed in consistently winning large amounts of money at gambling as well as achieving outstanding success in other areas of life and periods when they experience acute self-doubt, anxi-ety, and depression over experienced or potential failure.
- Pathological gamblers tend to view reward and achievement through grad-ual, sustained effort and delayed gratification as inferior means of financial self-support and accomplishment.
- Pathological gamblers typically have difficulty maintaining intimate, emotionally expressive, and supportive relationships with parents, sib-lings, spouses, children, and close friends.
- Many pathological gamblers have rather pronounced personality traits that are characteristic of specific personality disorders, especially narcissistic per-sonality disorder and several indicators of antisocial personality disorder.
- Pathological gamblers tend to view the outcomes of many life events as being externally controlled (McGurrin, 1992, pp. 11–14).

Lesieur (1993) outlines behaviors that are common signs of compulsive gam-bling (again, primarily action gamblers) that are observed in the workplace:

Misuse of Time

- Comes to work late (because of a late-night card game, casino venture, or bad night's sleep from worrying about gambling-related problems).
- Takes long lunches (goes to off-track betting parlor or meets bookmakers, loan sharks, or creditors).
- Mysteriously disappears in the afternoon (listens to sporting events or goes to the track, off-track betting parlor, or afternoon card or dice game).
- Uses vacation time in isolated days rather than in blocks.
- Takes sick days as they become available rather than allowing them to accumulate (uses sick days to gamble).
- Fails to take days off (obsessed with getting money to pay gambling debts or afraid fraud or embezzlement will be discovered).
- Uses the rest room excessively (reads sports pages or listens to the radio in the rest room).
- Spends an excessive amount of time on the telephone (talking to bookies, brokers, or creditors—including loan sharks and loan companies).
- Reads the newspaper and sports literature at work (such as scratch sheets from the racetrack, racing forms, or sports news).

Signs of Obsession with Gambling and/or Debts

- Unfinished projects.
- Irritability.
- Poor concentration.
- Moodiness and subsequent changes in productivity (mood depends on whether the gambler is winning or losing at the moment and whether money is available for gambling).
- An obsessive interest in the scores of sports events or the results of horse or dog races, lotteries, or illegal numbers.

Embezzlement, Employee Theft, and Other Illegal Activity

- Uses the corporate credit card for cash advances in gambling locations (this should be a red flag).
- Borrows money from the company.
- Steals items for resale to pay gambling debts.
- Sells items at work (either personal property or stolen goods).
- Sells drugs at work (may also have a drug problem).
- Defrauds customers or clients to increase commission sales (Lesieur, 1993, pp. 14–17).

Spouses or partners of problem gamblers are often fearful that the gambler is involved in some type of romantic affair or other legal problem. Employers or coworkers may believe that the gambler is experiencing emotional or family problems that are interfering with his or her work. There is very seldom a realization that gambling is the foundation of the problem behaviors, particularly since so few people are educated about the common signs and symptoms of problem gambling.

DIAGNOSIS OF PATHOLOGICAL GAMBLING

The diagnostic criteria used by most mental health professionals is outlined in the *Diagnostic and Statistical Manual of Mental Disorders,* fourth edition, text revision (*DSM-IV-TR*) published by the American Psychiatric Association (2000). The American Psychiatric Association did not formally recognize pathological gambling (the diagnostic term used in the *DSM-IV-TR*) as a psychiatric diagnosis until 1980. Under *DSM-IV-TR* criteria, pathological gambling is categorized as an impulse control disorder and defined as a progressive psychological disorder characterized by emotional dependence, loss of control, and accompanying negative consequences in the gambler's social, vocational, and family life.

Specifically, pathological gambling (312.31) is an Axis I disorder. To assign the diagnosis of pathological gambling, an individual must meet the criteria outlined in Box 5.3.

In diagnosing any disorders, clinicians are urged to consider the Pepe'-le-Pew dilemma. Since there are no medical markers or psychological tests that are 100% reliable in diagnosing pathological gambling (or any addictive disorders), the process is largely reliant on self-report, other's reports, and clinical observation. If it

---

BOX 5.3
Diagnostic Criteria for 312.31 Pathological Gambling

A. Persistent and recurrent maladaptive gambling behavior as indicated by five (or more) of the following:
  • Is preoccupied with gambling (e.g., preoccupied with reliving past gambling experiences, handicapping or planning the next venture, or thinking of ways to get money with which to gamble).
  • Needs to gamble with increasing amounts of money in order to achieve the desired excitement.
  • Has repeated unsuccessful efforts to control, cut back, or stop gambling.
  • Is restless or irritable when attempting to cut down or stop gambling.
  • Gambles as a way of escaping from problems or of relieving a dysphoric mood (e.g., feeling of helplessness, guilt, anxiety, depression).
  • After losing money gambling, often returns another day to get even ("chasing" one's losses).
  • Lies to family members, therapist, or others to conceal the extent of involvement with gambling.
  • Has jeopardized or lost a significant relationship, job, or educational or career opportunity because of gambling.
  • Relies on others to provide money to relieve a desperate financial situation caused by gambling.
B. The gambling behavior is not better accounted for by a "Manic Episode."

American Psychiatric Association. (2000). *Diagnostic and statistical manual of mental disorders* (4th ed., text rev.). Washington, DC: Author, p. 618.

"looks like a skunk, walks like a skunk, and smells like a skunk, it probably is a skunk." Clinicians always look for the pattern of behaviors that typify certain diagnostic criteria. There is, however, always some possibility that the "skunk" is a black cat that fell in a vat of Limburger cheese and walked underneath a white paintbrush.

Social gamblers may periodically experience enough of the symptoms noted to be assessed as a pathological gambler. A recreational gambler may occasionally spend more than they planned on gambling and try to win it back or hide their losses from family or friends. They may be irritable when they leave a gambling venue where they lost more than they anticipated and feel the urge to return and try to reclaim their losses. Social gamblers also enjoy the sense of escape or excitement that accompanies a trip to the track or casino. For pathological or compulsive gamblers, the pattern is the norm. Chasing their losses, feeling depressed over their behavior, becoming increasingly withdrawn from family, friends, and other activities and being highly irritable when they are not able to gamble becomes the rule, rather than the exception, for pathological gamblers.

THE CHASE

Pathological gamblers live in a state of chasing. The chase is one of the most problematic patterns that typically emerges in pathological gambling. Initially, chasing may involve pursuing the emotional high experienced when the gambler had a big win. A gambler chases the high; later, he or she is chasing to recoup the inevitable losses (Wexler & Wexler, 1993). The pattern of returning to gamble to win back losses from previous gambling is the more insidious chase that ensues as the gambling increases.

For some gamblers, the chase may be one of the factors that contribute to the compulsion to gamble in an irrational way. One gambler described going into a casino to play his favorite game: blackjack. When he was dealt an ace and jack on the first hand, he motioned the dealer to hit him with another card. The dealer pointed out that he had a winning hand—a 21, but the gambler insisted on another card. His rationale was that "it's no fun to hit right away, that takes the pleasure out of it" (McCown & Chamberlain, 2000, p. 62). The excitement of coming from behind and making up losses may be equally or more stimulating than winning.

Lesieur (1984) describes in detail the phenomenology of the chase. He highlights that a problem gambler doesn't quit when he or she is ahead. The thrill of previous success is a strong factor, particularly for action gamblers who describe the experience in terms typically used when people describe their first experience using cocaine or narcotics. A lottery gambler described it this way: "To me, buying that ticket and anticipating the announcement of the number—it's better than food, better than sex, better than anything you can imagine. I can only describe it as like a roller-coaster that goes on for a few hours before they do the daily lottery. . . . Frankly, it would be hard to imagine living life without this kind of thrill" (McCown & Chamberlain, 2000, p. 55).

The consequences of prolonged periods of chasing losses is often the factor that leads to hitting bottom. Spending more money trying to win money that was spent trying to win money is a pattern that digs a deeper and deeper hole. Problem gamblers sometimes report the awareness that it is impossible for them to win back their losses, but they continue to gamble in the hope that they can at least minimize the damage through recouping some winnings.

ASSESSMENT

There are comparatively few assessment tools specifically designed to measure gambling problems. Research and methodologies for both the assessment and treatment of gambling disorders are still being developed. There are, however, several public domain screening tools that can help you evaluate whether problem gambling may be a consideration with your clients.

SOUTH OAKS GAMBLING SCREEN

The South Oaks Gambling Screen (SOGS; Table 5.2) is probably the most widely known and utilized instrument for the general screening of gambling disorders. The SOGS was developed in 1987 by Lesieur and Blume (1987, 1993). The SOGS is used for initial screening and for indicating a possible diagnosis of problem gambling. SOGS results are highly correlated to *DSM-IV-TR* (APA, 2000) diagnostic criteria and it is used extensively in epidemiological studies. The authors of the SOGS have allowed it to be used freely by researchers and clinicians as long as the items are not revised.

The advantages to the SOGS are it's availability, ease of administration and scoring, and utility with both adult and adolescent populations. It has been used with subjects as young as age 11 with excellent results (Ladouceur, 1996) and in research with college students (McCown & Chamberlain, in press). Criticisms of the SOGS generally focus on the potential for false positives (people assessed to have a gambling problem when they do not) and that the SOGS fails to consider the frequency of gambling and, instead, focuses on the intensity of the gambling activity.

In clinical practice, the SOGS is an excellent addition to a screening battery for use with a variety of clients. Many substance abuse clinics, domestic violence treatment services, and general mental health services have added the SOGS to a comprehensive intake package. For therapists treating other addictions, family violence, depression, and forensic issues, inclusion of the SOGS is highly recommended.

MASSACHUSETTS GAMBLING SCREEN

Researchers at Harvard University (Shaffer, LaBrie, Scanlan, & Cummings, 1994) developed the Massachusetts Gambling Screen (MAGS; Table 5.3). The MAGS is a brief screening instrument that yields an index of nonpathological and pathological gambling. It is used with both adults and adolescents and was validated using *DSM-IV* criteria for pathological gambling. Like the SOGS, the MAGS is easy to administer and score and is openly available to clinicians and researchers. The MAGS is also designed to meet the *DSM-IV* criteria for diagnosing pathological gambling.

Table 5.2
The South Oaks Gambling Screen

1. Please indicate which of the following types of gambling you have done in your lifetime. For each type, mark one answer: "Not at all," "Less than once a week," or "Once a week or more."

	Not at All	Less than Once a Week	Once a Week or More	
a.	_____	_____	_____	Played cards for money.
b.	_____	_____	_____	Bet on horses, dogs, or other animals (in off-track betting, at the track, or with a bookie).
c.	_____	_____	_____	Bet on sports (parlay cards, with a bookie, or at jai alai).
d.	_____	_____	_____	Played dice games (including craps, over and under, or other dice games) for money.
e.	_____	_____	_____	Went to a casino (legal or otherwise).
f.	_____	_____	_____	Played the numbers or bet on lotteries.
g.	_____	_____	_____	Played bingo.
h.	_____	_____	_____	Played the stock and/or commodities market.
i.	_____	_____	_____	Played slot machines, poker machines, or other gambling machines.
j.	_____	_____	_____	Bowled, shot pool, played golf, or played some other game of skill for money.

2. What is the largest amount of money you have ever gambled with on any one day?
   _____ Never have gambled.
   _____ $1 or less.
   _____ More than $1 up to $10.
   _____ More than $10 up to $100.
   _____ More than $100 up to $1,000.
   _____ More than $1,000 up to $10,000.
   _____ More than $10,000.
3. Do (did) your parents have a gambling problem?
   _____ Both my father and mother gamble (or gambled) too much.
   _____ My father gambles (or gambled) too much.
   _____ My mother gambles (or gambled) too much.
   _____ Neither one gambles (or gambled) too much.
4. When you gamble, how often do you go back another day to win back money you lost?
   _____ Never.
   _____ Some of the time (less than half the time) I lost.
   _____ Most of the time I lost.
   _____ Every time I lost.
5. Have you ever claimed to be winning money gambling but weren't really? In fact, you lost?
   _____ Never (or never gamble).
   _____ Yes, less than half the time I lost.
   _____ Yes, most of the time.
6. Do you feel you have ever had a problem with gambling?
   _____ No.
   _____ Yes, in the past, but not now.
   _____ Yes.
7. Did you ever gamble more than you intended to? Yes _____ No _____

Table 5.2 *Continued*

8. Have people criticized your gambling?   Yes _____   No _____
9. Have you ever felt guilty about the way you gamble or what happens when you gamble?   Yes _____   No _____
10. Have you ever felt like you would like to stop gambling but didn't think you could? Yes _____   No _____
11. Have you ever hidden betting slips, lottery tickets, gambling money, or other signs of gambling from your spouse, children, or other important people in your life? Yes _____   No _____
12. Have you ever argued with people you live with over how you handle money? Yes _____   No _____
13. If you answered yes to question 12, have money arguments ever centered on your gambling?   Yes _____   No _____
14. Have you ever borrowed from someone and not paid them back as a result of your gambling?   Yes _____   No _____
15. Have you ever lost time from work (or school) because of gambling? Yes _____   No _____
16. If you borrowed money to gamble or to pay gambling debts, who or where did you borrow from? (Check "Yes" or "No" for each.)

	No	Yes
a. From household money.	( )	( )
b. From your spouse.	( )	( )
c. From other relatives or in-laws.	( )	( )
d. From banks, loan companies, or credit unions.	( )	( )
e. From credit cards.	( )	( )
f. From loan sharks (Shylocks).	( )	( )
g. You cashed in stocks, bonds, or other securities.	( )	( )
h. You sold personal or family property.	( )	( )
i. You borrowed on your checking account (passed bad checks).	( )	( )
j. You have (had) a credit line with a bookie.	( )	( )
k. You have (had) a credit line with a casino.	( )	( )

SOGS Scoring:

Scores on the South Oaks Gambling Screen itself are determined by adding the number of questions that show an at-risk response. Each scored question is assigned 1 point. There is a maximum score of 20 points.

Questions 1, 2, and 3 are not counted.
_____ Question 4: Most of the time I lost, or every time I lost.
_____ Question 5: Yes, less than half the time I lost, or yes, most of the time.
_____ Question 6: Yes, in the past, but not now, or yes.
_____ Question 7: Yes.
_____ Question 8: Yes.
_____ Question 9: Yes.
_____ Question 10: Yes.
_____ Question 11: Yes.
Question 12 not counted.
_____ Question 13: Yes.
_____ Question 14: Yes.

_____ Question 15: Yes.
_____ Question 16a: Yes.
_____ Question 16b: Yes.
_____ Question 16c: Yes.
_____ Question 16d: Yes.
_____ Question 16e: Yes.
_____ Question 16f: Yes.
_____ Question 16g: Yes.
_____ Question 16h: Yes.
_____ Question 16i: Yes.
Questions 16j and 16k not counted.

Total = _____ (20 questions are counted)
5 or more = Probable pathological gambler

Source: From "The South Oaks Gambling Screen (SOGS): A new instrument for the identification of pathological gamblers," by H. R. Lesieur and S. B. Blume, 1987, *American Journal of Psychiatry, 144*(9), pp. 1184–1188. Reprinted with permission.

Table 5.3
Massachusetts Gambling Screen

Please circle the response that best represents your answer.

	Responses	
1. Have you ever gambled (for example, bet money on the lottery, bingo, sporting events, casino games, cards, racing or other games of chance)?	1. No	Yes
2. Have you ever experienced social, psychological, or financial pressure to start gambling or increase how much you gamble?	2. No	Yes
3. How much do you usually gamble compared with most other people?	3. Less About the same More	
4. Do you feel that the amount or frequency of your gambling is normal?	4. Yes	No
5. Do friends or relatives think of you as a normal gambler?	5. Yes	No
6. Do you ever feel pressure to gamble when you do not gamble?	6. No	Yes

If you never have gambled, please skip to question #29 now.

7. Do you ever feel guilty about your gambling?	7. No	Yes
8. Does any member of your family ever worry or complain about your gambling?	8. No	Yes
9. Have you ever thought that you should reduce or stop gambling?	9. No	Yes
10. Are you always able to stop gambling when you want?	10. Yes	No
11. Has your gambling ever created problems between you and any member of your family or friends?	11. No	Yes
12. Have you ever gotten into trouble at work or school because of your gambling?	12. No	Yes
13. Have you ever neglected your obligations (e.g., family work or school) for two or more days in a row because you were gambling?	13. No	Yes
14. Have you ever gone to anyone for help about your gambling?	14. No	Yes
15. Have you ever been arrested for a gambling-related activity?	15. No	Yes
16. Have you been preoccupied during the past 12 months with thinking of ways to get money for gambling or reliving past gambling experiences (e.g., handicapping, selecting a number)?	16. No	Yes
17. During the past 12 months, have you gambled increasingly larger amounts of money to experience your desired level of gambling excitement?	17. No	Yes
18. During the past 12 months, did you find that the same amount of gambling had less effect on you than before?	18. No	Yes
19. Has stopping gambling or cutting down how much you gamble made you feel restless or irritable during the past 12 months?	19. No	Yes
20. During the past 12 months, did you gamble to reduce any uncomfortable feelings (e.g., restlessness or irritability) that resulted from having previously stopped or reduced gambling?	20. No	Yes
21. Have you gambled as a way of escaping from problems or relieving feelings of helplessness, guilt, anxiety, or depression during the past 12 months?	21. No	Yes

Table 5.3   *Continued*

Responses

22. During the past 12 months, after losing money gambling, have you returned to gambling on another day to win back your lost money?   22. No   Yes
23. Have you lied to family members or others to conceal the extent to which you have been gambling during the past 12 months?   23. No   Yes
24. Have you committed any illegal acts (e.g., forgery, fraud, theft, embezzlement) during the past 12 months to finance your gambling?   24. No   Yes
25. During the past 12 months, have you jeopardized or lost a significant relationship, job, educational or career opportunity because of your gambling?   25. No   Yes
26. During the past 12 months, have you relied on other sources (e.g., family, friends, coworkers, bank) to provide you with money to resolve a desperate financial situation caused by your gambling?   26. No   Yes
27. During the past 12 months, have you made efforts unsuccessfully to limit, reduce, or stop gambling?   27. No   Yes
28. How old were you when you placed your first bet?   28. _____
29. What is your sex?   29. Female   Male
30. What is your age as of your last birthday?   30. _____
31. How honest were your responses to each of the questions on this survey?   31. Not at all honest / Somewhat dishonest / Somewhat honest / Very honest

Thank you for your cooperation.

MAGS Scoring:

To classify according to the MAGS
Question #

6. No = 0   Yes = 0.63   _____
8. No = 0   Yes = 0.91   _____
10. Yes = 0   No = 0.56   _____
11. No = 0   Yes = 0.93   _____
12. No = 0   Yes = 1.51   _____
13. No = 0   Yes = 1.53   _____
15. No = 0   Yes = 1.63   _____
Subtotal = _____
Subtract   0.62
TOTAL 1   _____

To classify according to *DSM-IV*
Question #

16. No = 0   Yes = 1   _____
17. No = 0   Yes = 0.5   _____
18. No = 0   Yes = 0.5   _____
19. No = 0   Yes = 0.5   _____
20. No = 0   Yes = 0.5   _____
21. No = 0   Yes = 1   _____
22. No = 0   Yes = 1   _____
23. No = 0   Yes = 1   _____
24. No = 0   Yes = 1   _____
25. No = 0   Yes = 1   _____
26. No = 0   Yes = 1   _____
27. No = 0   Yes = 1   _____
TOTAL 2   _____

MAGS Classification Key

If the value on the TOTAL 1 line is a negative number, the respondent is classified as **Nonpathological.**

If the value on the TOTAL 1 line is between 0 and 2 (including 0 and 2), the respondent is classified as **In Transition.**

If the value on the TOTAL 1 line *is greater than 2*, the respondent is classified as **Pathological.**

DSM-IV *Classification Key*

If the value on the TOTAL 2 line is less than 5, the respondent is classified as **Nonpathological.**

If the value on the TOTAL 2 line is 5 or greater, the respondent is classified as **Pathological.**

(continued)

Table 5.3 *Continued*

Massachusetts Gambling Screen
Scoring Guide Instructions

Step One

Administer the Massachusetts Gambling Screen (MAGS) to the respondent.

Step Two

On the Scoring Guide, indicate the respondent's survey answers by circling the appropriate response option for each of the specified questions. The question numbers on the Scoring Guide refer to the question numbers on the MAGS survey. *Not all of the MAGS survey items are used on the Scoring Guide.*

Step Three

For each question, write the selected value on the corresponding line.

Step Four

Add the seven scores for the MAGS items. Enter the sum on the Subtotal line. Next, *subtract* the value 0.62. Enter the resulting value on the TOTAL 1 line. To classify the respondent according to MAGS criteria, refer to the MAGS Classification Key and select the category that corresponds to the value on the TOTAL 1 line.

Step Five

Add the twelve scores for the *DSM-IV* items. Enter the sum on the TOTAL 2 line. To classify the respondent according to the *DSM-IV* criteria, refer to the D*SM-IV* Classification Key and select the category that corresponds to the value on the TOTAL 2 line.

Source: From "Psychological Gambling among Adolescents: MA Gambling Screen (MAGS)," by H. J. Shaffer, R. LaBrie, K. Scanlan, and T. N. Cummings, 1994, *Journal of Gambling Studies,* pp. 353–358. Reprinted with permission.

GAMBLERS ANONYMOUS 20 QUESTIONS

Gamblers Anonymous (GA) uses a questionnaire (Gamblers Anonymous 20 Questions, Table 5.4) to help individuals determine whether they are compulsive gamblers. The questions focus on experiences that are commonly shared by problem gamblers and correlates with diagnostic criteria in the *DSM-IV-TR* (APA, 2000). Like the SOGS and MAGS, it is easy to administer and score and relies on face validity (the subject answering the questions honestly). All questions are answered either "Yes" or "No." If the subject answers yes to at least seven of the questions, they may be gambling compulsively. The GA 20 Questions is also used with family members or significant others to help them determine if someone they know is gambling problematically.

OTHER PSYCHOLOGICAL TESTS

Researchers and clinicians have studied a variety of standardized psychological tests for use with compulsive gamblers. These tests are available to trained clinicians only and should always be used in combination with interviews and other gambling specific questionnaires. While no single factor or configuration of results on these tests provides conclusive evidence of problem gambling, there are

Table 5.4
Gamblers Anonymous 20 Questions:
Do You Think You Might Have a Gambling Problem?

1. Did you ever lose time from work due to gambling?
2. Has gambling ever made your home life unhappy?
3. Did gambling affect your reputation?
4. Have you ever felt remorse after gambling?
5. Did you ever gamble to get money with which to pay debts or otherwise solve financial difficulties?
6. Did gambling cause a decrease in your ambition or efficiency?
7. After losing did you feel you must return as soon as possible and win back your losses?
8. After a win, did you have a strong urge to return and win more?
9. Did you often gamble until your last dollar was gone?
10. Did you ever borrow to finance your gambling?
11. Have you ever sold anything to finance gambling?
12. Were you reluctant to use "gambling money" for normal expenditures?
13. Did gambling make you careless of the welfare of yourself and your family?
14. Did you ever gamble longer than you had planned?
15. Have you ever gambled to escape worry or trouble?
16. Have you ever committed, or considered committing, an illegal act to finance gambling?
17. Did gambling cause you to have difficulty in sleeping?
18. Do arguments, disappointments, or frustrations create within you an urge to gamble?
19. Did you ever have an urge to celebrate any good fortune by a few hours of gambling?
20. Have you ever considered self-destruction as a result of your gambling?

Source: Retrieved from www.gamblersanonymous.org. Used with permission.

patterns that are often associated with gamblers. When used with the tests and questionnaires that are more specific to gambling, they can help indicate that a gambling problem might be indicated.

THE MINNESOTA MULTIPHASIC PERSONALITY INVENTORY

One of the most popular and widely used psychometric instruments is the Minnesota Multiphasic Personality Inventory (MMPI-2; Meyer & Deitsch, 1996). In research on the use of the MMPI-2 with gamblers (McCown & Keiser, 2000), two distinct clusters of chronic problem gamblers emerge. The first cluster is marked by persons who obtain elevated scores on Scales 1 (Hypochondriasis), 2 (Depression), and 3 (Psychopathic Deviate). They also generally score in the below-normal range on Scales 9 (Mania) and 0 (Social Introversion). This pattern reflects an anxious, highly aroused group of individuals who gamble primarily to relieve emotional distress. Depression is often the dominant internal state. Women and video gamblers are more likely to evidence this profile.

The second cluster involves elevations on Scales 9 (Mania) and 4 (Psychopathic Deviate) and a low score on scale 0 (Social Introversion). These gamblers are more

---

BOX 5.4
Sample Psychological Test Report

Name: Bob Jones

DOB: 11-22-57

Date of Evaluation: 07-14-03

Evaluator: Linda Chamberlain, PsyD

Procedures: Clinical Interview
Records Review
South Oaks Gambling Screen (SOGS)
Gamblers Anonymous 20 Questions (GA20)
Minnesota Multiphasic Personality Inventory,
   2nd edition (MMPI-2)
Rorschach Comprehensive System

REASON FOR EVALUATION:

Mr. Jones was evaluated at the request of his probation officer in order to assess the possibility of pathological gambling and to aid in developing an appropriate treatment plan.

HISTORY:

Bob Jones is a 37-year-old white male who is married and has two children. He
recently separated from his wife and is living independently. He completed
3 years of college; he currently is employed as a salesperson in a car dealership. He denies any significant use of alcohol or drugs. He and his estranged
wife, Ronda, were in marital therapy for 3 months prior to the separation 1
month ago. He denies any medical problems. He is currently on probation following an arrest for writing several bad checks on his wife's account.

Mr. Jones admits that the money he secured from his wife's checking account was used to place bets at a local casino. He states that he has gambled
regularly, 3 to 4 times per week for the past 2 years, at the Golden Boy
casino. He believes he is approximately $85,000 in debt to various casinos. In
addition to forging checks, he has used several major credit cards to finance
his gambling.

Mr. Jones describes an early interest in gambling through his family. He
participated in poker games with his father and father's friends beginning
at age 13 and has gambled regularly throughout his adult life. He primarily
plays poker and blackjack but states that he has played slots and roulette
more frequently in the past few years, mainly to try and win back loses from
his card playing. On several occasions, Mr. Jones spent entire weekends at
the casinos when he felt he was on a lucky streak.

Mr. Jones believes that his gambling became more problematic when the
Golden Boy casino opened near the car dealership where he is employed. He
began going to the casino during lunch hours and for a few hours after

work. During the last visit to the casino, Mr. Jones stopped after work to play poker and didn't leave the casino for 2 days. He described having a big win early the first evening, lost the winnings within a few hours on escalating bets, and began chasing his losses through the following day. He states that he wrote over $8,000 in bad checks on his wife's account on that day.

Mr. Jones admits to feeling extremely depressed and had considered suicide as a result of the recent losses. He believes that the marital separation is a direct result of his gambling. Mr. Jones is aware that his job is also in jeopardy due to the frequent unexplained absences while he was gambling and his poor sales record in recent months.

OBSERVATIONS:

Mr. Jones appears to be very depressed and distraught regarding the recent events related to his gambling. He denies any suicidal ideation or intent at present, but describes feeling overwhelmed and hopeless. He is well oriented, alert, and responsive to questions. He expresses an interest in completing the assessment and learning more about possible treatment.

RESULTS OF THE TESTING:

Mr. Jones was cooperative in completing the testing materials. He expressed a strong curiosity about the results. The test profiles indicate that he responded to the questionnaires in an open and honest manner.

On the SOGS, Mr. Jones received a score of 15, which indicates a probable gambling-related disorder. He admits to frequent lying to hide his gambling activity, depression related to the consequences of his gambling, and a strong pattern of chasing his losses.

The GA 20 Questions results echo the findings from the SOGS. Mr. Jones profile is typical of males who are experiencing a significant problem with gambling. He admits to relationship, financial, employment, and legal problems related to his gambling. Mr. Jones also confirms that he has experienced deep levels of depression with suicidal ideation as a result of his gambling.

On the MMPI-2, Mr. Jones answered the items in a manner, which indicated he is suffering from significant symptoms of depression because of his recent losses both financially and in his marriage. There is some evidence of manic tendencies in addition to the depression and a slight elevation on the scale that reflects antisocial tendencies.

On the Rorschach, Mr. Jones provided 21 responses of sufficient complexity to allow for interpretive statements. It appears that many of his behaviors will be formulated with little concern about social acceptability. It is likely that he perceives his environment as threatening, demanding, and rejecting. He is likely to be perceived as someone isolative and avoidant. His responses express a strong tendency to engage in fantasy and ruminate on his desired perception of reality. He may view his relationships in a rather

(continued)

manipulative manner, looking to others to fulfill his needs. There is also evidence of an overall hopeless and depressed approach to his life.

SUMMARY:

Mr. Jones appears to have a significant gambling problem with numerous symptoms commonly seen in the history and lives of pathological gamblers. Although he expresses a high level of hopelessness and despair about his current circumstances, he does have an interest in pursuing treatment for his gambling disorder and the associated depression.

DIAGNOSIS:

Axis I: Pathological Gambling
            Major Depressive Disorder
Axis II: None
Axis III: None
Axis IV: Financial Problems, Marital Problems, Employment Problems,
            Legal Problems
Axis V: GAF-75

RECOMMENDATIONS:

- Mr. Jones could benefit from regular participation in Gamblers Anonymous. He is encouraged to find a sponsor and pursue arranging a pressure-relief group meeting (a meeting with GA members to assist in establishing a budget and plans for repaying his gambling debt) when appropriate.
- Mr. Jones requires an evaluation for use of antidepressant medications to assist him in managing the symptoms of depression and to help avoid further decompensation.
- Mr. Jones, and his wife if they agree to reconcile, is encouraged to seek regular psychotherapy with a clinician who has training in working with problem gamblers and their families.
- Mr. Jones would benefit from attending educational and process groups with a focus on problem gambling and recovery. He appears very interested in gaining insight and a better understanding of the dynamics of his gambling problem and could benefit from the group support.

likely to be male, play action games (poker, blackjack, craps), and gamble for higher stakes. Gamblers with antisocial personality disorders are also associated with this profile.

Lowenfeld (1979) found gamblers to have similar patterns to alcoholics, but that gamblers tended to have even higher elevations on the Depression, Psychopathic Deviate and Mania Scales (a 4 to 9 profile). Other researchers have found response patterns on the MMPI that show elevations on Scales 2 (Depression), 7 (Psychasthenia), and 8 (Schizophrenia; Glen, 1979). "Profound feelings of inferiority and inadequacy, pervasive anxiety, difficulty relating to people, hypersensitivity, and depression relieved by gambling characterized this subgroup" (Galski, 1987, p. 126).

Although the MMPI-2 should not be used to screen for or provide a diagnosis of pathological gambling, it may be useful in helping to identify clients who might be engaged in problem gambling. It certainly can be helpful in planning treatment for individuals who have been diagnosed with gambling problems by identifying the patterns and associated emotional and behavioral problems that require attention. For example, if there is a high level of depression indicated in the MMPI-2 profile, that should be a focus in therapy.

THE RORSCHACH TEST

Like the MMPI-2, Rorschach results with pathological gamblers typically reflect two different patterns (McCown & Keiser, 2000). The first group of gamblers are people who are underaroused and gamble for sensation-seeking purposes. The second group represents pathologically overaroused individuals who gamble primarily as a distraction from internal dysphoria. On the Rorschach, it is common with low-arousal gamblers to find a high number of space responses, adequate human movement, excessive active movement, generally good form quality, an elevated affective ratio, and generally low shading or texture, indicative of deficient self-perception. Among the high-arousal gamblers, responses indicate impaired coping responses, aspirations that are lower than abilities and a desire for "getting something for nothing."

THE PSYCHOLOGICAL TEST REPORT

Box 5.4 on pages 154–155 is a sample of a psychological test report that addresses pathological gambling. The report provides an example of how psychological evaluation can help in assessment and treatment planning for problem gamblers.

CONCLUSION

Mental health professionals working with problem gamblers and their families will find they are pioneers in a territory with few maps or clear directions to follow in finding paths to wellness for those suffering from the dilemma of problem gambling. Unlike substance addictions, there are very few resources, a dearth of research, and an absence of sufficient numbers of trained clinicians to provide necessary services to this population. As gaming venues continue to expand and become even more accessible, particularly via the Internet, the numbers of people affected by problem gambling is certain to increase.

In the next chapter, Dr. William McCown explores the basics for effective treatment of problem gambling. It is our sincere hope that both clinicians newly entering the field and those who have decades of experience will incorporate the information in these chapters to ensure that those affected by problem gambling will find the help they so desperately need.

RECOMMENDED READING

The following books are a combination of scholarly work by researchers and clinicians and novels and autobiographies that focus on problem gambling.

Barthelme, F., & Barthelme, S. (1999). *Double down: Reflections on fambling and loss.* New York: Houghton Mifflin. Two brothers who are college professors and writers provide this heartbreaking reflection on the pull and power of illusions as they document their dual descent into compulsive gambling. This is a good description of the impact on both gamblers and their families.

Goodman, R. (1995). *The luck business: The devastating consequences and broken promises of America's gambling explosion.* New York: Free Press. A well researched, entertaining, and alarming look at the impact of the gambling industry on the towns and cities that invite casinos into their economy.

Lesieur, H. (1984). *The chase: Career of the compulsive gambler.* Rochester, VT: Schenkman Books. This is, deservedly, a true classic in the field—the one book that everyone who works with gamblers should read. *The Chase* is filled with brilliant images of problem gamblers and the lives they lead.

McCown, W., & Chamberlain, L. (2000). *Best possible odds: Contemporary treatment strategies for gambling disorders.* New York: Wiley. This book provides a comprehensive overview of the etiology, dynamics, and treatment of compulsive gambling. The book examines how current scientific theories involving nonlinear systems applies to patterns of problem gambling.

Milkman, H., & Sunderwirth, S. (1987). *Craving for ecstasy: How our passions become addictions and what we can do about them.* San Francisco: Jossey-Bass. This is a wonderfully written, fascinating examination of the basic dynamics at work in all addictions. These authors cleared the path that researchers and clinicians are now following.

Nelson, J. (1998). *Compulsive.* Ft. Collins, CO: Cheshire Moon. This is an excellent novel depicting the dynamics of compulsive gambling. In his forward the author writes, "After researching and writing the novel, I severely curtailed my own gambling activities. I scared myself."

O'Brien, T. (1998). *Bad bet: The insider story of the glamour, glitz, and danger of America's gambling industry.* New York: Random House. For those interested in the gambling industry and it's impact on our culture, economy, and psyche, this is a superb portrait of "America's love affair with gambling."

Shaffer, H., Stein, S., Gambino, B., & Cummings, T. (1989). *Compulsive gambling: Theory, research, and practice.* Lexington, MA: Lexington Books. A seminal work by pioneers in the research, theory, and treatment of problem gambling. This should be a basic reference for anyone working in the field.

REFERENCES

American Psychiatric Association. (2000). *Diagnostic and statistical manual of mental disorders* (4th ed., text rev.). Washington, DC: Author.

Boughton, R. (2002, April). *Voices of women who gamble in Ontario: A survey of women's gambling, barriers to treatment and treatment service needs.* Paper presented at the meeting of the Discovery 2002 Conference of the Responsible Gambling Council, Niagara Falls, Ontario, Canada.

Cambridge International Dictionary. (1996). Cambridge, England: Cambridge University Press.

Comings, D. E. (1998). *The molecular genetics of pathological gambling.* New York: CNS Spectrums.

Galski, T. (1987). Psychological testing of pathological gamblers: Research, uses and new directions. In T. Galski (Ed.), *The handbook of pathological gambling.* Springfield, IL: Charles C Thomas.

Glen, A. (1979, September). *Personality research on pathological gamblers.* Paper presented at the 87th annual convention of the American Psychological Association, New York.

Herscovitch, A. G. (1999). *Alcoholism and pathological gambling: Similarities and differences.* Holmes Beach, FL: Learning Publications.

Jacobs, D. F. (1986). A general theory of addictions: A new theoretical model. *Journal of Gambling Behavior, 2,* 15–31.

Jacobs, D. F. (1988). Evidence for a common dissociative-like reaction among addicts. *Journal of Gambling Behavior, 4,* 27–37.

Kusyszyn, I. (1980). Compulsive gambling: The problem of definition. *International Journal of the Addictions, 12*(7), 1095–1101.

Ladouceur, R. (1996). The prevalence of pathological gambling in Canada. *Journal of Gambling Studies, 12*(2), 129–142.

Lesieur, H. R. (1984). *The chase: Career of the compulsive gambler.* Rochester, VT: Schenkman Books.

Lesieur, H. R. (1993). *Understanding compulsive gambling: Revised.* Center City, MN: Hazelden.

Lesieur, H. R., & Blume, S. B. (1987). The South Oaks Gambling Screen (SOGS): A new instrument for the identification of pathological gamblers. *American Journal of Psychiatry, 144*(9), 1184–1188.

Lesieur, H. R., & Blume, S. B. (1993). Revisiting the South Oaks Gambling Screen in different settings. *Journal of the Addictions, 29*(12), 1611–1616.

Lowenfeld, B. H. (1979). Personality dimensions of the pathological gambler. *Dissertation Abstracts International, 40*(1-B), 456.

McCown, W., & Chamberlain, L. (2000). *Best possible odds: Contemporary treatment strategies for gambling disorders.* New York: Wiley.

McCown, W., & Chamberlain, L. (in press). *Gambling disorders: Experimental and empirical research.* Victoria, British Columbia, Canada: Trafford Publish House.

McCown, W., & Keiser, R. (2000). *Addiction, fantasy and perception: The role of projective techniques in assessment and treatment planning of addicted individuals.* Mahwah, NJ: Erlbaum.

McGurrin, M. (1992). *Pathological gambling: Conceptual, diagnostic, and treatment issues.* Sarasota, FL: Practitioner's Resource Series.

Milkman, H., & Sunderwirth, S. (1987). *Craving for ecstasy: How our passions become addictions and what we can do about them.* San Francisco: Jossey-Bass.

National Center for Responsible Gaming. (1999). *Annual report.* Kansas City, MO: Author.

National Council on Problem Gambling. (2000). *National Council on Problem Gambling* [Brochure]. Washington, DC: Author.

Nelson, J. (1998). *Compulsive.* Ft. Collins, CO: Cheshire Moon.

O'Brien, T. L. (1998). *Bad bet: The inside story of the glamour, glitz, and danger of America's gambling industry.* New York: Random House.

Pavalko, R. M. (1999). *Risky business: America's fascination with gambling.* New York: Burnham.

Peele, S. (1979). Redefining addiction: II. The meaning of addiction in our lives. *Journal of Psychedelic Drugs, 11,* 289–297.

Savage, D. (2002). *Skipping toward Gomorrah.* New York: Dutton.

Shaffer, H. J. (1989). Conceptual crises in the addictions: The role of models in the field of compulsive gambling. In H. J. Shaffer, S. A. Stein, B. Gambino, & T. N. Cummings (Eds.), *Compulsive gambling: Theory, research and practice.* Lexington, MA: Lexington Books.

Shaffer, H. J. (2002, December). *Rethinking addiction: How gambling and other behavioral addictions are changing the concept and treatment of alcohol and substance use disorders* [Abstract obtained from presentation materials], 4–6. Cambridge, MA: Harvard Medical School's Division on Addictions.

Shaffer, H. J., & Hall, M. H. (1996). Estimating the prevalence of adolescent gambling disorders: A quantitative synthesis and guide toward standard gambling nomenclature. *Journal of Gambling Studies, 12*(2), 193–214.

Shaffer, H. J., LaBrie, R., Scanlan, K., & Cummings, T. N. (1994). Psychological gambling among adolescents: MA gambling screen (MAGS). *Journal of Gambling Studies,* 353–358.

Stein, D. J., Hollander, I., & Liebowitz, M. R. (1993). Neurobiology of impulsivity and the impulse control disorders. *Journal of Neuropsychiatry and Clinical Neurosciences, 5*(1), 9–17.

Volberg, R. A. (1996). Prevalence studies of problem gambling in the United States. *Journal of Gambling Studies, 12*(2), 111–128.

Welte, J. W., Barnes, G. M., Wieczorek, W. F., Tidwell, M., & Parker, J. (2002). Gambling participation in the U.S.—Results from a national survey. *Journal of Gambling Studies, 18*(4), 313–337.

Wexler, A., & Wexler, S. (1993). *The counselor and compulsive gambling: The hidden addiction. Facts on compulsive gambling and addiction* [Clearinghouse fact sheet]. New Brunswick, NJ: Rutgers University Press.

CHAPTER 6

Treating Compulsive and Problem Gambling

WILLIAM G. McCOWN

C ONTRARY TO WHAT some people believe, problem gambling is not an un-treatable disorder. Consider the following case histories of two very different people.

The first client is a 57-year-old physician. In his high school days, he used to make considerably "more than pocket change" (his words) betting on the outcome of chess games played in a local park. By the time he was a college undergraduate he was, by his own account, "hanging around pool halls and hustling games while, let me stress to you, maintaining an excellent academic record." Interpersonally, he remembers that he avoided close relationships and sometimes appeared flat to those around him until he won money playing pool or was in one of his frequent episodes of playing poker.

"My roommates kind of wondered if I was interested in women. . . . I told them that my real mistress was the art of winning. Money made me excited."

By the time he was in medical school, Jerry (a pseudonym) had learned to use a mainframe computer to assist him in calculating racetrack odds. Racetracks set their odds by patrons' wagers. Therefore, Jerry's strategy was to look for situations in which the crowd's collective judgment was likely to discount a horse's true chance of winning. He found several situations where these collective errors often occurred. With the aid of a digital computer (which none of his fellow race fans could access), he was able to make several hundred dollars on a good weekend. By

The opinions expressed in this chapter are those of the author's and do not necessarily reflect those of the State of Louisiana. Special thanks are due to Robert Andreason, Sean Austin, Bob Abouee, Linda Chamberlain, John Chavez, Gordon Flett, Richard Gerald, Ross Keiser, Luciano L'Abate, Reece Middleton, Jerry Musick, Greg Stolcis, and, especially, Kimberly Zimmerman. Comments from four anonymous reviewers are also appreciated. I would also like to thank the International Gambling Treatment Internet Consortium for their ideas and encouragement. This chapter does not necessarily represent their views. Finally, I wish to thank our clients.

expanding his wagering to involve making bets at other race tracks with local book-ies, a good week for him might net several thousand dollars.

"You can imagine how I felt as a first-year medical student with that kind of cash. Suddenly, I was popular; I was noticed; I was someone. Although I still wanted to be a doctor, I wanted to be a doctor who gambled."

These successful days at the track continued until several other patrons with ac-cess to a mainframe computer began to recognize the same hidden patterns in rac-ing data that Jerry had painstakingly observed. While Jerry, an otherwise diligent medical student, should have been studying histology, he was either struggling at the computer, analyzing data, or betting increasing sums of money to compensate for the more frequent losses that he was now unexpectedly experiencing.

There was no doubt that Jerry was brilliant, but a close observer might have seen that he was on the way to developing a gambling problem. (See Box 6.1.) He did not stop with gambling at the race track but soon expanded to the casino. During a semester break, he learned the art of blackjack card counting, a mathe-matical procedure developed in the early 1960s. This method is every gambler's dream: a technique that allows people to beat the casino! However, it necessitates an excellent memory, great acting ability, and stoicism in the face of inevitable pe-riods of losses. Most important, it requires a firm understanding of the genuine probabilities and complexities of this card game.

Jerry possessed all of these abilities. He saw card counting as heaven on earth. In one vacation period, Jerry was able to win more money than many fully em-ployed and trained physicians made in a year. "I really felt like God back then!"

Jerry's luck at blackjack began to change when casinos quickly became wise to the methods of card counters. Casinos developed many ways to confuse the coun-ters and, if this failed, simply excluded them from wagering. When Jerry was barred from most of the casinos in Nevada, he went home and sulked. Then he re-sponded by betting more at a neighboring bar that had underworld connections.

Gradually, he realized that gambling was no longer merely a sideline for a medical student. Instead, it was the most incredible thrill imaginable, especially when he bet hundreds or even thousands of dollars. He felt in some strange way that gambling was his life's calling—even more than medicine. "There I was, just a kid out of college. And I was throwing around money like I had power. People treated me with respect!

"Win or lose, I felt incredible. When I won, I was king of the world. And when I lost, I was someone who figured he was classy enough, smart enough to win back anything that I had blown. Strange as it seems, losing was almost as much of a thrill as winning. Studying and gambling, life was crazy."

When Jerry tells his story, it is at this place in his narrative where he finally shows signs of sadness. "Any of my fellow students should have seen I had a problem. My life would have been so much better if someone could have stopped me then."

Jerry's sense that he was God was curtailed by limited gambling opportunities available during his residency in general surgery. "To me, not gambling was a pre-scription for a depressing day. I really wanted to be a doctor, but I really needed to gamble. Intellectually, I realized something was strange about me, but I didn't let that get in the way of a good bet."

Jerry was competent enough to squeak through his residency with less than a total commitment. "No one would have questioned my work. I was good—a very

---

BOX 6.1
Asking about Problem Gambling

A tactful way of inquiring of coworkers about their risks for problem gambling is to simply ask them, "Do you gamble much?"

This can be done in a friendly and nonthreatening manner. Often, this is an appropriate topic in conversations about sports, hobbies, or other activities.

If they say they gamble, then politely ask them how often?

If their reply is more than once a month, they have a high risk of developing a gambling disorder and further screening may be needed.

---

good resident. Surgery was exciting, but not as thrilling as playing a $10,000 hand of poker. Some of my friends used drugs, I guess because it was that time in life when they were popular. I always turned them down, telling them I'm already living on the edge. There is no drug like winning money.

"The funny thing was they thought I was so conservative, so hard working. No one knew I was living a double life. No one would have believed that Dr. Jerry stayed up all night gambling and taking care of patients during the day."

Jerry realized that he did not have time for both the completion of his intense residency and the time he needed for the racetrack. However, he knew many locations in town where he could play a quick, high-stakes round of poker. Success at poker was not related to Jerry's computer skills. Consequently, he found himself losing more than he was accustomed to. He responded in a fashion typical of many people developing a serious gambling problem. He abandoned some of the restraint that he had shown when he was losing. "I'd bet, even when I knew I shouldn't," he notes. Then, he adds somberly, "That should have been a sign that something was wrong."

As described in the previous chapter by Chamberlain (this volume), Jerry was showing a more serious sign. He began to chase his losses, responding to losing gambling periods by wagering more. Along with an attending physician who also had a gambling problem, Jerry even bet on the various patients' diagnoses! Later, he would amuse the other residents by developing gambling pools with the technicians and nurses' aids on an individual patient's likelihood of survival. "I was amazingly out of control," he notes, "but no one saw it. Looking back, it was really almost perverted—betting on whether patients would live or die. But you know, everyone thought it was funny, out of character maybe for this nerdish doctor, but really amusing."

Jerry completed his training and accepted a subsequent fellowship. His major criterion for accepting the fellowship was that it was near a particular bar that he knew took a great deal of sport gambling action. Returning to his old tool, the mainframe computer, he was able to maintain a slight advantage over the mob affiliates who ran the bar. Jerry's betting expanded to virtually all sports. It was common for him to make 100 wagers a day of $100 to $500 each. Inevitable periods of losses, which are dictated by the laws of chance, resulted in Jerry doubling and tripling his wagering. When police arrested a number of patrons, Jerry was ignored because he was a medical doctor, despite overwhelming evidence of his illegal gambling.

After Jerry completed his fellowship, he found employment in a distant suburban hospital with one of the first trauma units in the area. He was frequently on *pager call,* which means that he was not required to be physically present, but required to be in the area of the hospital and able to respond if needed. This provided him an opportunity to frequent a local restaurant that discretely accepted illegal sports betting. At about that time, his gambling triumphs were being sliced away because the bookies setting the odds were also using the services of people trained in using computers. Jerry's gambling successes at the racetrack took yet another plunge when personal computers became available. Jerry, who kept meticulous records, faced a bleak December, realizing that for the first time in his life he was in the red for the year, about $10,000.

The thought of a year's losses provoked an urge to gamble more irrationally, trying to recoup the previous year's missteps. "It was just a thing of pride," Jerry recalled. "I could have accepted a bad year, but my ego wouldn't allow it. So I went crazier." In desperation, Jerry returned to his first major success, the racetrack, for what he hoped would be an extended and lucrative vacation. But in just one day in Las Vegas, he lost $20,000 at a Sports Book—a facility for making multiple sports bets at different tracks. Jerry planned to use his computer advantage, but by now, many patrons had access to computer data because of the newly developed personal computers. This next year ended with Jerry as an even bigger loser.

"That was the first time it really occurred to me that one day I might have to quit gambling. But I didn't let it bother me long. After all, there was a basketball game to bet on. . . . I fooled myself into thinking I would catch up on my losses. That is a lie gamblers always tell themselves."

For the next year, between performing operations in his suburban hospital, Jerry would peruse every sports publication that he could find, looking for an edge. No one thought him odd, though. "My colleagues just thought I was a sports nut." By now he had found friendly contacts and he was betting on anything that he could, including political and world events. "I've operated and saved many people. That's a rush, but at that time in my life it was nothing like the rush of picking winners."

Jerry's addiction continued to grow. As he later said, "Gambling doesn't leave you with a smell on your clothes, but it does leave you with a hangover, an excitement or a feeling of depression, depending on how well you do. I can't believe that I would perform surgery with my mind on the odds of how many pitches were made in some obscure major league game." Ironically, the only one who recognized that he was a possible threat to the well-being of his patients was Jerry himself.

By the end of the year, Jerry was in debt to unsavory characters for more than $150,000. He also began having disabling panic attacks. For a while he simply stopped eating. A supervisor watched his deterioration in horror and thought he might be depressed. He recommended a psychiatrist with a good reputation. During his first attempt at treatment, the psychiatrist diagnosed him as having a bipolar disorder. This diagnosis resulted in a temporary suspension of his medical license, which resulted in more time to gamble. This allowed him more opportunities to lose and then recoup his losses with more irrational wagering. By the time he saw my colleague he was $425,000 in debt and being pursued by syndicated crime figures that needed to collect.

"What made me get treatment was when one of the loan sharks just showed up at the hospital. I didn't even work there at the time, but it didn't matter. The guy was pretty loud and threatening. Worse, he mouthed off to my boss that I had a gambling problem. More out of fear than concern, my boss looked into some treatment programs and found one on the Coast." (See Box 6.2.)

Jerry reluctantly accepted this referral, since his boss said that he would have to report Jerry's gambling problems to the state medical board. Psychological testing indicated that Jerry had substantial narcissistic tendencies and serious depression. At times he felt suicidal and he had perpetually low self-esteem. Psychiatric treatment with lithium was continued but was not effective.

"Every day was a struggle. Every day I wasn't gambling was just an utterly colorless day for me. I didn't know how to spend time except to gamble and be a good physician. Suddenly, both were taken from me. I went around for weeks in this fog of confusion, looking for something—anything—to bet on. It was a withdrawal as bad as any drug could ever be."

Jerry completed the inpatient program and continued in an outpatient treatment phase, four times a week. Nightly attendance at Gamblers Anonymous (GA) was also included as part of his treatment.

While in this phase of treatment a complicating personal issue emerged. Jerry faced the fact that he was gay and had spent his life attempting to avoid admitting his sexual orientation. This is an extremely important concern. However, the therapist treating his gambling problem realized that Jerry's addiction was more important at this time. She made a decision to concentrate on Jerry's most serious set of difficulties. Eventually, she referred Jerry to a therapist who specializes in gay men's issues.

Jerry had several rough years where he relapsed. Eventually, however, he achieved a degree of stability in his life that he thought was impossible. "I actually got to the point where I liked myself the way I was. For once, I was happy."

At the time of this writing, Jerry has not gambled in 4 years. He has also achieved comfort with his sexual orientation. After a time, he was again licensed to practice medicine and does so successfully, in another town. Jerry's major activities, apart from work and GA, involve lecturing groups of professionals about problem gambling.

The second case illustrates a woman on the other end of the socioeconomic ladder. However, she too was capable of benefiting from gambling treatment and achieving a meaningful recovery, despite the odds against her.

BOX 6.2
Successful Gambling Treatment Is Rare

Less than 10% of patients with gambling problems seek treatment. This contrasts with over 50% of people with substance abuse problems. Stigma, the lack of treatment options, and the desperation associated with gambling may be responsible for these statistics. Many mental health professionals fail to ask their patients about potential problem gambling. They simply lack the training.

Shandra is a 37-year-old Caucasian woman from a poor, largely rural Southern state. She began playing video poker when her state legalized this game and made it widely available. This was done in an effort to secure an income.

"I was shy the first few times I tried it," Shandra notes. "I was raised to believe gambling was a sin. Then, one day, I just could not get enough of it."

During the following 2 years, Shandra, a convenience store clerk who had not graduated from high school, lost "$40 or $50 thousand, maybe more" to the video machines. She did not earn this much money from her primary job. Therefore, to continue gambling, she took a second job, increasing tensions with her husband and three children. Eventually, her husband told her that she would have to decide whether their marriage was more important than her need to work another job to support her gambling.

"I tried to be nice about it, but I found the video machine much more interesting than he was." She moved out immediately, taking a third job. All of her spare money went to gambling. "I thought that was happiness for me. Work and gambling. But it was really mind numbing when I look back."

Despite this, Shandra remembers that she could not get enough money to gamble as frequently as she wanted. "It wasn't enough. So, not surprising, I started working at the truck stop." In this case, *working* is a euphemism for engaging in prostitution. Conveniently, the truck stop also had a room full of video poker machines.

"Every night I made several hundred pretty quickly. But as soon as I'd make it, it was gone. I'd turn a trick in a truck or something and then go into the truck stop and gamble as long as I could. This was my pattern. Trick and spend, just for hours, even for days. I just would lose track."

Shandra might have attempted this lifestyle indefinitely. However, her county and neighboring areas abruptly restricted the availability of gambling machines. This followed a change in the rules by the state legislature. Shandra responded first by increasing her smoking and eating. Then, she sunk into a serious depression. Like Jerry, she neglected her health and developed serious hypertension. Later she would find out that she was showing early signs of diabetes and also had a sexually transmitted disease. But, frankly, she did not care.

"Three, four times a week I would drive almost a hundred miles each way, just to play [gamble]. I was using [methamphetamine, a popular drug in her community] to stay awake. It was just part of the way things were. Life was really messed up. No kids, no husband, by then, the only job I had was at the truck stop.

"But I never sat back and said, 'This is a problem.' I couldn't admit I had a problem. Not as long as I could gamble."

Shandra finally realized that she had serious difficulties when her car was temporarily damaged and garaged for a week. She noticed that when she was not gambling every few days she would become very nervous, extremely excitable, and even overtly paranoid. She recalls that when she was not feeling agitated, she was constantly tearful.

"My car was out for a week. That meant no gambling, no working, no money to eat. I looked at myself in the mirror one day, all depressed because I hadn't gambled in four days. It was like a withdrawal, worse than when I quit cigarettes or Xanax. All I did was cry and want to hurt myself.

"So, I called the one person who still cared about me, my sister, who lived in [another southern state]. She came and picked me up. She had a friend who was a

---

The Lie/Bet Questionnaire

The simplest screening device for pathological gambling is the Lie/Bet Questionnaire. Developed by Edward Johnson and colleagues it consists of two questions:

1. Have you ever felt the need to bet more and more money?
2. Have you ever had to lie to people important to you about how much you gambled?

An affirmative answer to even one of these questions suggests the strong possibility of a gambling problem and warrants further evaluation.

These questions can be asked by mental health professionals or by people who care about someone who might have a gambling problem.

---

nurse and managed to get me on the waiting list [at a local substance abuse hospital with a small gambling unit attached]. I didn't have a cent, but they were okay saying, 'Pay us when you can.' And I really did.

"I stayed there for as long as I could, which was as long as treatment ran. I knew it wasn't good to go back home. I had no home, really. So I got a job as a waitress, something respectable and found a GA [Gamblers Anonymous] meeting I could go to. It's wasn't a great life, but it was a lot better than what I had. . . . It's slowly getting better."

At the time of this writing, Shandra has 3 years of gambling abstinence, no illicit drug use, and has completed her GED high school equivalency exam. She plans to attend a local college in the fall. Unfortunately, she has been unable to interest her children in visiting her, much to her disappointment. She continues in family therapy, with the hopes of understanding her children's needs. This is a sad spot in a life she sees as otherwise hopeful. In telling her story she wants one fact stressed above everything else. "People have to know that you can get better if you have a gambling problem. I'm living proof. No one wants to live the way we did. We were just too sick to understand that we needed to change."

PROBLEM GAMBLING: A TREATABLE DISORDER

Both cases, though different, share common properties associated with end-stage gambling. These two people had lost functional social ties. What families or friends they had were exhausted, angry, and bitter. Gambling had become their only reward. Furthermore, both clients had a frantic lifestyle that is common among serious gamblers (McCown & Chamberlain, 2004). Both were in poor health by the time they reached formal treatment.

Furthermore, each had complicating facets to his or her case involving employment and sexual concerns. Their lives were by all accounts, as Shandra noted, ". . . a hopeless mess—broken dreams and a real hopeless mess. . . ." Yet both of them improved and continue to improve even though the odds are against them.

Despite traditional pessimism, problem gambling *is* a treatable disorder. Part of our difficulty in current treatment is due to complex and contradictory social attitudes. It was merely 2 decades ago that pathological gambling was first recognized as an independent mental disorder, rather than as a symptom of a more primary psychiatric disease. Some social critics today even question whether a gambling disorder is merely a moral problem that has been recently medicalized to excuse decadent behaviors (Castellani, 2000). Not surprising, these attitudes, as well as a host of other difficulties, have stymied scientific research on problem gambling. For a useful comparison, over 7,000 readily accessible studies demonstrate the efficacious of various forms of psychotherapy. Yet, the number of double-blind, random assignment studies, which are the gold standard in psychiatric research, on the treatment of problem gambling fills less than half of a file drawer.

A clinician should not attempt to treat a client with a gambling disorder unless he or she has received adequate training and supervision. A referral to a practitioner with experience is generally the best strategy. Unfortunately, access to optimal treatment is often impossible. Too few clinicians have adequate training in the treatment of problem gambling. The realities of the mental health care delivery system make it likely that, at some time, most clinicians will treat a person with a gambling-related disorder (Estes & Brubaker, 1994).

My intention in writing this chapter is to provide a framework for understanding the processes, strategies, and therapeutic phases associated with successful treatment of gambling-related disorders. Hopefully, this chapter will provoke sufficient interest in clinicians that they will receive additional training and supervision. This commitment is extremely rewarding, but should not be made lightly. Mastery of this chapter does not guarantee competence in treating the problem gambler. It is not a substitute for training and supervision.

GAMBLING DISORDERS: WHY WE LACK NEEDED RESEARCH

One reason many people believe that gambling is untreatable is that very little research has been conducted in this area. There are several reasons for this. Until recently, for example, no one knew how common problem gambling is. Furthermore, many mental health practitioners viewed this behavioral syndrome as a symptom of a broader problem, such as antisocial personality disorder or extreme narcissism. For people who hold this belief, problem gambling is untreatable, at least until the real problem of personality is successfully resolved.

Political concerns may also have suppressed research, inasmuch as gambling is routinely promoted as a fiscally responsible and safe technique for enhancing government revenues (Castellani, 2000). This controversial issue bears note but is outside of the purpose of this chapter. Furthermore, neither drug companies nor practitioners can expect to make much money on the treatment of problem gambling. This has stymied research interests. McCown and Chamberlain (2004) suggest that clinicians who specialize in the treatment of gambling disorders are among the poorest paid mental health practitioners, regardless of their training or specialization. A convincing case can be made that very few people in the public or private sectors are interested in either treating or publishing treatment strategies for a group that perpetually cannot pay for psychiatric services.

Furthermore, gambling has a profound moral stigma that distracts researchers into other topics. Historically, gambling has been seen as something that good people did not do. Moral people do not gamble, or at least pretended this was the

Gambling Treatment Literature

Although the treatment literature is universally weak, there are a number of populations that are blatantly ignored in the gambling treatment literature. These include:

- Women.
- Minorities.
- Young people.
- The elderly.
- People with disabilities.
- The poor.
- People with respectable gambling habits, such as stock traders, high-risk financiers, and bingo players.
- Invisible gamblers on the Internet or people who wager in semilegal establishments.
- Problem gamblers in the helping professions.

case. When they do wager, unwritten rules state that they should do so in private and only in moderation. Problem gamblers are likely to be the objects of ridicule, people seen as sinners rather than as sick.

An additional impediment to research is that gambling does not cleanly fit the biological paradigm of addiction advocated by some primarily medically oriented clinicians of the previous decade (McCown & Keiser, 2003). Few practitioners can argue that a person with a gambling problem often shows behaviors that are indistinguishable from a person with a drug addiction. However, some mental health professionals insist that this similarity *has* to be superficial, since the gambler is not ingesting any specific drug. Their response is that problem gambling is merely a psychological addiction, somehow less serious than disorders that involve substance use.

Current official psychiatric terminology in the United States highlights this, as published in the *Diagnostic and Statistical Manual*, fourth edition, text revised (*DSM-IV-TR*; American Psychiatric Association [APA], 2000). The *DSM-IV-TR* classifies gambling as an impulse control disorder, grouped with such behaviors as fire setting and pica. The concept that gambling is an *addictive behavior* is deliberately sidestepped. Yet, as Table 6.1 illustrates, problem gambling and pharmacological addictions share substantial behaviors. Often, there effects are indistinguishable.

Equally confusing to researchers are suitable ways of measuring the effects of treatment on the problem gambler's family, social network, and society. Often, reductions in these harms are difficult to quantify. Clinicians need to be aware of all of the difficulties researchers face because they will also face similar problems in clinical practice (McCown & Chamberlain, 2004). Until these and other difficulties are answered, research in gambling will continue at a slow rate (Castellani, 2000).

Given this climate, it is not surprising that research-oriented clinicians are steered toward more friendly areas of psychiatric research. Certainly, there are

Table 6.1
Similarities between Gambling and Pharmacological Addictions

Property Associated with Addiction	Pharmacological Addictions	Gambling
Begins benignly in acceptable setting.	Usually	Usually
Requires higher threshold of substance or experience to achieve desired effect (produces tolerance).	Yes	Yes
Progresses insidiously.	Usually	Usually
Minimizes involvement with other previously enjoyed activities by addicted person.	Yes	Yes
Frequent desire to quit seen in addicted person.	Yes	Yes
Relapses are extremely common.	Yes	Yes
Results in biological dysregulation of neural circuits.	Yes	Yes
Effects personality and morality.	Yes	Yes
Usually involves experience that some can enjoy without addiction.	Yes	Yes
Possible genetic basis.	Yes	Yes
Results in withdrawal if abruptly ceased.	Yes	Yes
Denial of severity typical among addicted individual and family.	Yes	Yes
Results in personal ruin.	Frequently	Frequently
Can be eventually engaged in safely by addicted people.	Highly doubtful	Highly doubtful
Spontaneous cessation of behavior without treatment.	Extremely rare	Extremely rare
Impeded logic, judgment, and reasoning.	Yes	Yes
Successful treatment may require numerous attempts.	Yes	Yes

exceptions, including the work of outstanding clinician-researchers, such as Lesieur, Lorenz, Rosenthal, Schaffer, Taber, and Volberg to name a few Americans. Furthermore, research has flourished from clinicians in Britain, Australia, and other locations. However, most interventions for problem gambling that we presently use today have poor empirical validation. This forces the clinician to rely primarily on the experiences of other treatment providers. Often, this experience is contradictory, as I discuss next.

TREATING GAMBLING DISORDERS: A VARIETY OF OPTIONS

Despite pessimism because of the lack of literature, practitioners employ a number of common treatment strategies in clinical counseling and management of gambling-related disorders. The following sections review popular methods and recent clinical trends associated with these treatments. It is not an exhaustive literature review, but, as noted, a general introduction. Researchers interested in a more thorough background should consult Castellani (2000), McCown and Chamberlain (2000), or McCown and Chamberlain (2004), as well as the earlier chapter by Chamberlain (this volume).

Regardless of whatever methods clinicians and counselors employ, a consensus of contemporary treatment providers seems to be that successful outcomes are enhanced when both normal and problem gambling is destigmatized (McCown & Keiser, 2003).

This process can occur through exposure to GA, discussed later, but usually begins in individual counseling or therapy. After establishing themselves as nonjudgmental and credible sources of knowledge, therapists may begin the process of debunking the notion that gambling per se is an inherent evil. They are quick to indicate that at some time in their lives most people gamble. The overwhelming number of social gamblers continue to wager without any detectable harm, other than losing modest sums of money. For this majority, gambling is a pleasurable, respectable activity that can be combined with other life tasks. The increasing legalization of gambling venues has confirmed this, much to the delight of the governments and corporations who profit (McCown & Chamberlain, 2000).

My experience suggests that when clients believe that gambling is inherently evil, they return to this conviction at inopportune times throughout treatment. They may see their behaviors as a hopeless moral weakness that they should have successfully controlled. This adds to their guilt and frustration, which encourages more gambling or the acquisition of other dysfunctional behaviors. People who view gambling as a sin are also more likely to believe in quick fixes of sudden but insincere spiritual conversions. Consequently, they may be likely to resist more rational and potentially successful means of treatment, such as individual and group therapy and GA.

This does not discount the role of spiritual or religious conversion in helping the problem gambler change a pattern of destructive behaviors. However, shallow spiritual conversions, New Years resolutions, quick commitments made following an emotional crisis, or those made after nights of losing at a casino usually do not produce lasting changes. For gambling disorders, there are no quick fixes. The counselor must remember this, despite a client's overpowering fantasies that a brief treatment period can correct long standing life patterns (McCown & Keiser, 2003). Both clients and counselors desperately want to believe in the fantasy of a painless and effortless recovery. Reality, however, suggests that this is never the case.

Normalizing reasonable gambling—convincing the client that most people can gamble successfully without committing a moral transgression—is usually the first step in decreasing these fantasies of effortless healing. Morality, spirituality, and self-restraint are certainly important, even critical issues, but the therapist addresses them later, as recovery begins to unfold. However, if clients leave treatment at this time, not surprisingly, their gambling usually continues and is more dysfunctional (Johnson & McCown, 1997). They apparently rationalize that if gambling is normal, then they too are normal, despite their demonstrated inability to gamble in moderation. Unless clients are confronted with specific abnormalities of their own gambling, as compared to the moderate experiences of others, they are likely to interpret the previous therapeutic effort permission to continue in their destructive behavioral patterns.

The increasing availability of gambling opportunities provides undeniable evidence that gambling is not an appropriate leisure activity for everyone. Between 1.5% and 12% of people in North America, depending on which age, ethnic, and demographic groups are sampled, will eventually become *problem gamblers*. This means that they will lose control of their gambling behaviors and will not be able to quit when it is in their best interest (McCown & Chamberlain, 2000). It is important to realize that loss of control may not occur every time the person wagers. The problem gambler may be able to gamble on a limited basis, even doing so often. However, each gambling episode has the *potential* for a drastic loss of control, a qualitatively different experience than the social gambler ever encounters (McCown & Chamberlain, 2004).

In this preliminary phase of treatment, colleagues and I usually instruct clients that even though gambling is universal, some people cannot gamble safely in moderation. There should also be no shame in experiencing a loss of control over gambling behaviors. It is just a cruel fact and has nothing to do with moral factors. Most clients benefit immensely from understanding that their problem gambling is unrelated to individual morality, personal discipline, or self-control. Good people can and often do develop gambling problems. This is also a common message emphasized in GA.

SOCIAL COMPARISONS AS A FORM OF TREATMENT

Part of 12-Step recovery programs involves the addict constructing a *painful moral inventory.* A similarly useful exercise involves having clients construct *social inventories.* These are lists of local, community, familial, personal, and spiritual institutions that usually prevent most people from engaging in excessive gambling. Clients then work to identify why these naturally limiting feedback systems did not work for them. This assignment serves two functions. First, it illustrates to the client that his or her involvement in gambling is not normal. It is markedly excessive and problematic. This becomes obvious when the gambler looks at the frequency of his or her personal gambling behavior compared to those in the feedback network. Most people gamble moderately. Problem gamblers do not, and this exercise helps to break through their resistance about the extent of their problems.

Second, this exercise helps the client identify areas that he or she can draw on for support. Often, the client is shocked that there are so few people in this category. The client can then see how he or she has exhausted many personal resources. Occasionally, it becomes obvious that these resources may have colluded to deny that the client has a gambling problem. This method is often a powerful way to introduce the idea that problem gamblers need the assistance of groups like GA.

One case in which I employed this method, the client was able to use this self-generated information to see how normal people gambled. He was also able to see how his wife had failed in her attempts to limit his gambling and how gambling had reduced the influence of other community institutions on his behavior. He was finally able to admit that he had a problem with gambling and was amenable to attendance at GA. As an interesting follow-up, he has refrained from wagering for 5 years and states that he has no desire to return to gambling. At this stage, his treatment is considered a success. However, because of the chronic nature of relapse that seems endemic in gamblers, he has decided to remain active in GA for life.

Gambling as a Biobehavioral Disease

Even though, up until now, treatment has emphasized social networks that offer protection, it is helpful to integrate this knowledge with biological explanations of addiction. Failing to do so can cause the client to resent the feedback mechanisms that failed to limit the client's excesses. I have seen many clients terminate treatment at this time, convinced that their gambling was set up by a vicious coworker or vindictive spouses. They may also blame their children, ministers, or physicians. They usually quit therapy, feeling that they have new insight into their problem and now have an ability to resist problem gambling. The therapist may even share their optimism and agree to a quick termination to treatment.

Clients with any addiction are usually quick to try to blame others. This is part of a normal attributional process that people undergo when trying to understand their own behaviors. The reaction of many clients at this point is to think, "I do not gamble normally because people and groups around me did not limit me. It's their fault." With these presuppositions in mind, it is not surprising that client feel resentful and angry. Clients with this new insight may blame everyone from their parents to their present therapists. Rarely do they make sustained progress.

At this point, I suggest a step that some practitioners consider novel. I provide a biological basis for explaining the client's behaviors. Biological explanations emphasize that community feedback is a restraint that may help in prevention. Often, however, they fail to work because the client's vulnerability to problem gambling is extreme. I then introduce the client to various models of cerebral functioning that suggest that excessive behaviors cause permanent changes in neural activation. Whether the causes were failed social feedback, an angry family, or a lower vulnerability because of unknown genetic factors, the results are the same. Once clients show they have consistently lost control over a class of behaviors, they are at permanent risk to experience this loss again. The realities of biology make a return to social gambling impossible. (See box 6.3.)

My present view of treatment for all addictions is that biological explanations assist the client in resisting relapses, while simultaneously maintaining a necessary

---

BOX 6.3
What We Know about the Biology of Gambling

Gambling may release excessively rewarding neurochemicals or neurotransmitters.

Some people are especially sensitive to these neurochemical changes.

In response to these experiences, the brain's capacity to return to a normal state is impaired.

These changes affect reasoning, memory, and judgment.

There is no evidence that these changes are reversible.

destigmatization. I routinely explain that the client's addictive behaviors can be categorized as *biobehavioral disorders*. This is a class of diseases where both biology and behavior contribute to symptom severity and outcome. I present a clarification and updating of the classic disease model, incorporating advances in neurobiology with an understanding of the way behaviors can foster neurobiological changes. It is necessary for me to present a more detailed version on the disease of gambling.

Previously, theories of addiction postulated that each addictive substance involves a discrete neurotransmitter. This made it impossible that addiction resulted from psychological or biological responses to experiences. Emphasis was placed on substance dependence as primarily a discrete biological syndrome. By definition, nonpharmacological addictions were impossible. Now, however, it is obvious that addiction to endogenous (internal or self-generated) behaviors is common. Current evidence suggests that despite specific diverse neuronal actions through several neurophysiologic pathways, abused drugs and abused experiences ultimately produce similar chemical actions through a common brain reward circuit (Cooper, Bloom, & Roth, 2002).

Current neuronal circuits that have received the most attention concerning addiction have been referred to by a variety of names including the mesolimbic tract and the extended amygdala. Regardless, these pathways involve the mesolimbic dopamine system and specific subregions of the basal forebrain. Especially involved is the area known as the nucleus accumbens, often dubbed the *pleasure center* of the brain. Also of importance are the central nucleuses of the amygdala, with additional pathways involving the prefrontal lobes, the part of our cortex that is integral in motivation, planning, reasoning, and moral judgments. Dysfunction of this last circuit in the addict explains in part, why excessive pleasure is so blind to reason. It also explains why denial is so common and how the reward structure of addicts comes to be dominated by a single aspect of their environments (Bütz, Chamberlain, & McCown, 1996).

Present data indicates that rewards cause the release of dopamine at several sites, but with the most concentration at the nucleus accumbens (Cooper et al., 2002). It has usually been assumed by lay public and many less trained mental health personnel that addictions are voluntary behaviors and that free choice plays the major role in whether a person becomes addicted (McCown & Keiser, 2003). Even advocates of traditional disease models are unclear about what is under the individual's volitional control. However, I stress to clients that, for some people, the mesolimbic reward system does not and cannot respond to change through reasoning or will power. As reiterated earlier, clients resonate to the simple message that if will power alone were sufficient to control aberrant gambling, then they would not need treatment. Their life experiences have validated the inability of will or reason to control their wagering behaviors.

Once they realize that gambling disorders are biological disorders beyond their control, clients often become empowered to begin the arduous process of change. Their behaviors and attitudes begin to resemble people who cope with chronic hypertension or cardiovascular disease. They realize that the disease had many causes. However, once acquired, the disease is not willed away despite the patient's confidence. It is not a moral question. Furthermore, expectations of a cure are unreasonable. Still, there is much that the client must do to recover. Changes in attitudes and behaviors are essential for survival.

BIOBEHAVIORAL DISEASES AND THE RATIONALE FOR ABSTINENCE AS A TREATMENT GOAL

In the United States, most practitioners emphasize that gambling is a genuine addiction, no different from other addictions in its potential severity. At present, the consensus among most gambling clinicians in North American is that once gambling addiction develops, a goal of treatment is that the client must refrain from all gambling, including restricted or limited wagering (McCown & Keiser, 2003). As in the alcohol and other drug literature, conflict remains about whether the treatment of people with gambling disorders should focus on total abstinence. This contrasts with the goal of the client returning to a capacity for social gambling or controlled wagering. The literature is complex and conflicting and space does not permit reviewing it here. A conservative interpretation of existing studies suggests that it is not clear whether a return to social gambling is possible and if so, for whom and at what stage in their gambling histories. It is not a recommended goal at this time.

When clients with any addiction seek treatment, often they express a desire to be treated only enough so they can once again participate in their addiction in a safe manner. As we have argued elsewhere (McCown & Keiser, 2003), this belief usually represents a primitive fantasy that denies the seriousness of their chronic behaviors. Clients who want restoration of capacity for social gambling are usually people for whom gambling is the most important activity in their lives. They want to continue to use their poison, but somehow to do so in a moderation that has been proven to be beyond their capacities. These clients are essentially asking the therapist to collude with them regarding the fantasy that they can safely return to a behavior that was dreadfully harmful for them. In other areas of mental health, this degree of distortion of reality is usually associated with a delusional disorder. The early phases of treatment are forced to repeatedly confront these fantasies. (See Box 6.4.)

Consequently, most providers in North America treat the problem gambler with the goal of abstinence. (However, particularly in Australia, a limited but scientifically impressive literature has emerged that argues for controlled wagering.

BOX 6.4
Typical Client Fantasies Common in Gambling Treatment

I can quit any time I want.

I'll quit as soon as I have my next big pay off.

I can learn to gamble safely and moderately.

My problem is only due to temporary circumstances.

Once my real problems are treated, my gambling problem will vanish.

This is just a phase of my life that will pass on its own.

My therapist can fix me quickly.

My recovery will be painless and smooth.

Once I quit gambling, all my other problems will disappear.

Gambling once or twice more won't hurt me.

Reasons for these findings may be culturally specific and are outside of the framework of this discussion.) One rationale for total abstinence is that this goal may reduce the risk for relapse during episodes of unsuccessful controlled wagering. Furthermore, the communication of lower expectations of abstinence may allow clients to enter a self-fulfilling prophecy of failure. The client rationalizes treatment failure as an expectation. One client recently illustrated this to me after a relapse. "Come on, Doc. Don't be so concerned about my casino trip. You know most gamblers relapse. Why should I be any different? It won't make me any worse."

The goal of abstinence is naturally derived from biobehavioral accounts introduced earlier in treatment. The therapist can stress to clients that excessive pleasurable activities appear to involve progressive and chronic dysregulation of brain reward circuitry. This is probably true, regardless of specific biological vulnerabilities from genes or other sources (McCown & Chamberlain, 2004). Essentially, humans are not wired to experience prolonged periods of excessive pleasure without changes in neurochemistry and even microanatomy. The molecular mechanisms in these systems convey changes in reward set points, probably through numerous mechanisms that serve to back up each other. Regardless, once this dysregulation occurs, there is a chronic vulnerability to relapse. This line of theorization represents an updated disease model of gambling and other addictions (McCown & Keiser, 2003), congruent with advances in neuroscience.

INDIVIDUAL COUNSELING: THE LINCHPIN FOR CHANGING DYSFUNCTIONAL GAMBLING

Recently, a clinician at a national conference asked a colleague whether individual therapy for gambling disorders really worked? The respondent correctly hedged, recognizing that individual therapy is as diverse as the counselors who administer it are. Some counselors are committed Gestaltists, urging clients to get in touch with their feelings. Others operate out of the notion that traumatic experiences underlie gambling. Still others operate from classic psychodynamic theories. However, most counselors use an inconsistent set of methods and theories. Not surprisingly, given these heterogeneous techniques, there has been little consistent data to support the efficacy of individual treatment methods (McCown & Chamberlain, 2000).

The Multiple Uses of Individual Counseling   In problem gambling treatment, as in any other addiction treatment, individual counseling is used for a number of purposes. First, as illustrated previously, counseling is used to help confront the gambler that she or he has a problem. It is used to break down denial. It can be a strong motivational agent to inspire the client that major life changes are possible. A counselor can also model appropriate behavior in a number of areas. Individual counseling may be the first glimpses of hope that the client feels. Quite literally, it can be lifesaving.

Furthermore, a discussion of problem gambling with a nonjudgmental professional appears to have therapeutic and motivational values (McCown & Chamberlain, 2004). These nonspecific aspects include helping the client grieve the many losses that accompany a gambling lifestyle. Additionally, individual counseling may be the best place in the early stages of treatment to introduce the client to biobehavioral aspects of gambling. Often, these concepts are complex and more difficult to master from books or in groups. Furthermore, the counselor also can assist the family in adjustment and recovery, as well as helping them arrest behaviors in themselves that may provoke gambling in their loved one.

Another reason for individual counseling is that the counselor or therapist can also act as a barometer for measuring psychiatric disorders and psychological conditions that may interfere with progress. The counselor can help the client to monitor emotional states that are likely to lead to future problems. Particularly, in individual sessions, the counselor can best help inoculate the client to the likelihood of relapse, described later. If relapses do occur, the counselor can work with the client to minimize the potential for permanent return to dysfunctional wagering.

Attitudes Interfering with Individual Counseling   Often, a difficult problem for gambling counselors concerns the intensely negative feelings that problem gamblers can cause. As one nationally known counselor said recently, "If you don't want to work with clients who can routinely lie to you, then try counseling someone other than gamblers. It goes with the turf." One problem with individual counseling is that it can be an incredibly frustrating experience for the practitioner. Because of this, attrition by competent, well-trained gambling counselors is regrettably too common. Unless counselors are careful to manage their own feelings and stressors, it is likely that they will experience significant burn out.

Additionally, therapists may respond to gamblers in a less sympathetic light because chronic gambling violates a major social taboo. Very few of us feel we have enough money. An addiction that involves deliberately squandering money may seem more morally reprehensible than one where money is used to purchase a drug of abuse. McCown and Chamberlain (2000) suggest that as therapists find it harder to make a living in contemporary managed care market places, they will react more negatively to people who pathologically and injudiciously spend money. Furthermore, experience makes it much easier for therapists to empathize with substance abusers. Most therapists have or have known someone who has blatantly abused alcohol, drugs, food, cigarettes, or other substances. Although the same therapists may have family, friends, or coworkers with gambling problems, they often are unaware of these difficulties.

When therapists fail to destigmatize gambling in their own minds, they cannot be effective treatment providers. This is one reason that additional training for gambling counselors is so important! The feelings that a counselor may have regarding substance abusers may be quite more optimistic than those felt regarding a problem gambler. These negative feelings may be problematic at any point in the individual counseling process. Only training and supervision can assist the counselor in addressing, understanding, and overcoming these problematic attitudes.

In my clinical experience, these attitudes can develop into feelings that are most likely to interfere with treatment if the client relapses. At this time, counselors are likely to be confused about attributions of the cause of relapse. Large literature in social psychology involves different attribution people make for behaviors. Stout (1999) conducted a study to examine patterns of attributions among gamblers and their counselors following a gambler's *slip* and subsequent return to treatment. In brief, Stout's study suggests that gamblers and counselors do not share common attributions for these slips.

Counselors are much more likely to see slips as occurring from some inner disposition that the client possesses. They are more likely to respond angrily. The client is more likely to view a slip as a result of unfortunate circumstances or being "in the wrong place at the wrong time." Although gamblers in treatment and therapists may eventually reach concordance on reasons involving particular relapses, there is a decided lack of concordance in the attributions that are made soon after relapses occur.

Too frequently, this disparity results in friction within a therapeutic dyad, often at a time when tensions are already high because of the relapse (McCown & Keiser, 2004). To the relapsed gambler, who focuses on the situational factors that caused the relapse, the therapist's dispositional viewpoint often seems too punitive and insensitive. However, to the therapist, the gambler's tendency to look to situational factors, rather than take personal responsibility for the relapse, may seem particularly exasperating. Therapeutic dyads that work to reduce differences in beliefs prove beneficial at a crucial time in the recovery process—the period soon after a relapse. This may be one reason for the demonstrated successes of relapse prevention programs discussed later.

GROUP THERAPY AND ITS MULTIPLE USES

Group therapy is an incredibly popular modality for all addiction treatment. I strongly argue that clinicians who treat problem gamblers in group therapy must have specifically supervised experience with gamblers (Estes & Brubaker, 1994). Too often, counselors believe that generic group training in substance abuse is sufficient experience to qualify them to work with problem gamblers. While a general theme of this chapter has been that there are similarities between addictive behaviors, gamblers often present unique problems. Often, they inhabit a subculture that is not familiar to the typical addictions counselor. Furthermore, the shocking conditions of many gamblers' poverty and despair can overcome an untrained practitioner.

While clinical experience suggests that resistance, manipulation, and denial are commonly encountered in group therapies for any addiction, the creativity of gamblers to frustrate the best intentions of the well-meaning counselor are often astounding. Recently, I had to illustrate to supervisees that some of their mutual group clients were discretely wagering on who would speak next while the therapy session was in progress. Continued training and self-critiquing are ongoing requirements for conducting successful group therapies.

My sentiment is that good group therapy is probably as effective as good individual therapy. However, it is very difficult to be a good group therapist with gamblers. Since so much may occur in any group session, especially with gamblers, it is helpful if the therapists involved work in pairs. Additionally, they can maximally profit by recording their therapy sessions. Recently McCown and Chamberlain (2004) have experimented with off site, Internet supervision, with a video camera set up in one state or country and a supervisor hundreds or thousands of miles away. Sometimes this perspective from a different vantage may help the stuck group therapists realize obvious problems that they are missing.

One concern of group treatment resembles findings observed in the heroin addiction literature some years ago. Often, intense discussion about gambling will produce strong cravings for other group members to gamble. This phenomenon exists in a variety of addictive behaviors. In heroin addiction, the results are so strong that they are referred to as *shame addiction*. Discussion concerning arousal about gambling can often produce craving to wager in some individuals. These cravings can be a trigger for relapse. McCown and Chamberlain (2004) found that half of outpatient slips for gamblers in group therapy occurred within 2 hours after a gambling counseling group! Their theory is that sharing of feelings cues cognitions that are interlinked with cues for relapse.

Counselors who treat gamblers or other addicts in a group setting need to learn to monitor each group member for signs of relapse. These are often observed at the end of the group session. Therapy sessions usually should not end on an emotional end, but may best be wound down so that any cravings for relapse that may have been cued will extinguish. Often, it is useful to ask each member to comment on the mental status and the probability of relapse of other members in the group. Very often, group members are more attuned to the psychological conditions of their peers than the professional group leaders. Gamblers are often keen observers and may use these skills to help their recovering peers.

GAMBLER'S ANONYMOUS: THE BULWARK OF TRADITIONAL TREATMENT

Gamblers Anonymous (GA) remains the first line of treatment for problem gamblers in North America as noted by a recent survey of gambling counselors (McCown & Chamberlain, 2004). Adherents of GA staunchly advocate that compulsive gamblers cannot return to social gambling. The number of people who presently attend GA is hard to assess due in part to the organization's extreme insistence on anonymity. GA is similar to Alcoholics Anonymous (AA) in that it has related 12-Steps and traditions. It is also a nonprofessional and apolitical organization and does not take a stand on questions concerning wagering access and gambling expansion anymore than AA takes a stand on the appropriateness of liquor control laws. GA has often kept an even lower profile than many 12-Step self-help groups, largely because of the demands on its members for financial restitution as a necessary part of the recovery process.

Differences between AA and GA   There are major differences between AA and GA that are often mistakenly ignored or overlooked by well-meaning counselors (McCown & Chamberlain, 2000). These differences may disquiet clients expecting an AA experience from GA. In most GA groups, for example, meetings are closed, that is, they are not opened to someone who does not admit to a gambling problem. This has much to do with the private financial needs of gamblers, which are often desperate. However, this secrecy is in contrast to many AA groups, which often have a predominance of open meetings. However, this secrecy is necessary. It is common for people in GA to give advice to new members on how to placate a loan shark or other underworld figure. It is easy to see why confidentiality is even more prized than in other self-help groups.

GA is also very hands on in its approach to the individual in recovery, often more than AA groups. GA members are frequently openly intrusive concerning the finances of newcomers. Often, people who enter GA give up any vestiges of financial, medical, or psychological privacy. Not surprisingly, many of the stories of recovery in GA emphasize drastic changes in financial well-being, rather than the achievement of inner peace or personal harmony. Many of these testimonials also involve frank disclosures of suicide attempts or ongoing suicidal ideation. Often, they may ignore positive aspects a lifestyle committed to avoiding gambling.

These include enhanced family life, genuine friendships, and a greater sense of well-being and inner peace (McCown & Chamberlain, 2004).

Reliable statistics on the efficacy of GA are impossible to obtain. The most optimistic sentiment is that one-half of gamblers in treatment will have *no* significant period of abstinence. Slightly more than one-third will show a variable course, characterized by frequent relapses. According to GA lore, people in this group experience periods of gambling abstinence, but these periods are punctuated by severe lapses. A more common sentiment is that 5% to perhaps 20% of members will abstain from gambling. However, these numbers are not official or obtained in a scientific manner. As in the case of any 12-Step group, premorbid psychiatric factors, as well as a client's resources, such as the presence of supportive families and a job to return to, are positive indicators of success.

Criticisms of GA   GA has frequently been criticized for its lack of a spiritual emphasis as well as its overt behavioral orientation. For people familiar with other 12-Step groups, this is a serious concern. In part, this comparative lack of spirituality may be because one of its founders was an atheist. It also may be because most gamblers have made bargains with their God at various times during their addiction history and this has not helped them. It is not uncommon, for example, for gamblers to promise a tenth or a Biblical tithe of their winnings to the Almighty if they are afforded a winning opportunity.

GA is occasionally seen by members of AA and GA as being more confrontational and emotionally brutal. A growing sense is that GA is now becoming more holistic in addressing the emotional, spiritual, and psychological needs of its members (McCown & Chamberlain, 2004). GA is now less likely to worry about a person's finances alone, without considering their spiritual or emotional needs. Some practitioners feel that these changes are due in part to the increasing numbers of women who have joined GA and have subtly refashioned it to better meet their holistic needs.

A practical problem concerning GA is the lack of universally available meetings that are more common with AA and other 12-Step groups. Many towns simply do not have GA. Where GA is available, too often there are not a variety of meetings available for clients, as there would be for people interested in AA. For example, in a medium-sized town, if a recovering substance abuser is more comfortable with people of gay or lesbian orientations, he or she can usually find specialized meetings. Nonsmokers meetings are common as are meetings for younger people, seniors, the religiously orthodox, Christian Fundamentalists, minorities, or people who are comfortable with other diverse populations. While these meetings are usually open to everyone, they tend to take on a distinctive character, which is often therapeutic for people with special needs or life experiences.

Furthermore, AA groups also often have more varied personalities that may be lacking in GA groups. Clinical staff may be aware of AA groups that seem to be more introverted or outgoing and may informally match the client to the available groups in the area. GA rarely offers this diversity. As one client sarcastically stated, "GA is like a hamburger chain. Good but the same. AA is more of your local country kitchen, always good, but always different."

When there are more meetings, their nature will likely diversify to meet a variety of needs. As problem gambling becomes ubiquitous, GA meetings show more signs of responding to special needs and populations. In the meantime, the counselor probably does best by insisting that the client continue in GA, despite any difficulties. "If you don't like GA," one of my peers told a client recently, "then work hard to make it better for you and people like you."

Treatment Providers and an Understanding of GA   It is important that the treatment provider have an understanding of the process and limits of GA. A method to accomplish this (if the provider is not in recovery for gambling behavior) is for counselors to spend extensive time talking with GA members. A mistake that counselors who are recovering from another addiction, such as alcohol abuse and dependency, sometimes make is to believe that any 12-Step group is identical to the type of group that was helpful for them. As one counselor said, "AA worked for me, so why won't GA work for her? Don't they use just about the same 12 steps?" They do, but the process, social milieu, and pattern of member interactions are often radically different. I also recommend the outstanding book *Deadly Odds* by Estes and Brubaker (1994) as an introduction to the GA-based recovery processes.

GA may work splendidly for some people; while for others, it does not work at all. We have no way of predicting for whom or when it will work. Because responses to addiction treatment are not linear and dose-dependent (i.e., there is not a direct relationship between the number of meetings attended and the chance for abstinence), past failures are usually a poor index of the possibility of future change (Bütz et al., 1996). Therefore, if a person has been referred to GA and did not find it helpful, a subsequent referral is worth another try.

ADDITIONAL POPULAR TECHNIQUES TO TREAT THE PROBLEM GAMBLER

Other therapeutic techniques that are useful in individual counseling include classical methods of relaxation training, exercises that stress feeling awareness, anger management, and problem-solving training. McCown and Chamberlain (2000) have experimented with neurobehavioral biofeedback to reduce impulsiveness and they got positive results. Bütz et al. (1996) have argued that the science of nonlinear dynamics, or chaos theory, may furnish entirely new treatments for addictions based on developments in contemporary physics.

Less consistently positive results have been obtained with classical behavioral techniques, such as flooding, systematic desensitization, and aversion conditioning. However, additional research seems warranted with all of these and many more modalities. The cliché that more research is warranted seems appropriate at this time.

McCown and Chamberlain (2004) believe that the competent gambling therapist needs to have general clinical skills in a variety of mental health areas. They stress that training is necessary for people to understand and know their limitations. Too often, they argue, clients are treated with inappropriate modalities or are misdiagnosed by well-meaning, but ignorant professionals. They emphatically conclude that the counselor or therapist who has concerns should seek supervision and outside consultation. In combination with mastery of a variety of basic clinical skills, these authors believe that present-day treatment providers can perform more effectively. Most important, however, is to remember the maxim of doing the least harm possible.

Different treatment strategies need to be identified that will fit best with each set of these different clients' problems. Contrary to traditional lore, what works for the high-stakes gambler may not work for the nickel-slot player. As Estes and

---

BOX 6.5
Why Gambling Is So Treatment Resistant

"While gambling addiction shares many similarities with other addictions, there is one major difference. Everyone has to use money to live. An alcoholic can learn to avoid bars, stores, and restaurants that may be cues to relapse. A crack addict can avoid people, places, and things. Unfortunately, the gambler has to live with the reality that handling money is a part of life.

"The effectiveness of treatments for gambling is probably better compared to those for obesity than for substance abuse. Everyone has to eat and for the obese person each episode of normal hunger may be a powerful cue to eat to excess.

"Similarly, any time a gambler, whether in recovery or not, handles money there are strong cues to wager. The fact that money, like food, is a normal part of life may make the treatment of gambling disorders extremely difficult."

—Michael Brubaker, National Gambling Consultant

Brubaker (1994) note, most serious gamblers have one game that they really prefer and that is usually the one that is the riskiest for them. A therapy group addressing the realities of slot machine playing may simply reinforce the self-deluded image of the bankrupt day-trader that he or she does not have a gambling problem. Unfortunately, we are only beginning to tailor treatment to the type of gambling problem. (See Box 6.5.)

INPATIENT TREATMENT: BENEFITS AND RISKS

Following the pioneering work of Dr. Robert Custer (e.g., Custer & Milt, 1985) and his associates, inpatient hospitalization is often considered the treatment of choice for severe gambling disorders. This modality is so important and controversial that it deserves a separate discussion.

The casual observer notes that data is poor on the appropriate use of hospitalization for the treatment of problem gambling. Existing data is often skewed because this option is unavailable for most gamblers, at least in the United States. Usually, only those who have personal or family resources are able to use this option. These are hardly representative samples of typical people with gambling problems. As one client said, "If I had the cash to get inpatient treatment, I'd still be gambling."

The Veterans Affairs Hospital System has traditionally provided some free inpatient treatment. Too often, problem gamblers who were subjects for VA research have been middle-aged, mostly Caucasian males, many with other addictions. Data collected with these populations may not be applicable in other settings or to other groups (McCown & Chamberlain, 2000). In the United States, only Louisiana and a few other states are able to routinely offer inpatient options to the indigent gambler—the person with the most need. (Preliminary data concerning the efficacy of inpatient treatment in Louisiana is very encouraging.) However, proprietary or for-profit psychiatric hospitals have little use for treating gamblers since, by the time they seek treatment, gamblers are usually destitute, without insurance or cash for services.

THE DECISION TO HOSPITALIZE A PATIENT

Even if the option of inpatient treatment is available, the decision to hospitalize a client for a gambling problem should not be made in cavalier fashion. There are no documented rules of thumb or standards of care associated with the necessity of hospitalization. The standard of assisting the client in the least restrictive environment possible remains appropriate. This standard is often ignored in proprietary treatment facilities, in which the rare patient with insurance for inpatient coverage is likely to be admitted, regardless of genuine need.

Well-meaning addictions counselors, especially those who have experienced a personal recovery from another addiction, may also ignore the standard. Usually people making this error have drug and alcohol training, but not necessarily specific training in the treatment of gambling (Johnson & McCown, 1997). They may be more likely to think that since inpatient treatment was necessary for them, it is required for all addictions (McCown & Keiser, 2003). These counselors often forget that one reason they may have been hospitalized was that they needed medical detoxification. This medical process usually involved titration of a controlled substance and intensive behavioral monitoring. This is usually not necessary for problem gamblers unless they have a medical complication or additional psychiatric diagnoses. Regardless, because problem gamblers often live irregular lives filled with many health risks, a comprehensive physical examination by a medical doctor is indicated.

In general, as in other fields in psychiatry, it is necessary to consider hospitalization if the person is a risk to themselves or others. Inpatient hospitalization is otherwise most warranted when a problem gambler has a compounding severe Axis I diagnosis (such as a mood disorder, anxiety, or thought disorder), is otherwise at high risk for relapse, or has had a history of outpatient failures. Also, individuals who spend substantial portions of their time gambling during the day and who lack vocational and leisure skills appear most likely to benefit from a hospital program. As suggested earlier, people with physical problems from poverty or neglect can benefit from the enhanced medical care that is associated with inpatient treatment. Some clients may seek hospitalization because it offers them comparative safety from creditors or dangerous characters. Usually, their concerns are legitimate and not a product of imagination, fantasy, or delusional state.

Other Cases When Inpatient Treatment Is Desirable   Many people who have gambling problems also have experienced extreme traumatic stressors. For example, Shandra, described at the beginning of the chapter, was repeatedly raped while working for gambling money. The psychic scars from such events are serious concerns that often benefit from inpatient treatment. Often it is necessary to make a client face horribly traumatic memories. Uncovering therapies, including those designed to treat traumatic stress, need to be undertaken with great care, since the gambler in treatment is especially vulnerable. When necessary, therapists may demand an inpatient facility to secure the safety of the client who is undergoing an intense therapeutic period.

As we learn more about the comorbidity of gambling with other psychiatric disorders, the case for extended inpatient treatment becomes more compelling. Judicious use of medication, described later, may also require the intensive therapy of inpatient treatment. The absence of a support network that does not gamble is also a reason for inpatient treatment. Inpatient treatment may also be necessary when a spouse has a lifestyle or agenda that may interfere with out-patient counseling.

Issues concerning children may also prompt inpatient treatment. Zimmerman, a pediatric emergency specialist (unpublished communication, April 8, 2003) noted that women with gambling problems may be more likely to experience problems bonding with their children. She also noted that parents who are preoccupied with gambling may provide insufficient supervision for their children, making their children at risk for accidents and injuries. These issues may be more fruitfully addressed in residential treatment, when the client can gradually be reintroduced to his or her children under supervision. Reuniting a client with children may also be a powerful motive for completing successful treatment.

Psychiatric and Psychological Evaluations as Part of Inpatient Treatments

Regardless of whether the gambler is being treated on an in- or outpatient basis, a psychiatric evaluation is critical. Specifically, it is necessary to rule out both Type I and Type II bipolar disorders. Too often, patients who experience repeated treatment failures have a chemically controllable bipolar disorder. Unless this syndrome is regulated, successful gambling treatment is impossible. Depression and suicidal intentions also should be carefully evaluated. Suicidal thinking is quite common among gamblers in all stages of recovery. Similarly, coaddictions, including chemical dependencies, are common in gamblers. It is still surprising how frequent these basics are ignored.

Psychological evaluations are desirable, in part because they are very helpful for practical aspects of inpatient management and treatment planning (McCown & Keiser, 2003). It may be critical, for example, to realize that a particular client has an impulsive personality style making inhibition of behaviors difficult. This type of information can be obtained from psychological testing that is flexible enough to address suspected problems. Such testing should be problem focused rather than embrace practicing psychologists' common fault of having a fixed battery for all situations (Johnson & McCown, 1997).

Testing often is needed to screen for adult attention-deficit disorders, which may be commonly underdiagnosed. Furthermore, psychological testing should also address alexithymia, or difficulty in identifying subjective emotional states, since this is commonly underdiagnosed among problem gamblers but may be a causal factor in their behaviors (McCown & Chamberlain, 2000). Learning disorders are also common among problem gamblers for reasons we do not understand. Testing may also address problems the client is likely to have in treatment. For example, projective testing, using instruments such as the Rorschach, may be useful in predicting who will feel comfortable in self-help groups and who is likely to drop out of these groups quickly.

Furthermore, surveys done by Keiser and McCown (2000) suggest that clinicians and nonpsychologists of all varieties prefer a psychological report about addicts that is told in as close to the addict's own voice as is possible. As one clinician said, "While the examiner has a certain expertise, he is limited because his contact is usually a one-time thing. Addicts of all kinds like to try out new stories and new strategies on the examiner. It is often most helpful to the clinician if you document odd stories, strange words, verbal slips, and unexpected statements from the client in his or her own words. Then, perhaps weeks later, a word or phrase might unlock some therapeutic puzzle that you previously couldn't understand."

Genuine and Pseudo Inpatient Treatment Programs

Part of the difficulty about research concerning the effectiveness of inpatient gambling programs is that there is tremendous variability among these programs. Some gambling facilities are actually alcohol and substance abuse programs that treat all addicts identically. While there are common properties among addictions, there are also differences in treatment needs. For example, it is much more socially acceptable to be an alcoholic than a problem gambler. Programs that claim to have expertise in gambling but do not routinely treat the gambler should not be classified as an inpatient treatment program. I often refer to them as *pseudo inpatient gambling treatment programs.* Their success rates appear depressingly dismal.

Similarly, many addiction treatment programs claim to have gambling tracks in their inpatient programs. These usually involve a counselor or two who has additional training in the treatment of problem gambling. The client with a gambling problem usually sees this counselor, but the remaining treatment is essentially the same as other clients. While this is an improvement over an inpatient facility that erroneously claims to possess expertise in treating the problem gambler, it is not the best inpatient option. If inpatient treatment is necessary and there is a choice about where it will occur, preference should always be given to the facility with the most experience in treating problem gamblers.

My experience is that the most success is related to programs that have the most experience and training in the treatment of problem gambling. Unfortunately, demonstrating this empirically is difficult, since these programs tend to attract the most impaired patients. As a result, some older studies that compared the success of outpatient treatment to that of a comprehensive and lengthy inpatient program might as well have compared mortality rates in a general physician's office to those in an intensive care unit. The more impaired gambler—the person most likely to be treated in an inpatient setting—is most likely to relapse. (See Box 6.6.)

We desperately need well-designed research that clarifies what types of treatment programs are effective for what group of clients. However, interpretation of this research must be tempered by the changing symptoms of problem gambling. Twenty years ago, it was more common to see people with pure gambling problems. In one study I was asked to supervise, it was necessary to screen the histories of over 200 problem gamblers before we could find a single one who did not have concurrent and complicating psychiatric problems. Increasingly, gamblers are younger, more impaired, gamble for a greater variety of reasons, and are much more likely to have a number of complicating psychiatric diagnoses.

Because many people with gambling disorders have a variety of other psychiatric problems, any inpatient facility should also be able to treat a spectrum of psychiatric disorders. However, no program should attempt to succeed in all areas. Programs that do not realize their limitations harm their clients. Some clients need to be treated elsewhere before their gambling problems can be addressed. Clinical judgment is often necessary on the prioritization of a client's problems. Too often, this does not occur and makes inpatient treatment appear less effective than it is. Clients who are too depressed, manic, or agitated to

---

BOX 6.6
Gambling Treatment and Managed
Mental Health Care

"Often, people authorizing inpatient treatment for problem gamblers will deny payments. They claim that their assessment suggests that the problem gambler is too agitated, suicidal, or depressed to benefit from an inpatient gambling treatment. Sometimes this is true and a good care provider welcomes the help of other professionals.

"However, once these patients are stabilized, whether in the community or in an inpatient setting, there is a tendency to forget about their gambling problems. They slip through the cracks and soon begin gambling again.

"Not surprisingly, they become depressed, suicidal, agitated, and often manic. The cycle just repeats itself until these people receive help for their gambling problems or they succeed in suicide."

—John, a recovering gambler

---

effectively participate in treatment must have these disorders or symptoms successfully treated before serious interventions for problem gambling can be useful.

RELAPSE PREVENTION: AN EMPIRICALLY DEMONSTRABLE THERAPEUTIC PROGRAM

During the past decade, a number of new treatment strategies have emerged. In part this is because, despite many methods of treating the problem gambler, there is little evidence to indicate that any particular method is uniquely effective. One clear exception is the theoretically based cognitive behavioral treatment programs (e.g., Sylvain, Ladouceur, & Biksvert, 1997) loosely grouped under the heading *relapse prevention*.

Relapse prevention is not really new. It has been in existence for over 25 years for the treatment of alcohol and other drug abuse. It is unclear why relapse prevention methodology is not more popular with counselors who treat problem gamblers. In this treatment modality, problem gambling is assumed to be a chronic and recurrent collection of behaviors that have a very high probability of re-occurring. The relapse prevention model, though based in the literature of cognitive behavioral psychotherapy, is highly congruent with the biobehavioral paradigm that is advocated elsewhere.

In this treatment strategy, the therapist uses his or her experience and knowledge in attempting to *inoculate* the client to high-risk situations that lead to relapse (McMullan, 2000). He or she also uses any relapses that do occur constructively, so that a relapse does not mean the end of treatment. Instead, a relapse is an opportunity to help the client further understand her or his specific vulnerabilities. The following vignette illustrates this technique. It also shows the amazing lack of insight that is endemic in gambling and other forms of addiction.

THERAPIST: John, I don't get it. Eight months without slipping and suddenly your wife calls me and says you are in Las Vegas. What happened?

CLIENT: I can't figure it out. I know you don't understand it. I just messed up.

THERAPIST: Well, I've found it helpful to look at the process of how people slip because sometimes we can gain some insight to help them.

CLIENT: (Pause) Not here. You won't learn anything this time. I just did the same routines as usual. Just cashed my check and the next thing I knew I was in Vegas. There went my money. It was like I was someone else. I don't remember anything.

THERAPIST: Are you saying you blacked out?

CLIENT: No . . . I mean I didn't do anything unusual. I just cashed my check and waved to the guys who sit in the back of (the particular convenience store where he cashes his check).

THERAPIST: And then what happened?

CLIENT: Well, I mean, that's the part I guess I should be ashamed of. They had a card game in the back. I went to say "Hi" to some friends. Next thing I know, I was being dealt a hand and one turned into another.

THERAPIST: Hmmm. Then what?

CLIENT: I don't really know. I wound up in Vegas. Ran up my credit cards. It is all like a dream. I just don't understand what happened. I've got to figure it out. Just a blank, I guess . . .

In this case, the therapist was able to work with the client and assist him in finding a lower risk place to cash his paycheck, one where he would not be as likely to encounter cues that were conditioned with gambling. He would also be able to better anticipate high-risk situations so that he would not remain overconfident in his capacity to resist relapse.

Therapists are occasionally taken aback at the number of risky situations the client fails to recognize. In relapse prevention, it is important to avoid blaming clients for lack of insight. Denial, rather than being diagnostic of addiction, is seen as a normal part of the addictions recovery process. In this manner, relapse prevention is different from other therapies that attempt to break down denial through confrontation. A Socratic dialogue approach, similar to cognitive behavioral therapy for depression, is preferable.

If the cognitively behaviorally related and experimentally validated technique of relapse prevention works, why is it not more popular? Some practitioners argue that typical clinical cases are too complex for a single empirical model to have much usefulness. Others argue that treatment providers who excel in cognitive-behavioral techniques are not well trained in traditional counseling techniques. Data is needed to answer these questions and to assist the counselor in providing the best possible treatment. Unfortunately, in this new area of treatment possibilities, turf battles and professional interdisciplinary rivalries continue to dominate in inappropriate places.

LEARNING THE ODDS: NEW IMPROVEMENTS ON TRADITIONAL TREATMENT

During the previous decade, a number of treatment strategies emerged that were designed to teach clients that gambling is inherently an unbeatable game. However, one problem with this method is that it assumes that the gambler acts rationally. Often, problem gamblers will tell you before they enter a gambling establishment that they expect to lose (McCown & Chamberlain, 2004). Colleagues and I still include an educational component to treatment but have learned to modify it to make it more practical and successful.

As a methodology for prevention, there is reasonable evidence that programs that teach the odds of winning have some effectiveness. This is increasingly important, since gambling is increasing at epidemic proportions in young people and new users of the Internet. These programs often elucidate the manner in which casinos and other gambling venues work to maintain that the customer will be the ultimate loser. One particularly useful program has been piloted by Dr. Howard Schaffer and his group at the Harvard School of Addictions. It is listed as an Internet resource, at the end of the chapter.

However, there remains no convincing evidence that problem gamblers change their behaviors once they realize that the odds are against them. Often, a more fruitful solution than simply teaching the odds is to help problem gamblers examine what psychological factors cause them to compete in games they know they cannot beat. There are many possibilities, with the following discussion highlighting only a few that are currently developed.

LEARNING ABOUT LEARNING THEORY

Explanation of problem gambling and some aspects of treatment often begin with concepts from basic learning theory. A common explanation of gambling behavior is that gambling involves experience with a variable ratio (VR) of rewards (McCown & Chamberlain, 2000). As behaviorists have shown, animals placed on an elevated VR will act similarly to a frenzied slot-machine player. However, most people placed on a VR—meaning anyone who has ever played a slot machine—do not develop gambling problems. Other factors are, therefore, assumed to influence the development of problem gambling for all but the most vulnerable of individuals.

Still, the counselor can use the concept of VR as a powerful demonstration of the irrationality of gambling. What I have found useful is showing a client a video of a rat on a variable ratio, pressing a bar frantically, without receiving a reward. I run this illustration concurrently on a computer monitor that is also showing an equally frenetic video or slot player wildly spending hundreds of quarters or dollars. Often, this experience helps clients question the credibility of their behaviors. As one client said, "Damn, if I had known I looked like a trained rat, I'd have saved all my money."

TEACHING THE GAMBLER WHO REALLY PROFITS

In this class of interventions, we capitalize on many gamblers' fears of being taken for a sucker, a particular insult in the world of wagering. Whether or not a gambler has sociopathic tendencies as some have alleged, most abhor the notion that they are being exploited. Gamblers often romanticize their lifestyles by fostering the self-image that they are mavericks, individuals running against the grain. This may be one reason pioneer themes are common in Las Vegas. Often, the serious gambler wants to identify with the unfettered spirit of the American Western pioneers. The endless stream of gambling systems, racing methods, and inside information that is sold to the gambler often exploits these sentiments.

Often, it is therapeutic to educate the problem gambler about the realities of gaming. An entire industry exists to manipulate people into thinking that they can make money when they actually cannot. Gamblers hate to be manipulated! But our message is simple: For the casino industry, the race track, and the loan shark, you are nothing but a sucker, a mark.

Often, I refer to the ways in which people who win huge jackpots are repeatedly lured into losing this money. An initial big win early in a person's gambling history may often contribute to the risk for development of a gambling disorder (McCown & Chamberlain, 2000). Some casinos recognize this and habitually court players who have made a big score, knowing that they will soon return for more gambling. I have found it helpful to obtain testimony from a casino employee regarding the practices of soliciting people who have obtained a big win.

In general, most gamblers despise being controlled. The notion that someone is pulling their strings in a predictable manner infuriates them. It may even make them act more rationally. As one gambler in treatment said, "It's bad enough fighting off bad luck. But when you know that there's an entire industry just waiting to separate you from your money, it gets you so ticked off you can't stand the thought of gambling."

This intervention will not produce gambling abstinence. However, it may provide a therapeutic window that allows the client to question the reasonableness of his or her gambling behaviors. Sometimes the counselor can obtain a similar effect by teaching the client how much money states and municipalities are making from their patrons. One client's statements illustrate how effective this procedure can occasionally be:

> I used to go to Las Vegas every month. I'd spend half my paycheck and then spend the rest of it thinking about how I was going to win next time. Then I heard that Las Vegas has no state taxes. But they still have schools and police. So if that's true, where are they getting their money from? Suckers like me! That makes me angry. It's hard enough to win without someone taking their cut off the top.
>
> To me, it was like a wake-up call [when I realized] that someone was making money off of me. . . . I've been so disgusted since then that I've never gone back [to a casino]. But I miss it. I miss it every day. . . . I guess I started to realize that I had a problem when I knew that I was craving something that genuinely disgusted me. I was able to step back and say to myself, "Hey, maybe you do need help."

SKILL, LUCK, AND GAMBLING: EXPLAINING REALITY

Colleagues and I have had success in educating clients about the roles of skill and luck in successful gambling. When a gambler believes that skill can help him or her win, that person is apt to gamble more frequently and wager more. McCown and Chamberlain (2004) found that wagering increases as a log function of a gambler's belief that skill is important to payoff outcome. This is true only if gamblers feel they possess the specific skills necessary to win. One reason that sports betting may be particularly dangerous is that numerous handicapping methods are sold to convince the participant that he or she has an advantage of skill over fellow gamblers.

Problem gamblers begin to question their behaviors when they learn that no amount of skill can help them win on a consistent basis. Yet many gamblers still continue to play games that they know they will lose. Most gamblers clearly know the odds are not in their favor. Clever ruses from the gaming industry try to convince the gambler that he or she will be the exception. Problem gamblers do not need this convincing. Often, they engage in elaborate strategies for mentally denying the odds. My colleagues and I call this *maintaining the illusion of luck*.

Examples of this occur with all gamblers. People gamble irrationally when they feel lucky, a vague state that defies consistent description. Yet, all of us feel lucky at one time or another. This perception of luck makes people take chances. When the individual without a gambling problem feels lucky, he or she may go shopping, looking for an unadvertised sale. He or she may reach out to an estranged friend in the hopes of resolving differences. The person feeling lucky might even confront the boss, asking for a much needed raise.

However, people with gambling problems are apt to use irrelevant cues to believe that they can win against the odds. A problem gambler may have a dream, see her birthday on an auto license, or even read a horoscope and then be convinced that probability does not apply to her for a particular time. As one gambler said, "When I've got luck, I know I'd better play quickly. Luck doesn't stay with you forever."

Gamblers benefit from changing their perceptions about luck. One of our newer interventions involves *luck management*. This results in client-generated strategies for resisting the urge to gamble when clients feel lucky. Although data collection is incomplete, the technique appears to have some usefulness in preventing relapses.

FAMILY THERAPY: AN EMERGING TREATMENT OF CHOICE

Previously, McCown and Chamberlain (2000) argued that family therapy should be a treatment of choice for gambling disorders. GA has long pioneered the importance of the family in the recovery of the gambler. Yet as late as a decade ago, McCown and Johnson's (1993) case study of family therapy for problem gambling was criticized as being unnecessary.

However, in just a few years, family therapy for gambling disorders became a mainstream treatment (Ciarrocchi, 2001). There are a number of reasons for this. First, the family interactions of gamblers, if they indeed have intact families, are usually always pathological. Family roles are often skewed by pathologies that are well-known to structural family theorists. For example, the *parentified* child is commonly found in families whether father or mother has

---

Credentials and Competency

"The results of our research show that the more formal mental health training a professional has, the less they are likely to know about the effective treatment of gambling.

While certain professions, such as family therapy, can play an invaluable role in this treatment, they are critically handicapped unless they have appropriate training and supervision. The consumer and the therapist need to remember that credentials do not necessarily indicate competency!"

—William McCown and Linda Chamberlain, 2002

abdicated responsibilities and instead spends his or her time gambling. Variations of dysfunctional structure in families with problem gambling are infinite in their permutations.

As another example, one of our colleagues worked with a classic problem seen by family therapists. The mother had a gambling problem. Subsequently, to continue gambling, she turned over responsibility for her adolescent children to her sister. The sister was reticent to allow the children to return home. Consequently, the children allowed the mother and their aunt to compete for their affection. One way this occurred was by both parent figures offering progressively less supervision as an enticement for familial affect. During adolescence, this is a guaranteed disaster.

Classic strategic therapy may also be of particular value with the problem gambler, especially in the tricky world of paradoxical interventions and prescriptions of the problem. Although there is an extensive literature on strategic therapy of alcoholics and other substance abusers, there is almost no literature on this body of techniques and gambling disorders. Isolated case studies and clinical experience seems promising. However, well-controlled clinical trials, similar to those that established the effectiveness of other forms of therapy, are clearly needed.

The following case is an example of a family therapy case using structural/strategic therapy in an innovative manner. It also highlights the manner in which symptoms can substitute from one individual to another within a family system.

The identified patient was a 52-year-old separated Caucasian male named Donald. He was referred for counseling following discharge from a substance abuse facility and it was not clear how much education and treatment he received about gambling addictions. He had absorbed significant knowledge on the general process of 12-Step recovery, although it was unlikely that he had any other addictive disorders at this time.

The counselor, who had substantial training in strategic family therapy and systems theory, decided that the patient's best probability for staying abstinent was to involve the entire family in treatment. This is because early clinical work showed that Donald had an almost ruminative guilt concerning his addiction and the financial hardships it had placed on his family. He hoped, not so subtly, that his family could forgive him and he could return to live with them again, as he had before he was hospitalized. During his hospitalization, his wife moved their three adolescent children out of the house and into a small apartment. His wife, Tanya, was not very sanguine about the prospect of a reunion, noting, "He has lied to me about everything the whole time we were married. Why would a few weeks in a hospital change that?"

The therapist carefully confronted the group. He showed them how everyone in the family had become sicker and more pathological since their father had been released. "I don't understand it. He gets better and you all get worse? Help me out here."

"I guess we really don't want him back," one son admitted.

"The guy is a jerk, a real jerk when he is not gambling. He's an okay human when he is gambling, but otherwise, he's just a mean jerk."

With this revelation, treatment changed remarkably. Part of the focus was on restoring family unity and peace rather than on organizing the family to support the father's separation from gambling. When he was not gambling, the father made everyone else in the family miserable. Results were not surprising. Often symptoms seemed to be passed from one family member to another. For example, one individual would develop depression. It would remit as soon as another family member became depressed.

Treatment was not easy. The father relapsed many times. Eventually, however, the father was able to attain abstinence. He has not placed a bet in 2 years. The family remains intact, despite some occasionally rough emotional times. By any measure, the therapy has been effective, although the course of treatment was exhausting for both the family and the therapist.

MEDICATIONS AS A NEW AVENUE OF HOPE

In the past few years, the issue of medications for gambling disorders has become one of the most controversial aspects of treatment options. Medications are most helpful if the client has a bipolar disorder. However, once a bipolar disorder is controlled, the cues for dysfunctional gambling are not necessarily extinguished. The client or patient may have bipolar symptoms under control yet may have learned to engage in aberrant gambling so successfully that this behavior has a life of its own. If problem gambling occurs frequently, then it is unlikely to disappear when bipolar symptoms are under control. (See Box 6.7.)

It is controversial whether the selective serotonergic agents (SSRIs) or other antidepressants have any efficacy apart from increasing a sense of well-being in depressed people with gambling problems. Adherents to the belief that gambling is a compulsive action rather than an addiction have to be dismayed by the lack of specific therapeutic action of drugs known to decrease obsessive-compulsive behaviors. Such drugs may be helpful, though they are not a panacea.

Based on current knowledge on addictions (Cooper et al., 2002) it is hypothesized that use of dopamine agonists or partial agonists might reduce problem gambling. Case studies have suggested successful use of stimulant drugs, which all involve dopamine activity, but these have failed to control for attention-deficit disorder as a comorbid factor. Presumably, partial dopamine agonists like the antianxiety drug buspirone might have some effectiveness as well. More promising may be antidepressants that work through the dopamine system, such as buproprion.

BOX 6.7
Gambling as a Chronic Disease

Dr. Marc Porenza and associates at Yale University believe that pathological gambling is a chronic medical condition. They suggest that primary care physicians can treat pathological gamblers once these patients are stabilized.

Primary health care professionals can also be responsible for monitoring chronic gamblers and recommending more intensive interventions when necessary. Furthermore, when medications are indicated, the primary care physician may be the most appropriate professional to encourage medication compliance.

While controversial, this proposal may help with early detection of gambling problems. Moreover, it may assist the chronic gambler in remaining motivated to stay in treatment.

CONCLUSION

Our overall observation is that gamblers are, in general, very clever people with very complex problems. Gamblers want to know as much as they can about their addiction. They are people who are oriented toward the odds. The therapist must respect the intellect of the gambler and use their curiosity in a creative and affirming fashion. This may result in the most important innovation in treating gambling disorders during the past few years, that of making the gambler a therapeutic ally in the treatment of his or her own disorder.

Research on gambling disorders needs to be addressed from all perspectives by a variety of orientations and theories. Research is needed from the sociological and economic specialties, social and clinical psychology, personality theory, and neuropharmacology. What is most needed at this phase is a commitment to broad-based psychosocial and medical research that allows clinicians to enhance methods that are already assumed to possess therapeutic possibilities.

This chapter opened with the frank admission that we know too little about the effectiveness of treating gambling-related disorders. This remains true; and as gambling opportunities spread throughout society, this lack of knowledge is likely to become more problematic. A concerted effort by government, the academic community, and legitimate gambling venues, with an impetus provided by the public, will help unravel the most effective treatment strategies for problem gambling behaviors. My hope is that in the next edition of this book, basic empirical questions concerning the treatment of gambling can be answered by empirical data. Until then, the clinician will remain challenged in trying to provide the best possible odds for his or her clients.

RECOMMENDED READING

BOOKS

Anonymous (1994). *Gamblers Anonymous.* This is an essential recovery tool for compulsive gamblers. Comparable to the *Big Book* in Alcoholics Anonymous, the section "A Day at a Time" offers hope, support, and guidance throughout the year, which many people in recovery consider essential.

Ciorrochi, J. (2001). *Counseling problem gamblers and their families: A self-regulation manual for individual and family therapy.* This is a very readable textbook that offers a novel approach to the treatment of gambling disorders.

Fedderman, E., Drebing, C., & Krebs, C. (2000). *Don't leave it to chance: A guide for families of problem gamblers.* This is an excellent cognitive behavioral guide for clients, families, and therapists in training.

WEB SITES

www.gamblersanonymous.org. This is the official site of Gamblers Anonymous. It explains how the international group provides support and recovery tools. It is an excellent overall resource.

www.ncpgambling.org. This is the official site of the National Counsel on Problem Gambling. This group seeks to increase public awareness of pathological gambling and promote treatment programs. It provides a service where potential clients can find a counselor online or receive additional information.

www.hms.harvard.edu/dua. Harvard Medical School, Division on Addictions offers timely research topics concerning gambling, as well as other addictions. They also publish the online interdisciplinary journal the *Wager*, dedicated to a multidisciplinary understanding of problem gambling. Under the leadership of Howard Schaffer, MD, they have become one of the premiere research and clinical institutions. They also offer an empirically validated prevention program for young people.

www.mayoclinic.com/findinformation/diseasesandconditions. This site, run by the Mayo Clinic, presents a guide of comprehensive resource on gambling addiction covering its signs and symptoms, causes, and risk factors, especially useful in its discussion of complications associated with problem gambling. It is a must for family members.

REFERENCES

American Psychiatric Association. (2000). *Diagnostic and statistical manual of mental disorders* (4th ed., text rev.). Washington, DC: Author.

Bütz, M., Chamberlain, L., & McCown, W. (1996). *Strange attractors: Chaos, complexity, and the art of family therapy.* New York: Wiley.

Castellani, B. (2000). *Pathological gambling: The making of a medical problem.* Albany: State University of New York Press.

Ciarrocchi, J. (2001). *Counseling problem gamblers and their families: A self-regulation manual for individual and family therapy.* New York: Academic Press.

Cooper, J., Bloom, F., & Roth, R. (2002). *The biological basis of neuropharmacology* (8th ed.). Oxford, England: Oxford University Press.

Custer, R., & Milt, H. (1985). *When luck runs out: Help for compulsive gamblers and their families.* Washington, DC: Facts on File.

Estes, K., & Brubaker, M. (1994). *Deadly odds: Recovery from compulsive gambling.* New York: Fireside.

Johnson, J., & McCown, W. (1997). *Family therapy of neurobehavioral disorders.* New York: Haworth.

Keiser, R., & McCown, W. (2000). Personality characteristics of professionals who abuse addictive substances. *Abstracts of the Annual Spring Scientific Conference, Society for Personality Assessment.* [Abstract], 34.

McCown, W., & Chamberlain, L. (2000). *Best possible odds: Innovative theory and treatment of gambling disorders.* New York: Wiley.

McCown, W., & Chamberlain, L. (2005). *Gambling disorders: Experimental and empirical research.* Victoria, British Columbia, Canada: Trafford.

McCown, W., & Johnson, J. (1993). *Therapy with treatment resistant families: A consultation/crisis intervention approach.* New York: Haworth.

McCown, W., & Keiser, R. (2004). *Addiction, fantasy, and perception: The use of projective testing in the assessment, treatment planning, and understanding of addictive disorders.* Mahwah, NJ: Erlbaum.

McMullan, R. (2000). *The new handbook of cognitive therapy techniques.* New York: Norton.

Stout, T. (1999). *Attribution comparisons of gambling clients following a relapse and their counselors' responses.* Unpublished manuscript, University of Louisiana at Monroe.

Sylvain, C., Ladoucuer, R., & Biksvert, J. (1997). Cognitive and behavioral treatment of pathological gambling: A controlled study. *Journal of Consulting and Clinical Psychology, 65,* 727–732.

PART IV

SEX ADDICTION

CHAPTER 7

Understanding and Diagnosing Sex Addiction

JENNIFER P. SCHNEIDER

DIAGNOSIS AND TREATMENT of psychosexual disorders have traditionally focused on problems caused by *decreases* in sexual desire or an inability to carry out the sexual act (hyposexuality), or on *abnormalities* in the person's sexual desire (paraphilias). Yet, as an addiction counselor you are undoubtedly aware of the increasing public attention and professional perplexity about sexual problems that appear to result from *uncontrolled* or *excessive* sexual behaviors (hypersexuality) . You have no doubt read newspaper accounts or seen TV reports about:

- Sexual harassment in the workplace.
- Sexual misconduct or misbehavior by clergy, health professionals, and public figures.
- The increasing use of sex on the Internet, sometimes leading to loss of jobs and even to life.
- The contribution of high-risk sexual behavior to the HIV epidemic.

Because these sexual behaviors are not inherently abnormal (i.e., they are non-paraphilic), they have been addressed punitively rather than clinically, with the result that the behavior often continues. You have surely seen clients who not only are addicted to more than one drug but who also have both drug addictions and compulsive behaviors. A failure to address these concurrent problems is a common cause of chemical dependency relapse. Chapters 7 and 8 describe the recognition, assessment, and treatment of excessive sexual urges and behaviors. These are often best viewed as behavioral addictions.

You may be asking, "How can a behavior be an addiction?" I remember asking the same question 20 years ago, as a young internal medicine physician, when I came across the following letter in a Dear Abby column:

I do not know what is the matter with me. I am a 25-year-old, respectable, unmarried, churchgoing woman. I have many good friends and have never had trouble getting dates. My problem: If I am physically attracted to a man, I will go to bed with him the first minute he wants to. . . . Sex for me is an addiction, like alcohol or gambling. I cannot seem to control it. Is there help for me?

Abby replied:

In 1979, a small group of men and women who realized that their lives were out of control because of their addiction to sex formed an organization they named Sexaholics Anonymous based on the 12 Steps of Alcoholics Anonymous. They are people who admit their lives have become unmanageable because of their compulsive sexual behavior. . . . For information, write to SA. . . . ("Decent woman," 1983)

This concept was new to me then, but in the intervening 20 years, as an addiction medicine specialist, I have come to know many sexually addicted men and women and have seen first hand that they have the same disease as people who are addicted to drugs or to gambling and other behaviors. I have also seen these people recover by following Abby's advice to attend 12-Step meetings. Today, fortunately, many counselors are familiar with behavioral addictions and can hasten recovery. The following sections clarify the reasons for understanding excessive sexual behaviors as addictive disorders.

UNDERSTANDING EXCESSIVE SEXUAL BEHAVIORS AS ADDICTIVE DISORDERS

Although the term *sexual addiction*—or any type of addiction for that matter—does not appear in the *Diagnostic and Statistical Manual of Mental Disorders*, fourth edition (*DSM-IV*; American Psychiatric Association [APA], 1994) you can extrapolate a framework for the use of the term from the *DSM-IV*'s diagnostic criteria for substance dependence. According to the *Manual* (p. 181) 3 of 7 criteria must be met for a diagnosis of substance dependence. If the term *sexual fantasy, sexual urge,* or *sexual behavior* is substituted for *substance use,* the same diagnostic criteria can be used to define addictive sexual disorders. Two of the 7 criteria for substance dependence (tolerance and withdrawal) describe physical dependence. In the category of "substance dependence without physiologic dependence," 2 of the 5 criteria refer to decreased control, 1 of obsession with obtaining and using the substance, and 2 of continued use despite negative consequences. These 5 criteria all refer to *behaviors,* and, thus, you can logically apply them to behaviors such as sex or gambling (see Part III in this volume).

Any behavior can be viewed as an addiction if it is characterized by:

- Loss of control.
- Continuation despite significant adverse consequences.
- Obsession or preoccupation.

Any sexual behavior can be taken to excess or used addictively, including otherwise healthy activities, such as masturbation or sexual intercourse. The crucial issue is not the *frequency* of the sexual behavior, but rather the *consequences* of the sexual behavior to the person's health, relationships, career, or legal status. When explaining this to clients, a good one-word summary is *unmanageability*. An addictive disorder eventually creates unmanageability in the person's life.

An attractive 47-year-old man who had had multiple affairs that eventually cost him two marriages, recalled:

> I never thought of myself as one of those one-night-stand kind of guys. I prided myself on getting to know the people I slept with. I conned myself that the latest affair was really the last one. In reality, what I found was that once I had sex with her, she lost that mysterious quality and I began to get restless.
>
> I had a set of rules regarding my playing around. At first I had affairs only on business trips out of town. I had vowed not to have an affair in my own city, certainly not with someone at work or in my own social circle. And I set myself a minimum age limit for the women I would come on to. But I broke each of those rules as I began to take more and more risks. Soon being seen in public places with other women didn't seem so dangerous—I somehow thought that my wife would not find out. Then, I began having girlfriends visit me at work even though my coworkers knew my wife. I finally realized how out of control I was when I made a play for the 18-year-old daughter of one of my friends. After being confronted by my friend, I realized I needed help. (J. P. Schneider, 1988, p. 80)

PREVALENCE OF SEXUAL ADDICTION

Sex addiction is common in the American population. Although no formal population studies have yet been done, its prevalence has been estimated to be approximately 6% (Carnes, personal communication). There is no information yet on the prevalence on sex addiction in other cultures. Because the definition of sex addiction depends on consequences, the particular array of addictive behaviors may differ in different cultures. For example, it is socially acceptable in some cultures for married men to have multiple affairs, so that adverse consequences may be fewer. Nonetheless, although sex addiction may be expressed as different behaviors in different cultures, sex addiction itself is likely to be found in many parts of the world.

In a recent study of sexual compulsivity in 294 HIV-positive men and women, 16.6% of them scored high on a standardized sexual compulsivity measure (Benotsch, Kalichman, & Pinkerton, 2001). This prevalence is at least threefold greater than in the general population. Additionally, 33% of the sexually compulsive group had used cocaine in the previous 3 months, compared with about 10% of the noncompulsive group. There were no significant differences between the two groups in the recent use of alcohol or marijuana. The authors suggest that sexual compulsivity may be a potent risk factor for transmission of HIV disease and that traditional HIV risk-reduction interventions will likely be ineffective for this group, who need treatment for their sexual compulsivity as well.

COEXISTING ADDICTIONS

A few years ago, I knew a young physician who was found drunk in his house one morning by a colleague when he didn't show up for work. He had already been through inpatient treatment for alcoholism and had just passed his sixth birthday of sobriety from alcohol. Here's how he explained the relapse to me:

My real problem isn't alcohol—it's my sex addiction. I've been feeling so bad about what I was doing sexually [having frequent anonymous sex in parks with unknown men, a part of his life he'd kept hidden from his friends and family] that I started drinking to feel better. If I could get that part of my life straightened out, I know I'd have no trouble staying away from alcohol.

This time he was sent to a treatment program that assessed and treated his sexual problem as well as his drinking problem. After this he was able to sustain long-term recovery from both addictions.

Addictive disorders tend to coexist. You may already have noticed that alcoholics are more likely to be smokers than are nonalcoholics. Las Vegas hotels that attract gamblers have learned that it pays to offer them inexpensive food and plentiful alcoholic drinks. Studies show that sex addiction is more prevalent among those with other addictions than in the general population. Conversely, other addictions are often found among sex addicts. In a study of cocaine addicts entering an outpatient treatment program, 70% were also engaging in compulsive sex (Washton, 1989).

A 44-year-old businessman reported:

Cocaine was a lure to get a woman to come back to my apartment with me. Once there, we would get a little high, and I knew she would probably have sex with me. But later on, it got to be where I couldn't have sex without it. I remember once being with a woman I was very attracted to, and we went to the bedroom to have sex. I was really excited. But as soon as we started to make love, I realized my coke was in the living room. I jumped out of bed to get it. Coke was more important than sex. But after I did a couple more lines, I couldn't get an erection. (B. H. Schneider, 1992, p. 6)

Edlin et al. (1992) compared the sexual behaviors of over 500 young street women less than 30 years old, 55% of whom were current regular crack cocaine smokers, whereas the others had never smoked crack. They found that 70.5% of the crack smokers had sold sex, versus 4.3% of the nonsmokers; 37% of the crack-smoking women had had more than 100 lifetime sex partners, versus 3% of the nonsmokers. It is likely that many of the crack cocaine-addicted women were also sexually compulsive.

During a 4-year period in one addiction facility that specialized in treating patients who had relapsed, approximately 33% of the chemically dependent non-physicians and 25% of the chemically dependent physicians were also found to be sexually compulsive (Gordon, Fargason, & Kramer, 1995).

In a survey of 289 persons admitted for inpatient treatment of sex addiction (Carnes, 1991), fewer than 17% reported that sex was their only addiction. Coexisting addictions and compulsions are shown in Table 7.1.

Similar results were obtained in an anonymous survey of 75 recovering sex addicts who were not in inpatient treatment (J. P. Schneider & Schneider, 1991). In a group of health professionals assessed for sexual impropriety, those who were diagnosed with addictive sexual disorders were almost twice as likely to have concurrent chemical dependence (38%) than those who were not sexually addicted (21%; Irons & Schneider, 1994).

These studies suggest that in the presence of concurrent drug and sexual dependence, relapse or failure to treat one of the addictions is likely to lead to relapse to the other.

Table 7.1
Concurrent Addictions
Reported by Inpatient Sex Addicts

Addiction	Percentage
Chemical dependency	42
Eating disorder	38
Compulsive working	28
Compulsive spending	26
Compulsive gambling	5

VALUE OF THE ADDICTION MODEL

When people read about some famous person who self-destructs (or nearly so) because of his sexual conduct, they shake their heads in confusion. Why did he take those risks when he had so much at stake? The addiction paradigm gives a new way of understanding some previously inexplicable behaviors and leads to a different treatment model for compulsive sexual behaviors, which will be described in Chapter 8. The addiction model is useful for anyone whose sexual behavior is out of control but is particularly useful in the following situations:

- Clients who have been unable to stop their behaviors despite insight-oriented and other treatment efforts.
- Clients whose behavior is sufficiently risky that stopping the behavior must be the immediate top priority. Examples are:
  —Repeated unprotected sexual encounters where there is risk of transmitting or becoming infected with the HIV virus.
  —A pattern of sexual exploitation by professionals of vulnerable persons, such as medical patients, counseling clients, and parishioners.
- Immediate risk of job loss because of having been warned about the behavior.
- Engaging in illegal sexual behaviors that are likely to lead to arrest.
- Risk of loss of the primary relationship because of continuation of the sexual behaviors.
- Clients with chemical dependency who have relapsed to drug use and are found to have a coexisting compulsive sexual disorder.

An addiction psychiatrist learned about the nature of addiction from his own experiences. In childhood, he was sexually abused by his father. At age 12, when an 18-year-old neighbor introduced him to pictures of nude women, "I had found my 'drug'; I felt excited and energized as never before." In college, his pornography collection became famous in the dorm. Although money was tight, he spent large sums on porno magazines. After getting married while in medical school, his addiction escalated to multiple affairs as well as many hours masturbating. He recalled:

I had sex at my place of work, out of town at conferences, and spent thousands of dollars on pornography and other women. Work was something I did between escapades. By the time I entered my sexual addiction recovery program, my life was completely out of control. My wife had thrown me out after confronting me for the third time about my sexual acting out with other women. My work life was reduced to a zombie-like automatic task in which there was no pleasure. Couples therapy, psychiatric consultation, and church had not helped one bit to reduce my sexual acting out. The irony was that I was a psychiatrist who treated addictions, but to me that meant only chemical dependency; I was totally unaware that I suffered from an addiction myself. . . .

When I am out of town and there is no sexual addiction fellowship meeting, I am most comfortable in an AA or NA meeting. Our stories are similar. AA and NA members are often amazed by the similarities after hearing my story. Their initial response of course is one of disbelief about how I could suffer from an addiction to sex. Many of them have discovered their own cross addiction in the sexual area. (J. P. Schneider, 1994)

HEALTHY SEX VERSUS ADDICTIVE SEXUAL BEHAVIORS

As mentioned previously, the *DSM-IV* considers certain sexual behaviors to be psychosexual disorders (e.g., voyeurism, exhibitionism, or frotteurism [touching others for sexual gratification without their permission]), whereas others are considered psychologically normal (e.g., sex with multiple partners or masturbation). However, a person can carry out even normal sexual activities in relatively healthy or unhealthy ways. A sexual behavior can be considered healthy if the person doing it answers "Yes" to the following questions, which were posed by Hunter (1992):

- Does the behavior agree with the person's values?
- Is it safe?
- Is it respectful of self and others?
- Is it honest?
- Is it spontaneous and playful?
- Does it increase intimacy?
- Are both partners free to choose?

Carnes (1991) contrasted addictive and healthy sexuality. When you work with clients who have difficulty recognizing that their sexual behaviors are unhealthy despite significant adverse consequences, you might find it helpful to review questions in the previous list and the comparisons in Table 7.2.

CHARACTERISTICS OF SEX ADDICTION

In his original work on sex addiction, Carnes (1983) proposed three levels of sexually addictive behaviors. These are:

1. *Level One:* Behaviors regarded as normal, acceptable, or tolerable (e.g., masturbation, viewing pornography, prostitution, or multiple affairs).
2. *Level Two:* Illegal behaviors that are clearly victimizing and are regarded as nuisance crimes (e.g., exhibitionism, voyeurism, or obscene telephone calls).
3. *Level Three:* Illegal behaviors that have grave consequences for the victim and severe legal consequences for the offender (e.g., rape, incest, or child molestation).

Table 7.2
Comparison of Addictive and Healthy Sex

Addictive Sex	Healthy Sex
Feels shameful.	Adds to self-esteem.
Is illicit, exploitative.	Has no victims.
Compromises values.	Deepens meaning.
Draws on fear for excitement.	Uses vulnerability for excitement.
Reenacts childhood abuse.	Cultivates sense of being adult.
Disconnects one from oneself.	Furthers sense of self.
Creates world of unreality.	Expands reality.
Is self-destructive and dangerous.	Relies on safety.
Uses conquest or power.	Is mutual and intimate.
Is seductive.	Takes responsibility for needs.
Serves to medicate and kill pain.	May bring legitimate suffering.
Is dishonest.	Originates in integrity.
Becomes routine.	Presents challenges.
Requires double life.	Integrates most authentic parts of self.
Is grim and joyless.	Is fun and playful.
Demands perfection.	Accepts the imperfect.

Source: From *Don't Call It Love*, by P. Carnes, 1991, New York: Bantam Books. Reprinted with permission.

Addictive disorders tend to progress, meaning that with time the addict needs more to get the same effect. However, this does *not* mean that addicts are likely to progress from Level One to Level Two or Three. Sex addicts are more likely to intensify their preferred activity rather than switch to an unrelated one. For example, a sex addict who has multiple affairs is more likely over time to have more affairs and to take greater risks of discovery and is less likely to begin to make obscene phone calls or engage in rape.

Addicts who are compulsive at Level Three usually are also compulsive at Levels Two and One; Level Two addiction is generally accompanied by addictive behaviors at Level One as well. Although one specific behavior type may precipitate the crisis that brings a sexual addict to intervention, experience has shown that when a thorough sexual history is taken, an average of three compulsive sexual behaviors is found. Sexual behaviors tend to be used addictively in various patterns. For example, a voyeur is likely also to view pornography and to masturbate compulsively. The lesson here is that when assessing a person who has come to grief because of one particular behavior, it is crucial to obtain a thorough sexual history to identify all compulsive behaviors in which the person engages.

Based on an extensive survey of nearly 1,000 patients (81% male, 19% female) admitted for inpatient treatment of addictive sexual disorders, Carnes (1991) identified 10 patterns, each of which has a specific sexual focus with common characteristics. The 10 patterns and some examples of each (adapted from Carnes & Schneider, 2000) are listed in Box 7.1.

BOX 7.1
Addictive Sexual Behavior Patterns

- *Fantasy sex (an obsessive sexual fantasy life):* Arousal depends on sexual possibility. Neglecting responsibilities to engage in fantasy and/or prepare for the next sexual episode is common among fantasy sex addicts (e.g., reading romance novels, spending much time on computer e-mails and chat rooms, or corresponding on romantic or sexual themes), and is often associated with masturbation.

  Example: Alan, a 36-year-old divorced man, said, "Fantasy was my first drink. I would see an ad for scanty underwear in a magazine and I would drink in the image. Then, when I was alone and in need of comfort, I would replay in my mind, over and over, the image of that girl in the ad. Masturbation just fueled the flame, and next thing I'd be on the phone calling a girl to set up a lunch date. I would then fantasize about what we might say to each other and how we might end up in bed" (Schneider, 1988, p. 79).

- *Seductive role sex (seductive behavior for conquest):* Arousal depends on conquest and diminishes rapidly after initial contact. Arousal can be heightened by increasing risk and/or number of partners. Much time spent on making yet another conquest (e.g., multiple relationships, affairs, or flirtation).

- *Voyeuristic sex (visual arousal):* The use of visual stimulation to escape into an obsessive trance. Arousal may be heightened by masturbation, or risk, such as peeping (e.g., pornography, window peeping, secret observation with cameras or telescopes), which is associated with excessive masturbation, even to the point of injury.

- *Exhibitionistic sex (attracting attention to body or sexual parts of the body):* Sexual arousal stems from reaction of viewer shock or interest (e.g., exposing oneself in public or from home or car or wearing clothes designed to expose).

  Example: Janelle, a 28-year-old single woman, lived in a first-floor apartment that had a large picture window in the living room. She would deliberately undress seductively in front of the picture window and felt powerful and in control as she repeatedly was able to make a man stop in his tracks and look at her beautiful body.

  Ironically, one evening her doorbell rang. It was a policeman, who said to her, "Ma'am, we've caught a peeping Tom outside your window." Undoubtedly some innocent bystander was being labeled a voyeur, whereas the real miscreant was the woman who was an exhibitionist.

- *Anonymous sex (high-risk sex with unknown persons):* Arousal involves no seduction or cost and is immediate. The arousal has no entanglements or obligations and is often accelerated by unsafe or high-risk environments (e.g., one-night stands or sex with strangers in restrooms, beaches, bars, or parks).

- *Paying for sex (purchase of sexual services):* Arousal is connected to payment for sex and, with time, arousal becomes connected to money itself (e.g., prostitutes, phone sex, or Internet sites).

- *Trading sex (selling or bartering sex for power):* Arousal is based on gaining control of others by using sex as leverage (e.g., being a sex worker).

- *Intrusive sex (boundary violation without discovery)*: Sexual arousal occurs by violating boundaries with no repercussions (e.g., touching others without permission [frotteurism]).

    Example: Every young woman who frequently uses public transportation is likely to be the victim of a frotteur. When I (JPS) was a teenager, I traveled on the New York City subway daily to get to and from an after-school job. On several occasions when the train was crowded, I felt a hand running along my body. The first few times I tried to wiggle away, but on a crowded train that is often not possible. More effective was to shout loudly, "Get your hands off me!" That usually resulted in several pairs of hands immediately rising upwards where they could seen by others (and, by presumption, couldn't possibly be guilty of feeling up another passenger).

- *Pain exchange (causing or receiving pain or humiliation to enhance sexual pleasure)*: Arousal is built around specific scenarios or narratives of humiliation and shame. It is associated with use of animals.

- *Exploitative sex (exploitation of the vulnerable. Arousal is based on particular targets of vulnerability)*: Such a use of force or partner vulnerability to gain sexual access (e.g., using professional position of power, physician, psychologist, priest, or teacher, for sex or child molestation, incest, or rape).

GENDER DIFFERENCES

Carnes and colleagues (Carnes, Nonemaker, & Skilling, 1991) observed significant gender differences in the prevalence of these behavior patterns. Men tended to prefer activities that objectified their sexual partners and required a minimum of emotional involvement, including voyeuristic sex, paying for sex, and anonymous or exploitative sex. Women have a relatively higher prevalence of behaviors that distort power—either gaining control over others or being a victim including fantasy, seductive role, or trading sex and pain exchange. Women sex addicts use sex for power, control, and attention, as Kasl (1989) had earlier observed.

A women's workshop participant who likened herself to the title role of the film *The General's Daughter* declared:

> I'll lie in wait like a snake in the grass and watch for my victim. Or if I'm in a particularly vicious mood, I'll slither around until I find someone. I'm not interested in an affair like some of you girls. I get off on knowing that this time, I'm in control. I have the power. If anybody gets hurt this time, it for sure won't be me. (Ferree, 2001, p. 295)

Based on her work with women sex addicts, Ferree (2001) writes of six myths about such women. They are:

1. Females are not sexually addicted.
2. Even the females who might be addicted are only relationship or love addicts, not sex addicts.
3. The motivation of females who act out is neediness.

4. Females' presenting problems can be taken at face value.
5. The life consequences of addiction are the same for men and women.
6. The same diagnostic questions are employed with women and men.

In addition to the usual work and relationship consequences of excessive sexual behavior that men experience, women have the added problems of unwanted pregnancies and sexually transmitted diseases. Among women who attended Ferree's workshops, 25% to 50% had at least one abortion because of an unplanned pregnancy that resulted from their addictive behavior. She suggests that when assessing women, some questions should be asked using different language from that used for men. For example, instead of asking "Do you engage in anonymous sex?" a better inquiry would be, "Are you sexual with someone you've just met?" Rather than ask about cruising, inquire about bar hopping and flirting.

HOMOSEXUAL SEX ADDICTS

In the United States and other Western countries, most prehomosexual children and adolescents conceal their same-sex feelings because these feelings are not acceptable by many heterosexuals. These young people feel great shame about an important part of who they are. The typical addict characteristics of isolation, poor self-concept, secrecy, and compartmentalization may have more firmly established developmental roots in the gay male sexual addict population (Weiss, 1997). Turning to drugs, alcohol, and sex is one way to medicate the shame. There is a significantly higher prevalence of substance abuse in the homosexual population than in the general population, 30% versus 10% to 12% according to one study (Cabaj, 1992). It is likely that gay men also have a higher prevalence of addictive sexual disorders. In addition to the increased shame, a second reason is that for many within the urban gay community public social activity remains tied, in large extent, to the use of alcohol and the seeking of sex and/or romance, an outlook that nourishes chemical and sexual addiction (Weiss, 1997). It was only in the 1980s, with the arrival of the HIV epidemic, that some gay men found they had great difficulty stopping their pattern of multiple unsafe sexual encounters.

CONSEQUENCES OF SEX ADDICTION

Addiction counselors who are well aware of the diverse consequences of drug dependence may nonetheless be less familiar with the adverse effects of sex addiction. Table 7.3 contains a partial list of consequences, which are described in greater detail by Carnes and Schneider (2000).

PROFESSIONAL SEXUAL EXPLOITATION

Professional sexual exploitation is the abuse of power and professional position to further the sexual agenda of the person with greater power. Examples of professionals with greater power are physicians, psychotherapists, dentists, and priests and other clergypersons. (When employers use their position of power to obtain sexual gratification with employees, this is termed *sexual harassment*.) Some of the behaviors are "consensual" sexual intercourse, molestation, inappropriate touching, voyeurism, or exhibitionism. What makes this behavior by professionals so

Table 7.3
Consequences of Addictive Sexual Behaviors

A. Physical consequences
1. Acquisition of HIV and other sexually transmitted diseases (when the addict has had unprotected sex with others). Compulsive sex is often unsafe sex. Sex addicts in the midst of their rituals (regular methods of preparing for sexual activity to take place) are in an altered state of mind, focused on gratifying their urges. In this state, they are on automatic pilot and often do not even think about safe versus unsafe sex.
2. Unplanned pregnancies and complications of abortions.
3. Rape and/or physical abuse.
4. Physical injuries to genitals, breasts, colon, and so on.
5. Motor vehicle accidents (while preoccupied with sexual thoughts or activities).
6. Unnecessary surgeries to enhance appearance (especially true for women sex addicts).
7. Abuse of drugs reputed to be sexual performance enhancers or facilitators of sexual activity (amyl nitrite, butyl nitrite, sildanefil [Viagra], flunitrazepam [Rohypnol]).

B. Psychological and emotional consequences
1. Shame and guilt, especially if there is public exposure.
2. Depression.
3. Anxiety.
4. Fear of being discovered.
5. Posttraumatic stress disorders.
6. Divorce or marital discord.
7. Difficulty maintaining sobriety from drug dependence and other addictions.

C. Financial, legal, and employment consequences
1. Job loss as a result of poor work performance and/or acting out on the job.
2. Arrests as a result of illegal sexual activities.
3. Financial costs of legal defense, psychotherapy, job loss, and money spent on the addiction.

---

egregious is that the patient, client, or parishioner believes that the person with power is acting at all times in their best interest. When they are taken advantage of sexually, it feels like a significant betrayal by someone they trust. The relationship between the professional and the person with lesser power is analogous in many ways to a parent-child relationship (Irons & Schneider, 1999) and the betrayal may feel like incest.

Even when the patient, client, or parishioner initially believes that the sexual relationship with the professional is consensual, often they later feel exploited and betrayed. In many states, a sexual relationship between physician and patient, or psychotherapist and client, is considered a felony and the professional is subject to arrest. The licensing boards of several helping professions consider such a relationship to be a reason to revoke the professional's license.

Clergy sexual misconduct has been subject to increasing attention in the past few years. You can hardly read a newspaper without coming across another story about a priest who has been charged with, or has acknowledged, some inappropriate sexual activity. A good review of this subject was written by McCall (2002). In

2002, under a new policy of zero tolerance, Catholic priests who had molested parishioners in the past were removed from their positions and no longer allowed to practice their profession. Later in the same year, Cardinal Richard Law, head of the Boston diocese, was forced to resign his position amidst evidence that over many years he had participated in cover-ups of sexual abuse by priests. The biggest outcry was over the finding that many of these priests were repeat offenders; but, rather than being removed from contact with their target victims, their superiors shuffled them from one parish to another, where they continued their sexual exploitation, often of minor children.

Irons and Schneider (1994) reported the results of an intensive, multidisciplinary assessment of 137 health care professionals, 85% of whom were physicians, referred primarily by state licensing bodies because of allegations of professional sexual impropriety. The most common diagnosis was an addictive sexual disorder. Of the 137 (97% male), 54% had an addictive sexual disorder, and 30% were chemically dependent. Those who were sexually addicted were almost twice as likely to have a concurrent chemical dependence (38%) than did those who were not (21%). The remaining professionals were diagnosed with an adjustment disorder related to some life crisis or with a personality disorder or other psychiatric disorder. A few had simply not had adequate education about appropriate professional boundaries.

The standard way of disciplining sexually exploitative professionals is no longer to simply suspend their license, fine them, and suggest psychotherapy—as used to be the case. It appears that about half of sexually exploitative professionals have an addictive sexual disorder, many of these with concurrent chemical dependence. Addictive disorders are chronic diseases with a tendency to relapse. The addicted professional needs addiction treatment, ongoing relapse prevention strategies, and monitoring if he or she returns to work. When allegations of professional sexual impropriety are made, it is essential for the professional to undergo intensive evaluation so that appropriate treatment will be forthcoming.

CYBERSEX

By February, 2002, more than half of all Americans were using the Internet, with more than two million going online for the first time each month. Nine out of 10 school-age children had access to computers, either at home or at school ("Internet Use," 2002). The explosion of Internet availability in the past decade has changed the way sex addiction is played out. Cybersex is any form of sexual expression that is accessed through the computer. Cybersex is widely accessible, inexpensive, legal, available in the privacy of one's home, apparently anonymous, and does not put the user at direct risk of contracting sexually transmitted diseases. It is also ideal for hiding the activities from the spouse or significant other because it does not leave obvious evidence of the sexual encounter. Most people who access the computer for sex are *recreational users,* analogous to recreational drinkers or gamblers, but a significant proportion (6%) have preexisting sexual compulsions that are now finding a new outlet. In an additional 9%, cybersex is the first expression of an addictive sexual disorder (Cooper, Delmonico, & Burg, 2000). Cybersex is to sex addiction what crack cocaine has been to cocaine addiction—easy to obtain, rapidly progressive, and traps people who did not have a significant addictive problem before they found this new source of pleasure.

Pornography addicts now view pictures on the Internet, in the privacy of their own home, rather than in movie theaters or on rented videotapes. They can easily download and save thousands of porno images of every possible type. People can also spend hours in sexually oriented chat rooms, having real-time sexual conversations with each other, often while masturbating and describing what they are doing. Advances in technology now enable people to have sex via the computer which can include everything except skin-to-skin contact. Using digital cameras mounted on the computers, someone can have real-time sex with a stranger. They can transmit and receive photos of each other while typing with one hand and touching themselves with the other.

In a survey of male and female sex addicts (J. P. Schneider, 2000b), a significantly higher proportion of men than women reported downloading pornography as a preferred activity. Women tended to prefer sex within the context of a relationship or at least e-mail or chat room interactions rather than accessing images. However, several women did enjoy pornography, and two women with no prior history of interest in sadomasochistic sex discovered this activity online and came to prefer it.

Although a similar proportion of cybersex-addicted men (27%) and women (30%) engaged in real-time online sex with another person, significantly more women than men (80% versus 33.3%) stated that their online sexual activities led to real-life sexual encounters. Women are more likely than men to seek romance rather than just sex on the Internet. Some women spend many hours at the computer chatting with an idealized partner and also many additional hours fantasizing about him. Believing they are in love, these are the women who will risk their marriage or primary relationship by flying to a distant city to meet the stranger they believe they already know intimately.

Consequences of Cybersex Addiction   In their large-scale study of cybersex users, Cooper and colleagues (Cooper, Putnam, Planchon, & Boies, 1999) defined problem cybersex users as those who spend at least 11 hours per week on computer sex. However, cybersex addicts usually report engaging in sexual activities on the Internet for several hours per day. When this is done in the home, it is often in the evening, at night, and on weekends. As with all types of computer addiction, the time element alone results in adverse consequences, especially loss of time with partner and children. Also, heavy cybersex users, like other Internet addicts, give up other activities and friends to spend time on the Internet. They become very isolated, spending most of their time sitting alone in a room staring at a computer screen. They may sacrifice sleep for the computer, resulting in poor job performance.

In addition to the time consequences, there are specific problems resulting from the sexual content of the addiction, which are summarized next (J. P. Schneider & Weiss, 2001).

LOSS OF INTEREST IN SEXUAL ACTIVITIES WITH THE PRIMARY PARTNER   Pornographic images are often more exciting and more attractive than one's usual sexual partner. In chat rooms, people can pretend they are younger and more attractive than they really are and are willing to engage in, or talk about, sexual activities they would never actually do in real life. Sex with the primary partner may come to seem boring. Male sex addicts may be physically unable to have more sex after a session on the computer.

A survey of partners of cybersex addicts found that among 68% of the couples, one or both had lost interest in relational sex: 51% of addicts had decreased interest in sex with their spouse, as did 34% of partners (J. P. Schneider, 2000a).

A 33-year-old woman, married one year, became aware that her husband was online in sex chat rooms, porno sites, and was exchanging nude pictures with others. She related:

> Because of the things he looks at and what he chats about to others, our sex life has become almost nonexistent. Because of his fantasy world, reality is very boring to him. The normal, romantic things that couples do for each other do not interest him. He is much more satisfied with masturbating alone. Like a drug addict, the more you subject yourself to, the more you need each time to satisfy your craving. We are now at the point that I am completely unable to compete with what he's involved with. It sickens me to see what he is looking at or searching for, and I am now indifferent to our sex life. (J. P. Schneider, 2000a, p. 125)

A 31-year-old woman, married 3 years, reported:

> The kinky and perverted behaviors shown all over the Internet fuel his beliefs and give him ammunition to say that I am the "weird one" for not wanting anal sex. "See all of the women out there on the Internet who are just crazy about it." (J. P. Schneider, 2001, p. 127)

NORMALIZATION OF ILLEGAL OR DEVIANT SEXUAL ACTIVITIES   The Internet has chat rooms and support groups for every type of sexual activity imaginable. Users who never would have carried out unusual sexual thoughts find others who support and encourage these activities, including sex with children and various fetishes. Men who had never had sex with children, some of whom had never even fantasized about this before encountering it on the Internet, have gotten arrested in child porn stings. Other people become so comfortable with deviant sex on the computer that regular sex loses all its appeal for them, and they may ask their primary partner to participate in such activities. Usually they receive a very negative reaction.

A 30-year-old man with a previous history of preoccupation with sex and masturbation with pornography, explained what happened when he got on the Internet (J. P. Schneider, 2000b):

> In the last couple of years, the more porn I've viewed, the less sensitive I am to certain porn that I used to find offensive. Now I get turned on by some of it (anal sex, women urinating, etc.). The sheer quantity of porn on the Internet has done this. It's so easy to click on certain things out of curiosity in the privacy of your home, and the more you see them, the less sensitized you are. I used to only be into soft-core porn showing the beauty of the female form. Now I'm into explicit hardcore.

A 36-year-old woman with no reported history of compulsive sexual behaviors is now about to separate from her husband. She explains why:

> After venturing into computer chat rooms, one day I stumbled into my first BDSM [bondage and discipline, sadomasochism] room. Amazing! I learned about D/s

[dominance and submission] and I studied it. I binged there. I have become a presence in the BDSM community. My focus has been on D/s. I was molested by a pedophile as a child. It's interesting that I would see myself as a sub [submissive] and not a domme [dominant]. . . . In retrospect, my life was so damn normal, straight, vanilla. Now I have a Dom.

She is considering meeting her Dom face-to-face. Despite her husband's request for a separation, she is not ready to stop her online sexual activities or leave the BDSM community she now feels a part of. Her priorities have shifted so that these activities are more important to her than her marriage.

DECREASED WORK PRODUCTIVITY, OR LOSS OF JOB (SOMETIMES WITH PUBLIC SHAME) Most large companies have policies against use of company computers for sex. Some of them forbid *any* personal use of the computer, but they tend to be particularly punitive when the computer is used for sex. Some users spend hours on Internet sex at work, sometimes downloading thousands of pornographic pictures on the company computer. They may not realize that the employer has the right (and the ability) to access the employee's computer. Many have lost their jobs. High-profile figures have received adverse media publicity and great embarrassment and shame when their on-the-job cybersex use was discovered.

A 36-year-old married lawyer states (J. P. Schneider, 2000b):

My work productivity was cut by probably 75%. I would spend on the average 3 hours per day at work behind my closed door cybering and masturbating. I would sit there at work masturbating as secretaries were knocking on my door. I once got called to court during a cybersex encounter just as I was ejaculating. I was flushed and sweaty, but did that stop me? *No!!*

ARREST FOR ILLEGAL ONLINE SEXUAL BEHAVIORS Exchanging in child pornography or sexual activities with minors online, or using chat rooms to arrange offline meetings with minors, is illegal. Many people have been arrested and imprisoned for these activities. In May 2002, Congress expanded wiretap authority to target molesters who find young victims online ("House Approves," 2002). Two months later, the FBI arrested over 100 people nationwide for viewing and trading pornographic images of children 12 and younger on one particular web site, and that the FBI had obtained the e-mail addresses of 3,400 people who were subscribers ("10 Arrested," 2002). In August 2002, it was reported that 10 Americans and 10 Europeans were arrested for sexually molesting their own children, photographing them, and swapping their pictures over the Internet. One of them, who pleaded guilty, was sentenced to 20 years in prison ("Indictment," 2002).

Some men who have never had real-life sexual contact with minors have been caught up in new sexual fantasies on the computer and underage chat rooms and web sites and then experienced severe consequences to their freedom and career.

A 35-year-old divorced man wrote:

I am a lawyer and lost my job with a law firm. I would spend up to 8 hours online trying to escape from my problems by getting a porn and sexual fix. I would not eat or drink during this time. Emotionally, I was as detached as though I were in a coma. Nothing else mattered. I didn't think about the illegality of what I was saying or doing on the computer.

My online activities created some serious trust issues between my wife and me. I got divorced so that my wife and children would not have to deal with my sexual addiction. When we were separated, it was easier for me to act out with cybersex, and I continued to do so. Right now, I am at one of the lowest points in my life. I may be indicted on felony criminal changes. I don't have much contact with my family. I feel worthless and shamed. I am in a group for sexual offenders. (Schneider, 2002, p. 251)

Risk to Emotional Health, Physical Health, and Life   A telephone survey of 1,500 youths aged 10 to 17 who were regular Internet users found that, in the previous year, 19% had been targets of unwanted sexual solicitation, and 25% of this group experienced high levels of distress after solicitation incidents (Mitchell, Finkelhor, & Wolak, 2001). Many people use the Internet as a means of planning offline sexual encounters. A major outbreak of syphilis in 1999 in San Francisco was traced directly to a gay chat room, where offline meetings were being arranged (Klausner et al., 2000). Marriages have ended when cybersex users left their home to meet a long-distance sexual partner. Adolescents have been molested and people killed as a result of meetings with strangers that were arranged online. A news article described a 13-year-old girl who was an exemplary student, but on the Internet she routinely had sex with partners she met in chat rooms. She was strangled by a 25-year-old man whom she originally met on the Internet and then got together with offline ("Altar Girl Slain," 2002).

Adverse Effects on the User's Children   In addition to the most common effect—children spend less time with a parent who devotes many hours to the computer—children may perceive tension in the home, overhear arguments between the parents about cybersex use, encounter pornographic images or sex talk on the computer, or even observe the parent masturbating while on the computer.

According to a 42-year-old man, married 17 years:

I know my sons have gotten into my "special photos" file on the PC. They've walked in when I was chatting and saw the sexual chat rooms where I spend time. They've even told me to take those pictures off the computer, that "it's gross." I told them it was none of their business, but I think they've lost respect for me. Now I try to be more discreet about it with the kids, but I'm sure they've heard my wife and me arguing about it.

Effect of Cybersex Addiction on the Partner   Even when it does not extend to offline encounters, cybersex addiction can be very damaging to the spouse or partner (J. P. Schneider, 2000a). A 36-year-old woman responded to a survey question, "What's the big deal about online sex?" Her husband was addicted to simply viewing online pornography, but as a result he was rarely interested in relational sex. She wrote:

I have very strong feelings about this. My husband's Internet porno-only use has affected us:

- The pornography is the other woman. He would rather be with her than with me.
- Our ability to have a child has been impacted significantly!
- If he is satisfied by the Internet, he feels he has no need for a true emotionally connected relationship.

- When will he get tired of being caught and begin to get this need met outside the home—perhaps at work?
- When will his acting out escalate because computer sex is not enough?
- If it is so harmless, why is he ashamed, why does he lie, and why does he hide it?

A man's online sexual activities included sexual chat rooms, pornography, and exchanging pornographic images. His wife related:

> To me, the computer is the other woman. He lies and sneaks behind my back to get on it. He waits for me to leave each morning and jumps on the computer until it's time for him to leave. He comes home for lunch to get on it. It is the same thing as physically cheating. He may not have physical sex with them, but he thinks about it and it consumes him all the time.

Counselors who are not familiar with the sexual smorgasbord available on the Internet tend to underestimate the significance of the client's involvement in computer sex:

> Before our marriage, I knew something wasn't quite right with our love making. I questioned him about why he didn't feel desire for me, why he didn't care if we made love, and why he didn't care if he had an orgasm. His answers were vague. . . .
>
> One month after our marriage, I caught him at the computer secretly viewing pornography. My first question was, "Are you addicted to this?" Of course, his answer was no. I went to my male therapist immediately. He told me emphatically, "No, this is not an addiction. Just tell him he has to stop using it to stay in the relationship with you." Well, he kept the craziness going for the next six months. My husband lied constantly and just hid his usage more cunningly. We started into a cycle of his shame and embarrassment; my anger and feelings of betrayal, rejection, and abandonment; and him promising to try to change. . . .
>
> After six months, I left the male therapist and started working with a woman therapist who totally understands sexual addiction. I am still pissed off at the first therapist—he is well respected and effective, but he had no clue about the reality of sex addiction. (36-year-old woman, married 3 years)

It is crucial for the professional to obtain a detailed history of the client's activities, including the range of activities on the computer, the content of web sites accessed, the amount of time involved, and the consequences to the client's life, including the effects on the sexual and emotional relationship with the partner, on the social network, and on the job. For additional resources on cybersex addiction, see Box 7.2.

ADDICTION INTERACTIONS

Milkman and Sunderwirth (1987), early students of the neurochemistry of addictions, divided addictions into three categories:

1. *Satiation:* alcohol and benzodiazepines, opiates, food.
2. *Arousal:* cocaine, amphetamines, gambling.
3. *Fantasy:* psychedelic drugs, workaholism, compulsive religious practice.

BOX 7.2
Cybersex Resources

WEB SITES

www.sexhelp.com.
www.onlinesexaddict.com.
www.cybersexualaddiction.com.
www.sexualrecovery.com.

BOOKS

Schneider, J. P., & Weiss, R. (2001). *Cybersex exposed: Simple fantasy or obsession.* Center City, MN: Hazelden Educational Materials.

Carnes, P., Delmonico, D., & Griffin, E. (2001). *In the shadows of the Net.* Center City, MN: Hazelden Educational Materials.

Cooper, A. (Ed.). (2002). *Sex and the Internet: A guidebook for clinicians.* New York: Brunner-Routledge.

Satiation is currently associated with the neurotransmitters gaba-amino butyric acid (GABA) and endorphins, arousal with norepinephrine and dopamine, and fantasy with serotonin. Sex can fit into any of these categories, making it a very powerful mood-altering activity. However, sex addiction is primarily an arousal activity, as satiation or sedation occurs only at the very end of what may be hours of arousal. Addictions interact with each other in various ways. Cocaine and sex, for example, are both arousal-type addictions and combining them gives a more powerful euphoric experience.

A high-powered salesman in his thirties, reported (B. H. Schneider, 1992, p. 5):

Sex while high on cocaine was incredible. It was like pouring gasoline on a fire. I'd get into this cycle of using cocaine and drinking beer, and I'd get so wired that I'd have to masturbate to come down. Then I'd feel terrible. The only way to take care of the pain was to start the cycle again by fantasizing and doing coke.

I had a lot of shame about what I did sexually. A part of my acting out was to get really high and drive to the university where there were sorority houses and apartments. I would find a bathroom window and wait for hours for a glimpse of a woman stepping out of the shower. It was a miracle I wasn't arrested.

As noted earlier, the majority of cocaine addicts include sex in their addictive ritual. Cocaine and sex each acts as a strong trigger for the other, making it difficult to recover from one addiction while continuing the other. Cigarettes and alcohol are two other addictions that are strongly correlated.

Another type of addiction interaction is switching addictions. Addiction counselors are very familiar with the tendency of drug addicts who stop one drug to switch to addictive use of another. This is the reason chemical dependency treatment strongly promotes abstention from *all* mood-altering drugs. (Sex addiction recovery, in contrast, teaches *healthy* sex rather than *no* sex.) Some recovering alcoholics who attend AA practice the *thirteenth step,* a euphemism for sexually pursuing other AA members. Having stopped their drinking, some of them switch to compulsive sexual behaviors.

A 65-year-old woman was admitted to a psychiatric hospital for evaluation of paranoia because her husband said she was constantly accusing him of ogling other women. Here is her version of events:

> During the first years of our marriage, we often had arguments about Marty's excessive drinking. Then, when I was pregnant with my second child, I became very ill and nearly died. Marty made a vow to God that if I survived, he'd never drink again. I recovered, and Marty kept his word. Right after that he became involved in a new business venture, and, all of a sudden, he started working much harder than he'd ever done before—12-hour days, 6 days a week, and hardly ever took any vacations. I basically brought up our two sons by myself. Last year, after 30 years of hard work, Marty retired and we moved here to our retirement community. For the first time in all these years, Marty has some free time, and he uses most of it flirting with every woman he sees. When we're in the car and he's driving, he keeps his eyes on the women rather than on the road, and we've nearly gotten in an accident three times already in the two months we've been living here in Green Valley. When we sit in a restaurant eating dinner, he hardly hears a word I say, because he's so preoccupied with ogling the waitresses and the female customers. I feel completely ignored.

Based on this history, the psychiatrist immediately discharged Anne from the hospital. What she had related was a coherent account of a man who had repeatedly switched addictions in response to changes in his life circumstances: He drank excessively until he made the vow to God to stop, then worked excessively for many years until he retired and is now obsessively involved with ogling and flirting with the bevy of women who surround him, despite the negative consequences on his relationship with his wife.

FAMILY OF ORIGIN AND CHILDHOOD EXPERIENCE OF SEX ADDICTS

The majority of sex addicts have other family members with addictions. In his study of sex addicts at an inpatient treatment facility, Carnes (1991) found that 87% identified another addict in their family of origin (alcoholics, sex addicts, etc.). For any type of addiction, the addiction holds a primary place in the life of the addict. As a result, children of addicts tend to get inadequate nurturing. In a large study of sex addicts getting inpatient treatment, 81% of the addicts had been sexually abused in childhood, 72% physically abused, and 97% emotionally abused (p. 109). The more severe the abuse, the greater impairment of the self that predisposed an individual to addictive behaviors. In a study of 290 recovering sex addicts including 57 women, Carnes and Delmonico (1996) found that the greater the frequency of sexual and/or physical abuse in childhood (from 1 = Once to 5 = Very often on a 5-point Likert Scale), the greater the number of addictions they later developed. In addition to sex, these included drug dependency, eating disorders, smoking, gambling, spending, working, and coaddiction.

Olson's circumplex model (Olson, Sprenkle, & Russell, 1979) classifies families along two axes, one describing their degree of cohesion, or emotional involvement, which ranges from disengaged to enmeshed, the other describing their adaptability, or style of interacting, from chaotic to rigid, each with four possibilities. This model classifies the families into 16 cells. A study of sex addicts' families (Carnes, 1991) found that 68% of the families were of one type—rigid and disengaged. In this type of family (prototypical rigidly religious), what is important is for everyone to look good to the outside world. Rules of behavior are rigid, feelings are not discussed, and there is little warmth and emotional nurturing.

PROGRESSION OF THE ADDICTION

Carnes (1989) described the progression of untreated sex addiction. This progression will be familiar to chemical dependency counselors, with the sexual experience replacing drug use:

- *Initiation phase:* The impact of sexual observations and/or experiences during adolescence and young adulthood is unusually intense. At some point, sex becomes the drug of choice used to escape or cope.
- *Establishment phase:* There is repetition of an addictive cycle of preoccupation, ritualization, and sexual acting out, then despair, shame, and guilt, which is alleviated by renewed preoccupation.
- *Escalation phase:* Over time, the addiction may escalate and acting out becomes more frequent, more intense, more risky, and occurs with greater loss of control.
- *De-escalation phase:* Many addicts never experience this phase, but for some the behavior may intermittently decrease, at times by substituting another addictive behavior such as heavy drinking or drugging, at other times by sheer will power.
- *Acute phase:* The addict is constantly preoccupied with the addiction cycle and becomes isolated and alienated from family and friends. Some addicts are stopped only by physical consequences or incarceration or by complete absence of opportunity.

Progression from the initiation to the acute phase usually takes years, but with the advent of the Internet, the process is often accelerated to months or even weeks. This is why cybersex is often called the *crack cocaine of sex addiction*. For example, J. P. Schneider (2000b) describes a 35-year-old woman, married since her teens, who had a long history of compulsive masturbation. However, her life spun out of control only after she accidentally found a pornography site on the Internet:

> I stumbled across a porn site by typing in a business address wrong. I went back out of curiosity. Within days, I was doing it on a daily basis; within weeks, that is all I did. It literally took control and consumed my life. I went from joining all the free stuff, to anything I could to feed my addiction. I began to lie to my husband about working overtime just so I could continue to feed it. I didn't want to go home. I lost my mind in such a short time that I could not function at work or at home. The pictures I placed before me would haunt me day and night. I became very withdrawn and depressed. Cybersex will take a person down a road they never dreamed they would go. It sucks them into it and [there is] hell to pay to get out.

THE SPOUSE OR PARTNER OF THE SEX ADDICT

Like substance addictions, sex addiction directly or indirectly affects the entire family. Partners of sex addicts (sexual coaddicts), whether male or female are often intensely fearful of abandonment and are overly invested in the relationship. They may be aware of serious family problems but often believe that they are responsible for the problems and that if they tried harder or were better partners, they could solve the problems. They may tolerate unacceptable behaviors from their spouse. By covering up their feelings (e.g., their pain over an affair), they enable the addict to continue the behavior without consequences. Children may receive inconsistent nurturing while one parent is focused on the addiction and the other is intensively involved with the addict's behavior and the relationship. It is common for such families to have many secrets from each other and from others outside the family (Corley & Schneider, 2002).

Sexual coaddicts tend to have the following core beliefs (J. P. Schneider, 1988) summarized in Box 7.3:

I Am Not a Worthwhile Person   A wide gap often exists in the coaddict between the kind of person she appears to be and the person believes herself to be. Despite outward appearances and accomplishments, the spouse feels that he is deeply flawed, worthless, and does not deserve to be happy. He measures her worth by what others think. She is so dependent on someone else that she has little or no sense of self.

No One Would Love Me for Myself   The coaddict believes she must earn love and confuses being needed with being loved. She is drawn to a man who is needy, and she makes her indispensable to him. Believing that the more she can do for him, the less likely he is to leave her, she assumes increasing responsibility for his life. Fearful of abandonment, the sexual addict's partner does anything she can to maintain the relationship, ignoring her own feelings and needs, excusing his hurtful behavior, and avoiding conflict and confrontation.

I Can Control Other People's Behavior   Believing she can manipulate those around her to carry out her wishes, the partner typically helps others do things they should do for themselves (enabling). Her continuing involvement in the addict's behavior, however, works only to perpetuate the status quo rather than to stimulate change because it prevents the addict from experiencing the consequences of the compulsive thinking and behavior.

BOX 7.3
Core Beliefs of the Sexual Coaddict

- I am not a worthwhile person.
- No one would love me for myself.
- I can control other people's behavior.
- Sex is the most important sign of love.

It may be that the controlling behavior of the coaddict is a defense against feelings of helplessness and powerlessness. In childhood, the coaddict often felt helpless to influence events around her; in adulthood, she tries to control and manipulate her environment in order to avoid feeling helpless.

Sex Is the Most Important Sign of Love   The coaddict tends to confuse sex with love, and assumes that when a man is intimate with her, it indicates he loves her. She also believes that sex is the price of love and will often accede to her partner's request for sexual activities that are uncomfortable for her—in some cases, this may even involve other sexual partners.

Many sexual coaddicts report having been sexually abused as children, which Carnes (1997) hypothesized may have led to a hyposexual or aversive desire disorder, which he termed *sexual anorexia*. Such persons may either tacitly encourage their partners to find sex elsewhere, or may consider sex simply the price to pay for maintenance of the relationship rather than something to be enjoyed.

Carnes (1991) described nine traits that characterize partners of sex addicts. These are shown in Table 7.4. According to Carnes (1991), these characteristics contribute to the dysfunction of the relationship and may lead to a vicious circle in which the sex addict perceives the partner as being controlling, critical, and overly responsible for the addict's well-being. In turn, the partner feels emotionally abandoned, pursues the addict, and views the addict as irresponsible, distant, erratic, and self-destructive.

Partners of sex addicts may go to any length sexually to avoid abandonment by the addict. As a result, some female coaddicts resemble sex addicts in their behavior. A key distinction between sexual addiction and coaddiction, however, is the goal of the behavior. For example, a woman who explains, "The sex was always to hold on to the guy" is describing coaddictive behavior, while the woman who seeks a sense of power over another person is describing addictive behavior. Kasl (1989) observed that "[T]the potential addict denies her neediness and seeks power, while the potential coaddict denies her anger and searches for security." To complicate the picture, however, some women behave like sex addicts when they are single but develop behaviors typical of coaddiction when in a committed relationship.

The core belief of the coaddict result in low self-esteem and fear of abandonment. The coaddict engages in constant efforts to control the addict and to manage

Table 7.4
Characteristics of Coaddicts of Sex Addicts

1. Covering up for the sex addict and keeping secrets (collusion).
2. Obsessive preoccupation about the sex addict.
3. Denial of reality and ignoring the problem.
4. Emotional turmoil.
5. Manipulation (including using sex to control).
6. Excessive responsibility (blaming themselves for the problem).
7. Compromise or loss of self (e.g., making a constant series of compromises that erode the sense of self).
8. Blame and punishment (i.e., becoming self-righteous and punitive).
9. Sexual reactivity (e.g., shutting down sexually to numb self-needs).

his or her addiction. A common assumption is that "If I only have enough information, I can control the situation and prevent disaster."

For example, an attractive but very insecure woman who worked as a dental assistant to her dentist husband believed that she was ideally suited to keep track of his activities:

> I loved working in Peter's office because I thought I could monitor every woman. If I was in the reception room and saw the best-looking patient who came in that day, or a woman of the type that he was usually attracted to, I'd go to her chart and I'd look up how old she was and whether she was married. Then I'd start up a conversation with her. I was very good at getting people to reveal things about themselves. I never let them know I was his wife. I would also try to stay in the room while he was treating her so I could see what the interaction was and if it was a threat or not. If I couldn't be there, I'd find out from the other dental assistant how he acted around the patient.
>
> I did much the same thing at parties. I'd look around the room and find the woman that he'd be most attracted to and I'd watch them carefully. I'd look at his eyes to see if he met hers. I was so consumed with his behavior, it was like a prison. (J. P. Schneider, 2001, p. 98)

Partners of sex addicts often attempt to control the addict through sex. One woman, the mother of seven, related:

> If there was going to be a problem, I knew I could smooth it over by having sex with him. If I had to tell him the checkbook was all out of whack or I'd overspent our budget, then I could ease into it with sex. I'd get him into a good mood. If one of the kids did something wrong, which he always thought was my fault, I would always try and not tell him about that until after we'd had sex. (J. P. Schneider, 2001, p. 98)

Surveys of sex addicts and coaddicts (Carnes, 1991; J. P. Schneider, 1988) found that partners of sex addicts come from a family background very similar to that of a sex addict—a dysfunctional family replete with addiction or other problems, such that their emotional childhood needs were not met. Just like sex addicts, the majority of their future partners (62.5%) come from rigid, disengaged families (Carnes, 1991). They grow up with a great need for approval from others and have difficulty setting appropriate boundaries. They often have a history of relationships with addicts or other emotionally unavailable people. Leaving an unsatisfactory or emotionally abusive relationship is often difficult for them.

A 34-year-old woman was married for 4 years when her husband left her to be with a woman he met online in a dominance/submission web site. She related:

> He was always too tired for real sex with me. I felt lonely and paranoid. He always told me I needed to initiate sex more; but, when I would, he'd *always* turn me down. I felt so confused. I would constantly look for proof of his acting out, find it, confront him, threaten to leave, and then he'd promise me he'd stop. I'd believe him, but also continued snooping and would find out he'd never stopped. Of course, when it came right down to it, I never would have left. I was too terrified to be alone and I was desperate to keep him. . . . After he left, if it weren't for my son, I know I would have

killed myself. I honestly did not think I could exist without my husband's presence in my life.

Many future spouses of sex addicts were sexually abused or grew up in a sexually charged or sexually repressive atmosphere. This may have consisted of excessive sexual comments or sexual materials in the home, or, on the contrary, sex may have been considered a dangerous and evil activity to be constantly deplored and guarded against. Many grew up believing that sex is the most important sign of love or that love must be earned with sex. Others fear sex and have problems with sexual desire, arousal, or orgasm. Choosing a sex addict for a relationship is generally no accident (J. P. Schneider, 2001). An example of a couple whose dysfunctions complement each other is the addict who prefers prostitutes to marital sex, and his wife, who was sexually abused in childhood, who has no interest in sex and is grateful for her husband's lack of sexual interest in her.

THE MALE COADDICT

Male partners of female sex addicts face particular challenges. Men's self-esteem is often so bound to their sexuality that learning that their wife has been unfaithful is an intense source of shame for them and in some countries has even been considered a justifiable reason for homicide. Also, there is less societal acceptance of female sex addicts and less support for men who decide to stay with their partners. Male partners of male sex addicts also have difficulty finding support because many gay men consider it the norm to have multiple sex partners.

Several factors contribute to increasing the amount of shame men feel when their wife acts out sexually. In Western culture, there is much more shame to be a man than a woman with an unfaithful partner. There is even a pejorative name for such men—cockolds—but not for women. Moreover, having been cockolded has for centuries been considered a valid legal defense in some countries for killing one's wife and/or her lover.

Second, men's self-esteem is so rooted in their sexuality that having an unfaithful wife strikes at the core of their manhood. In dealing with a partner's affair, men are much more distressed if the affair involved sexual activity than love and romance without sexual intercourse, whereas women are more distressed if the relationship included emotional intimacy (Glass, 2003). Thus, for example, a man's one-night stand or visit to a prostitute is less disturbing to most women than a long-term intimate emotional relationship that did not include sexual intercourse; the opposite is true for the way most men react.

Another societal problem for male coaddicts results from a paradox that women tend to be blamed no matter who has the affair: When a man has affairs, many people wonder if perhaps his wife was not a good sexual partner; when a woman has affairs, the usual assumption is that it's her fault—she's a slut, a home-breaker, and so on. One consequence of this double standard is that women whose husbands have problems are supported for a stand-by-your-man attitude, whereas men whose wives are alcoholic or sexually addicted are not faulted for leaving them (many of these men are themselves sexually addicted and/or chemically dependent).

One difference between men and women who learned of their partner's infidelities was that the men were generally more able to express their anger and wanted to lash out. One man described his reaction to the disclosure:

One night she told me she wanted to talk with me. She said she had been molested by her brother when she was a kid and that that was the start of her preoccupation with sex. She proceeded to tell me about several affairs, including one with a guy who had just built a bookcase for us.

I immediately went into deep anger and sadness and crying and rage at the same time. I pulled the bookcase off the wall and threw it off the balcony. Then I got my ax and chopped it into small pieces. The next day I built a fire and burned the pieces. Looking back, I realize that that helped me get rid of a lot of anger. (J. P. Schneider, 1990, p. 244)

A study of 24 heterosexual couples in which the woman was sexually addicted and the man chose to stay in the marriage (J. P. Schneider & Schneider, 1990) found that most of the husbands were sexually addicted themselves and/or were alcohol or drug dependent. The remaining husbands appeared to suffer from depression and were emotionally very dependent on their wives. They had great difficulty expressing their feelings and tended to flee into denial of problems. Underlying their depression was a great deal of unexpressed anger.

Husbands were more likely to be supportive of their wives if (1) the husband was a sex addict himself and (2) if the wife had not had sex with other men. Husbands who had no addiction had the most difficult time coping because they tended to deny or minimize the problem. One man explained:

I accept the therapist's explanation that she had a compulsion for relationships more than she had for sex. The sex was not the driving force. I think that if my wife had been really interested in sex, she'd have had affairs with more than five men in 7 years (J. P. Schneider, 1990, p. 246).

DIAGNOSIS OF ADDICTIVE SEXUAL DISORDERS

Treatment for any disorder depends on the diagnosis. Before embarking on a treatment plan, the clinician must have formulated an explanation for the excessive or inappropriate sexual behavior. It is not always sex addiction. Table 7.5 lists diagnoses from the *Diagnostic and Statistical Manual of Mental Disorders*, fourth edition (*DSM-IV*; APA, 1994) which must be considered.

Sex addiction is the most prevalent diagnosis, but it does not appear directly on the above list because it is not cited in the *DSM-IV*. However, addictive sexual behaviors can most commonly be classified as one of three *DSM-IV* categories: paraphilia, sexual disorder NOS (not otherwise specified), or, less commonly, impulse control disorder. A *paraphilia* is defined as "recurrent, intense, sexually arousing fantasies, sexual urges, or behaviors generally involving (1) nonhuman objects, (2) the suffering or humiliation of oneself or one's partner, or (3) children or other nonconsenting persons, that occur over a period of at least six months and which cause clinically significant distress or impairment in social, occupational, or other important areas of functioning." Examples given in the *DSM-IV* are exhibitionism, fetishism, frotteurism, pedophilia, sexual masochism, sexual sadism, cross-dressing, and voyeurism.

Looking back to Carnes' 10 patterns of addictive sexual behavior, five of the categories can be readily identified in the *DSM-IV* as specific paraphilias. These include voyeuristic sex, exhibitionistic sex, pain exchange, some types of intrusive

Table 7.5

Differential Diagnosis of Excessive Sexual Disorders

---

1. Paraphilia.
2. Sexual disorder not otherwise specified (NOS), that is, nonparaphilic excessive sexual disorder.
3. Impulse control disorder.
4. Bipolar affective disorder.
5. Cyclothymic disorder.
6. Post-traumatic stress disorder (PTSD).
7. Adjustment disorder.
8. Dissociative disorders.
9. Delusional disorders (erotomania).
10. Substance-induced disorder.
11. Obsessive-compulsive disorder.
12. Delirium, dementia, or other cognitive disorder.
13. Personality disorder such as antisocial or narcissistic personality disorder.

Source: From "Differential Diagnosis of Addictive Sexual Disorders Using the *DSM-IV*," by J. P. Schneider and R. R. Irons, 1996, *Sexual Addiction & Compulsivity: Journal of Treatment and Prevention, 3,* pp. 7–21.

sex (frotteurism), and exploitative sex (pedophilia). Four of the remaining categories sometimes involve paraphilias: Fantasy sex may be associated with paraphilic urges that are not acted on, anonymous sex may be used to act out a paraphilia with less likelihood of consequences, and paying for and trading sex are means of purchasing a partner who might permit acting out some paraphilia (J. P. Schneider & Irons, 1996).

Compulsive masturbation, multiple affairs, compulsive viewing of pornography on the Internet, and related behaviors are generally nonparaphilic and can be diagnosed as sexual disorder NOS, 302.9. The *DSM-IV* describes this as "a sexual disturbance that does not meet the criteria for any specific Sexual Disorder and is neither a Sexual Dysfunction nor a Paraphilia. Examples include . . . distress about a pattern of repeated sexual relationships involving a succession of lovers who are experienced by the individual only as things to be used" (APA, 1994, p. 538).

Since March 2001, a group of experts on sexual excess, who come from various points of view, have been working on recommendations for the future *DSM-V* for the diagnosis that we have been calling *sex addiction* (Berlin, 2002). Their opinions were published in 2002 in the journal *Sexual Addiction & Compulsivity.* One of them was Martin Kafka, a researcher and clinician at Harvard Medical School. Kafka and Hennen (1999) studied 206 men who had nonparaphilic hypersexuality disorders. In 2002, noting the similarities between paraphilias and nonparaphilic hypersexuality disorders, they proposed a *DSM-V* diagnosis of "paraphilia-related disorders" (Kafka, 2002). This diagnosis would include "compulsive masturbation, protracted promiscuity, pornography dependence, cybersex dependence, telephone sex dependence, severe sexual desire incompatibility, and paraphilia-related disorder not otherwise specified."

There are other diagnoses that need to be considered before sex addiction is diagnosed:

- *Bipolar affective disorder* is frequently characterized by sexual excess in the manic phase. Increased sexual drive, fantasies, and behavior are often present.
- *Cyclothymic disorder* is a scaled-down version of bipolar illness. Hypersexuality may be seen during the hypomanic periods.
- *Substance-induced mood disorder* such as anxiety or euphoria may result in sexual preoccupation and activity, which should then be considered secondary to the substance use rather than an independent diagnosis. The challenge then is to sort out the role of the chemical use in the sexual compulsivity.
- *Obsessive-compulsive disorder* (OCD) consists of recurrent intrusive thoughts or impulses, which cause anxiety. The person engages in various compulsive behaviors in an attempt to prevent or reduce anxiety or distress, not to provide pleasure or gratification. Obsessive sexual imagery and/or sexual behaviors may be part of OCD symptoms, but the person usually has several others that can help make the diagnosis.
- *Adjustment disorder* is a temporary mood or behavior resulting from either a single event (such as ending of a relationship or being fired from a job) or multiple stressors. It begins within 3 months after the stressor's onset and lasts no more than 6 months after the consequences of the stressor have ended. In contrast, an addictive disorder is an ongoing, pervasive part of the person's life.
- *Delusional disorder* is the presence of one or more nonbizarre delusions that persist for at least a month. This may be of having a romantic relationship with a prominent person (erotomania) or that the person has a bad odor or insects on the skin. The person's behavior appears normal in other aspects of his or her life.
- *Cognitive disorder,* such as delirium or dementia, can result in loss of the ability to judge the appropriateness of various behaviors such as inappropriate sexual touching, uninhibited language, or public masturbation.

In addition to the disorders just mentioned, which are all listed in what the *DSM-IV* terms Axis I Clinical Disorders, the book has an additional set of 11 psychiatric problems called Axis II Personality Disorders, including narcissistic, dependent, and antisocial personality disorders. Because addicts are so focused on their addiction, their behavior may appear narcissistic, dependent, or antisocial. In most of them, these personality traits diminish or resolve as they work a recovery program. However, some addicts have a coexisting personality disorder that is an entrenched part of their character, even if they stop their addictive behavior. If a client appears to be having great difficulty becoming engaged in addiction recovery work, it may be because he has a dual diagnosis. For example, if he has concurrent narcissistic personality disorder, his feelings that he is special, unique, and can only be understood by other special people and his lack of empathy for others can prevent him from opening up to the counselor and the self-help group.

In another cohort of people with excessive sexual behaviors, their personality disorder, rather than sex addiction, may be their primary disorder. This is particularly true for persons with antisocial personality disorder, who readily see other people as objects to be used for one's own sexual pleasure, and who have no empathy for them and are not deterred by the consequences of their behavior. Their behavior is not compulsive—it may be planned carefully and deliberately. These people are rarely amenable to treatment.

In summary, when you assess a new client who has some problem with excessive sexual behavior, you need to rule out the following possible causes of the behavior:

- Direct physical effect of some medical condition.
- Effect of substance abuse, medication, or toxin.
- Presence of psychosis, bipolar illness, or other Axis I disorder.
- Presence of an Axis II personality disorder.

Remember, however, that some people do have two primary psychiatric disorders—an addictive disorder and an Axis I or a personality disorder. These people are said to have a *dual diagnosis,* both of which must be treated.

SEX OFFENDERS VERSUS SEX ADDICTS

You might understandably be confused about the definition of sex addict and sex offender. As is evident from the earlier description of various addictive sexual behaviors, some are against the law. *Sex offense* is a legal term, indicating that the particular behavior is illegal. However, not all sex addicts are sex offenders, and not all sex offenders are sexually addicted. Among 109 imprisoned sex offenders, Blanchard (1990) determined that 55% were sexually addicted. This included 71% of child molesters and 39% of rapists. According to Delmonico and Griffin (1995), sexual addicted offenders have more prior offenses and fewer intrusive offenses, engage in rituals rather than impulsive actions, have more shame about the offense, use more pornography, are more likely to be chemically dependent, feel unworthy and out of control (whereas nonaddicted offenders feel angry, frustrated, and hateful), and are more in touch with their own past history of victimization. Many sex offenders repeatedly reoffend, despite incarceration and despite going through various sex offender treatment programs. Mental health professionals need to assess sex offenders for the presence of addictive sexual disorders. Sexually addicted sex offenders need concurrent addiction treatment to help them avoid relapses.

COUNSELOR PREPARATION FOR WORKING WITH THIS POPULATION

If you are considering working with the population that I've been describing, you first need to be sure your own house is in order. This means becoming educated about the following areas of the counselor-client relationship that are important for all types of practices, but in particular when the content of the interaction is the client's sexual behavior:

1. *Concepts of a power differential, professional boundaries, and the ethical issues of counselor-patient personal relationships:* These concepts include boundaries, transference and countertransference in the therapeutic relationship, recognition that it is normal to be attracted to some clients, but inappropriate to act on it, the nature of a fiduciary relationship, the power differential between counselor and client, gender issues, and state laws about sexual exploitation by counselors and about reporting others.

2. *Factors that increase a counselor's risk of sexual misconduct:* Modeling of sexual boundary blurring during training, lack of appropriate community ethics, personal vulnerability, client's vulnerability, and risks for same-sex offending.

3. *Maintaining appropriate nonsexual boundaries in the office:* Some guidelines are: Post your professional society's code of ethics in your office. Set appropriate interpersonal tone in the workplace. Avoid giving the client an impression that he or she has special status. Avoid excessive self-disclosure. Don't accept anything other than money for your services. Avoid dual relationships—Don't accept friends, family members, or office staff as clients. Avoid a personal relationship with a former client. Avoid getting seduced by a client's appreciation and admiration. Don't ask a client to do personal favors for you. Don't undertake any business deals with patients. Don't accept valuable gifts from patients.

4. *Maintaining appropriate sexual boundaries in the office:* Here are some guidelines: Be sure that any sexual question you ask is for the client's benefit, not your own. Avoid self-disclosure other than for the client's benefit. Do not comment on a client's body. If you are sexually attracted to a client, discuss it with a supervisor, not the client. Avoid touching the client unless it is clearly therapeutic and only in a nonsexual area.

Some helpful resources for learning more about these areas include the books: *The Wounded Healer: Addiction-Sensitive Approach to the Sexually Exploitative Professional* by Irons and Schneider (1999), *The Ethical Use of Touch in Psychotherapy* by Hunter and Struve (1998), *Sex, Power and Boundaries* by Rutter (1996), *Breach of Trust: Sexual Exploitation by Health Care Professionals and Clergy,* edited by Gonsiorek (1995), *Boundaries and Boundary Violations in Psychoanalysis* by Gabbard and Lester (1995), *Sexual Feelings in Psychotherapy* by Pope, Sonne, and Holroyd (1993), *Sex in the Forbidden Zone* by Rutter (1991), and *Ethics for Addiction Professionals* by Bissell and Royce (1987).

CLINICAL ASSESSMENT OF SEX ADDICTION

In the next chapter, Robert Weiss describes in detail how a person who presents with an excessive sexual behavior is assessed clinically, from the moment he or she arrives at the counselor's office. Here I give a brief overview. Figure 7.1 (Carnes, 2000) provides a decision tree for the diagnosis and treatment of clients who present with problems of compulsive sexual behaviors.

As shown in the decision tree, the first decision for the clinician is whether the sexually excessive behavior is situational or part of a pattern. If the behavior has been repetitive, you must determine whether the cause is compulsivity or other mental disorders. If the behavior fits the criteria for sex addiction, you must then decide the level of intervention required, whether inpatient or outpatient. In either case, as described by Carnes (2000), treatment is divided into three phases:

1. Intervening in the cyclic compulsive process: education, referral to 12-Step programs, and confrontation of denial.

2. Attendance at 12-Step programs: completion of Step One of the program; preparation of a written abstinence statement, a relapse prevention plan,

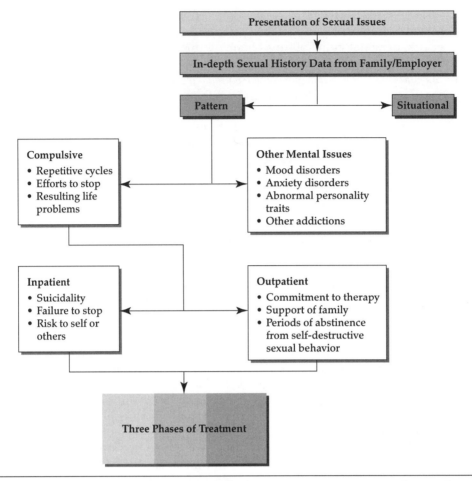

Figure 7.1   Diagnosis and Treatment Plan for Compulsive Sexual Behavior. *Source:* From "Sexual Addiction and Compulsion: Recognition, Treatment, and Recovery," by P. J. Carnes, 2000, *CNS Spectrums, 5*(10), pp. 63–72. Reprinted with permission.

abstinence period, sex plan; involvement of partner and family; assessment for multiple addictions, group therapy, and shame reduction.

3. Understanding underlying development issues and family-of-origin issues.

Drug dependence professionals are increasingly recognizing the need for screening for multiple addictions. Especially at inpatient programs, brief screening tests for pathologic gambling, sex addiction, and eating disorders need to be included as part of the initial evaluation. The classical screening instrument for sex addiction is the Sexual Addiction Screening Test, a 25-item yes-or-no questionnaire designed and statistically validated by Carnes (1989). The test is reproduced in Table 7.6.

A score of at least 13 yes answers identified 96% of the addicts who were given this survey (Carnes, 1989). Notice, however, that this test was designed for adult heterosexual men and was written before the cybersex era. Newer versions are now available for women, for gay men, and for adolescents. The screening test for

Table 7.6
Sexual Addiction Screening Test (SAST)

---

1. Were you sexually abused as a child or adolescent?
2. Have you subscribed or regularly purchased sexually explicit magazines?
3. Did your parents have trouble with sexual behavior?
4. Do you often find yourself preoccupied with sexual thoughts?
5. Do you feel that your sexual behavior is not normal?
6. Does your spouse (or significant other) ever worry or complain about your sexual behavior?
7. Do you have trouble stopping your sexual behavior when you know it is inappropriate?
8. Do you ever feel bad about your sexual behavior?
9. Has your sexual behavior ever created problems for you or your family?
10. Have you ever sought help for sexual behavior you did not like?
11. Have you ever worried about people finding out about your sexual activities?
12. Has anyone been hurt emotionally because of your sexual behavior?
13. Are any of your sexual activities against the law?
14. Have you made promises to yourself to quit some aspect of your sexual behavior?
15. Have you made efforts to quit a type of sexual activity and failed?
16. Do you have to hide some of your sexual behavior from others?
17. Have you attempted to stop some parts of your sexual activity?
18. Have you ever felt degraded by your sexual behavior?
19. Has sex been a way for you to escape your problems?
20. When you have sex, do you feel depressed afterwards?
21. Have you felt the need to discontinue a certain form of sexual activity?
22. Has your sexual activity interfered with your family life?
23. Have you been sexual with minors?
24. Do you feel controlled by your sexual desire?
25. Do you ever think your sexual desire is stronger than you are?

Source: From *Contrary to Love: Helping the Sexual Addict* (pp. 218–219), by P. J. Carnes 1989, Minneapolis, MN: CompCare. Reprinted with permission.

gay men (S-SAST, Box 8.1) will be described in the next chapter. The Women's Sexual Addiction Screening Test (W-SAST, Box 8.2) differs in 10 of the 25 questions of the SAST. These changes are shown in Table 7.7. Neither the S-SAST nor the W-SAST has been statistically validated.

Because cybersex addiction is becoming such a significant aspect of sex addiction, I have included a checklist (Table 7.8) specifically for this problem. This tool has not been statistically validated; it is merely a list of useful questions for determining how significant is the client's involvement with Internet sexual activities. If the client answers yes to more than five or six questions, this is clearly an area of concern.

The most important part of your clinical assessment is to obtain an in-depth sexual history. Because shame is usually present, new clients may initially conceal or deny some aspects of the behavior. The client may fail to report other sexual behaviors may not be reported because he or she doesn't recognize them to be problematic or perceives them to be unrelated to the behavior that brought him or her in for treatment. You need to ask specific and detailed questions about the nature of the behaviors, the time frames, and the consequences to self and others. If there have been legal, employment, or medical consequences, ask for legal or medical records, written complaints at the client's place of work, and talk with the spouse

Table 7.7
Women's Sexual Addiction Screening Test*

1. Do you regularly purchase romance novels or sexually explicit magazines?
2. Have you stayed in romantic relationships after they have become emotionally or physically abusive?
3. Do you often find yourself preoccupied with sexual thoughts or romantic day dreams?
4. Have you ever participated in sexual activity in exchange for money or gifts?
5. Do you have times when you act out sexually followed by periods of abstinence (no sex at all)?
6. Do you find yourself having multiple romantic relationships at the same time?
7. Has sex or romantic fantasy been a way for you to escape your problems?
8. Do you regularly engage in sadomasochistic behavior?
9. Do you feel controlled by your sexual desire or fantasies of romance?

*Changes only.
Source: From *Cybersex Exposed: Simple Fantasy or Obsession?* (pp. 194–195), by J. P. Schneider and R. Weiss, 2001, Center City, MN: Hazelden. Copyright by Patrick Carnes and Sharon O'Hara. Printed with permission of Sharon O'Hara.

or partner if appropriate. Screen for other addictions as well as concurrent mental health disorders.

Also consider obtaining psychiatric testing, such as the Minnesota Multiphasic Personality Inventory (MMPI) or the Millon. It is also valuable for you to obtain a family history of addictions and other psychological problems from the client.

Table 7.8
Cybersex Addiction Checklist

1. Are you spending increasing amounts of online time on sexual or romantic intrigue or involvement?
2. Have you been involved in multiple online romantic or sexual affairs?
3. Do you prefer online sex to having "real" sex with your spouse or primary partner?
4. Have you tried unsuccessfully to cut back on the time you spend online in sexual and romantic activities?
5. Has the time you spend online sex or romance interfered with your job or other important commitments?
6. Have you collected a large quantity of Internet pornography?
7. Have you engaged in fantasy online acts or experiences which would be illegal if carried out (e.g., rape or sex with children or adolescents)?
8. Has your online sexual or romantic involvement resulted in spending significantly less time with your spouse/partner, dating life, or friends?
9. Have you lied about the amount of time you spend online or the type of sexual or romantic activities you experience online?
10. Have you had sexual experiences online that you wish to keep hidden from a partner or spouse?
11. Have your family or friends increasingly complained or been concerned about the amount of time you have spent online?
12. Do you frequently become angry or very irritable when asked to get off the Internet or off the computer?
13. Has the computer become the primary focus of your sexual or romantic life?

Source: From *Cybersex Exposed: Simple Fantasy or Obsession?* (pp. 196–197), by J. P. Schneider and R. Weiss, 2001, Center City, MN: Hazelden.

When assessing physicians and other professionals, you need to probe for cognitive distortions that support their sexual misconduct. According to Sealy (2001), these include:

1. *Denial:* This is the most common distortion. The client might tell you, "I'm not doing any harm," "What's the big deal?" or "The patient didn't say anything, so it must be okay." Physicians may deny the power differential between them and their patients.
2. *Entitlement:* "After all I've done for other people, I deserve some rewards for myself."
3. *Negotiable boundaries:* "If the patient is under anesthesia, then I'm not harming her by molesting her."
4. *Minimization:* "I'm not the only one doing these things."
5. *Narcissism:* "I'm so needed around here, nobody would report me and they wouldn't dare fire me."

After gathering information, you need to decide whether the client's behaviors were temporary or constitute a recurrent pattern. Problems of recent onset, without a related history, may reflect the client's temporary way of coping with a particular situation and might be an adjustment disorder. Persistent and recurrent behaviors are likely to reflect an addictive disorder, although, as discussed earlier, they may be secondary to other psychiatric disorders. The client may also have a dual diagnosis.

The next decision is the level of treatment that the client needs. The Patient Placement Criteria of the American Society of Addiction Medicine (2001) is used by addictionists to determine whether a chemically dependent person requires inpatient treatment or can be treated as an outpatient. The same guide can be used for addictive sexual disorders. Inpatient treatment should be considered if the client:

- Is unable to stop high-risk sexual behaviors that may be dangerous to him- or herself or others.
- Has a concurrent psychiatric disorder, such as severe depression, that makes it desirable for him or her to be in a safer environment.
- Has no support system (family, friends, or employer).

If outpatient treatment is appropriate, one additional decision is whether the client would benefit from medications. The most commonly used drugs are the SSRI antidepressants, which are useful not only for depression but also to decrease obsessive sexual thoughts and compulsive behaviors. If medication management is under consideration, the client should be referred for psychiatric consultation.

RECOMMENDED READING

Carnes, P. J. (1983). *Out of the shadows: Understanding sexual addiction.* Minneapolis, MN: CompCare. The classic book about sex addiction is written for people with the problem.
Carnes, P. J. (1991). *Don't call it love: Recovery from sexual addiction.* New York: Bantam Books. Written for professionals, this book describes the results of research on a large number of sex addicts treated in an inpatient setting.
Carnes, P. J., & Adams, K. M. (Eds.). (2002). *Clinical management of sex addiction.* New York: Brunner-Routledge. The latest and most complete guide for clinicians on treatment of sex addiction, including special populations (women, pastors, gays, homeless, etc.).

Carnes, P. J., Delmonico, D. L., & Griffin, E. (2001). *In the shadows of the Net.* Center City, MN: Hazelden. A book for people who are hooked on Internet sex.

Cooper, A. (Ed.). (2002). *Sex and the Internet: A guidebook for clinicians.* New York: Brunner-Routledge. An up-to-date scholarly text for understanding Internet sex, both healthy and problematic.

Corley, M. D., & Schneider, J. P. (2002). *Disclosing secrets: When, to whom, and how much to reveal.* Wickenburg, AZ: Gentle Path Press. Information and exercises for all types of addicts who are keeping secrets from spouses and families.

Earle, R., & Earle, M. (1995). *Sex addiction: Case studies and management.* New York: Brunner/Mazel. An excellent guide for clinicians who treat sex addicts and their families.

Schneider, J. P. (1988). *Back from betrayal: Recovering from his affairs.* Center City, MN: Hazelden. (Second edition, 2001, Tucson, AZ: Recovery Resources Press.) The classic book for spouses of sex addicts. It describes the steps of recovery for the partner.

Schneider, J. P., & Schneider, B. H. (1991). *Sex, lies, and forgiveness: Couples speak on healing from sex addiction.* Center City, MN: Hazelden Educational Materials. (Second edition, 1999, Tucson, AZ: Recovery Resources Press.) Based on research with many couples who have dealt with sex addiction, this book describes how to rebuild trust, forgive, and rebuild the relationship. Written for couples who are going through the process.

Schneider, J. P., & Weiss, R. (2001). *Cybersex exposed: Simple fantasy or obsession?* Center City, MN: Hazelden. This book provides an explanation of how and when computer sex becomes an addiction, and the steps to recovery.

REFERENCES

Altar girl slain in Net crime led a double life, police say. (2002, May 22). *Arizona Daily Star,* p. A5.

American Psychiatric Association. (1994). *Diagnostic and statistical manual of mental disorders* (4th ed.). Washington, DC: Author.

American Society of Addiction Medicine. (2001). *ASAM patient placement criteria for the treatment of substance-related disorders* (2nd ed., rev.) [ASAM PPC-2R]. Washington, DC: Author.

Benotsch, E. G., Kalichman, S. C., & Pinkerton, S. D. (2001). Sexual compulsivity in HIV-positive men and women: Prevalence, predictors, and consequences of high-risk behaviors. *Sexual Addiction & Compulsivity: Journal of Treatment and Prevention, 8,* 83–99.

Berlin, F. (2002). The Vanderbilt symposium—In my opinion. *Sexual Addiction & Compulsivity: Journal of Treatment and Prevention, 8,* 187–190.

Bissell, L., & Royce, J. E. (1987). *Ethics for addiction professionals.* Center City, MN: Hazelden.

Blanchard, G. (1990). Differential diagnosis of sex offenders: Distinguishing characteristics of the sex addict. *American Journal of Preventive Psychiatry and Neurology, 2,* 45–47.

Cabaj, R. P. (1992). Substance abuse in the gay and lesbian community. In J. H. Lowenson, P. Ruiz, & R. B. Millman (Eds.), *Substance abuse: A comprehensive textbook* (2nd ed., pp. 852–860). Baltimore: Williams & Wilkins.

Carnes, P. J. (1983). *Out of the shadows: Understanding sexual addiction.* Minneapolis, MN: CompCare.

Carnes, P. J. (1989). *Contrary to love: Helping the sexual addict.* Minneapolis, MN: CompCare.

Carnes, P. J. (1991). *Don't call it love: Recovery from sexual addiction.* New York: Bantam Books.

Carnes, P. J. (1997). *Sexual anorexia.* Center City, MN: Hazelden.

Carnes, P. J. (2000). Sexual addiction and compulsion: Recognition, treatment, and recovery. *CNS Spectrums, 5*(10), 63–72.

Carnes, P. J., & Delmonico, D. L. (1996). Childhood abuse and multiple addictions: Research findings in a sample of self-identified sexual addicts. *Sexual Addiction & Compulsivity: Journal of Treatment and Prevention, 3,* 258–267.

Carnes, P. J., Nonemaker, D., & Skilling, N. (1991). Gender differences in normal and sexually addicted populations. *American Journal of Preventive Psychiatry and Neurology, 3,* 16–23.

Carnes, P. J., & Schneider, J. P. (2000). Recognition and management of addictive sexual disorders: Guide for the primary care clinician. *Lippincott's Primary Care Practice, 4,* 302–318.

Cooper, A. C., Delmonico, D. L., & Burg, R. (2000). Cybersex users, abusers, and compulsives: New findings and implications. *Sexual Addiction & Compulsivity: Journal of Treatment and Prevention, 7*(1/2), 5–30.

Cooper, A. C., Putnam, D. A., Planchon, L. A., & Boies, S. C. (1999). Online sexual compulsivity: Getting tangled in the Net. *Sexual Addiction & Compulsivity: Journal of Treatment and Prevention, 6*(2), 79–104.

Corley, M. D., & Schneider, J. P. (2002). Disclosing secrets: Guidelines for therapists working with sex addicts and co-addicts. *Sexual Addiction & Compulsivity: Journal of Treatment and Prevention, 9,* 43–67.

Decent woman wants to end addiction to sex. (1983). *Arizona Daily Star,* "Dear Abby" column.

Delmonico, D. L., & Griffin, E. (1995, March 24). *Yes, Virginia, there are sexually addicted offenders.* Talk presented at the annual conference of the National Council on Sexual Addiction and Compulsivity, Atlanta, GA.

Edlin, B. R., Irwin, K. L., et al. (1992). High-risk sex behavior among young street-recruited crack cocaine smokers in three American cities: An interim report. *Journal of Psychoactive Drugs, 24,* 363–371.

Ferree, M. C. (2001). Females and sex addiction: Myths and diagnostic implications. *Sexual Addiction & Compulsivity: Journal of Treatment and Prevention, 8,* 287–300.

Freeman-Longo, R. E. (2000). Children, teens, and sex on the Internet. *Sexual Addiction & Compulsivity: Journal of Treatment and Prevention, 7,* 75–90.

Gabbard, B., & Lester, E. (1995). *Boundaries and boundary violations in psychoanalysis.* New York: Basic Books.

Glass, S. (2003). *Not "just friends."* New York: Free Press.

Gonsiorek, J. (Ed.). (1995). *Breach of trust: Sexual exploitation in health care professionals and clergy.* Thousand Oaks, CA: Sage.

Goodman, A. (2001). What's in a name? Terminology for designating a syndrome of driven sexual behavior. *Sexual Addiction & Compulsivity: Journal of Treatment and Prevention, 8,* 191–214.

Gordon, L. J., Fargason, P. J., & Kramer, J. J. (1995). Sexual behaviors of chemically dependent physicians and nonphysicians in comparison to sexually compulsive chemically dependent physicians and non-physicians. *Sexual Addiction & Compulsivity: Journal of Treatment and Prevention, 2,* 233–255.

House approves online-predator bill. (2002, May 22). *Arizona Daily Star,* p. A17.

Hunter, M. (1992). *Joyous sexuality.* Minneapolis, MN: CompCare.

Hunter, M., & Struve, J. (1998). *The ethical use of touch in psychotherapy.* Thousand Oaks, CA: Sage.

Indictment: Adults abused own kids, e-mailed photos. (2002, August 10). *Arizona Daily Star,* p. A9.

Internet use rises to 54% of Americans. (2002, February 6). *Arizona Daily Star,* p. A8.

Irons, R. R., & Schneider, J. P. (1994). Sexual addiction: Significant factor in sexual exploitation by health care professionals. *Sexual Addiction & Compulsivity: Journal of Treatment and Prevention, 1,* 198–214.

Irons, R. R., & Schneider, J. P. (1999). *The wounded healer: Addiction-sensitive approach to the sexually exploitative professional.* Northvale, NJ: Aronson.

Kafka, M. P. (2002). The paraphilia-related disorders: A proposal for a unified classification of nonparaphilic hypersexuality disorders. *Sexual Addiction & Compulsivity: Journal of Treatment and Prevention, 8,* 227–240.

Kafka, M. P., & Hennen, J. (1999). The paraphilia-related disorders: An empirical investigation of nonparaphilic hypersexuality disorders in outpatient males. *Journal of Sex and Marital Therapy, 25,* 305–319.

Kasl, C. D. (1989). *Women, sex, and addiction: A search for love and power.* New York: Ticknor and Fields.

Klausner, J. D., et al. (2000). Tracing a syphilis outbreak through cyberspace. *Journal of the American Medical Association, 284,* 447–449.

McCall, D. (2002). Sex and the clergy. *Sexual Addiction & Compulsivity: Journal of Treatment and Prevention, 9,* 89–96.

Milkman, H., & Sunderwirth, S. (1987). *Craving for ecstasy: How our passions become addictions and what we can do about them.* San Francisco: Jossey-Bass.

Mitchell, K. J., Finkelhor, D., & Wolak, J. (2001). Risk factors for and impact of online sexual solicitation of youth. *Journal of the American Medical Association, 285,* 3011–3014.

Olson, D. H., Sprenkle, D., & Russell, C. (1979). Circumplex model of marital and family systems. I: Cohesion and adaptability dimensions, family types and clinical application. *Family Process, 18,* 3–28.

Pope, K. S., Sonne, J. L., & Holroyd, J. (1993). *Sexual feelings in psychotherapy.* Washington, DC: American Psychological Association.

Rutter, P. (1991). *Sex in the forbidden zone.* New York: Fawcett Crest.

Rutter, P. (1996). *Sex, power, and boundaries.* New York: Bantam Books.

Schneider, B. H. (1992). *The cocaine-sex connection: Understanding our sexual acting out.* Center City, MN: Hazelden.

Schneider, J. P. (1988). *Back from betrayal: Recovering from his affairs.* Center City, MN: Hazelden.

Schneider, J. P. (1994). Sex addiction: Controversy within mainstream addiction medicine, diagnosis based on the *DSM-III-R,* and physician case histories. *Sexual Addiction & Compulsivity: Journal of Treatment and Prevention, 1,* 19–44.

Schneider, J. P. (2000a). Effect of cybersex addiction on the family: Results of a survey. *Sexual Addiction & Compulsivity: Journal of Treatment and Prevention, 7,* 31–58.

Schneider, J. P. (2000b). A qualitative study of cybersex participants: Gender differences, recovery issues, and implications for therapists. *Sexual Addiction & Compulsivity: Journal of Treatment and Prevention, 7,* 249–278.

Schneider, J. P. (2001). *Back from betrayal: Recovering from his affairs* (2nd ed.). Tucson, AZ: Recovery Resources Press.

Schneider, J. P., & Irons, R. R. (1996). Differential diagnosis of addictive sexual disorders using the *DSM-IV. Sexual Addiction & Compulsivity: Journal of Treatment and Prevention, 3,* 7–21.

Schneider, J. P., & Schneider, B. H. (1991). *Sex, lies, and forgiveness: Couples speak on healing from sex addiction* (2nd ed.). Center City, MN: Hazelden.

Schneider, J. P., & Weiss, R. (2001). *Cybersex exposed: Simple fantasy or obsession?* Center City, MN: Hazelden.

Sealy, J. R. (2001). Physician sexual misconduct. *Sexual Addiction & Compulsivity: Journal of Treatment and Prevention, 9,* 97–112.

10 arrested in Federal investigation of Internet child pornography. (2002, July 10). *New York Times,* p. A21.

Washton, A. M. (1989). Cocaine may trigger sexual compulsivity. *Journal of Drug and Alcohol Dependency, 13*(6), 8.

Weiss, R. (1997). Special populations: Treatment concerns for gay male sexual addicts. *Sexual Addiction & Compulsivity: Journal of Treatment and Prevention, 4,* 323–334.

CHAPTER 8

Treating Sex Addiction

ROBERT WEISS

I masturbate multiple times daily to pornography that I find on the Internet. My activities primarily consist of going into web cam sites to watch live sexual acts and exchange sexually graphic pictures in chat rooms. I am a lawyer and I lost my job with a law firm, as I would spend up to 8 hours online during and after work trying to escape from my problems and trying to get a porn and sexual fix. I don't eat or drink during this time. Emotionally exhausted, I feel detached as if I am in a coma. When I am into my sexual high, nothing else matters. I don't think about the insanity of what I am saying or doing on the computer. (45-year-old male, recently divorced)

I would go to work, race through my appointments, and as soon as possible, I would leave and go home. I'd get on the phone with one of my sex buddies, meet for sex, go back to work, and again go home and get back online as soon as I could. This went on for years. I was shut down emotionally. Sometimes, I'd get in a chat room looking for a man with whom I could have sex. I'd meet him at a hotel or at my house and have sex. When I traveled, I'd set up meetings in towns where I knew I would be staying. None of these meetings were ever romantic interests. I was clear from the beginning that this is about sex and nothing else. (37-year-old executive never married)

THE CHALLENGE OF TREATING SEX ADDICTION

As therapists, we may find ourselves at a loss when presented with clients who bring us stories like the ones just mentioned. Often these clients come to therapy following some severe consequence, such as a job loss or marital separation. Sometimes it can be difficult understand why someone would put their livelihood or family life at risk for the sake of a shallow, two-dimensional online sexual experience or momentary sexual interaction. Some of us who have come to understand the nature of working with substance addictions feel confident

Special thanks to Jennifer Schneider, MD, for her outstanding help with the spouses section of this chapter, Christine Cook, MSW, ATR, for her clinical art therapy contribution, and Jon Westerman for his continuing support and understanding.

when confronting or intervening on an alcoholic or drug addicted client but feel at a loss when a client's apparently volitional sexual activity has brought them repeated negative consequences. Those familiar with harm reduction might also find themselves challenged by having to negotiate the intricacies of a sexual acting-out history. Working with sexual addicts requires a new skill set—one that combines the empathy, insight, and relational abilities of a good psychotherapist with the limit setting, confrontation, and cognitive-behavioral strategies of an addiction specialist.

For many professionals, the idea of providing sexual addiction treatment can provoke responses ranging from curiosity and intrigue to outright fear. Many chemical dependency counselors and mental health professionals, while expressing interest in furthering their understanding of such work, are understandably anxious and uncomfortable at the thought of actually working with client issues such as compulsive masturbation, exhibitionism, anonymous sex, and the frequenting of strip clubs. Quite often clinicians are faced with having to treat those whose lives are compromised by having been cheated on or lied to rather than treating those who are themselves engaging in acting-out behaviors. It is generally more familiar and comfortable to provide treatment for victims rather than victimizers and not everyone is prepared to do this work. Personal qualities that seem most helpful to the clinician in providing effective sexual addiction treatment include:

- The ability to tolerate your own discomfort and even disbelief (at times) at the content and information being presented.
- The willingness to avoid openly judging and shaming a client for his or her sexual behavior choices.
- The courage to confront and challenge clients' existing belief systems, even in the face of client disapproval or anger.
- The clarity to organize a clear set of treatment guidelines with the client and hold the client accountable to those commitments.
- The consistency to maintain the guidelines of treatment despite client manipulations and despite your own feelings (positive or negative) about the client.

In many ways, the process of sexual addiction treatment does not vary significantly from addressing a chemical addiction or most dual diagnoses. The basic tools and principles of sound addiction and mental health assessment followed by a cognitive-behavioral approach, including 12-Step social support, provide the most effective and successful strategy for helping sexual addicts eliminate self/other destructive sexual behavior patterns and introduce healthier means of coping and relating. This chapter gives specific direction and means to provide such treatment to sex addicts, giving the prospective treating clinician a taste, a flavor, and a direction for the treatment process. Not every aspect of the treatment of sexual addiction can be outlined in this chapter. Materials on the subject are provided at the end of the chapter for those needing a more complete description of the treatment of sexual addiction.

INITIAL CONTACT: PHONE CALL TO INTAKE

By the time clients make contact with a professional or organization to discuss their addictive sexuality, they are often filled with shame and fear of discovery, sometimes even unconsciously projecting their shame on those they call. As much as they want help, they are also seeking to avoid their intense embarrassment and shame. Making the discussions and assessment of sexual concerns as comfortable and matter-of-fact as possible facilitates information gathering and gaining trust. The way a therapist or agency presents itself to these issues goes a long way toward winning over clients who are already predisposed to minimize and avoid their sexual problems.

When saying his goodbyes at his graduation from the sexual addiction therapy group—more than 3 years since first entering treatment—Jeff had the following comment for his therapist:

> If it weren't for that advertisement you put in the phone book I never would have made it here. There I was, having acting out for the millionth time, filled with shame, looking through the counseling section for someone who could help me. When I saw those words in your ad, "We treat sex addiction and compulsive Internet porn use" I cut it out and carried it with me for 3 months, using it for hope and support that change was possible, until I finally got up the courage to call for an appointment.

THE SELF-HELP TEST

Once it is clear that a client is seeking help for a sexual addiction problem, it is important to be completely open in discussing the concerns that engendered the call or visit. It is helpful to have a standard set of screening questions when clients first call. In addition to the standard intake questions of age, marital status,

---

BOX 8.1
The Male Sexual Screening Addiction Test

The Male Sexual Screening Addiction Test (G-SAST) is designed to assist the assessment of sexually compulsive or addictive behavior. The G-SAST provides a profile of responses that help to identify men with sexually addictive disorders. Answer each question yes or no. Depending on the particular pattern of symptoms:

- *1 to 3 positive answers:* This may indicate an area of concern and should be openly discussed with a friend or family member.
- *More than 3 positive answers:* This indicates the need to consider more professional addiction support, such as Sexual Addicts, a 12-Step support program.
- *6 or more positive answers:* This indicates a problem with potentially self-abusive and/or dangerous consequences. The client should seek treatment.

1. Were you sexually abused as a child or adolescent?
2. Have you subscribed or regularly purchased/rented sexually explicit magazines or videos?
3. Did your parents have trouble with their sexual or romantic behaviors?
4. Do you often find yourself preoccupied with sexual thoughts?

(continued)

5. Has your use of phone sex lines, computer sex lines, and so on exceeded your ability to pay for these services?

6. Does your significant other(s), friends, or family ever worry or complain about your sexual behavior (not related to sexual orientation)?

7. Do you have trouble stopping your sexual behavior when you know it is inappropriate and/or dangerous to your health?

8. Has your involvement with pornography, phone sex, computer board sex, and so on become greater than your intimate contacts with romantic partners?

9. Do you keep the extent or nature of your sexual activities hidden from your friends and/or partners (not related to sexual orientation)?

10. Do you look forward to events with friends or family being over so that you can go out to have sex?

11. Do you visit sexual bath houses, sex clubs, and/or video bookstores as a regular part of your sexual activity?

12. Do you believe that anonymous or casual sex has kept you from having more long-term intimate relationships or from reaching other personal goals?

13. Do you have trouble maintaining intimate relationships once the "sexual newness" of the person has worn off?

14. Do your sexual encounters place you in danger of arrest for lewd conduct or public indecency?

15. Have you spent time worrying about being HIV positive, and continue to engage in risky or unsafe sexual behavior anyway?

16. Has anyone ever been hurt emotionally by events related to your sexual behavior, for example, lying to your partner or friends, not showing up for event/appointment because of sexual liaisons, and so on (not related to sexual orientation)?

17. Have you ever been approached, charged, arrested by the police, security, and so on because of sexual activity in a public place?

18. Has sex been a way for you to escape your problems?

19. When you have sex, do you feel depressed afterward?

20. Have you made repeated promises to yourself to change some form of your sexual activity only to break them later (not related to sexual orientation)?

21. Have your sexual activities interfered with some aspect of your professional or personal life, for example, unable to perform at work, loss of relationship (not related to sexual orientation)?

22. Have you engaged in unsafe or "risky" sexual practices even though you knew it could cause you harm?

23. Have you ever paid for sex?

24. Have you ever had sex with someone just because you were feeling aroused and later felt ashamed or regretted it?

25. Have you ever cruised public restrooms, rest areas, and/or parks looking for sexual encounters with strangers?

Source: Developed by Patrick Carnes, PhD and Robert Weiss, LCSW.

referral, and so on, questions specific to sexual acting out, asked at the initial call, serves the dual purpose of qualifying the client's appropriateness for treatment while putting them at ease. These questions, if not asked by phone, should be answered on arrival when the client fills out the admission paperwork. One alternate way of asking these questions is to utilize the Generalized Sexual Addiction Screening Test (G-SAST, see Box 8.1) for male clients or the Women's Sexual Addiction Screening Test (W-SAST, see Box 8.2), which are screening tools commonly used at intake.

The answers to the intake questions and the completed forms help clarify the nature of the sexual behavior problems that brought the client into treatment. These assessments list pertinent questions; they do not qualify as a formal psychological test but are used to gather personal data and to normalize the content of the upcoming interview.

The First Session

The needs of this particular patient population require that a great deal be accomplished in the initial session. For that reason, the initial introduction/assessment process is best organized into a 2-hour block, either at one session or in two consecutive sessions. Suggest that the client arrive early for the first session to locate parking, find the office, fill out initial paperwork, and so on. Office policies, rules and boundaries of treatment, fees, and so on, must be clearly discussed as these may come up later when the client tests the limits and boundaries of the treatment process, as addicted clients often do.

Most clients first come in with feelings of great shame, holding many secrets awaiting disclosure. While many have been in previous therapy experiences, it is nonetheless essential, especially when sexual issues are going to be discussed, to review the laws of Informed Consent, explaining the limits and boundaries of confidentiality. This is a time-intensive process since the clients' shame and anxiety about previous sexual behaviors often leave them fearful of further consequences. Most enter their first session in an emotional crisis, having recently gotten in trouble for betraying a spouse, violating the law or another person. These fears require detailed discussion during the process of gathering a thorough assessment and history and making initial recommendations for further treatment. There is much to accomplish from the beginning.

Assessment

Although patients come into treatment seeking help for sexual addiction, other psychological problems might be driving their hypersexual activity. Untreated mental illnesses can trigger, maintain, or mimic the signs and symptoms of sexual addiction. Some patients, initially appearing to be sexual addicts, may, under closer analysis, be diagnosed with an obsessive-compulsive, attention-deficit, or bipolar disorder. For example, some bipolar patients demonstrate what might appear to be sexually addictive behaviors, but they differ from sex addicts as they only act out sexually during their periods of mania. Attention-deficit disorder or attention-deficit/hyperactivity disorder clients might also engage in *impulsive* sexual acting out, but their patterns do not have the same addictive or *compulsive* patterns and features that a sex addict exhibits.

BOX 8.2
Women's Sexual Addiction Screening Test

The Women's Sexual Screening Addiction Test (W-SAST) is designed to assist the assessment of sexually compulsive or addictive behavior. Answer each question yes or no. Depending on the particular pattern of symptoms:

- *1 to 3 positive answers:* This may indicate an area of concern and should be openly discussed with a friend or family member.
- *More than 3 positive answers:* This indicates the need to consider more professional addiction support, such as Sexual Addicts, a 12-Step support program.
- *6 or more positive answers:* This indicates a problem with potentially self-abusive and/or dangerous consequences. The client should seek treatment.

1. Were you sexually abused as a child or adolescent?
2. Do you regularly purchase romance novels or sexually explicit magazines?
3. Have you stayed in romantic relationships after they became emotionally or physically abusive?
4. Do you often find yourself preoccupied with sexual thoughts or romantic daydreams?
5. Do you feel that your sexual behavior is normal?
6. Does your spouse (or significant other[s]) ever worry or complain about your sexual behavior?
7. Do you have trouble stopping your sexual behavior when you know it is inappropriate?
8. Do you ever feel bad about your sexual behavior?
9. Has your sexual behavior ever created problems for you and your family?
10. Have you ever sought help for sexual behavior you did not like?
11. Have you ever worried about people finding out about your sexual activities?
12. Has anyone been hurt emotionally because of your sexual behavior?
13. Do you participate in sexual activity in exchange for money or gifts?
14. Do you have times when you act out sexually followed by periods of celibacy (no sex at all)?
15. Have you made efforts to quit a type of sexual activity and failed?
16. Do you hide some of your sexual behavior from others?
17. Do you find yourself having multiple romantic relationships at the same time?
18. Have you ever felt degraded by your sexual behavior?
19. Has sex or romantic fantasies been a way for you to escape your problems?
20. When you have sex, do you feel depressed afterward?
21. Do you regularly engage in sadomasochistic behavior?

22. Has your sexual activity interfered with your family life or desire to have one?
23. Have you been sexual with minors?
24. Do you feel controlled by your sexual desire or fantasies of romance?
25. Do you ever think your sexual desire is stronger than you are?

Source: Developed by Patrick Carnes, PhD and Sharon O'Hara, MA.

Biopsychosocial History   It is essential to obtain a good biopsychosocial assessment from the client (review Chapter 7). That includes any previous history of psychotherapy, mental health or addiction treatment, or hospitalizations, including any medications prescribed for any purpose. Ideally, clients should be evaluated by utilizing a multiaxial *DSM* diagnosis to make as complete an overview as possible of the presenting concerns and past history. This also helps point out additional diagnoses, such as depression, anxiety, or relational problems that need to be added and organized into the treatment plan.

The case in Box 8.3 outlines the outpatient assessment. While not an actual person, this case is a composite of many and is typical of the sexually addicted client coming into treatment. The bolded words at the beginning of each section indicate the assessment question being covered.

TREATMENT PLANNING

The immediate treatment plan logically flows from the assessment. Immediate and longer term goals can be laid out based on the information provided in Box 8.3. The multiaxial assessment and overall picture provides the direction for laying out an effective treatment plan. Some sexual addiction treatment is consistent from patient to patient; other concerns and focuses vary with each individual. You can begin to pick out concerns that are individual to this patient and then move on to more general treatment planning for sexual addicts.

Immediate Presenting Concerns   The case discussed in Box 8.3 offers some specific and immediate concerns to be addressed with Michael immediately. This is accomplished at the end of the initial assessment almost as a form of intervention. Confronting this patient's denial, perhaps raising his anxiety in the short term, bonds him to the therapist and the process, helping him understand the serious nature of his situation and underscores his need for treatment.

Here is a list of the pressing concerns about Michael's case:

1. Possibility of sexually transmitted diseases (STDs):
   —Does Michael currently have any?
   —Has Michael passed any on to his wife?
2. Is Michael currently acting out sexually with any other women?
3. Does Michael abuse alcohol and is he an alcoholic?
4. Is Michael currently acting out online?
5. What was the nature of the images Michael was viewing online?

BOX 8.3
Case Example

Patient Name: Michael Smith

Therapist: Robert Weiss MSW

Referred By: Friend at local Sex Addicts Anonymous meeting

Date: 06/23/01

Presenting Problem

Michael is a 38-year-old heterosexual Caucasian married man, self referred to treatment after having been placed on suspension by his employer for downloading porn on the Internet at work 3 to 4 weeks ago. He has worked as a special events and catering manager of a large hotel chain for the past 12 years. His suspension occurred after several verbal and written warnings where Michael was clearly notified of the policy but continued to engage in this behavior anyway.

Presenting Appearance and Mood

Michael presented as a casually and appropriately dressed man of average weight and size who appeared his stated age. He appeared mildly depressed evidenced by tearfulness when discussing difficult issues in the session. His affect was full, ranging from tearful to angry at times, his mood was depressive. He evidenced no psychosis or delusional thought. Since his recent job suspension, he reports interrupted sleep, with frequent anxious awakening (terminal insomnia). He reports having lost approx. 8 lbs since this job loss occurred.

Suicidal Ideation or Plan

Some ideation when first suspended. No plan. "I would never leave my kids like that, I know what it would do to them."

Current Stressors

1. Possible loss of job, status, and income.
2. Fear of financial crisis: Michael is currently on unpaid suspension and might lose his job.
3. Marital problem: Wife is very angry and disappointed in him; she was unaware of the warnings or problem sexual behaviors.
4. Two children at home under the age of 6.

History of the Problem

1. Compulsive masturbation 2 to 4 × weekly often for 1 to 2 hours at a time from adolescence to the present, utilizing print media, video, or Internet pornography.
2. Constant sexual fantasy when at work, frequent flirtation with guests and other staff.

3. Anonymous sex with guests at hotels 3 to 4 × yearly past 5 years, "not always with condom!"
4. Depression: "I have felt bad about myself for many years. I never seem to enjoy the good things I have in my life like other people do. Even my kids don't make me happy."

SOCIAL SUPPORT

Michael reports working long days at the hotel, has maintained few friends since school, and, other than his wife, is socially isolated. He has occasional contact with his older brother, does not talk to his parents "except to see them on the holidays."

FAMILY HISTORY

Wife: Jennifer, 35 years old, couple married 9 years.

Children: Caitlin, female, 2 years old; Alan, male, 5 years old.

Brother: James, 31 years old, lives in New York City, gay man, single, no children.

Mother: 63 years old, lives in Arizona.

Stepfather: Nice guy, good to mom.

Father: Deceased 1994, heart attack.

HISTORY OF PREVIOUS TREATMENT.

1. Marital therapy prior to conceiving second child (Marlee Justine PhD, phone # xxx-xxx-xxxx). Treatment focus was lack of intimacy and distance in the marriage. Michael never disclosed any of his sexual behavior or masturbatory activity to the marital therapist. When his wife brought up his masturbation and pornography it was dismissed as, "all guys do that." The couple left after 11 sessions and conceived their daughter.
2. No individual treatment.
3. No previous 12-Step attendance.

HISTORY OF PROBLEM SUBSTANCES OR BEHAVIORS

Alcohol: Patient drinks two to three 6 oz. glasses of wine several nights a week with dinner, also up to one and one-half six packs of beer on weekend afternoons.

Recreational drugs: Marijuana. Patient smoked several joints weekly ages 17 to 24. None since. Some use of cocaine in his late 20s. No hallucinogens. No current drug use.

Prescription drugs: None, no history of abuse.

(continued)

OTHER

Work: Rule out addictive work as a means to avoid intimacy, family life, and feelings. He works 45 to 55 hours weekly, several nights home after 8 P.M.

Exercise: No.

Spending: No.

Smoking: Patient smoked approx. 1 pack of cigarettes daily ages 17 to 27 and quit at that time.

Eating: No.

Gambling: No.

VIOLENCE CURRENT OR HISTORY

Some verbal abuse to wife, sarcastic and devaluing at times. No hitting, throwing objects, yelling, and so on.

DIAGNOSIS

Axis I
Rule out Dysthymia
Sexual disorder NOS—With addictive and compulsive patterns.
Relational concern.
Rule out alcohol dependence.

Axis II
Narcissistic and dependant traits (by interview).

Axis III
Rule out STDs.
None stated.

Axis IV
Job suspension, possible job loss.
Marital conflict.
Financial concerns.
Loss of role.

Axis V
Current GAF 70

6. Does this family have any immediate pressing financial crisis because of Michael's being out of work longer term?

LONGER TERM ISSUES

In addition to these immediate and pressing concerns, there are lesser concerns, specific to this case, that need to be addressed as quickly as possible with Michael. Some of these include:

1. Discussing with Michael what role, if any, he would like you (the therapist) to play in speaking to his employer or EAP on his behalf. Does he wish a letter stating he is in treatment for his sexual acting out?
2. Getting a signed release if such communication is requested.
3. Are there any further concerns about the severity of Michael's depressive symptoms, and do they require further assessment by a psychiatrist?
4. When was the last time Michael had a full physical exam?

Taking the most pressing (and overlooked) concern first, potentially sexually transmitted diseases, what follows is a dialog that challenges the patient's denial and steps forward the treatment plan:

THERAPIST: I noticed when we were speaking earlier in the session that, in addition to your sexual behavior online, you have had sex with a number of women without a condom.

MICHAEL: Yeah, but mostly it was oral sex, only a very few times intercourse.

THERAPIST: When was the last time you had any testing for sexually transmitted diseases?

MICHAEL: I had an HIV test about 8 months ago and it was negative.

THERAPIST: What about testing for other STDs?

MICHAEL: What other STDs?

THERAPIST: Like chlymidia, herpes, and venereal warts.

MICHAEL: No, I think just HIV.

THERAPIST: When was the last time you had sex with anyone other than your wife?

MICHAEL: About 6 weeks ago—but it was oral sex.

THERAPIST: When was the last time you had sex with your wife?

MICHAEL: About 2 weeks ago.

THERAPIST: Do you use a condom when you have sex with your wife?

MICHAEL: No.

THERAPIST: Why not?

MICHAEL: Well, then she would know that I was cheating on her.

THERAPIST: I see. So then by your actions you are saying that it is more important to keep your wife in the dark about your infidelity than it is to protect her health?

MICHAEL: I wasn't thinking of it that way.

THERAPIST: How were you thinking of it?

MICHAEL: I just didn't want to hurt her.

THERAPIST: What do you mean hurt her?

MICHAEL: Well if she found out I was cheating on her she would be devastated and so hurt.

THERAPIST: Michael, who were you really protecting by not telling your wife about your sexual liaisons? Was it her or was it you?

BREAKING THROUGH DENIAL

The previous conversation covers much ground. It is an opportunity to break through the client's denial about the potential to contract and pass on not only HIV but also a whole variety of problematic health disorders. It confronts Michael on his narcissism and apparent lack of empathy and remorse about his sexual acting out and the possible consequences for those he cares about. Plus, this intervention lays groundwork for the treatment plan: getting Michael and his wife a full battery of STD tests and bringing Michael's wife in for a consultation session to begin to disclose the immediate concerns around his sexual behavior. The material presented is also diagnostic since it offers the clinician a chance to gauge Michael's emotional health based on how he responds to this potentially shameful and difficult conversation. A client who responds to the previous questions by being hostile and defensive is in a very different emotional and psychological place from a client who responds with tearful remorse. This is all useful information for the treatment planning process.

Accepting Healthy Responsibility

For change to take place, there has to be an honest self-acknowledgment of the existence of the problem. Ask the sex addict what effect his or her sexual behavior has had on others. Understanding that there is a genuine addictive behavior problem and that this problem may have truly harmed others (friends, lovers, children, etc.) helps to combat the natural resistance to following through on these steps to recovery. Even a grudging willingness to make new choices complimented by a superficial early sense of guilt or remorse can be a starting point toward change.

Hierarchy of Treatment Concerns

A thorough assessment like the one just discussed lays out treatment planning groundwork for the most pressing needs of the addicted client. Some clients who enter treatment for sexual addiction have other concerns that must be addressed prior to managing their sexually addictive behaviors.

Psychiatric Disorders   Clients who have any type of active, undiagnosed, or untreated psychotic or delusional disorders are unlikely to be good candidates for any type of addiction treatment until their thinking is more linear and stable. They require psychiatric intervention and stable medication management as a precursor to addiction treatment. There are clients whose mood disorders are so distracting that they render them emotionally unavailable to follow the structure of a cognitive-behavioral of program. These clients may also be considered pretreatment cases.

A Pretreatment Case: Jon's Story

Jon, a 26-year-old graduate student came to sexual addiction treatment after campus security caught him having anonymous sex in a university-center men's restroom. When brought into the school security office for questioning, Jon was so clearly distraught that, rather than prosecuting him, security referred him to the student psychological center for evaluation. He presented as clearly depressed and was tearful throughout much of the interview. He disclosed that since the arrest he had been sleeping very poorly, awakening several times nightly. Jon's appearance was unkempt and drawn. He admitted losing weight over the past several weeks and not really caring much about how he looked. He has been socially isolated and has some thoughts of not living. Lately Jon has been avoiding classes, feeling like he does not have enough energy to attend or do the work. Jon offered a lengthy history of anonymous sex with men going back to late adolescence. Although he felt comfortable as an out gay man and had enjoyed several stable long-term relationships with men, he always maintained what he calls a "double life" of anonymous sex on the side. He needed help but was not hopeful that anything would really work.

In his current state, Jon is unlikely to have the energy or focus to begin a coordinated plan of recovery (12-Step meetings, readings, homework, therapy, accountability, etc.) because he is so very depressed. Jon needs help becoming stabilized before he can fully throw himself into treatment. However, there are some very helpful pre-treatment steps that can help stabilize him, guiding him toward behavior change and recovery:

1. Create a written and signed contract with him, defining:
   —No self-harm.
   —No sexual acting out in any public place that might involve security, arrest, or strangers (important to define this in detail with Jon).
   —Going to see a psychiatrist.
2. Instill hope that there will be improvement.
3. Build a supportive relationship with him working to reduce his shame by educating him about sex addiction.
4. Monitor the status of his depression, adding tasks and commitments as he improves.

Multiple Addictions   Another area suggesting a hierarchy of treatment choices is a patient who presents with multiple addictions. These patients require some assessment on how their other addictions interfere with sexual addiction treatment. Substance addictions are primary and must be treated first for recovery from behavioral addictions such as sex, gambling, and so on to be successful.

There are some exceptions to this rule; there are those for whom sexual acting out and substance abuse are so related that they cannot stop abusing substances without also addressing their sexual behavior. Consider the patient who is trying to get sober from alcoholism and cocaine abuse but is addicted to seeing prostitutes. He refrains from these substances only to relapse time and time again when the prostitute he hires either has drugs on her or is drug seeking. Another example might be the gay patient addicted to going to bath houses for anonymous sex, but, once there, consistently gets involved in the use of crystal-meth or ecstasy. For these types of people, it may be necessary to address both the substance addiction and the addictive sexual behavior problem simultaneously.

Sexual Offenders   While most sexual addicts have no history of sexual offenses, sexual addiction by definition is a behavior that is repetitive, often escalating and out of control. Inevitably some sexually addicted patients have engaged in sexual offending behaviors to varying degrees. This chapter provides a very loose definition of sexual offending: any sexual behavior carried out without the full consent and understanding of the sexual object or partner. Therefore, exhibiting yourself naked to someone from a car is a sexual offending behavior because you didn't have the consent of the person forced to see you. Voyeurism is offending because you didn't have permission to look in someone's window or dressing room. Child porn is offending because a child could not consent to or fully understand the outcome of the pornographic images being taken of them. Professionals who cross boundaries for sex are included in the offender category. Physicians, therapists, or attorneys who are sexual with their clients or clergy who are sexual with their congregants are violating a trusted power relationship, which by definition is nonconsensual. *Violent sexual offending* is obtaining a nonconsensual sexual experience by means of violence. This would include rape and some forms of child molestation.

With all the different categories of problematic sexual behavior, it can be difficult to determine whether or not someone is appropriate for sexual addiction treatment, especially if they have a history of sexually offending. Here are some ways to think about this:

1. Violent offenders are not candidates for outpatient sexual addiction treatment. Though they may have addictive patterns to their activities, their sociopathy and lack of remorse is generally too profound to include with the sexual addicts. Most sex addicts have not engaged in any criminal acts, and extreme violence would be too great of a treatment distraction. The offenders would become marginalized in treatment.
2. Sexual offenders who do not act out addictively or compulsively but act out in a highly impulsive or random sexual behavior patterns are not candidates for sexual addiction treatment. They are not addicts and will not gain from a traditional cognitive-behavioral, relapse prevention model.
3. Sexual offenders who are resistant or unmotivated or those with severe character pathology should not be offered outpatient sexual addiction treatment. (They may require other forms of therapy first.) Severe character pathology distracts from the treatment process and usually becomes a primary focus.
4. Child/adolescent sexual offenders are best served in their own offender groups (even those with sexual addiction problems) and do not get their recovery needs met fully in sex addiction groups. Child offenders can become marginalized in sexual addiction groups and tend to avoid talking about their offending actions and desires.

Sexual addicts with offending behaviors require additional tasks and levels of accountability than do nonoffending sexual addicts. They need written behavior inventories, victim empathy exercises, and self-monitoring activities challenging them to consistently maintain sexual sobriety and cause no further harm to anyone. Even the sexual addict who admits to only a few offending experiences has to fully acknowledge this behavior, and the clinician has to provide treatment accordingly. The sexual addiction counselor has to reassess whether this patient is an addict who has occasionally strayed into some offending behavior for the higher high, or whether this person has an additional or separate sexual offending disorder. It is incumbent on the counselor who takes these offenders into group or individual therapy to get the proper training and education on the most effective forms of outpatient treatment for sexual offenders. Some expert places to gain knowledge and training in this area are the Safer Society Foundation Inc. (www.safersociety.org) and the Association for the Treatment of Sexual Abusers (www.atsa.com). David Delmonico and Elizabeth Griffin have written extensively in the area of classification of sexual addiction versus sexual offending including an excellent article titled "Classifying Problematic Sexual Behavior" published in the *Clinical Management of Sexual Addiction* (2002).

Cases Requiring More Intensive Treatment   Occasionally clients presenting for assessment are not appropriate candidates for an outpatient setting. Clients presenting with a severe diagnosis, such as suicidality or a crisis in life circumstances, or an ongoing compulsion to carry out life-threatening sexual behaviors demonstrate a persistent failure to succeed in outpatient care and, as such, may require more intensive and aggressive forms of intervention. Other levels of care beyond outpatient treatment are:

1. *Intensive outpatient treatment (IOP):* Similar to a hospital day-treatment or partial hospitalization program, patients attend treatment programming 6 to 8 hours daily but go home or to a hotel at night. More restrictive than a few hours a week, IOP treatment encourages patients to take time off from work and other life distractions focusing entirely on his or her sexual addiction recovery, leaving only time for 12-Step meeting attendance, meals, homework, and rest.
2. *Inpatient treatment:* Clients participate in treatment programming throughout the day and remain in the hospital at night. This is the most restrictive form of care. Unlike a traditional psychiatric hospital stay, inpatient treatment for sexual addiction is a predesigned program, usually 14 to 35 days where patients voluntarily choose to remain inpatient to work on their sexual addiction concerns. Hospital-based treatment provides the support and containment of 24-hour psychiatric counseling and nursing care in addition to the treatment programming.

TASK-CENTERED TREATMENT PLANS

Beyond initial crisis considerations there is a general treatment template that is more or less common to working with all sexually addicted clients. All clients have common goals related to:

- Defining sexual sobriety.
- Achieving and maintaining sexual sobriety.
- Building peer support systems.
- Reducing shame.
- Exploring family history.
- Improving relationship intimacy.
- Introducing healthy sexuality.
- Encouraging play and creativity.

These goals are accomplished in treatment by applying a standard list of tasks. The work of reading, homework assignments, attendance at support groups, and other mandatory routine tasks are part of the individual and later group therapy sessions. These tasks organize and funnel the clients toward the goals listed earlier, and offer all patients a common language. Somewhat standardized in form, these assignments can be tailored to the individual's abilities or situation.

THE IMPORTANCE OF THE TASK

In his recovery workbook, *Facing the Shadow,* Patrick Carnes lays out a step-by-step action plan for treatment of sexual addiction. He outlines the specific recovery tasks designed to take a sexually addicted individual through the processes of internal awareness and external behavior change required for recovery. As one of the preeminent experts in the sex addiction field, Dr. Carnes is clear and deliberate in his emphasis on the use of *task-centered* programming in order to provide a successful outcome to addiction treatment. In addition to the need for a solid relationship with a counselor, clients being treated for addictions should to be taken through certain tasks to successfully achieve long-term sobriety and personal/relational growth. A large contributor to relapse in all addictions, Carnes asserts, is recovery tasks missed, incompletely accomplished, or left aside by the therapist or recovering person.

This general chapter on the treatment of sexual addiction allows room to consider only the most essential treatment tasks for sexual addiction recovery. *Facing the Shadow: Starting Sexual and Relationship Recovery* (Carnes, 2001) offers a complete discussion of these tasks in a workbook format. Sex addiction treatment is staged, in part, through the accomplishment of these tasks. Each task or assignment is discussed in the course of the therapeutic hour or group session, often using the task as a jumping off point toward the client's primary concerns.

Sexual Addiction Treatment Tasks

12-Step Attendance   From the very first intake call suggest that the caller consider attending an Sex Addicts Anonymous, Sex and Love Addicts Anonymous, Sexual Compulsives Anonymous, Sexaholics Anonymous, or an equivalent support group. Participation in 12-Step groups is built-in to all sex addiction/recovery treatment planning, though not every patient is ready to attend when they first arrive in treatment. Some clients resist attending sexual recovery meetings in fear of being seen at such a meeting. This is a good time for a gentle reminder to the client of all of the risks of being seen or exposed that they took in their sexual acting out and that a recovery meeting is a place of anonymity. Getting some clients to attend even one meeting after the initial session is a fantastic start. Other clients are off and running from the very beginning, seeking out and attending multiple weekly meetings.

Sex addicts are unlikely to engender ongoing behavior change without the help of others. The very nature of addiction implies that addicts suffer from a kind of distorted thinking. Recovery requires both the insight and accountability that others can provide. Unfortunately, often spouses and partners are not the best people to turn to as a primary resource for the recovery process. The issues are too painful and close to home for the partner of an addict to be objective no matter how much they care. The best people to provide support and guidance are those with similar problems who are in the process of getting better. These people are most readily found in 12-Step sexual recovery programs and through therapists and professionals who specialize in sexual addiction. These outsiders are necessary as a resource for phone calls, outreach, and support. (See Box 8.4.)

Written Sobriety Plan   For addiction recovery to take place, there must be some bottom-line definition of sobriety. For an alcoholic, this definition is clear: Sobriety is the total abstention from the use of alcohol and other mind-altering chemicals. The *sobriety date* occurs when they gave up drugs and alcohol or when they entered into 12-Step recovery. The time spent continuously away from using these substances is the recovering person's sobriety period. For example, a recovering

---

BOX 8.4
12-Step Meeting Information

There are 12-Step recovery meetings daily in numerous cities throughout the United States for sexual addicts and their partners. The following list gives a brief description of these programs, their focus, and attendance. Local information hotline numbers can provide specific meeting information.

How to Contact and Attend a 12-Step Sexual Recovery Meeting

Some meetings are open to anyone who wishes to attend, while others are closed to members only or are gender specific. It is best to check ahead by calling a local hotline number. This will help determine the best choice of meeting. The hotline numbers will usually confidentially take your name and call you back with meeting information or provide a recorded announcement. Be aware that phone numbers and postal and web addresses are subject to change.

Fellowships

Sexual Addicts Anonymous (SAA)
(713) 869-4902
P.O. Box 70949
Houston, TX 77270

This is a national 12-Step program that encourages participants to define their sexual sobriety through the boundaries of a Sexual Boundary Plan, which is evolved by working with other recovering members. The population is mixed, primarily men, bi-, homo-, and heterosexual with some female attendance. They also have a program for partners of sexual addicts called COSA.

Sex and Love Addicts Anonymous (SLAA)

The Augustine Fellowship
(781) 255-8825
P.O. Box 650010
West Newton, MA 02165-0010
E-mail: slaafws@aol.com

This is a national 12-Step program focused on addictive sexual and romantic relationships and is helpful for people who consistently involve themselves in abusive, nonnurturing relationships as well as sexual addicts. This program tends to attract more women and mixed male/female groups.

Sexaholics Anonymous (SA)
(615) 331-6230
Fax: (615) 331-6901
P.O. Box 111910
Nashville, TN 37222

This is a national 12-Step program that employs the most restrictive definition of sexual recovery. Sobriety is defined as "No sexual behavior outside of

(continued)

a committed marital relationship." The population is primarily heterosexual men, although some women do attend. They have a program for spouses of sexual addicts and offenders called S-Anon.

Sexual Recovery Anonymous (SRA)
3579 E. Foothill Blvd. #191
Foothill/Rosemead Shopping Center
Pasadena, CA 91107
Call and Leave Message: 24-hour recording
Information: (213) 243-9438
E-mail: info@sexualrecovery.org

Sexual Recovery Anonymous is for the person who is suffering from compulsive obsessive sexual addiction and wishes to find release from this destructive behavior. Their site is also for the helping professionals who want to become better acquainted with the SRA 12-Step Program Sexual Recovery Anonymous (SRA).

Sexual Compulsives Anonymous (SCA)
P.O. Box 1585, Old Chelsea Station
New York, NY 10011
(212) 606-3778
(800) 977-HEAL
E-mail: info@sca-recovery.org

12-Step program found in major urban areas primarily attended by gay and bisexual men and some women. Participants define their sexual sobriety through the boundaries of a Sexual Boundary Plan, which is evolved by working with other recovering members. They currently have no formal partners program.

GROUPS FOR PARTNERS AND FAMILY MEMBERS

Codependents of Sex Addicts (COSA)
P.O. Box 14537
Minneapolis, MN 55414
(612) 537-6904

S-Anon International Family Groups
P.O. Box 111242
Nashville, TN 37222-1242
(615) 833-3152

Co-Sex and Love Addicts Anonymous (CO-SLAA)
P.O. Box 6500010
West Newton, MA 02165-0010
(617) 332-1845

Recovering Couples Anonymous (RCA)
P.O. Box 11872
St. Louis, MO 63105
(314) 830-2600
Fax: (314) 830-2670
E-mail: rca-wso@aol.com

12-Step program that helps partners who are addicts or co-addicts work on issues of commitment, intimacy and mutual recovery, with a focus on improving the significant other bonds. All couples—married, nonmarried, homosexual or heterosexual—are welcome.

GROUPS FOR SEXUAL TRAUMA SURVIVORS

Survivors of Incest Anonymous (SIA)
P.O. Box 21817
Baltimore, MD 21222
(410) 282-3400

Incest Survivors Anonymous (ISA)
P.O. Box 17245
Long Beach, CA 90807
(562) 428-5599

Sexual Assault Recovery Anonymous (SARA)
P.O. Box 16
Surrey, BC, V35 424 Canada
(604) 584-2626

alcoholic might say: "I stopped using drugs and alcohol on June 15, 1987; therefore, I am 14 years sober." A definition of sobriety for the recovering sex addict can be challenging. Unlike sobriety from the use of substances, sexual sobriety is rarely considered to be complete abstinence from sex although some recovering persons may take short periods (30 days to 6 months) of complete sexual abstinence (celibacy) to get a more balanced sense of themselves with sexual activity temporarily taken out of their daily lives (see Table 8.1).

Sexual Sobriety Planning is a contract between a sex addict and his or her 12-Step recovery support group or therapist. These contracts or *Sexual Boundary Plans* are always written to clearly define concrete behaviors from which the sex addict has committed to abstain in order to define his or her sobriety. These definitions are always reviewed first with at least one other recovering person, therapist, or clergy person and are not changed at a later date without thorough discussion and understanding of the reasons for the change. A concisely written sexual recovery plan provides the addict with a tool as an ongoing recovery reminder, even in the face of challenging circumstances. One characteristic of addiction, particularly for sex addicts, is difficulty maintaining a clear focus on personal beliefs, values, and goals when faced with situations of intensity, arousal, stimulation, and impulsive acting

Table 8.1
Writing a Sexual Boundary Plan

A sexual boundary plan or "sex plan" clearly defines healthy, sober sexual behavior for the sex addict. This is usually done in the form of columns or pages representing the areas needing attention and focus. This plan should always be completed and signed off by another recovering person or experienced therapist before implementing to guard against denial or further acting out.

Column I	Column II	Column III
These are actions that I know are shameful, problematic, or hurtful to others and myself. In this column are all of the most concerning sexual or related behaviors that need to be stopped immediately. *These behaviors (not thoughts or fantasies) are used to define* sobriety *and aid the person seeking help in defining a sober date or amount of time they have without sexual acting out.*	A list of people, places, and experiences that can lead me toward wanting to act out sexually (not necessarily directly sexual things). *This column is used to define all of the situations that can set up a person to engage in their problematic sexual activity.* This is not the sexual activity itself but more a definition of warning or danger signs.	These are the positive rewards of maintaining sobriety. *This final column lists examples of all the positive things that are encouraged by not sexually acting out.* It offers the sex addict something to do with the time and energy created by stopping the compulsive behaviors and a vision toward positive things to come.

EXAMPLES

Bottom-Line Sobriety	Warning and Danger Signs	Healthy Activities of Recovery
Going online to observe any kind of pornography (soft or hard). Buying, renting, reading, or using paper, video or computer porn. Sex outside my marriage. Contacting former girlfriends or sex partners. Contacting prostitutes or escorts or going to sexual massage.	Getting online when no one is home. Flirting with women. Scanning TV channels hoping to catch something exciting or distracting. Unresolved fights with spouse. Lying to myself, others, or keeping secrets. Isolating. Working more than 45 hours a week. Not getting enough sleep or exercise. Skipping my support group meetings or therapy. Excessive sexual fantasy and objectification of others. Wanting to call or write former sex or dating partners.	More time with loved ones and friends—better relationships. Returning to hobbies and creative activities that bring me pleasure. Rediscovering romance with my wife. Taking some classes toward a possible new career. Feeling clean and good about myself. More time for relaxation and fun. Going to movies and ball games. Not having to worry about sexual disease or getting caught lying.

out. The words, "Trust me just one more time . . ." and promises like, "I really will be good this time" will not hold up in an impulsive moment.

Without the clearly defined boundaries of a recovery plan, the sex addict is vulnerable to deciding in the moment what action is best for him or her. Unfortunately, most addict's impulsive decisions do not lead them toward their long-term goals and beliefs. Following a sexual boundary plan helps to maintain a clear focus on recovery choices regardless of situation or momentary motive. Sexually addicted people have to clearly determine when, how, and under what circumstances they will again be sexual in a healthy manner. Some will say that these steps make life too difficult and get in the way of their relationships or life circumstances. This may be true. Some of the steps may seem trivial, a pain, or just silly. These clients need to be reminded of the larger goal of creating long-lasting change.

Books and Articles   Because sexual addiction is so poorly understood and readily given to dramatic misinterpretation, it is important for addicted patients and their spouses to read clear, well-organized materials from the beginning of their healing process. Books provide credibility and shame reduction, giving the patient a I-guess-I-am-not-the-only-one kind of experience, and spouses with some understanding what is happening to their families. Patients need to read about people with problems like themselves, identifying with the consequences and getting hope from the recovery. Not only are there books on the nature and diagnosis of sexual addiction but also workbooks for journaling and self-discovery, daily meditation books for self-reflection, books for women who sexually act out, and a range of useful materials. (See the Recommended Reading list at the end of the chapter.)

Completion and Reading of a Sexual Inventory   All sexually addicted patients have behaviors and histories of sexual shame and sexual secrecy. No matter how much bravado or lack of embarrassment patients may demonstrate in the initial disclosures of their sexual history, there are activities and experiences they would rather forget or leave in the past. These are the very experiences that they need most to reveal and discuss openly. To organize this discussion, the therapist must use a lengthy and organized sexual inventory tool. In his groundbreaking book, *Don't Call It Love*, Patrick Carnes offers a diagnostic inventory called the Sexual Dependency Inventory (SDI) of over 200 questions related to sexual history and interests. The focus of the questionnaire is sexual addiction, and it forces the client to consider both the degree of interest that they may have had in any particular sexual activity and the frequency with which they may have acted out that particular behavior. The SDI also offers an opportunity to review a client's sexual childhood and adolescent sexual history, offering a chance to look at the historical pieces that engendered the behavior problems.

Psychoeducational Programming   Many treatment programs for sexual addiction, both inpatient and outpatient, have an educational component, providing clear instruction on the nature of addictive sexual disorders, their underlying psychological concerns, relapse prevention, family systems, and so on. Patients are active in the educational process, taking notes, offering insights, and comparing histories. In many situations, spouses and partners are invited into the psychoeducational programming, or they have their own track. Education is taught separately from group or individual therapy, sometimes in evenings or weekends.

This programming is usually mandatory, underscoring its value to the recovery process. Similar to education for substance addictions, psychoeducational programming for sex addicts is generally broken down into three parts:

1. *Understanding the sexual addiction process:* This includes addictive cycles, distortions in thinking, denial, and so on, and discussions of patterns and levels of sexual acting out.
2. *Issues underlying sexual addiction:* This includes lectures about family systems dynamics, family history, self-esteem, and moods and the psychological characteristics of sex addicts and their partners.
3. *Relapse prevention:* This includes self-care, relapse patterns, distorted thinking leading up to a relapse and how a couple might deal with a slip or relapse.

Homework   For a variety of reasons, homework comes in varying forms. One way to view homework is as small tasks given to a patient to help them focus on particular issues as they arise in therapy. These assignments may be given in addition to the larger, ongoing tasks of completing sexual inventories or attending 12-Step meetings. Some examples are:

1. *Written:* Write a break-up letter to the woman you are having the affair with and bring the letter to group, but don't contact her in the process.
2. *Verbal:* Talk to your wife about your feelings on her new job and bring the results of that conversation back to the group.
3. *Reading:* Read Chapter 6 in the *Hope and Recovery* book and highlight the reading so that we can discuss it.
4. *Assignment:* When you get paid this week, go out and buy that new shirt you mentioned liking at the store. Be aware of all the thoughts and feelings that occur to you as you purchase it. Wear the shirt to your next group.

Tasks for Those in Committed Relationships   There are several tasks that absolutely must be accomplished in treatment by those in committed spousal relationships, whether married or long term. These tasks involve sexual addicts taking responsibility for the lying, secrets, and sexual acting out behaviors that have gone on during the course of the relationship and being absolutely accountable—first to themselves and later to their spouse—for how those actions have affected the relationship. These partnership tasks are:

1. *A list of lies or secrets held from a partner or spouse:* Very early in treatment, usually in the second or third session, the sex addict is asked to make a complete list of any sexual behaviors that have been kept secret from his or her partner. This list might also include family monies spent on sexual activity, drugs used, or any activity that has been kept a deliberate secret.
2. *A letter of atonement:* The patient is asked to begin to write a letter to the spouse, that they will not send or communicate to the partner for some time but will use as an exercise in therapy. The focus of this letter is to be accountable to the partner for how their sexual betrayal of the relationship, lies, and so on has affected them and the relationship. Apology or the seeking of forgiveness is not the focus of this letter but, rather, accountability.

Because of the underlying shame and fear of abandonment that patients understandably feel, it may take some time to help them get to a neutral stance on this task. There will likely be several versions of this letter written before a workable version is created that might be ready to be shared at some point with a partner.

3. *Disclosure:* Disclosure is the simple act of telling the truth. It occurs when a sex addict sits down with a spouse or partner and tells him or her his sexual history, particularly secret, openly answering any subsequent questions about his or her past activities. For a relationship to go forward in a healthy manner, the past must be revealed, and the addict cannot be allowed to continue to hold the power of those secrets. Provided that the patient's spouse wishes to have this information and is offered some direction for support and guidance, the real healing for the relationship begins only with disclosure. The task work of atonement letters and secrecy lists is working toward disclosure, to allowing the sex addict to offer his or her sexual history, often validating the partner's long denied past suspicions and beliefs.

In their book on disclosure, Jennifer Schneider and Deborah Corley provide extensive background and reasoning for the disclosure process along with many stories of partners and sex addicts who have been through the process themselves. Corley and Schneider (2002) found that both addicts and their partners recommend disclosure, despite the pain that accompanies it:

> George, a 51-year-old manager, explained, "The truth only helps. Honesty is essential in a healthy relationship and recovery. It was very cleansing and seemed to take away some of the power of the addiction as it always thrived on secrets and lies. Had I not told the truth, I would have stayed on a destructive course for longer—perhaps until I destroyed everything. Because I have been honest, now I have nothing to hide." (p. 88)

> Misty, a 45-year-old accountant had been married 23 years to a sex-addicted husband who covered up his behavior by casting doubts on her emotional state. After he disclosed, she related, "I needed to know what kind of risks I was taking. Knowing he could relapse with men and prostitutes let me know how to protect myself from STDs. I also had suspicions about when he was active in his addiction in the past. By finding out that I'd been accurate in my hunches about his behavior, I learned I can trust myself and I'm not crazy, or at least I wasn't making things up or being overly suspicious. It started us off on a footing of greater honesty." (p. 89)

Addicts need to be prepared for negative consequences of disclosure. After admitting her affairs to her husband, Suzy, 37, reported:

> My husband wanted to "reclaim" me sexually. I felt so guilty that I let him consume me sexually for weeks. He then became vigilant about my behavior, thoughts, and actions for several months. He started to judge me and try to manage my program. Now when he is feeling insecure or mad, he brings up my history and throws up to me certain situations or individuals. I don't know what to say at these times; I just feel worse, guiltier. (p. 90)

It is best to disclose the basic outline of *all* the acting out behaviors, rather than only what the partner already knows or what the addict thinks is most acceptable. Staggered disclosures cause a lot of damage. One woman told:

> There were several major disclosures over six months. I was devastated. He continued to disclose half-truths—but only when the lies didn't make sense and he was backed to the wall. This only increased my pain and anger and made the whole situation worse. Each new disclosure was like reliving the initial pain all over again. I felt lied to and didn't trust him. All I wanted was the truth. I wish the truth had been disclosed all at once and not in bits and pieces. (p. 67)

It is best initially not to disclose all the "gory" details. Ben, 31, explained:

> I hope it wasn't just "dumping," but I felt cleaner, relieved. But I shouldn't have shared so much; it was hurtful to her. Now it's hard for her to have so much information. The knowledge doesn't help her and seems only to cause pain as dates roll around or if we drive past a particular place. She can't stop thinking about it. (p. 64)

CONFRONTING SEXUAL SLIPS AND LIMIT TESTING

The primary goal of sexual addiction treatment is for the client to stop their sexual acting out. While clients may be making great use of therapy by gaining insight into their history, working through transference, or stabilizing a chaotic relationship, if they are not getting sexually sober, then treatment is not working. Clients desiring to focus primarily on other issues might be better referred out to other, less directive treatment settings.

Sexually addicted clients often test the limits of the treatment and the treating therapist to determine if the boundaries being set keep them emotionally safe. They unconsciously introduces distracting and stimulating material to occupy the treatment sessions while avoiding talking about their sexual acting out and distractions. They arrive late for sessions, come up with issues around payment, forget or skip homework assignments, and so on. All of this must be dealt with in the sessions and not overlooked if the treatment is to be successful. It is the responsibility of the therapist to monitor this and respond appropriately.

Many of these clients come from backgrounds where their early emotional needs were neglected or completely dismissed. On some level, they test to see if the therapist really does care enough to keep them on track and focused on the work at hand. For this population, the therapist must carefully manage and often lead the early therapy sessions, making sure that assignments are accomplished and any treatment boundaries and agreements are responsibly discussed, particularly those having to do with the patients' sexual sobriety.

Sexual sobriety as a goal should be accomplished fairly quickly, often by the end of the first or second session, following guidelines set through the sexual sobriety plan (see earlier discussion). The therapist should see slips into a return to sexual acting out as a need for more support and accountability. Perhaps the patient might need to be seen more often or to check in daily by phone for a week or so. They might need to increase their attendance at 12-Step support group meetings or even considered for a higher level of therapeutic care. When working with sex addicts, we confront limit testing, validate any and all accomplishments, and add as much containment and support as needed. If the client acts out sexually, always keep in mind that sexual sobriety is the primary goal of the work.

THERAPEUTIC BOUNDARIES AND COUNTER TRANSFERENCE

It is more important in working with sexual addicts than perhaps with any other patient population that the counselor is cognizant and actively managing his or her own personal boundaries in regard to patient interactions. Not only in physical contact, but also in the more subtle emotional and verbal exchanges, the counselor needs to be aware of his or her own feelings, attitudes, and attractions toward the client, utilizing that information to guide his or her words and actions. Sexually addicted patients are not only extremely emotionally needy but also very consciously and unconsciously blocked about any healthy way of getting their needs met. This is a population that is more comfortable being seductive and manipulative to get attention than by being vulnerable or openly asking for validation or support.

The counselor needs to have clear physical boundaries from the very beginning. The treating clinician must carefully judge his or her use of hugs or physical contact particularly within the first 90 days, remembering that this is a patient population that is in treatment for using physical and sexual seduction in an attempt to meet concealed dependency needs. Carefully drawn therapeutic boundaries can easily be pulled back later in treatment if appropriate, but lax boundaries are always problematic. Those providing treatment to sex addicts should carefully consider their work attire, understanding that this client actively objectifies and sexualizes them. Only under the most unusual of circumstances should a counselor working with this population disclose any of their own feelings of attraction toward a client. Though it is not unusual to have feelings toward this client population, that information should be strictly reserved for discussion in professional supervision and never acted on. When clients make comments that can be perceived as seductive or openly inviting a sexual or romantic situation with the therapist, handle these by reframing the comment in a way that validates the client for being willing to bring this information into the light, while at the same time keeping the session on task.

CLIENT: I have wanted to tell you for a while that I have some feelings about you that I have been keeping to myself.

THERAPIST: I am glad you decided to bring them up. What kinds of feelings have you been having?

CLIENT: Well, I need you to know that I think you are really attractive, especially your hair and your eyes when you look at me like that (long stare). I feel like we have a special kind of connection and I haven't felt this way about anyone in a long time (long direct stare).

THERAPIST: I have noticed you might be having some of these feelings and I am glad you brought that up (very directly and matter of fact). It is not unusual at all for clients, especially sex addicts, to sexualize or romanticize their therapist. As you have told me, you tend to objectify many of your relationships in this way, isn't this the kind of thing that brought you into treatment in the first place?

CLIENT: No doubt.

THERAPIST: It seems like you can get into the bubble or trance of your objectification really easily. Even in therapy, the very place where you are seeking help for this issue, you can find yourself lost in these feelings. I wonder what that is like for you?

CLIENT: (Becoming more genuine, less seductive now.) Wow (sigh), I guess when you put it that way, it's scary (looking down). I guess I can get lost in these feelings just about anywhere and I don't even know why. Sometimes I am not even really attracted to someone and I find myself romanticizing or fantasizing about him or her.

THERAPIST: Then maybe it's about something else, something other than sex or romance.

CLIENT: I never really looked at that.

Note that in the preceeding dialog the therapist has taken a potentially uncomfortable situation for both and turned it into an opportunity for the client to begin to observe how his seductive defenses may serve to protect him from some underlying feelings that are, as yet, unexplored. If followed, this would likely lead to the client getting in touch with his fear of being vulnerable and his use of seduction and sexualization as a means of gaining control and power over an emotionally threatening situation.

THE ROLE OF THE INDIVIDUAL THERAPIST

The role of the therapist changes over time at a rate determined by the progress of the patient. Initially the individual therapist serves a role much like a sponsor in a 12-Step program: The therapist or counselor sets limits, provides guidelines and contracts, confronts denial and distorted thinking, and serves as a solid, stable resource. The role is active, directive, and somewhat authoritative, allowing the client to have a place to be known, an unmovable, safe environment, where the client cannot manipulate, be seductive (sexually or emotionally), or get away with pushing boundaries.

Over time, as most clients get sober from their sexual acting out and their life circumstances begin to stabilize (or at least become less chaotic) the clients themselves begin to integrate that self-stabilizing role, allowing the therapist to transition to a more reflective, empathic, and traditionally psychodynamic role. The rate at which the client makes this transition from needing the therapist to being more structured to allowing the relationship to be less authoritative depends in great part on the emotional health of the patient. The patient's mood stability, motivation to make the best use of treatment, current life circumstances, his or her degree of character pathology and amount of past trauma all work to determine how well he or she is able to make use of the treatment relationship.

GROUP TREATMENT

Some reasons to keep a client out of the group setting might be:

1. Strong narcissistic impairment that would either interfere with the group process or his or her own ability to gain from the group (e.g., they would take everything personally).

2. Deep depression or anxiety that needs to be stabilized before the patient could tolerate a change into group.
3. The patient is not committed enough to suggest that he or she will remain in the group once started.
4. The patient demonstrates a great deal of resistance following through with assignments, is frequently late, and so on, and may not remain in treatment.

The individual therapist can initially serve as a filter for a group, predetermining whether a client is ready for a group process.

Group is by far the preferred method of therapy for all addiction treatment and this is clearly the case with a sexually addicted population. By the time they reach some form of treatment, sex addicts are generally quite isolated, often have some social deficits, have great shame about their sexual acting out histories, and require a great deal of support to maintain their sexual abstinence. A successful group offers clients the opportunity for improved socialization, shame reduction, and support for all stages of recovery. Group treatment for sexual addiction is most successfully carried out in an atmosphere that promotes absolute safety and confidentiality in sharing past sexual behaviors combined with advocacy and willingness to change. While short- and long-term groups serve different functions and potentially differing populations, the availability of therapists, number of potential clients, and direction of the treatment program all help to determine the best choice.

Short-Term Groups Short-term groups offer large numbers of mixed populations the chance to gather a great deal of information about the problems they face, while at the same time gaining the sense that they are not isolated with these concerns. These tend to be closed groups of 8 to 12 sessions. Short-term groups often run about 2 hours with the first part of this time being devoted to a psychoeducational topic area for all the attendees. After the general discussion, this larger group may be broken up for more personal and confidential sharing and discussion. In this way, spouses, family members, and sex addicts all might attend the educational portion of the sessions, later to be broken into smaller groups by population. The spouses' group then takes the second hour alone to support each other and focus on their feelings and losses related to the sexual addicts' behavior. The addicts' group then separate to focus on sobriety and peer support concerns. When this group is completed, the attendee has to make a new choice about the next step for therapy. This situation can be problematic at times since once the group has bonded after 8 to 12 sessions it can be difficult to get members to move on to a longer term situation. Often, these members are offered the opportunity to stay together and turn the group into a long-term situation. Another concern with the short-term group is that some sex addicts perceive themselves to be cured once the 8 to 12 sessions are completed and may be resistant to receiving treatment.

Long-Term Groups Long-term sex addiction groups focus on small numbers of similar people gaining awareness and intimacy. For sex addiction treatment, these are open groups—clients going from start to completion generally in 1½ to 3 years. Group size is best at seven to eight patients and same sex, though mixed hetero- and homo-sexual groups are useful and share more similar than dissimilar concerns. These groups are structured but tend to be more interactive than the short-term sessions and are best at 2 hours. Patients are encouraged to be non-shaming but open to confront each other's thinking about any minimizing or denial about past or future sexual acting out. The key to the success of the long-term sexual addiction group is accountability. Each member must present weekly check-ins to the group about the amount of time they have been abstinent from their sexual acting out, frequency of their attendance at 12-Step support groups and other related concerns. Group members are responsible for written task work as assigned. Accountability extends to overall and timely attendance, payment for sessions, and the handling of absences. The group participants are encouraged to meet and call each other outside of the group for support. Gossip and cliques can be confronted within the group framework.

Once the safety and rhythm of the group is established, as with all group processes, the work of deeper family concerns, underlying character disorders, and authority relationships are worked out. However, the primary directive is and always remains sexual sobriety, honesty within the group, and accountability. This frame creates the common bond, safety, and support necessary for the maturing of the individuals and the group to take place. The leader is an active member of the group, role modeling appropriate feedback and confronting where necessary, encouraging the clients to identify and manage affect, educating and encouraging the healthy communication of those feelings to other group members.

ANCILLARY THERAPIES

At some point in the patient's development, it can be helpful to offer differing therapy modalities to facilitate greater insight and access to feelings. Provided the patient has maintained some period of stable sexual sobriety and that his or her life circumstances are also constant, the utilization of additional therapy techniques can help the patient become more integrated and self-contained. Ancillary therapies can be offered in both the individual and group settings. Patients can be sent out to alternative therapists or the therapists can be brought into the primary therapy. The primary therapist, if properly trained, may carry out some of these experiences themselves, integrating them into the addiction treatment. Art Therapy, Eye Movement and Desensitization and Reprocessing (EMDR), and Psychodrama are the most commonly used alternative therapy processes for patients undergoing inpatient or outpatient sexual addiction treatment. Each of these offers nonintellectualized methods to help break through a patient's defenses, working to unblock static emotional states. EMDR is traditionally provided on an individual basis and is most helpful with specific trauma memory or charged emotional experience. Psychodrama has proved most useful in the group setting, with different group members playing the roles of important figures in the patient's experience both past and present.

THE USE OF ART THERAPY IN SEX ADDICTION TREATMENT

Art therapy can be used as a primary or adjunctive form of treatment in addressing issues of sex addiction. The use of art materials offers entrée to unconscious material that may not be accessible through verbal therapy. Once the information is revealed in the art, it can be further explored verbally. Similarly, problem solving is possible through exploration of the images concretely visible on paper. One can see how large obstacles are or how long the journey ahead is perceived to be. Most sex addicts have difficulty identifying their feelings since their sexual acting out has served to keep them numb. In art therapy, a client is encouraged to draw emotional experiences without the initial pressure of naming them or understanding them. During the discussions that follow, clients can often see how they feel by the colors, expressions, and images that they depict thus assisting them in identifying and connecting to their feelings (Figures 8.1 and 8.2). They can then feel freer to communicate those feelings to others, validate their feelings, and get support or help in coping with those feelings. Some other treatment goals, which align with art therapy, are increasing insight into the self, recognizing distorted thinking, clarifying unresolved issues, improving self-esteem, and connecting with others.

Figure 8.1 A client in a weekly sexual addiction outpatient group produced this artwork. The group assignment was for each man to draw or paint a depiction of his emotional baggage. This drawing reveals the client's heavy emotional burdens of the past. He holds them on his back as he bends at the waist and kneels to hold up the load. Abandoned as an infant, being overpowered by a sibling, watching animals be killed, and religious education are all subjects represented as areas of unresolved trauma, confusion, or hurt. The drawn face of the client expresses how it feels to be weighed down by his past: He appears exhausted, sad, anxious, and pained. Life seems depressing and hopeless as evidenced by the chosen colors which are brown, gray, and mustard. Overall, the drawing provides a view into the life of the client revealing what it has been like to manage these overwhelming issues and feelings on his own. *Note:* Thanks to Christine Cook, MSW, ATR, for providing this artwork and description.

Figure 8.2   This art therapy work was created in an outpatient intensive session. The assignment directed the client to draw the path that he saw leading from his sexual addiction toward a life lived in recovery and sexual health. The client chose the metaphor of a bridge to show movement and transition from active addiction to healing. Anticipation of hope and alliance are revealed in the image as the figures move from darkness into light becoming more articulated and literally brighter as they are helped over into recovery. The client sees the ongoing nature of the recovery process as people getting over the bridge and then going back to help others across. This speaks to the service portion of the 12-Step beliefs. In the distance, there is the faint image of a structure or house, which the client sees as the potential for a healthy relationship and family life if he remains on this path.

CYBERSEX AND SEX ADDICTION

Cybersex—any form of sexual expression accessed through the computer or the Internet—is now one of the biggest industries on the Internet. Currently, over 70% of all visits on the Internet involve a sexual purpose. These days cybersex activities include not only viewing pornography but also exchanging sexually explicit messages and e-mail, placing ads to meet people for sex dates, hanging out in sexually oriented chat rooms, engaging in interactive online affairs and sometimes even utilizing digital cameras for real-time mutual viewing and sex acts. Many people engage in online activities they might never do in the real world, yet harm themselves and their relationships through online affairs or engaging in workplace cybersex. The intensity, easy availability, anonymity, and relatively low cost of this new sexual medium have opened the door to playful experimentation for some and confusion and loss for others. These consequences include:

- Lonely and constricted lives where many hours are spent alone with the computer involved in fantasy sexual activities. Real-life friendships and social contacts fall away.
- Relationships where partners or spouses or children often feel lonely, unimportant, neglected, or angry.
- Children exposed to pornography and graphic sexual content.
- Poor productivity and boundaries in the workplace with risk of being written up or terminated.
- Risks of acquiring HIV and other sexually transmitted diseases.
- People putting themselves in physically vulnerable or dangerous situations with strangers.
- Risk of arrest and imprisonment for downloading illegal pornography.
- Lying and hiding in relationships and mistrust and betrayal.

Why Cybersex?

Through the pioneering work of Dr. Al Cooper at Stanford University, we have come to understand that the anonymity, affordability, and accessibility of Internet sexual resources, a phenomenon called *The Triple A Engine* (Cooper et al., 1998), the computer can both initiate and accelerate the progression of sexual addiction. For those with a prior history of addictions and compulsive sexual behaviors, the Internet can escalate their addiction and the unmanageability of their lives. For most cybersex users, the Internet provides a fascinating new venue for learning about and experiencing sex. Some users, however, perhaps 8% to 10%, become hooked on the neurochemical arousal produced by repetitive involvement with cybersex and experience significant life problems as they compulsively engage in online sexual activity. These people can be considered cybersex addicts. For those who become hooked on the intensity of the cybersex experience, the consequences are serious; some resulting from the many hours the user spends on the Internet and others specifically caused by the sexual content of the user's activities. For couples, the emotional impact of a cybersex affair is described by many spouses as similar to those of a real or offline affair. The partner's self-esteem is damaged, leaving him or her with strong feelings of hurt, betrayal, abandonment, loneliness, and shame. Relationships suffer as isolation and jealousy become the norm. Spouses (and often the user) begin to compare their bodies and sexual performances to those of the online fantasy partners. Many couples lose interest in intimacy and mutual sexuality.

Managing Cybersex Problems at Home

In some instances, maintaining home use of the computer online is necessary. Some examples are a home office, using the Internet for travel, helping kids with homework, or managing finances. If patients need to continue using the computer online at home, here are some simple, helpful guidelines:

1. *Move the home computer.* Isolation and the potential for getting away with illicit actions feed the addiction. Cybersex addicts who live with others should not keep their home computer in an isolated location. Moving it to a

family room or other public area prevents secret keeping and can also help partners feel less suspicious and uncomfortable.

2. *Go online only when someone else is home.* Utilize the accountability provided by having others around. Make a commitment not to go online when alone.

3. *Online providers:* There are several online Internet service providers (ISPs) offering access only to sites that their evaluation team has determined are appropriate for children and families. Such providers exclude sexual content sites.

4. *Go online for e-mail only.* If there is no reason to be searching online—don't. Make a written and verbal commitment to avoid any online searching activity. Let others gather information or data if that becomes necessary.

5. *Purchase blocking software.* Blocking software designed to eliminate access to sexual content and other specific types of sites can be purchased and downloaded over the Internet or purchased in computer stores. This software is a *must have* for cybersex addicts who intend to go back to using the computer online. Although this software does not provide a screen for all problem sites, it will present an initial challenge to the addict and slow down their initial impulsivity problem. Although, with enough effort, the software can be defeated, it provides the cybersex addict with time to reflect before logging onto an inappropriate site. It is essential when loading this software to *give the access code to someone else* (preferably someone else in cybersex recovery—not a spouse or partner). Without the access code, someone who wants to act out sexually cannot remove the blocking software.

6. *Utilize bookend online activity.* One of the keys to any successful recovery program is to use support. When going online, make it a habit to call a friend first, or better, someone from a support group—this is *book ending*. By making a commitment to another person to stay out of problem online sites and calling them back when offline, accountability is created.

MANAGING CYBERSEX PROBLEMS IN THE WORKPLACE

Acting out by going to sexual content or relationship sites while at work creates a good possibility of being embarrassed, written-up, or losing a valued job. Most companies have now adapted a zero tolerance policy for this kind of behavior in the workplace. When the latest e-mail joke or an employee's baby picture is being passed around the office, company policies are often easily forgotten or minimized. The cybersex addict may think, "Everyone is looking at something personal from their computer, what's the big deal?" But sexual activity in the workplace *is* a big deal. Many cybersex addicts try to avoid being observed by staying late to access sexual content, unaware that in the workplace they are continuously being monitored. In a networked system, every site and piece of mail accessed from an individual workstation has the potential to be observed by management through programs designed to follow him or her as they traverse the Internet. By the time they formulate a recovery plan, some cybersex addicts have already used the office computer to access online sexual content. Even if only the home computer has been used, the office computer constitutes a significant risk for recovering cybersex addicts. If online work in the office is a necessity, the following steps may be helpful:

1. *Go online only during work hours.* Don't stay late to work on projects and take on assignments involving Internet use. Avoid being alone in the office.
2. *Move the position of the computer screen.* If the office computer screen faces away from people walking by or entering your workstation, move the screen so that others can view what is being accessed or worked on.
3. *Install blocking software on a work PC.* In a nonnetworked system, this should be a fairly simple task.
4. *Remove any files or history of past sexual activity* from the computer.
5. *Display inspirational photos around the computer screen.* Family photos are reminders of the reasons to avoid sexual content at work.
6. *Find a safe person in the workplace to turn to for help when needed.* It is unlikely that anyone goes to the boss to disclose a history of sexually acting out at work, unless having been caught. However, others can be recruited for support and help.
7. *Take breaks when feeling tempted.* Go for therapeutic walks; get out of the workplace. Find a quiet place to meditate or perform breathing exercises. A little time and distance goes a long way toward avoiding old behavior.
8. *Use the telephone.* Call other recovering people to check in for support during the workday.

Offering tools or worksheets to help clients change and monitor their behavior offers a manageable guide for editing out their most problematic and potentially dangerous computer related concerns.

TREATMENT CONCERNS OF PARTNERS AND SPOUSES

Sex addiction affects not only the sex addict but also ripples through the entire family. Like the sex addict, spouses and partners also need healing and can benefit from a treatment and personal recovery program. Helen, a 45-year-old woman, had been married for 11 years. Two years into her marriage, Helen discovered over 3,500 child pornography photos on her husband's (Damon) computer. He claimed he knew nothing about them, but over the next 2 years similar photos kept appearing on his computer. He finally disclosed that he'd been a sex addict since his early teens and had been a compulsive consumer of Internet pornography for at least 6 years:

> I was horrified! I could not believe I had married this man! I'd thought I had married 'the man of my dreams.' After attending counseling and promising that he would not use Internet porn again, he resumed its use. This continued over and over, broken promise after broken promise, until we ended up separating. After several months we got back together, only to find that he had issued yet another false promise.

Partners Are Isolated

Feelings of shame, self-blame, and embarrassment about having sexual problems accompany the early days of dealing with a partner's sex addiction. These feelings often prevent the spouse from talking with others and appealing for help.

The resulting isolation only worsens the situation. Much like the partner of an alcoholic will cover up for the drinker, denial, making excuses and covering up for the sex addict is part of this stage. A 46-year-old woman, involved for many years in an abusive marriage describes why she finally left:

> His behaviors would have been public knowledge had I not shielded and protected him. I kept friends from knowing the truth about my marriage and husband, so that they would continue our friendship. I ended friendships with people who got too close and knew too much. I allowed him to choose my friends and to tape my phone calls by not confronting him about it. I allowed him to explore three extramarital affairs.

Based on the experience of many partners of cybersex addicts, we recognize three stages of prerecovery.

STAGES OF PRERECOVERY

Stage One: Ignorance and Denial   Although the partner recognizes there is a problem in the relationship, he or she is unaware of the role of sexual acting out. "I knew something was wrong the first two years of our relationship, but I could not identify it." They believe the sex addicts' denials, explanations, and promises. They tend to ignore their own concerns and may blame themselves for sexual problems in the relationship. When sex addicts do seem interested in relational sex, partners may try to enhance their own attractiveness through purchasing seductive clothing, buying sexual toys, or even attempting weight loss or cosmetic surgery. Self-esteem is clearly suffering, but spouses are unlikely to seek help at this point as they are attempting to control the problem themselves, often seeing themselves as being at fault. Later in Stage One, suspicions may increase and detective work begins, snooping or detective behaviors leading toward Stage Two.

Stage Two: Shock: Discovery of the Sex Addiction   At some point, the partner learns about the true nature of the sexual acting out activities. The partner may discover this by accident or as the result of deliberate investigation. Discovery of the addictive sexual activities usually evokes strong feelings of shock, betrayal, anger, pain, hopelessness, confusion, and shame. Many spouses describe cycles of discoveries, fights, promises made, and, later, more painful discovery. During Stage Two, the partner's ignorance and denial come to an abrupt end.

Stage Three: Problem-Solving Attempts   The partner now begins to take action to resolve the problem, perceived as sexual acting out. At this stage, the classic sexual coaddictive behaviors peak—becoming a personal library of information for the addict on sex addiction and addiction recovery, snooping, bargaining, controlling access to the cell phone, computer, and so on, having ultimatums, asking for full disclosure after every episode, and (early in this stage) increasing the frequency and repertory of sexual activities with the addict in hopes of decreasing the addict's desire to sexually act out. A partner in Stage Three believes that additional information will help them to manage the situation.

Recovery begins when partners of addicts are aware that they are in crisis and need help. Partners enter into crisis when their problem-solving efforts are unsuccessful and the costs of remaining in the status quo become intolerable. Symptoms include depression, isolation, loss of libido, a dead marriage, dysfunctional behaviors in some cases (affairs, excessive drinking, or violence), and awareness of the effects on the children. In the recovery stage, spouses learn that they are not the cause of the problem and cannot solve it. Once the spouse of the sex addict is in therapy and getting help the marriage or relationship most likely ends unless the sex addict also becomes committed to the recovery process.

Some of the activities listed in the following checklist can help spouses or partners of sex addicts to identify behaviors of their own that may have developed in relationship to the problem of living with a sexual addict. These are issues beyond their own grief and anger that they may begin to address for themselves.

Partner Checklist

- Attempting to compete with sexual images or experiences through dress or in sexual behavior.
- Agreeing to uncomfortable sexual activities.
- Spying on a spouse's sexual activities or images.
- Taking care of everyone around them, losing focus on their own needs, wants, and self-care.
- Covering up for a spouse's sex activities or absences.
- Beginning to dislike themselves for consistent whining, criticizing, fighting, or nagging.

First Steps for the Spouse   Spouses cannot control their partner's computer behavior or loss of interest in having relational sex; the spouse can only become empowered by *getting help and support for themselves.* Shame and fear of being blamed can keep spouses isolated and sometimes unable to seek counseling or talk with close friends. Spouses should be encouraged to confide in at least one friend, relative, or professional who is accepting and nonjudgmental. There are also 12-Step support groups for spouses of sexual addicts (similar to Alanon for spouses of alcoholics), called S-anon or C-osa (see Box 8.4).

TREATMENT OF PARTNERS AND SPOUSES

Many professionals who treat sex addicts find spouses and partners to be a difficult population. Much of the partner's focus is on the one who has sexually acted out; they often have little interest in addressing their own concerns or seeking support for themselves. Looking at just a few of the issues that a partner faces—betrayal, violation of trust, or possible disease concerns—it is easy to understand why partners can be so challenging. Partners come to treatment at a variety of stages:

1. Those who have had some knowledge all along that their spouse was sexually acting out.
2. Those who have just recently found out about their spouses sexual acting out.

3. Those partners who are completely in the dark and have yet to find out about the sexual acting out.

Despite the complex issues presented in each individual situation, the basic needs of the spouse or marital partner entering treatment are very similar. Partners of sex addicts entering treatment need:

1. *Validation for all of their feelings:* Partners of sex addicts enter treatment filled with anger, hurt, and betrayal. It is essential that each partner have his or her say for as long as they need and to do so in as many ways as they need to during the therapeutic session. Partners need to vent and grieve. It is better for them to bring this to treatment than to bring this into their families.
2. *Education about sex addiction:* Spouses thrive on gaining information about the addictive process and sex addiction. They need access to books, articles, and educational sessions to help contain their anxiety and provide hope and information for the future (see the end of this chapter for some materials).
3. *Support groups:* Like the addicts, partners need a safe, confidential place for support and guidance. Facilitated partner's or 12-Step groups provide room for them to vent their hurt and gain support toward their own personal growth.

SEX ADDICTION THERAPY THAT WORKS: THE CLIENT'S VIEW

A recent survey of patients who had been treated for their online sexual addiction behavior problems (Schneider, 2001) showed many respondents were pleased with the professional help they obtained for their sexual addiction problems. Those who saw knowledgeable counselors were given an appropriate diagnosis, guidance about how to stop the behaviors, and referral to 12-Step sexual recovery programs; however, several respondents reported less positive experiences. The most reported problem was that therapists seemed to lack understanding about the power of the actual experiences of sexual addict. Therapists who were less than helpful lacked information about types of sexual acting out activities and tended to underestimate their tremendous effect on the user. This led to diversion of the therapy into attempts by the underinformed therapist to make the user more accepting of the activity or an attempt by the therapist to get the client to decrease the behavior by willpower and simple decision making. The behavior was not acknowledged for the all-encompassing addiction it really was. Therapists needed to ask probing questions giving them a full picture of what the client is doing and how it is affecting his or her life.

A second problem was a failure by the therapist to make it an absolute priority for the patient to stop self-destructive or illegal sexual behaviors. In some cases, sessions ended up focusing in an insight-oriented fashion about the underlying causes of the behavior, while the client continued activities that harmed self/others (family members, coworkers) at great risk to the client. Therapists need to independently assess the risk of the behaviors. When high, sessions should urgently focus on practical ways to stop the behavior.

A third problem was the failure to consider that the behavior had consequences for the spouse or partner. Issues of trust, betrayal, anger, decreased intimacy, and loss of self-esteem by the significant other greatly impact the relationship. Significant others must be involved in the therapy, whether with the same or a different counselor, and it is suggested that they attend support groups, if available.

SUMMARY

Therapists treating sexual addiction and addictive cybersex problems need to be aware that special training is required to adequately manage these ongoing, challenging concerns. As hypersexual behavior can appear in several differing psychiatric and substance abuse diagnoses, an extensive and clear assessment and lengthy sexual history taking is required. Clients who sexually offend must also be carefully assessed for their appropriateness for inclusion in sexual addiction treatment. Because of the compulsive nature of their sexual behaviors and shameful content, patients tend to minimize and avoid being truthful or responsible about their histories and actions, which must also be taken into account in the assessment phase. Therapists working with sex addicts need to place considerably more emphasis on personal boundaries, accountability, and behavioral tasks than when working with many other client populations. The therapist leads the course of treatment utilizing confrontation as a modality along with a somewhat proscribed treatment approach, working to ensure a level of accountability and structure that these clients are often lacking internally.

Treatment as a whole is cognitive-behavioral and also encourages 12-Step involvement. Patients remaining in longer term treatment who have become sexually abstinate often evolve in therapy to use more traditional psychodynamic psychotherapy technique. Sex addiction group therapists act as role models for the group, providing active confrontation and support toward affect exploration and management. A major goal of the group work is engaging the members toward increasing levels of healthy intimacy. Spouses and partners of sexual addicts require treatment along with the addict, but their needs differ in the treatment. Partners of sexual addicts require support in working through their anger, grief, and betrayal, while also being offered information about the process of addiction and recovery. Ancillary therapies, such as Psychodrama, Art Therapy, and EMDR, can often be helpful as an adjunct to the primary cognitive-behavioral work once stable sexual sobriety has been established. These therapies can help elicit subconscious motivations and concerns, often uncovering blocks to therapy and recovery.

Finally, effective sexual addiction treatment requires the therapist to fully understand the cycle of addiction as specifically applied to sexual acting out, making it a treatment priority for the problem sexual behaviors to stop and also taking into account the challenges and needs of any involved partners or spouses.

My first professional work after graduate school was providing inpatient sex addiction and offender treatment at a national treatment center. Patrick Carnes, PhD, was the clinical director. After several years of working with sex addicts and offenders in a hospital setting, I set out on my own in 1995 and started the Sexual Recovery Institute, a Southern California outpatient sexual addiction treatment center. I find moments of joy in working with sex addicts. This treatment population that many would prefer to avoid, seems ideal to me. Motivated, truly in need of genuine help, and often having many more strengths than failings, these people have always brought more professional and personal rewards to me than disappointments. I never cease to be amazed at the explosion of inner and outer growth that our clients experience, once we help them recover from their destructive sexual acting out. They grow; they heal; they move on. Over what seems like a natural evolution of a professional career, I have gone from providing intensive clinical work and treatment programming to doing more administration, supervision, writing, and lecturing, but I never forget the value of working with the unrecovered addict, walking in the door for the first time, looking for support and direction.

RECOMMENDED READING

FOR THE ADDICT

Carnes, P. J. (2001). *Facing the shadow: Starting sexual and relationship recovery.* Center City, MN: Hazelden. Dr. Carnes' task-centered treatment book designed to take people through the recovery process with written assignments and psychoeducation.

Carnes, P. J. (2001). *Out of the shadows: Understanding sexual addiction,* third edition. Center City, MN: Hazelden. This is the third edition of Dr. Patrick Carnes' groundbreaking work that first introduced the idea of sex addiction into the popular culture. In its current form, it is as helpful as ever. This is a must read for every recovering sex addict.

Kasl, C. (1989). *Women, sex and addiction.* New York: Ticknor and Fields. This is an excellent resource for women struggling with addictive disorders with or without a sexual problem.

Schneider, J. P., & Weiss, R. (2001). *Cybersex exposed: From fantasy to obsession.* Center City, MN: Hazelden. This is a helpful guide through the problems of addictive sexuality on the Internet with some practical solutions for addicts and their partners.

FOR THE PARTNER

Beattie, M. (1987). *Codependent no more.* Center City, MN: Hazelden. This fundamental book is for written those in a close relationship to addicts and alcoholics. This book shifted the addiction field by balancing the focus of treatment toward both the addict and the partner. While the book is focused toward substance addicts and their partners, the themes are useful for all addictions.

Schneider, J. (1988). *Back from betrayal: Recovering from his affairs.* New York: Ballantine. This book was one of the first written about how a spouse survives and thrives beyond the discovery that her husband is a sex addict. Dr. Schneider offers examples and practical information that can guide partners and spouses in their own recovery.

Spring, J. A. (1996). *After the affair: Healing the pain and rebuilding trust when a partner has been unfaithful.* New York: HarperCollins. An extraordinary read, sensitive to the betrayal and wounding present in a sex-addicted relationship. It is very helpful to the couple seeking to rebuild their partnership.

FOR THE THERAPIST

Carnes, P. J. (1989). *Contrary to love: Helping the sexual addict.* Minneapolis, MN: CompCare. This helpful understated book is a good read for any clinician wishing to better understand how to approach the treatment of a sex addict.

Carnes, P. J. (2001). *Facing the shadow: Starting sexual and relationship recovery.* Center City, MN: Hazelden. Dr. Carnes' task-centered treatment book is designed to take people through the recovery process with written assignments and psychoeducation.

Carnes P. J., & Adams, K. M. (2002). *Clinical management of sex addiction.* New York: Brunner-Routlege. This text is a compendium of articles about sexual addiction gathered from the experts in the field. Many of these are practical and helpful toward day-to-day management and patient care.

Cooper, A. (2002). *Sex and the Internet: A guidebook for clinicians.* New York: Brunner-Routlege. This book provides practical, research-based material on how cybersex is affecting our clients and how we can help.

Corley, M. D., & Schneider, J. P. (2002). *Disclosing secrets: When, to whom, and how much to reveal.* Wickenburg, AZ: Gentle Path Press.

BIBLIOGRAPHY

Allen, P. (1985). Integrating art therapy into an alcoholism treatment program. *American Journal of Art Therapy, 24,* 10–12.

American Psychiatric Association. (1994). *Diagnostic and statistical manual of mental disorders* (4th ed.). Washington, DC: Author.

Carnes, P. J. (1983). *Out of the shadows: Understanding sexual addiction.* Center City, MN: Hazelden.

Carnes, P. J. (1989). *Contrary to love: Helping the sexual addict.* Minneapolis, MN: CompCare.

Carnes, P. J. (1991). *Don't call it love: Recovery from sexual addiction.* New York: Bantam Books.

Carnes, P. J. (2001). *Facing the shadow: Starting sexual and relationship recovery.* Center City, MN: Hazelden.

Carnes, P. J., & Adams, K. M. (2002). *Clinical management of sex addiction.* New York: Brunner-Routlege.

Carnes, P. J., Delmonico, D. L., & Griffin, E. (2001). *In the shadow of the Net.* Center City, MN: Hazelden.

Cooper, A. C. (2002). *Sex and the Internet: A guidebook for clinicians.* New York: Brunner-Routlege.

Cooper, A. C., Delmonico, D. L., & Burg, R. (2000). Cybersex users, abusers, and compulsives: New findings and implications. *Sexual Addiction & Compulsivity: Journal of Treatment and Prevention, 7*(1/2), 5–30.

Corley, M. D., & Schneider, J. P. (2002). *Disclosing secrets: When, to whom, and how much to reveal.* Wickenburg, AZ: Gentle Path Press.

Earle, R., & Crow, G. (1989). *Lonely all the time: Recognizing, understanding and overcoming sex addiction for addicts and co-dependents.* New York: Simon & Schuster.

Earle, R., & Earle, M. (1995). *Sex addiction: Case studies and management.* New York: Brunner/Mazel.

Hunter, M. (1990). *Abused boys: The neglected victims of sexual abuse.* New York: Fawcett.

Isley, P. J. (1992). A time limited group therapy model for men sexually abused as children. *Group, 16*(4), 233–246.

Kasl, C. D. (1989). *Women, sex and addiction: A search for love and power.* New York: Ticknor and Fields.

Milrad, R. (1999). Coaddictive recovery: Early recovery issues for spouses of sex addicts. *Sexual Addiction & Compulsivity: Journal of Treatment and Prevention, 6,* 125–136.

Money, J. (1986). *Lovemaps: Clinical concepts of sexual/erotic health and pathology, paraphilia, and gender transpositions in childhood, adolescence, and maturity.* New York: Irvington.

Parker, J., & Guest, D. (1999). *The clinician's guide to 12-step programs: How, when and why to refer a client.* Westport, CT: Auburn House.

Schneider, J. P., & Schneider, B. H. (1990). *Sex, lies, and forgiveness: Couples speaking on healing from sex addiction.* Center City, MN: Hazelden.

Schneider, J. P., & Weiss, R. (2001). *Cybersex exposed: From fantasy to obsession.* Center City, MN: Hazelden.

Sex Addicts Anonymous. (1997, November). *Getting started in sex addicts anonymous* (11th ed.). Houston, TX: Author.

Sexual Compulsives Anonymous. (1995). *Sexual compulsives anonymous.* San Diego, CA: Author.

Turner, M. (1990). Long-term outpatient group psychotherapy as a modality for treating sexual addiction. *American Journal of Preventative Psychiatry and Neurology, 2*(3), 23–26.

Weiss, R. (2000). *Cyber-addiction checklist.* Available from http://www.sexualrecovery.com /sri_docs/cyber.htm.

Wilson, M. (2000). Creativity and shame reduction in sex addiction treatment. *Sexual Addiction & Compulsivity: Journal of Treatment and Prevention, 7*(4), 229–248.

Yalom, V. J., & Yalom, I. (1990). Brief interactive group psychotherapy. *Psychiatric Annals, 20*(7), 362–367.

Young, K. (1998). *Cybersexual addiction quiz.* Available from http://www.netaddiction.com /resources/cybersexual_addiction_quiz.htm.

PART V

EATING DISORDERS

CHAPTER 9

Understanding and Diagnosing Eating Disorders

DAVID M. GARNER and ANNA GERBORG

A NOREXIA NERVOSA IS a common and deadly disorder in adolescents. It is estimated to be the third most common chronic medical illness in girls aged 15 to 19 years. It is associated with significant medical complications and mortality rates exceed the expected incidence of death from all causes among women 15 to 24 years of age by 12-fold (see Fairburn & Brownell, 2002). The mortality rates for bulimia nervosa are much lower; however, the negative effects on quality of life are enormous. Moreover, eating disorders during adolescence are associated with elevated risk for a broad range of physical and mental health problems during early adulthood (see Boxes 9.1 and 9.2).

Eating disorders have been designated for many years as psychiatric disorders; however, only in the past 15 years have they gained interest in mainstream psychology. One of the factors responsible for the growing attention to eating disorders is that they provide a model of the complex interaction between cultural, somatic, and psychological factors in abnormal functioning. The varied psychological features associated with eating disorders contribute to their heterogeneity on presentation. Finally, there are potentially serious physical and psychological consequences of starvation that must be addressed in the understanding and the treatment of the eating disorders. These factors, as well as the increasing prevalence of eating disorders among adolescent and young adult women, have led to a rapid increase of research on eating disorders and their treatment. The past two decades have led to divergence in etiological formulations as well as convergence of opinion on the utility of certain practical intervention principles (Garner & Garfinkel, 1997). In spite of these advancements, current knowledge has yet to yield conclusive support for any one theoretical viewpoint or treatment modality.

On a very basic level, it is difficult to understand why anyone would willingly engage in self-starvation or how control over food intake could become such a powerful reward that it could be thought to be an addiction. However, the addiction

---

BOX 9.1
Mortality and Morbidity in Eating Disorders

ANOREXIA NERVOSA

- Estimated to be the third most common chronic medical illness among girls aged 15 to 19 years old.
- Mortality:
  —Two times higher than any other psychiatric disorder.
  —Rates vary between 2% and 18%.
  —10 to 17 times higher than age-matched controls.
  —Treatment has major effect on mortality rates.

BULIMIA NERVOSA

- High morbidity, low mortality.

---

model is one theoretical framework that has been broadly applied to those with eating disorders. Most often, it is associated with binge-eating behavior within the context of bulimia nervosa, anorexia nervosa, or compulsive overeating. The addiction model is appealing since studies have shown that both substance abuse and poor impulse regulation are common features in bulimia nervosa. However, it has also been applied to self-starvation since periods of sustained calorie restriction can activate powerful neurochemical reward systems that may fuel further dietary restriction. Moreover, applying the addiction model to eating disorders makes sense since eating disordered behaviors appear to conform to the following three

---

BOX 9.2
Eating Disorders in Adolescence Predict Physical and Psychological Disorders in Early Adulthood

Anxiety disorders.

Depressive disorders, suicide attempts.

Cardiovascular symptoms.

Neurological symptoms.

Chronic fatigue.

Chronic pain.

Infectious disorders.

Insomnia.

Limitations in activities due to poor health.

Source: From "Eating Disorders during Adolescence and the Risk for Physical and Mental Disorders during Early Adulthood," by J. G. Johnson, P. Cohen, S. Kasen, and J. S. Brook, 2002, *Archives of General Psychiatry, 59,* pp. 545–552.

Cs often used to define addiction (i.e., compulsive use, loss of control, and continued use despite adverse consequences).

In this chapter, we review diagnostic features and defining characteristics of eating disorders. We also explain some of the more popular ways of understanding eating disorders, with an emphasis on the cognitive-behavioral model. Possible origins of eating disorder symptoms, both distant and proximal to the onset of symptoms, are discussed. Finally, we summarize the treatment implications for the major models for understanding eating disorders.

DEFINING FEATURES

A key feature of anorexia and bulimia nervosa is a persistent overconcern with body size and shape indicated by behavior such as prolonged fasting, strenuous exercise, and self-induced vomiting. These behaviors are intended to decrease body weight, shape, and fat. The obsessive concern with weight in anorexia nervosa was described in various ways by several theorists who have been pioneers in the field. Hilde Bruch portrayed anorexia nervosa as a "relentless pursuit of thinness"; Gerald Russell characterized it as "a morbid fear of fatness" and Arthur Crisp described it as a "weight phobia" (Garner & Garfinkel, 1997, for a detailed discussion of diagnosis). The term *bulimia nervosa* was proposed by Gerald Russell in 1979 to define a syndrome where the patient suffers from powerful and uncontrollable urges to overeat. These urges lead to bouts of binge eating followed by extreme efforts to control weight through self-induced vomiting, laxative abuse, fasting, and/or vigorous exercise. Bulimia nervosa shares many features in common with anorexia nervosa; however, the patient is not emaciated.

There is general disagreement in the literature about the psychological and developmental significance of eating disorders and their symptoms. Both individual and family theorists have emphasized that eating disorders often represent a developmental struggle for autonomy, independence, and individuality. Accordingly, these normal developmental hurdles become flashpoints in adolescence, when the vulnerable individual, parents, or entire family are forced to deal with emergent developmental realities. For instance, in those who present with eating disorders, it is not uncommon for them to have mothers so overinvolved in their daughters' lives that the daughters express a morbid fear of growing up, fearing that their mothers would be left alone. This separation anxiety may be an unconscious reason for physically remaining a child, that is, not gaining weight to a normal level for an adult woman. Other women are terrified of getting their menstrual period. Some say they are afraid of the connotation of menstruation. Rather than being a marker of fertility, for some women with eating disorders it is an indicator that they now have enough body fat to be capable of giving birth. In these cases, body fat takes on powerful surplus meaning underlying extraordinary efforts to maintain a body weight that the hormones require for normal menstrual functioning. This focus on fat may serve additional functions such as shielding the women from thinking about the real issues bothering them. For example, fat may be linked to menstruation, which symbolizes adulthood and specific aspects of adulthood (e.g., mature sexual functioning or separating from parents) are viewed as threatening and to be avoided at all costs. In this way, developmental issues can play a significant role in the development and maintenance of eating disorders in certain patients.

The occurrence of eating disorders cannot be fully appreciated outside the context of culture values (Garner & Garfinkel, 1997). In recent years, intense pressure has been placed on women to diet to conform to ultraslender role models for feminine beauty. However, very few women will ever achieve this admired physical form through restrictive dieting, largely owing to biological limits to achieving permanent weight loss. Nevertheless, traits such as competence, control, attractiveness, self-worth, and self-discipline continue to be associated with dieting and weight control in our culture. It is impossible to walk down the frozen food section of the grocery store without being bombarded with bright red, attractively labeled diet entrees. Magazine ads show women with donut-shaped buttocks who are urged to eat nutritious breakfast bars so that they can "respect themselves in the morning." Television commercials for diet products are followed immediately by fast-food ads imploring the viewer to order the supersized meal. The consequence of the conflict between cultural imperatives to lose weight and biological and genetic realities related to body weight has led to widespread dissatisfaction with body shape and weight that has even infected prepubescent young girls. However, as has been pointed out by researchers looking at anorexia nervosa in non-Western cultures, the fear of fatness may play less of a role in the development of the disorder. For example, in China, many cases of anorexia nervosa seem to be motivated by a sense of virtue that comes with self-denial.

Another characteristic of eating disorders is the ego-syntonic nature of certain symptoms. In contrast to patients with other psychological disorders, such as depression or anxiety, most anorexia nervosa patients actively embrace their eating disorder symptoms. Because a defining feature of this disorder is denial of the significance of a low body weight raises the question of the nature and degree of free choice or will that the patient has to decide to enter treatment. For example, one woman, looking back at the worst stages of her anorexia nervosa, agreed that the eating disorder would never have allowed her to seek treatment—at least not any form of treatment that involved weight gain. Historically, involuntary treatment has been characterized as inhumane by some; however, in this case, without involuntary treatment, delivered in a compassionate and humane manner, death would have been an almost certain outcome. In addition to minimizing symptoms such as a low body weight, restrictive dieting, excessive exercise, and other weight controlling symptoms, patients are often proud of actually achieving a diagnosis of anorexia nervosa. Thirty years ago, patients usually developed anorexia nervosa with no prior knowledge that such a disorder existed. Since that time, the fashion industry has relentlessly promoted an ultrathin image of beauty. Anorexia nervosa itself has developed a positive meaning because of the disorder's association with celebrity status and socially desirable traits, as well as the aforementioned traits of intelligence, self-control, and self-discipline. This placement of the disorder in the limelight has resulted in some patients developing an anorexic identity and enjoying what they perceive as a sense of self that is controlled. We have found that numerous patients will say that they do not know who they are without the disorder and are convinced that they cannot function without it. It resembles the self-defeating process of substance abusing patients who need the disorder to feel okay about themselves and whose attempts to inhibit symptoms produce often overwhelming anxiety. While most women with an eating disorder think they are exerting control by extreme monitoring of their bodies, the eating disorder is in control of them and, without help from experts who are trained in eating disorders, is bound to eventually take control of their lives.

BOX 9.3
Major Medical Complications in Eating Disorders

ANOREXIA NERVOSA

- Chronic renal insufficiency.
- Amenorrhea and infertility.
- Osteoporosis and associated fractures.
- Chronic constipation.
- Anemia, leukopenia.

BULIMIA NERVOSA

- Electrolyte abnormalities dehydration.
- Enlarged parotid glands.
- Destruction of dental enamel.
- Gastrointestinal complications.
- Renal failure.

The medical complications seen in eating disorders are another defining feature. Symptoms, such as hypotension, hypothermia, bradycardia (low heart rate), and overall reduced metabolic rate are common for anorexia nervosa. Self-induced vomiting and purgative abuse may cause various symptoms or abnormalities, such as weakness, muscle cramping, edema, constipation, and cardiac arrhythmias. Additionally, general fatigue, constipation, depression, various neurological abnormalities, kidney and cardiac disturbances, swollen salivary glands, electrolyte disturbances, dental deterioration, finger clubbing or swelling, and dehydration are common. Anorexia nervosa has the highest mortality rates of any psychiatric disorder (see Box 9.3).

DIAGNOSTIC FEATURES

The resistance to change seen in anorexia has obvious implications for treatment and has been a major focus of therapeutic strategies recommended for this disorder. The prevailing diagnostic system in the United States, namely the *Diagnostic and Statistical Manual of Mental Disorders,* fourth edition (*DSM-IV-TR;* American Psychiatric Association [APA], 2000) formally defines as well as distinguishes the two major eating disorders, anorexia nervosa and bulimia nervosa. By drawing the boundaries for these eating disorders, the current *DSM-IV-TR* diagnostic criteria have substantial implications for clinical care and research.

ANOREXIA NERVOSA

The requirements for diagnosis of anorexia nervosa according to the *DSM-IV-TR* (APA, 2000) are summarized as (1) refusal to maintain a body weight over a minimally normal weight for age and height (e.g., weight loss leading to maintenance of a body weight less than 85% of that expected or failure to make expected weight gain during a period of growth), (2) intense fear of gaining weight or becoming fat, even though underweight, (3) disturbance in the way that body weight, size, or shape is experienced, and (4) amenorrhea in females (absence of at least three consecutive menstrual cycles).

The *DSM-IV-TR* divides anorexia nervosa into two diagnostic subtypes: restricting type and binge-eating/purging type. The restricting type is defined by rigid restriction of food intake without bingeing or purging, while the binge-eating/purging type is defined by stringent attempts to limit intake, followed by episodes of binge eating as well as self-induced vomiting and/or laxative abuse. This definition differs from earlier descriptions of anorexia, in which the disorder was simply subdivided based on the presence or absence of binge eating. Patients who regularly engage in bulimic episodes report greater impulsivity, social/sexual dysfunction, substance abuse, general impulse control problems, family dysfunction, and depression as part of a general picture of more obvious emotional disturbance than patients with the restricting subtype of anorexia nervosa. Those with the restricting type of anorexia nervosa are often characterized as not only overly compliant but also obstinate, perfectionistic, obsessive-compulsive, shy, introverted, interpersonally sensitive, and stoical.

BULIMIA NERVOSA

The criteria for the diagnosis of bulimia nervosa according to the *DSM-IV-TR* (APA, 2000) are summarized as (1) recurrent episodes of binge eating (a sense of lack of control over eating a large amount of food in a discrete period of time); (2) recurrent inappropriate compensatory behavior in order to prevent weight gain (i.e., vomiting, abuse of laxative, diuretics or other medications, fasting, or excessive exercise); (3) a minimum average of two episodes of binge eating and inappropriate compensatory behaviors per week for the past 3 months; (4) self-evaluation unduly influenced by body shape and weight; and (5) the disturbance does not occur exclusively during episodes of anorexia nervosa. Bulimia nervosa patients are further subdivided into purging and nonpurging types based on the regular use of self-induced vomiting, laxatives, or diuretic (APA, 2000).

EATING DISORDERS NOT OTHERWISE SPECIFIED

The *DSM-IV-TR* (APA, 2000) delineates a large and diverse diagnostic category, eating disorder, not otherwise specified (EDNOS), for individuals with clinically significant eating disorders who do not meet all of the diagnostic criteria for anorexia nervosa or bulimia nervosa. Unfortunately, the term *not otherwise specified* could be interpreted as meaning that these eating problems have minor clinical significance. This assumption is incorrect since the clinical picture for many individuals with EDNOS can be as complicated and serious as the two main eating disorders. For example, to qualify for this diagnosis, binge eating must occur, on average, at least twice a week for a 6-month period. This means that a patient who is normal weight and who does not engage in objective binge-eating episodes but vomits 20 times following subjective binges (small amounts of food), would be classified as EDNOS rather than bulimia nervosa. Many patients complain that having a diagnosis of *not otherwise specified* discounts their level of suffering and makes them feel like they do not have a real problem.

RELATIONSHIP BETWEEN DIFFERENT
EATING DISORDERS

Current systems of diagnosing the two main eating disorders into mutually exclusive categories, based largely on body weight, present some limitations. This distinction overlooks the overlap between these eating disorders. Bulimia and anorexia nervosa can have virtually identical cognitive, clinical, psychological, and behavioral symptoms. Binge eating is the hallmark for bulimia nervosa; however, it is also a common symptom in anorexia nervosa. The major difference between the disorders is that in anorexia nervosa (binge-eating/purging subtype), these symptoms occur at a low body weight. Nevertheless, the body weight threshold used to define anorexia nervosa is arbitrary. Some patients move between the diagnostic categories of anorexia and bulimia nervosa at different points in time based only on variations in body weight; thus, it is counterintuitive to suggest that these diagnostic entities are not shared to some extent. Moreover, the extraordinary variety within each of the anorexia and bulimia nervosa diagnostic subclasses emphasizes the need to be careful about generalizations based only on diagnosis. Body weight is not likely to be the ideal marker for differentiating between eating disorders.

Extraordinary variability exists within each of the diagnostic subgroups, in terms of demographic, clinical, and psychological variables. Since people with anorexia and bulimia nervosa can move between the diagnostic categories at different points in time, some patients may alternate between the two subtypes of anorexia nervosa (restricting and binge-eating/purging types). However, it is more common for restricters to move toward bulimia (and purging) than for bulimic patients to move to an exclusively abstaining mode. Some women vacillate between the two subclasses for years (Garner, Garner, & Rosen, 1993).

Although distinctions between diagnostic subgroups have been emphasized in research, recognizing that the different subclasses share numerous features is important. For example, even though persons with anorexia are differentiated into restricter and binge-eating/purging subtypes, virtually all eating disorder patients restrict their food intake, diet, and probably fast for abnormally long periods of time. Some do this in association with binge eating, some with vomiting, and/or purging, and others with neither of these symptoms. For some persons, these symptoms occur at a statistically normal body weight (bulimia nervosa) and for others it occurs well over the body weight norms (e.g., binge-eating disorder).

The classic case of anorexia nervosa has historically been known for the restricting eating pattern rather than for binge eating and some have emphasized the relative similarity of this restricting anorexia nervosa (RAN) subgroup. The RAN subgroup has been described as perfectionistic, obsessional, inflexible, socially introverted, emotionally reserved, conflict avoidant, rule-minded, and overly compliant. The RAN subgroup also has been distinguished from individuals with more temperamental personalities who have the typical bulimic symptom pattern. These people are generally characterized as having greater impulsivity, interpersonal conflict, and mood instability, regardless of whether they are at a normal body weight in bulimia nervosa or at a suboptimal weight in anorexia (binge-eating/purging subtype). However, as mentioned earlier, inferring specific psychological traits from the behavioral symptoms of an eating disorder is overly simplistic and does little to explain meaningful distinctions between patient subgroups.

DIFFERENTIAL DIAGNOSIS

Patients without anorexia nervosa, bulimia nervosa, or some variant can superficially resemble patients with an eating disorder diagnosis. Patients with a severe depression can display marked weight loss (because of loss of appetite) or have periods of marked overeating that is different from a classic eating disorder. People with schizophrenia may have an aversion to eating because they are afraid of being poisoned and occasionally engage in binge eating or purging. A range of physical illnesses producing weight loss, such as inflammatory bowel disease, chronic hepatitis, Addison's disease, Crohn's disease, undiagnosed cystic fibrosis, diabetes mellitus, hyperthyroidism, tuberculosis, malignancies, or malabsorption diseases, should be ruled out as the primary diagnosis.

GENDER CONSIDERATIONS

Eating disorders have been consistently found to be more common among women than men. Clinical samples support this finding, saying that only 5% to 10% of patients are men. Other studies in the United States suggest the incidence of anorexia nervosa among males may be as little as 0.02% per year and the prevalence of current bulimia nervosa in men is between 0.1% and 0.5% (Hoek & van Hoeken, 2003). The differences in gender rates for eating disorders are generally attributed to cultural factors; however, biologic and psychodynamic factors may also play a role. Eating disorders are less common in men, but, when they occur, they have symptoms very similar to those observed in women.

HAVE EATING DISORDERS CHANGED OVER TIME?

Anorexia nervosa was once believed to occur only in the higher socioeconomic classes; however, now there is plenty of evidence of its occurrence in middle- and lower-class households. The most dramatic evidence for a change in the psychopathology of anorexia nervosa seems to be the increased appearance of binge eating, both in anorexia nervosa and eating disorder patients who are not emaciated. However, the actual extent to which binge eating has become more common in anorexia nervosa is unclear since the symptom may have been identified less reliably in earlier reports.

The theme of asceticism associated with weight loss is common in anorexia nervosa but may play less of a role in modern cases than a drive for thinness as in pursuit of a thin ideal image of beauty. The theme of asceticism was common in early writings on anorexia nervosa and is expressed in the conceptions of dieting as purification, thinness as virtue, and fasting as an act of atonement. Some eating disordered patients are motivated by a belief in the virtue of oral self-restraint. This trait is generally applied to areas other than food. These patients often report that they feel powerful because they are able to overcome all physical gratifications. Control of bodily urges is associated with spiritual ideals such as self-discipline, self-denial, self-restraint, and self-sacrifice. By conquering her bodily urges, the woman with anorexia nervosa temporarily feels better and feels that she has achieved control over her body; ironically, the reality is that the eating disorder has total control of her.

Since the earliest descriptions of anorexia nervosa, considerable controversy has emerged on whether eating disorders represent discrete psychological entities or are simply manifestations of other illnesses. For instance, anorexia nervosa and bulimia nervosa have both been considered variants of affective disorder, obsessive-compulsive disorder, or borderline personality disorder. Traits such as hostility, social maladjustment, rigidity, interpersonal sensitivity, anxiety, poor self-esteem, external locus of control, and confused sex-role identity have been observed repeatedly in eating disorder patients. Although there is general acceptance that eating disorders are best considered as separate clinical entities, an increasing number of researchers are becoming interested in psychological features that may define meaningful subclasses of eating disorders.

HOW COMMON ARE EATING DISORDERS?

Incidence rates are defined as the number of new cases in the population per year; prevalence rates refer to the actual number of cases in the population at a certain point in time. Prevalence rates are determined most commonly on high-risk populations such as college students and athletes. Estimates of the incidence and prevalence of eating disorders have serious limitations, since most have been derived only from self-report instruments and on samples that may not reflect important demographic differences. In general, estimates based exclusively on questionnaires yield much higher rates of eating disorders.

Estimates of incidence based on detected cases in primary care practices resulted in rates of 8.1 per 100,000 persons per year for anorexia nervosa and 11.5 per 100,000 persons for bulimia nervosa (Hoek & van Hoeken, 2003). The most sophisticated prevalence studies using strict diagnostic criteria report rates of about 0.3% for anorexia nervosa and about 1% for bulimia nervosa among young females in the community. In contrast, surveys using questionnaires find that as many as 19% of female students report bulimic symptoms. Interestingly enough, prevalence studies of higher risk samples indicate that serious eating disorders occur in as many as 4% of female high school and college students. Suspected cases of clinical eating disorders are even more common among groups exposed to heightened pressures to diet or maintain a thin shape, such as ballet students and professional dancers, wrestlers, swimmers, skaters, gymnasts, and distance runners.

SCREENING AND CASE FINDING FOR EATING DISORDERS

There is evidence that effective treatment exists for both bulimia and anorexia nervosa; however, findings from community studies indicate that only a minority of cases are in treatment. Following are some of the factors that led researchers to employ various screening strategies to estimate the prevalence of eating disorders and to detect cases for earlier interventions.

Screening versus Case Finding

Screening and case finding are based on the assumption that early identification of a disorder can lead to earlier treatment, thereby reducing morbidity and mortality. Screening for a variety of medical disorders has become routine in a range of different settings and involves testing presumably healthy volunteers from the general population for the purpose of separating them into groups that have either a high or a low probability of having a particular disorder. An example of screening would be a national program aimed at identifying those who are HIV positive or who have breast cancer in a particular population. In screening, the initiative is taken by the health care professional rather than volunteered by the patient.

In contrast, case finding involves testing patients who have voluntarily sought health care or information as part of a comprehensive assessment of health. Health care workers may screen for certain disorders during routine physical examinations in patients who are at risk or in community-based voluntary settings. An example of case finding would be blood pressure assessment in a shopping mall or mammographies offered at community centers. The routine practice of a primary care physician closely resembles this definition of case finding, since it is common for a complaint-related or noncomplaint-related illness to be identified in the course of the patient seeking care.

NATIONAL EATING DISORDERS SCREENING PROGRAM

In 1998, the National Eating Disorder Screening Program (NEDSP, www.mental-healthscreening.org) was initiated in the United States. The aim of the NEDSP was to determine the effectiveness of a national effort to identify those suffering from eating disorders and to encourage them to seek professional help. In February 1998, the NEDSP conducted screening for eating disorders at 1,083 sites in the United States. A total of 69,374 individuals attended the screening and 35,897 individuals were screened for eating disorders. More than half of those screened were college students. Follow-up by telephone interview was conducted 2 months after the initial case finding on a representative sample of 937 participants. The screening (case finding) instrument used by the NEDSP was the Eating Attitudes Test (EAT-26), which was originally developed by one of us (DG). The EAT-26 is a standardized, self-report measure of symptoms and concerns characteristic of eating disorders. It is designed to be economical both in administration and scoring time. The EAT-26 has been used as a screening and case finding instrument in nonclinical populations (see Table 9.1).

Of those screened in the NEDSP and then interviewed at follow-up, 34.5% scored positively (20 or more) on the EAT-26, and 89% of these individuals were not in treatment at the time of screening. Of those interviewed, 15% reported vomiting in the preceding 6 months to control their weight, 15% reported abusing laxatives, 33% used diet pills, and 11% took diuretics. Results from the follow-up indicated that 38% of the sample was referred for further treatment. Of those who scored positively on the EAT-26 and were referred to a clinician, 42% actually followed through and saw a clinician and 76% of this group continued in further treatment. Of those interviewed, 82% felt that the screening program was helpful in at least some way and 32% noted an improvement in their eating attitudes or behaviors following the NEDSP. The EAT proved to be a psychometrically sound and useful screening instrument, particularly when supplemented by behavioral questions asking about eating disorder symptom frequencies. It was concluded that voluntary screening for eating disorders was an effective way to bring certain untreated individuals to treatment. The behavioral questions used in the

Table 9.1
Eating Attitudes Test (EAT-26)

Age ____ Sex ____ Height ____ Current Weight ____ Highest Weight (excluding pregnancy) ____ Lowest Adult Weight ____ Level of Education Completed: Grade School High School College Post-College Please check a response for each of the following questions.	Always	Usually	Often	Sometimes	Rarely	Never
1. Am terrified about being overweight.						
2. Avoid eating when I am hungry.						
3. Find myself preoccupied with food.						
4. Have gone on eating binges where I feel that I may not be able to stop.						
5. Cut my food into small pieces.						
6. Aware of the calorie content of foods that I eat.						
7. Particularly avoid food with a high carbohydrate content (i.e., bread, rice, potatoes).						
8. Feel that others would prefer if I ate more.						
9. Vomit after I have eaten.						
10. Feel extremely guilty after eating.						
11. Am preoccupied with a desire to be thinner.						
12. Think about burning up calories when I exercise.						
13. Other people think that I am too thin.						
14. Am preoccupied with the thought of having fat on my body.						
15. Take longer than others to eat my meals.						
16. Avoid foods with sugar in them.						
17. Eat diet foods.						
18. Feel that food controls my life.						
19. Display self-control around food.						
20. Feel that others pressure me to eat.						
21. Give too much time and thought to food.						
22. Feel uncomfortable after eating sweets.						
23. Engage in dieting behavior.						
24. Like my stomach to be empty.						
25. Have the impulse to vomit after meals.						
26. Enjoy trying new rich foods.						

Source: From "The Eating Attitudes Test: Psychometric Features and Clinical Correlates," by D. M. Garner, M. P. Olmsted, Y. Bohr, and P. E. Garfinkel, 1982, *Psychological Medicine, 12,* pp. 871–878. ©1998 D. M. Garner. Reprinted with permission.

Table 9.2
EAT-26 Behavioral Questions

EAT-26 Behavioral Questions *In the past three months* have you:	Never	Once to Several Times a Month	Once a Week	2 to 6 Times a Week	Once a Day	More than Once a Day
1. Gone on eating binges?*						
2. Made yourself sick (vomited) to control your weight?						
3. Used laxatives to control your weight or shape?						
4. Been treated for an eating disorder?						
5. Thought of or attempted suicide?						

*A binge is defined as eating much more that most people would eat under similar circumstances with a feeling of a loss of control over eating during the episode.

Source: From "The Eating Attitudes Test: Psychometric Features and Clinical Correlates," by D. M. Garner, M. P. Olmsted, Y. Bohr, and P. E. Garfinkel, 1982, *Psychological Medicine, 12,*

1998 NEDSP were further modified for the 2000 NEDSP. The EAT-26 behavioral questions as well as the scoring instructions are reproduced in Tables 9.2 and 9.3.

RISK FACTORS THAT CAUSE OR MAINTAIN EATING DISORDERS

A complete understanding of anorexia nervosa and bulimia nervosa must take into consideration factors that predispose individuals to each of the eating disorders. A variety of developmental experiences interact with these factors, resulting in the initiation of symptoms. They also account for the maintaining variables (biological, psychological, and interpersonal) and the range of symptoms. Although current models do not specify all of these elements in precise detail, research and clinical observations in the last 2 decades have improved the understanding of eating disorders, which, in turn, has led to more sophisticated treatment recommendations.

During the past several decades, the idea that eating disorders are caused by a single factor has been replaced by the view that eating disorders are multidetermined. More than 20 years ago, we proposed a model in which symptom patterns represent final common pathways resulting from the interplay of three broad classes of predisposing factors shown in Figure 9.1 (see Garner, 1997). Accordingly, environmental, cultural, individual (psychological and biological), and familial causal factors combine with each other in different ways leading to the development of eating disorders. The precipitants of eating disorders are less clearly understood except that dieting is invariably an early element. As discussed in detail later in this chapter, one of the most practical advancements in treatment came

Table 9.3
Scoring Instructions and for the EAT-26

Responses for each item are weighted from 0 to 3, with a score of 3 assigned to the responses furthest in the "symptomatic" direction ("always" or "never," depending on whether the item is keyed in the positive or negative direction. *Item 26 is the only negatively keyed item on the EAT-26*).	Always	Usually	Often	Sometimes	Rarely	Never
1. Am terrified about being overweight.	3	2	1	0	0	0
2. Avoid eating when I am hungry.	3	2	1	0	0	0
ALL OTHER ITEMS EXCEPT #26	3	2	1	0	0	0
26. Enjoy trying new rich foods.	0	0	0	1	2	3
To compute the total EAT-26, add all of the item scores together.						

Interpretation: If a respondent scores 20 or more on the EAT-26, it is very likely that he or she has eating disorder symptoms of clinical severity. The behavioral questions have been added to the EAT-26 based on the experience of the 1998 NEDSP in the United States.

Source: From "The Eating Attitudes Test: Psychometric Features and Clinical Correlates," by D. M. Garner, M. P. Olmsted, Y. Bohr, and P. E. Garfinkel, 1982, *Psychological Medicine, 12,* pp. 871–878. ©1998 D. M. Garner. Reprinted with permission.

from increased awareness of the perpetuating effects of starvation with its psychological, emotional, and physical consequences. Symptoms can be connected to remote origins of behavior that may stem from inherited personality features, genetic vulnerabilities, and variations in family predispositions. These historical origins may represent specific vulnerabilities to the disorder itself; more likely, they are general risk factors that are associated with dieting, perfectionism, and certain thinking styles, which predispose someone to the development of an eating disorder. It's important to point out that it may not always be clear along the time line that an individual risk factor exerts its influence. Once the disorder develops, certain psychological traits, such as perfectionism, overcompliance, low self-esteem, grandiosity, and preference for certainty and exactness, may be interpreted as preceding conditions that can be directly linked to personality; however, they may be attributed to more distant genetic influences. Similarly, family factors may exert their influence as distant or immediate predecessors, as well as maintaining factors

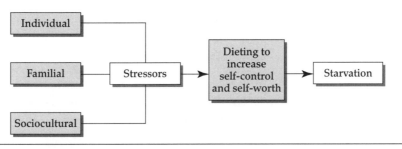

Figure 9.1 Pathogenesis of Eating Disorders. *Source:* Garner & Garfinkel (1997).

of eating-disorder symptoms. The multiple points of influence and the variety of pathways operating with different people must be kept in mind in the following discussion of cognitive vulnerability to eating disorders. The distinction between environmental and individual risk factors is not always completely clear. Most often, the true risk is attributable to a blending of several risk factors from the environment, the individual, and the family.

ENVIRONMENTAL FACTORS

Taken together, the increase of eating disorders over time and their prevalence in Western cultures and females (especially during adolescence, when conspicuous changes occur in a woman's physical appearance) all point to the environment as an important contributor to the development of eating disorders. Although a number of environmental risk factors have been identified (see Box 9.4), we review two that have been points of recent emphasis.

CULTURAL FACTORS

Eating disorders involve an intense preoccupation with fatness, leading to extreme attempts to control body weight. A strong concern about physical appearance appears to predate the appearance of anorexia nervosa. The role of culture in the development of eating disorders has been debated for years; however, there is little debate about the magnitude of more than 40 years of exposure to the fashion, entertainment, and publishing industries that have bombarded women with an image of physical attractiveness by featuring role models of a so-called ideal physical form, who are so gaunt as to represent virtually no women in the actual population. The pernicious effects of the current image of feminine beauty has left most women feeling insecure about their bodies and has resulted in a wide array of products aimed at achieving the desired physical form. Restrictive dieting to achieve this skeletal desired look has become the norm. Most evidence points to the link between cultural influences and vulnerability to eating disorders. Although this may seem obvious to most readers today, Garner (1997), along with other colleagues, remembers intense skepticism in response to the theory (and some data) advancing culture as a major determinant of eating disorders. In one of our studies (Garner & Garfinkel, 1997), we reported that ballet dancers and fashion models had a dramatically elevated risk of developing anorexia nervosa. In another study, we documented and quantified the changing expectations for thinness by reporting that *Playboy* centerfolds and Miss America

---

BOX 9.4
Environmental Factors

Sociocultural emphasis on thinness.

The association between dieting and self-control and self-discipline.

Sports emphasizing thinness (gymnastics).

Sexual/physical abuse.

Attention from others.

contestants had become significantly thinner over time. The implications of these changing ideals was further magnified by a steady *increase* in the actual weights for women the same age and height as the magazine models. At the time, just over 5% of female life insurance policy holders between the ages of 20 and 29 were as thin as the average Miss America Pageant winners. This trend has continued, with the greatest weight increases for both women and men in recent years. Thus, the prevailing shape standards do not even remotely resemble the actual body shape of the average woman consumer.

The norm for women in recent years has been dissatisfaction with their own weight and shape. However, research has shown that the gulf continues to broaden between actual and preferred shapes. One survey of eighth- and tenth-grade students indicated that 61% of female students and 28% of male students reported dieting during the previous year. Moreover, there is convincing evidence that restrictive dieting actually does increase the risk of developing an eating disorder. Another study found that the risk of developing an eating disorder is 8 times higher in 15-year-old girls who diet compared to those who do not diet. Other crosscultural studies demonstrated that young women from other more weight-tolerant cultures become more fearful of fatness and develop eating disorder symptoms as they are assimilated into thinness-conscious Western culture. In Western culture, those exposed to more pressure to diet, such as athletes in sports that emphasize leanness for performance or appearance, are at greater risk of eating disorders. There has been a proliferation of women's fitness magazines that are oriented much more toward achieving the slender shape ideal than performance and health. The irony is that countless women sacrifice health through compulsive exercise aimed at unrealistic weight loss. We treated many women at our clinic who described being so addicted to exercise that they cannot imagine a day without it. Actually inhibiting exercise creates such severe states of guilt and panic that some will sneak out of the residence for a nightly walk even if it means exhaustion the next day.

One of the most jarring expressions of our culture's view of thinness is the media's fascination with anorexia nervosa by shamelessly glamorizing the disorder through its association with celebrities. The text highlights the dangers of the disorder; however, the sentimental subtext invariably emphasizes the tragic decline of a beautiful, intelligent, and self-disciplined young woman who turns to thinness to express her psychological distress. It is rare for the media to chronicle the plight of a more average-looking young woman with average achievements who will gradually decline into invalidism without family supports, insurance, or hope for recovery. The glamorizing of anorexia nervosa may constitute a specific risk factor since some patients report beginning self-induced vomiting as a weight control method following exposure to media articles describing the practice. The cultural attitudes toward anorexia nervosa not only increase risk for the disorder but also make recovery more difficult. Another obstacle to recovery is the cultural stigma associated with obesity. Many formerly obese patients who develop an eating disorder as a complication due to weight loss remain unambiguous in their determination to endure the life-threatening illness.

One of the keys to overcoming an eating disorder is relaxing strict and extreme forms of dietary restriction. To accomplish this task, it is important to have some understanding of the factors motivating individuals' attempts to control body weight. In some cases, the motivation involves complex emotional and interpersonal problems that need to be addressed to make progress. In other cases, the primary motivation is the individual's acceptance of the cultural message that a thin body is crucial to personal happiness. Either way, recovery involves swimming against the cultural stream. Patients are continually besieged by messages from the media that glorify the virtues of dieting and thinness.

The gradual recognition of the unreasonable stresses on women to conform to the contemporary gaunt look provides the basis for urging those suffering from eating disorders to reframe their disorder in cultural terms. The simple exercise of collecting appearance-oriented images from women's magazines can lead some women struggling with eating disorder symptoms to develop a healthy sense of indignation at the confining definitions of feminine attractiveness promoted in the media.

SEXUAL ABUSE

Another area that has gained interest in recent years concerns the role of sexual abuse as a risk factor for the development of eating disorders. Some accounts reveal a high incidence of sexual abuse among eating disorder patients, while other findings come to the exact opposite conclusion. The prevailing view is that childhood sexual abuse is more common in those with bulimia symptoms than those who do not engage in binge eating. One of the most respected studies in the field analyzed rates of childhood sexual abuse in those with eating disorders, those with other psychiatric diagnoses, and nonpatient controls. The results indicated that childhood sexual abuse was definitely more common among those with eating disorders; however, it was not a specific risk factor for eating disorders since those receiving other psychiatric diagnoses had a similarly elevated rate of childhood sexual abuse. Other studies indicated that a more sophisticated approach to the definition of sexual abuse can lead to better prediction of later disturbances in eating. Generally speaking, studies that looked at different forms of childhood sexual abuse as a predictor of eating disorders found a greater association with the most severe forms of abuse. It is important to recognize that the relationship between childhood sexual abuse and disordered eating may hold true only for certain subgroups of women. In one study, investigators found that childhood sexual abuse predicted disordered eating, but not dieting or weight satisfaction, for a group of middle-aged females aged 45 to 49 years. However, for young women, aged 18 to 22 years, who participated in the same study, childhood sexual abuse was predictive of weight dissatisfaction but not dieting or disordered eating. Regardless of the conclusions that can be drawn from the statistical analysis of the relationship between eating disorders and childhood sexual abuse, it is important to emphasize that a significant proportion of women with clinical eating disorders have been sexually abused. Regardless of the linkage, for those who have been abused, treatment must focus on the nature of the sexual abuse, the meaning that it has for the patient, and the implications for ensuring the victim's safety. Moreover, a significant element of treatment needs to focus on the process of dealing with feelings of shame, distrust, and anger.

INDIVIDUAL RISK FACTORS

There are a wide range of individual risk factors that have been attributed to eating disorders. The most frequently mentioned are listed in Box 9.5. A number of these individual risk factors are described in greater detail next.

BOX 9.5
Individual Risk Factors

Genetic vulnerability.

Depression, obsessive-compulsive traits.

Cognitive style preferring order, exactness, precision, and sameness.

Impulse control problems.

Low self-esteem.

Extreme need for approval.

Perfectionism.

Early onset of puberty.

Sexual maturation.

Restrictive dieting.

Fear of psychosexual maturity.

Extreme need for control.

Harm and risk avoidance.

Pursuit of an eating disorder identity.

GENETIC FACTORS

Recent evidence points to genetic factors in the expression of eating disorders. In recent twin studies, heritability estimates for anorexia range from 54% to 80%. Similarly, twin studies meant to determine the contributions of genetic versus environmental influences on abnormal eating attitudes for those without anorexia nervosa have shown that between 40% and 60% can be attributed to genetic influences.

Much evidence also exists that genetics contribute to obsessionality, perfectionism, rigidity, harm avoidance, and depression. Even after recovery from the disorder, many patients remain rigid, perfectionistic, and obsessional. People with restricting anorexia nervosa were found to be particularly conscientiousness, prone to over self-control, behavioral constraint, as well as inhibition of emotionality. Again, we found that reframing anorexic symptoms as symbols of a *lack* of control and as a handicap that sets a very low limit on performance or meaningful interpersonal relationships can sometimes help people with anorexia nervosa see their eating disorder as undesirable and self-limiting. Some patients view their obsessional tendencies as positive and fear that they may not only lose control of eating if they recover but also may not be as rigorous in other areas of daily living. For these patients, it can be helpful for the therapist to emphasize that obsessional traits will not necessarily diminish once the patient gains weight; however, the content may change to more functional topics. There are some important distinctions between the types of obsessional symptoms seen in anorexia nervosa compared to those who have obsessional symptoms alone. Those with eating disorders typically do not seem to have the types of obsessional symptoms, such as compulsive checking or sexual obsessions, commonly reported for people with ego-dystonic obsessive-compulsive (OC) disorder. Rather, the OC symptoms in anorexia nervosa tend to focus on the obsessive need for order, symmetry, exactness, and arranging. One of those OC symptoms that we found to be common is the obsessive need to weigh oneself. As mentioned earlier, the compulsive need to check one's weight can be paralleled to an addict's repetitive, ritualized acts and the inability to limit or resist inner urges that form the more typical pattern of addiction. Other such rituals that we witnessed included compulsive checking of body parts, by touching them, gazing at them in a mirror, measuring them directly or using certain clothing as a gauge of size. For instance, one patient reported not being able to use the rest room without checking her stomach. She explained that she was hoping it would be flatter than the last time she looked. Since she was in treatment and eating on a regular basis, this hope was hardly ever realized. The ritual was self-defeating in several ways. First, it almost always resulted in more anxiety and in a negative mood. Second, the body checking was partly tied to the superstitious belief that failure to check would lead to weight gain. Third, the body checking, like all obsessive rituals, actually increased her anxiety levels. Thus, it was very difficult to convince her that her anxiety would actually decline if she could inhibit body checking. Although she was able to understand these issues on an intellectual level, she persisted with this behavior, which is similar to the continued use despite adverse consequences, or the third C, in the addiction framework.

Another genetic factor involves variance in body weight. Early maturation and a tendency toward adolescent obesity may play a major role in the development of anorexia nervosa. Dieting is relatively rare among the small minority of women who are naturally underweight. According to this theory, dieting leading to weight loss and anorexia nervosa represents a defensive strategy for reversing the entire pubertal process that is seen as a threat. Often, body fat is seen as the marker for the threat associated with puberty and this leads to restrictive dieting. Dieting in response to a higher body weight may play a more general role in vulnerability.

ANXIETY

The most common anxiety symptoms documented in anorexia nervosa are obsessive-compulsive in nature. Obsessive-compulsive symptoms occur in anywhere between 11% and 83% of people with eating disorders, either during the active phase of the disorder or after weight restoration. For instance, in a poll of 93 women with either anorexia or bulimia nervosa, 37% met diagnostic criteria for obsessive-compulsive disorder. These women also had higher average scores on five of eight Eating Disorder Inventory subscales (Garner, 1991). Likewise, in another study, 11% of 151 women with obsessive-compulsive disorder had a history of anorexia. Underlying personality disorders tend to predict poor outcome. We saw several women with anorexia nervosa whose obsessive-compulsive rituals are sufficiently intractable that they seem virtually addicted to carrying them out. For instance, one woman was so compelled to weigh herself every morning that, despite having her scale confiscated numerous times and each time providing good-faith assurances not to purchase another scale, she would relapse even knowing that the result would be yet another donation to her therapist's scale museum. This urge fits the conceptual framework of addiction in that the behavior represents repetitive, ritualized acts seen in compulsive use, as well as that the addicted person may abstain for brief periods but cannot stay stopped. We found that this woman's anxiety skyrocketed when initially abstaining from weighing herself. She described her heart rate increasing, her hands shaking, and her thoughts racing. She felt as if she had no way of judging or evaluating herself without a number on the scale. As she was able to consistently refrain from weighing herself, she did report her anxiety somewhat dissipating, but her urges to weigh herself remained strong. These feelings seem very similar to those of an addict going through withdrawal.

DEPRESSION

Depression is often a theme in eating disorders, but its precise role is controversial. Originally, bulimia nervosa was described as a variant of depression based on evidence that eating disorder patients exhibit (1) a high prevalence of depression, (2) a family history of depression, (3) biological markers of depression, and (4) a positive response to antidepressant medications. However, other researchers have suggested that assuming that eating disorders are variants of depression is simplistic and theoretically limiting. Although depression may play an important predisposing role in eating disorders, current evidence shows that eating disorders are not simply depressive equivalents. Nevertheless, we have found that depression is still one of the most common experiences of those with eating disorders, and to minimize the significance of this experience would be misleading. Moreover, bulimia nervosa patients with a history of affective disorder or substance abuse disorder report significantly more suicide attempts, social impairment, and previous treatment both before and after the onset of the eating disorder. One study found no suicide attempts among the group of patients with bulimia alone; however, 26.5% of those with concurrent affective disorder and 32.4% with substance abuse had attempted suicide. Bulimia nervosa patients with a history of substance abuse also report a high incidence of stealing, which may indicate a more general problem with impulsivity.

Some studies suggest that depressive states of varying intensities foreshadow the development of anorexia nervosa. In one sample of severely ill anorexia nervosa patients, for instance, 68% were found to have major depression throughout their lives. However, as will be discussed later in detail, depression may also be secondary to starvation and will improve following nutritional rehabilitation. Another population study found that depression typically did not precede the eating disorder; however, it did come with onset. In a 6-year follow-up study, affective disorders were found to be common throughout the follow-up period rather than before the disorder. Thus, a history of affective disorder may foreshadow a subgroup of eating-disordered patients who may be particularly resistant to treatment efforts. Unfortunately, this subgroup of patients does not seem to respond any more favorably to antidepressant therapy than those without a history of mood disorder. Thus, the mechanism of action of the antidepressants is unclear, since we do not know when they do lead to a reduction in eating disorder symptoms.

FEARS OF PSYCHOSEXUAL MATURITY

Several theorists conceptualized anorexia nervosa as an adaptive strategy to avoid having to deal with psychological and biological threats associated with normal adulthood. Entering adolescence can produce new challenges and problems. It is not uncommon for young women to feel insecure or distressed during this time and to decide that dieting and weight loss might be a solution. Following this viewpoint, weight loss becomes a mechanism to prevent psychobiological maturity, since it results in a return to a prepubertal appearance and hormonal status. Discomfort and conflicts associated with the move to adulthood no longer seem relevant and are replaced by feelings of control and confidence. In addition to the obvious physical changes that occur as a girl enters into puberty, research has shown that there are important changes in thinking and overall experience that occur with the onset of puberty. Certain patients for whom this theme applies show remarkable insight about this process. They openly state that following weight loss they experience themselves as younger, which may be attributed to the reversal of mature adolescent hormonal profiles that form the biological substrata for psychological experience. They are able to articulate this fear quite clearly and can openly discuss fears of growing up. For others the developmental significance of weight loss and regain remain incomprehensible until they begin to approach a normal weight during refeeding. At this point, the developmental fears or conflicts begin to emerge and can lead to resistance to further weight gain.

FAMILY RISK FACTORS

Some of the earliest descriptions of anorexia nervosa emphasize the role of the family in the development of the disorder. There are many paths by which the family could impose vulnerability to anorexia nervosa (Fairburn & Harrison, 2003; see Box 9.6). For example, the family environment could foster low self-esteem and/or poor self-image, which could prompt an adolescent to engage in other risk factors, such as highly restrictive dieting. Perceived parental control, a critical family environment, and frequent talk about weight may also cultivate eating disorder symptoms. As indicated earlier, fears associated with psychobiological maturity may threaten some adolescents, but the same developmental milestones can also impact the psychological equilibrium of other family members. This shift in the family dynamics perceived by other family members may lead to conflicts, vulnerabilities, and dysfunctional communication patterns.

BOX 9.6
Family Risk Factors

Eating disorder in a family member.
Disorder evokes extreme caring.
Emphasis on fitness/weight in family.
Passive anger in response to family conflicts.
Avoidance of family conflicts.
Emphasis on fitness/weight.
Overprotective family style.
Difficulty in establishing parental authority.
Ineffective parenting.
Fears related to emancipation from parents.

Dysfunctional communication patterns within the family were the focus of family theories of anorexia and now are integrated into the cognitive theory of anorexia. Enmeshment, overprotectiveness, rigidity, and poor conflict resolution are examples of these patterns. One functional role of anorexia nervosa may be to divert attention away from deeply rooted familial distress and conflict. In this case, the identified patient serves an essential stabilizing role within the family. Many family theorists emphasized that anorexia nervosa typically represents a developmental struggle for autonomy, independence, and individuality. These issues are very likely to surface in adolescence, when the vulnerable individual, parents, or entire family are forced to deal with emergent developmental realities.

Although families may play a role in the development of eating disorders, it is important to take a cautious view on this topic. Patients and their family members arrive at an initial assessment suffering from needless guilt fostered by simplistic psychological theories and uninformed therapists who generalize far beyond the existing data and attribute the disorder to family dysfunction. Unfortunately, in the history of psychological theory, there have been other examples of disorders in which the family (usually the mother) has been considered the major cause. Schizophrenia was attributed to the schizophrenogenic mother and of infantile autism to the refrigerator mother. These glaring misunderstandings aside, it's naive to deny the potency of the family in the expression of functional as well as dysfunctional beliefs, values, and interactional patterns of anorexia nervosa.

Starvation as a Maintaining Factor

One of the most important advancements in the understanding of eating disorders is the recognition that severe and prolonged dietary restriction can lead to serious physical and psychological complications. Many of the symptoms once thought to be only features of anorexia nervosa are actually symptoms of starvation and can exert a powerful role in maintaining an eating disorder (see Figure 9.2) by changing the way that the individual thinks, feels, and behaves. Given what we know about the biology of weight regulation, what is the impact of weight suppression on the individual?

A classic experimental *starvation study* (as it is commonly known) conducted more than 50 years ago and published in 1950 by Ancel Keys and his colleagues at

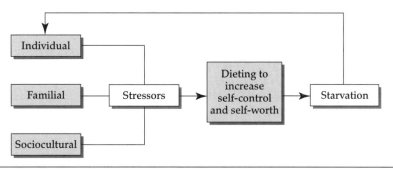

Figure 9.2 Starvation as a Maintaining Factor for Eating Disorders. *Source:* Garner & Garfinkel (1997).

the University of Minnesota (see Garner, 1997, for a synopsis of the Keys et al., 1950 study) involved carefully studying 36 young, healthy, psychologically normal men while they restricted their caloric intake for 6 months and lost a significant amount of body weight. More than 100 men volunteered for the study as an alternative to military service. The 36 men selected to participate had the highest levels of physical and psychological health, as well as the most commitment to the objectives of the experiment. What makes this study so important is that many of the experiences observed in the volunteers are the same as those experienced by patients with eating disorders.

During the first 3 months of the experiment, the volunteers ate normally while their behavior, personality, and eating patterns were studied in detail. During the next 6 months, the men were restricted to approximately half of their former food intake, consuming, on average, about 1,550 calories per day. This restriction resulted in an average weight loss of approximately 23% of their former weight over the 6-month period. The weight loss phase of the experiment was followed by 3 months of nutritional rehabilitation, during which the men were gradually refed. A subgroup of men was followed for almost 9 months after the refeeding began. Most of the results were reported for only 32 men, since 4 men were withdrawn for various reasons either during or at the end of the semistarvation phase. Although the individual responses to weight loss varied considerably, the men experienced dramatic physical, psychological, and social changes. As indicated next, in most cases, these changes persisted during the renourishment phase.

ATTITUDES AND BEHAVIOR TOWARD FOOD

One of the most of the striking changes that occurred in the volunteers was a dramatic increase in food preoccupations. The men found concentration on their usual activities increasingly difficult because they became increasingly plagued by thoughts of food and eating. During the weight loss phase of the experiment, food became a main topic of conversation, reading, and daydreams for the men. While they experienced a steady increase in thinking about food, they also showed a declining interest in both sex and activity during the weight-loss phase.

In addition to cookbooks and collecting recipes, some of the men even began collecting coffeepots, hot plates, and other kitchen utensils. According to the original report, hoarding even extended to nonfood-related items such as "old books, unnecessary second-hand clothes, knick knacks, and other 'junk.' Often after making such purchases, which could be afforded only with sacrifice, the men would be puzzled as to why they had bought such more or less useless articles" (Garner, 1997, p. 837). One man even began rummaging through garbage cans. This general tendency to hoard even nonfood-related items has been observed in starved anorexic patients and even in rats deprived of food.

The Minnesota subjects were often caught between conflicting desires to gulp their food down ravenously and consume it slowly so that the taste and odor of each morsel would be fully appreciated. As indicated previously, toward the end of the starvation phase of the experiment, some of the men would linger for almost 2 hours over a meal that previously would have been consumed in a matter of minutes. According to the report, they spent an extraordinary amount of time planning how they would handle their day's allotment of food. The men demanded that their food be served hot; and as noted previously, they mixed their foods together in unusual combinations. There was also a marked increase in the use of salt and spices. The consumption of coffee and tea increased so dramatically that the men had to be limited to 9 cups per day. Similarly, gum chewing became excessive and had to be limited after it was discovered that one man was chewing as many as 40 packages of gum a day and "developed a sore mouth from such continuous exercise" (Garner, 1997, p. 835).

Refeeding did not lead to an immediate return of normal attitudes and behavior around food. During the 12-week refeeding phase of the experiment, most of the men continued to experience abnormal attitudes and behaviors in regard to food. During the first 6 weeks of refeeding, a small number of men found that their difficulties in this area remained quite severe.

BINGE EATING

In the area of eating disorders, many theories emphasize emotional factors in the etiology and maintenance of binge eating. Binge eating is often considered functional in regulating mood, numbing a person from unpleasant affect, or otherwise expressing underlying psychological conflicts. While binge eating may serve many of these or other psychological functions, the experiences of the Minnesota experiment indicate that the best explanation of increased hunger and episodes of binge eating are directly linked to undernutrition and weight loss. During the restrictive dieting phase of the experiment, all of the volunteers reported increased hunger. Some appeared able to tolerate the experience fairly well, but for others it led to episodes of binge eating that were indistinguishable from those seen among patients with eating disorders. Several men were unable to adhere to their diets and reported episodes of binge eating along with feelings of loss of control and guilt. During the eighth week of starvation, "one volunteer flagrantly broke the dietary rules, eating several sundaes and malted milks; he even stole some penny candies. He promptly confessed the whole episode, [and] became self-deprecatory" (Garner, 1997, p. 884). Working in a grocery store, another man experienced an episode of uncontrollable overeating and ate several cookies, a sack of popcorn, and two overripe bananas before he could regain control of himself. He immediately suffered a severe emotional upset, with nausea, and upon returning to the laboratory, he vomited. He reported being self-deprecatory, expressing disgust and self-criticism.

It is significant that the tendency toward binge eating persisted or even became worse during the refeeding phase of the experiment. Many of the men reported that they "ate more or less continuously" (Garner, 1997, p. 843). Even after 12 weeks of refeeding, the men frequently complained of increased hunger immediately following a large meal. One of the volunteers ate immense meals estimated to be between 5,000 and 6,000 calories, yet he began snacking an hour after he finished a meal. During the weekends, in particular, some of the men found it difficult to stop eating. Their daily intake commonly ranged between 8,000 and 10,000 calories, and their eating patterns were described as follows:

> Subject No. 20 stuffs himself until he is bursting at the seams, to the point of being nearly sick and still feels hungry; No. 120 reported that he had to discipline himself to keep from eating so much as to become ill; No. 1 ate until he was uncomfortably full; and subject No. 30 had so little control over the mechanics of "piling it in" that he simply had to stay away from food because he could not find a point of satiation

even when he was "full to the gills." . . . "I ate practically all weekend," reported subject No. 26. . . . Subject No. 26 would just as soon have eaten six meals instead of three. (p. 847)

After about 5 months of refeeding, the majority of the men reported some normalization of their eating patterns, but for some the extreme overconsumption persisted. Factors distinguishing men who rapidly normalized their eating from those who continued to eat prodigious amounts were not identified. Nevertheless, the main findings here are as follows: Serious binge eating developed in a subgroup of men, and this tendency persisted in come cases for months after free access to food was reintroduced. However, the majority of men reported gradually returning to eating normal amounts of food after about 5 months of refeeding. Thus, because binge eating was experimentally produced in some of these normal young men, speculations should be tempered about primary psychological disturbances being the cause of binge eating in patients with eating disorders. These findings are supported by a large body of research indicating that habitual dieters display marked overcompensation in eating behavior that is similar to the binge eating observed in eating disorders.

EMOTIONAL AND PERSONALITY CHANGES

Although the subjects were psychologically healthy prior to the experiment, most experienced significant emotional deterioration as a result of semistarvation. Almost 20% experienced extreme emotional deterioration that markedly interfered with their functioning.

Irritability and frequent outbursts of *anger* were common, although the men had quite tolerant dispositions prior to starvation. *Anxiety* became evident for most subjects and, as the experiment progressed, many of the formerly even-tempered men began biting their nails or smoking because they felt nervous. *Apathy* also became common, and some men who had been quite fastidious neglected various aspects of personal hygiene.

Depression was common and became more severe during the course of the experiment. *Mood swings* were extreme for some of the volunteers with occasional periods of elation inevitably followed by low periods. During the refeeding period, emotional disturbance did not vanish immediately but persisted for several weeks, with some men actually becoming *more* depressed, irritable, argumentative, and negativistic than they had been during semistarvation. After two weeks of refeeding, one man reported his extreme reaction in his diary:

I have been more depressed than ever in my life . . . I thought that there was only one thing that would pull me out of the doldrums, that is release from C.P.S. [the experiment] I decided to get rid of some fingers. Ten days ago, I jacked up my car and let the car fall on these fingers . . . It was premeditated. [Several days later, this man actually did *chop off three fingers of one hand* in response to the stress.] (Garner, 1997, pp. 894–895)

During semistarvation, two subjects developed disturbances of psychotic proportions. One of these was unable to adhere to the diet and developed alarming symptoms:

[He exhibited] a compulsive attraction to refuse and a strong, almost compelling, desire to root in garbage cans [for food to eat]. He became emotionally disturbed enough to seek admission voluntarily to the psychiatric ward of the University Hospitals. (p. 890)

Standardized personality testing with the Minnesota Multiphasic Personality Inventory (MMPI) revealed that semistarvation resulted in significant increases on the Depression, Hysteria, and Hypochondriasis Scales. For one man who scored well within normal limits at initial testing, but after 10 weeks of semistarvation and a weight loss of only about 4.5 kg (10 pounds, or approximately 7% of his original body weight), gross personality disturbances were evident on the MMPI. Depression and general disorganization were particularly striking consequences of starvation for several of the men who became the most emotionally disturbed.

SOCIAL AND SEXUAL CHANGES

The extraordinary impact of the experiment was reflected in the social changes experienced by most of the volunteers. Although quite gregarious prior to the experiment, as they continued to lose weight, the men became progressively more withdrawn and isolated. Humor and the sense of camaraderie diminished amidst growing feelings of social inadequacy. The general retreat was evident in the sharp decline in the volunteers' social contacts with women during the experiment. Those who continued to see women socially found that the relationships became strained.

Sexual interests were likewise drastically reduced. Masturbation, sexual fantasies, and sexual impulses either ceased or became much less common. One subject graphically stated that he had "no more sexual feeling than a sick oyster." Keys observed that "many of the men welcomed the freedom from sexual tensions and frustrations normally present in young adult men" (Garner, 1997, p. 840). That starvation perceptibly altered sexual urges and associated conflicts is of particular interest, since it has been hypothesized that this process is the driving force behind the dieting of many anorexia nervosa patients. Some psychological theories of anorexia nervosa have emphasized the adaptive function of the disorder in the sense that it curtails sexual concerns for which the adolescent feels unprepared. During rehabilitation, sexual interest was slow to return. Even after 3 months, the men judged themselves to be far from normal in this area. However, after 8 months of renourishment, virtually all of the men had recovered their interest in sex.

COGNITIVE AND PHYSICAL CHANGES

The volunteers reported impaired concentration, alertness, comprehension, and judgment during the experiment; however, formal intellectual testing revealed no signs of diminished intellectual abilities. As the 6 months of semistarvation progressed, the volunteers exhibited many physical changes, including gastrointestinal discomfort, decreased need for sleep, dizziness, headaches, hypersensitivity to noise and light, reduced strength, poor motor control, edema (an excess of fluid causing swelling), hair loss, decreased tolerance for cold temperatures (cold hands and feet), visual disturbances (i.e., inability to focus, eye aches, spots in the visual fields), auditory disturbances (i.e., ringing noise in the ears), and paresthesias (i.e., abnormal tingling or prickling sensations, especially in the hands or feet).

Various changes reflected an overall slowing of the body's physiological processes. There were decreases in body temperature, heart rate, and respiration, as well as in basal metabolic rate (BMR), the amount of energy (in calories) that the body requires at rest (i.e., no physical activity) to carry out normal physiological processes. BMR accounts for about two-thirds of the body's total energy needs, with the remainder being used during physical activity. At the end of semistarvation, the men's BMRs had dropped by about 40% from normal levels. This drop, as well as other physical changes, reflects the body's extraordinary ability to adapt to low caloric intake by reducing its need for energy. More recent research has shown that metabolic rate is markedly reduced even among dieters who do not have a history of dramatic weight loss. During refeeding, Keys found that metabolism sped up, with those consuming the greatest number of calories experiencing the largest rise in BMR. The group of volunteers who received a relatively small increment in calories during refeeding (400 calories more than during semistarvation) had no rise in BMR for the first 3 weeks. Consuming larger amounts of food caused a sharp increase in the energy burned through metabolic processes.

The changes in body fat and muscle in relation to overall body weight during semistarvation and refeeding are of considerable interest. While weight declined about 25%, the percentage of body fat fell almost 70%, and muscle decreased about 40%. On refeeding, a greater proportion of the new weight was fat; in the eighth month of rehabilitation, the volunteers were at about 110% of their original body weight but had approximately 140% of their original body fat!

How did the men feel about their weight gain during rehabilitation? "Those subjects who gained the most weight became concerned about their increased sluggishness, general flabbiness, and the tendency of fat to accumulate in the abdomen and buttocks" (Garner 1997, p. 828). These complaints are similar to those of many eating disorder patients as they gain weight. Besides their typical fear of weight gain, they often report feeling fat and are worried about acquiring distended stomachs. However, the body weight and relative body fat of the Minnesota volunteers were at the preexperiment levels after about 9 months of rehabilitation.

The various effects of starvation on the thinking, emotions, and physical functioning of these men are summarized in Box 9.7. A review of the list in Box 9.7 makes it evident that weight suppression has the capacity to make normal people experience changes that could be interpreted as clinically significant and disordered.

SIGNIFICANCE OF THE STARVATION STUDY

As is readily apparent from the preceding description of the Minnesota experiment, many of the symptoms that could be considered specific to anorexia and bulimia nervosa are actually the results of starvation. These are not limited to food and weight but extend to virtually all areas of psychological and social functioning. Since many of the symptoms that have been thought to cause these disorders may actually result from undernutrition, it is absolutely essential that weight be returned to normal levels so that psychological functioning can be accurately assessed.

The profound effects of starvation also illustrate the tremendous adaptive capacity of the human body and the intense biological pressure on the organism to

---

BOX 9.7
The Effects of Semistarvation from the
1950 Minnesota Study

ATTITUDES AND BEHAVIOR TOWARD FOOD

- Food preoccupation.
- Collection of recipes, cookbooks, and menus.
- Unusual eating habits.
- Increased consumption of coffee, tea, and spices.
- Gum chewing.
- Binge-eating.

EMOTIONAL AND SOCIAL CHANGES

- Depression.
- Anxiety.
- Irritability, anger.
- Lability.
- Psychotic episodes.
- Personality changes on psychological tests.
- Social withdrawal.

COGNITIVE CHANGES

- Decreased concentration.
- Poor judgment.
- Apathy.

PHYSICAL CHANGES

- Sleep disturbances.
- Weakness.
- GI disturbances.
- Hyperacuity to noise and light.
- Edema.
- Hypothermia.
- Paresthesia.
- Decreased BMR.
- Decreased sexual interest.

Adapted from "Cognitive-Behavioral Therapy for Anorexia Nervosa" (pp. 94–144), by D. M. Garner, K. Vitousek, and K. Pike, in *Handbook of Treatment for Eating Disorders*, D. M. Garner, and P. E. Garfinkel (Eds.), 1997, New York: Guilford Press.

maintain a relatively consistent body weight, which makes complete evolutionary sense. Over hundreds of thousands of years of human evolution, a major threat to the survival of the organism was starvation. If weight had not been carefully modulated and controlled internally, early humans would simply have died when food was scarce or when their interest was captured by countless other aspects of living. The starvation study illustrates how the human being becomes more oriented toward food when starved and how other pursuits important to the survival of the species (e.g., social and sexual functioning) become subordinate to the primary drive toward food.

One of the most notable implications of the Starvation Study is that it challenges the popular notion that body weight is easily altered if one simply exercises a bit of willpower. It also demonstrates that the body is not simply reprogrammed at a lower set point once weight loss has been achieved. The volunteers' experimental diet was unsuccessful in overriding their bodies' strong propensity to defend a particular weight level. Again, it is important to emphasize that following the months of refeeding, the Minnesota volunteers did not skyrocket into obesity. On the average, they gained back their original weight plus about 10%; then, over the next 6 months, their weight gradually declined. By the end of the follow-up period, they were approaching their preexperiment weight levels.

Providing eating disorder patients with this account of the semistarvation study can be very useful in giving them an explanation for many of the emotional, cognitive, and behavioral symptoms that they experience. Eating disorder patients often suffer from misconceptions about the factors that cause and then maintain symptoms. Patients may be less likely to persist in self-defeating symptoms if they are made truly aware of the scientific evidence regarding factors that perpetuate eating disorders. The educational approach conveys the message that the responsibility for change rests with the patient and is aimed at increasing motivation and reducing defensiveness. The operating assumption is that the patient is a responsible and rational partner in a collaborative relationship.

THE ADDICTION MODEL OF EATING DISORDERS

Eating disorders have been compared to addictions, which is understandable because there are many similarities between these two behavioral problems (see Box 9.8). First, it is well documented that substance abuse and poor impulse regulation are very common among a subgroup of patients with eating disorders. Second, the experience of loss of control is a common experience, particularly among patients who engage in binge eating and purging. Third, those with eating disorders show a marked preoccupation with the abused substance. Fourth, those with eating disorders use the abused substance to cope with stress and negative

---

BOX 9.8
Addictions and Eating Disorders: Shared Features

Substance abuse and poor impulse regulation.

Loss of control.

Preoccupation with the abused substance.

Use of the abused substance to cope with stress and negative feelings.

Secrecy about the behavior.

Maintenance of the addictive behavior despite the adverse consequences.

feelings. Fifth, those with eating disorders maintain the addictive behavior despite adverse consequences.

One of the problems with the addiction model has been its translation into treatment. The addiction model has become the framework for Overeaters Anonymous (OA), one of the most popular self-help programs for bulimia nervosa and for other commercial eating disorder programs patterned after the OA or 12-Step approach to chemical dependency. Benefits of the OA approach to eating disorders include reliance on group support, sponsorship by someone who has achieved some measure of success, and a guiding philosophy that has been very effective in its application to alcoholism through Alcoholics Anonymous (AA). Generally, OA programs are aimed at achieving abstinence from compulsive overeating, which is accomplished by adhering to several axioms. Although there is a lot of variability in the way OA programs are implemented, participants are usually advised to adhere to specific dietary guidelines aimed at holding the addiction in check. For example, participants are advised to eat nothing beyond three meals a day, based on the premise that certain foods are addicting and will trigger bouts of compulsive overeating.

Although parallels exist between eating disorders and chemical dependency, the comparison has serious theoretical and practical limitations. A major problem with the OA approach to understanding eating disorders is that abstinence from alcohol is possible, but this concept is obviously unrealistic when applied to food. It would seem that recommending controlled eating is analogous to recommending controlled drinking, which is antithetical to the abstinence model applied to substance abuse. The parallel breaks down further when trying to understand the nature of the compulsive overeater's addiction. Empirical evidence is lacking for the assertion that specific foods are addicting. Moreover, the OA explanation of compulsive overeating is completely inconsistent with the far more parsimonious understanding of binge eating, food preoccupations, and food cravings as biological adaptations to chronic undernutrition (Garner, 1997). Thus, to the degree that OA programs encourage control by avoiding certain foods while not deviating from three small meals a day, they may inadvertently collude with the bulimia nervosa patient's restrictive eating patterns.

Treatment based on the OA version of the addiction model may also reinforce the fear that normal eating will result in inordinate weight gain. Moreover, encouraging participants to avoid forbidden foods is inconsistent with the evidence from the treatment literature on the effectiveness of incorporating these foods into a daily eating plan. While strongly encouraging abstinence from bingeing or vomiting is consistent with recommendations of other treatment approaches, the relative intolerance for slips in some abstinence-oriented eating disorder programs may exacerbate the harsh, self-critical, and dichotomous thinking patterns that are already prominent among these patients.

The OA model also has been criticized for presenting compulsive overeating as an incurable illness, a characterization that contradicts the growing literature on treatment success. Finally, whereas some patients find the spiritual orientation of the OA approach appealing, others may find it incompatible with their religious or moral beliefs. In summary, the addiction model of eating disorders has several flaws: (1) it does not address the core clinical features of eating disorders, (2) it fails to account for the effects of dieting on behavior, and (3) it may seriously undermine the effectiveness or treatment. Despite these criticisms, it is important to acknowledge that many find the OA model useful and effective. What is needed is research extending the one uncontrolled report in the literature.

While translating the addiction model into treatment has limitations, there still is compelling evidence for an addictive component to some aspects of eating disorders, particularly the connection between compulsive exercise and extreme dietary restriction. Hyperactivity is a salient feature of anorexia nervosa. Research has shown a period of high-intensity aerobic exercise precedes the onset of any eating-disorder symptoms in about 60% of anorexia nervosa patients. Traditionally, hyperactivity in anorexia has been viewed as a method of expending unwanted calories. However, some have argued that it occupies a more central role in the pathogenesis of the disorder. In a series of studies, Epling and Pierce (Davis & Claridge, 1998) at the University of Manitoba reported on "activity-induced weight loss syndrome" with experimental rats. They found when food was restricted to 60 to 90 minutes per day and the animals were given free access to a running wheel, they began to increase their running (see Garner, 1997). Typically, they exhibited decompensated eating behavior within 1 week with exponentially increasing activity and decreasing food intake, these animals literally ran themselves to death.

Results from studies comparing anorexia nervosa patients with women who exercise at either moderate or high levels have indicated that obsessive compulsiveness, weight preoccupation, and pathological aspects of exercise are significantly related of the level of physical activity. These findings can be understood in terms of a model in which physical activity, starvation, and obsessive compulsiveness each contribute to a destructive bidirectional feedback loop that is difficult to break. This self-perpetuating loop may be a significant influence in the development and maintenance of eating disorders. The combination of excessive weight preoccupation and obsessive-compulsive tendencies is likely, in women, to increase the frequency and duration of physical activity and to exacerbate the obligatory nature of their commitment to this behavior. In turn, increased physical activity itself may foster greater food restriction by virtue of its appetite-suppressing effects and by encouraging a heightened focus on appearance, weight, and performance.

The idea that activity induces anorexia is a controversial subject, and much research is still needed in this area. In any case, as indicated earlier, excessive physical activity often precedes an onset of the eating disorder. Overachieving and athletic young women are particularly prone to developing an eating disorder. Coaches, physical education teachers, and athletes must be aware that excessive exercise *combined with* excessive dieting can be harmful. This combination may be perceived as perfectly normal in the sports environment; however, coaches and athletes need to know that while dieting may seem to go hand in hand with training, the resulting feeling of success because of weight loss can become very addictive. In fact, beta-endorphins were found to be released in athletes after heavy physical activity. These beta-endorphins may then have an appetite-suppressing effect, while they also make people feel good. In turn, these athletes can become addicted to overtraining. This overexertion results in even more fatigue; while athletes may be able to continue training, the quality of their performance declines. Initially, these athletes may feel elated because, with some weight loss, their times may temporarily decrease and they may experience a runner's high since serotonin levels are temporarily increased after exercise. Furthermore, they may apply similar cognitive strategies used to keep themselves on track in training toward keeping their weight in check. The no-pain-no-gain strategy usually reserved for sports is now applied by these athletes to weight control. However, soon their bodies will no longer be able to perform at the same level as before, which leads many of these high-achieving people to become extremely depressed and even suicidal. Thus, while they initially aim to overachieve with the aid of dieting, performing to their utmost in dieting ironically causes the exact opposite effect: Their performance suffers and they end up underachieving.

Coaches need to know that students who are high-achieving, perfectionistic, and persistent are very likely to apply the same kinds of demands on themselves toward eating recommendations as they do toward their running and academics. In other words, they will do their absolute best in this area as well; unfortunately, the absolute best performance in dieting often leads directly to an eating disorder, which eventually leads to poor or no performance in athletics.

THE COGNITIVE-BEHAVIORAL MODEL OF THE DEVELOPMENT AND MAINTENANCE OF EATING DISORDERS

More than 20 years ago, cognitive-behavioral models of eating disorders were applied to anorexia nervosa by Garner and Bemis (1982) and to bulimia nervosa by Fairburn (see Garner et al., 1997 for a review). The Garner and Bemis formulation was intended to fit with the understanding of eating disorders as multidetermined and expanded on the cognitive-behavioral model of treatment that has been offered for other disorders such as depression and anxiety disorders. This approach to understanding eating disorders relies mainly on the assumption that eating disorder symptoms are maintained by a typical set of beliefs about the importance of weight and shape. These beliefs are then believed to lead to stereotypic weight controlling behaviors. According to the cognitive view, this dogma becomes the central factor of self-evaluation. For instance, we have many women who decide how they feel about themselves every day based on the number on the scale. Other women believe they are better human beings if they refrain from eating things with sugar or fat. This concept can become so essential to their sense of self that they experience severe distress at the mere thought of having to eat something outside their comfort zone. For example, one woman's heart rate increased dramatically when simply reading the word *fat* or seeing a high-calorie item. She then had a panic attack when told that she would have to eat cream cheese. She reported feeling as if her entire sense of identity would disappear if she ate anything that contained more than one gram of fat. Basic reasoning and information processing errors, such as selective attention, confirmatory bias, and cognitive rigidity may cause these beliefs to remain extremely ingrained. The result is that certain idiosyncratic beliefs become tied to the feelings of positive and negative reinforcement associated with success or failure at weight controlling behaviors. Once weight loss is achieved, the process is further maintained by starvation symptoms (as will be discussed in detail later) that tend to sustain particular beliefs and behavior about weight control.

Cognitive-behavioral approach to anorexia nervosa does not disclaim the role of biologic, genetic, constitutional, developmental, personality, and family variables, but also it does not require taking a strong position on the contribution of these factors. The cognitive approach to eating disorders is distinguished not by the specific content or timing of a presumed variable but rather by the methods used in evaluating their importance. The cognitive approach to therapy does not make assumptions about the relevance of historical variables; however, their relevance is determined by how much they are currently influencing eating-disorder symptoms and overall functioning. Moreover, the cognitive approach is distinguished by focusing on proximal factors that maintain the disorder while gradually working back to explore distal belief systems that may have played a role in the actual development (Garner et al., 1997). This model allows the exploration of historical themes relevant to the meaning system of a particular person without compelling all cases to fit into one explanatory system.

The cognitive-behavioral theory of anorexia also emphasizes the cultural context in which these disorders occur. Given the current cultural pressures for thinness, it's not hard to understand how women, particularly those with persistent self-doubts, could conclude that personal failings are to some degree related to weight or that the attainment of thinness would improve their self-esteem. However, only a small fraction of the population has an eating disorder. Thus, personality and temperamental traits, such as obsessionality, perfectionism, rigidity, and avoidance of danger, as well as variations in neuronal systems that influence cognitive style and information processing, are thought to be the main causes of eating disorders.

REINFORCEMENT CONTINGENCIES AS MAINTAINING FACTORS

NEGATIVE REINFORCEMENT

As indicated earlier, anorexia nervosa has been conceptualized as a retreat from the psychosocial demands of adulthood. Various theories have described anorexia nervosa as a retreat from fears associated with adolescence, such as sexuality, high performance expectations, separation from the family, and family conflicts. However, it is important to consider that these explanations can be understood in reinforcement terms without being wedded to one theory of the meaning that this has for every patient, such as the eating-disorder patient's sense that the reward system conforms closely to the fulfillment of psychic needs and rewards (i.e., blocking out painful feelings) described in addictions.

Negative reinforcement can be understood on a purely cognitive level. Cognitive contingencies may be represented by beliefs that are propelled by the anxiety reduction they create. For the patient with an eating disorder, exposure to feared stimuli, such as certain foods or a higher weight on the scale, creates such anxiety that rigid rules are adopted to guard against encountering the feared consequences. We have found that some persons with anorexia nervosa will literally do whatever it takes to avoid fear foods and, especially, a higher weight. For example, it is not uncommon for patients who are normally risk avoidant to engage in extremely dangerous behaviors to maintain their eating disorder in the face of social pressures to change. For example, it is not uncommon for patients to consume vast quantities of water before they are weighed so they can satisfy both their need to maintain a particular body weight while convincing the therapist they actually weigh more. The potency of the internal reinforcement system is illustrated by one patient whose water loading resulted in an almost fatal series of seizures. Shortly after being discharged from intensive care, this patient engaged in water loading again in a desperate attempt to avoid weight gain. This self-defeating behavior can be understood if you can examine the situation from the patient's perspective. Her identity rested primarily on her low body weight and the pressures to gain within the context of therapy were sufficiently threatening that the negative medical consequences of her actions paled in comparison to the terror set off by weight gain. However, it was the positive reinforcement associated with maintaining her eating disorder that was at the core of the obdurate clinging to symptoms. To relinquish her coveted low body weight meant that she had lost the sense of personal meaning associated with her eating disorder. It was not until this patient could redefine her personal meaning or identity in terms other than her disorder that she could begin to see the disorder accurately as a deadly threat to her life as well as an impediment to achieving other interpersonal goals that gradually became apparent. It is critical for caretakers to be aware of the powerful nature of the internal reinforcement driving the disorder to take necessary measures to protect the person against herself.

A unique aspect of the fear and avoidance seen in anorexia nervosa is that the patient cannot distance herself very much from the feared stimulus since it is *herself* at higher weight levels. Since total escape from the aversive stimulus is impossible, it may be controlled only through constant vigilance. Unlike other disorders in which avoidance plays a major role, the anorexia nervosa patient may not want to be relieved of anxiety about food and weight gain. These aversive experiences are *functional*, in that they assist the patient in the difficult task of oral self-restraint, despite voracious hunger.

Positive Reinforcement

In addition to being motivated by a phobic fear of fatness, people with anorexia are driven by positive reinforcement characterized by a sense of triumph, mastery, self-control, and superiority at successful weight loss. Early clinical accounts of patients portray them as exhilarated, elated, delighted, triumphant, powerful, and proud; weight loss is viewed as an accomplishment, achievement, virtue, source of positive pleasure, and sensuous delight. Because most patients extol the virtues of their pathological state, actively pursuing ego-syntonic symptoms, distinguishes anorexia nervosa from a simple weight phobia. A claustrophobic patient typically panics in closed spaces but does not typically report euphoria or a sense of power in an open field.

In the early stages of the disorder, there also may be considerable social reinforcement for initial weight loss and the self-control required to adhere to a diet. An adolescent, struggling with extreme feelings of ineffectiveness, might embrace the idea that a thinner shape could enhance her value. As indicated earlier, the resounding media message is that ultra-thinness is a sign of beauty, success, self-control, and social competence. In turn, the media portrays thinner ideals. The weight loss industry and the folk culture surrounding dieting provide the remedies. In addition, social positive reinforcement may take other forms. Initial weight loss may win parental concern or attention, and patients often strive for and then cling to an anorexic identity because of the associations with celebrity status and socially desirable traits. However, social reinforcement fails to account adequately for the development of anorexia, since the emaciated state reached by most patients goes beyond the societal standards for shape. Once initiated, *cognitive self-reinforcement* becomes a key factor in regulating the disorder.

It is important to realize that some women with anorexia nervosa may erroneously feel superior to those diagnosed with bulimic symptoms, since anorexia nervosa may be perceived as more pure and is often characterized as rigid rather than impulsive. However, symptoms exhibited by many patients belie this perfectionistic stereotype. Hiding food, wearing weights under clothing to avoid pressures to gain weight, and engaging in other dishonest activities to protect their eating disorder are inconsistent with the value system applied to other areas by many of these patients. By gently conveying that these frantic attempts to hide the truth are much more consistent with the desperate and impulsive acts of drug addicts, skillful therapists can gently convince patients to apply their high valuation of integrity and honesty to reporting of eating disorder symptoms. Gradually, patients are able to reframe their symptoms as impulsive, undisciplined, out of control, and dishonest while resisting self-blame. These symptoms are part of the disorder; however, the motivation to correct them can sometimes be tied to a higher-order value system based on honesty that is applied to other areas of their life.

Most cases of anorexia nervosa are characterized by a seemingly endless pursuit of a very thin bodily form. According to cognitive theory, anorexia is crystallized when the belief that "[I]t is absolutely essential that I become thin" becomes inexorably tied to the regulation of self-esteem. Therefore, weight, shape, or thinness serve "as the sole or predominant referent for inferring personal value or self-worth" (Garner & Bemis, 1982, p. 142). The development of the disorder can be understood within the context of real-life experiences. Thus, the persistence of anorexic symptoms, even in the presence of severe emaciation, is neither bizarre nor irrational. Rather, it is perfectly compatible with an organized system of beliefs, attitudes, and assumptions about the meaning and importance of body weight and is explained by the strong reinforcing properties that being and remaining thin can acquire. The cognitive model suggests that the general vulnerability to the disorder is propelled by the particular meaning that symptoms serve for the person. Cognitive vulnerability to anorexia nervosa can be linked with faulty beliefs and assumptions (both those closely associated to food, weight, shape, and core beliefs reflecting overall negative self-evaluation), as well as faulty thinking processes. Some examples, about which we will go into further detail, include (1) self-statements, automatic thoughts, and underlying assumptions that reflect concern with food, eating, weight, and shape; (2) core beliefs that reflect general negative self-evaluation; and (3) dysfunctional styles of reasoning and biases about food, eating, weight, and shape issues.

CORE BELIEFS REFLECT GLOBAL NEGATIVE EVALUATIONS OF THE SELF

The cognitive theory of eating disorders holds that the behavioral patterns are maintained by general core beliefs related to the self, such as guilt, poor self-esteem, and biological maturity fears. They tend to express more depressive beliefs about the self and the future than controls. The cognitive model for anorexia nervosa suggests that the belief systems associated with these aspects of self provide the connection between the general vulnerabilities and the final common pathway of symptom expression.

DYSFUNCTIONAL STYLES OF REASONING OR INFORMATION PROCESSING

The theories described thus far highlight the importance of disturbed information processing errors and unusual assumptions, beliefs, or attitudes about weight, shape, and food in anorexia. Disturbed information processing errors are caused by cognitive style and distortions in the processing and interpretation of events. Again, empirical evidence for the support of these theories has been limited to clinical observations and self-report measures, which may be influenced by a person's own denial and distortion.

For more than 20 years, one way the cognitive style has differentiated subclasses of eating disorder sufferers is by the variety of impulse control ability. Persons with bulimic symptoms have been characterized as emotionally outgoing and impulsive, in contrast with restricting anorexia nervosa patients who tend to be more emotionally inhibited and obsessional. Those with bulimic anorexia nervosa made significantly more errors and had significantly longer response latencies on a test compared to restricting anorexia nervosa patients. Restricting anorexia nervosa patients took longer but did not differ in errors compared with a small group of bulimia nervosa patients. Thus, these studies indicate that the relatively slow and accurate cognitive style of restricting patients is consistent with their reflective and careful ways of analyzing new information. Bulimic patients, meanwhile, tend to be cognitively more impulsive in their approach to problem solving tasks.

The cognitive theory of the development of anorexia also points out that systematic errors in information processing, such as selective attention, confirmatory bias, and selective memory around weight-related issues may play a role in maintaining symptoms in a relatively automatic manner. In recent years, a handful of researchers have tested different aspects of these cognitive theories. They have used modified versions of an inventory task test developed by Stroop to assess errors in information processing related to food, weight, and shape concerns in people with eating disorders. The premise is that people with eating disorders spend large amounts of time preoccupied with thoughts of food, weight and shape, and base their personal value and self-worth on these concepts. The Stroop task aims to measure whether people with eating disorders selectively process such information. In the Stroop test, participants are presented with cards that contain words printed in different colors and are asked to name the colors in which the words are printed while ignoring the meaning of the words. In the original experiments, words of particular importance to some respondents caused more color-naming interference for these respondents than for the control groups. Therefore, if anorexic patients are concerned with thoughts of weight, food, and shape, we would expect they will take longer to name the color of words related to their concerns. In the first study using the Stroop test, six color-naming tasks were administered to a sample of 20 anorexic and 20 female controls of normal weight. Results indicated that anorexic patients were more preoccupied with food by being slower to color-name food and body words as compared to the controls.

Another series of studies has been conducted using dieters with and without a history of eating disorders and patients with anorexia nervosa, bulimia nervosa, and controls. Normal dieters were similar to controls by failing to show selective processing information related to eating, shape, and weight. However, anorexics, bulimics, and dieters with a history of eating disorders did show selective attention for eating, shape, and weight concerns. Furthermore, one study displayed selective attention among anorexics, bulimics, and recovered anorexics indicating that a cognitive bias may remain even when recovery is reached. In an interesting twist, some researchers have found selective processing when participants were categorized according to their Drive for Thinness scores on the EDI rather than patient characteristics, thus indicating that this selective processing is not exclusive to patients with eating disorders.

CONCLUSION

A variety of risk factors can be identified for eating disorders. We described individual, family, and sociocultural influences that may place a person at greater risk of developing an eating disorder. Cognitive-behavioral theory is one of the most influential theories applied to eating disorders today, focusing mainly on the beliefs, underlying assumptions, and behavior of the individual. However, emotions, motivational issues (particularly the role of positive and negative reinforcement), interpersonal conflicts (including family communication patterns), and the influence of starvation symptoms must be included in a complete analysis of anorexia nervosa. The addiction theory is another model that has been applied to eating disorders. Central to this theory is the resemblance between eating disorders and other addictions. Patients with eating disorders often are characterized by substance abuse and poor impulse regulation, loss of control, preoccupation with the abused substance, symptomatic behavior around food to cope with stress, and negative feelings and secrecy about the behavior. Certainly, they maintain their behavior despite the adverse consequences. However, the addictions theory of eating disorders has not translated into as clear a set of recommendations for treatment as has emerged from cognitive-behavioral therapy.

We hope this chapter provides you with a greater understanding of the various factors that contribute to the development and the maintenance of eating disorders. If you are a person with an eating disorder, we hope this information shows that symptoms, including restricting and overexercise, do not show self-discipline and purity, but instead display a poor sense of self and often lead to dishonesty. However, with the proper help from knowledgeable and experienced experts in the eating-disorders field, the future can be a bright road ahead, free from the constraints inherent with an eating disorder.

RECOMMENDED READING

Garner, D. M. (1997). "Psychoeducational Principles in Treatment." In D. M. Garner & P. E. Garfinkel (Eds.), *Handbook of treatment for eating disorders* (pp. 145–177). New York: Guilford Press. This chapter provides a comprehensive review of the inherent conflict between cultural pressures on women to diet to achieve standards for physical attractiveness risk factors on the one hand and biological factors that resist permanent weight loss on the other hand. It is useful reading for therapists who have not had specific training in eating disorders, as well as patients who need to be informed about these issues. The chapter also provides a review of the complications of eating disorders.

Garner, D. M., & Garfinkel, P. E. (1997). *Handbook of treatment for eating disorders.* New York: Guilford Press. This book provides an in-depth presentation of the major theories of eating disorders, as well as chapters on diagnosis and treatment of both anorexia and bulimia nervosa.

Garner, D. M., Vitousek, K., & Pike, K. (1997). "Cognitive-behavioral therapy for anorexia nervosa." In D. M. Garner & P. E. Garfinkel (Eds.), *Handbook of treatment for eating disorders* (pp. 94–144). New York: Guilford Press. This chapter provides a detailed presentation of the theory and the treatment of eating disorders from a cognitive behavioral perspective. It describes a broad-based cognitive approach that integrates interpersonal therapy, family therapy, and motivational approaches to treatment. It also includes a comprehensive reference list to earlier work in this area. .

REFERENCES

American Psychiatric Association. (2000). *Diagnostic and statistical manual of mental disorders* (4th ed., text rev.). Washington, DC: Author.

Davis, C., & Claridge, G. (1998). The eating disorders as addiction: A psychobiological perspective. *Addictive Behavior, 23,* 463–475.

Fairburn, C. G., & Brownell, K. D. (2002). *Eating disorders and obesity: A comprehensive handbook* (2nd ed.). New York: Guilford Press.

Fairburn, C. G., & Harrison, P. J. (2003). Eating disorders. *Lancet, 361,* 407–416.

Garner, D. M. (1991). *Eating Disorder Inventory-2 professional manual.* Odessa, FL: Psychological Assessment Resources.

Garner, D. M. (1993). Pathogenesis of anorexia nervosa. *Lancet, 341,* 1631–1635.

Garner, D. M. (1997). Psychoeducational principles in treatment. In D. M. Garner & P. E. Garfinkel (Eds.), *Handbook of treatment for eating disorders* (pp. 145–177). New York: Guilford Press.

Garner, D. M., & Bemis, K. M. (1982). A cognitive-behavioral approach to anorexia nervosa. *Cognitive Therapy and Research, 6,* 123–150.

Garner, D. M., Garner, M. V., & Rosen, L. W. (1993). Anorexia nervosa "restricters" who purge: Implications for subtyping anorexia nervosa. *International Journal of Eating Disorders, 13,* 171–185.

Garner, D. M., Olmsted, M. P., Bohr, Y., & Garfinkel, P. E. (1982). The Eating Attitudes Test: Psychometric features and clinical correlates. *Psychological Medicine, 12,* 871–878.

Garner, D. M., Vitousek, K., & Pike, K. (1997). Cognitive-behavioral therapy for anorexia nervosa. In D. M. Garner & P. E. Garfinkel (Eds.), *Handbook of treatment for eating disorders* (pp. 94–144). New York: Guilford Press.

Hoek, H. W., & van Hoeken, D. (2003). Review of the prevalence and incidence of eating disorders. *International Journal of Eating Disorders, 34,* 383–396.

Johnson, J. G., Cohen, P., Kasen, S., & Brooks, J. S. (2002). Eating disorders during adolescence and the risk for physical and mental disorders during early adulthood. *Archives of General Psychiatry, 59,* 545–552.

Johnson, J. G., Cohen, P., Kotler, L., Kasen, S., & Brooks, J. S. (2002). Psychiatric disorders associated with risk for the development of eating disorders during adolescence and early adulthood. *Journal of Consulting and Clinical Psychology, 70,* 1119–1128.

Keys, A., Brozek, J., Henschel, A., Mickelsen, O., & Taylor, H. L. (1950). *The biology of human starvation* (2 vols.). Minneapolis: University of Minnesota Press.

Wilson, G. T. (1991). The addiction model of eating disorders: A critical analysis. *Advances in Behavior Research and Therapy, 13,* 27–72.

Walsh, B. T., & Garner, D. M. (1997). Diagnostic issues. In D. M. Garner & P. E. Garfinkel (Eds.), *Handbook of treatment for eating disorders* (pp. 25–33). New York: Guilford Press.

CHAPTER 10

Treating Eating Disorders

JEAN PETRUCELLI

SCOPE OF THE PROBLEM

TREATING ADDICTIONS FROM the interpersonal perspective involves the interplay between attending directly to the addiction and disengaging from the pull to do so. This becomes the inevitable interplay between the therapist and the patient. The emphasis is on how relational interactions contribute to and maintain addictive patterns. The addict progressively either withdraws from, or never really develops, intimate relationships with others. With eating disorders, this withdrawal or avoidance for the eating-disordered patient may be seen as a false outward presentation of sociability to the world at large that belies his or her inner secret retreat to that singular most important relationship—their relationship to the world of food.

The eating-disordered patient may present with an array of symptoms ranging from anorexic starvation and compulsive eating to bingeing and purging behaviors characteristic of bulimia. Eating disorders, as other issues of addiction, provide an extremely complex terrain to negotiate. The interpersonal dyad between therapist and patient is immediately fraught with issues of control, questions about intervention, and anxieties that permeate the very physical being of whom we are. As therapists, we face the challenge of how to intervene.

One-third of eating-disordered patients will never recover, one-third will become asymptomatic with partial recovery, and one-third will experience a full recovery. The highest reported caloric intake in a single binge is 55,000 calories with an average of 3,400 to 4,800 calories per binge. Regardless of presentation, disordered eating may be a sign that the patient is locked in a narrow, isolating world of preoccupation, obsession, and despair. The superficiality of dieting and bodily concern may hide a severe withdrawal from intimate and interpersonal interactions.

The psychotherapeutic treatment of eating disorders requires an acute respect for the power that bodily concerns can hold over patients. The patients we encounter are compelling, either drawing us into their suffering or pushing us out.

312

At times, the patient's focus on eating and weight can be so captivating that the therapist has to fight tooth and nail to find a way in. As therapists, we are immediately engaged, fascinated, and sometimes horrified as we view their struggles and the underlying terror of relatedness, which is obscured by their varying symptoms.

The awakening of my fascination with eating disorders, addictions, and creativity can be traced to my pre-analyst days as a player in the world of sex, drugs, and rock and roll. Having a prior career in the music business with all its excess, allowed me to bear witness to the often tragic link between the creative mind and addiction. Emerging relatively unscathed, I switched careers and attained my doctorate degree, wanting a career for later life. When I began analytic training at the White Institute, in the late 1980s, I was looking for a way to combine my specialization in eating disorders and addictions with analytic thinking. While my instincts told me that long-term treatments were a necessity for this population, I grew increasingly concerned that the general consensus was that these types of disorders were considered unanalyzable in the analytic realm at large. Never willing to accept the status quo and relying on my growing experience with the so-called unanalyzables, I found that indeed it was possible to do analytic work with this population. It required engaging the symptom in an active way—the symptom arriving announced or unannounced by the patient. Sometimes the symptom would need to be invited by the therapist into the room. Regardless of the way in, from there, the work would begin. It simply took longer to create the environment for meaningful work to take place. The relationship to food or drugs may be thought of as a patient's secret love affair—the challenge for the therapist to unravel the language and mysteries of the romance. The relational aspects of the patient to the substance plays out and is understood in the treatment room during the course of therapy.

In 1995, I became cofounder and codirector of the Eating Disorders, Compulsions and Addictions Service, with Dr. Catherine Stuart, at the William Alanson White Institute with the hope of broadening thinking about eating disorders and addictions in the analytic community. I will never forget being told by an eminent psychoanalyst, "Eating disorders, there's no trauma there. . . . They just need to sidle up to a salad bar and lose weight." I believe the Service has made dramatic inroads in changing once prevailing attitudes toward this population, and there is much promising work and discovery on the horizon.

The specific treatment with each patient varies; but, whether a patient suffers from anorexia, bulimia, or compulsive overeating/binge eating disorder, the concerns that the therapist stays mindful of remain relatively the same. This chapter presents a paradigm for working with the eating-disordered patient from a psychodynamic perspective where active behavioral interventions are integrated into the therapeutic model. The clinical vignettes highlighted in this chapter are reflective of interpersonal dynamics and, hopefully, may provide an orientation that will serve as a useful guide in how to think about working with this population regardless of the type of eating disorder.

EATING DISORDERS DEFINED

According to the *DSM-IV*, anorexia nervosa, bulimia nervosa, compulsive/binge-eating, and eating disorders not otherwise specified are defined as follows:

I. Anorexia Nervosa
   A. Characterized by self-starvation and excessive weight loss.
   B. *DSM-IV*-specific criteria include:
      1. Two physiological criteria:
         a. Body weight is 15% below minimally normal for height and age.
         b. Primary or secondary amenorrhea greater than 3 months.
      2. Two psychological criteria:
         a. Intense fear of gaining weight or becoming fat.
         b. Distorted body image or extreme concern with body weight and shape.
      3. Two subtypes:
         a. Binge/purging:
            i. Binge/purging types can use laxatives, vomiting, or exercise to purge.
            ii. Purging anorexics can be the most severe and most medically unstable because of vital sign instability as well as electrolyte disturbances.
         b. Restricting: Restricting types only restrict their intake.
II. Bulimia Nervosa
   A. Characterized by a pattern of bingeing and purging. Bulimia includes eating large amounts of food, usually in secret, in short periods of time, followed by the expulsion of food and calories through vomiting, laxative abuse, or overexercising.
   B. *DSM-IV*-specific criteria include:
      1. Binges/week for 3 months.
      2. Recurrent purging behaviors such as vomiting, laxatives, diuretics, fasting, severe dieting, or overexercising to prevent weight gain.
      3. Overconcern with and disturbance in body image.
      4. Lack of control around binge eating behavior.
      5. Two subtypes: purging (i.e., using laxatives, vomiting, diet pills, or overexercising) and nonpurging (i.e., fasting after a meal for days).
III. Compulsive Overeating/Binge Eating
   A. Characterized by periods of uncontrolled, impulsive, or continuous eating beyond the point of feeling comfortably full. While there is no purging, there may be sporadic fasts or repetitive diets and often feelings of shame or self-hatred after a binge. People who overeat compulsively may struggle with anxiety, depression, and loneliness, which can contribute to their unhealthy episodes of binge eating.
   B. Body weight may vary from normal to mild, moderate, or severe obesity.
IV. Eating Disorders: Not Otherwise Specified
   A. Many people have disordered eating but do not fulfill criteria for anorexia nervosa, bulimia, or compulsive/binge eating. Other eating disorders can include some combination of the signs and symptoms of anorexia, bulimia, and/or compulsive overeating. Eating disorders, not otherwise specified, do not fit into either of the previous categories, for example, a person who vomits but does not binge.
   B. While these behaviors may not be clinically considered a full syndrome eating disorder, they can still be physically dangerous and emotionally draining.

A MULTIDISCIPLINARY APPROACH
TO OUTPATIENT TREATMENT

It is generally agreed that eating disorders are multifaceted in nature and are viewed as being multidetermined. Several factors such as individual psychodynamics, family interactional patterns, cultural values, and genetic predisposition seem to all contribute in varying ways to the development of an eating disorder. The treatment may be thought of as multidimensional, combining the individual, group, and family and marital, pharmacology, and nutritional counseling, and medical consultation (sometimes a referral is made for a dental consultation as well). In utilizing a team approach, the growth of a new external foundation can concurrently be addressed with the psychological issues.

THE TEAM APPROACH

The Therapist   For most patients, individual psychotherapy is the cornerstone of treatment. The therapist should have specialized training and knowledge in the field of eating disorders and/or addiction. The patient meets with the therapist alone for a 45-minute session at a minimum of once a week. Ideally, sessions may be held more frequently ranging from two to three times a week. It is easier to work with the patient when he or she does not have to hold what has transpired in the session for a whole week.

The therapist is responsible for the psychological aspects of treatment, setting up the treatment team, and determining when group, marital, family, and nutritional therapy is appropriate as an adjunct to the individual treatment. Regardless of theoretical orientation, therapists have recognized the importance of working with the visible symptoms of starving, bingeing, purging, and the invisible psychological factors. The work in therapy is to discuss the eating behavior itself, understand the role that eating or purging serves in the person's life, help find alternative behaviors, and foster the development of healthier coping mechanisms. While focusing on changing the eating behaviors of the patient, the therapist should never lose sight of the reasons that food was used in the first place. The goal of treatment is never merely behavioral change but a deeper understanding of how and why the individual uses food to attempt (in an illusory way) to meet developmental and emotional needs.

The individual therapy should include treatment of the immediate symptom as well as a focus on the inner world and dynamics of the patient. One without the other is doomed to failure. The one-on-one relationship with the therapist provides an arena where the patient can acknowledge, formulate, and explore his or her feelings and thoughts. This aids the process of differentiating feelings from physiological sensations, such as hunger or satiation. Eating-disordered patients tend to misinterpret internal emotional experiences as hunger and respond by eating or deciding not to eat as a way of feeling in control.

Group Therapy   Group therapy usually consists of 5 to 10 people who meet with a therapist on a weekly basis for 1½ hours. Group therapy can be a crucial aspect of treatment and is particularly helpful in countering feelings of isolation, providing feedback, support, and education. It is also a safe place for members to learn and practice new ways of relating, to express feelings, to share in the experience of being vulnerable, and to develop trusting relationships that can substitute for the self-destructive relationship to food. Group member relationships to other members in the group may provide the transferential backdrop for family relationships to be played out, practiced, and better understood.

There are different types of groups, for example, segregated/homogeneous, mixed/heterogeneous, open or closed, support, educational, insight-oriented, psychodynamic, and short-term/long-term. Group treatment is not appropriate for every person (especially severe anorexics) but those for whom it is appropriate seem to benefit greatly from sharing the pain and the promise of hope.

Overeaters Anonymous   As an adjunct to treatment, Overeaters Anonymous (OA) and other 12-Step programs are often helpful. Look for a local listing in your telephone directory.

Nutritionist   A nutritionist is a professional who not only specializes in nutrition therapy but also has an understanding of the psychodynamics of eating disorders, is comfortable collaborating and communicating with the treating therapist and team, and is accustomed to working within his or her treatment domain as an integral part of the team. It is not uncommon for a person who makes an appointment with a nutritionist for nutrition and weight regulation to be surprised when the nutritionist informs him or her that he or she has an eating disorder and subsequently makes the recommendation that the person seek psychological treatment. Some of the responsibilities of the nutritionist include:

- Evaluating the current food intake patterns of the individual.
- Educating the individual with the eating disorder about normal and abnormal food intake patterns.
- Identifying hunger patterns, somatic sensation, satiation, or symptoms for each.
- Educating the individual about metabolism and metabolic rate.
- Estimating or determining the individual's set point for weight.
- Monitoring weight gain or loss (individuals often request to be weighed facing away from the scale and do not want to know the actual number).
- Developing a meal plan and strategies to balance the various food groups based on a system of food exchanges or caloric intake.
- Collaborating with the individual on incremental changes in food behaviors in a step-by-step fashion.
- Providing interpersonal support and acknowledgment of the fear of the anticipated change in behavior around the food.
- Using a food chart.
- Clarifying the physical and emotional consequences of maintaining a weight significantly below or above the individual's weight range set point (or ideal body weight range).
- Supporting the connection between emotions and behaviors by identifying food behaviors in response to emotions.
- Helping the individual to normalize his or her eating.

The communication and collaboration from the nutritionist to the therapist should include any behavioral changes the individual makes or any reversals in progress. For example, with an anorexic patient, if a nutritionist sees weight gain not warranted by the patient's food intake, the nutritionist might be concerned about water loading, which would be important information to convey to the therapist and/or internist.

Initially, the eating-disordered patient may meet with the nutritionist once a week or once every two weeks, for several months, gradually reducing the frequency of visits. Although many eating-disordered patients are obsessively knowledgeable about various aspects of nutrition and may resist making changes in food and weight-related behaviors, the educational phase of nutrition therapy is important as a first step. As with the therapist-patient dyad, the development of a trusting relationship with the nutritionist becomes an integral part of the recovery process as the individual develops the capacity to talk about the food and food related behaviors.

The Internist   The internist is responsible for the medical management of the eating-disordered patient. This entails assessing and detecting the medical aspects of eating disorders. Sometimes there is a need for a referral to a gynecologist, especially with anorexic patients. This may begin the introduction of talking about body issues and sexual apprehensions in the therapy.

The frequency of appointments will vary depending on the person's health. Communication and collaboration with the treating therapist is essential especially involving the following issues:

- Determination of whether the individual is at medical risk requiring inpatient treatment.
- Monitoring electrolyte levels.
- Advising the individual and informing the therapist if the person stops exercising and when it would be reasonable and safe to resume.
- Detecting medical complications of the following review of systems:
    1. Abdominal pain, bloating, constipation, and esophagitis.
    2. Cold intolerance.
    3. Hair loss and hair texture change.
    4. Fatigue, weakness, or fainting.
    5. Delayed puberty or short stature.
    6. Stress fractures.
    7. Laboratory examinations: CBC with differential, ESR, UA, Electrolytes, Ca++, Mg++, Phos, BUN, Creat, thyroid function tests, EKG (check QT, arrhythmia), CNS imaging in all boys or if symptoms warrant.

The Dentist   The dentist may be involved in the treatment of a person with bulimia because of the complications from purging by vomiting. The role of the dentist is to determine the extent of enamel erosion that has occurred or to conduct restorative work. Sometimes the dentist can diagnose bulimia nervosa during a dental examination before the person has told anyone about his or her eating disorder and then can be instrumental in helping the person seek treatment.

The Psychiatrist: Psychopharmacological Assessment   Sometimes, a psychiatrist may be the treating therapist for the eating-disordered patient. In other situations, the psychiatrist is solely utilized for psychopharmacological assessment. In this scenario, the psychiatrist is responsible for evaluating whether the individual with the eating disorder has a mood disorder and is usually looking for signs of clinical depression or anxiety. The psychiatrist's responsibilities include making the diagnosis, prescribing the appropriate medication, monitoring the medication for possible side effects, and resolving issues related to medication management. Again, the importance of communication with the primary therapist is essential to avoid the possibility of splitting dynamics or offering unilateral treatment decisions outside of the professional's realm of expertise.

FAMILY HISTORY AND ASSESSMENT

Check the family history for eating disorders, obesity, depression, anxiety, alcoholism, substance abuse, and other mental illness. Adolescents have a higher rate of eating disorders when there is a primary relative with an eating disorder.

ASSESSMENT AND HISTORY QUESTIONS

The following is a list of some questions that could be included when taking a history. Some of these questions are important from the onset of treatment; some will be answered as the treatment develops.

- What is your height? What is your weight now?
- What was your highest weight? Your lowest weight? When?
- What would you like to weigh?
- How often do you weigh yourself?
- Is there any particular part of your body that you feel is overweight?
- Do you consider yourself to be too thin, too heavy, or just about right?
- Have you had trouble maintaining your weight lately?
- Do you ever or have you ever purged, used laxatives, diuretics, or dieted? When?
- Do you drink caffeine? If so, how much and when?
- Have you ever taken diet pills, ephedrine, or steroids?
- Do you exercise and how much?
- How much water do you drink daily?
- Do you drink diet soda? How much?
- When was your last menstrual period? What is the regularity of your cycle?
- Have you been dizzy when you stand up or have you fainted?
- Do you take any drugs (substance use or abuse) or alcohol? How often and how much?
- What foods do you binge on? What foods do you purge?
- Do you eat large amounts of food when you are not hungry?
- Do you feel that food controls your life?
- Do you stay at home or avoid social situations to maintain your eating or exercise schedule?
- Do you skip two or more meals a day?
- Do you eat a very large amount of food within a 2-hour period while feeling out of control?
- Who knows about your eating disorder?

- What are your known triggers to your disordered eating?
- Is there a history of being teased about your weight?
- Was there a change in your family constellation?
- What age did your disordered eating start?
- Do you feel disgusted with yourself, depressed, or very guilty after overeating?
- What brought you into treatment now?

CLINICAL APPLICATIONS IN THE INTERPERSONAL TREATMENT OF EATING DISORDERS

How do therapists attempt to create safety in the eating-disordered patient's world of chaos where out of control or over control are the only known staples of their diet? We recognize that patients with eating disorders and addictions need the experience of a safe, real relationship with a therapist to ultimately enable them to acquire more tenable solutions to their body image and eating problems. But what actually makes one treatment safe and another not?

Therapists often report an accumulation of tension in themselves when working with multiple eating-disordered patients. There is a challenge that presents from the onset beyond that of deciding the order in which you schedule a series of eating-disordered patients in any given day. For example, you never want to schedule three patients with anorexia back to back before lunch—too much deprivation and starvation. I sometimes feel ravenous and end up eating for all three. Or, conversely, after lunch, seeing too many bulimic patients in a row can make me feel like I'm on a roller coaster, trying to hold everything they are unable to take in, leaving me exhausted and even nauseated.

The therapist's tension is connected to the eating-disordered patients' feeling an urgent need to gain immediate control over their lives. These are patients who seek immediate gratification, even if gratification is deprivation (which after all, can be a gratification of another pain). So, to advocate that the patient participate in a psychoanalytically oriented psychotherapy, which requires delayed gratification, is a challenging task in and of itself because it involves the patient's sense of urgency, some of which is inevitably contained within the therapist.

Most clinicians who specialize in the treatment of eating-disordered patients agree that engaging anorexic, bulimic, or compulsive/binge eaters in a psychoanalytically oriented treatment is a daunting task. The difficulty stems from several factors, most notably, a disturbance in body image and a general disregard for their inner psychic life. Eating-disordered patients tend to be preoccupied with their physical and somatic selves. Their need for nourishment is a foreign concept since emotional as well as nutritional needs are denied. Eating-disordered patients are plagued with delusions of fatness and experience profound dissatisfaction and disturbances in their body image. As Rabinor (1991, p. 93) has saliently noted, "Patients treat their own bodily needs cruelly, or at best indifferently, a symbolic reenactment of how they treat their emotional needs as well."

The patients may aptly be viewed as wholly consumed by concrete, somatic concerns to the detriment of their inner psychic life. Thinness becomes the Holy Grail; its pursuit marked by somatic rituals (i.e., starving, bingeing, vomiting, dieting, and relentless exercising). They appear lifeless, immune to introspection, insight, and analysis, the touchstones of psychotherapy.

BRIEF HISTORY AND THEORETICAL BACKGROUND

Not surprising, the historical underpinnings of the understanding of eating disorders began with Freud. Freud conceptualized eating disorders of anorexia and bulimia as hysterical symptoms resulting from unconscious sexual conflict. He theorized that bulimia, or psychogenic vomiting, was representative of an oral-sadistic, cannibalistic sexual fantasy. This fantasy emanating from the young, eating-disordered girl's point of view was that she could eat her father's penis and be impregnated with his baby. Psychogenic vomiting was the girl's neurotic hysterical symptom resulting from this unconscious sexual conflict and subsequent compromise formation (Freud, 1953). Freud's ideas were modified by Hilde Bruch in the 1960s and 1970s. Hilde Bruch, a psychoanalyst influenced by Frieda Fromm-Reichmann and Harry Stack Sullivan, described how she eagerly looked for such oral impregnation fantasies in the anorexic patient assigned to her when she was a resident. When Bruch was unable to discern these fantasies, she told herself that she hadn't stayed long enough at the clinic for them to be discovered because she was sure they must be there somewhere. The literature demonstrates that other experienced analysts offered similar explanations when failing to observe "these specific psychodynamics," so firmly established was their supposed "factual" existence (Bruch, 1973).

Over time, Bruch began to shift away from the drive-defense model entailing unconscious sexual conflict and began to emphasize self-development. She observed that anorexic patients displayed major deficits in their sense of self-continuity and autonomy. Bruch discovered that, prior to their symptoms, these patients felt helpless and ineffective in living. The severe discipline over their bodies represented a desperate effort to ward off panic about feeling completely powerless. In Bruch's view, anorexic symptomatology represented a defensive reparative maneuver against the underlying sense of powerlessness and ineffectiveness associated with major deficits in the personality development of the individual. She chose what she called "a fact-finding, non-interpretative approach" over interpretation. Bruch coined the phrase *constructive use of ignorance* to describe her therapeutic approach to anorexic patients. Put simply, Bruch meant that the therapist should listen closely to discern the patient's story, pay attention to the discrepancies in a patient's recall of her past, and look for the misperceived or misinterpreted events that would often be responded to in an inappropriate way. When patients are held to a detailed examination, as opposed to hiding behind expressions like food addiction or compulsive eating, they will uncover the when, where, who, and how of real or fantasized difficulties and emotional stresses. More often than not, they were completely unaware of these stressors.

Bruch identified a very important concept in the work with eating-disordered patients with her recognition of their inability to identify bodily sensations accurately. Feeling states are inaccurately perceived or conceptualized. This misperception is often associated with the inability to recognize the implications of interactions with others.

Bruch (1985) advocated that the therapist and patient act as true collaborators. The therapist should not act in such a way as to mislead the patient into thinking that he or she has a secret store of knowledge that is purposely withheld. It is noteworthy how many eating-disordered patients hold on to this notion while also holding on to their own secret contemptuous place that they try to keep hidden from others. Working with the therapist in a collaborative way is often a new type of experience for these patients. To be listened to as opposed to being told by someone else what they really feel or mean becomes an important step in the process of patients' experiencing their contributions as meaningful. Having experienced emotions and bodily sensations in an unformulated way, without the words to describe them, patients thrive when given help and are able to identify and formulate meaning to their previously unknown feeling states and, thus, learn how to control them.

According to Bruch, the therapeutic goal was to make it possible for the patient to uncover her own abilities—her resources and inner capacities for thinking, judging, and feeling. So Bruch, a true interpersonalist, promoted a "naive" stance that emphasized listening to the patient and guiding her in defining her internal experiences as they unfold in treatment. Bruch was influenced by Harry Stack Sullivan's ideas of the *detailed inquiry* and the concept of *participant/observer*. She considered him her most influential teacher. Her work focused on the therapeutic task of empowering her patients to face the realities of their lives and problems in living as opposed to providing insight about the symbolic significance of symptoms and behavior.

Bruch found that each eating-disordered patient faces the challenge of constructing a new personality after many years of a faked existence. Because patients with eating disorders are eternally preoccupied with the image they create in the eyes of others, they invariably question whether they are worthy of self-respect. An attitude of basic mistrust tends to permeate their self-concept and their relationships. Every anorexic, for example, fears that they are inadequate, mediocre, inferior, and despised by others. All their efforts to be outstanding or perfect are motivated by the necessity of cloaking their perceived inadequacies. Bruch asserts that anorexics are convinced that all people look on them with scorn and criticism. They respond to the imagined contempt with mistrust masked from the therapist under the veneer of pleasing cooperation.

The Role of the Mother   Bruch focused her work on the impact of the failure of the mother to respond appropriately (in a reasonable and consistent fashion) and affirmingly to child-initiated behaviors resulting in difficulties in the child's sense of initiative and active self-experience. From a developmental perspective, the eating-disordered symptoms (self-starvation, bingeing, and vomiting) emerge because of chronic disturbances in the empathic interplay between the growing child and the facilitating environment.

Deficiencies in mirroring, idealizing, and a wholly inadequate holding environment conspired to deprive the growing child of the necessary transitional experiences that foster cognitive and affective growth, self-cohesion, and object relatedness (Goodsitt, 1983; Rabinor, 1993). Bruch (1973) demonstrated how food addictions are defensive interpersonal patternings specifically related to the patient's interrelational world. From this perspective, eating disorders provide the patient with a means of taking charge of his or her own life in an environment where doing so more directly would threaten established, stabilized interpersonal connections (Brisman, 1995a).

Bruch believed that eating-disordered patients often adopt the position that "Mother always knew what I needed" and that this feeling is unrealistic and needs to be reexamined. In fact, the opposite is often true. Their mothers disregarded their feelings and, through the experience of therapy, these patients begin to discover their own needs and values. In the early caretaking environment, when the subtle needs of the dependent child are not recognized correctly or ignored, food may be substituted for an emotional need such as physical tenderness. A mother or caregiver may use her own needs to interpret a child's distress instead of distinguishing those of the child. The unintentional maternal neglect of eating-disordered patients is a complicated picture that fosters a difficulty in identifying internal emotional experience. These children are left with a pervasive feeling of mistrust, unable to have their needs met by external sources. This promotes a sense of ineffectiveness, reflected in their failure to take care of themselves and in having their needs met elsewhere.

Given this dynamic, it is not surprising that eating-disordered patients often feel overpowered by the judgments of others and have not learned to trust their own decisions. They present a facade of compliance while secretly maintaining the conviction, "I really know better, I'm different and for me I know things are different." In living so long with a self-belittling assumptive reality, they hold the conviction that they cannot change. The result is a compensatory attitude of grandiose aspirations for their low self-esteem. The idea of reducing their ambitious dreams of glory to human proportions with human limitations is experienced as a sacrifice of pride and ultimate failure. For the anorexic, the disavowed need to be super special is so compelling, that any conclusion based on human limitations or on the observation of others is rejected and simply does not apply to them. Anorexics want to be human in a way that is different from the rest of mankind, to the point of feeling inhuman in their demands.

The psychological influence mothers have on their daughters is unquestionably profound. All too often, however, the mother is unfairly castigated as the sole cause of psychopathology without due respect being paid to the multitude of factors: interpersonal, relational, intrapsychic, familial, and cultural that truly determines the nature of eating disorders (Rabinor, 1993). Rather than focus on mother blaming or the feminist perspective of mother affirming, a deeper understanding of the role of interrelational aspects of the mother-daughter relationship can be a fruitful area of exploration.

The Object Relations Point of View   Winnicott (1975) and McDougall (1974) provide a framework for understanding eating disorders from an object relations point of view. They theorize that psychosomatic illnesses are a somatic expression of something the person cannot experience psychologically because it is not represented symbolically. The body is exploited to express what the mind cannot. There is deficient symbolic representation. Chewing, for example, may be especially important in understanding how the sensory aspects of eating disorders function. In reporting a case, a supervisee once told me that he couldn't "stomach hearing his patient talk about the nuances of chewing each morsel into teeny tiny bites, swishing it around her mouth, swallowing, and regurgitating," until he was able to understand the significance of the aspects of chewing as a soothing, regulatory mechanism for his patient.

The patient who suffers from anorexia, bulimia, or compulsive overeating or binge eating relates strangely to her body. Sensations of hunger or other bodily states are often suppressed or ignored. At the same time, sensations of hunger, fullness, and other sensations seem very important. Patients will say they vacillate from extreme hunger to extreme fullness and they cannot tolerate any inbetween state. Gray is not a state these patients feel comfortable in. So, for example, when an eating-disordered patient caves in to hunger, she cannot stop after she is satisfied; she must eat until she is painfully stuffed. Without an accurate reading of one's own experience—food—the taking in or the not taking in becomes the vehicle for allowing a sense of control over needs and identity. The compulsive or binge eater turns to food to meet unacknowledged needs. In her drive for thinness, the anorexic attempts to retake control over an otherwise relinquished self. The loss of weight is the only means of assuming autonomy—of being in control of one's self without threatening tentative relational connections (Brisman, 1995a). However, this attempt to use food fosters an illusion of control or short-lived gratification. Ultimately, the eating disordered patient experiences the same emptiness with unfulfilled needs from her history repeated with her therapist.

BUILDING A BRIDGE OVER THE MIND-BODY DIVIDE

The split of mind/body functioning is enacted in many arenas in the patient's life. Concretely, these patients expect that through discipline over the body they can establish interpersonal effectiveness. One may conceive of an eating disorder as an attempt at self-cure, which fails and leads to further isolation and helplessness. When you begin to work with an anorexic, bulimic, or compulsive/binge eater, you soon discover the deep level of entrenchment that the eating disorder has in their lives. You also begin to see the varying capacities these patients have to self-soothe and tolerate emotional experience. The question then arises: How do you enter into their world, learn to speak their language, and aid them in learning self-regulation? These patients have a deficient capacity to self-regulate. With limited ability to self soothe, self-regulate, and self-enliven, patients are then vulnerable to feelings of depletion, fragmentation, and overstimulation (Goodsitt, 1983; Kohut, 1971, 1977, 1984; Sands, 1991).

In the psychoanalytic arena, psychosomatic symptoms are considered failures of thought with unthinkable thoughts becoming stuck in the body. The work of treatment in dealing with bodily symptomatology and bodily preoccupation thus focuses on creating the link, or building the bridge of understanding, over the body-mind divide.

The eating-disordered patient challenges us to consider how one works to build that bridge, when psychosomatic symptoms may represent another way of thinking. In the treatment of the anorexic, bulimic, or compulsive/binge-eating patient, words alone don't work. Eating-disordered patients don't believe in the efficacy of words. To them, words are tools that are used to manipulate or hide, not to communicate or effect exchange or change in a relationship (Brisman, 1995b).

Real needs are expressed through acts such as eating or vomiting. Therefore, a genuine respect for the action in the initial phase of treatment may be one of the most important ways that a therapist lets a patient know that she is being heard. The initial phase of treatment involves a focus on the patient's direct food involvement rather than providing them with interpretations. To these patients, receiving interpretations in the traditional setting painfully represents a reexperience of being told what to feel and think, confirming their sense of inadequacy and interfering with the development of a true self-awareness and trust in their own psychological abilities. If the therapist does not take seriously the patient's wish for direct support and communication concerning the disordered eating and talk about the food directly, another unspoken, potentially destructive interchange is immediately set into play. That is, the therapist unintentionally gives the patient the message that his or her needs are to be dismissed and a relationship founded on control and subtle coercion is initiated (Brisman, 1995a).

Anorexic patients, who are often historically described as being unusually good, compliant, and successful in school and at home become negativistic, angry, and distrustful as they become entrenched in their disorder. Onset of eating disorders is usually marked by negative behaviors as previously compliant children now stubbornly reject the help and care that is constantly offered to them, claiming not to need it and insisting on their right to be as thin as they want to be. In therapy, these patients reveal that underneath this self-assertive facade, they experience themselves as acting only in response to demands coming from others and not doing anything they want. Perceptions of their bodily and emotional sensations are often inaccurate; they do not trust themselves to identify their own needs and feelings accurately. When this idea becomes known to them and is shared between us in the room, I often say to the adolescents or young adults, "Why should you trust your own feelings at this point . . . when is the last time you made your own decision about something? When is the last time your parents let you fail or make a mistake, so you could learn that you could actually live through it?"

To highlight this, Jesse, a 23-year-old woman with multiple issues, such as bulimarexia, an addiction to Klonapin, cutting, and alcohol abuse with occasional slips, came into my office for a consultation because her psychiatrist believed he was at an impasse in her treatment. I felt she was close to hitting rock bottom and recommended that she go to an inpatient-eating-disorder treatment facility when she had expressed a willingness to do so. I described two different facilities to her and then met with her and both of her parents. One of the treatment centers was strictly an eating disorders facility and the other a hospital with a specialized small unit that accepts the more severe cases, especially if there is a medical component. I watched what happened in the room:

MOTHER: Honey, you can't have your cell phone or your lap top if you go to Place X.

FATHER: If you see Place X, I'm afraid you won't go in at all.

JESSE: But Dr. P. suggested that it might be a good idea for me to see both places so I could get my own feel and see which one I want.

MOTHER: But, how could you feel good, sweetheart, at Place X if they won't even let you bring a walkman?

FATHER: If you don't like Place X, this will be just another thing you start and stop.

As this dialog went around and around, I watched Jesse sink into her chair becoming frustrated and overwhelmed as she failed to experience her body as being her own. This exchange represented a microcosm of the many events wherein she experienced her body as something extraneous, separate from her psychological self, a possession of her parents.

SHIFTING THE FOCUS FROM FOOD AND WEIGHT TO THE INTERPERSONAL EXCHANGE

When you begin to present the eating-disordered patient with the possibility that there is more to the picture than food, you have to be willing to begin the formidable process of gaining passage into the patient's psychic and interpersonal life.

The goal is to shift the focus for the patient from food and weight toward that of an interpersonal exchange, something alien to the eating-disordered patient. The eating-disordered patient denies his or her need for relatedness and invents a restitutive system as Sands (1991) described, where disordered eating patterns rather than people are utilized to meet self-object needs. This occurs, in part, because previous relationships brought disappointment, frustration, and/or sometimes abuse. Therefore, offering the patient a relationship with a therapist will understandably be met with inevitable ambivalence. The therapeutic task is to encourage the eating-disordered patient in his or her search for autonomy and self-directed identity through the setting of a new intimate interpersonal relationship, where what he or she has to say, is heard, and made the object of exploration.

From the interpersonal perspective, areas of concern are not based on issues of internal conflict, urges, wishes, or damage. Rather, the emphasis is on how relational interactions contribute to, and maintain, dysfunctional patterns. The eating-disordered patient portrays a dichotomous, seemingly contradictory picture. He or she is someone who has, at once, repudiated relationships, yet at the same time relinquishes self-care, integrity, and empowerment, and turns him- or herself over to others in a frantic search for nurturance, direction, definition of self, or the quieting of tension, anxiety, and stress (Brisman, 1995a).

Despite the seeming abandonment into the arms of those outside, the eating-disordered patient is afraid of people. Interactions imply manipulation and control, profound disappointment, and anxiety. Direct communication, in which there is a movement toward intimacy and growth, is sacrificed. In its place, communication becomes organized to deceive, control, frighten, or placate rather than to express an honest thought or feeling. Thus, the eating-disordered patient progressively either withdraws from, or never really develops, intimate relationships with others (Brisman, 1995a).

THE DETAILED INQUIRY

Listening to what is said and to what is not said helps the therapist explore the unspoken agendas of the patient. The therapist's task involves obtaining data, asking the questions that aid in the understanding of the patient's experience, not only in terms of his or her attempts to manage symptomatic behavior but also his or her experience of other aspects of him- or herself, experience of others, and experience of the therapist as well. Paying attention to what is not said magnifies the possibility of revealing the unspoken agendas that interfere with patients' attempts to self-regulate their eating. For example, does changing eating behavior interfere with a patient's sense of security by increasing the opportunity for involvement with others (Brisman, 1995b)?

Questions

- What do you like about bingeing?
- Why is it that food is safer than turning to people?
- Why does nothing feel as soothing as bingeing or purging?
- What keeps getting in the way of the resolve to stop bingeing or purging?
- What would be on your mind if you weren't worried about your weight?

DIRECT ACTION-ORIENTED TECHNIQUES

Two direct action-oriented techniques that can be utilized in therapy with eating-disordered patients are the creation of verbal contracts and the writing of a food journal. One verbal contract I often enter into with a patient, if he or she is willing, is that the patient must agree to place a phone call to me before he or she binges or purges and wait until I return that call before he or she can binge or purge. After the phone call, if he or she still feels like bingeing and purging, he or she may do whatever he or she wants, having my blessing. The purpose is twofold: first, the patient learns to entertain the idea of an alternative behavior and second, a delay is put in place, where only impulse existed before. A difficulty with tension regulation occurs because the internal psychic mechanisms of self-regulation are not reliable.

Sometimes patients experience contracting pressure as deterring, not facilitating therapeutic action. In these cases, I come to a decision with the patient not to use contracts. Other patients cling desperately to any concrete bit of structure they are afforded. In utilizing the notion of readiness, a patient will decide whether he or she is ready to enter into this kind of contract. When a patient is able to enter into this contract, he or she begins a process of taking me in, digesting the words, holding the feelings, and using me as an alternative to using food. The work over time involves weaning the patient from the contracts and the dependent hold on the structuring aspects of treatment by embracing the external structure of choice.

What tends to ensue when a patient chooses to call is a discussion about what it feels like to hold the idea of an agreement in his head, especially when she is feeling that calling me is the last thing in the world she wants to do. When the patient doesn't call and she tells me about it in the next session, we end up talking about why she didn't call, the feelings before the binge, planning, timing, what was imagined if she had called, how it was done, who was told, and so on. I had one patient who said to me, "I didn't call because I was afraid you would talk me out of it."

I replied, "Well, tell me how I would have done that," ready to file that info in my head.

The patient replied, "Oh no, I can't tell you . . . then you would know what to say."

To which I retorted, "Oh, you mean there is something I really could say to you" and the conversation continued on and on in that vein.

Before we knew it, we were actively involved in some new negotiation centered on what the patient was actually feeling about our interaction around the issue of food as well as looking at the concept of alternative behaviors.

Alternative behaviors are necessary to allow the patient the opportunity to better assess what she requires at that moment other than bingeing, purging or starving. Alternatives might include self-care, self-soothing behaviors, such as resting, taking a walk, and meditation. It may involve vehicles for encouraging the patient to channel her experience into words, for example, using food charts or writing in a journal where the patient may begin to struggle to formulate and name her feelings, before, on, and after an incident with food.

In the initial part of treatment, I will often suggest that patients fax me lists of their weekly food and other ingested substances (alcohol, laxatives, diuretics, drugs, etc.) as a journal or food chart before their session. The food charts involve recording the time, place, foods, and/or substances, feelings, and eating disorder behaviors. (See Box 10.1 and Tables 10.1 through 10.8 for illustrations of various food charts.)

Writing, in and of itself, may be thought of as a vehicle for connecting the patient to his or her internal process. It facilitates the knowing and then ultimate trusting of one's self. For an eating-disordered patient, the initial experience of writing down the time she eats, what she eats, how much she eats, bingeing and purging behavior, and what she may be feeling around food can be excruciatingly painful. I offer these patients the opportunity to write as much or as little concerning their affective experience.

BOX 10.1 Journal/Food Chart			
Time of Day	Food, Amount, Quantity	Hunger Scale 0–10 0 = Not Hungry	Mood, Thoughts, Feelings, Eating Behaviors

Table 10.1
A 19-Year-Old Anorexic Patient Beginning Her Food Charts[a]

Friday		Saturday		Sunday		Monday	
Time	Food	Time	Food	Time	Food	Time	Food
8:00 A.M.	Breakfast	9:00 A.M.	Breakfast	9:00 A.M.	Oatmeal with dried fruit, vitamins, tea	7:45 A.M.	Breakfast
12:30 P.M.	Pita with lettuce, mustard, pickles, apple	5:00 P.M.	2 toast with tomato	2:00 P.M.	White kidney beans with salt and pepper, pickles, carrots, apple	12:30 P.M.	2 toast with soy cheese, mustard, apple
5:00 P.M.	Apple	7:00 P.M.	Pasta with sauce, peas, bread, pear, and frozen yogurt	5:15 P.M.	Dried fruit	4:30 P.M.	Apple
7:00 P.M.	Veggie burger with ketchup, lettuce, apple			7:00 P.M.	Tofu steak with rice, mushrooms, broccoli, dried fruit	7:30 P.M.	Beet soup (homemade), salad with potatoes, 2 toast, dried fruit
10:00 P.M.	2 pretzels						

Thoughts for the Week[b]

. . . the idea of restricting food goes way back . . . the more I think about it. "Like mother . . . like daughter" . . . I always remember her claiming she was on a diet . . . becoming vegetarian . . . RESTRICTING was always something good . . . something with benefits. . . . My mother always bought low fat or no fat . . . kitchen was usually empty . . . I remember using my stomach as a way to eliminate eating . . . wanting very early on to go to the gym with mom because I associated exercising with feeling less hungry. . . . I felt shame if I ate too much . . . felt their eyes watching me eat, especially when I was heavier.

Mom and Dad and my older brother have always been so involved with the things they do. I guess I was tired of trying to constantly get their attention on their turf. . . . I wanted THEM to see ME on my own ground. . . . "SEE" . . . a bit ironic.

Problem—they still don't see me, but they now see a disease instead. They accurately understand that this reflects on them, therefore the sooner "I pack on pounds" the sooner they can displace the guilt and shame they feel . . . the disease . . . I am a bit embarrassed and afraid that this is ALL that people see when they look at me. . . . It certainly was the case when I was at school—people couldn't even talk to me, let alone look at me like a normal human being.

I think my MOTHER is embarrassed by me, by the ANOREXIC. . . . I hate this label . . . I hate that she can't see past how I have tainted her perfect family by not becoming that independent, self-sufficient daughter. . . . Somehow I don't get mad at Dad because I know he is not even aware . . . but Mom is almost hyper-aware. . . . She won't even tell her own mother that I'm on medical leave from school. . . . I guess I have always felt that I was imperfection in a world of perfection . . . where nothing else is acceptable. WHY CAN'T I JUST ACCEPT THAT THIS IS THE WAY SHE IS AND WILL BE???????

[a]This patient writes her feelings in a stream of consciousness manner, which she then uses to organize her thoughts in the session.
[b]*Authors note:* These thoughts are written randomly on a page, scribbled in different directions as if it were the collage of thoughts in her brain.

Table 10.2

Journal/Food Chart of a 26-Year-Old Woman Who Binge Eats*

Friday		Saturday		Sunday	
Time	Food	Time	Food	Time	Food
4:45 A.M.	Coffee: brewed	12:30 A.M.	4 oz. chicken	10:00 A.M.	½ cup cottage cheese, 1 cup Fiber One and Wheaties
5:30 A.M.–8:00 A.M.	GYM	1:45 A.M.	1½ cups cottage cheese, 2 cups Fiber One and Wheaties	11:15 A.M.	Pretzels (20) with hummus
8:00 A.M.	Coffee: instant	3:30 A.M.	4 oz. chicken	12:00 P.M.	1½ cups cottage cheese, 2 cups Fiber One and Wheaties, 4 pieces of candy
9:30 A.M.	Coffee: decaf	5:30 A.M.	1 drink of Grand Marnier	1:30 P.M.	1 glass of wine
10:30 A.M.	1½ cups of low fat cottage cheese, 1½ cups of Fiber One cereal	5:45 A.M.	Pretzels (40) with hummus, 5 oz. chicken	2:30 P.M.	1 slice of bread, 1 Bloody Mary, small cup of noodle soup, salad, slice of bread, broiled flounder with spaghetti, 1 glass of wine

Time	Food
8:30 A.M.	Tea, ice tea, coffee, water, gum
9:20 A.M.	½ glass Sambuca
9:30 A.M.	½ glass Sherry
10:45 A.M.	Tons of kale, 8–9 oz. chicken, broccoli, orange sauce
1:00 P.M.	5 oz. chicken, collard greens, spinach, ½ cup of Fiber One, coffee, soda, water, tea, gum
1:30 P.M.	1 grapefruit, 2–3 oz. of chicken
3:30 P.M.	DISASTER: 5 pieces of cake, 2 servings Ambrosia, 7 brownies, 2 cheese cake cup cakes with whipped cream, 2 large peanut butter and chocolate chip cookies, 1 chocolate covered cream puff
4:00 P.M.	1 carton egg beaters, kale, onion, green beans, water chestnuts, shredded cabbage
4:30 P.M.	10 Tootsie Rolls
5:30 P.M.	10 pieces of candy
6:30 P.M.	1 protein shake
7:30 P.M.	2 tablespoons of cool whip, 1 fig, 10 pieces of candy, 10 chocolate chip cookies, 3 brownies, 3 hot chocolates
8:30 P.M.	In bed asleep

*During the week this woman eats the exact same thing every day and exercises compulsively. On Saturday and Sunday she binge eats.

Table 10.3

Journal/Food Chart of a 32-Year-Old Woman Who Night Binges in Secret: Day 1*

Time	Food	Feelings
10:00 A.M.	Banana	Hungry, satisfying until I have time for a meal.
1:30 P.M.	Falafel wrap	Terrible choice . . . now I know I don't like falafel . . . but I eat enough to get full.
6:00 P.M.	Grilled chicken, chutney, wild rice and mashed potatoes	Delicious, very enjoyable.
1:00 A.M.	½ turkey sandwich	Defiant thoughts . . . I know what I should be doing but I don't want to.
1:30 A.M.	3 packs of M&Ms	Don't even really remember . . . I never thought about it. . . . It's too hard to bring myself to consciousness.

*The progression from day 1 through day 3 highlights this woman's struggle to learn to be conscious.

Eating-disordered patients, for the most part, are not adept at communicating in words, since their distress is communicated through the food rituals. There is a part of them that doesn't want to know that part of themselves—at least not on paper and surely not shared with someone else. These patients suffer from *alexithymia*; they have no words to describe their affect and often feel completely overwhelmed by their feelings (Barth, 1994, p. 70). Food journaling is an attempt by the patient to begin to name the feelings and formulate what he or she is

Table 10.4

Journal/Food Chart of a 32-Year-Old Woman Who Binges in Secret: Day 2

Time	Food	Feelings
1:00 P.M.	Tomato, mozzarella on foccacio	I know it's late for breakfast.
6:00 P.M.	Meatloaf, mashed potatoes, string beans	Felt hungry.
8:00 P.M.	Chocolate lite ice cream cone	Tortured by thoughts of having something before I go to bed.
12:30 A.M.	2 pieces of meatloaf	Woke from sleep in bed. Just kept thinking I wanted it. Knowing all along how miserable it would make me feel.
1:00 A.M.	1 slice of pizza	Automatically go right to the fridge. It's as if I'm programmed. I don't even think about it. . . . I eat ½ first . . . then go back for the other ½.
2:30 A.M.	3 bags of M&Ms	Devour them in seconds . . . find extreme comfort, then fall back asleep.

Table 10.5
Journal/Food Chart of a 32-Year-Old Woman Who Binges in Secret: Day 3

Time	Food	Feelings
9:30 A.M.	English muffin with cream cheese and jelly, grapefruit	Determined to lose weight and cut out night eating completely.
1:30 P.M.	Seared chicken with salad	Happy when making healthy, delicious choices.
3:00 P.M.	Grapes	Happy, satisfied, but feel fat.
5:00 P.M.	Salmon, baked potato, broccoli	I'm going to try really hard not to binge tonight.
9:30 P.M.	Few spoonfuls of vanilla ice cream	
1:00 A.M.	Water	FIND MYSELF OUT OF BED STANDING IN THE MIDDLE OF MY BEDROOM. . . . DAWNS ON ME . . . THAT I DON'T WANT TO BE DOING THIS. LOOK AT MY HUSBAND SLEEPING. IMMEDIAT-EDLY GO BACK TO BED. TAKE A SIP OF WATER. VERY RESTLESS NIGHT. WAKE WITH A HEADACHE. BOTTOM LINE—I GOT THROUGH!!!!

experiencing. Food journaling may also begin to serve as a container for the out-of-control feelings related to food.

The experience of writing also connects the patient to others by facilitating interpersonal trust. However, for the eating-disordered patient, revealing one's secret world to the therapist may elicit myriad feelings of being judged, shame, disgust, self-loathing, and often relief. It is also an attempt to gain access to a place untraveled within oneself. To put something on paper requires the person to develop the ability to stand back and observe—the hallmark of an observing ego. The process of journaling food and behaviors teaches self-monitoring, while serving as a transitional object providing the patient ultimately with a feeling of safety.

Journal writing may facilitate, as Winnicott (1975) terms it, *the capacity to be alone*. Several Winnicottian principles inform the understanding of the value of journal writing. The anticipated reading and sharing of one's thoughts and feelings concerning food with the therapist offers the patient the "ability to be alone" in the (anticipated) presence of another. Journal writing also facilitates "potential space," a place from which to become aware (Rabinor, 1991). The writing provides the opportunity to access cut-off aspects of one's own self-experience. The hope is that a patient may initially open up to herself and then may later share this awareness with the therapist.

As you begin to address and put in place direct interventions or action-oriented techniques to help structure and repair out-of-control feelings or rituals, patients experience the therapist as some figure in their world, and their stuff is played out with you. For example, you may become the controlling parent or the overprotective mother. The psychodynamic material is always present even as you directly focus on the eating and food issues. The back-and-forth process of negotiation rather than the techniques themselves becomes the arena for growth and change.

The question of who is really present in the therapeutic arena at any given moment is prominent in the psychoanalytic literature. The issue is particularly pronounced with a population whose characteristic mode of interaction is to hide, defer, and secretly control interactions through submersion of self.

How to allow the possibility of two ever-emerging people into a relationship is the work of therapy. With an eating-disordered patient, the attempt is to tenaciously redirect the patient out of the world of food and into the arena of human interaction. The overt and ongoing negotiation of the patient's experience with that of the therapist's is ever present.

FOOD LANGUAGE AS METAPHOR

Treatment of the eating-disordered patient is an ever-evolving interplay between the language of the therapist and that of the patient. One thing that I find useful in this work involves the incorporation of the use of metaphor with food and the therapeutic process as a way of shifting the focus for the patient from food and weight toward that of an interpersonal exchange. For example:

- The issue of regulation of connection between the patient and myself = How much of my words can the patient take in?
- Overwhelmed = Stuffed, dissociated.
- When the patient needs more interaction from me = She feels starved by me.
- When the patient chooses to starve herself = Her punishing silence.
- Processing overwhelming feelings = Digestion.
- Small steps = Small bites . . . how to define them.
- Stopping, identifying the nameless but powerful emotional experiences that had been not attended to before that moment = Deciding together how one might go about breaking it into small pieces, chewing each morsel.
- The concept of choice = Deciding consciously what to spit out.
- Changing the concept of spitting out = Dissociation to choice.
- Holding conflicting thoughts or tolerating the ambiguity of a moment is = Mixing two foods on a plate, allowing for their separateness but knowing they can be contained and held in one stomach.
- Letting new ideas bubble in one's head = Percolating.
- Mulling thoughts = Brewing.
- Overloading one's emotional system = Bingeing.
- The impulsive expulsion of words or feelings = A purge.
- Getting rid of all feelings or being numb = Purging.
- New thought = The taste of a new food.

Using various food metaphors to talk about your relationship concretely enables the eating-disordered patient to build the bridge to integrate the various aspects of his or her self-experience. As one patient told me, "It's like being able to sit down and enjoy a seven-course Italian meal."

THE INITIAL CONSULTATION

Michael Strober (1991), in his writings on engaging the severe anorexic, stresses that the initial consultation is the most important encounter between patient and therapist. I usually address the vexing tension of conflicting agendas hanging over the consultation by telling the patient that he or she enters my office having one foot in and one foot out before even sitting down. As Bruch (1974) stated, the treatment of anorexia creates its own unique conundrum. If the patient's physical health is restored—the undeniable hope of all who gaze on her with revulsion and panic—she is left feeling profoundly inadequate and psychologically imperiled by comparison. As the therapist, internist, and/or nutritionist keep striving to add one small increment of weight gain, the patient shudders, feeling vanquished and cowed as she loses the one facet of her life where she misguidedly thinks she excels. She may genuinely come to treatment seeking relief from the misery created by the forces working to actively discourage her from realizing this goal.

Strober (1991) believes that if by the end of the consultation, the patient senses or is otherwise aware of the therapist's intuitive ability to decode the hidden meaning of her illness, a prerequisite for establishing therapeutic partnership will have been met, and both parties will better understand the shared commitment that is imperative to confront the daunting task that lies ahead.

Most important, the patient must be given reason to hope for a less painful alternative to the forbidding prospect of continuing her life as it is.

The Case of Lucy

This is an example of an exchange where issues were stirred up from the first session with a patient. Lucy was a very bright, hardworking, creative, 30-year-old anorexic woman with a beautiful face on a skeleton's body. She was 5'8" and weighed 83 pounds. Lucy had a history of two previous therapies that she maintained were bad experiences. One was, as she put it, "an Italian psychiatrist who didn't have a sense of the language so I ended up controlling her." I remember thinking to myself . . . okay . . . Italian . . . Petrucelli . . . Boy, she's letting me know I better be on target with her from the get go.

Lucy's nutritionist referred her to me because she didn't feel comfortable treating her unless she was in therapy. Her bone density test revealed that she had the bones of an 85-year-old woman. Lucy had seen an internist who recommended hospitalization for total parenteral nutrition (TPN; an intravenous line inserted directly into an artery that leads to the heart) or peripheral parenteral nutrition (PPN; an intravenous line inserted into the vein in the arm). She came straight from his office and refused the treatment options. Lucy was coming to me in the hopes that I would support her wish to avoid hospitalization. I would not. It was a very difficult session and I told her we would only begin treatment if she would agree to become medically stable first.

In the consultation, I came on pretty strong, giving her two options about eating-disorder inpatient centers posthydration. I explained that I could help coordinate her follow-up care, which would be twice weekly outpatient sessions and weekly nutritionist and internist appointments. Lucy appeared shocked that three professionals were in agreement that she should be admitted. At the end of the session, she neared the door, but didn't leave.

Throughout the session, I was aware of having two sets of thoughts: The undercurrent was that I was not getting through to her, not even coming close to penetrating her wall. She had been hostile and not engaging. I was also cognizant that I was throwing some serious choices and information at her that I knew would be hard for her to digest.

When she paused at my door, I knew I had to address this. I said, "I feel like I've really hit you with a lot in this session. This isn't the way a first consultation *typically* goes." As the words slipped out of my mouth, I immediately thought: What an odd thing for me to say . . . typical . . . there's no such thing. I realized I was feeling frustrated, worried, exhausted, and concerned about taking her on. I was already feeling worn down by her and by the lack of interpersonal connection.

Lucy, while standing at the door, grabbed on to the word typical. "Well," she said, "how would a first consultation *typically* go? I know I've been hostile here with you."

I retorted back to her, *"Typical?"*

She quickly asked, "Am I different than other patients that walk in through this door?" I paused and replied, "When I think about what you are up against, I would say that this consultation went the way it should."

Lucy became honest with me and revealed, "It seemed to bottom out at some point here." I told her I felt that as well and that she was hoping I would give her an alternative that would feed into the part of her that believes that she can still manage this on her own terms. To which she responded in a huff, "Well . . . did you expect that I would just take what you said and agree just like that?"

I smiled and replied, "I was hoping but not counting on it. If we had an established relationship, this still might be a really tough decision, but we would have had a history and the decision might emerge from a place of trust. That's not possible now; all you have is your fear and my hope. I wouldn't feel comfortable telling you things would be okay for you if you do nothing."

To which Lucy replied, "I'm hoping you'll be able to tell me what's my window, and I would like you to speak with my internist and nutritionist." I told her I would. Now she put her hand on the doorknob and said sadly, "You know, it's not easy for me to trust people, but I'll look forward to your call. Thank you."

In this consultation, I engaged some aspect of Lucy's self-experience as she was already asking me how she was alike or different from other patients. Although I was cognizant of how difficult this work would be with her, there was nonetheless something appealing, compelling, and likeable in Lucy's tenacious feistiness. Lucy was starving, but I could feel the potential for her aliveness and it engaged me.

The manner in which Lucy stopped at the door became an important piece of information in her treatment. That moment, an ending, a transition, a loss, a switch, helped me understand a dynamic that was mirrored in her relationship with food. Lucy delays eating for as long as she can in a day and when she begins to eat her bagel she must be reading or walking. She reads a paragraph then takes two bites and with each bite becomes fearful of the ending of the bagel, which represents a transition into something else. She cuts her bagel into 12 pieces, to use her words, "skins" off the top, "skins" off the bottom, then eats the "flesh" in the middle. Between top, bottom and middle, inside, outside, skin, and flesh, her unintegrated aspects of self-experience are enacted with her bagel.

She takes over an hour to eat it in this ritualistic way. Terrified of the food ending, which represents the terror of the "black hole" and "nothingness of time"; she becomes fixated on the saving process and holds off on eating until she is beyond exhaustion. She told me, "I can't just finish something and go on. . . . When I'm done with my bagel, I become totally unfocused. . . . I save the last bites to help me transition. I call it 'ramping up.' If I don't have the food to use as an organizing principle, I don't feel like I'm a functioning human being. That's why the first thing I purchase in the morning is the last thing I eat at night."

I understood this better as time went on. But at the beginning of the relationship, the sense of safety had to be negotiated between us. My awareness of Lucy's level of anxiety made me wonder: Did I ask the question at the door to engage Lucy and stir up her anxiety while paradoxically thinking I was helping her not become overwhelmed? Does the key to maintaining safety require the therapist to back off when the anxiety rises too high? Or is there safety when the situation does not feel too safe for the patient or the therapist and they together negotiate the unexpected? It certainly fosters the chance of a more alive, spontaneous moment emerging. Does safety then involve inculcating the awareness that not knowing may become predictable and the collaboration for safety a possibility?

Safety may be felt as a protection from experiences. Safety may aid in the ability to deal with experiences. The safety issue is something of a paradox. While a patient has to feel a sense of safety to work in treatment, too much safety (e.g., a feeling of overprotection) may be experienced as too dangerous. Therefore, the issue of balance is critical when dealing with safety. With an eating-disordered patient, ultimately, a goal is not to feed but to facilitate the process of helping the patient learn how to feed herself.

Lucy entered the hospital the next day after the consultation. She weighed 81 pounds and was placed on a PPN. We spoke by phone during her hospital stay and began twice weekly sessions on her discharge. She also agreed to see the nutritionist and internist on a weekly basis. Working in conjunction with the nutritionist, Lucy faxed me weekly food charts with paragraphs and paragraphs of feelings around the food. Her relationship to food (especially her daily bagel and donut) read like a clandestine, taboo love affair, anticipation fueling excitement, intimacy enveloped in secrecy, and disappointment and emptiness when it was over.

Treatment revealed that intimacy enveloped in secrecy was the norm in Lucy's family history. At age 15, she discovered her mother had been married before and that her sister, 14 years senior, had a different father. He had been killed in a car crash, a powerful family secret held long and hard. This information was first revealed to Lucy during a fight when she, ironically said to her parents in anger, "I don't feel like I am your real child." Although, she is the biological child of her parents, her experience of not being their real child may reflect some of her feelings concerning belonging (or connection). In the consultation, the word *typical* made Lucy question my impressions of her and her impact on me. Difficulties surrounding Lucy's ability to trust her connection to me continued to become

Table 10.6
The Case of Lucy: Journal/Food Chart 1

Time	Place	Food	Feelings
4:00 P.M.	Desk	Yogurt	"I've made you fight and you've won your right to start your food. After your early meeting, which made you late for your dentist appt., after which left too little time to eat before your conference call, which led you right into your big client meeting. Now, that that's over with, take a breath and have some yogurt. But, make it last the whole rest of the day because you can have your bagel when you get home."
9:00 P.M.	Home	½ of bagel	"It's been a long hard week. You're tired. And I know you're saying you need to use the fact that it's Friday, you can relax, don't have to rush and don't have the excuse that you have no time to 'fit all your food in.'"
		1 c. cottage cheese with honey and sesame seeds	"But I'm telling you that it's Friday and you can take it easy and enjoy your food the way you want. And since you can putsy enough to put off eating until 9:00 anyway, you can get away with just your bagel. Then you won't have to deal with dinner."
12:00 A.M.		Toasted coconut cake donut	"You should have thought of that when you were arguing with me before. So now you have to suffer. It's not my fault you can't enjoy your donut. It's your fault for listening to me in the first place. So eat and weep on your own time, not mine."

Author's note: On this chart, Lucy is using her other voice to talk to herself. It is a conscious dissociation because she cannot own the battle at this point.

enacted in the treatment room. Being a real person in the room involved Lucy's capacity for feeling that she was in a safe enough arena to be able to access, recognize, and give voice to the dissociated aspects of her self-experience. Lucy would often tell me in her food charts that she "needed to tell me something by talking in her other voice." To Lucy, this other voice represented her self-labeled *self-destructive* part. I would relabel that with her as "a part of her that just needed a voice." With Lucy, an approach was needed that not only allowed dissociated aspects of self-entry into the treatment room but also took me out of the room and into her subjective space—into the very moments that her body was most vocal—the moments of her starvation and deprivation.

After 7 months of treatment, Lucy, who came into treatment weighing 83 pounds, now weighed 116. Six months later she stabilized at 111 pounds and remained there for over 2 years. Through the work in treatment, Lucy learned that the eating rituals served a psychological function for her. Food was being used to communicate needs, stabilize her relationships, subdue her tensions, and was an

Table 10.7
The Case of Lucy: Journal/Food Chart 2

Time	Place	Food	Feelings
2:45 P.M.	Park	Bagel with 3 tsp. of peanut butter	"So what if you are feeling uncomfortable sitting there eating a bagel like it's the last one on earth. You've got privacy, you've got time and you'll make it to your appointment. And you are eating, so it should make all the powers that be—yours, your boyfriend's, your doctors, and everyone else happy."
9:30 P.M.	Writing at the computer	Yogurt, grilled banana, and cheese on rye	
11:15 P.M.	Reading	Frosted whole wheat donut	"You're having feelings about tomorrow. Sleeping in sounds good, but getting up and going to work before your TPN insertion is what you think is the right choice. Because you can't decide if 'sleeping in' is being used as a way to take care of yourself, which needs to be the priority, or if it's a cop out to deal with going back to work—where my food structure and your work flow don't see eye to eye. So what if it's a cop out? Everyone says that you need to start making yourself a priority—taking time to eat, get the rest you need, etc. But you think you're making it a priority for the wrong reason. It's only a priority when it's convenient for me. Which is true. It's a lot easier to deal with the food plan you've got me forced to fight when I can have it on the terms that make it most enjoyable. Just like I make this donut your daily communion. It's all that you believe in. You get disgusted by the fact that your entire life revolves around donuts and what not. Like it's the only thing that really matters. Like an earthquake could occur and the first thought that would enter your head is, 'I wonder if my donut cart survived.' And if not, you'd be panicking about where you'd find one for eating that night. You think that's irrational. I think of it as a way to somehow put order into an otherwise unmanageable chain of events. If I were in an earthquake, I'd want some kind of grounding to know that everything will be all right. If my lifesaver happens to fry in oil and get some frosting on the top, then so be it. After all, if it floats to the top after taking the plunge in all that grease, you gotta give it some credit."

Table 10.8
The Case of Lucy: Journal/Food Chart 3

Time	Place	Food	Feelings
Noon	Desk	Yogurt	"I actually lost track of time and seeing it was passing 11:15 A.M., at once I felt an urge to get my yogurt, then thought twice about it. But got the will to get it by noon. But didn't finish it till much later. And only when forced to, since I had to leave for a meeting. But I got it down before the meeting, not after, which is what I usually do—that is, just wait and wait and wait."
4:30 P.M.	Desk	Toasted bagel with peanut butter	"I was at a meeting and before returning to the office went OUT to get this bagel to avoid the anxiety of having to prepare it myself. I was much calmer compared to last Monday. And was able to eat it at a normal pace and even decided to eat the second half (which I thought was saving) and not feel overwhelmed or out of control about it. I also noticed that everybody was gone for the day. Except for another coworker—so the solitude, I think, has something to do with feeling more relaxed about eating. Because it's 'my time' at the office—without anyone else there to make me feel self-conscious or interrupted."
9:45 P.M.	Working at computer	Bagel with 2 tsp. tahini	"No deli had cottage cheese, but I didn't freak out. I just substituted. And was a little bit glad that I didn't have to go through the cottage cheese ritual as usual. Maybe this is a sign of growing tired of the old and growing into new things—more 'safe' foods. Tired but not cranky tired and in a much better disposition overall when I got home. No 'transition' problems. I found myself wondering where they were and was expecting them. Too much silence always makes me feel like disaster is lurking around the corner ready to catch me when I least expect it."
11:15 P.M.	Reading	Coconut cake donut	"I ALWAYS get the most pleasure from this and at the same time, the most panicked, when I realize when the donut is coming to an end, so is the day, and there's nothing to hold onto to help me with tomorrow. Instead of looking forward to the adventure of every day and the possibilities it brings. Maybe feeling better and feeling better about myself will make me want to forge ahead because I'll have the energy and self-esteem to feel like it's not the losing battle that I feel it is now."

attempt to regulate the chaos of her inner and outer world. She learned that my message to her was that there was more to the picture than just food and weight. A goal of the treatment was to help her find better ways of recognizing and addressing her needs rather than turning to food or diet as solutions. Allowing me to know her was both rewarding and terrifying for her. Lucy was afraid the ante of intimacy would be upped beyond what she believed she could tolerate. However, her intellectual curiosity surrounding this conflict permitted us to play around with words, and we were able to explore the multitude of feelings this crossroads presented. With Lucy's boyfriend, there seemed to be a parallel process evolving, where, to use her words, "We physically play and fool around more . . . and do everything sexually, but intercourse." Penetrating her wall in therapy would only occur in an arena of relational safety.

An exploration of how food and bodily focus were used to negotiate and paralyze internal experience and interpersonal exchange was crucial in Lucy's treatment. However, symptom change or alleviation never feels like the hardest part of this work. Recovery from the acute phase alone does not remedy all the pervasive aspects of this disorder. When Lucy was able to transcend the day-to-day involvement with food and could begin to translate the dynamics involved, the nonacute work began.

With Lucy, our talks and struggles deepened because the power of this approach did not merely affect behavioral change. Celebration of change is sure to collide with a patient's narrowed view of herself as contained in her body. Behavioral intervention is critical, not solely as a means of alleviating the symptom but as a means of speaking the patient's language, while integrating the therapist's language into the treatment.

After 2 years, Lucy and I entered into a new phase of treatment that was challenging in a different way than the initial acute crisis. She decided to stop all her adjunct therapies (nutritionist and internist) and the writing of her food journals. She openly complained about the meaninglessness of engaging in therapy and was no longer interested in any comments I would make about our relationship. She became irritated with me whenever I tried to make such interjections. Lucy's stance was that I was exaggerating the importance of our relationship and that, in any case, she was not open to exploring it. My understanding of Lucy's position with me, as in all her relationships, was that it was necessary "not to need too much." Therefore, she sought to keep the therapy on as impersonal a basis as possible.

There were two opposing currents in the transference: There was the rigid control Lucy exercised over the structure and the emotional distance of the relationship. However, within these parameters, she was relatively open, connected, and spontaneous.

I would directly comment on these opposing currents by playfully capturing her attention. (I had a 50/50 success rate.) When she would inform me in each session that she didn't want to come to therapy, she would pose the question in a kiddish voice, "Do I have to come?" as if it were up to me. Playing around with her, I would reply that she was asking me a *typical* kind of question for someone who wouldn't own her own commitment to her recovery and that her fear of becoming more connected to me was very strong. So strong, that she might have to terminate therapy to preserve her private space.

I was attempting to do several things here. I knew that in brandishing the word *typical*, I would at least momentarily stop her in her tracks. In addition, I was attempting to help her hold two interests in mind. The first involved recognizing the part of her that felt fearful and stuck in the moment; the second was recognizing that staying in therapy meant ultimately risking Lucy's loss of private space. Allowing me in would inevitably foster the growth of our connection. Lucy also needed permission to feel that she could leave treatment.

Playing on the concept of uniqueness, I had also hoped to dare her to become curious enough to begin to think that she might be able to do it differently. This intervention falls in the class of what Sullivan called *double statements* and Havens referred to as *balancing techniques,* which would hope to allow a fresh element added to the mix (Havens, 1976). Lucy could potentially make a choice without having to just do the opposite, namely, to distrust and disavow her needs and feelings. This opened up a new series of negotiations and resistances.

When I was not successful in playing around with Lucy, we engaged in a struggle in which Lucy would tell me repeatedly that she didn't want to talk to me about her work life, her relationship, how she felt about food, or how she felt about anything. In these moments, Lucy deprived me of herself and this defense served as a security operation that protected her from the underlying terror of relatedness. There were many instances where she could not hold on to the history of the relationship and by walking out my door she would inform me that the relationship stops until the next appointment.

Often, I felt worn down by her and confided to her that I was close to giving up. We would then renew the dance: Lucy would back down from her rigid position, take a step forward, feel hopeful, become scared, and back away. We inevitably continued to repeat this pattern. Each time, taking a small bite or baby step forward, learning something new in the process. This enactment repeated Lucy's problems in living and provided us with rich encounters that expanded our consciousness. One has to be mindful, though, that an enactment may retraumatize a patient if it simply repeats an old hurtful pattern or if the therapist's countertransference creates difficulties and blind spots that are critical to the growth of the therapeutic process. Given the tension between Lucy's need to defend herself from an intimate experience and the intimacy involved in working through an enactment, there was a heightened need to be sensitive to Lucy's concerns about relatedness as we struggled to create a different experience between us.

Lucy's battle was long and hard fought, but each small victory became a cherished moment. One time, she laughingly said, "I feel like I'm 21 instead of 31. There's an immaturity in everything I do, my relationships, my job, the food. I feel like you've scared me . . . Ha! . . . You don't really scare me . . . into thinking if I don't do this work I won't reach my potential. It's like that saying, 'An unexamined life is not worth living.' Uh oh . . . Did I say that? . . . Now I know I'm in big trouble! . . . Ha!"

COUNTERTRANSFERENCE

Eating disorders can induce strange and curious countertransference responses that are difficult to tolerate. The profound pain and mix of trauma, sexual abuse, battering, demands for perfection, unreachable expectations, verbal abuse, alcohol or drug addiction, garbage eating, laxative and/or diuretic abuse, bingeing, purging, self-mutilation, and other insufferable pains are so perplexing that it is difficult for a therapist to determine what to explore or how to resolve the many complexities that often present simultaneously. Therapists may leave sessions feeling confused, angry, frustrated, despairing, and worried. These feelings often may reflect conscious or unconscious identifications with the patient's own intense struggles. Even the most empathic, caring therapeutically attuned therapist will often fail. It is through these failures that we gain rich tools in understanding the meanings of our countertransferential responses and then utilize that knowledge in treatment.

In a dynamic interactive matrix of treatment, there is an ever-changing interpersonal field that acknowledges the inevitable affective input of therapist and patient alike. This two-person psychological model involves the patient and the therapist influencing one another in a rich feedback loop—any one, narrow, therapeutic stance is ill fated. Therapists must remain vigilant to the problems inherent in effectuating this model. We face several dilemmas in this regard: How do you contain the patient when you are having trouble containing your own emotional responses? How to use our emotional responses to the patient as a key to furthering treatment? And, most important, how to acknowledge the dynamic and mutual nature of the therapeutic dyad, ensuring the safety of the vulnerable patient while remaining attuned to using our countertransferential responses, without imposing them in ways that feel intrusive, over-stimulating, or self-serving?

THE DISREGULATION OF AFFECT OF THE THERAPIST AND ITS IMPACT ON A BULIMIC PATIENT

The Case of Carla

Carla was a 28-year-old woman with a 15-year history of bulimia. She would binge and purge three times daily, regardless of the quantity of food actually ingested. When Carla was 13, her older brother, then 17, began showing prodromal signs of schizophrenia, resulting in a series of hospitalizations and medications. Carla had two previous therapy experiences, both she described as "bad and baddddddest." In her last therapy experience at a clinic, the therapist (according to the patient), accused her and her boyfriend of being alcoholics, referred Carla for a psychiatric consultation, and then accused her of being drunk at the consultation. When Carla adamantly denied these accusations in her last session, the therapist "screamed" at her, "You can go through the charade and find a therapist who will listen to your lies!"

These were her first words to me and the backdrop of how we initiated our work together. Carla described herself as a demanding child with a sweet tooth. Her mother would not give her sweets, so she would eat sweets daily at her friend's house. Carla's mother was secretly bulimic, which Carla claims to have known then, but only consciously as an adult. When Carla was 13 years old, her best friend taught her how to throw up. The best friend's mother killed herself that year. Carla did not begin to menstruate until she was 19; she was a virgin until age 23. At the time she entered treatment with me, she was in her first long-term positive relationship with a man named Michael, although, he had a problem with social drinking.

Carla finished law school, had several jobs as a lawyer, determined she hated it, and decided on a new career in the media arts. For one year, we struggled with food charts, the nutritionist, and the internist. Slowly, bit by bit, she began to put the delay in calling me where only impulse existed before. The binges and the purges became a conscious choice when she made the decision that she couldn't deal with the moment. In therapy, she became aware of her emotional triggers— boredom and loneliness—and developed a greater motivation to look good but be healthy at the same time.

It was around this time that she reported this dream:

> I'm sitting in a car with Jennifer Aniston and Kevin Costner is in the back seat. I was needling him about how bad he was in the film *Message in a Bottle.* (I thought that was good reality testing.) We were all going to eat and when it came to dessert, I had to choose between chocolate and strawberry. I thought if Jennifer Aniston is not going to get the chocolate then I'm not going to get any either. I then ordered a salad smaller than hers.

Carla's associations concerned the idea of flirting, putting men down, the experience of envy, and being obsessed with Jennifer Aniston, thinking she's beautiful and sexy. In the next session, she decided to bring in old family pictures. As I was looking at them, one jumped out. It was a picture of Carla on her father's lap, which I believed had a very strong sexual overtone to it. In the picture, Carla was about 13 or 14, but appeared much older and sexy wearing short shorts. Being somewhat startled, I said, "Wow, you look like you could be your father's mistress here." I continued, "Does it seem odd to you? What do you see when you look at this picture?" I wasn't exactly having a neutral reaction. However, we continued to discuss it in what I thought was a fairly normal session.

I was wrong. She was furious. In the next session, she strode in angrily, denouncing me for insinuating that there might have been something sexual in her father's relationship with her. She screamed, "I feel I can't trust you now . . . that you would even think of asking me that question . . . if you thought I had been abused . . . why didn't you just ask me that directly?"

Carla continued, "Are you inventing a problem where there isn't one? Even though you explained to me how things can be stimulating and sexualized to a child even if it's not intended to be sexual. . . . This was a favorite picture of my father and me, especially since he wasn't so open with me. Now, I feel it's ruined." She continued on and on and ended with, "This is reminding me of how I felt with the other therapist, the more I talk, the more I fear that I will not be believed. I feel like I'm the accused now and I have to defend myself."

I believed we were finally getting somewhere. Carla was touching on something very important and I knew we were involved in a powerful enactment. I told her I was struck by how much she was protesting about this and quoted Shakespeare: "The lady doth protest too much." She responded with, "You mean you think I'm overcompensating for something?"

I thought that might be true. Carla retorted, "I've heard that therapists can help create false memories of abuse."

I reassured her that was not my intent but questioned whether there was a link to her issues around sexuality and her eating disorder. She became silent in the room. Feeling curious, I said, "Given your strong reaction, which has an element of panic in it, maybe there's something in this for us both to better understand."

In a hushed voice she told me, "You know, I was really a prude in my house."

"Oh," I replied.

"My parents got the *Playboy* channel and once I found a sexual book of my mother's."

"Oh. . . . How did you find it?" I asked.

"Well, I used to search through all my mother's underwear drawers. My mother was a very sexual being. I was 9 years old and would hear my parents having sex and my mother would be screaming. In fourth grade, I asked my mother if she had sex more than twice (for me and my brother) and I was shocked when she answered me, 'Well, *of course*' . . . like I was stupid. I couldn't figure out why our television had the *Playboy* channel. I always thought it was a mistake. It never occurred to me that my parents subscribed to it until we moved and it showed up on that television, too. Once I tried to embarrass them in front of their friends and announced, 'I suppose you are now going to watch the *Playboy* channel.' "

This history was information Carla had never revealed to me before. Carla continued with her history, "My brother and I would watch the *Playboy* channel whenever we could. At age 5 or 6, I used to masturbate on this horse and my father used to tell me all the time with a smile or chuckle, go ride your horsie. Once when I was 7 my teacher commented on me rubbing myself . . . you know where . . . on the chair. What do you want? My mother used to walk around naked in front of me. Once I saw this string hanging down and I asked her what it was. She told me it was her tampon but never told me what a tampon was. I ended up reading my mother's Nancy Friday book, *Men in Love* to learn about stuff."

Feeling touched by Carla's story and empathically attuned to the vulnerability she was now sharing with me, I conveyed how it seemed that sexuality was spilling out all over the place in her home as a child growing up. That it seemed like a flood with no dam and there were no words to help explain the multitude of unformulated feelings she must have experienced. I suggested that I was right and wrong with my disregulated comment about the picture. The sex wasn't necessarily between her and her father, but I was responding to the precociously sexual little girl in her that on some level had taken on her mother's sexuality.

Carla responded, "You know, my boyfriend and I watch porno whenever we have sex. I'm the one who puts it on and needs it to feel aroused. I've overcompensated my whole life for the lack of the spoken word by being so direct and blunt that my style is often abrasive to people. It's like I'm missing the filter, I can't regulate my words at times . . . just like I couldn't regulate my food. I would binge to not feel, not make sense of things . . . and without the filter or ability to sort out and make sense of my chaos, I would have no choice but to purge. . . . It was the only way to get it out of my system."

This vignette highlights how the therapist's disregulation of affect, bluntly commenting on the patient's picture, provided her access to feelings that had been stuffed or hidden inside. Ultimately, this patient utilized this exchange to understand how linking the chaos of her early emotional life contributed to an inability to process affective experience as an adult. It raised interesting questions that we explored about the body and its boundaries or lack there of, the negative and positive identification with her mother's sexuality as a way of separating herself from her mother, the patient's envy, desire, and shame. We explored the adaptive value of Carla's compensation as the immature, but necessary, processing of an untenable conflict and how this manifested with her food as well.

THE REGULATION OF RELATEDNESS

The regulation of relatedness is a constant factor in treatment issues with the eating-disordered patient. Relating on the patient's level is essential. Regulating the relatedness in a manner that feels manageable to both the patient and the therapist is often a struggle. Meeting points between patient and therapist can occur in a split second exchange, where the level of involvement and/or relatedness will shift back and forth between patient and therapist.

There are powerful moments that often happen spontaneously and jolt us into a heightened state of consciousness that can set the stage for therapeutic change. By seizing these moments that catch us by surprise, we are offered an opportunity to see something from a new angle, a view not ordinarily seen. There is a distinction that can be drawn between how much work is involved to create these moments and how these moments occur naturally with some patients. Sometimes the patient invites you into a moment. Sometimes you invite the patient. Sometimes these moments just occur by chance.

These moments afford us an opportunity to move toward greater shared intimacy where the relational field shifts into a momentary new configuration. Being able to sustain the shift is a far-reaching question and entails a struggle for all patients, but it is particularly compelling for the eating-disordered or addictive patient who struggles with pervasive issues of regulation.

The therapeutic action concerns the negotiation and the interpersonal use of the relationship as a method of mutual and self-regulation (Petrucelli, 2001). Bromberg (2001) maintains that the eating-disordered patient is someone who is totally at the mercy of his or her own feelings, someone who is enslaved by the felt inability to contain desire as a regulatable affect. The renunciation of desire is what we see as the hallmark of anorexia, and in a different way, of bulimia. But at its core, it is a loss of faith in the reliability of human relatedness (Bromberg, 2001). The work in treatment becomes a process of redirecting the eating-disordered patient out of the world of food and into the arena of human interaction.

SUMMARY

A person with an eating disorder faces an arduous road to recovery. The therapist must enable the patient to view the journey as a possible one as they undertake to forge a new path through the thicket of failed relationships. All too often, the eating-disordered patient has lost faith in the ability to enter into meaningful relationships. Connections that support a sense of self are grievously lacking. Starving, bingeing, and purging behaviors are a way to communicate failed emotional needs. Therapists must help translate the raw and undigested material into a new conscious palatable form. To experience authenticity within intimacy, patients must learn a new way to be with others. It is the mutuality of the therapeutic relationship that provides the vehicle for changing and understanding deleterious behaviors. Relating to the person, not the eating disorder, becomes the stepping stone for growth, healing, and the possibility of renewal. It is a process that calls for taking small bites, creating a safe haven that allows the patient to become conscious in a world previously marked by dissociation and trauma. Disengaging from the eating disorder by understanding what has kept the patient so involved and developing healthier relationships sets the stage for a world of new possibilities where faith in human relatedness is reliably restored and eating can be just eating.

RECOMMENDED READING

Fairburn, C. (1995). *Overcoming binge eating.* New York: Guilford Press. 1995. This book offers a comparison between binge eating and overeating, including discussions of associated psychological, social and physical problems, research study outcomes, and treatment approaches. It presents an accessible self-help program for individuals with binge eating-problems that can best be used in conjunction with professional help.

Garfinkel, P. E., & Garner, D. M. (Eds.). (1985). *Handbook of psychotherapy for anorexia nervosa and bulimia.* New York: Guilford Press. This comprehensive handbook covers many topics including treatment advancements in assessment, epidemiology, diagnosis, complications, psychological and biological factors and research on treatment outcomes.

Petrucelli, J., & Stuart, C. (Eds.). (2001). *Hungers and compulsions: The psychodynamic treatment of eating disorders and addictions.* Northvale, NJ: Aronson. This anthology, which includes 26 prominent contributors, offers a wise, creative and often inspired guide to the treatment of patients who present with eating disorders and other addictive behavior, such as compulsions, alcoholism, and erotic attachments. Clinician can learn from this inside view the demands that working with this difficult group of patients place on their therapies. This book is particularly appropriate for anyone treating patients with addictions who wants a deeper understanding of the fundamental questions about human desire, will, and our need to live authentically and creatively.

Siegal, M., Brisman, J., & Weinshel, M. (1997). *Surviving an eating disorder: Strategies for families and friends.* New York: Harper Perennial. This book is a comprehensive analysis of the complexities of eating disorders in the familial context and helps to demystify this disorder for family members. The authors discuss the psychological and behavioral aspects of eating disorders and family therapy, with an emphasis on developing healthier relationships and guidelines for making the situation better—now.

Zerbe, K. (1993). *The body betrayed: A deeper understanding of women, eating disorders and treatment.* Carlsbad, CA: Gurze Books. The author presents a feminist perspective on parent-child relationships, family dynamics, abuse issues, medical complications, the biology of nutrition, pregnancy, athletics, and treatment. This book covers important aspects of diagnosis and treatment interlaced with stories about individuals engaged in treatment.

RESOURCES

Eating Disorder Awareness and Prevention (EDAP)
603 Stewart St, Suite 803
Seattle, WA 98101
(206) 382–3587

Sponsors Eating Disorders Awareness Week in February with a network of state coordinators and educational information. EDAP includes the following: conference, newsletter, nationwide referral listings for eating disorder professionals, and development of educational and prevention programs. EDAP merged with ANRED and NEDO in 1999.

International Association of Eating Disorder Professionals (IAEDP)
427 Whooping Loop #1819
Altamonte Springs, FL 32701
(800) 800-8126

A membership organization for professionals, they provide certification, education, local chapters, and a newsletter and annual symposium.

Overeaters Anonymous Headquarters (OA)
P. O. Box 44020
Rio Rancho, NM 87174
(505) 891-2664

A 12-Step self-help program with free local meetings that are listed in the phonebook nationwide.

WEB SITES

www.edp.org
Eating Disorders Awareness and Prevention

This nonprofit organization provides educational materials for schools and health professionals that deal with various forms of eating disorders.

www.something-fishy.org
Something Fishy

A comprehensive resource center for patients and family members coping with anorexia, bulimia, and binge eating. Also included is a geographic list of treatment providers.

www.wawhite.org
Eating Disorders, Compulsions, and Addictions Service at the William Alanson
   White Institute in New York City.

This clinical service offers in-depth treatment for eating-disordered patients who want to go beyond behavioral change to deep shifts of character. Interpersonal perspective and techniques offer analytic opportunities to patients with a history of addiction who want to attain the deepest level of change. Individual, group, family, and couples treatment as well as referral to ancillary services are offered. A moderate-level, sliding fee scale is available for financial need.

REFERENCES

Barth, D. (1994). The use of group therapy to help women with eating disorders differentiate and articulate affect. *Group, 18*(2), 70.

Brisman, J. (1995a). Addictions. In M. Lionells, J. Fiscalini, C. Mann, & D. Stern (Eds.), *Handbook of interpersonal psychoanalysis* (pp. 301–316). New York: Analytic Press.

Brisman, J. (1995b). Psychodynamic psychotherapy and action-oriented technique: An integrated approach. In I. Yalom & J. Werne (Eds.), *Treating eating disorders* (pp. 31–70). San Francisco: Jossey-Bass.

Bromberg, P. (2001). Treating patients with symptoms—and symptoms with patience: Reflections on shame, dissociation and eating disorders. *Psychoanalytic Dialogues, 11*(6), 891–912.

Bruch, H. (1973). *Eating disorders: Obesity, anorexia, and the person within.* New York: Basic Books.

Bruch, H. (1974). Perils of behavior modification in treatment of anorexia nervosa. *Journal of the American Medical Association, 230,* 1419–1422.

Bruch, H. (1985). Four decades of eating disorders. In D. Garner & P. Garfinkel (Eds.), *Handbook of psychotherapy for anorexia and bulimia* (pp. 7–18). New York: Guilford Press.

Freud, S. (1953). Three essays on the theory of sexuality. In J. Strachey (Ed. & Trans.), *The standard edition of the complete psychological works of Sigmund Freud* (Vol. 7, pp. 135–230). London: Hogarth Press. (Original work published 1905)

Goodsitt, A. (1983). Self regulatory disturbances in eating disordered patients. *International Journal of Eating Disorders, 2*(3), 51–60.

Havens, L. (1976). *Participant observation.* New York: Aronson.

Kohut, H. (1971). *The analysis of the self.* New York: International Universities Press.

Kohut, H. (1977). *The restoration of the self.* New York: International Universities Press.

Kohut, H. (1984). *How does analysis cure?* Chicago: International Universities Press.

McDougal, J. (1994). The psycho-soma and the psychoanalytic process. *international Review of Psycho-Analysis, 1,* 437–459.

Petrucelli, J. (2001). Close encounters of the regulatory kind: An interpersonal/relational look at self-regulation. In J. Petrucelli & C. Stuart (Eds.), *Hungers and compulsions: The psychodynamic treatment of eating disorders and addictions* (pp. 97–111). Northvale, NJ: Aronson.

Rabinor, J. R. (1991). The process of recovery from an eating disorder: The use of journal writing in the initial phase of treatment. *Psychotherapy in Private Practice, 9*(1), 93–106.

Rabinor, J. R. (1993). Mothers, daughters, and eating disorders: Honoring the mother-daughter relationship. In P. Failon (Ed.), *Feminist perspectives on eating disorders* (pp. 272–286). New York: Guilford Press.

Sands, S. (1991). Bulimia, dissociation and empathy: A self-psychological view. In C. Johnson (Ed.), *Psychodynamic treatment of anorexia nervosa and bulimia* (pp. 34–50). New York: Guilford Press.

Strober, M. (1991). Disorders of the self in anorexia nervosa: An organismic-developmental paradigm. In C. Johnson (Ed.), *Psychodynamic treatment of anorexia nervosa and bulimia* (pp. 354–372). New York: Guilford Press.

Winnicot, D. W. (1975). Mind and its relation to the psycho-soma. In *Collected papers: Through paediatrics to psycho-analysis* (pp. 243–254). New Youk: Basic Books. (Original work published 1949).

PART VI

WORKAHOLISM

CHAPTER 11

Understanding and Diagnosing Workaholism

BRYAN E. ROBINSON and CLAUDIA FLOWERS

THERE WAS A time when I (BR) took my work everywhere. While driving, I made business calls, wrote case notes, or revised manuscripts—once broadsiding another vehicle while in a work trance or driving while working (DWW). The day of my father's funeral, I sequestered myself in my university office to work at my desk. I didn't realize it at the time but I was medicating myself, using my work to numb the pain. In work, I found my salvation, my Nirvana—or so I thought. While protecting me, my workaholism kept people out, making intimate relationships impossible. Although it was something over which I thought I had complete control, it actually had control of me.

Despite my own bout with workaholism and the desperate clients I saw in my private practice who, like me, learned to drug themselves with compulsive overworking, I was doubly hurt to realize that the public and many well-meaning clinicians didn't take us seriously. Early in my career, I committed myself to take the term *workaholic* from the realm of pop psychology to the academic arena where it could be examined scientifically. Along the way, I teamed with colleague, Dr. Claudia Flowers, a skilled psychometrician who collaborated with me on numerous scientific studies and was instrumental in developing a reliable and valid test to measure workaholism in these studies. This chapter charts the course of our journey to foster more understanding of workaholism in the mental health field and the public domain.

HITTING THE BIG LEAGUES

Early in my recovery, I decided to write a small book describing my personal experience with workaholism and some of the identifying characteristics observed firsthand in my psychotherapy practice. The outcome was a book called *Work Addiction* (Robinson, 1989), in which I tried to distinguish working to *succeed* from working to *excess*. After all, hard work built this country. It put us on the moon and helped us discover vaccines for diseases that have saved countless lives. I didn't want readers to think that they were workaholics if they worked long hours, worked overtime, or eagerly took on additional job tasks.

In that book, I included a test that contrasted the hard worker in the office looking forward to being on the ski slopes to the workaholic on the ski slopes dreaming about being back at the office. The test distinguished between hard workers who can turn off their work appetites and insatiable workaholics who see themselves as underfunctioning, when others see them as overfunctioning—much like anorexics who sees themselves as fat when others see them as thin. I wanted a name for the test that would expose the underbelly of the condition, so I called it the Work Addiction Risk Test (WART; see Box 11.1).

The book caught the attention of a reporter who conducted an interview for a feature-length article on workaholism that appeared in the *Charlotte Observer*. The article was a thorough description of the characteristics of workaholics with case examples and the simple test I had developed for the book. The newspaper story was picked up by the Associated Press and I was inundated with hundreds of telephone calls, e-mails, and letters from California to the Carolinas from men and women recounting their agonizing battles with workaholism and the devastation left in its wake. Detailed personal stories in San Diego resembled accounts of those in Atlanta—similar patterns of work highs reminiscent of the alcoholic euphoria that runs a cycle of adrenaline-charged binge working, followed by a downward swing. Claire described her euphoric binges that eventually gave way to work hangovers including withdrawal, depression, irritability, and anxiety:

> When I used to binge, I would take on a project and stay up until three or four in the morning to get it finished, just compulsively thinking that morning's not going to come and that if something happened to me, I have to have it done today. That binge would go into 14 and 16 hours, and then I'd have two or three hours of sleep and then go on a roll and do this for two more days. Then I'd be exhausted and sleep it off. It's almost like I've heard alcoholics talk about sleeping off a drunk. I would sleep off that binge of work. Sometimes I would sleep in my clothes, and I hated it! I just hated it!

Many of the people who responded said they worked incessantly until they hit bottom before they could admit they had a problem that they couldn't control. Some became so depressed they couldn't get out of bed. They found themselves alone, unable to feel, and cut off from everyone they cared about. Marriages shattered and health problems swelled to crisis proportions. As one man said, "It finally reached a point that I hit a wall, and I couldn't escape it anymore. I was either going to deal with it or I was going to die."

The correspondence that was pouring in also validated another pattern that I had observed clinically—that workaholism casts a long shadow and infects other family members, causing them to experience a set of mental health problems of their own—disgruntled wives and husbands dragging their workaholic spouses kicking and screaming into the office to force them to start investing in the marriage. Spouses of workaholics in the Midwest described, almost in exact detail, the sentiments of spouses in the Northeast. While friends, family, and management glorified the workaholics, the spouses often described their lives as living nightmares because they had little support from the mental health system, outside

BOX 11.1
Do You Fit the Workaholic Profile?

To find out if you are a workaholic, rate yourself on the WART, using the rating scale: 1 = Never true, 2 = Sometimes true, 3 = Often true), or 4 = Always true. Put the number that best describes your work habits in the blank beside each statement. After you respond to all 25 statements, add the numbers in the blanks for your total score. The higher your score (highest possible is 100), the more likely you are to be a workaholic; the lower your score (lowest possible is 25), the less likely you are to be a workaholic.

_____ 1. I prefer to do most things rather than ask for help.

_____ 2. I get impatient when I have to wait for someone else or when something takes too long.

_____ 3. I seem to be in a hurry and racing against the clock.

_____ 4. I get irritated when I am interrupted while I am in the middle of something.

_____ 5. I stay busy and keep many irons in the fire.

_____ 6. I find myself doing two or three things at one time, such as eating lunch and writing a memo while talking on the telephone.

_____ 7. I overcommit myself by biting off more than I can chew.

_____ 8. I feel guilty when I am not working on something.

_____ 9. It's important that I see the concrete results of what I do.

_____ 10. I am more interested in the final result of my work than in the process.

_____ 11. Things just never seem to move fast enough or get done fast enough for me.

_____ 12. I lose my temper when things don't go my way or work out to suit me.

_____ 13. I ask the same question over again without realizing it after I've already been given the answer once.

_____ 14. I spend a lot of time mentally planning and thinking about future events while tuning out the here and now.

_____ 15. I find myself continuing to work after my coworkers have called it quits.

_____ 16. I get angry when people don't meet my standards of perfection.

_____ 17. I get upset when I am in situations where I cannot be in control.

_____ 18. I tend to put myself under pressure from self-imposed deadlines when I work.

_____ 19. It is hard for me to relax when I'm not working.

_____ 20. I spend more time working than socializing with friends or on hobbies or leisure activities.

_____ 21. I dive into projects to get a head start before all the phases have been finalized.

(continued)

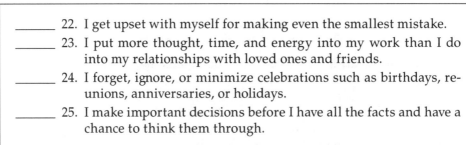

_____ 22. I get upset with myself for making even the smallest mistake.

_____ 23. I put more thought, time, and energy into my work than I do into my relationships with loved ones and friends.

_____ 24. I forget, ignore, or minimize celebrations such as birthdays, reunions, anniversaries, or holidays.

_____ 25. I make important decisions before I have all the facts and have a chance to think them through.

For clinical use, scores on the WART are divided into three ranges: those scoring in the upper third (67 to 100) are considered highly workaholic. If you scored in this range, it could mean that you are on your way to burnout, and new research suggests that family members may be having emotional repercussions as well. Those scoring in the middle range (57 to 66) are considered mildly workaholic. If you scored in this range, there is hope. With acceptance and modifications, you and your loved ones can prevent negative lasting effects. Those scoring in the lowest range (25 to 56) are considered not workaholic. If you scored in this range, you probably are a hard worker instead of a workaholic. You needn't worry that your work style will negatively affect yourself or others.

Source: WART reprinted from _Chained to the Desk: A Guidebook for Workaholics, Their Partners and Children, and the Clinicians Who Treat Them_ by B. E. Robinson, 1998, New York: New York University Press. Copyright 1998 by Bryan E. Robinson.

family or friends, and, least of all, the workplace (see Box 11.2). However, among the many phone calls and letters, some of the most touching came from the children of workaholic parents (see Box 11.3).

I heard myself echoed over and over again with these descriptions. My own attempts to be unlike my alcoholic father had made me a clone. I had become a chain-smoking, caffeine-drinking work junkie, hiding my work as my father had hidden his bottle. I numbed my feelings by intoxicating myself with work, as my father had with booze. I slept off work highs in my sweats, just as my father slept off his alcoholic binges in his coat and tie.

On vacations when close friends would ask me to join them for a stroll on the beach, I would say that I was tired and wanted to take a nap. While they swam and played in the surf—which I considered a big waste of time—I'd pull out my concealed papers and secretly toil over a makeshift desk in the empty house until I heard them returning. Then I'd hide the papers again, stretch out on the bed, and pretend to be asleep.

During the mid-1970s, hardly a vacation passed that a stuffed briefcase of work didn't accompany me as part of my luggage. I never spent a Thanksgiving or Christmas Day without working. Uninterrupted 12- and 13-hour days were the norm. I continued racing against the clock, shaking my fists at the heavens, and moaning about the shortage of time. Compulsive work thoughts shackled me when I strolled the beach, beat me to the office in the morning, and haunted me in my sleep. They nagged me at social gatherings and during movies. They lurked

---

BOX 11.2
Outcries from Spouses of Workaholics

Dorothy described her isolation and loneliness and the vilification inflicted on her if she dared speak her feelings:

> When the kids were small and we went on picnics, I carried the blanket and picnic basket and my husband carried his briefcase. To everyone else my husband can do no wrong. He denies there's anything wrong and gets hostile if I bring up his workaholism. Our friends want to know why I'm always complaining. I have become the bitchy wife in the eyes of our friends, but they don't understand what it's like being alone. Sometimes I think that maybe it's just me, so I keep my mouth shut and go on.

Of the many e-mails, the most sobering came from Judy who wrote:

> I know how pathological it sounds, but my feelings of rage, confusion, and abandonment were such that I often wished that my husband would bruise my face or break my arm. That would confirm my suspicions, would make me stop doubting myself, would enable me to say to myself and everyone else, "See, he really is hurting me. He's doing something terrible to this marriage, and it's not my fault." But as it stood, everyone praised him for his work ethic and suggested that I was nagging, impatient, and ungrateful. I started to believe it myself.

---

over my shoulder when I tried to have heart-to-heart talks. I coped with the panic of unplanned Saturday mornings and holidays by packing free time full of tasks. The challenge of finishing a project under a ridiculously short deadline or getting three or four things done at once was thrilling because my adrenaline surged and I felt an enormous sense of accomplishment (or fix).

SOCIETY'S DENIAL

Despite media attention and personal anecdotes across the country that validated my personal experience, workaholism had become the acceptable replacement drug for the politically incorrect substance abuse of nicotine and alcohol. Advertisers, using the glamour of workaholism to sell their wares, depicted it as alluring and sexy in the same way the tobacco industry used to promote cigarette smoking as sexually provocative in the 1940s and 1950s. Rarely did adults boast about playing Black Jack for 48 hours nonstop or proclaim that they binged on an entire chocolate cake. But organizational managers who eschewed cigarettes and booze bragged about their chronic workaholism. Corporate climbers proudly wore their workaholic name tag, as I had done, to underscore their tireless efforts and loyalty to the company.

A radio commercial for a truck praised the versatility of the "Workaholic 4 by 4." An automobile advertisement boasted: "Workaholics you call us? We're flattered!" Larry King, on one of his nightly talk shows, extolled Lucille Ball for being a workaholic. "That's why she was so good," he said. Workaholism got light-hearted

BOX 11.3
"Daddy Gone": Growing Up with a Workaholic Parent

Desperate for love and attention, Charles pulled every antic his child's mind could dream up to get his father to notice and spend time with him. Those futile antics, leaving him feeling lonely and angry as a child and empty as an adult, are common among children of workaholics. He wrote, "The second words I learned to say were, 'Daddy gone.' That indicates to me that I was missing my dad at a very young age and it shocks me that I am doing the same thing to my kids."

Children, like Charles, hungry for attention from their psychologically absent parent, complained about their parents' mental absenteeism. But their natural way of handling the disappointment was to defer their emotional needs by joining in the workaholic pattern to get their parents' approval. This involved working alongside the workaholic parents or accompanying them to the workplace in hopes of stealing a few moments of attention. Charles remembered going with his father to his office just to be in his company.

Cindy's workaholic mother ran the household by the motto, "Your best is always better yet." Cindy's mother believed that no matter how hard you work, you could work harder, earn more, do better. Marsha shutters at the memory of traveling home after her high school graduation—not just because there had been a late spring snow and it was cold outside but because of her mother's chilly attitude toward her. Despite the fact that Marsha had been honored for the second highest grade-point average out of 2,000 students, her mother had been distant and unenthusiastic all day. As tires crushed the icy road beneath them, Marsha's mother broke the ice inside the car: "Why couldn't you have been number one?" she demanded.

The messages many children of workaholics introject are, "I cannot measure up" or "I need to be someone other than who I really am." Expectations are often out of reach for children of workaholics who internalize their failure as self-inadequacy. At 35, Nell described how she smuggled memos and contracts into her dying father's hospital room: "It was the only way I could be with him," she said fighting back tears. "The only time he'd pay attention to me was around the subject of his work." Desperate for connecting with the unavailable workaholic parent, children unwittingly become enablers. Nell sneaked work to her father as one might sneak a drink to an alcoholic. He died working, a pen still in his hand. Nell says she lives with the guilt of hastening his death.

portrayal in the media—often the target of ridicule and the butt of jokes. One newspaper cartoon showed a huge, empty meeting room with a sign posted at the front that read, "Workaholics Anonymous" and a caption that said, "Everybody had to work overtime."

A book on workaholics by Marilyn Machlowitz (1985) applauded the workaholic lifestyle as being as much a virtue as a vice and suggested that workaholics are surprisingly happy because they are doing what they love: working. Then there were the cynics, such as Daniel Seligman (1994) writing in a *Fortune* magazine commentary, who ridiculed workaholics for inventing another pop psychology *ism* on which to pin their problems:

> Along with heroin, gambling, sex, and sniffing model airplane glue, work is now taken seriously as something people often get addicted to, in which case they need to get cured. . . . The references to work addiction are instantly psychiatric. The phrase is enveloped in psychobabble about inner insecurities, lives destroyed, and—could it be otherwise?—support groups needed. How did work addiction make it to the social-problem big leagues? Plowing through our mound of articles, we posit that one source of support has been the universe of corporate human resourcers, always on the lookout for workplace woes. . . . Finally, the specter of widespread work addiction—an article in *Vibrant Life* puts the number of addicts at 12 million—appeals to unionists and others looking for excuses to impose legal limits on hours worked. And coming any day now: massive support from Donahue and Oprah. (p. 133)

I felt fortunate enough to have a condition that was respectable and not to be taken seriously. But I was concerned that cynicism prevented workaholism from receiving the serious attention it deserved and perpetuated dangerous myths (see Box 11.4). Although a household word, *workaholism* had not been accepted into the official psychiatric and psychological nomenclature. Even some therapists prescribed work immersion as a solution to emotional maladies rather than diagnosing it as the cause of a problem.

These shocking practices and the media ridicule, in light of the living hell so many had described, compelled me to investigate more about the condition known

---

BOX 11.4
Ten Myths about Workaholism

There are 10 myths about workaholism that mislead families and businesses into enabling workaholism instead of seeing the damage it creates (Robinson, 1998):

1. Workaholics are motivated out of loyalty to their companies to provide a decent living for their families or to make contributions to society.
2. Workaholism occurs because of high-pressure jobs that demand more than a nine-to-five commitment.
3. Workaholism is a positive addiction.
4. Workaholism is a secondary addiction to the more serious, primary addictions.
5. Workaholism is not a legitimate addiction because it doesn't have a physiological base, as do the chemical and food addictions.
6. If one is not gainfully employed, he or she cannot be a workaholic.
7. Recovery from workaholism will impair work quality and productivity.
8. Recovery from workaholism simply requires cutting back on work hours.
9. Workaholics must enjoy their jobs to be workaholics.
10. The solution to workaholism is to cut back on work hours.

as workaholism. These personal accounts, while not scientific in the quantitative sense, carried their own reliability. Geographically separated individuals documented their stories in matching detail and in such high numbers that the emerging profiles could not be attributed to chance alone. In this respect, it was a qualitative science of workaholism derived from parallel themes.

STUDIES ON WORKAHOLICS: SLIM PICKINGS

Still, personal anecdotes and clinical case studies wouldn't convince the cynics. A body of research was needed comparable to the controlled studies on other addictions and compulsive disorders. For the next 6 months, determined to find hard evidence, I ransacked the university library for every magazine and professional journal I could get my hands on. I discovered that Wayne Oates coined the term *workaholism* in 1971 as an analogy to the term *alcoholism* to demonstrate how some people become addicted to work as others do to alcohol. And, although it had become a household word, workaholism was not an official psychiatric label. Clearly, it was a better addiction to have—a character strength, compared to alcohol and drug addiction, which were viewed as character defects. Alcoholism was associated with skid-row bums, instability, and irresponsibility. Workaholism was associated with status, power, and material gain.

So naturally, it had been understudied, compared to hundreds of studies on alcoholism, substance abuse, and eating disorders. The information that I unearthed was mostly in newspapers, popular magazines, and self-help books and reflected the thinking of the mental health field and scientific community. Only a handful of scientific studies were available. One study sampled 193 attorneys and physicians and concluded that, although more attorneys fell into the classification of workaholic, there were no differences in the incidences among men and women (Doerfler & Kammer, 1986).

The second study by psychiatrist Anthony Pietropinto (1986) polled a national sample of 400 physicians about their impressions of workaholics as marital spouses. The survey showed that workaholics devoted an inordinate amount of time to work versus marriage, and they had higher than normal expectations of marital satisfaction. Their behavior in marital disagreements was to avoid confrontation and to maintain silence or sulk. They were perceived as more demanding of achievement in their children than nonworkaholics and their typical approach to leisure time was to fill it with work.

Over the next several years, more studies began to appear in the scientific literature. Several studies examined the harmful consequences of workaholism on the physical well-being of the workaholic (see Box 11.5 for a profile of the workaholic). The first national study on workaholics was a survey of 291 (134 men and 157 women) social workers, median age 43 years. The researchers (Spence & Robbins, 1992) administered questionnaires to assess workaholism defined as high scores on measures of Work Involvement and Drivenness and low scores on a measure of Enjoyment of Work. Workaholism was contrasted with *work enthusiasm*, which was defined as high work involvement and enjoyment and low drivenness. A major difference between work enthusiasts and workaholics was that workaholics perceived themselves as having more job stress, perfectionism, and unwillingness to delegate job responsibilities to others. In addition, workaholics reported more health complaints, more difficulty delegating, and felt more stressed in their jobs than work enthusiasts.

BOX 11.5
A Profile of the Workaholic

The handful of studies that have been conducted on workaholics indicate that, compared with nonworkaholics, workaholics tend to have more:

- Health complaints.
- Difficulty delegating.
- Stress from the job.
- Perfectionism.
- Anxiety.
- Anger.
- Depression.
- Difficulty feeling than thinking.
- Hours at work per week.
- Families that they perceive as dysfunctional.
- Difficulty with intimacy.
- Self-inadequacy.
- Impaired social functioning.

A study of 253 college males reported that workaholics exhibited greater anxiety, anger, and depression than nonworkaholics (Haymon, 1993). These findings corroborated the anecdotal reports that I had collected and observed in my own clinical work. Another parallel body of work in Japan also confirmed these findings, going even further to indicate that workaholism can be deadly (see Box 11.6).

THE WORKAHOLIC FAMILY: A REVIEW

In my search I found nothing that described the kinds of life-changing events family members had shared with me. And, although I had clinically observed the breakdown in family functioning, brittle relationships, and marital conflict in workaholic families, no study had ever measured these factors. So I teamed with Dr. Claudia Flowers to launch the first studies examining the relationship between family functioning and workaholism. While Claudia oversaw the statistical analysis of the data and the refinement of the WART as a reliable and valid measure of workaholism (e.g., Flowers & Robinson, 2001, 2002, 2003a, 2003b), I spearheaded the studies (e.g., Robinson, 2001; Robinson & Flowers, 2003; Robinson, Flowers, & Carroll, 2001; see Box 11.7).

We set out to study workaholics and their families in the same way researchers studied alcoholics and their families. We discuss some of our findings in this chapter.

The first study from the University of North Carolina at Charlotte to directly investigate the relationship between workaholism and family functioning provided evidence suggesting that workaholism can lead to brittle family relationships, contribute to marital conflict, and create dysfunction within the family (Robinson & Post, 1995b, 1997). We mailed surveys to chapters of Workaholics Anonymous across the United States and Canada. Although the sample was self-selected, it was groundbreaking because it was the first time self-professed workaholics had been studied. We received completed surveys from 107 participants (average age 44)

BOX 11.6
Karoshi: Death from Overwork

The Japanese have the term, *karoshi,* to refer to the 10,000 workers a year who drop dead from putting in 60- to 70-hour workweeks. Otherwise healthy, they keel over at their desks after a long stretch of overtime or after consummating a high-pressured deal, usually from stroke or heart attack. Karoshi among corporate workers in their 40s and 50s has become so common that the Japanese workplace has been called *a killing field* (Ishiyama & Kitayama, 1994). Karoshi victims are believed to work in excess of 3,000 hours a year—roughly twice the norm for people in France, Germany, and Sweden (Kato, 1995).

According to Japanese social scientist Uehata (1993), in Japan it is widely known that, in addition to death from overwork, chronic, excessive work habits and work-related stress can result in various mental, physical, and interpersonal problems. Although Japan enjoys an international reputation for strong work ethics, various medical and psychosocial problems have surfaced associated with workaholism. Helping professionals and social critics stress the necessity for improvements and reevaluation of how individuals, employers, society, and the government deal with workaholism and job stress (Ishiyama & Kitayama, 1994).

Research with Japanese workers indicated a significant impact of workaholism on health complaints and job stress among Japanese male employees (Kanai, Wakabayashi, & Fling, 1996). Workaholism has been linked with high work stress reactions such as depression, anxiety, anger, and irritability, as well as behaviors such as absenteeism, withdrawal, low productivity, mistakes, and accident proneness on the job (Haraguchi, Tsuda, & Ozeki, 1991). Workers with high stress reactions tended to work more hours per week (over 70 hours) and more overtime (50 hours per month) than workers with low stress reactions.

In Japanese families, workaholic men are often referred to as *7-11 husbands*—a term for marginal fathers who work from dawn to dusk, have extricated themselves from family life, and live on the fringes of their families (Ishiyama & Kitayama, 1994). Japanese wives use the derogatory term *nureochiba* (a wet fallen leaf stuck to the bottom of their shoes) to refer to retired workaholic husbands who do not know what to do with themselves when they are not working and who hang around the house expecting their wives to be in charge of their spare time (Ishiyama & Kitayama, 1994).

---

representing five regions of the United States and Canada. Of our sample, 14.2% came from the Northeast; 23.6% from the Southeast; 38.7% from the Northwest; 18.9% from the Southwest; and 0.09% from Canada.

The findings showed that the more severe the participants' workaholism, the more severe the dysfunction in their families. Greater workaholism was linked to greater confusion of family roles, lower family communication, less effective problem solving, less expression of feelings, lack of interest in and value for other family member's activities and concerns, and overall problems in daily family functioning.

BOX 11.7
Refining the Work Addiction Risk Test

The Work Addiction Risk Test (WART) is a 25-item, self-report inventory drawn from clinical observations and anecdotal accounts. Respondents rate each item on how well the item describes their work habits on a four-point Likert Scale. Higher scores indicate greater tendency toward workaholic behaviors.

For scientific study, however, we tested the reliability and validity of the test before it was used as a viable tool for research. We reported a number of short studies providing psychometric information on the WART. They indicated a high test-retest reliability over a 2-week period in a sample of 151 university students of .83 (Robinson, Post, & Khakee, 1992) and a high split-half reliability (Robinson & Post, 1995a). Face validity and criterion-related validity were also established (Robinson, 1999; Robinson & Phillips, 1995).

We also examined underlying dimensionality and the accuracy in discrimination of the WART scores (Flowers & Robinson, 2002). The results suggest that workaholism, as measured by the WART, is not a unidimensional construct. Five subscales were developed from the factor analysis: (1) Compulsive Tendencies, (2) Control, (3) Impaired Communication/Self-Absorption, (4) Inability to Delegate, and (5) Self-Worth. A discriminant analysis that used the subscale scores as independent variables and group membership (workaholic or control group) as the dependent variable indicated that the first three subscales provided the greatest distinction between the groups, with a 88.5% correct classification rate. A discriminant analysis that used the total WART score as the independent variable and group membership as the dependent variable had an 86.4% correct classification rate.

Another study empirically evaluated the construct validity of scores from the WART with the Workaholic Inventory developed by Spence and Robbins (1992). Results of the study suggested that the WART is a tenable measure of workaholism (Flowers & Robinson, 2003a).

Although children were not targeted in this study, the family climate that emerged from these findings made us suspect that they lived in risk of psychological maladjustment, not unlike children of alcoholics. Plus, the correspondence I received validated the pattern that I observed clinically—workaholism casts a long shadow, causing other family members to experience a set of mental health problems of their own.

We conducted the first study on adult children of workaholics by giving a battery of tests to 211 college students (average age 24) at the University of North Carolina at Charlotte (Robinson & Kelley, 1998). Using the WART, we asked them to rate their parents on workaholic tendencies and to rate themselves on measures of depression, anxiety, self-concept, and locus of control.

Adult children from workaholic families had higher levels of depression and anxiety and felt less in control of the events in their lives compared to adults from homes where parents carried an average workload. Although our sample was a select group of university students, two other studies followed on the heels of our research and replicated our findings with two different populations. One study conducted at the California Graduate Institute in 1998 surveyed a sample of 107 working nurses (Navarette, 1998). The other study from the University of South Australia in 2000 tested 125 first-year university students (Searcy, 2000). When compared to children from nonworkaholic parents, both studies reported that children of workaholic parents had significantly higher depression and anxiety levels, more incidences of obsessive-compulsive tendencies, rated their families as more dysfunctional, and were at higher risk for workaholism themselves.

A second sample of 207 students who grew up with a workaholic parent (average age 25) from the University of North Carolina at Charlotte found that adult children of workaholics had higher depression levels and higher rates of parentification than adult children from alcoholic homes (Carroll & Robinson, 2000).

Although the research on adult children of workaholics is still embryonic, results to date suggest that children are affected by parental workaholism in negative ways that are mentally unhealthy and that might cause problems well into young adulthood. The statistics matched the stories I received from readers who described patterns of failed marriages and anxiety and depression with no obvious causes—adults who seemingly came from picture perfect childhoods. Most lived under the unspoken adage that workaholism not only looks good on workaholics but also is becoming on their offspring. At the heart of their troubles was a well-meaning but absent parent who taught them that you are judged by what you do, not who you are. They tend to be motivated by what people think of them rather than their own sense of value and to have an emotional framework that seems to collapse like a house of cards once they reach adulthood. They are self-critical, accommodating, and chameleon-like and fumble badly in relationships (see Box 11.8).

An excerpt from a letter from Steve, the son of an Arizona politician, is a sample of the extent to which children of workaholics gauge their emotions and behaviors to win the attention and praise of emotionally absent and neglectful parents:

> Everything I did as a kid was based on accomplishment and goals. I tried hard and got awards for everything: outstanding academic scholarship, top awards in band and choir, captain of the football team. But the one award I never won was my dad's love and attention. "I'm proud of you" would have been nice. I just wanted him to play catch with me or hit me on the head with a pillow and say, "How ya doing?" To this day it's hard for me to sit in a room without having a project or a product. I guess something in me is still trying to grab my dad's attention.

In alcoholic families, children can point to the bottle as a source of their discontent. But in workaholic families, there is no tangible cause for the feelings of confusion, guilt, and inadequacy. If Dad drank too much, the child could point to the bottle; if Mom was strung out on pills, the drugs might explain her unusual mood swings. But the American work ethic prohibits children from faulting their parents for perceiving hard work or workaholism as a good thing. The logical conclusion that children of workaholics draw is that "Something must be wrong with me." After all, workaholic parents are usually highly successful, responsible, and may even hold leadership positions in the community. Their overachieving is sanctioned by society, the community, and, often, the church. So why should the

BOX 11.8
Confessions of an Adult Child of a Workaholic

My father had two loves: work and bourbon. He also loved his two sons, but we learned at an early age that being close to our father required entering his world of ambitious interests and endless cycles of working, drinking, and sleeping. Our house ran on our father's energy. When the phone rang, as it frequently did just as we sat down to an already delayed, late evening family dinner, it was usually a graduate student or colleague calling for my father. "Oh damn!" he'd say as he jumped to his feet and raced from the dining room into his study. Sometimes I would groan as he made his quick exit, but usually my mother, sister, and I would just sit in silence, staring and continuing to eat until he returned with the latest tale of upheaval in the department or of the almost nervous breakdown his advisee was having over an oral comprehensive.

Childhood pleasures like the state fair, shooting basketballs through a new goal, picnics, going fishing or to the pool, learning to ride a bike without training wheels, or carving the Halloween pumpkin were all scheduled around Dad's work and often were simply endured by him in a state of irritation, or worse, exhaustion after long hours at the office. It was clear from the start that family life and traditional family activities came second and were actually rather trivial compared to the adult world of work, politics, ambition, and collegiality. Even vacations to the beach involved taking along favored graduate students. If students couldn't come with us, my father would make contacts with colleagues and former students in a nearby town to come visit. Over shrimp and beers, they would give him the latest scope on the local school system or reminisce with him about his early years as a bachelor high school chemistry teacher in this same nearby beach town.

My father's (and thus also my mother's) friends were his students and former students. I realize now that his mentoring of these young, admiring professionals occupied his time and energy and left me, his oldest son, competing with handsome bright male graduate students for his love and attention.

When he brought home his favorite students or colleagues to drink and talk shop late into the evening, he was at his best: happy, lively, and eloquent. As a small boy on these nights of discussion and drinking, I would run rambunctiously in and out of the living room where he was holding forth, and, in childish ways, would compete for his audience's attention (or perhaps actually for his attention) by asking questions, making noises, or hiding and jumping out from behind the sofa to scare everyone. Usually Dad would just give me a hug and then firmly direct me out of the room to find Mom (who was sequestered in her bedroom) so she could give me a bath and put me to bed, usually well past the designated hour. These were the fun nights in the house filled with my father's business company, their laughter and serious and meaningful conversation. I remember nights like these throughout my entire childhood and adolescence.

(continued)

As I grew older, I learned to sit quietly and listen, watching Dad as he related to his students and colleagues. If I was quiet and didn't interrupt, I could stay in the same room with him, and this was very important to me since it was often the only contact I would have with him for days at a time except when he would sleepily drive me to school (almost late) the following mornings. I learned to make strong percolated coffee and serve it to him in his study when he would write until two, three, or four in the morning. My bedroom was next door to his study, and I loved to try to stay awake reading as late into the night as his light was still on; and I would get out of bed, go to his study door, and see him sitting focused intensely at his desk wearing his black horn-rimmed glasses. It seemed as if I was constantly interrupting him and distracting him from something very important.

My father was always at work whether at the office, hovering over his desk at home, or entertaining his students, and talking shop. When I was very little, I would beg him to play with me in the evenings when he would come home from his office without his students. "Daddy's tired," he'd say as he slumped in a chair. I would grab his arm and pull him to get up to play cowboys with me, which at times he would agree to begrudgingly; and then in a less than enthusiastic tone, he would respond to my piercing war-cries with a distracted "bang, bang." Even then, I remember feeling mad at him for being so tired and disinterested in my childhood fantasies and dramas.

I was always the little warrior in our family. I raged and cried at canceled camping trips; at my father's out-of-town consulting jobs, which took him away for days; and at his sleeping till noon on the weekends when I wanted him up to be with me. At a very young age, I would follow him to his university office on Saturdays and Sunday afternoons to play alone in the science lab with the hamsters and gaze at anatomy books while he labored in a nearby office. It was lonely, but it was a way to be near him so I always behaved and was trusted fully to take care of myself and not interrupt him too often. When he'd take a coffee break, we'd walk to the soda shop across the street and I'd get a vanilla ice cream cone and, in our return to the office, would ask him to "Watch!" as I balanced myself walking along the ivy-covered stone wall lining the sidewalk. I was happiest when I was with my dad even if it meant learning the importance and priority of his work over my childish whims and wishes.

When I cried and yelled at him for always working, my little brother just sucked his fingers and watched quietly. Dad's work cycles of all-night writing binges, teaching, and long hours with students at home or at the office were always followed by periods of intense exhaustion when he would sleep for long periods or sluggishly mope around the house, relax with his bourbon, and sleep more.

Dad had his first heart attack at 42. In my 15-year-old eyes he seemed so old, even fragile. His doctors told him to quit smoking his four packs per day, stop drinking caffeine, and stop eating the New York strips he loved to cook and serve generously to his protégés during those late-night sessions after bourbon rendered them ravenous at 10 o'clock without dinner. His doctors also told him to exercise more, work less, reduce stress, and consume no more than two alcoholic beverages daily. At 42, my father was told to change just about every aspect of his life that had so much been the source of his greatest success and pleasure: hard work, hard drinking, smoking, and late-night talking and dining. Although then, in my usual fashion, I was so angry at him and his failed attempts to reform himself, I realize now how very sad it was to watch his feeble efforts to smoke less, drink less, and be with his students less.

He died at 51 of a coronary after a full day at the office. My grandmother, his mother, said my father would have wanted it that way—to have worked fully every day of his life until he died. I was 24 when he died. I'm now 42 and 51 doesn't seem all that old. Sometimes I go to professional baseball games and watch the fathers with their sons and daughters. The kids are so excited, and the fathers buy them things, hold them on their laps, and talk to them about the game, pointing, whispering in little ears, with them jumping up, arms waving, with loud joyous cheers. When I watch those children, I get a glimpse of what it means to have lost the moments childhood offers us all, however so briefly, to know pure excitement over something simple and playful. I don't really like ball games now. I find them boring, no fun, and a waste of time. But when I was a child, I wanted so much for my father to take me to ball games like other dads. But he was either too busy or too disinterested in sports and the heroes like Mickey Mantle and Roger Maris whom I, as an 8-year-old, adored. Who knows? Maybe if he had taken me to some of those games before the age my stodgy boredom set in, I would know how to enjoy baseball now. My father worked through most of my childhood. And, he hasn't been around for any of my adulthood.

family member complain about an upstanding contributor to society? Acknowledging a problem can make children feel guilty and disloyal because they are complaining when everything is so perfect. Children of workaholics often silently reprimand themselves for being the unappreciative bad guy who has nothing to complain about. If you think this profile sounds like adult children of alcoholics, it does—which further confirmed our belief that family workaholism is a systemic problem.

But there was still one last member of the workaholic family to be heard—the disgruntled wives and husbands. While friends, family, and management glorified workaholics, husbands and wives often described their lives as living nightmares because they had little support from the mental health system, outside family or friends, and, least of all, the workplace.

We wanted to verify these anecdotes by conducting the first scientific study of marital relationships of spouses of workaholics. So we surveyed a random national sample of 1,000 women in the American Counseling Association and received questionnaires from 326 women with an average age of 47 (Robinson, Carroll, & Flowers, 2001). We found that workaholism had negative effects on marital relationships. Spouses of workaholics reported a significantly lower degree of caring, attachment, and desire for emotional intimacy with their partners than spouses of nonworkaholics. Spouses of workaholics also reported a significantly lower level of positive feelings toward their partners than spouses of nonworkaholics. The workaholic marriages had far more marital estrangement, typically indicating deterioration in the marriage, often leading to apathy and indifference between husband and wife. All participants had a minimum of a college degree and most had personal incomes of $20,000 or higher. A total of 77% of the women were married an average of 18 years. Their workaholic spouses had an average age of 50 years and worked an average of 56 hours per week, compared to the nonworkaholic spouses who worked an average of 46 hours per week. Not surprising, marriages with workaholic spouses had a much higher divorce rate (55%) than marriages where workaholism was nonexistent (16%). Wives of workaholics were more likely to report that external events controlled their lives, whereas the nonworkaholic group said they felt in control of the events in their lives. Using structural equation modeling, we conducted a second analysis of the data (Robinson, Flowers, et al., 2001). Our findings supported the body of literature that suggests that strength and cohesion of a marriage is associated with the presence or absence of excessive working on the part of one spouse.

In our most recent study, we surveyed a national random sample of 1,000 husbands to determine the influence of wives' workaholic behaviors on the marriage (Robinson & Flowers, 2003). The results suggested that the workaholism of the wives was positively related to marital estrangement and negative affect. The most important workaholism domains for predicting marital disaffection were overcontrolling behaviors and impaired communication.

WORKAHOLICS IN THE WORKPLACE

The cost of health-related problems associated with workaholism in corporate America is $150 billion per year. That figure does not account for costs of inefficient workaholic behaviors, none of which have been evaluated by researchers, that can add millions to organizational debt (Robinson, 2000b). While corporate America has failed to underscore problems resulting from workaholism and to extol its virtues, organizational psychologists have continually emphasized that workaholism leads to inefficiency and erodes trust in throughout the organization (Burke, 2000; Porter, 2001). While we were conducting research on workaholics and family dynamics, organizational psychologists Dr. Kay Porter at Rutgers University and Dr. Ronald Burke at York University in Ontario, Canada, were studying the workplace. Their findings of workaholism in the workplace paralleled what we were finding in the home.

It is not uncommon for workaholics to generate a crisis and get attention and praise for resolving it. Porter (1996, p. 74) described this phenomenon in the workplace:

> During a crisis, everyone's attention goes to its resolution. Rarely is time taken to reexamine the history of decision points at which the crisis might have been averted, but the cost of meeting crisis conditions is significant. All organization members should be concerned about the possibility that someone in their midst may contribute to or create crises. Indeed, managers focus on praise for those who function well during that time. The same person could be playing both roles, and this person may be a workaholic.

Porter further suggests that workaholics struggle with low self-esteem to such an extent that they distort patterns of working with others because they focus on how interactions enhance their self-esteem, not on how they can enhance the quality of the task itself.

Because of their sense of time urgency, workaholics can take the most inefficient avenue for completing tasks. Their compulsions to push themselves and to impulsively jump in over their heads without planning and forethought can make it difficult for them to complete projects in a timely manner. As workaholics continue to overinvest in their jobs, fatigue sets in and rates of errors and accidents increase. Eventually, the amount of effort workaholics put into their jobs exceeds their level of productivity (Porter, 1998). Thus, many workaholics are less efficient than their coworkers who put in fewer hours planning and working toward a job goal (see Table 11.1).

Workaholic managers, instead of seeking advice, asking for input, or showing vulnerabilities, tend to rule with an iron fist, using intimidation as a defense against their own insecurities and unwittingly undermining rather than supporting subordinates to reinforce their own, more powerful position. They tend to pressure employees to match their own inhuman standards, long hours, and frantic pace (Robinson, 1998). They are overly critical, overly demanding, and unable to tolerate mistakes, becoming roadblocks to productivity and quality in the workforce and causing disharmony, absenteeism, mistrust, and conflict. Their leadership style lowers productivity and morale and destroys team playing and creative brainstorming.

Porter (2001) argued that managers need guidelines to identify workaholic employees and their ineffective behaviors that previously have gone unnoticed or have been rewarded to reduce prohibitive costs related to absenteeism, burnout, lower creativity, health problems, and waste of human potential. She recommended that four widely held but untested beliefs about workaholics in the workplace be clarified by future research (Porter, 1996, p. 80):

1. Workaholics will choose a new course of action that requires as much or more work rather than a potential solution that meets organizational goals but is actually less work.

Table 11.1
Characteristics of Healthy versus Workaholic Workers

Healthy Workers	Workaholic Workers
Good collaborators and delegators.	Unable to delegate or work as a team; works best alone.
Socially gregarious.	Employees with few or no friends.
Employees who enjoy the process of working.	Employees who work for the sake of working.
Motivated by intrinsic needs and creative contributions.	Motivated by fear and loss of status.
Efficient: They see the whole picture and step toward the goal.	Inefficient: They get bogged down with details.
Creative risk takers who stretch beyond customary bounds.	Reluctant to take chances to achieve creative outcomes.
Masters of self-correction; when they make mistakes they learn from them.	Unable to tolerate mistakes; they try to avoid them or cover them up.

2. Workaholics will resist or even sabotage efforts to impose more balance between work and nonwork involvements.
3. Workaholic managers will choose to maintain control rather than delegate work or rely on others to set standards of performance.
4. Workaholics will respond to both success and failure by working more.

Burke (2000) recommended that employers pay attention to the performance and work habits of employees and alert themselves to warning signs of workaholism. Instead of rewarding addictive behaviors, they should recognize employees who lead balanced lives. To reduce workaholism, it is important that employers minimize the impact of job insecurity, work overload, and limited career opportunities—all of which can compel employees to work longer hours.

More aggressive companies are beginning to mandate shorter working hours and goal-setting sessions that include leisure objectives; however, initiatives of this type will not cure the workaholic, although they may help reveal those individuals whose work excess is self-inflicted (Porter, 2001). Porter concurs with my colleagues and I at the University of North Carolina at Charlotte that the intersection of workplace and family functioning will continue to be destructive to personal relationships until workaholism is more effectively recognized and treated as an addictive behavior.

WORKING WITH WORKAHOLIC FAMILIES: SOME CASE EXAMPLES FROM ROBINSON'S CLINICAL WORK

When an individual or couple comes to me for help, I use my own personal and clinical experience with workaholism. First of all, I screen for workaholism much as other therapists screen for a present or past history of alcoholism. In the first session, I ask questions designed to elicit whether there is a problem with workaholism. Instead of asking about the numbers of hours worked, I ask the couple or individual to describe the dinner hour, which is a significant time for families to communicate and connect emotionally. I also ask couples how they spend their free time together and who is in charge of what at home. Asking questions about how couples spend time and getting sound bites of their daily lives lets the problem, if it exists, naturally emerge. The workaholic or spouse is going to say that they don't have any spare time, that they don't do anything together, that they don't share common interests, or that they never see each other because one of them is always working.

So, when I probe about how time is spent in the relationship, I am particularly interested in knowing whether the workaholic has significant relationships, whether he or she makes genuine efforts to spend time with loved ones, and whether there is a degree of balance among exercise and health, hobbies, leisure, and social relationships. I try to discern whether clients can turn off the work faucet or if it runs constantly, elbowing other thoughts, people, and activities out of the way. I ask these dynamic questions rather than directly asking about hours because the number of hours worked doesn't tell me if there is a problem or not.

Many who come to see me work above-average hours but are not workaholics, so asking about the number of work hours doesn't tell much. There are people like Gary, a 34-year-old, high-powered attorney, who works many hours but who also cannot wait to get home to his family and to his son's soccer games. Although he is stressed from the demanding job, he is constantly thinking of ways to spend more time at home. He wants to be successful and earn enough money to provide a decent standard of living for his loved ones but is committed to putting his family first. Much of his stress comes from how to be successful without sacrificing time with his family. When push comes to shove, he would change jobs in a heartbeat in order to protect his valuable time with his wife and son. For people like Gary, the number of work hours alone doesn't accurately reflect their work motives.

Instead of hours worked, my strategy is to listen for extreme thought patterns—all-or-nothing thinking, perfectionism, or catastrophic thinking—the kinds of addictive thinking that undergirds all addictions and frames the workaholic's world. I check for the origins of workaholism to see if there is a family-of-origin history of parentification, workaholism, or alcoholism that could serve as a blueprint for the present workaholism. I look also for the meaning workaholics get from their work and their underlying motivations. I'm interested in knowing the clients' histories of overloading themselves and how has it served them over time. For example, I want to see if perhaps overworking helps workaholics with tension reduction.

Another reason I focus on what's happening in the context of the relationship instead of on number of work hours is to keep a neutral position with the couple instead of shifting blame to the workaholic. Many workaholics enter therapy already having tried unsuccessfully to cut back their hours and feeling inadequate for having failed. Some carry into therapy the all-or-nothing fear that they'll be asked to change or quit their present jobs or cut back on work hours. They are like the coal miners who took canaries into mines to test for deadly methane gas. When the birds stopped singing (because of a lack of oxygen), the miners fled. Dyed-in-the-wool workaholics are on guard and will not come back to therapy if they feel ganged up on or unduly examined. They will hang on to their work more tenaciously if their overworking becomes the main focus, unless they have already identified it as a problem themselves. I don't recommend that workaholics change jobs because the workplace doesn't create workaholics anymore than the bar creates alcoholics or the casino creates compulsive gamblers. Suggesting any kind of geographic escape, such as job change or additional vacations, does not get at the root of the problem, and the workaholism will only crop up again at another time. I attempt to get workaholics to come to the place where they gradually recognize they have a problem and to help them arrive at that place on their own.

Although all workaholics work excessively, they do not all act alike. Workaholism has many faces. Some workaholics are too careless; some are too ploddingly scrupulous; some can't get started; others plunge in on a dozen projects and finish little. The end result of these differing work styles may look the same on the surface—an unbalanced life dominated by long hours at the office—but each style expresses a different set of emotional and cognitive vulnerabilities and requires a different therapeutic approach (see Box 11.9). So, one of the things I try to do if workaholism is an issue is to determine the category of workaholism based on a typology of workaholics that I have observed clinically (Robinson, 2000a).

When it comes to working with couples, many therapists only see workaholic couples in terms of the pursuer-distancer dynamic. For example, Henry was the 42-year-old head of a national, family-owned restaurant chain. He and his live-in fiancee of 5 years had been in couples therapy for 6 months, where they worked on the pursuer-distancer issue, but the workaholism had not surfaced. He came

---

BOX 11.9
The Many Faces of Workaholism

It is possible to classify workaholics by type based on their level of work initiation in proportion to their level of work completion. *Relentless workaholics* are dyed-in-the-wool workaholics who are high work initiators and are high in work completion. They work compulsively and constantly, day and night, and holidays and weekends, with no let up and no periods of downtime. They are hurried and relentless in meeting deadlines often weeks ahead of schedule.

Bulimic workaholics are low in work initiation and high in work completion and have extreme work patterns that vacillate from bingeing to purging. This is the procrastinating workaholic who waits until the last possible minute and then binges for hours on end to complete a project, sometimes sleeping in clothes, just as an alcoholic sleeps off an alcoholic binge.

Attention-deficit workaholics are adrenaline-seeking workaholics who are easily bored and constantly seeking stimulation. They are high work initiators but are low in work completion. They have many bright ideas and creative solutions but have difficulty focusing on the task before them, get bored, and jump ahead to the next item on the agenda, leaving many projects unfinished.

Savoring workaholics are slow, deliberate, and methodical. Consummate perfectionists, they are afraid that the finished project is not going to be good enough. They savor their work just as alcoholics savor a shot of bourbon. They are low in work initiation and low in work completion because they prolong and create additional work when they realize that they are nearly finished with a project. They are nitpickers who overanalyze, get bogged down in detail, and reexamine tasks to the point that it impedes their ability to initiate and complete work in a timely fashion.

---

to see me because of pressure from his fiancee to set a wedding date and his anxiety over it. Although he deeply loved his fiancee and wanted to be with her forever, his tentative approach to their relationship kept him emotionally distant and unwilling to propose marriage.

Every significant woman in his life had left him. His mother's death at age 7 turned his world upside down; she was replaced by two consecutive stepmothers, the first he hated and the second he tolerated; his older sister committed suicide at age 20; and he was divorced from his first wife with whom he had one son after 10 years of marriage. Henry's theory was that people change and are undependable and that you cannot count on them being there. It was through this lens that he saw his fiancee.

Because of family money, Henry didn't have to work but confessed that work gave his life structure. And, since he liked to be in control, it gave him a sense of knowing what's going to happen. He announced to his fiancee that she had to understand that work is number one in his life. But he complained that she packed their weekends with social engagements, and he got dragged along when he just wanted to stay home and rest. But at home she was always pulling on him, wanting to have deep conversations, and talk about their future together. The more he feared closeness, the more his fiancee pulled on him, and the more anxious he got—retreating into his head to work or think about being back at the office, or he would go into another room to work on the computer. Many therapists might see this couple strictly in terms of the pursuer-distancer synchrony, much like a Ginger Rogers-Fred Astaire dance routine. They might instruct workaholics to stop working so much and start spending more time with their loved ones, as though they ought to be able to do this. But I saw more; I saw workaholism in the dance steps. The safety of distancing himself through his work soothed Henry's anxiety, and the anxiety relief became a more powerful payoff than a close, loving relationship that is unpredictable and uncontrollable. Henry's fear of getting too close to yet another female and recreating his worst nightmare—another loss—raised his anxiety level. Escaping into constant work soothed his anxiety because it gave him the predictability and control he craved and a framework to handle any surprises. His relationship did the opposite. It brought up his worst fears because relationships are slippery, unpredictable, impossible to control, change over time, and are full of surprises.

Henry felt guilty that at work he dashed past people as if they were cardboard figures because he was constantly rushing to his next appointment. Driving home from work, he turned over problems of the day in his mind. Sometimes, as he neared their house, he could feel his anxiety thermometer rise, thinking that she was going to bring up the subject of marriage again. As soon as he walked through the door at 7:30 P.M., she was ready to talk. But, because his mind was still back at work, he reacted by snapping at her. Feeling constantly pushed away and that he always set the agenda, she accused him of treating her like one of his employees.

The solution was for Henry to get the same comfort and safety from the relationship that he got from compulsive working. These changes began during the work day, not at the end of it. For example, I suggested that he reduce his anxiety by avoiding unrealistic deadlines or putting self-imposed time limits on important projects and that he build time cushions between appointments and meetings so that he could stretch, get a drink, go to the restroom, or chat with a colleague. He could give himself extra driving time to arrive at a destination. I recommended that he schedule time cushions in his Daytimer with the same importance he scheduled his appointments. Slowing down his pace could help him feel less stressful at the end of the day and be more receptive to his fiancee. And changing his reentry pattern from work to home could help him arrive in a calmer mood. Instead of waiting until he hit the front door, I suggested he start his descent on the drive home by playing relaxing music and doing deep breathing. Instead of work thoughts, I recommended he reframe his attitude about being with his fiancee at the end of the day from thinking of her as someone who created anxiety in him to someone who wanted to comfort and love him, from being with her as an obligation to being with her because it was his choice. I even suggested that he choose to initiate discussions of their future together and the possibility of marriage, instead of waiting for these conversations to be imposed on him, thus, lowering his anxiety.

Another couple was on the verge of separation when they came to see me. The husband complained his 34-year-old childhood sweetheart and computer executive, Shelia, put her work before the marriage, and he wanted his wife back. He described himself as a family man who wanted children, family mealtimes, and a partner to share life together. Shelia wasn't sure she wanted children and felt restricted by these demands. Just the thought of cutting back on work and sitting at the dinner table every night with her husband and children made her feel trapped. Although this is not an unusual refrain among contemporary women, I saw something else there. Shelia deeply loved her husband, but her work was more important. This is one of the differences approached in early sessions. I have a finely tuned radar to work-related issues that helps me assess balance, spot all-or-nothing thinking, and check how clients use their work to reduce tension.

Being able to come and go to work at will and to throw all-nighters with her staff to get the monthly billing done by deadline gave her a sense of freedom. But, because of the marital strife, Shelia consented to a curfew of 7:00 each night, usually not making it home until 7:30 or 8:00. And, although she wasn't hungry, she would sit begrudgingly at the table in silence, drum her fingers, and watch her husband eat the now-cold meal that he had prepared for them. She tried to have decent conversations, but all she could think about was all the work piling up at the office. After dinner, feeling she'd paid her dues, she'd go back to the office and work all night. Trying to adapt to her husband's request for a closer relationship created tremendous tension for Shelia, and her half-hearted attempts frustrated and angered him.

Even though she worked 24/7, Shelia had no clue she was a workaholic. I suggested that her work patterns sounded extreme and asked about her manager's view of forcing employees to work all night. She confessed that, although she was highly productive, he suggested that she find a better way to get the work done over a gradual period. She prided herself because she didn't take lunch breaks, using the time instead to get more work done. I asked her if others took lunch breaks and if they were getting their work done. She acknowledged they were. So I asked her, "As smart and capable as you are, why can't you take lunch?" Shelia had no friends, was estranged from her parents, and her marriage hung by a thread. I asked her who would be an emotional support if she separated from her husband. Tears in her eyes, she shook her head as if to say nobody. I recommended that she make this a goal, and she was able to repair her relationship with her mother and find comfort in being able to confide in her.

With each session, Shelia was gradually able to see that workaholism had made her life unmanageable and she became convinced of the need to make healthy changes. Her big breakthrough came the day she was leaving for lunch and caught herself feeling guilty, believing that management would think she was goofing off. Then the absurdity of the thought hit her as she reminded herself that everybody in the building, management included, always took lunch breaks. Now, depriving herself of lunch no longer felt honorable but abusive.

Workaholics recreate within themselves the psychological environment of their childhoods. They treat themselves the way they were treated. Jim, a 39-year-old newspaper journalist grew up with well-to-do parents who didn't believe in him. Nothing he did as a child was ever good enough. Today, he uses that same yardstick to judge himself. Riddled with self-doubt, he constantly questions his judgments, which increases his anxiety. He throws himself into a quandary, worrying for 10 hours over an editorial piece that a colleague would write in half the time. His colleagues and editor rave about his work, but when he looks at it, it's never good enough. The discontent and self-doubt his critical voice creates causes him to dig his heels in deeper and work harder and longer. His perfectionism raises a bar of success that no human being could meet; and, even though his "failures" receive accolades from the public and journalism awards from the news media, he berates himself for the flaws. Anxiety from falling short of his standard causes him to devalue his worth and drive himself with, "Next time I'll work twice as hard and get it perfect!" This self-doubt and criticism causes him to live with a false sense of failure that fuels his workaholism.

In these cases, I work with helping clients see how they are recreating similar feelings by using old, outdated images of themselves. I have them consider discarding the childhood image and starting to see themselves as others see them and to let the evidence—instead of the inner critic—speak for itself. The goal is to substitute a nurturing voice to create a dialog with the critical voice so that, eventually, the validating voice and the day-to-day evidence win out. The self-acceptance helps clients see themselves more realistically and lowers their anxiety and their need to overcompensate through workaholism.

I asked Jim to think of himself as a bank account and weigh the emotional withdrawal (stress, self-imposed demands, and put-downs) with the deposits (spare time, self-praise, recreation). He decided he was emotionally bankrupt. The withdrawals far exceeded the deposits. The goal then became keeping the bank account in the black. Every time he has self-doubt, he makes a withdrawal; every time he gives himself pep talks and confident thoughts and treats himself to leisure time, he makes a deposit.

Gradually, Jim started to believe in himself the way others did. The self-care carried over into a weekend golf trip with four other men, which he'd never done before. He started to notice that the more he supported himself emotionally this way, the more he felt like the golf trip was a huge investment in his bank because there was more of him to go around and he had more to give his family and work. These short-term investments that workaholics often resist at first give them such huge payoffs that they are eager to make them. Jim started completing editorial assignments in half the time and looking forward to time off with his wife and children. Instead of seeing family time as a waste, he saw it as a well-deserved and valuable investment that he approached with enthusiasm instead of dread.

I often employ family-of-origin work with both partners present to help break a negative circular pattern that keeps them apart. This happens when, in the course of therapy, each party starts to see the deeper reasons for the workaholism and when nonworkaholic partners start to feel compassion—instead of resentment—toward the workaholic.

For example, Judy, a 48-year-old real estate broker, came to see me because of marriage problems. She said her husband was supposed to be with her for their first session, but he claimed he was sick at the last minute. Her biggest problem was that she couldn't trust this man who kept secrets from her. She complained that he bought a $200 golf club and didn't tell her and that when he flew from North Carolina to Seattle to his son's wedding, his ex-wife just coincidentally happened to be on the same airplane.

Judy's husband came in alone for the second session and if ever a man loved his wife, this man did. He said he craved affection from her but felt she kept pushing him away with her anger and suspicion. He said he felt unloved by her and that her work was more important than anyone or anything in her life. He said she had no friends, no hobbies, and was estranged from her ex-husband and two grown daughters. He described a mistrustful wife who constantly watched over his shoulder and who hit the roof when he made spontaneous purchases like the bargain $200 golf club that he found in the golf shop's discontinued bin. He described her as having financial wealth but acting as if she were impoverished. His secrecy, which had become a passive way to protect himself against her anger and hopefully gain her affection, inadvertently fueled her suspicions, causing her to distance herself further from him and find solace in her work.

In the first joint session, Judy described her upbringing on a farm in central Florida as traumatic. Her alcoholic parents drank away the lunch money, so she had to work full time raking yards and picking tobacco so she could eat—becoming self-sufficient by age 12. "It was sink or swim," she said, "I learned early that I can't depend on anybody but myself, and I still feel that way today." When watching TV, she finds it hard to relax unless she's also reading a book or magazine, working on an appraisal, and simultaneously carrying on a conversation with her husband. "I still feel like that little girl who has to cover all the bases and if I let up, I'll die," she said. She described her work as the safest place in the world because she was aggressive, knew the job inside out and felt she could manage all possible outcomes. As Judy spoke of her fight for survival, putting work before personal relationships, and her painful ulcers, tears welled up in her husband's eyes. Although stalwart as she spoke, I could tell by her tone that Judy too was starting to understand how that deep-seated fear still motivated her need to keep busy and work nonstop, becoming suspicious of situations or people she couldn't control. I could tell that his empathy neutralized his previous anger as he gently put his hand on top of hers and interjected that he just wanted to be close again. It was clear that Judy had gained insight too, when, at the conclusion of the session, she softened: "So basically what I've been doing is reacting to my husband the way I did to my parents in feeling I couldn't trust him to manage money, pay bills, and put food on the table."

This was only the beginning of Judy coming to her own realization that her deep fear of not having enough resources had caused her to put work before personal relationships. And although overworking reduced her insecurity, it blocked her affection-craving husband from emotional entry, causing him to feel rejected and to compensate by spending. The goal for Judy was to find emotional security (i.e., tension reduction) within the marriage as she had in workaholism. That shift started in the joint session when Judy started to understand herself and her husband's reaction to her insecurities. And the husband's reframing of "his rejection" to "Judy's insecurity," enabled him to respond with more sensitivity and honesty so that Judy felt more secure and took down the emotional walls that kept him from hurting her the way she had been hurt as a child. Thus, the circular pattern was broken.

Once clients know they have a problem, I introduce a variety of ways that they can begin, gradually and gently, to modify the way they think about themselves at work and how they behave. For example, Ward's underlying reasons for not having a vacation in 10 years was a fear that if he took a week off, his multimillion dollar business would crumble. When he struggled with the thought of a vacation, this 38-year-old heart surgeon teetered between either building his business by working nonstop or losing it by taking a week's vacation. Working through vacations won out for 10 years. To help him become aware of his all-or-nothing thinking, I used an approach that I call *accessing your graydar*, which focuses on the shades of gray. I asked him to draw a line across a sheet of paper with the two extreme beliefs on each end: "I must work nonstop to build my business" on one end and "If

I take a vacation, my business will crumble" on the opposite end. Writing extreme thought patterns down helps clients see that neither is true and that the truth lies somewhere in between. Using his graydar, Ward considered an option at the midpoint, "It is possible for me to take a week's vacation *and* for my business to continue to grow." Sensitivity to words like *always, all,* and *everybody,* or *nobody, never,* and *none* alerts workaholics to access their graydar, giving them a broader scope of the issues that translates into more balanced actions.

Most workaholic clients need help setting boundaries. For example, Mildred, a 43-year-old psychotherapist, needed help in setting clearly defined limits on her eating and work patterns because she found it easy to wiggle around poorly defined or vague boundaries. When she opened the fridge, she found herself overeating because she drank from the milk jug and ate from the food container. Instead of keeping regular work hours, she worked 6 days a week from 8:00 A.M. to 8:00 P.M. I recommended she contain both eating and working activities. For example, instead of eating from containers, I suggested she pour a glass of milk and spoon a serving of potato salad onto a plate. I challenged her to use a different daily planner. She discarded her Daytimer that showed daily times starting at 7:00 A.M. and ending at 11:00 P.M. and purchased one that stopped at 5:00 P.M. These simple changes automatically limited Mildred's overeating and overworking and led to dramatic results. She expressed a sense of accomplishment and security with automatically having these lines in place—knowledge that had been erased in her childhood when she became her mother's emotional caretaker at 10 years of age. Her early caretaking became a template for her professional and personal relationships and blurred for her the difference between self-care and selfishness. This led to her inability to say, "No" to clients and friends when her plate was already full and to putting her on a self-destructive course toward compassion burnout.

Not everyone (e.g., medical personnel, tax accountants, or flight attendants) can limit work to 8-hour days, 5 days a week with no weekend or holiday work. Work moderation or abstaining from excessive work is the goal, and these boundaries must be tailored to the individual lifestyles and unique jobs of the clients.

In some cases, I have clients focus on intrusive thoughts that sometimes elbow their way into every waking moment, inhibiting their ability to function. Neal, a 34-year-old investment broker, needed immediate relief from his obsessive-compulsive working. During dinner with his wife, Neal mentally strategized how he would meet his quota. Tossing his toddler in the air, he worried how he'd present this quarter's loss to his best client. Tossing and turning at night, he agonized over what the stock market would do the next day, often getting up at 3:00 A.M. to work, which relieved his anxiety.

To allay his worry while he worked from 5:00 A.M. to 9:00 P.M., 7 days a week, he insisted that his wife keep her cell phone with her at all times, so he could always reach her. She adamantly refused his unreasonable request, which he took as rejection. His overbearing need to control his wife and work were destructive ways to reduce his anxiety, and they were tearing him apart. After many sleepless nights and desperate pleadings from his wife, who felt imprisoned by his control, Neal came to see me. He informed me that even as a child, he had approached his jobs in the same relentless manner.

I referred him for a medical evaluation and an antidepressant to help relieve the obsessive-compulsive tendencies. And I taught him to compartmentalize his intrusive thoughts by mentally putting each one in a box, placing a lid on the box, and putting it on a storage shelf in a basement or attic. He was to take the thoughts off the shelf and out of the box only when he planned to give them his full attention. If one got loose, I suggested *thought stopping*—wearing a thick rubber band around his wrist and snapping it every time he had an intrusive work thought and saying, "Stop!" in his mind. You would have thought that this simple rubber band was a miracle cure. He proudly wore it to each session, proclaiming the dramatic change in his life. Combining these simple strategies with an antidepressant and basic relaxation and breathing techniques, Neal slept better, was more present with his loved ones, and tackled work problems with more clarity and energy.

I often assign homework because I want clients to experiment with doing something fun that has no product and that teaches them spontaneity and flexibility. These are usually process-oriented versus goal-oriented activities, such as painting something artistic where you have to flow, digging in the garden, soaking in a hot bath, or walking barefoot in a rain shower. I have them choose a hobby, sport, or pastime that they can do imperfectly and that immerses them in the process instead of the outcome.

Richard, a 62-year-old bank president, took up golf to achieve this balance in his pressure-cooker schedule. He was committed to not keeping score, not hurrying from hole to hole, and keeping the emphasis on the process of having a good time instead of the winning score—the opposite of who he was at the office. When he played with business associates, they marveled that he was like a different person on the golf course. For the first time, they saw Richard's fun, light-hearted, and playful side. What started off as a task for Richard became a joyful event that he treasured and looked forward to—all because of experimenting with the process.

I try to help spouses of workaholics see that their natural response to workaholism (as with any addiction) might unwittingly enable it (Robinson & Chase, 2001). Examples of enabling include building the family schedule around the impossible workaholic schedule, putting dinner on the table at midnight for the umpteenth time after the workaholic promised to be home by seven o'clock, making alibis for the workaholic's absenteeism or lateness at family gatherings, taking over the workaholic's household chores, covering for the workaholic in business meetings or social gatherings, participating in rigorous work schedules just to spend time with the workaholic, and returning phone calls meant for the workaholic.

Sometimes spouses of workaholics create a double bind for their partners by complaining about the overworking in one breath and making unreasonable financial demands in the next. In some cases, spouses must be willing to accept financial disadvantages in return for the workaholic's work reduction and increased presence and participation at home. By taking over child rearing and household responsibilities, spouses often give workaholics the necessary freedom to work endlessly. Shielding workaholics from domestic worries and working alongside them has the effect of enabling the workaholism.

Family members often become just as obsessed with trying to get workaholics to cut back their workload as workaholics are obsessed about working. The more pressure family members put on them to take a break, a day off, a vacation, slow down, or come home early the more threatened the workaholics feel and the more tenaciously they resist because they interpret these pressures as efforts to undermine their control. The key is for partners of workaholics to detach with love. Workaholics and family members can also contact Workaholics Anonymous for help. Workaholics Anonymous is a nonprofit, 12-Step group dedicated to helping men and women stop working compulsively through fellowship and support. For more information contact: Workaholics Anonymous World Service Organization, P. O. Box 289, Menlo Park, CA 94026-0289.

FUTURE DIRECTIONS: RECOMMENDATIONS

It is important that future research consider the subject of workaholism so that a better working knowledge of the condition can be accrued. The attention given to the study of workaholism pales in comparison to the hundreds of investigations that exist on alcoholism and other compulsive behaviors. One exhaustive search of the literature using *Psychological Abstracts, Sociological Abstracts,* and the *Guide to Periodical Literature* revealed only a handful of articles containing the word *Workaholism* in the title or abstract (Seybold & Salomone, 1994).

Researchers made a compelling case for devoting more scientific attention to the study of workaholism (Burke, 2000). An increase in the sheer quantity of studies on workaholism is needed—studies that include the direct assessment of workaholics and their spouses instead of polls of physicians (e.g., Pietropinto, 1986) or magazine readers. More empirical research is needed on the psychological problems and adjustment of family members. Currently, only five studies exist on the perceptions of the children (Carroll & Robinson, 2000; Navarette, 1998; Robinson & Kelley, 1998; Searcy, 2000). Moreover, only two studies have ever been performed assessing the attitudes, feelings, and psychological adjustment of spouses of workaholics (Robinson & Flowers, 2003; Robinson, Carroll, et al., 2001).

Progress needs to be made on the measurement of workaholism. Three measures of workaholism (Haymon, 1993; Robinson, 1999; Spence & Robbins, 1992) warrant further attention. Burke (2000) recommends that more effort be devoted to validating these workaholism measures:

> First, workaholism must be shown to predict validating job and work behaviors (e.g., perfectionism, non-delegation). Secondly, workaholism must be shown to predict extra-work satisfactions (e.g., family satisfaction and family functioning). Thirdly, workaholism must be shown to predict psychological well-being (e.g., emotional health). Fourthly, self-reports of workaholism must be shown to predict other reports (spouse, coworkers). Fifthly, measures of workaholism must be shown to be stable over time. (p. 13)

The instruments currently used to measure workaholism utilize relatively small samples and to date no instrument contains norms developed from large representative samples. Our most recent work at the University of North Carolina at Charlotte involves the development of norms for the Work Addiction Risk Test and a study that examines gender differences on workaholism (Flowers & Robinson, 2003b).

The information we have on workaholics is based predominantly on self-report data, namely self-administered questionnaires or face-to-face interviews with convenient samples. These limited approaches, although useful for building a knowledge base, have led to a need for more sampling and methodological specificity. It is important that future research studies are well-planned and include randomized, representative samples. These samples should extend beyond convenient college student populations or professional groups to the larger world of the gainfully employed in a variety of businesses.

A multimethod approach to data collection in which observational techniques are used in conjunction with the traditional self-report and interview techniques will yield more reliable data and lead to a better understanding of workaholic family functioning. No study has ever employed this approach in its investigation of workaholic families. Moreover, it is essential that future research employs a systems-oriented approach and assesses perceptions and behaviors of spouses and children of workaholics. Other researchers have emphasized the importance of collecting data from family, friends, and coworkers to provide a more reliable indicator than the self-reports of workaholics (Burke, 2000; Porter, 1996).

Maintaining an ecological focus is crucial as workaholics are observed interacting in the workplace or in the family. Researchers need multivariate designs with larger samples that will provide data on the interaction of significant variables that impact workaholics and their entire families. Longitudinal studies also are needed to follow workaholics over time to assess the progression of the disorder in terms of psychological, attitudinal, and behavioral changes and family dynamics, work relationships, and on-the-job satisfaction and performance. It has been noted that a major drawback of studies involving one-time data collection cannot address issues of casualty in a meaningful way (e.g., Does workaholism cause dissatisfaction or does dissatisfaction cause workaholism? Burke, 2000).

We believe that workaholism is this decade's cocaine; it is "problem without a name." The time has come for our profession to stop relegating workaholism to pop psychology bookshelves and take a hard, scientific look at this problem. It is our hope that future research and clinical reports will no longer perpetuate workaholism's masquerade as the best-dressed addiction. The goal of our work has been to expose this insidious disorder for the damage it unleashes on individuals, families, and the workplace. It has been our goal to attach a negative stigma to the term *workaholism* in hopes that the profession will open its eyes to this problem and develop strategies for intervention.

RECOMMENDED READING

Killinger, B. (1992). *Workaholics: The respectable addicts*. New York: Fireside. This book provides an insightful look at workaholics, including psychological motivation and solutions for recovery.

Robinson, B. (1998). *Chained to the desk: A guidebook for workaholics, their partners and children, and the clinicians who treat them*. New York: New York University Press. This book is the first comprehensive portrait of the workaholic, presenting an inside look into the impact on those who live and work with workaholics—partners, spouses, children, and colleagues—as well as appropriate techniques for clinicians who treat them.

Robinson, B., & Chase, N. (2001). *High-performing families: Causes, consequences, and clinical solutions*. Washington, DC: American Counseling Association. Through theoretical frameworks and case examples, the authors uncover the negative consequences of the societal phenomenon of overwork and overdedication to careers. Topics addressed include family patterns in the lives of overachievers, the parentification of children, and the relationship between high performance in the workplace and family relationships.

Sotile, W., & Sotile, M. (1996) *The medical marriage: A couple's survival guide.* New York: Birch Lane Press. The first book to address the intimate lives of medical couples, it presents sound advice, dramatic case studies, and cutting-edge information on preventing careers from consuming a medical marriage and how to make it work in today's society.

REFERENCES

Burke, R. (2000). Workaholism in organizations: Concepts, results and future research directions. *International Journal of Management Reviews, 2,* 1–16.

Carroll, J., & Robinson, B. E. (2000). Depression and parentification among adults as related to paternal workaholism and alcoholism. *Family Journal: Counseling and Therapy for Couples and Families, 8,* 33–41.

Doerfler, M. C., & Kammer, P. P. (1986). Workaholism, sex, and sex-role stereotyping among female professionals. *Sex Roles, 14,* 551–560.

Flowers, C., & Robinson, B. E. (2001). Review of the Work Addiction Risk Test. In J. Maltby, C. A. Lewis, & A. Hill (Eds.), *Handbook of psychological tests* (pp. 81–92). Wales, U.K.: Edwin Mellen Press.

Flowers, C., & Robinson, B. E. (2002). A structural and discriminant analysis of the Work Addiction Risk Test. *Educational and Psychological Measurement, 62,* 517–526.

Flowers, C., & Robinson, B. E. (2003a). *Construct validity study of scores from the Work Addiction Risk Test.* Unpublished manuscript, University of North Carolina at Charlotte.

Flowers, C., & Robinson, B. E. (2003b). *Gender differences and workaholism.* Unpublished manuscript, University of North Carolina at Charlotte.

Haraguchi, M., Tsuda, A., & Ozeki, Y. (1991). The current status of stress among information-related industry workers. In M. Tanaka & A. Tsuda (Eds.), *L'espirit d'aujourdhui* [The spirit of today] No. 290: *Stress and karoshi* (pp. 75–86). Tokyo: Shibundo.

Haymon, S. (1993). The relationship of work addiction and depression, anxiety, and anger in college males (Doctoral dissertation, Florida State University, 1992). *Dissertation Abstracts International, 53,* 5401B.

Ishiyama, F. I., & Kitayama, A. (1994). Overwork and career self-validation among the Japanese: Psychosocial issues and counseling implications. *International Journal for the Advancement of Counseling, 17,* 167–182.

Kanai, A., Wakabayashi, M., & Fling, S. (1996). Workaholism among employees in Japanese corporations: An examination based on the Japanese version of the Workaholism Scales. *Japanese Psychological Research, 38,* 192–203.

Kato, M. (1995, February). Workaholism: It's not in the blood. *Look Japan,* 1–4.

Machlowitz, M. (1985). *Workaholics: Living with them, working with them.* Reading, MA: Addison-Wesley.

Navarette, S. (1998). *An empirical study of adult children of workaholics: Psychological functioning and intergenerational transmission.* Unpublished doctoral dissertation, California Graduate Institute, Santa Barbara.

Oates, W. (1971). *Confessions of a workaholic: The facts about work addiction.* New York: World Publishing.

Pietropinto, A. (1986). The workaholic spouse. *Medical Aspects of Human Sexuality, 20,* 89–96.

Porter, G. (1996). Organizational impact of workaholism: Suggestions for researching the negative outcomes of excessive work. *Journal of Occupational Health Psychology, 1,* 70–84.

Porter, G. (1998). Can you trust a workaholic? How work addiction erodes trust throughout the organization. *Journal of Contemporary Business Issues, 6,* 48–57.

Porter, G. (2001). Workaholics as high-performance employees: The intersection of workplace and family relationship problems. In B. Robinson & N. Chase (Eds.), *High-performing families: Causes, consequences, and clinical solutions* (pp. 33–45). Washington, DC: American Counseling Association.

Robinson, B. E. (1989). *Work addiction*. Deerfield Beach, FL: Health Communications.

Robinson, B. E. (1998). *Chained to the desk: A guidebook for workaholics, their partners and children and the clinicians who treat them*. New York: New York University Press.

Robinson, B. E. (1999). The Work Addiction Risk Test: Development of a tentative measure of workaholism. *Perceptual and Motor Skills, 88*, 199–210.

Robinson, B. E. (2000a). A typology of workaholics with implications for counselors. *Journal of Addictions and Offender Counseling, 21*, 34–48.

Robinson, B. E. (2000b). Workaholism: Bridging the gap between workplace, sociocultural, and family research. *Journal of Employment Counseling, 37*, 31–47.

Robinson, B. E. (2001). Workaholism and family functioning: A profile of familial relationships, psychological outcomes, and research considerations. *Contemporary Family Therapy, 23*, 123–135.

Robinson, B. E., Carroll, J., & Flowers, C. (2001). Marital estrangement, positive affect, and locus of control among spouses of workaholics and spouses of nonworkaholics: A national study. *American Journal of Family Therapy, 29*, 397–410.

Robinson, B. E., & Chase, N. (2001). *High-performing families: Causes, consequences, and clinical solutions*. Washington, DC: American Counseling Association.

Robinson, B. E., & Flowers, C. (2003). *The relationship between workaholism and marital estrangement, locus of control, and positive and negative affects: A national study of husbands*. Unpublished manuscript, University of North Carolina at Charlotte.

Robinson, B. E., Flowers, C., & Carroll, J. (2001). Work stress and marriage: A theoretical model examining the relationship between workaholism and marital cohesion. *International Journal of Stress Management, 8*, 165–175.

Robinson, B. E., & Kelley, L. (1998). Adult children of workaholics: Self-concept, anxiety, depression, and locus of control. *American Journal of Family Therapy, 26*, 223–238.

Robinson, B. E., & Phillips, B. (1995). Measuring workaholism: Content validity of the Work Addiction Risk Test. *Psychological Reports, 77*, 657–658.

Robinson, B. E., & Post, P. (1995a). Split-half reliability of the Work Addiction Risk Test: Development of a measure of workaholism. *Psychological Reports, 76*, 1226.

Robinson, B. E., & Post, P. (1995b). Work addiction as a function of family of origin and its influence on current family functioning. *Family Journal: Counseling and Therapy for Couples and Families, 3*, 200–206.

Robinson, B. E., & Post, P. (1997). Risk of work addiction to family functioning. *Psychological Reports, 81*, 91–95.

Robinson, B. E., Post, P., & Khakee, P. (1992). Test-retest reliability of the Work Addiction Risk Test. *Perceptual and Motor Skills, 74*, 926.

Searcy, E. A. (2000). *Adult children of workaholics: Anxiety, depression, family relationships, and risk for work addiction*. Unpublished master's thesis, University of South Australia.

Seligman, D. (1994, March). The curse of work. *Fortune, 7*, 133.

Seybold, K. C., & Salomone, P. R. (1994). Understanding workaholism: A review of causes and counseling approaches. *Journal of Counseling and Development, 73*, 4–9.

Spence, J. T., & Robbins, A. S. (1992). Workaholism: Definition, measurement, and preliminary results. *Journal of Personality Assessment, 58*, 160–178.

Uehata, T. (1993). *Karoshi no kenkyu* [Research on Karoshi]. Tokyo: Nihon Planning Center.

CHAPTER 12

Treating Workaholism

STEVEN BERGLAS

Hello, My Name Is RAM . . . and I'm a Workaholic.
— Advertising Campaign for the Dodge Ram heavy-duty truck, 2002

Work gives them the comfortable illusion of existing, even of being important.
   If they stopped working, they'd realize they simply weren't there at all, most of them.

— Aldous Huxley, *Point Counter Point*

THE MOST VEXING aspect about designing treatment strategies for workaholism is the lack of consensus that exists about whether or not the syndrome needs to be treated. As illustrated by the quotes that open this chapter, on one hand workaholism is deemed a virtue while on the other hand it is thought to be a disorder that can mask overwhelming feelings of dissolution. This disparity about what workaholism is pervades the halls of academia as well. Among those scientists who first identified and studied the concept of workaholism, there is a huge difference of opinion about what this syndrome is and what it implies about the mental health of those who exhibit it.

Oates (1971), for example, who takes credit for inventing the word *workaholism*, defines it as an addictive disorder in a person "whose need for work has become so excessive that it creates noticeable disturbance or interference with his bodily health, personal happiness, and interpersonal relationships" (p. 4). Conversely, Machlowitz (1985), another founder of the workaholism phenomenon, does not see it as a disease at all. To her, those labeled workaholic are earning "psychic income" defined as "responsibility, meaning, opportunity, [and] recognition" (p. 119) from a job that affords them more satisfaction than home life or social interactions. This may be why workaholics bring an incredible amount of resistance to a treatment setting, presuming, that is, that they are willing to accept the need to modify a lifestyle that Spruell (1987) referred to as "the addiction most rewarded in our culture" (p. 44). In bottom-line terms, workaholics resist psychotherapy with more well-entrenched denial than those suffering any other addictive disorder because workaholism not only thrives within our culture; to some, it is the embodiment of our materialistic ethos.

WORKAHOLICS: THE POSTER CHILDREN FOR MATERIALISM

Workaholism is rewarding, not only in terms of the *secondary gains* that it affords (cf. Berne, 1964), but also in real-world *material ways*. Despite being judged odd or, at worst, deviant, workaholics are rarely subjected to the social censure or ostracism directed at those who suffer from addictive disorders that involve an overindulgence in psychoactive substances or vices. Typically, workaholics evoke the sort of wariness-mixed-with-appreciation that is captured by a joke Woody Allen tells about a man who consults a psychiatrist out of concern for his brother who thinks he is a chicken. When the doctor asks why no one has disabused the man of his delusion, the concerned brother replies, "We can't; we need the eggs."

Workaholics are definitely "egg-layers" within the business world, and the value placed on productivity affects how their behavior is construed. There is no doubt that, over time, most workaholics begin to exert excessive control and devolve from being loners into mistrustful and hostile people who seek solace in isolative activity. Yet, because the early stages of a workaholic's career trajectory blends so well with the defining features of our culture, we accept their oddities longer than we should—for their good and ours.

Proof of this overacceptance is seen in the lengths that one set of researchers went to bend the definition of workaholism to accommodate a cohort of careerists (so-called *work enthusiasts,* Spence & Robbins, 1992) who reported experiencing high levels of enjoyment as a consequence of engaging in what others would judge to be an obsessive devotion to work. It would be unthinkable, regardless of self-reports provided by alcoholics, to propose a subtype of chemical dependency such as ego-syntonic alcohol dependence. But, because the manifestations of workaholism can appear to be extremes of role-prescribed behavior, researchers accept claims that this syndrome has a non- or subpathogenic presentation.

From my perspective, workaholism exists in definitional limbo because our ethos is materialism: The belief that a healthy lifestyle is achieved and prolonged through the acquisition of wealth and consumer goods, along with the commensurate social status that such "ownership" affords (Csikszentmihalyi, 1999) (see sidebar on p. 385). Although we trace our capitalistic roots to the Protestant work ethic—a doctrine that emphasized the importance of diligence, self-sacrifice, and achievement as means of attaining *spiritual improvement*—the current application of this principle bears only the most peripheral resemblance to its original formulation.

Over time, both the Protestant work ethic and Puritanism have suffered an affliction that bedevils many organized religions: Sacraments became dissociated from what was once held to be sacred. A primary case in point is how the doctrine of valuing work became transformed.

According to Calvinists, every Christian had two callings: The first, a general calling, was to serve the Lord Jesus Christ. The second, a personal calling, required employment by which a man's usefulness in his neighborhood is distinguished. Specifically, in his personal calling—what we, today, would call a

---

If We Are So Rich, Why Aren't We Happy?

"Aristotle noted that although humankind values a great many things, such as health, fame, and possessions, because we think that they will make us happy, we value happiness for itself. Thus, happiness is the only intrinsic goal that people seek for its own sake, the bottom line of all desire."

Source: From "If We Are So Rich, Why Aren't We Happy?" by M. Csikszentmihalyi, 1999, *American Psychologist, 54*(10), pp. 821.

---

career—Calvinism maintained that every good Christian should see to it that his business glorified God by *doing good for others* (Huber, 1971).

According to Weber (1920/1958), who examined the manner in which Protestant religious orthodoxy became transformed into capitalist philosophy, over time there was a juxtaposition of philosophical ends and means on the value of work. Rather than remaining true to the *end* of getting closer to God through habits of industry, self-discipline, and contempt for self-indulgence, our capitalist society became obsessed with the *means* of securing wealth or profit. The most damaging consequence of this juxtaposition was that the spiritual goal of Puritanism—*striving for a sense of fulfillment through labors that benefited and strengthened ties to one's community*—was ignored. As a consequence, Americans acquired a preoccupation with reaching for an ever-higher standard of living that, in turn, spawned pathologies such as status-driven consumerism and workaholism.

WORKAHOLISM: COPING WITH A FAILURE TO ACHIEVE PSYCHOSOCIAL INTEGRATION

Support for the argument that workaholism is a disorder and not merely *hyperbolic capitalism* comes from two observations: (1) Workaholics respond to leisure time (being blocked from access to work) in precisely the same manner that those who meet the criteria for substance dependence disorders recognized by the American Psychiatric Association do, by exhibiting classic symptoms of withdrawal (including craving, anxiety, and depression) and (2) over the course of their careers, workaholics also develop a tolerance to the rewards of work manifest by a need for markedly increased amounts of their intoxicant of choice (work) to achieve a desired effect.

Since vocational pursuits are not generally assumed to be physically addictive (some argue that you can become addictive to the adrenaline highs that ensue from achievement), the underlying cause of the withdrawal suffered by workaholics, particularly those whose labors do not evoke euphoria (or even pleasure following achievement) must stem from the emergence of repressed psychological pain. From my perspective, the pain workaholics endure during withdrawal is elegantly captured by the Huxley quote used to open this chapter: When unable to engage in their coping strategy, workaholics suffer a near nihilistic delusion that they have no connection to others in the world or, at worst, do not exist. Thus, given their inability to achieve satiation and their vulnerability to symptoms of withdrawal and fears of dissolution, it is safe to assume that workaholics are suffering a legitimate psychological disturbance, regardless of how it is classified.

"I am doomed to an eternity of compulsive work. No set goal achieved satisfies. Success only breeds a new goal. The golden apple devoured has seeds. It is endless."

Source: Bette Davis, *The Lonely Life.*

PSYCHOSOCIAL INTEGRATION

From my perspective, the fear of dissolution suffered by workaholics is the hallmark of the disorder. While many researchers posited a correlation between workaholism and the failure to achieve intimacy, questions about cause and effect abound. For example, Machlowitz (1985) stated that "intimacy is incompatible with workaholism" (p. 77), but views workaholism as causal because of the way in which self- or externally imposed work expectations lead to a diminution of a workaholic's sex drive. Others have argued that in response to living with workaholics spouses suffer great emotional pain and disengage from their mate since a workaholic's devotion to work supercedes their desire for involvement with a spouse, family, community, or religion.

I see a different cause-and-effect relationship. As one set of researchers argued, "A workaholic is anyone who uses busyness to avoid getting in touch with personal feelings, to stay clear of intimacy" (Minirth, Meier, Wichern, Brewer, & Skipper, 1981, p. 49). Based on my clinical experience, a person who lacks the capacity to form authentic intimate ties with others is drawn to workaholism as a lifestyle because it enables him to block out the emotional pain caused by his lack of connectedness. In the final analysis, workaholics fail to invest in work for the right reasons—striving for a sense of fulfillment through labors that benefit and strengthen ties to one's community.

From a psychiatric perspective, the ability to establish and continually renew relationships with a family, community, and a belief system that gives meaning to life, is the core component of psychological health. According to Erikson (1963, 1968) who has called this process "psychosocial integration," those who fail to achieve it are doomed to search for ways to mask or cope with the pain this failed status causes. Alexander (2000) argued that all forms of addictive behavior stem from the failure to achieve psychosocial integration, something he calls *dislocation:* "[w]henever substitute lifestyles are the best adaptation that people are able to achieve (to cope with dislocation), they cling to them with a tenacity that is properly called 'addiction'" (p. 503). While there may be cause to question Alexander's premise when it comes to accounting for the etiology of addictive disorders that involve a dependence on psychoactive substances, holding that the emotional consequences of a failure to achieve psychosocial integration leads to the development of a workaholic lifestyle is compelling.

Although people can cope with the pain of dislocation by engaging in antisocial lifestyles ranging from the eccentric (e.g., avante garde artist or high-tech wizard)

"It is impossible to escape the impression that people commonly use false standards of measurement—that they seek power, success, and wealth for themselves and admire them in others, and they underestimate what is of true value in life."

Source: Sigmund Freud, *Civilization and Its Discontents.*

to the less adaptive (drug addict or gang member), considering the unique role that professional success plays in defining a sense of self in America it is not coincidental that a dominant response to the pain of dislocation is workaholism. The beauty of this lifestyle is that the single-minded pursuit of professional success through a compulsive dedication to work has all the earmarks of connectedness with none of the authentic interpersonal ties that define it, and can make it threatening. Workaholism appears to be the quintessential mode of making it in America when just the opposite holds true.

TOWARD DESIGNING TREATMENT STRATEGIES FOR WORKAHOLISM

For the purposes of the analysis that follows, workaholism is considered to be a maladaptive lifestyle that emerges when an individual attempts to cope with the failure to achieve psychosocial integration. It is also postulated that the failure to achieve psychosocial integration will likely result from either of two patterns of child rearing: (1) parental abuse that makes a child shrink from human contact or (2) parental overindulgence that instills a child with an unrealistic sense of superiority, which makes him insufferable to others. While there are degrees of damage that precipitate workaholic lifestyles and, as such, varying degrees of impairment within the population of workaholics, all workaholic lifestyles are deemed maladaptive for the purposes of this analysis.

In operational terms, workaholism can be construed as a strategic negotiation of advantageous status ("I'm really a fully functioning adult; I'm just too busy to spend time with my family; I've got to put food on the table"). As such, one would presume that any therapeutic program that enhanced social skills would be a good point of departure for the treatment of workaholism. Based on my experience, however, while this approach is an effective short-term palliative, it has few, if any, lasting benefits.

To be effective, a treatment program for workaholism must initially address the consequences of the developmental histories that give rise to this disorder. More specifically, the symptoms of a failure to achieve psychosocial integration (compensatory narcissism, isolation, shame-induced anger, control-seeking behavior) are the symptoms of a workaholic's behavioral repertoire that must be the primary focus of treatment. Not coincidental, these same symptoms are the manifestations of a workaholic's disorder that emerge in the workplace over the course of his or her professional career to disprove the claim that devotion to work is healthful.

In light of the preceding considerations, the treatment approaches presented next focus primarily on addressing the emotional consequences (disturbances) of the failure to achieve psychosocial integration and secondarily on the symptoms of workaholism (behavioral change leading to a so-called "balanced life"). The justification for this is simple: If the psychic damage that promotes workaholism is resolved, the pursuit of balance will be a natural propensity. Failure to address the antecedents of the disorder will render all balance-seeking directives inefficacious.

That said, it is not necessarily easy to help workaholics experience authentic emotional pain. Because of the fit with societal norms that workaholism enjoys (or suffers from, depending on your perspective), the best outcome one often expects from psychotherapy is an amelioration of the emotional problems that threaten a workaholic with the loss of his job.

To do the work necessary to treat workaholism, it is imperative for you to keep in mind three goals, operationalized as a set of shared assumptions:

1. First and foremost, those suffering from workaholism lack the capacity to exploit *social support,* be it from coworkers, family members, or clinicians in a healthful manner. The examination and ultimate resolution of this issue should be tied to an demonstration of how the workaholic failed to become involved in collaborative work endeavors and, ultimately, in humanistic development or spiritually satisfying pursuits that Erikson (1968, p. 138) called *generativity*—the concern for establishing and guiding the next generation, which grows out of the mature, reciprocal need to be needed and cared for.

2. You and your client must ultimately agree on an unambiguous cost-benefit analysis of the gains accrued from a compulsive devotion to work or the rewards it provides, relative to the interpersonal and spiritual losses this concern causes.

3. On the "gains accrued from work," therapy must, as early as possible, expose the causal connection between narcissistic injury and consequent shame, anger, self-esteem deficiencies (e.g., inadequacy) and how the accrual of professional rewards serve to mollify those feelings.

The manner in which these goals are achieved through a combination of psychotherapeutic techniques—selected on the basis of "goodness of fit" with each client's circumstances—are illustrated in three case histories that follow.[1] Each case highlights a different aspect of psychotherapeutic work, and none address all of the issues relevant to this population. This is so for two reasons:

1. Workaholics typically do not enter individual psychotherapy. Most find their way into marital therapy because of the disruptive consequences that workaholism has on spousal relationships. For this reason, I will not discuss

---

[1] The three cases used in this chapter were men that I treated between 1989 and 1999 while I was working in the Department of Psychiatry at Harvard Medical School. Identifying data has been changed in ways that ensures anonymity for the men described and their significant others. The aspects of the cases that were altered do not affect the clinical elements of the problems described.

how marital therapy alone can help workaholics resolve their problems and restrict my discussion to those cases where marital therapy was either contraindicated or impossible because of the patient's lack of a spouse.

2. Because of the nature of my research and clinical and consulting practices (Berglas, 2001), the workaholics I am familiar with have all enjoyed significant career success; and, by the time they see me, their lifestyle is well entrenched. For this reason, I found that helping my clients function in a healthy manner while sustaining a successful lifestyle is more often than not a major goal of therapy. This may not be the case for clinicians who see clients who have achieved less real-world success, but I believe that despite the nature of the cases presented, the techniques employed will generalize to workaholics of all social statuses.

Finally, before addressing the particular therapeutic choices appropriate for the treatment of workaholism, it is crucial to raise one concern about a strategy that is *never appropriate* for workaholics because of the nature and strength of the resistances they bring to psychotherapy: A workaholic can never be forced to withdraw from his or her professional life; and, at the outset of therapy, the mere suggestion of modifying his or her work-life to accommodate more than the inclusion of psychotherapy may precipitate hostile termination.

Most workaholics do not accept the need for psychotherapy unless or until they are subjected to an event that prevents them from working (e.g., termination or a disease such as a myocardial infarction attributed to work stress). As a rule, they cling to their lifestyle with a tenacity befitting someone who fears dissolution if unable to indulge in it. During the process of building a therapeutic alliance with a workaholic, all discussions of balance (e.g., adding recreational pursuits to one's life or cutting down on overtime) should be avoided. I have found that the paradoxical technique of *adding work* that forces a workaholic into collaborative relationships is of far greater value in heightening his awareness of the dynamics of his disorder than seeking to limit his involvement in professional pursuits. When this end can be achieved with the cooperation or collaboration of a patient's employer, the likelihood of successful treatment outcome is enhanced significantly.

Sean

The first time I met Sean, he was a 43-year-old entrepreneur brought to me for psychotherapy (as many workaholics are) by his spouse, over his protests.

"Any program that 'coaches people on the joys of the real world' is virtually guaranteed to keep job-related psychological problems flourishing at epidemic proportions because interventions based on a *predetermined notion* of what will make mankind happy are prone to backfire to one degree or another."

Source: S. Berglas, 2001, *Reclaiming the Fire: How Successful People Overcome Burnout,* New York: Random House.

Because of the strength of Sean's initial resistances to therapy and odd tenure as a client of mine, his case serves to highlight many of the difficulties involved in working with a workaholic.

Sean was the first of three children born to a socially prominent and extremely successful liquor wholesaler-distributor and his homemaker wife. Sean's parents were both of first-generation Irish Americans actively involved in the affairs of the Irish cultural ghetto in which they spent their entire lives. After earning a bachelor's degree in business studies, Sean immediately enrolled in the Marines to serve in the Vietnam War. During two tours of duty, he was combat decorated and received two Purple Hearts. Although Sean considered a career in military service, at the end of his second tour, he opted to return to Boston, get married, and begin building a business.

Professionally, Sean was an entrepreneur who refurbished ailing businesses by providing what he called "new wrinkles to old wash-ups." To his credit, he had many good ideas including the mass-market pairing of espresso bars and booksellers, long before Barnes & Noble teamed with Starbucks to do it. As his career progressed, many of the businesses he acquired in receivership were later sold for a huge profit, and Sean became known as a take-over specialist.

Sean would have happily continued to turn around distressed business holdings had his wife, a religious woman, not insisted that he stop ignoring the development of his four daughters, two of whom were in their teens. To get his attention, she initiated divorce proceedings but, while consulting a priest to get help for what was expected to be an inordinately stressful move in light of how the Catholic Church views divorce, the priest persuaded her that psychotherapy might be a preferable option. With that in mind, Sean's wife prevailed on him to see me.

Like most workaholics who have no idea of how their lifestyle is driven by compensatory needs, Sean assumed that since he had made millions of dollars and believed that he loved his wife and his family, he could easily withdraw from his business pursuits and satisfy his wife's demand that he return to church life. He also adamantly challenged the contention that he needed help. At our second session, he bragged that he had already returned to church and appointed his CFO as acting president of his business while he began to assume a chairman's oversight role—proof of his powers of self-control. With that, Sean cancelled our third session and terminated our relationship, which did not surprise me. What did surprise me was when his wife called me 9 months later to say she and Sean were divorced. She asked, despite their estrangement, that I see Sean again along with her, assuring me that this time he would be more amenable to therapy.

When I saw Sean and his then ex-wife, I learned that immediately after he withdrew from actively running his businesses to assume a role in his family, life for his wife and daughters was a living hell. He immediately embarked on a home-remodeling venture that disrupted everyone in the family. When that effort led to calamitous battles, his wife reported that he started going to church with what appeared to be "an obsessive devotion." As it turned out, Sean was obsessed, but not with prayer. When he returned to his congregation, he couldn't stand how things were being run, felt a need to rejuvenate the parish, and in a matter of months was appointed deacon.

In effect, as I later explained to Sean, he attempted to do to his home and church what he had done to bankrupted businesses—refurbish them. But he failed miserably at becoming a member of either of the two organizations his wife wanted him to be part of. Moreover, in the course of attempting to integrate within his family, Sean clashed violently with his eldest daughter because she was dating a Black Muslim. A month before his divorce became final, Sean's daughter married the man. This broke through Sean's defenses, given his bigotry. Somehow he knew he precipitated his daughter's acting out (my term, not his) and felt a genuine sadness that opened him up to the process of self-examination in the context of psychotherapy.

BREAKING THE DEFENSES OF WORKAHOLICS BY INVOLVING SIGNIFICANT OTHERS

To some, my willingness to include Sean's wife in each of the two first sessions we had is both a violation of clinical protocol and a barrier to forming a therapeutic alliance with my patient. With any other population, I would agree. But with workaholics I *always* involve significant others willing to provide me with data on the patient's flawed interpersonal relationships. The rationale for this unorthodox technique rests on the following three assumptions:

1. Since a workaholics' disorder stems from a failure to achieve authentic psychosocial integration, it would overwhelm him to be the focus of the traditional intervention used to break the resistance to treatment of an alcoholic. That said, many workaholics do marry and do achieve a quasiconnectedness with a spouse whom, to the extent possible, they trust. For this reason or to preserve an image of social competence (many business executives believe that they need a spouse to function in the world of work), I have found that even highly resistant workaholics will allow me to gather data from spouses.
2. Prior to consenting to even consider psychotherapy most workaholics will try to self-regulate their problem behavior, as Sean did, with disastrous consequences. Most family systems mount strenuous resistances to the intrusion of workaholic's attempting to reform, and it is not uncommon to find horrific battles erupting in response to their attempts to do so. Getting reports of these battles obtained from a significant other are invaluable aids in helping a patient begin to understand the trade-offs made in pursuit of his or her lifestyle and what the consequences of this controlling behavior are likely to be in any context.
3. Families of workaholics are typically organized in ways that have accommodated to the patient's disorder long before psychotherapy is ever considered. Thus, rather than risk an exacerbation of stress on a new workaholic patient, I ask that the sum total of his efforts to effect integration within his family be limited to having them support him in his *therapy* and leave his career pursuits and existing role in the family unaffected.

BREAKING DOWN RESISTANCES ONCE THE PATIENT ENTERS PSYCHOTHERAPY

Sean's decision to terminate our therapeutic relationship after two sessions the first time is not unusual because of how disruptive the process of self-assessment can be for this type of person. For this reason, I spend a number of sessions allowing a workaholic patient to acclimate to the process of self-focus before initiating what many would recognize as conventional psychotherapy. I use these preparatory sessions for what I call *"illustrated history gathering,"* a technique that I find invaluable in facilitating discussions of a patient's history that are invariably painful and actively suppressed. The way I conduct *illustrated history gathering* as follows:

1. Rather than risk an assault on workaholics' defenses or the possibility of a discussion that would shake their tenuous sense of self-worth, I ask new patients to help me understand their current status and background by "filling suitcases with memorabilia" from their immediate and distant past that highlight their achievements. I request photographs, yearbooks, awards, certificates, and the like, and tell them that I would like to hear stories about each item in what amounts to an adult form of Show-and-Tell. An added benefit of this exercise is that it makes me a supporter of their sole source of self-esteem—work achievements.
2. After a minimum of three sessions spent delving into the particulars of the events and affects the patients report when describing the items they have selected, I begin to probe for what is missing from their treasure troves of memorabilia and from their descriptions of them.
3. Without fail there are two significant "omissions" in the Show-and-Tell sessions: (1) group experiences of joy and (2) experiences of avocations. Invariably, the items chosen to represent the highlights of workaholics' history show no proud moments with families, proud moments with "team members," joyous vacations, souvenirs from family trips, hobbies, or the like. Items that most people would include for a presentation of the sort I ask patients to conduct (e.g., a wedding album, golf outings, club president's plaques, or a picture of their boat) are few.

Once patients come to understand my surprise at the dearth of depictions of achievements that have enabled them to share joy, entrench interpersonal bonds, or contribute to familial or community development, I typically have enough data to begin probing for a traditional psychohistory (see Box 12.1).

Initial Stages of Psychotherapy with Sean   Because workaholics fail to form healthy interpersonal attachments, my treatment of choice for the initial stages of a therapeutic relationship is psychodynamic insight-oriented or supportive therapy. Regardless of the school of thought a psychotherapist subscribes to, this work can achieve the following goals:

- Understanding and some resolution of the conflicts precipitating the workaholic's maladaptive behavior.
- A clarification of interpersonal events in the real world. Specifically, a cost-benefit analysis of workaholism and barriers to intimate relationships and feelings of belonging to groups.
- An alliance with a therapist who can become a "good parent" capable of helping the person analyze and cope with real-world issues. The evocation and resolution of a so-called transference neurosis is not necessary for this to

occur in most forms of psychotherapy commonly called *relationship-oriented psychotherapy.*

During sessions devoted to illustrated history gathering with Sean, I was able to help him see that none of the items he included for discussion were depictions that included his father. He had photographs that included his mother and siblings, yet when I asked where his father was (e.g., at his college graduation) he said, "He was the guy telling us where to stand, complaining that the light was wrong . . . you know, the King Photographer." After evoking a number of similar references to his father's controlling and critical nature, Sean was ready to discuss how his father constantly demeaned him.

BOX 12.1
The Berglas Diagnostic Inventory for
Serial Entrepreneurism

The following tongue-in-cheek assessment tool is designed to help workaholic clients see the errors of their ways.

How well do the following statements describe your typical behavior. Award yourself 5 points if the behavior is something you *always do,* 4 points if it is something you *usually do,* 3 points if it is something you *have done on occasion,* 2 points if it is something you *believe you have done,* 1 point if it is something you *feel you should do,* and no points if it is something *you cannot picture yourself* ever doing.

1. When on vacation at a seaside resort, I kick over sand castles in the hope that I will be asked to repair them or rebuild them with the children who created them.
2. I turn down tickets to concerts if I have heard the music (e.g., a Beethoven symphony) before.
3. I cry on Christmas day after all the presents have been opened.
4. When shopping for household goods, I get far more excited when I see the words *some assembly required* than when I see *50% Off Sale.*
5. The only cars I will own and drive are Edsels or DeLoreans.
6. My motto is, "Anyone can win at solitaire when they have 52 cards; I'll win with no more than 50 if it's the last thing I ever do."

If you scored:

- Between 0 and 12 points, you are not a workaholic!
- Between 13 and 18 points, you might be able to build a "Mom & Pop" business but will likely sell to the first person who makes you an offer.
- Between 19 and 24 points, start befriending Venture Capitalists now.
- Between 25 and 30 points, dissolve that retirement fund; you're working until the day you die.

© Dr. Steven Berglas.

THE SHAME UNDERLYING WORKAHOLISM

Virtually all of the workaholics I have treated work to excess in a vain attempt to validate either a precarious or flawed sense of self-worth. As noted, they often achieve the accolades that should afford them a sense of satisfaction and quiescence but never do. Despite external indices of objective success in their professional lives they cannot feel secure unless constantly rebuilding, revalidating, or replenishing their stores of accrued self-worth (a process that, not coincidentally, Sean did for a living). The simple reason for this is that they are often driven by feelings of shame born of abusive parenting. In Sean's case, shame was evoked from the receipt of chronic feedback from a hypercritical father whose preferred mode of correcting Sean's behavior was to call him a "dummy" and allege that he would "never amount to anything." This, in turn, prevented Sean from ever truly bonding with his father and left him with an emotional void he tried to fill with work success.

As Lewis notes in his analysis of shame, "The phenomenological experience of [a shamed] person is that of a wish to hide, disappear, or die" (1992, p. 75). I believe that there is also the fear that unless a person can somehow negate the feedback that generates the sense of shame, the shamed person will feel that he or she may die of it. While shame also induces feelings of powerlessness, it often, as Miller (1981) notes, renders those who suffer from it prone to adopting retributive behaviors. In Sean's case, and as is the case with so many workaholics, the compulsive striving for success is actually a socially sanctioned mode of beating a parent into the recognition that they were wrong. Moreover, since the many sons of high-achieving men are shamed by their father's attempts to instill high expectations for achievement in their offspring, the linkage between shame and a propensity to be driven to demonstrate, through behaviors that garner rewards, "See, you bastard, I'm not a piece of crap," is common and quite strong among workaholics.

Another consequence of shame, apart from a drive to disprove it, is rage. Shamed individuals are made to feel like pariahs and, in turn, feel rage toward those they assume have rejected them. In Sean's case, he was contemptuous of most people (as evidenced by his bigotry and subsequent estrangement from his oldest daughter), and at one point in his life found that he was rewarded for it. Items Sean included in his illustrated history gathering sessions were his medals from the Vietnam War. When describing the commendations he received, he told me in expletive-filled detail of killing "Charlie" with a passion and wanting to go on doing so but could not "because peace was at hand." When I casually noted that he seemed to have no outlet for his anger in the world or work, he laughed and reminded me, "I'm screwing people daily. When you help pull someone out of bankruptcy, you nail their ass to a wall because you have all the control."

THE LIMITATIONS OF INDIVIDUAL PSYCHOTHERAPY

Individual psychotherapy with Sean on his need to understand how work provided a facade that could mask his shame as well as provide an outlet for his rage was effective up to a point. Sean developed enough of an observing ego to gain distance from the damage done by his father's abuse. He was also able to feel appropriate pain that while his career choice—an essentially solitary pursuit of salvage operations—served to disprove his father's condemnation and refurbish both businesses and an image of selfhood, these efforts did nothing to build bonds with others. Despite this insight, I found that what our work could not alter was Sean's functional capacity to form healthy attachments. Sean even came to understand that much of his bigotry was a function of projection, but our work did not give him the skills to form meaningful attachments. Thus, after almost two years of working with him, I referred Sean to a psychotherapy group for workaholics.

I recommend referrals of this sort for a majority of workaholics I treat because our society suffers from a dearth of opportunities for people to become part of a group solely on the basis of who they are as people. Many psychotherapists believe that marital or family therapy is an appropriate resource to address this need, but, in my experience, the organization of spousal and family units is incredibly entrenched and highly maladaptive by the time a workaholic is open to addressing the emotional underpinnings of his disorder. For these reasons, I learned that attempts to integrate a workaholic into these systems is often impossible without the full cooperation of others who may be motivated to exact some form of revenge against a workaholic who has, for years, punished them. In contrast, a group psychotherapy situation comprised of workaholics allows a patient to enter, de novo, and have his disordered interaction patterns exposed without the burden of negative history to overcome. With that barrier to entry removed, a workaholics-only therapy group seems to provide the social network that can re-create for a patient the experience of close interrelationships that he failed to master en route to feeling a lack of belongingness.

The other reason I recommend group therapy for workaholics who have gained insight into their problems is that it is a form of psychotherapy ideally suited to exploring techniques for the behavioral resolution of suppressed feelings. *Suppression* (the conscious withholding of information about the self that evokes shame, anger, or anxiety) is attended to quite well by members of psychotherapy groups and ameliorated by one of the central benefits of well-structured groups: a same-boat empathy.

When a person like Sean is able to reveal that he was driven to find validation in professional pursuits to silence the ghosts of his father's demeaning harangues and discovers that other members of the group suffered comparable histories or feel inadequate or feel rage at being subjected to chronic criticism, it affords the type of support that no individual therapeutic relationship can match. Moreover, with the support of a group, workaholics can feel part of a sharing process that, historically, they were wholly deprived of.

Finally, groups re-create family settings for patients without (as noted previously) well-entrenched historical resentments to overcome. While it is expected that workaholics will all engage in maladaptive attempts to exert control over the workings of the group and will display isolative tendencies, the process of reality testing that is a core component of group work serves to demonstrate to the patient how he must separate his reactions to the group born of a flawed worldview and past conflicts. When this occurs, the feedback he receives from group members about his interaction style helps him learn healthy patterns of bonding with peers who need to be judged in real time, not because of schemata developed when the workaholic was a child.

In Sean's case, his investment in group therapy had the desired outcome. When we spoke last, he was engaged to be married and had mended fences with his eldest daughter. While he never abandoned his career as a turn-around artist,

I did receive a Christmas card from him that included a picture of him with friends on a fishing trip.

Ken

In contrast to Sean's workaholism, which was born out of a need to defend against and attempt to avenge a pattern of abuse that shamed him, many workaholics are abused by *parental overindulgence* that instills them with a disruptive sense of superiority. I often hear workaholics report that the seed of their disordered lifestyle was something one or both parents told them was a "gift"—superior intellect, a skill, or both. Unfortunately, making a child the focus of inordinate attention because he has the ability to secure materialistic rewards causes two forms of damage: (1) the belief that the child is loved only for *what he does* and cannot secure love for *who he is* and (2) the derivative conclusion that the only sort of love or approval one need seek in life derives from achievement.

What is lost to the person raised in this manner beyond the ability to achieve psychosocial integration is self-actualization: Joy from pursuing a vocation for intrinsic satisfaction alone. Actually, a developmental history that establishes an inextricable link between achievement and love ensures that work will never be intrinsically rewarding because it is always used to secure love and, hence, for extrinsic gain. Whenever you deal with a workaholic who professes that he must be the top salesman, top rainmaker (revenue generator) in a law firm, or sit atop whatever hierarchy he belongs to, you can be certain that his work is a means of securing love. Regrettably, the dogged pursuit of love via achievement striving is a fool's errand. As an old German proverb cautions, "What's the use of running when you may not be on the right road?"

For reasons not entirely clear to me, workaholics raised by parents who abuse them by generating narcissistic expectations is more amenable to psychotherapy than those who have been demeaned. While both antecedents to failed psychosocial integration doom children to have, at best, utilitarian relationships with others, It seems that workaholics who are taught that they can receive love if they achieve success familiarizes them with the process of being coached, pushed, or egged on to achievement by significant others. Because of the misinterpretation of what psychotherapy is and does, these workaholics are less resistant to working with an expert whose job it is to make them better than workaholics whose main goal is to negate felt shame. Thus, it is incumbent on the therapist, with referred grandiose workaholics, not to disabuse them too quickly of the notion that psychotherapy will lead to any and all forms of improvement they desire.

Adhering to that guideline is what made it possible to work with Ken, the most driven person I have ever been involved with in psychotherapy. When I met him he was a 44-year-old management consultant referred to me by his partner out of concern that Ken would "suffer a second heart attack and die" or be fired from the consulting firm where he worked. The friend's concern was well founded.

According to Ken's friend (who provided me with data about Ken prior to our first psychotherapy session with Ken's approval), Ken suffered a myocardial infarction when he was only 42 years old. The event occurred moments after he engaged in a screaming match with two other partners in his consulting firm, a familiar interaction pattern. Months after recovering from this event, Ken returned

"Illness is the most heeded of doctors: to goodness and wisdom we only make promises; pain we obey."

Marel Proust cited in *Life and Death in the Executive Fast Lane: Essays on Irrational Organizations and Their Leaders* by M. F. R. Kets de Vries, 1995, San Francisco: Jossey-Bass, pp. 181–182.

to work in total denial of the need to change his behavior. He argued bitterly with all members of his firm; worked a minimum of 12-hour days as he always had in the past; and, when most of his partners were having dinner, Ken would nurse single malt Scotch and wait for client meetings held at night.

The other reason Ken was being referred to me was because his firm had considered firing him. While he was invaluable as an analyst, his abusiveness was taking an incredible toll on morale. Two female staffers filed sexual harassment suits against the firm claiming that Ken's tirades created a hostile work environment, and many partners complained that they could not be on project teams with him because of his tyrannical demands to control every aspect of the assignment, including their work schedules. The managing partner of the Ken's firm decided that there was a 6-month window for Ken to turn himself around; and, armed with that knowledge, Ken's friend persuaded him to see me.

When we met, Ken's presenting complaint was, "I cannot lose my job; you must help me to learn how to deal with incompetents." He was fully cognizant that his tirades were the reason his job was in jeopardy. He realized as well that verbal assaults were not appropriate in the workplace. Unfortunately, the notion of his undergoing change to effect a rapprochement with his colleagues was alien to him. According to Ken, his tirades were the product of righteous indignation. One of his favorite phrases was, "How can I soar like an eagle when surrounded by turkeys?" Because his sense of entitlement was so extreme; because he was aware of a need, albeit the wrong one; and because Ken had 6 months to improve at work or be shown the door, I felt that Ken could tolerate the initiation of therapy without an illustrated history gathering. It turns out that I was both correct and incorrect.

The form of self-assessment in which Ken was able to participate involved his developmental history because he was acutely aware of his circumstances and quite proud of having overcome what he called his horrific start in life. In one discussion of his past Ken told me, "I could have as easily ended-up in Alcatraz as here, a success, were I not blessed with what it took to overcome the hell I was born into." What he was referring to was that Ken was the only child of immigrant parents from Poland who raised him in near poverty in New York City. His father, an alcoholic, abandoned the family when Ken was 5. Following that trauma, Ken's mother fell into a profound depression that, when she wasn't hospitalized and physically absent, left her emotionally unavailable to Ken. Like so many workaholics raised by emotionally unavailable parents, one of the earliest messages Ken received in life was of being unwanted (the message internalized by a child when a parent dies, departs, or is emotionally incapacitated). However, when Ken's mother was not hospitalized, appropriately medicated, and at least physically available to him, she spent all the time she could telling him how smart he was, how he could be her "little savior," and drilling him in academic exercises.

From Ken's perspective, his mother's "confidence in my genius" was his salvation. As it turned out, from the time Ken began the first grade he knew he could garner praise from teachers for his mental acuity. Thus, although there was never a time in his life when Ken wasn't receiving kudos, every bit of positive feedback he received was linked to performance. Unfortunately, every incremental gain in attention he accrued from the world was attributable to academic prowess. And, while academic honors and overindulgence from caring teachers is gratifying, it is a poor substitute for a proud father's smile or a loving mother's hug. As Lasch (1978) points out, child rearing that leads to a sense of narcissistic grandiosity and entitlement always results in bland, superficial, and deeply unsatisfying interpersonal relationships.

Another factor that contributed to Ken's inability to form interpersonal ties was that he was delicately built and never participated in organized athletics. He was also terribly shy (a pattern of isolation that persisted through adulthood), which prevented him from engaging in other extracurricular activities available to him. He attended City University of New York, always made the dean's list, but made no friends. After graduating, he married a girl whose interest in accounting paralleled his affection for economics and formed a childless, functional union. Ken moved to Boston to join a premiere consulting firms and after 6 years of putting in 12-to-14-hour days, made partner.

In all likelihood, Ken's life would have proceeded along this uneventful path without interruption had it not been for the economic boom of 1980s. Like so many egg heads who were transformed into powerhouses during the decade of the yuppie, Ken went from relative anonymity at his consulting firm to become a $1 million-a-year economic strategist. Under the supervision of a charismatic dealmaker, Ken's economic forecasting abilities and limitless capacity to absorb economic data made him an invaluable in-house resource.

After three sessions of exploring his history up to the time he suffered his heart attack, I asked Ken, "So what's the problem? You're doing well, why the concern?" Not surprising, he was at a loss to explain how and why folks were mad at him except to say he demanded of others what he demanded of himself. After two sessions of not getting past this remark—and seeing it strengthen every time he reiterated it—I asked Ken if I could interview members of his firm's management committee, and he said I could. As noted earlier, traditional psychodynamic psychotherapies would not condone boundary violations of this sort. That said, I find it both necessary and useful when dealing with workaholics who, because their productivity is so high, have no sense their disruption of firm morale detracted from a bottom-line calculation of how valuable they are to an organization as a whole.

I interviewed three of Ken's partners and, to a man, they professed amazement that the moment Ken experienced wealth and incremental social status he became actively abusive of others. While he was always treated as an odd-duck (like the butt of Woody Allen's joke) and a loner notorious for never attending the social events held during firm retreats, Ken was not actively problematic until he became a star. Once he recognized that he was among the top money earners in the firm, it was as though the resentments he harbored over being loved only for his work

"One of the symptoms of an approaching nervous breakdown is the belief that one's work is terribly important."

Bertrand Russell

began to emerge with a vengeance. Although Ken was accustomed to working overtime to ensure he would always be first in his class, once he was overtly successful his need to be seen as number 1, be treated as he assumed stars were treated, and to beat actual or imagined competitors for top status led to bullying and berating anyone who interfered with his perfectionistic pursuits.

As noted, my initial judgment that Ken was capable of self-assessment was half-wrong. It turned-out that I erred when it came to his capacity to look at the causal role he played in the problems at his firm; it was nonexistent. He argued that the claims of the "turkeys" were being validated only because "Some [expletives] exploited the law" and in so doing jeopardized the firm. He became adamant about his right to demand excellence of himself and others and angrily rejected suggestions I made about his need to understand his impact on others. Reminding him of the mandate to change or be fired within 6 months seemed to heighten his entitlement: "The [expletive] turkeys can hire lawyers; so can I. Plus, I'll always find work given my last five years [of being behind some headline-grabbing deals]."

Because all of the pain Ken felt was externalized into rage and because his denial was growing stronger each time my attempts at having him adopt a self-reflective stance failed, I concluded that *paradoxical intervention* (Seltzer, 1986) would be my only hope of helping him modify his interpersonal style. I should note, parenthetically, that when I worked with Ken I had never used paradoxical techniques in contexts other than inpatient behavior settings where they worked quite well with treatment-resistant patients. I knew, however, that no technique other that paradoxical intention had a chance of moving Ken, so I gave it a shot.

Rather than searching for a patient's insights, or trying to help him to interpret the emotions that entrench his resistance, a paradoxical intervention hopes to break through resistances by, essentially, pulling the patient in the direction of his resistance. Rather than trying to decrease symptomatic behavior, the symptom is "prescribed" or the patient is told not to change. On occasion, you can even encourage an increase in symptomatic behavior in the hope that by encouraging maladaptive symptoms patients will recognize the adverse consequences that arise from them.

My approach to Ken's grandiosity and need to elicit chronic validation was highly paradoxical since, given that he was a workaholic striving to achieve perfectionistic goals, he would resist assuming professional burdens external to the ones that defined him and gave validation to his narcissism. But following his mantra that he was thwarted from soaring with eagles by the "turkeys" in his firm, I thought that suggesting he devote time to a source of work in another, high-status context would both enable him to garner extra kudos and, in the process, generate a de facto withdrawal from the fray in his consulting firm.

As luck would have it, my work with Ken commenced in May, and at the time a friend of mine who was the dean of continuing education at a Boston-area business school was able to add adjunct faculty to a new MBA program for the fully employed that he was rolling out in September. I convinced him that Ken would make an ideal lecturer and Ken accepted the challenge of this new endeavor. It proved to be a match made in heaven that enabled Ken to indulge in his pathological pursuit of the spotlight in a new venue and in a healthier way.

By putting Ken in front of an audience of aspiring business executives who tolerated his braggadocio about how his insights helped structure some of the biggest deals of the decade, Ken soon lost enough of his need to demand star treatment from his consulting-firm colleagues to make his presence in the firm tolerable without directly addressing the source of his demandingness. Moreover, by spending more time involved in teaching and less time berating others (although the total hours he worked per week actually increased), Ken inadvertently allowed colleagues to operate more freely and the number of clashes he got into dropped dramatically.

GENERATIVITY VERSUS STAGNATION: THE UNIQUE PROBLEM THAT WORKAHOLICS HAVE EXPERIENCING CONNECTEDNESS

Ideally, an ancillary benefit of introducing Ken to teaching was to enable him to experience the joys inherent in what the Protestant work ethic argued that the purpose of work should be: Doing good for others. Erikson called this *generativity*. As far as I know, this never occurred. Once Ken's work conflicts went into remission, he terminated therapy in an appreciative way but without effecting a true cure. My guess is that Ken is enjoying a life today filled with what most workaholics endure: professional success (or at least clear indications of competence within a restricted realm), and pseudointimacy, or what Erikson (1968) called *stagnation*.

Stagnation, akin to what social scientists call *identity dependence,* is the belief that My job = My self, whether conscious or not (Berglas, 2001). The major problem born of this symptom of workaholism is that it renders a person so dependent on gaining chronic reaffirmation of self-esteem that overwhelming anxiety and fears of dissolution threaten the person's sanity when divorced from the source of one's identity for a period as brief as a weekend. To protect against these lapses of identity maintenance, Erikson argues that people learn to achieve pseudointimacy with others—modes of keeping people near you in contexts that will ensure that you can use them to validate your sense of self. The workaholic project leader who keeps direct reports around him working overtime or Ken conducting discussion groups for interested students ad nauseum are examples of the ways in which workaholics achieve pseudointimacy.

The problem you are likely to confront when seeking treatment strategies to help workaholics achieve authentic generativity is that their modus operandi—controlling anxiety, masking shame, and structuring self-worth through overwork—corrupts the process. In my experience with workaholics, this has been my greatest source of frustration: being thwarted in my efforts to help them experience and understand the distinction and experiential difference between authentic generativity and what Erikson (1968) called *overextension.* Simply stated, overextension is an excessive desire to be the most extraordinarily giving or involved individual one can be. Stated another way, overextension is an impediment to generativity that arises when an individual pursues generativity as an end, not as a means. When workaholics *learn* as opposed to *feel* that there is value in creating interpersonal alliances, they engage in overextension as a means of building a coterie of "yes-men" who will validate their worth. When healthy people engage in generativity, they nurture others or give of themselves for the joy it generates.

Next is an example of one of my workaholic patients whose progress in psychotherapy was almost undone by overextension but who ultimately came to experience feelings of generativity. Jacob had a developmental history that was similar to Ken's but was complicated by a problem that proved to be his salvation: hypochondriasis.

Jacob

Jacob was referred to me for psychotherapy by his physician who diagnosed him as suffering from depression. In reality, I believe that in addition to being a workaholic, Jacob suffered from *anhedonia,* the absence of pleasure or the ability to experience it. Anhedonia, a concept first identified in the 1890s has been largely ignored in favor of more obvious, quantifiable symptoms of depression. But for a number of workaholics that I have treated, this absence of pleasure from all life activities—particularly from the experience of the joy that success should engender—seems a better depiction of their dominant mood.

Many workaholics who have been raised to expect success find that achieving it is merely attaining good-enough status, hence, the festering rage in people such as Ken and the manifestation of depression in people such as Jacob. Parenthetically, I find that workaholics I diagnosed as anhedonic are only minimally responsive to psychopharmacological treatments that relieve depression in most other patients. Anhedonia seems to stem from a cognitive schemata that does not include components that recognize joy. (See Box 12.2.)

When I met Jacob he was a 33-year-old tax attorney with a major firm. Despite his youth, Jacob's work led to his referral to the most complex, and important, tax matters dealt with by the transactional attorneys in his firm. The only other remarkable aspect of this never-married man with no interests apart from work was that he suffered from hypochondria (a problem suffered by many stressed workaholics) his entire life. The event that precipitated Jacob's visit to his physician, which led to his referral to me, was the death of Jacob's mother who, for most of his life, was his only living relative. After three clinical work-ups that revealed no medical disorders, his physician informed Jacob that his complaints were psychogenic in origin and that he needed psychotherapy.

Jacob was raised in a predominantly Jewish suburb of Boston in lower class circumstances by two very strict parents. Jacob's father died he was 11 and his mother doted on him to excess (a common antecedent of hypochondria). In addition to monitoring every sniffle and cough he emitted, Jacob's mother hovered over him like a hawk when he did his homework and was intolerant of anything less than a straight-A report card. She extolled his academic prowess, while demanding that he actualize it or be guilty of committing what she said was a sin. Jacob obliged by graduating from Harvard College and Harvard Law School. He then joined a law firm and made partner in five years—three below the average.

Jacob was surprisingly cognizant of how his upbringing led him to a lifestyle of workaholism. At the outset of our work together he told me, "I have never done anything but work since childhood; it's all I have ever known." Yet try as I

BOX 12.2
Alice Miller's Analysis of Workaholics Like Jacob

When a child is made the focus of inordinate attention because he has the ability to secure materialistic rewards, two forms of damage occur: (1) the belief that the child is loved only for *what he or she does* and cannot secure love for *who he or she is* and (2) the derivative conclusion that the only sort of love or approval one need seek in life derives from achievement.

Alice Miller analyzed another consequence of this incredibly damaging pattern of child rearing: alternating phases of grandiosity and depression. According to Miller, "They are two sides of the medal that could be described as the 'false self,' a medal that was actually once given for achievements For these people, success brings no psychological satisfaction but, only, the need to keep performing."

Source: From *The Drama of the Gifted Child: How Narcissistic Parent Form and Deform the Emotional Lives of Their Talented Children* (revised edition, p. 43) by A. Miller, 1981, New York: Basic Books.

---

would, I could not find a way to help him perceive that a sense of satisfaction is something that typically derives from pursuit of a vocation. In a very real sense, the only way Jacob could allow himself not to work was to experience psychosomatic symptoms—a dynamic he developed with his mother whose sole ministrations of caring were contingent on his illnesses. Because success was an expected, unrewarding, pro forma enactment of a duty; and caring was a consequence of illness, with his mother gone the only human contact he knew how to solicit was with doctors—first his physician and then me.

I felt that Jacob's workaholic lifestyle was intractable unless I was able to maneuver him into a new role in life. At the time I met Jacob, I had begun working for the nation's largest legal consulting firm and as a consequence became familiar with the alarming rates of workaholism within the legal profession. Moreover, because lawyers traditionally suffer extremely high rates of burnout, I reasoned that a call to the managing partner of Jacob's firm (with his permission) would give me a chance to help him. In what proved to be a discussion that was enthusiastically welcomed by Jacob's managing partner, I detailed a plan to have the firm sponsor an initiative that would give partial credit toward the minimum number of billable hours expected of partners (in this case, 2,200 per year) for pro bono work done on behalf of recognized community programs.

With the cooperation of his firm, the paradoxical intervention I structured involved Jacob providing pro bono tax assistance (like a one-man H&R Block) to the members of the Boston chapter of B'nai B'rith (a Jewish community service group) that expressed financial need. While the work he was asked to do for this group was technically unchallenging for a man with his skill and experience, I knew that the interactions his clients would have with him would be qualitatively different from those he was accustomed to. For people in need who can rarely access professionals of Jacob's status, there is a tendency is to bring him every manner of concern that is on their minds.

As expected, people who asked Jacob for help preparing their taxes also solicited advice for concerns such as navigating the morass of red tape involved in helping a relative emigrate from Russia, getting a scholarship for a child, finding affordable insurance, and the like. In contrast to the routine requests of corporate clients who turned to Jacob for state-of-the-art techniques of sheltering money, his new clients saw him as an emporium of advice.

The paradoxical intervention worked like a charm, for a while, until Jacob's workaholic tendencies took over. Rather than savoring client contact, Jacob began filling every available waking moment with new cases. This, on top of his firm-related work, served to distract him from hypochondria, but did nothing, as would be predicted from an understanding of overextension, to help him begin the process of forging relationships. When I discussed this with Jacob and suggested that involvement in group psychotherapy would be helpful, he explained, "I can barely carve out the time to see you."

Sensing that my paradoxical intervention misfired, I was ready to admit having failed Jacob until I received a call from the supervisor of volunteer services at B'nai B'rith expressing concern over problems Jacob was causing. As luck would have it, Jacob's overextension was interfering with the work of other volunteers. Jacob was accused of stealing cases from volunteer attorneys and a CPA and publicly criticizing the efforts of these professionals. In one instance, Jacob caused a split between the son of one of his clients and a psychologist working with the client's son when Jacob scheduled a meeting with the boy to discuss his academic underachievement.

When I brought this issue to Jacob's attention, he became furious. He accused me (with some justification) of fostering his role in pro bono work and now recanting. My response was that I wasn't concerned with his work but his failure to derive joy from his labors and his inappropriate efforts to control the work relationships of others. As expected, as Ken and so many workaholics are wont to do, Jacob claimed that his superior intellect mandated his involvement in the relationships of others "when fools might foul things up."

In response to this crisis, I employed a second paradoxical intervention: Sensing that Jacob had forged a therapeutic alliance with me I said, "Well, I seem to have screwed up by placing you in a context where you have encountered problems, so I guess you should end our relationship as you seek to end the relationships of B'nai B'rith counselors who err in their work with their clients." Jacob's overt distress over the prospect of losing me allowed me to help him process—for what seemed to be the first time in his life—how an interpersonal relationship may have value apart from any performance outcomes related to it.

RATIONAL-EMOTIVE THERAPY

Most workaholics do not present themselves to psychotherapists with symptoms amenable to rational-emotion therapy (REBT; or cognitive-behavioral therapy, the two of which are often confused), because of their history of being rewarded for what they do. Moreover, the societal mandate for their work product makes it hard to have them see adverse consequences emerging from their behavior. Just the opposite holds true. Whereas it is easy, using the A-B-C (Ellis, 1962; Ellis

& Dryden, 1987) model favored by many therapists (A = Antecedent or activating event; B = Beliefs or thoughts the patient has about A; C = Consequences, or what the patient feels, thinks, or does as a result of A and Bs), to see that triggers to excessive alcohol consumption lead to adverse consequences, the same cannot be said, traditionally, for work.

The classic exception to this occurs when workaholic patients form alliances—typically with therapists or, in some circumstances, with family members—and the patient Bs (a belief that they must control interactions, do stellar work, and ensure that incompetent behavior is not allowed to go uncorrected) can be seen as having an adverse consequence, namely, a threat to a relationship. My paradoxical threat to have Jacob control our psychotherapeutic relationship by ending it allowed me to conduct an intensive course of REBT (exploiting Ellis's classic list of cognitive distortions) and help Jacob examine the schemata or automatic thoughts that led to his problems at B'nai B'rith:

1. *Demandingness:* When workaholics are amenable to REBT, the presence of "shoulds" and "musts" are the cognitive distortion that will emerge first. In Jacob's case, the feeling that he "must help people with all problems" because of his intellectual prowess was the easiest to exploit. The greatest gains he experienced in therapy came from being able to see that knowledge was not necessarily a precursor to the establishment of a good relationship. For the first time, Jacob came to see that caring resulted in bonding. Through this, he was also able to see the etiology of his hypochondria—the outgrowth of bonding even though his mother had no medical skills to ease his ailments.

2. *Low frustration tolerance:* Jacob had zero tolerance of the counseling efforts of others at B'nai B'rith that, in his mind, were not 100% on target. I used my "errors" in working with him to help him see how, as relationships develop and people bond, errors may be self-correcting.

3. *All-or-nothing thinking:* This distortion is also common among workaholics who, as noted, fear dissolution if not working. In my experience, workaholics merge all-or-nothing thinking with what cognitive-behavioral therapists call "catastrophizing" ("If I don't get an A the world will end"). Jacob and I were able to examine his "If I don't work, I'm nothing" schemata with great success.

In traditional REBT, once a patient is capable of seeing how triggering events have adverse consequences, the therapist adds D and E to the ABC model: D = Disputations of the irrational belief ("Just because I'm the smartest, it does not mean I'm the best counselor") and E = Effective rationales ("Even if others can bond better with some clients than I can that does not mean I am bad, won't have clients who need me, or am not valuable to B'nai B'rith"). After several months of rehearsing and reworking the ABCDE model with Jacob, there was a marked dissipation of his attempts to control the counseling program and a broadening in his role with B'nai B'rith. He experienced an end to his anhedonia to the extent that he actively enjoyed the kudos he received from his pro bono work. Armed with this gain, I was able to refer Jacob to a workaholic's therapy group. Three years after Jacob began working with me, as a result of his joining a Jewish Singles group sponsored by B'nai B'rith, he got married.

CONCLUSION

Workaholism is a disorder that is difficult to treat, but it is not intractable. Flexibility in terms of acceptable treatment goals and appropriate techniques is key to sustaining a therapeutic relationship with a cohort of patients who, by definition, do not form healthy bonds with others but who are talented, successful, and very often intelligent—all double-edged swords in terms of helping them achieve desirable life goals.

As evidenced in the cases presented, the therapist's willingness to acknowledge failure or, at minimum, accept it and regroup without hesitation proves invaluable when treating workaholics for several reasons: (1) It demonstrates good parenting to a person who has never received it; (2) it creates the perception that being momentarily out of control does not precipitate disaster; and (3) it generates new work within the therapeutic context that, at minimum, enables the patient to feel that he can earn an A in psychotherapy—a very significant feeling for these sorts of individuals.

I must also reiterate the need for you not to fear stretching the boundaries of psychotherapy to involve significant others, employers, or if appropriate, executive coaches (trained in psychiatry, see Berglas, 2002) who now proliferate in the workplace. In contrast to psychotherapy with chemically dependent people, you cannot divorce a workaholic from vocational pursuits. Exploiting them for the patients' benefit can be achieved if you accept that the therapeutic alliance will be enhanced—not threatened—by the inclusion of adjunctive resources.

On the other hand, clinicians must be alert to a set of problems not addressed in this chapter (because of the myriad logistical problems that each individual case presents) born of workaholics losing their jobs because of down-sizing or other economically mandated cutbacks. In essence, these forced withdrawals from workaholics primary coping strategies will, in all likelihood, generate a set of symptoms (typically, agitated depression) that should be treated with a combination of both pharmacological interventions, supportive therapy and what the business world calls *outplacement counseling*—helping careerists land new jobs. The facilitative role that trained outplacement counselors can play in providing symptomatic relief to a workaholic may—to the chagrin of the psychotherapist—not only be more highly valued by workaholics than the ministrations that clinicians afford, but may actually be more important to clients' short-term mental health. Being flexible enough to cede control to nonclinicians when treating workaholics is something most clinicians are loathe to do, but must, with this unique population, when clients are traumatically deprived of their compensatory lifestyle.

Finally, because our understanding of workaholism and workaholics is constantly evolving, I would suggest that you not fear adding to state-of-the-art theorizing about the syndrome and client population by assuming that there is no definitional dogma to restrain you in developing novel treatment strategies of your own. For example, while not described, one of the more interesting types of workaholics I see (and still, to this day, get referred to my executive coaching practice) are those whose success is predicated on the active falsification of work-related credentials. To some extent, these individuals are driven to work out of a fear of being exposed as liars, but at bottom they are far more concerned with having a fabricated sense of narcissistic entitlement torn away from them. For this population, an understanding of compensatory narcissistic drives is critical.

The clinician who is versed in that literature, as well as existential psychiatry, can work wonders with a subset of workaholics who are just beginning to be understood as differing from those suffering a narcissistic personality disorder and workaholism, while manifesting features of both disorders.

RECOMMENDED READING

Because our understanding of workaholism is only in the pupal stage of development, I believe books that describe the syndrome are incomplete. I recommend that those wishing to do additional reading examine the context within which workaholism flourishes and the desired resolution of the syndrome, which will shed light on the subject.

Berglas, S. (2001). *Reclaiming the fire: How successful people overcome burnout.* New York: Random House. This book is for clinicians who want a better understanding of how I coach workaholics. Although most of the case presentations do not fall within the rubric of workaholic, the analysis of how people cope with narcissistic injuries through work is, nonetheless, relevant.

Csikszentmihalyi, M. (1975). *Beyond boredom and anxiety.* San Francisco: Jossey-Bass.

Csikszentmihalyi, M. (1997). *Finding flow.* New York: Basic Books. These books are ideal places to start if you want to understand the ultimate treatment goal for workaholics.

Lasch, C. *The culture of narcissism: American life in an age of diminishing expectations.* New York: Norton. To understand the context within which workaholism flourishes, nothing is better than this book. The most far-reaching analysis ever written of how and why Americans behave as they do. Although ostensibly dated, it rings true—and will for decades.

Miller, A. (1979). *The drama of the gifted child.* New York: Basic Books. To understand the antecedents of workaholism, nothing is better than this book. This work is a must-read for anyone who treats workaholics (or those suffering from any form of narcissistic injury). It is the best analysis on record of how being raised to assume that one has high-potential or special strengths can prove to be a double-edged sword.

REFERENCES

Alexander, B. K. (2000). The globalization of addiction. *Addiction Research (8)*6, 501–526.

Berglas, S. (2001). *Reclaiming the fire: How successful people overcome burnout.* New York: Random House.

Berglas, S. (2002, June). The very real dangers of executive coaching. *Harvard Business Review,* 86–92.

Berne, E. (1964). *Games people play.* New York: Grove Press.

Csikszentmihalyi, M. (1999, October). If we are so rich, why aren't we happy? *American Psychologist,* 821–827.

Ellis, A. (1962). *Reason and emotion in psychotherapy.* Seacaucus, NJ: Citadel.

Ellis, A., & Dryden, W. (1987). *The practice of rational-emotive therapy.* New York: Springer.

Erikson, E. H. (1963). *Childhood and society* (2nd ed.). New York: Norton.

Erikson, E. H. (1968). *Identity, youth and crisis.* New York: Norton.

Huber, R. M. (1971). *The American idea of success* (pp. 11–12). New York: McGraw-Hill.

Lasch, C. (1978). *The culture of narcissism: American life in an age of diminishing expectations.* New York: Norton.

Lewis, M. (1992). *Shame: The exposed self.* New York: Free Press.

Machlowitz, M. (1985). *Workaholics: Living with them, working with them.* Reading, MA: Addison-Wesley.

Miller, A. (1981). *The drama of the gifted child* (rev. ed.). New York: Basic Books.

Minirth, F., Meier, P., Wichern, F., Brewer, B., & Skipper, S. (1981). *The workaholic and his family: An inside look.* Grand Rapids, MI: Baker Book House.

Oates, W. (1971). *Confessions of a workaholic: The facts about work addiction.* New York: World Publishing.

Seltzer, L. F. (1986). *Paradoxical strategies in psychotherapy: A comprehensive overview and guidebook.* New York: Wiley.

Spence, J. T., & Robbins, A. S. (1992). Workaholism: Definition, measurement, and preliminary results. *Journal of Personality Assessment, 58,* 160–178.

Spruell, G. (1987). Work fever. *Training and Development Journal, 41*(1), 41–45.

Weber, M. (1958). *The protestant ethic and the spirit of capitalism.* New York: Charles Scribner's Sons. (Original work published 1920)

PART VII

COMPULSIVE BUYING

CHAPTER 13

Understanding and Diagnosing Compulsive Buying

HELGA DITTMAR

MANY OF US enjoy shopping and buying consumer goods. We get a buzz out of browsing through shops and stores that sell our favorite things and satisfaction from buying new goods that we really desire—at least some of the time. In the current consumer culture of North America and also Europe, it is often not so much economic and utilitarian value we are interested in but rather psychological benefits. Almost all of us have purchased goods at some time to cheer ourselves up, and many see money and material possessions as tangible signs of personal success. We use consumption to improve our image, self-esteem, or relationships with others. Buying impulses are normal and frequent and can help people feel better about themselves, at least temporarily. So what could possibly be wrong with a bit of retail therapy? Why not buy things that make you feel special and distinctive, particularly after a bad day at work or a row at home? Retail therapy has become normalized in mass consumer societies like ours, and to some extent we all negotiate our sense of identity and our relationships with others through money and material goods. Material goods can give people the means of creating valued experiences, enhancing interpersonal relationships, and maintaining a sense of identity and self-continuity. For example, it is important for elderly people to take treasured personal possessions into nursing homes or sheltered accommodations to counteract the trauma of relocation (Wapner, Demick, & Redondo, 1990) because the possessions symbolize their life experiences and relationships and, thus, the historical continuity of self. I first became interested in the psychological meanings and functions of material goods when I wrote my doctoral thesis on material possessions and identity, later published as a book (Dittmar, 1992b). I became convinced that material goods can be genuinely important and healthy for our sense of who we are, but that they

411

also can be unhealthy. We can become preoccupied with material goods, trying to use them as remedies for underlying difficulties within ourselves—an attempt usually doomed to failure. This concern led me to use my insights on having material possessions on researching the process of and motivations for buying consumer goods.

There is a dark side of buying material goods—consumption can dominate individuals' lives and become an addiction. We are talking about much more than the occasional shopping extravaganza when we spend just a little bit too much or when people respond to the topic by saying, jokingly, "I'm a little bit of a shopaholic myself, you know." It is time that compulsive buying is taken seriously as an addiction, rather than smiled on as the fashionable pastime of affluent people who frequent the boutiques and designer shops out of boredom. Imelda Marcos's voluminous shoe collections or Elton John's spending sprees come to mind as epitomizing this (misconstrued) stereotype. In contrast to fantasies conjured up about affluent people, there is really nothing amusing about the reality of "shop until you drop." Mass media has picked up on the problem of compulsive buying and the life stories, experiences, and confessions of shopping addicts and shopaholics have become commonplace. The danger is that by seeing shopping addiction and addicts everywhere, we may trivialize what can be a very serious disorder. In Box 13.1, there is a summary of an interview with Nancy, who took part in one of my research studies and who, at that time, was just recovering from compulsive buying. She is not an extreme example, particularly as far as her level of debt is concerned, and her experience gives a flavor of what is typical and common in compulsive buying.

In contrast to seeing shopping addiction everywhere, there is a widely shared assumption in the clinical literature that compulsive buying is a deviant and

---

BOX 13.1
Summary of an Interview with a
Compulsive Buyer

For Nancy, aged 35, there is only impulse buying; there is no planned buying apart from food. If she sees something in a shop she likes, she must have it. She can't stop herself. It is always clothes and jewelry, smart clothes mainly, a size 12, which she desires to be. Shopping is an excuse to go outside the house. It does lift her up for a few hours. When home, she does not try on the clothes, but puts them away in the loft for fear her husband will find out. It is all her fault, she thinks. She feels guilty. She has driven the family into debt. She says that she cannot tell her husband because he would walk out on her. She started overspending after the birth of her daughter about 8 years ago. Since she did not have money of her own, she applied for credit cards. She complains that it is too easy to get them and that credit limits are increased without consideration of whether the applicant can pay. When she had about $13,500 worth of debt on her credit cards, she decided to go to a bank and take out a loan. She is paying back $399 per month, and now has two years and approximately $9,000 to go. With the interest, her repayments will add up to about $22,500.

abnormal activity that is qualitatively distinct from ordinary consumer behavior. Yet, simply dichotomizing individuals into those who are compulsive in their buying and those who are not may also miss important aspects of the phenomenon. Compulsive buying may well constitute a more extreme form of a continuum with particular kinds of everyday shopping. There may be similarities as well as differences between ordinary and compulsive buying. This is the view that I explore in this chapter.

Let's consider some of the similarities first. An increasing part of our shopping is psychologically motivated. That is rather different from the traditional rationality assumption that casts us as economic actors and consumers who carefully, systematically, and dispassionately collect and weigh information in our attempts to get the best possible goods and services for ourselves. Taking a number of studies together (Babin, Darden, & Griffin, 1994; Dittmar, Long, & Meek, in press; Lunt & Livingstone, 1992), we can identify three main dimensions of buying motivations. In addition to the *functional* and utilitarian aspects of shopping (convenience, good value for money, and practical use), there are two sets of psychological motivations: *emotional-social* and *identity-related*. Emotional-social concerns include emotional involvement in shopping (buzz or enjoyment), direct contact with the good (touching or trying on), and social interaction, both with family or friends and sales personnel. Identity-related dimensions refer to self-expression and buying to move closer to a better or ideal self. Different aspects of buying may be important for different goods—you probably buy saucepans for functional reasons and clothes for self-expression—or be more salient at certain times—a leisurely weekend browse through your favorite shops has probably more to do with emotional, social, and identity-related concerns than a trip to buy tools and material to redecorate your bathroom when you are short of both time and money.

It is worth stressing that there are systematic gender differences in overall buying orientations. Enjoying shopping and browsing, the atmosphere and buzz in the street and social interaction while shopping are all much more important to women than to men (Dittmar & Drury, 2000). Campbell (2000) also reports that women have highly positive attitudes, associating buying with a "leisure frame," while men tend to have negative attitudes, seeing buying as work that they want to accomplish with minimum input of time and effort. Women tend to focus on the (often enjoyable) *process* of buying, whereas men focus on the *outcome*. This general tendency might be less strong or even reversed for particular types of goods, such as tools or computer equipment, which are predominantly bought by male consumers. Notwithstanding such exceptions, it can be plausibly argued that, overall, buying consumer goods is more integral to the personal and social identity of women, at least in terms of traditional gender identity, and, therefore, plays a stronger emotional, psychological, and symbolic role for them compared to men (Fischer & Gainer, 1991). Notwithstanding this current gender difference, psychological involvement in shopping may be increasing for young men. This gender issue is picked up again in the next section of this chapter, with particular reference to compulsive buying.

In addition to psychological motivations, there is a second, related area of similarity between compulsive and ordinary buying. Many of our purchases are made impulsively, rather than in a planned fashion, where we have selected the exact good that we will buy before we go out shopping (often after extensive information searches and price comparisons). Impulsive purchasing has three main characteristics: (1) It is spur of the moment, done with little deliberation and prior planning; (2) our emotional and psychological involvement is high, we *really* want this particular good or goods; and (3) our desire is so strong that we disregard financial constraints and consequences (Dittmar & Drury, 2000; Verplanken & Herabadi, 2001). Impulse buying is common in at least half of the general population (Lejoyeux, Adés, Tassian, & Solomon, 1996; Rook & Fischer, 1995), and there is emerging evidence of impulsive buying in compulsive consumers (DeSarbo & Edwards, 1996; Dittmar, 2001). This is how one compulsive buyer, a woman, put it: "Impulse buying is if I go to buy something like grocery and I come back with a £300 [~$450] suit" (Dittmar & Drury, 2000, p. 123).

Notwithstanding these similarities in psychological motivations and impulsive buying, there are differences between ordinary and excessive buying. It is possible that these differences are more a matter of degree rather than kind and this is probably what German psychologist Scherhorn had in mind when defining addictions as us becoming "dependent on our habits" (1990, p. 42). Buying becomes an addiction when it takes on excessive dimensions: in terms of frequency, financial costs (credit abuse and debt), and subjective importance, leading to impairment in personal, social, and occupational functioning. Sufferers experience urges to buy as irresistible. The subjective experience is one where shopping takes over, having control over you rather than you having control over your buying habits. Regardless of what they can afford, sufferers carry on despite inflicting harm on themselves and those around them. The distinction between compulsive and healthy buying behavior is also explored in the next chapter on treatment (see Box 14.5 in particular).

An alarmingly high number of individuals engage in repetitive impulsive and excessive buying that results in serious personal, social, and financial consequences. They experience psychological distress over being out of control, their functioning in relationships and at work is impaired, and they get into serious debt, or even bankruptcy. In defining compulsive buying, there is a lack of agreement on specifics, but we find a common consensus in characterizing the core problem as buying that is impulsive and uncontrolled, with negative outcomes for the individual concerned. Compulsive buying is used here in a wide sense, given that it may involve "compulsive purchasing" of goods, "compulsive spending" of money or "compulsive shopping" without necessarily purchasing anything (Nataraajan & Goff, 1991).

LIVING IN A MASS-CONSUMER SOCIETY

Buying-mania (the literal translation of the Latin *oniomania*) is not altogether new, but was identified and described by both Kraepelin and Bleuler in the early part of the twentieth century. Their work on categorizing psychiatric syndromes was highly influential, and, in that sense, had an impact on the conceptualization of psychiatric symptomatology feeding into the development of the *Diagnostic and Statistical Manual,* the main clinical tool in diagnosing psychiatric disorders that, currently, is in its fourth revised version *DSM-IV-TR.* Yet, it was not until the mid-1980s that research publications started to appear on compulsive buying—first in the United States and Canada and then in Europe.

The Figure 13.1 shows the number of published articles in scientific journals from 1985 onward, demonstrating an accelerating interest in compulsive buying, particularly marked in the past 8 years or so. While research interest does not simply equate with prevalence, it is plausible to assume that there is a link, where clinicians and psychologists found themselves confronted with increasing numbers of people whose shopping is causing them sufficient problems to seek help. The argument that compulsive buying has recently and swiftly emerged as a mass phenomenon also is supported by the sudden attention in the mass media, as well as by the finding reported in several studies that excessive buying tendencies are stronger among younger rather than older people (Dittmar, 2003). Taken together, this points strongly toward the importance of social context and social causation for an understanding of compulsive buying. While it is individuals who suffer from compulsive buying, they do so in societies that are characterized by mass consumption, materialism, and an obsession with "to have is to be" (Fromm, 1976). We have to understand compulsive buying as an addictive disorder that is embedded in the major economic, social, and cultural changes that have transformed consumer behavior in Western developed economies.

Our thoughts, feelings, and behaviors as consumers have changed dramatically over the past two or three decades. People now have more money to spend than ever. Since the mid-1970s, personal disposable incomes in the United States and European countries have risen enormously. Between 1990 and 2000, the increase per person was 45% in the United States and 27% in the United Kingdom. In addition, it is now easier than ever to spend money that you do not have. During that same 10-year period, the amount of outstanding consumer credit (in real terms, taking inflation into account) has roughly doubled in the United States to a staggering $1,561 billion, and the average amount of personal debt per U.K.

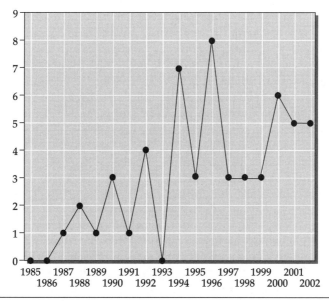

Figure 13.1 Published Research Studies on Compulsive Buying from 1985 Onward. *Note:* This graph excludes conference papers, dissertations, and books. The research studies appeared in journals that are abstracted by PsychInfo.

resident in 2002, including man, woman and child, was over $17,000. From 1970 to 1990, the number of credit cards in use in the United Kingdom has multiplied more than fourfold. In the United States, the average number of credit cards per family just exceeded one in 1989, a comparable figure to the U.K. household in 1992. By 1998, the U.S. average had risen to almost one and a half credit cards per family, and the U.K. average for 2002 was just under two and a half credit cards per household. A recent television documentary screened by the United Kingdom's BBC followed a young man who spent one afternoon going to banks, stores, and shops to get as much credit as possible in the form of unsecured loans, in-store accounts, credit cards, and so on. He gave truthful information on his current income (around £11,000 or $16,500) and found himself with no-questions-asked credit worth £40,000 ($60,000) after just a few hours.

Credit facilities have mushroomed and, while consumer choice has clearly increased, people also experience the easy availability of credit as a negative pressure to spend and consume (Lunt & Livingstone, 1992). This is where sufferers of shopping addiction lay blame, at least in part, for the extent of their overspending:

> I got into difficulties because it's so easy to run up debts. Oh, you know, in the past if you wanted a bank loan you had to say what it was for . . . Now you get showered with letters inviting you to take out bank loans and . . . consolidation loans . . . [to] pay off all your debts. So, you get a bank loan and pay off all your credit cards and then, of course, you've got nothing outstanding on all your credit cards, so you start again. (Dittmar & Drury, 2000, p. 132)

In terms of social and cultural changes, consumption has assumed a more central role in everyday life (Featherstone, 1991; McCracken, 1990). While French social theorist Baudrilliard's description of contemporary life as "perpetual shopping" is probably exaggerated, it is fair to say that leisure activities increasingly involve consuming, that shopping itself has become a leisure and lifestyle activity, and that shopping malls are becoming centers of socializing and socialization. For example, U.S. adults spend most of their time in shopping malls after home and work, going there to eat or drink, meet friends, or take the kids out, as well as browse and buy (Bloch, Ridgway, & Nelson, 1991). Material goods have come to play a stronger psychological role for us, and we value and buy them as means of regulating emotions, gaining social status, and as ways of acquiring or expressing self-identity and aspiring to an "ideal self" (Dittmar, 1992b, 2001). The link between material goods and identity is used frequently in advertising, where goods are marketed as symbols of an ideal self. When we buy consumer goods, we consume not only the product, but also the symbolic qualities associated with it. In fact, a recent therapy approach developed in Spain (see Chapter 14) includes explicit consumer education, where compulsive buyers are aided in their recovery by being taught to understand the cues given by television commercials and print advertisements, and thus being able to resist them.

Brands of consumer goods have also changed in meaning. Originally, manufacturers and advertisers used the branding of mass-consumed goods as nothing more than a way to communicate to consumers that their product is of high and dependable quality. With the recent glut of *parity products* (goods that are identical in their functional qualities), branding is now primarily used to add value to consumer goods by constructing, manipulating, and exploiting the symbolic meanings associated with them. Partly echoing psychological functions of material goods, brands can be seen as performing two roles, in addition to their practical role, for consumers' identity: an *emotional role* by providing a means of identification, *self-expression*, or link to the past, and a *social role* by providing shorthand communication of who we are (Franzen & Bouwman, 2001). There is emerging evidence that brands may be more strongly linked to identity construction for young people, in particular teenagers, than adults (Dittmar, in press); and, therefore, brand buying may become excessive for the next generation.

Given that consumer culture has an increasing impact on our psychological well-being and our sense of identity, compulsive buying has to be considered as a significant modern or postmodern addiction, not only because of its potential severity but also because it seems to have increased so rapidly over the past two decades. As we will see, there is some indication that it may become even more prevalent if recent trends among adolescents are any indication. Therefore, I am particularly pleased to see compulsive buying included in this *Handbook of Addictive Disorders* among addictions that have longstanding recognition such as alcoholism and gambling. I wholeheartedly agree with the authors of Chapter 14 that it is timely for compulsive buying to assume "its rightful place" among the addictive disorders characterizing this century.

HOW WIDESPREAD IS COMPULSIVE BUYING?

When it comes to definitions, compulsive buying is complex. And when it comes to causes, it is likely to be multidetermined. But before starting to tackle these issues, I address a more basic question first: Just how big is the problem? How widespread is compulsive buying in the United States, Europe, and other countries? The direct answer is: We do not know, at least not exactly. The reason is that no epidemiological studies exist as yet that profile the prevalence in the population through controlled sampling. But, it is possible to give a more indirect answer by examining previous research studies on compulsive buying. In a recent review, I identified 25 empirical studies and classified them into four types, according to the samples and sampling strategies used (Dittmar, 2003). First, there are studies that use psychiatric in- or outpatients, who often presented initially with a different problem, such as depression. The second type compares compulsive buyers with (usually matched) samples of ordinary buyers, but there are two different approaches to identifying compulsive buyers. They are either self-identified, in the sense that they have sought help from support services (debt, psychiatric, or general social), or self-help groups, or have responded to advertisements asking for people with buying problems to come forward; or, they have been identified through an assessment tool, such as a screener questionnaire, specifically designed to diagnose compulsive buyers. The most commonly used screeners are described in the next section of this chapter. For the moment, it is sufficient to understand that these assessment tools can measure an individual's tendency toward compulsive buying, as well as offer a cut-off score for classifying individuals as compulsive as opposed to ordinary buyers. Third, there are studies that focus exclusively on compulsive buyers to study their thoughts or behaviors in some depth. Forth, some investigations examine compulsive buying tendencies as a continuous variable in nonclinical samples (e.g., school-aged adolescents). This classification of studies is important for two reasons: It helps us to identify the kinds of studies from which prevalence estimates can best be made, and the sampling strategies used are key when consid-ering demographic profiles of compulsive buyers in terms of income, age, and—most significantly—gender.

PREVALENCE

The best estimates about the prevalence of compulsive buying can be made from studies on general population samples that use a diagnostic screener to identify compulsive buyers. The classic large-scale survey in the United States carried out by Faber and O'Guinn (1992) identified just over 8% of their adult sample as com-pulsive buyers. Two later, smaller U.S. studies on younger samples give figures as high as 16% (Magee, 1994) and over 12% (Hassay & Smith, 1996). In my own re-search project on compulsive buying in the United Kingdom, 13½% of respondents were classified as compulsive buyers among a subsample of adults who returned a postal questionnaire sent to addresses that were selected so that they residentially matched (by town and street) those of respondents who contacted a self-help group (Dittmar, 2003). All other respondents in the project were contacted either through a self-help organization, advertisements, or snowballing (individuals suggest peo-ple they know personally who may have problems with uncontrolled buying, and these individuals are then contacted by the researchers). Not surprising, when using sampling strategies explicitly aimed at people with shopping problems, the proportion of compulsive buyers identified among this subsample was much higher at almost 46%. Thus, estimates from general population samples using a diagnostic screener to identify compulsive buyers range from 8% to 16%. These figures are alarmingly high, but it is possible that they present a slight overestimate because they rely on people willing to take part in research on shopping, which may include a greater number of individuals who have a psychological involvement in consump-tion, and hence have compulsive buying tendencies. Clinicians who treat psychi-atric patients tend to give more conservative estimates. Black (1996) suggests that 2% to 5% of adults are affected. It is likely that the truth lies somewhere in the middle. Yet, turned into actual numbers, even the lowest estimate of 2% translates into more than 10 million sufferers in the United States, about half a million in the United Kingdom and a million in Germany. Even the most restrictive preva-lence estimates demonstrate the need to understand such prominent excessive forms of behavior.

THE GENDER QUESTION

In terms of demographic profile, an obvious expectation is that compulsive buying is linked to a person's financial circumstances because individuals who are less af-fluent are likely to run up debts beyond their means more quickly than people who have money. Surprisingly, my review found little evidence of such a link: Compul-sive buying was not associated with either income or number of credit cards in the great majority of studies that had collected such data. Thus, it appears to afflict in-dividuals at all levels of income. However, there is a systematic difference with re-spect to age: Compulsive buyers are younger on average than comparison samples. They are usually in their 30s, while their ordinary buyer counterparts tend to be in their 40s or older. This age difference, as well as the negative correlations between age and compulsive buying tendency reported in a number of investigations, are all consistent with the proposal that rapid increases in excessive buying are recent and have to be understood in the context of the economic, social, and cultural changes in Western mass-consumer societies outlined earlier where buying consumer goods now fulfills a stronger psychological function for identity and emotions, while it has become progressively easier to spend money, particularly money one does not have.

More dramatic than age, and consistent across all studies, is the strongly lop-sided gender ratio in compulsive buying.[1] Not only do women have higher scores than men on scales that measure compulsive buying tendencies but also reports of the percentage of women among samples of compulsive buyers range from 74% to over 93%, with the great majority around 90%. If we take this percentage at face value, we have to conclude that compulsive buying affects almost exclusively women.

However, there are two sets of arguments that urge caution. Almost two-thirds of studies seeking to recruit compulsive buyers used sampling strategies that are more likely to reach women than men, such as appeals on breakfast television or talk shows or contacting people who wrote to self-help organizations advertised in women's magazines. This is further compounded by the common reliance on respondents who sought help for their compulsive buying from support services, psychiatrists, or self-help groups or who have responded to advertisements asking for people with buying problems. Thus, individuals likely to seek help for personal problems are overrepresented and known to include more women (Travis, 1993). In addition, women may also perceive less stigma attached to admitting that they have problems with shopping than men. Thus, it is possible that male excessive buyers are systematically underrepresented as a consequence of these sampling strategies. Previous research studies appear to be gender blind, in the sense that this is treated as incidental, although there is agreement that the majority of compulsive buyers are female. While recognizing the difficulties that all researchers face in recruiting compulsive buyers, this state of affairs nevertheless highlights the need for a study that, in addition to women, explicitly targets male populations.

My U.K. project tried to explore the gender ratio in the incidence of compulsive buying as a research issue in its own right. Given the aim of reaching male compulsive buyers, we engaged in a range of activities aimed at persuading men to participate in the study, particularly those with a strong interest in shopping. Advertisements were placed in popular men's lifestyle magazines, flyers were distributed to men at local shopping malls, and a number of radio interviews were arranged, aimed at male audiences. Snowballing was also used, with the expectation that a number of men would provide contacts for further male participants.

In the general population sample (i.e., residentially matched with respondents who contacted a self-help organization for compulsive buying), the gender ratio was extremely skewed with 92% women and 8% men, consistent with findings in previous studies. Of more interest for the gender issue are the respondents recruited through contacts with self-help groups, advertisements, and snowballing, where we made special efforts to target men. This is likely to have some success,

---

[1] The only exception is one study of depressed patients that failed to find a statistically significant difference in gender ratio (Lejoyeux, Haberman, Solomon, & Adés, 1999), but this was because of the small sample size ($n = 21$ compulsive buyers), given that 45% of depressed women were compulsive buyers compared to 20% of depressed men.

given that the percentage of male compulsive buyers was more than twice as high as among the general population sample, at almost 18%. However, this still means that the great majority of sufferers (82%) were women. Thus, a person identified as a compulsive buyer in our U.K. project was six times more likely to be a woman than a man.

Compulsive buying was assessed through a diagnostic screener, and this gender imbalance can be examined further by scrutinizing the distribution of scores among women and men classified as compulsive buyers. All of these have scores above the cut-off point, but the scale end in the compulsive buying range nevertheless indicates different levels of severity in the sense that scores just above the cut-off point indicate a milder form of compulsive buying than scores that lie at the extreme end of the scale. Indeed, the distribution of male compulsive buyers' scores is radically different from that of female compulsive buyers. Men had a significantly lower average total score than women, and their scores were concentrated at the lower end of the scale's compulsive range. The compulsive range of the scale was divided into four equal parts, with the first indicating the lowest quartile of compulsive buying and the fourth the highest quartile of compulsive buying. Men scored predominantly in the lowest quartile (69%), and none at all scored in the highest quartile. In contrast, more than 70% of women score higher than the lowest quartile, with over 30% in the third quartile, and over 18% at the top of the scale in the fourth quartile. The preliminary conclusions drawn from these findings are that the proportion of men who are compulsive buyers is not only very small, but their total scores vary little and have a strong tendency to fall just above the cut-off point. Therefore, these few men show a homogeneously mild form of compulsive buying compared to their female counterparts.

Given that the U.K. project collected extensive demographic information, we can ask the interesting question: Who are these men? Comparisons with women compulsive buyers and the whole U.K. sample showed that this group of men had three special characteristics: They were significantly younger, more highly educated, and had a higher income. Thus, their profile indicates that these are young, professional, and financially stable men, who may well constitute a new group of compulsive buyers, with an interest in grooming and fashion, and whose gender-role identification is less likely to be traditionally male compared to older or less educated men.

Thus, at this time, compulsive buying seems atypical in men in three ways: First, it appears to occur rarely; second, if it does occur, it is in a mild form; and third, it is specific to a young, highly educated, high-earning subpopulation of men. Thus, while not gender exclusive, compulsive buying behavior affects women predominantly. The findings reported here fit with the proposed cultural link between shopping and women's gender-role identification, given also that men identified as compulsive buyers have characteristics associated with a less traditional male-gender identity, such as being very young or highly educated. It is important to emphasize that a gender explanation of compulsive buying should not be misunderstood as an essentialist account of differences between male and female consumers. Rather, I argue that buying behavior is likely to remain gendered as described earlier only as long as cultural norms and socially shared representations continue to frame shopping as closely linked to women's social, personal, and gender identities (Dittmar et al., 2003). In addition, there may also be social-structural reasons why shopping is a more likely compensation strategy for women than men, who might have better opportunities for engaging in different activities, such as excessive sports or going down to the bar with their friends. For instance, primary caregivers and homemakers—who are still predominantly women—may well be able to bring their children along on shopping trips but not on excursions to the gym. However, with changes in the occupational and domestic roles of women and men, and the recent, increasing emphasis on appearance, body image, and consumption of goods also for men, it seems likely that compulsive buying may become more common in men. To clarify whether this is the case, future studies should systematically study the gender ratio in compulsive buying in different age cohorts. Moreover, there is clearly also a need for crosscultural research, to address two further questions about prevalence. It would be informative to study non-American and non-European mass consumer societies, such as Hong Kong or Japan who are highly developed economies, but have a different, more collectivist cultural heritage. Also, there is benefit in examining countries that have engaged with global consumerism only relatively recently, such as the posttransition Eastern Block countries, which appear to be characterized by a frantic hypermaterialism.

WHAT IS COMPULSIVE BUYING?

To date, clinical models constitute the main perspective, which use the terms *compulsive buying* or *shopping addiction* and treat this behavior as similar to other types of psychiatric disorders, such as impulse control, compulsive-obsessive, or substance abuse disorders. Some believe that compulsive buying is directly induced by depression (e.g., Lejoyeux, Tassian, Solomon, & Adés, 1997). In the current diagnostic manual *DSM-IV-TR* (American Psychiatric Association [APA], 2000), compulsive buying is included in the residual category Disorders of Impulse Control Not Otherwise Specified. While there is not a definition that all would agree with in every detail, there is agreement on three core features of compulsive buying: The impulse to buy is experienced as irresistible, individuals lose control over their buying behavior (although the nature and extent of this loss remains a matter of debate), and sufferers continue with excessive buying despite adverse consequences. These three core features are addressed in turn next, although there is some conceptual overlap between them, particularly between the notion of irresistible impulses and controllability.

When discussing prevalence, it was mentioned that compulsive buying is assessed and diagnosed with various screeners and scales. Invariably, these include items that refer to the three core features identified. The two most widely used screeners are the compulsive buying scales developed by Valence, d'Astous, and Fortier (1988) and by Faber and O'Guinn (1992).[2] The items of these scales are given in full in Table 13.1. You can use these scales for self-assessment if you follow the instructions given at the bottom of the table on completing and scoring each of the two screeners.

In the validation study of their screener, Faber and O'Guinn published a scoring equation for their scale as well as a cut-off point for classifying somebody as a compulsive buyer. The validation study by Valence et al. (1988) compared how

---

[2] Two other scales used less widely, but worth mentioning, are the Yale-Brown Obsessive-Compulsive Scale-Shopping Version (Goodman et al., 1989) and the Edwards Compulsive Buying Scale (Edwards, 1993).

Table 13.1

The Two Most Commonly Used Diagnostic Scales for Compulsive Buying

Compulsive Buying Scale[a]

1. Please indicate how much you agree or disagree with the statement below. Place an X on the line which best indicates how you feel about the statement.

	strongly agree	somewhat agree	neither agree nor disagree	somewhat disagree	strongly disagree
a. If I have any money left at the end of the pay period, I just have to spend it.	___	___	___	___	___
	(1)	(2)	(3)	(4)	(5)

2. Please indicate how often you have done each of the following things by placing an X on the appropriate line.

	Very often	Often	Sometimes	Rarely	Never
a. Felt others would be horrified if they knew of my spending habits.	___	___	___	___	___
	(1)	(2)	(3)	(4)	(5)
b. Bought things even though I couldn't afford them.	___	___	___	___	___
c. Wrote a check when I knew I didn't have money in the bank to cover it.	___	___	___	___	___
d. Bought myself something in order to make myself feel better.	___	___	___	___	___
e. Felt anxious or nervous on days I didn't go shopping	___	___	___	___	___
f. Made only the minimum payments on my credit cards.	___	___	___	___	___

Calculating your score:

Please use the equation given below, and substitute the question number (e.g., *Q*1a) with the number given for the line where you placed your X. So, for example, if you had placed your X on the line for "neither agree nor disagree" for question 1a ("If I had any money left at the end . . ."), then you would replace *Q*1a in the equation with 3. And, to carry on, if you had placed your X for question 2a on the line indicating "never," then you substitute *Q*2a in the equation with 5. You repeat this process until you have replaced all question numbers. You can then calculate your score.

$$\text{Equation} = -9.69 + (Q1a \times .33) + (Q2a \times .34) + (Q2b \times .50) + (Q2c \times .47) + (Q2d \times .33) + (Q2e \times .38) + (Q2f \times 0.31)$$

If your score is −1.34 or lower, you are classified as a compulsive buyer.

[a] From "A Clinical Screener for Compulsive Buying," by R. J. Faber and T. C. O'Guinn, 1992, *Journal of Consumer Research, 19,* p. 468. ©1992 by R. J. Faber and T. C. O'Guinn.

Table 13.1   *Continued*

Compulsive Buying Scale[b]

Please express the extent to which you agree or disagree with each of the following statements. Please place an X on the line which best indicates how you feel about each statement.

	(5)	(4)	(3)	(2)	(1)
When I have money, I cannot help but spend part or all of it.	—	—	—	—	—
I am often impulsive in my buying behavior.	—	—	—	—	—
For me, shopping is a way of facing the stress of my daily life and relaxing.	—	—	—	—	—
I sometimes feel that something inside pushed me to go shopping.	—	—	—	—	—
There are times when I have a strong urge to buy.	—	—	—	—	—
At times, I have felt somewhat guilty after buying a product, because it seemed unreasonable.	—	—	—	—	—
There are some things I buy that I do not show to anybody for fear of being perceived as irrational in my buying behavior.	—	—	—	—	—
I often have an unexplainable urge, a sudden and spontaneous desire, to go and buy something.	—	—	—	—	—
As soon as I enter a shopping center, I have an irresistible urge to go into a shop and buy something.	—	—	—	—	—
I am one of those people who often respond to direct mail offers.	—	—	—	—	—
I have often bought a product that I did not need, while knowing that I have very little money left.	—	—	—	—	—
I am spendthrift.	—	—	—	—	—
I have sometimes thought, "If I had to do it over again, I would . . ." and felt sorry for something I have done or said.	—	—	—	—	—

Calculating your score:

Each X that you placed correspond to a number: 5 for "strongly agree," 4 for "somewhat agree," 3 for "neither agree nor disagree," 2 for "somewhat disagree," and 1 for "strongly disagree." Please add together the 13 numbers for your Xs to get your total scale score. If your score is 42.2 or higher, you are classified as a compulsive buyer.

[b] From "Compulsive Buying: Concept and Measurement," by G. Valence, A. d'Astous, and L. Fortier, 1988, *Journal of Consumer Policy, 11,* p. 426. ©1988, G. Valence, A. D'Astous, and L. Fortier. The original measurement scale as given in the source contains three additional items, which were later eliminated. The modified version published in d'Astous, Maltais, and Roberge (1990) was shortened to 11 items ("I am one of those people who often respond to direct mail offers" and the last item "I have sometimes thought . . ." were deleted) and uses simpler formulations for a few items. For instance, "I often have an unexplainable urge, a sudden and spontaneous desire, to go and buy something" becomes "I often have a real desire to go shopping and buy something." Thus, these two scales are very similar to each other. The criterion score on the modified scale is a total score of 36 or above (Elliott, 1994). Reprinted with permission.

ordinary and compulsive buyers scored on their scale. The average total score of the compulsive buyer sample can be, and has been, used as a criterion cut-off point for classification. The Valence compulsive buying scale or a later modification (d'Astous, Maltais, & Roberge, 1990) has been used in Canadian and European studies and focuses on both psychological and financial aspects of buying behavior. The Faber and O'Guinn screener has been employed predominantly in U.S. research and has a relatively stronger focus on financial aspects. Clinical interviews are also used to verify a compulsive buying diagnosis, and these often use the draft diagnostic criteria proposed for inclusion in the next version of the *DSM*, which are reproduced in Table 13.2. Example items, one each from the two screeners outlined in Box 13.2, that address each of the three core addictive features of compulsive buying are:

1. *Irresistible impulses:* "If I have any money left at the end of the pay period, I just have to spend it" and "As soon as I enter a shopping center, I have an irresistible urge to go into a shop and buy something."
2. *Loss of control:* "Bought things even though I couldn't afford them" and "I sometimes feel that something inside pushed me to go shopping."
3. *Continuing with excessive buying despite aversive consequences:* "Felt others would be horrified if they knew of my spending habits" and "When I have money, I cannot help but spend part or all of it."

The ways that compulsive buyers themselves talk about these three core addictive features is illustrated through interview excerpts in Box 13.2, which gives typical expressions and accounts.

IRRESISTIBLE IMPULSE

In research that focuses on the perspective of the sufferers' own experience, compulsive buying is described as an "inability to control an overpowering impulse to buy" (O'Guinn & Faber, 1989). The first three excerpts from in-depth interviews with compulsive buyers in Box 13.2 capture the sense of "I've got to have that" (A) and not being able to walk out of shops without having bought something (B and C). Some researchers see this behavior as belonging to the spectrum of obsessive-compulsive disorders (OCDs), characterized by intrusive thoughts, uncontrollable urges to perform a particular behavior, and negative affect (Black, 1998). A compulsion is "an unwelcome pressure which the person experiences as *alien to himself*" (Scherhorn, 1990, p. 34, emphasis in original). Maybe, for most people, the best-known manifestation of this type of behavior is compulsive hand washing and an obsessive fear of dirt and contamination. From this perspective, the irresistible impulse to buy is seen less as a matter of intense desire (an internal force) and more a matter of being driven by forces outside the individual.

However, it is commonly reported that compulsive buyers have feelings of excitement and relief while shopping and purchasing goods, although they may well feel dejected, regretful, or guilty after they get home. This means that they experience a mix of both positive *and* negative emotions rather than feeling negative emotions throughout the different phases of the entire shopping episode: before, during, and after buying. This led some researchers to question whether excessive buying can be meaningfully understood as a compulsion (e.g., Scherhorn, 1990).

BOX 13.2
Excerpts from In-Depth Interviews with Sufferers to Illustrate Core Addictive Features

IRRESISTIBLE IMPULSE

A. You see something and you think, "I've got to have that" and you buy it.

B. I like to see the new things in the shop and I like to tempt myself to see whether I can actually walk by the shop and not go in and buy anything, but I usually can't [laugh]. I have to go in and I almost feel that I can't go out of the shop without having got something.

C. No, I can't tell you how bad it is. . . . I can't walk out without buying it.

LOSS OF CONTROL

D. I couldn't go home with money left in my pocket. It became a habit.

E. If I saw something I liked, I had to have it. Financial considerations didn't enter my head.

F. You're not [pause] in control. I suppose it's a hunger, it's like kind of, really hungry [pause], not hungry in food in that sort of, symbolic, but you're hungry for something. So I must have, go home, heavy [laughs], got bags to carry. So, it's like I've filled my life with something that day and I need a good feeling every day.

G. I'll check that I've got my credit cards, and I'll be saying to myself . . . . It's like having a split personality. Go away, walk away, get on a bus, get a taxi home even. Get a taxi, go straight home, think about it. . . . Well, one side of me's saying, "So what, it's only money, it's my money, I can spend it as I wish, I've got no other pleasures. I don't go out, I don't mix with people, I don't drink, I don't smoke." And then the rational side of me'll be saying, "No, don't spend it, but save it until next week and you'll have twice as much to spend."

CARRYING ON DESPITE ADVERSE CONSEQUENCES

I. I could not cut that card up. It was like cutting my wrist. . . . It's like losing, it's like cutting my toe off really. It's a life line. It is just like losing a part of me.

J. I might be going past the dress shop and I see something in the window and I say, "That looks nice." I go into the shop, then I see something else. And then I say, "That looks nicer than the ones in the window." And I go in and I am saying, "I am not going to buy these things, I am just going to try them on." So, I go in and try them on and I say, "Mmh that looks all right, I wonder whether there is anything else that goes with it." So, then I try on other things that would go with it, and I might go in interested in one thing and I will come out with three or four others. And I

(continued)

can come out with three or four or five things all the same, just different colours. . . . I have to go in and I almost feel that I can't go out of the shop without having got something.

K. But I blame these credit card companies for making it so easy to get the credit card. 'Cos if they know that you had trouble in the beginning, why do they let you? Even now I've blacked my name, they still send me leaflets about credit cards. And I've told them that I don't want any credit cards, but they still send them to you. Not so many, but they still send them. If you, if you've got, say, a two thousand pound limit and you, you get up to that, well, they say, "Oh, would you like another thousand?" don't they? And they keep bringing your limit up and then you keep spending.

There are good arguments that it is more like an addiction than a compulsion because behavior that is pleasurable, at least initially, is used to discharge tension and negative affect. Excerpt B explicitly refers to the pleasure of seeing new goods and to temptation. Anxiety, feeling bad about oneself, and depression are all common mood states for which buying and spending becomes a form of self-medication (needs and rewards in compulsive buying are discussed in more detail in a later section of this chapter). In fact, if compulsion is understood in the narrow and specific sense just outlined, the very term *compulsive* buying is likely to be a misnomer, and *shopping addiction* may well capture the nature of the disorder. I argue that the term *excessive buying* may be best of all (e.g., Dittmar, 2003) because it avoids built-in assumptions about how this behavior should be conceptualized. However, I will nevertheless continue to use compulsive buying in this chapter because this term is used predominantly in the clinical literature.

The proposal that compulsive buying has strong impulsive elements is at the core of clinicians' perspectives who see it as an impulse control disorder: the failure to resist the impulse to behave in a way that is ultimately harmful but is pleasant at the time and relieves a sense of tension (e.g., Faber, Christenson, de Zwaan, & Mitchell, 1995). Pathological gambling is a widely known example of an impulse-control disorder. However, a conceptual criticism of proposing compulsive buying as a form of impulse-control disorder is that the impulsive nature of this behavior has hardly been studied so far. All we have at the moment is some evidence concerning general impulsiveness in compulsive buyers, and—for the first time to my knowledge—I have examined impulsive buying specifically in the U.K. research project. A French study of depressed patients reported a higher level of impulsivity among compulsive buyers (Lejoyeux et al., 1997), and an examination of predictors of compulsive buying tendencies failed to find any links with a measure of general compulsiveness from the Minnesota Multiphasic Personality Inventory (MMPI) but established impulsiveness as a strong predictor (DeSarbo & Edwards, 1996). We have found in the United Kingdom that compulsive buyers engage in more impulse buying compared to ordinary consumers, but they do so in a goods-specific way, which means that they are high on impulse buying particularly for clothes, appearance-related goods (shoes or make-up), and music items (Dittmar, 2001). Recently developed draft diagnostic criteria combine both compulsive-obsessive and impulsive elements by emphasizing a maladaptive preoccupation with buying or shopping impulses and behaviors, which results in serious consequences for sufferers, causing "marked distress, are time-consuming, significantly interfere with social or occupational functioning, or result in financial problems" (see Table 13.2). These draft diagnostic criteria were developed for inclusion in the next revision of the *DSM*, thus making the case that compulsive buying should be regarded as a distinct and clearly identifiable disorder in its own right.

LOSS OF CONTROL

When discussing an irresistible impulse as a core feature of compulsive buying, the question of losing control over one's behavior is clearly implicated. While already touched on, it is worth discussing issues around loss of control as the second core addictive aspect. Compulsion would imply a loss of volitional control, that is, individuals become incapable of exercising their wills. This is a perspective that is somewhat different from the idea that people have a strong desire to shop or buy and then fail to resist this impulse. This impulsive notion of loss of control is quite similar to ordinary impulse buying, characterized by a lack of planning and deliberation, emotional and psychological involvement, and disregard for financial consequences. Almost all of us have experienced this kind of impulsive buying, which is captured by this man, who is an ordinary consumer:

> For me, an impulse purchase is something generally—it'd be more expensive than I wanted to purchase or . . . it's deciding that you want something and going for it, and then worry about the consequences afterwards. (Dittmar & Drury, 2000, p. 124)

It seems that impulsive buying can become more extreme for compulsive buyers in just "having to have it" no matter what, but it still seems similar rather than radically different in kind, as shown by two sufferers' interview responses, the first from a woman and the second from a man (excerpts D and E in Box 13.2). Even if their behavior (or some part of it) can be meaningfully described as extreme impulse

---

Table 13.2
A Draft of Diagnostic Criteria for Compulsive Buying

A. Maladaptive preoccupation with buying or shopping or maladaptive buying or shopping impulses or behavior as indicated by at least one of the following:

  1. Frequent preoccupation with buying or impulses to buy that is/are experienced as irresistible, intrusive, and/or senseless.

  2. Frequent buying of more than can be afforded, frequent buying of items that are not needed, or shopping for longer periods of time than intended.

B. The buying preoccupations, impulses, or behaviors cause marked distress, are time-consuming, significantly interfere with social or occupational functioning, or result in financial problems (e.g., indebtedness or bankruptcy).

C. The excessive buying or shopping behavior does not occur exclusively during periods of hypomania or mania.

Source: "Compulsive Buying: a Report of 20 Cases," by S. L. McElroy, P. E. Keck, H. G. Pope, J. M. Smith, and S. M. Strakowski, 1994, *Journal of Clinical Psychiatry, 55*(6), pp. 242–248. Reprinted with permission.

buying, excerpt F indicates that there is a common subjective experience of losing control in the sense that shopping comes to dominate one's life—at least at particular times. You become preoccupied with thoughts and feelings about shopping, with the sense that you *need* to go shopping, and you actually spend a lot of time browsing and buying goods—sometimes even when you should be working or devoting time to your family or friends. It is as if the binoculars through which you look at life have narrowed in focus where buying has assumed center stage, and all other concerns are a blur at the periphery of your field of vision.

Yet, despite this subjective experience of shopping being in control of you rather than the other way around, there is some control left. Sufferers often describe internal dialog and struggles (see excerpt G) about whether to go shopping or not, and many manage to refrain from buying on some occasions. During recovery, it is important that treatment programs emphasize compulsive buyers' responsibility for learning to handle their money and buying behavior to empower them to regain control (see Chapter 14). Notwithstanding this, it is also important, at the same time, to combat feelings of self-blame, shame, and guilt if you suffer from compulsive buying, and to remind yourself that we live in a mass-consumer society that fosters excessive buying and debt. We need to be careful that the medicalization of compulsive buying does not lead us to focus exclusively on the individual as the cause of the problem while overlooking the social context as a cause.

Earlier, I identified impulse buying as a similarity between ordinary and compulsive buying, but it is important to remember that ordinary buying also does involve planned and deliberate purchasing, not only impulse buying. However, the argument that there are similarities between compulsive buying and ordinary consumer behavior—when people buy impulsively—questions the assumption in much of the clinical literature that compulsive buying is a deviant activity, qualitatively distinct from our everyday behavior. Instead, there may be a *continuum of uncontrolled buying* with varying degrees of extremity (e.g., d'Astous, 1990; Scherhorn, 1990), where "consumer behavior falls on a normal-abnormal continuum with an ill-defined middle that is culture and context specific" (Hassay & Smith, 1996, p. 742) and where "compulsive buying may be considered a progression from normal to impulsive spending, to a means of escape from stress and anxiety, and finally to gross addiction" (DeSarbo & Edwards, 1996, p. 232). Thus, the extent of losing control is a problematic issue, and it seems reasonable to think of this loss as progressively increasing along the continuum from ordinary to impulsive to addictive buying. Yet, while the proposition of a continuum is not new, there is, as yet, little research on underlying motivations that may be common to both ordinary and compulsive buying. As you will see, motivations related to mood and identity seem particularly important, and they are discussed in the next section.

CARRYING ON DESPITE ADVERSE CONSEQUENCES

As made clear in the draft diagnostic criteria in Table 13.2, and as already suggested in the two core features discussed so far, compulsive buying does have serious consequences for sufferers. Thus, the third core addictive feature is that they carry on with their behavior in the face of a range of adverse consequences. What may be most useful here is a simple list of examples that fall into four different categories of consequences: finances, time, distress, and functioning in diverse areas of one's life (personal, social, and occupational). People who engage in some excessive buying some of the time could use this list as potential warning signals that they may be moving toward the addictive end of the continuum.

Finances   This is the most obvious adverse consequence we think of with respect to compulsive buying. Buying more than you can afford may be relatively mild at first—dipping into savings earmarked for a large purchase or project (e.g., car or holidays), making increasing use of one's credit or store cards, or extending limits on these cards. Unfortunately, it is too easy to get more credit and store cards, and once you are on the mailing lists of one or more companies, offers of further or new cards come unsolicited through the mail. Unless customers are credit black-listed, there are few company policies to check or ensure that they are financially capable of making payments. Statements that tend to emphasize the minimum payment for that month, and many people find that they focus on this piece of information rather than on the amount of debt that is accumulating. As one compulsive buyer put it: "You don't think about paying back later; it only looks like $5.00 a month."

In addition to store and credit cards, there are numerous unsecured personal loans available, and there is no thorough, routine check by companies or banks on whether customers are already committed to repaying loans elsewhere. Some people try borrowing money from family, friends, and then acquaintances to get them through a repayment bottleneck, which they describe to their lenders as temporary. They may even manage to convince themselves that the financial bottleneck is only of a short duration, but—as they increasingly get into debt—juggling cards, loans, and accounts will eventually fail. Debts of tens of thousands of dollars, or even hundreds, can accumulate frighteningly fast, and repayment schedules become impossible. Some sufferers end in extreme financial ruin: Their houses are repossessed or they have to declare bankruptcy. However, although the most obvious, money is not the only problem.

Time   The preoccupation with buying and impulses to buy can become time consuming, starting to take up a significant space in people's lives. This can take the form of thinking about shopping, fantasizing longingly about new goods and the benefits that they will bring, or visualizing in detail shopping trips and how it feels to browse, touch, or try goods. This can reach such an extent that it is hard to concentrate on one's everyday affairs at home and at work; attention slips and commitments or planned transactions get forgotten. In place of such preoccupation in thoughts and feelings, or in addition to it, people may actually find themselves spending a large part of their time shopping, whether it is walking through the high streets or malls or looking through and ordering from catalogues or Internet retail web sites. Excessive time can take the form of frequency, where people engage in shopping much more often than they like, or length, where they spend much longer on individual shopping trips than they really wanted or can afford.

Distress   It is no great surprise that sufferers become distressed over such expenses of money and time. People begin to sense progressively losing control over their affairs and lives, interspersed with firm intentions to stop, pay back the money, and get off the shopping merry-go-round. Such struggles are emotionally and psychologically draining. People's experience of losing control and finding themselves on yet another shopping spree gives rise to a range of negative emotions: shame, self-blame, guilt, anxiety, and—not least—depression. The studies carried out by Lejoyeux and colleagues in France showed that compulsive buyers are likely to suffer from depressive symptoms. His research strategy was derived from the conviction that depression gives rise to compulsive buying as a way of relieving the symptoms (feeling low, sad, or dejected). He studied depressed patients, finding in one study that over 40% could be clinically diagnosed with compulsive buying (Lejoyeux, Haberman, Solomon, & Adés, 1999). However, this model of depression as the cause and compulsive buying as the effect does not find unequivocal support when considering recent treatment trials that use antidepressant medication (see discussion of Black's SSRI trials in Chapter 14). It makes intuitive sense also to consider the opposite cause-effect relationship: Depression and dejection are an outcome of compulsive buying. We will see in the discussion of evidence cited in support of psychiatric perspectives, that a range of mood and anxiety disorders are regularly found in a number of compulsive buyers. This documents that there is a link between mood and compulsive buying, but it is difficult to assess whether extreme emotional states are cause or consequence. Let us just conclude that compulsive buyers' distress can and does involve a range of negative emotions, which are likely to come to dominate more and more over the momentary high that shopping affords.

Functioning   Given the consequences outlined so far, it is easy to see that an individual's functioning becomes impaired. The more sufferers become one dimensional in their concerns, the more other interests are likely to be neglected. These may include leisure pursuits that usually offer some satisfaction and fulfillment, thus supporting personal well-being, either physical, artistic, or academic. Commitments and arrangements may be broken. And impairment in personal functioning will invariably have an effect on your immediate family. Children, partners or spouses, and other family members may experience sufferers' preoccupation as a form of withdrawal from them, giving them the feeling that they receive little attention and care. Marriages and long-term relationships where partners live together may come under severe strain. Part of this may be that partners feel neglected emotionally and psychologically, but there is also the real, hard-hitting effect of excessive spending on joint finances. Sufferers often try to hide their purchases and the bills from their partners, but with escalating debts, discovery looms increasingly larger. The fear of discovery and intense guilt about spending money that should be devoted to the partnership or family adds to sufferers' distress. In some cases, relationship breakdown or divorce results, but it is encouraging that in many others spouses or partners are understanding and come to play a supportive role in the recovery from compulsive buying. Families and partners can be invaluable in helping sufferers to regain a sense of self-esteem so that they become able to put the buying addiction behind them, gradually.

Friends and social activities may also suffer as individuals focus on their shopping addiction and carefully built-up and maintained networks may start to crumble and need rebuilding. Finally, in addition to personal, familial, and social functioning, compulsive buyers may start to experience difficulties in their work, whether at home or in an occupation. Lacking motivation and concentration in paid employment, being late, having lunch breaks that are too long (because of spending too much time in the shops), using Internet access at work to browse and shop are just some of the signs that occupational functioning is affected. Compulsive buyers' sense of confidence and efficiency at work lessens and colleagues and superiors are bound to notice changes in attention and behavior at some stage.

Despite negative effects, sufferers find it extremely hard to part with their addiction. One compulsive buyer made this case dramatically by likening cutting up her credit card to cutting her wrist, and losing a part of herself (excerpt I in Box 13.2). Another's narrative casts her as a double victim of her own compulsion and of the pulling power of shops and goods (excerpt J), and the complaint that credit companies keep thrusting offers on you, irrespective of financial situation and credit record, is common (excerpt K). Not every compulsive buyer will experience all of the consequences outlined in this section, and there is also variability in severity. Yet, having considered the possible consequences, I think the message has to be that if you feel any doubt about your buying behavior, get advice and help now—it is never too early!

PSYCHIATRIC DISORDER OR SEARCH FOR A BETTER SELF? CLINICAL AND SOCIAL PSYCHOLOGICAL PERSPECTIVES

When it comes to explaining the causes of compulsive buying, psychiatric and clinical perspectives are the main approaches to date, which tend to treat it as a specific manifestation of general psychiatric disorders. These approaches tend to focus on four main types of psychiatric problems, all of which have been touched on already. Compulsive buying is seen as belonging to the spectrum of compulsive-obsessive disorders, impulsive control disorders, addictions, or depression. The main evidence used to support these models is comorbidity between compulsive buying and these other disorders. *Morbidity* means suffering from a clinically diagnosed disorder and associated symptoms, and comorbidity in this context refers to an individual suffering simultaneously from more than one such disorder. *Current comorbidity* means that a person has more than one disorder at this time, for instance he or she buys compulsively and is bulimic, while *life-time comorbidity* means that somebody who is a compulsive buyer right now has had another disorder at some stage in the past. Life-time comorbidity rates are higher than current comorbidity rates, given that they include a much longer time span. So, when it comes to assessing how compelling the comorbidity evidence is, using life-time rates is more generous.

Some view compulsive buying as an obsessive-compulsive spectrum disorder, characterized by intrusive and uncontrollable thoughts and behaviors that are accompanied by negative affect. Their accounts of the etiology, the causation, of compulsive buying propose biological and genetic predispositions, and the proffered evidence focuses on demonstrating generalized compulsive personality traits in compulsive buyers as well as comorbidity with OCDs. Several studies document that compulsive buyers have higher scores on general obsessive-compulsive scales (e.g., Faber & O'Guinn, 1992), and one reports a comorbidity rate of 22% with obsessive-compulsive personality disorder (Schlosser, Black, Repertinger, & Freet, 1994). Yet, the most direct evidence, concerning comorbidity with OCDs, is more mixed. It appears that the sample and sampling strategy used make a large difference to the findings. While the rate of comorbidity with a life-time OCD diagnosis was 35% in a sample of psychiatric patients (McElroy et al., 1994), percentages were very low in two samples of nonpsychiatric, self-identified compulsive buyers who responded to advertisements: 3% and 4%, respectively (Black, Repertinger, Gaffney, & Gabel, 1998; Schlosser et al., 1994).

A number of clinicians focus on the similarity with impulse-control disorders (ICDs) or addictions, and many examine comorbidity with a range of other psychiatric conditions, most commonly mood and anxiety disorders, substance abuse, and eating disorders. Life-time comorbidity with mood and anxiety disorders is particularly high in psychiatric samples, in some studies reaching 80% or more (McElroy et al., 1994) but still sizeable in samples of self-identified compulsive buyers, ranging from 40% to over 60% (e.g., Black et al., 1998). In addition, a number of studies report more negative affect, depression, or anxiety among compulsive buyers, using specifically developed scales to measure these emotions (see review in Dittmar, 2003). Notwithstanding this link between mood and compulsive buying, it is difficult to assess whether extreme mood states are cause or consequence. Even studies that document more mood change during buying for compulsive buyers compared to a comparison group of ordinary buyers cannot address this question (e.g., Faber & Christenson, 1996). Substance abuse comorbidity rates—also fairly high—are equally uninformative with respect to causality and are inflated by the inclusion of smoking (nicotine dependence) in some studies. Again, comorbidity rates for eating disorders are higher in psychiatric samples (35%) than in self-identified compulsive buyers (17% and 21%), and this pattern is repeated for comorbidity with a life-time ICD diagnosis, where 40% in a psychiatric sample compare to about half that rate in self-identified compulsive buyers (21% in Faber et al., 1995; 11% or 20%, depending on diagnostic tool, in Schlosser et al., 1994).

In summary, the evidence for comorbidity of compulsive buying with other psychiatric disorders is probably less compelling than claimed by proponents of these clinical models. Sampling from psychiatric populations is likely to lead to overestimates of comorbidity because it overrepresents individuals who suffer from a range of psychiatric difficulties, and this is supported by consistently lower rates in compulsive buyer samples that are self- or screener identified. Additional evidence to support this interpretation comes from a rare study that compares comorbidity rates in a sample of compulsive buyers with those in a comparison sample of ordinary buyers (Black et al., 1998). To my knowledge, there are no empirical studies of comorbidity in general population samples, which would address the question of whether the rate of associated disorders is higher than normal in compulsive buyers. So, this study is the best available source of relevant evidence. Compulsive buyers were about twice as likely to suffer from depression (60.6%) than ordinary buyers (27.3%), and this is a statistically significant difference. This is the only category-specific difference between compulsive and ordinary buyers, and the high life time comorbidity rate with any psychiatric disorder among compulsive buyers, 78.8%, was not significantly higher than that for the ordinary buyer comparison sample, which was 54.6%. The lack of statistical significance means that this difference may be due to random sample fluctuation so that we cannot be confident that this difference would actually occur in other samples. It is likely that the rate is so high among comparison respondents due to sampling strategy because they were recruited through an advertisement in the newsletter of a psychiatric hospital for a family study on obsessive-compulsive disorder. Thus, respondents who currently had contact with psychiatric services were overrepresented, and this may mean that they were likely to be particularly high in psychiatric diagnoses. Psychiatric and related samples may produce overestimates of comorbidity. With respect to compulsive buying, the safest conclusion is that, while there clearly are some individuals for whom uncontrolled buying is just one facet of generalized psychiatric impairment, there are others, including successful professionals (Elliott, 1994), for whom excessive buying is the main or only troubling aspect of their lives.

While the mainstream clinical and psychiatric approaches are clearly valuable, they have a number of blind spots. It is these blind spots that are worth addressing because they may both deepen and widen our understanding of compulsive buying, and, hence, improve our chances of successful treatment. Clinical models do not really offer an account of underlying motivations. Because they tend to assume a radical disjunction between pathological buying and ordinary consumer behavior, they do not set out to examine underlying motivations that may be similar or common in both. Furthermore, they fail to account for a striking aspect of impulsive and compulsive buying. Only certain goods (such as fashionable clothes) are typically bought, whereas others are not (such as basic kitchen equipment), and this list of favorites is quite typical of compulsive buyers: "I like clothes. Well, I've always liked clothes. I think most women like clothes. . . . And makeup—I always used to buy a lot of makeup. And jewelry's always been one of my favorites."

Several of my studies empirically confirm that clothes, shoes, appearance-related goods, and accessories are the favorite purchases of compulsive buyers, followed by music and electronic items at some distance. While this is also consistently reported in clinical research, it is not seen as an important aspect of compulsive buying that deserves explanation. When asked in interviews why they buy these goods, both compulsive and ordinary consumers spontaneously refer to the link between the symbolic meanings of these goods and their sense of self. This excerpt shows that this (recovering) compulsive buyer believed that consumer goods are an important route toward success, identity, and happiness, and that she purchased these goods to bolster her self-image:

> I probably wanted to make myself feel that I was something better than I was. And so, to do that I bought expensive clothes, expensive makeup, expensive perfumes, and things. Got it all on the [pause] store cards from a big department store. So, you know, by buying those things I felt . . . , 'cos I used to dress up really smart and, you know, I used to think "Oh the shop assistants probably think I've got loads of money and I'm this sort of person," and I enjoyed getting them because of that really. [*Interviewer:* What kind of person?] I think it was a kind of, sort of, a smartly dressed, young, trendy woman that you see around the places, can afford to wear designer labels and show them off and have Chanel makeup and that kind of thing. The sort of image that they portray . . . (Dittmar & Drury, 2000, p. 135)

This quote is not an idiosyncratic view of a particular individual, but it is typical in the sense that it reflects the beliefs and motivations of many compulsive buyers. A number of the research studies that include a wider set of factors—beyond a narrow clinical focus—commonly report two sets of nonpsychiatric correlates (i.e., factors that are associated with compulsive buying). The first set concerns consumers' self-concept, most often low self-esteem, but also accounts of an empty self, distorted self-beliefs, and a proneness to fantasize. The second set concerns the importance of, and attachment to, material goods and money. For example, one study found that compulsive buyers had a stronger commitment to money as a symbol of power and image (Hanley & Wilhelm, 1992). I developed these two characteristics into a social psychological two-factor theory of impulsive and compulsive buying (Dittmar, 2001), which is intended to extend and complement received clinical wisdom. This is detailed in the later section on identity-seeking as an important psychological motivation in compulsive buying.

Together, identity and materialism are consistent with the proposal that people "impulse buy to acquire material symbols of personal and social identity" (Dittmar, Beattie, & Friese, 1996, p. 187). In the U.K. survey, we examined the motivations involved in buying high-impulse goods, such as clothes and accessories, which are favorites of compulsive buyers. We selected four buying motivations, which were value for money, usefulness, mood change ("to cheer myself up"), and ideal self, and respondents rated them on scales. The ideal-self motivation asks respondents to indicate the extent to which they buy these goods on impulse because it "makes me feel more like the person I want to be." The relative importance of the four different motivations to ordinary and compulsive buyers is shown in Figure 13.2.

The pattern is significantly different for compulsive and ordinary buyers. By comparison, price and utility are less important to compulsive buyers, and both mood and ideal identity more. This shows that the motivational strength of compulsive buyers' wanting to cheer up and move closer to their ideal identities characterize compulsive buying. When it comes to comparing mood with identity, it is interesting to note that the difference between the two groups of shoppers is greatest with respect to the ideal-self motivation, outstripping mood. While these findings need replication before we can be certain, they do suggest two things. First, moving closer to an ideal identity is a strong motivation for all consumers

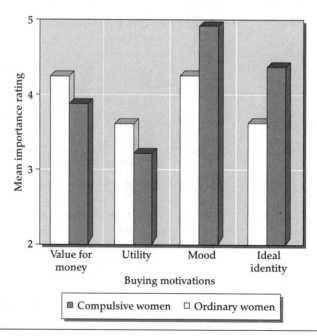

Figure 13.2   In Search of the Ideal Identity: Compulsive and Ordinary Buyers' Motivations

when buying compulsive buyers' favorite goods, thus supporting the idea that people seek identity through consumption. And, second, the strength of wanting to move closer to their ideal selves as a buying motivation is particularly strong for compulsive buyers. Thus, there is good initial empirical support for the argument that searching for a more ideal identity plays an important role in compulsive buying. With respect to the question of compulsive buying as a psychiatric disorder or a search for a better self, it is likely that our understanding is enhanced and deepened if we broaden the focus to include social-psychological perspectives on identity.

WHY DO PEOPLE DO IT?

At various times in this chapter, we touched on needs of consumers and rewards through shopping—real or merely hoped for—that can lead to, and then help maintain, addictive buying. This section takes up these various issues and tries to develop them in more detail and depth by organizing them into three sets. The first concerns hedonic pleasure: the recreation, fun, and enjoyment associated with shopping. The second focuses on the instrumental gains and achievement people can derive from having material goods. The third set discusses psychological motivations: two central concepts of mood and identity. Excerpts from interviews with compulsive buyers that illustrate these three sets of needs and rewards are given in Box 13.3. It will become apparent very quickly that all of these are interlinked: The pleasure aspect of shopping can be used to change mood when we try and cheer ourselves up through retail therapy, and we feel that designer labels can give us both social status and a sense of being somebody different and special—a new identity. Notwithstanding these links, I provide a useful conceptual map by discussing the range of need and rewards in shopping addiction under the three categories: hedonic, instrumental, and psychological.

RECREATION, FUN, AND ENJOYMENT

At the beginning of this chapter, we looked briefly at hedonic aspects of shopping, the experience of enjoyment, excitement, and fun, and that people have started to use shopping as a leisure and recreation pursuit. Notwithstanding that shopping can be exhausting and stressful, this interview excerpt captures the possible thrill of ordinary impulse buying:

> It is some kind of excitement. It is sort of, you give yourself a little thrill as if you were younger, when you were a child or a teenager having a ride at one of those merry-go-rounds at the fair. It is sort of a little bit like that. It can be exhilarating. (Dittmar & Drury, 2000, p. 124)

There is clearly a sense of a shopping buzz, which many of us may experience occasionally. Compulsive shoppers also talk about that buzz but as something that they experience all the time (see excerpt A in Box 13.3), and as at least one of the factors that keeps them shopping. A high emotional charge is also captured in the next excerpt (B), but here we do not get a pure sense of hedonic pleasure but a more mixed account of feelings and strong bodily reactions, which seem to resemble the high one might experience from a drug. I chose these two excerpts

BOX 13.3
Excerpts from in-Depth Interviews to
Illustrate Addictive Needs and Rewards

RECREATION, FUN, AND ENJOYMENT

A. I just got a buzz out of it all the time.

B. It's like a taste in my mouth, a dry, dry mouth, a ringing in my ears, believe it or not. Sometimes my vision will . . . , I'll be swaying a bit, I'll
have to reach out, something to steady myself. And I've often thought
I'm having an attack, an anxiety attack, or whatever, but it can't be because it seems to be every time I'm going in to spend money. . . . And
then when I've spent the money, I start to come down a bit.

INSTRUMENTAL GAINS AND ACHIEVEMENT

C. When I start to wear them [clothes], I am really glad that I have them,
you know. Oh, that is great, especially if people make comments about
how nice they are, how nice they look.

D. It's a range [pause]. Sometimes, it's just the buying. 'Cos, as I said, the,
the items, sometimes I can buy anything. It's the actual buying, not the
items. Apart from the clothes that we're talking about, the actual items
that I have bought lately are not that important, you know. But it was the
actual buying. Now, the ritual, ritual of actually buying. The sort of
gratification of buying something. Of course, I wouldn't buy pipes or
guns or things like that, you know. But I mean, I tend to more or less buy
things that give me some sort of pleasure, you know. But, it is for me
more important, the buying than the actual items.

PSYCHOLOGICAL NEEDS AND REWARDS

Mood

E. Oh, when I'm, you know, when I'm depressed I'll go out shopping to
cheer myself up. And when I feel happy I'll go out shopping for fun.

F. It's like some people might eat when they feel miserable. You know, it's
comfort. Comfort shopping.

Identity

G. 'Cos sometimes I will see something and I think, "That is absolutely
me." I'm having it and I don't care whether I can afford it or not
[coughs]. And I buy it with, with great pleasure and bring it home feeling really pleased with myself and never regret having spent the money,
you know, debts or no debts.

H. Because that was what it was [pause], my sort of ideal thing of how I'd
like to be was formed by the fantasies that we had, but they in turn were
formed from images on the telly and in the magazines 'cos there was
nowhere else I could have got them from.

> I. I'm somehow thinking, you know, that if I get the right things I'd project the right image if you like, you know. I'd feel right about myself. Sometimes I feel I'm there but, as I say, you know every so often I have this feeling if only, I just need such and such a thing, you know, and then it'll be right. . . . I think it's all to do with, you know, how I think of myself, . . . there's always one more thing I need and then I'll have everything I need.

because I think they illustrate a shift from recreational aspects of shopping, relaxation, and leisure to a more frantic hedonism (buzz all the time) that may, for some individuals, develop into an experience akin to substance abuse. Some compulsive buyers do talk about withdrawal symptoms, both bodily and psychologically, when they do not go shopping. So, while enjoyment and emotional involvement play an important role in both ordinary and compulsive buying, excitement can take on extreme forms for compulsive buyers. As we will see in the section on identity later, the shopping high is a rather short-lived experience for compulsive shoppers, which tends to give way to regret and other negative emotions soon after, particularly after getting home with the purchases. The hedonic dimension of shopping is also linked to mood, in the sense that people try to manage and change negative feelings.

INSTRUMENTAL GAINS AND ACHIEVEMENT

Regardless of the pleasure and excitement that people may or may not experience during shopping, there is a real sense in which buying goods can provide instrumental gains and act as an outward signal of achievement. I couldn't put it better than this woman in her interview:

> Great, I'm buying this item. People think I've got money to buy clothes. I haven't really, but people think I've got money to buy clothes. So I think it was also a case of how I looked to society . . . You know, and did I look like, not a wealthy person but somebody who could afford to buy clothes. . . . It was all me trying to say to people "I'm not only a housewife." I am somebody and I can go and buy myself these clothes and I can do this and I can just . . . , I'm not only a housewife [laughs], you know. I think that's what it all came down to. . . . I think I thought clothes were going to give me confidence [laughs]. (*Interviewer:* And they never did?) No [laughs], no they didn't, no [laughs]. No. But you always think that they're going to when you're buying them (Dittmar & Drury, 2000, p. 135).

While identity is clearly implicated here with this woman's feeling that she made a statement about not only being a housewife through buying particular goods, I chose this excerpt because it highlights social status gains through material goods. This may be an important underlying theme in compulsive buying. An early case report in the *British Journal of Addiction* describes a 24-year-old sufferer who primarily purchased clothes, especially leatherwear, because she was trying to impress her friends (Glatt & Cook, 1987). A more recent study found that compulsive buyers were more likely to make purchases to increase their social status and to impress others (Lejoyeux et al., 1999). A typical comment from compulsive buyers concerns other people's complimentary reactions to new clothes (see excerpt C in Box 13.3).

It is worth emphasizing at this point that the belief that expensive goods increase social status and are seen by others as a tangible sign of achievement is not erroneous. Experimental studies confirm that the very same individual is evaluated rather differently, depending on the material goods he or she has. For example, I carried out one such study, where I made short videos showing young adults in their homes. I filmed the same person, but in one setup the person (either a young man or a young woman) was shown with material possessions that indicated a lack of affluence, such as an inexpensive stereo, a small car, and basic kitchen appliances. In the other setup, the same person was shown with an expensive stereo, a large car, and a designer kitchen. These videos (one at a time) were shown to various groups of adolescents, allegedly to study their first impressions of the person depicted. The findings showed that the same person is seen as more educated, intelligent, successful, in control, and assertive when shown with expensive goods (Dittmar, 1992a). This implies that the association between a person and certain goods can indeed increase others' perceptions of their social status and achievement.

This line of argument would imply that the types of goods that compulsive buyers purchase are important. In the clinical literature and in clinically informed consumer research, compulsive buyers are often portrayed as hooked on the thrill of the shopping experience and spending money and as less concerned with the actual goods they obtain (e.g., Faber & O'Guinn, 1992). Indeed, many purchases are never used and even hidden so that the compulsive buying stays undetected by others as long as possible. Notwithstanding this, my model of buyers as identity seekers suggests that the goods bought are as important as the shopping experience, if not more so. Social status and identity concerns can be significant at the point of purchase, when buyers fantasize about their new, improved identity, even if they then do not actually use the goods later on. In our in-depth interview study, we asked directly which was more important: the actual buying process or having the goods. Over half (70%) answered similarly to ordinary women shoppers, by emphasizing that both the goods *and* the shopping experience are important. However, a minority (30%) described the act of buying itself as giving a high like a drug (as typified in excerpt B). Yet, even when compulsive buyers talked in this way, there is evidence that they would not just buy anything but are still selective. This is typified in excerpt D, which seems to suggest indiscriminate buying, at least at first sight. Yet, the fact that only particular goods are bought is so obvious and self-evident that it is added as an afterthought, "Of course, I wouldn't buy pipes or guns or things like that." Thus, the actual goods bought are seen as important as or even more important than the shopping experience itself. Only a minority of compulsive buyers reported that the buying activity itself was more important, and even then there was clear indication that certain types of goods were nevertheless selected.

This qualitative finding is validated and supported further by quantitative results from the mail survey. In the questionnaire, respondents were not asked directly for a decision about which of these two aspects of impulse buying was more important to them. Instead, they responded on two independent rating scales: one asking them to indicate the extent to which they got enjoyment from goods bought and the other about enjoyment from the shopping experience. There was a systematic difference between ordinary and compulsive buyers. Compulsive buyers gave higher ratings for both goods and shopping experience. However, all shoppers—ordinary and compulsive, women and men—reported getting significantly more enjoyment out of the products they bought rather than out of the shopping atmosphere and experience. Thus, it seems that people want material goods because of their symbolism; and, at least in part, this symbolism communicates a positive image, social status, and achievement.

PSYCHOLOGICAL NEEDS AND REWARDS: MOOD AND IDENTITY

In terms of psychological processes underlying excessive buying, two focal concepts emerge in the literature: mood and identity. While mood is discussed prominently in clinical approaches, the notion that individuals are identity-seekers in search of a better self when they buy is more prominent in social psychological perspectives.

Mood   The idea that mood states and emotions are important in shopping comes out clearly in the excerpt below, where a noncompulsive woman buyer talks about impulse buying as a consequence of both positive emotions (happy or jolly) and negative feelings (miserable):

> I seem to buy things on impulse if I feel really happy. You know, if I'm feeling quite jolly, I might buy things. I might buy things to cheer myself up. But it's not all, I mean it's not always the case. If I feel miserable, I'll buy something . . . . And I, you know, might try and cheer myself up by buying things. (Dittmar & Drury, 2000, p. 129)

This woman also talks about buying things to cheer herself up. Mood enhancement, managing negative affect, and escape from painful feelings are seen as psychological drivers of compulsive buying in the clinical literature. Mood directly caused by depression is central to Lejoyeux's perspective on compulsive buying, where sufferers use the hedonic aspects of shopping as self-medication to alleviate their depressive symptoms. Indeed, sufferers do mention buying when feeling "depressed" (see excerpt E in Box 13.3). However, this same excerpt also refers to positive moods that translate into shopping, and I chose it because this is not an uncommon response. In the addiction framework, mood is also central because the basis of the addiction is seen as individuals' dependency on the relief from negative mood states that they experience when shopping, such as anxiety—at least in the short term. This sense of relief is captured by the notion of "comfort shopping" in excerpt F. Indeed, there is overwhelming evidence that mood plays a significant role in compulsive buying, and we have already looked at the high comorbidity rates between compulsive buying and mood disorders in the previous section. If we accept that mood is important, we are still left with the question of exactly how mood plays a role in compulsive buying. Here, relevant evidence is much thinner, and I see the development of a better understanding of mood-related processes as an area for more future research. Compulsive buyers report more intense negative and positive emotions than ordinary buyers, and they experience more mood change from before to just after purchase (Faber & Christenson, 1996).

As part of my U.K. project, a group of women—both ordinary and compulsive buyers—kept a shopping diary for one month, recording each impulse purchase of durable consumer goods. For each purchase, they gave factual information (good, price, etc.), as well as their thoughts and feelings just before the purchase, just after, and then after getting home with the good(s). They gave global evaluations of how they felt about themselves on a rating scale ranging from "Very bad" (1) to "Very good" (6). They also wrote open-ended accounts of their thoughts and feelings during the same three phases of their impulse buy. Four types of buying motivations before the purchase were mentioned often enough that they could be analyzed: wanting to buy something because it has good value for the money spent, useful, likely to change one's mood, and improve self-image. As an explicit motivation, wanting to change one's mood or cheering oneself up was stated less frequently, compared to the other motivations. On average, respondents mentioned mood change for only 7% of their impulsive purchases, whereas they reported the other three motivations for just under 20% of their impulse buys: buying because the good is useful (18%), because it has good value for the money spent (18%), and because it improves self-image (17%). It is interesting to note that, when respondents were not prompted in any way, self-image was stated more often or as often as other buying motivations, except mood. This is especially remarkable, given that concerns with economy and utility are the dominant discourse about good consumers: They are rational, socially desirable, and prominent in both expert and commonsense narratives about shopping.

Possibly, the argument that (English) people are reluctant to talk about mood and their feelings and that this reluctance explains why they do not admit to mood enhancement as a strong driver of their buying behavior does not hold water, since mood was mentioned frequently in the diary accounts. Usually, respondents simply stated whether their mood and feelings were positive or negative at various stages of the buying process. Many respondents stated both positive and negative feelings in their diaries, sometimes even for the same purchase. To assess the relative presence of positive mood, statements of negative mood were subtracted from statements of positive mood. This was done at each of the three stages of impulse buying to be able to track mood change. This means that respondents had a single score at each stage, averaging across all of their impulse buys, which can range from −1 (indicating only negative feelings), through 0 (indicating an equal amount of positive and negative feelings), to +1 (indicating only positive feelings). The findings are shown in the top graph of Figure 13.3. The pattern is striking and very different for compulsive compared to ordinary buyers. Compulsive buyers experience more extreme emotions, and they report greater positive mood shifts during buying than ordinary buyers. To this extent, these findings are consistent with the U.S. study by Faber and Christenson already mentioned. However, the shift toward more positive feelings, which is much steeper for compulsive women who report predominantly negative feelings before impulse buying, is one that ordinary women can sustain until after they get home with their new purchase, and even enhance, given that positive feelings increase further. In contrast, the mood gain peaks for compulsive buyers just after purchase, but it is rather short-lived because they feel worse by the time they get home with their purchases.

There is clearly a gap between mood changes that actually happen when shopping and mood change when given as a reason for going shopping by respondents. This may suggest that people are not aware of the extent to which mood changes

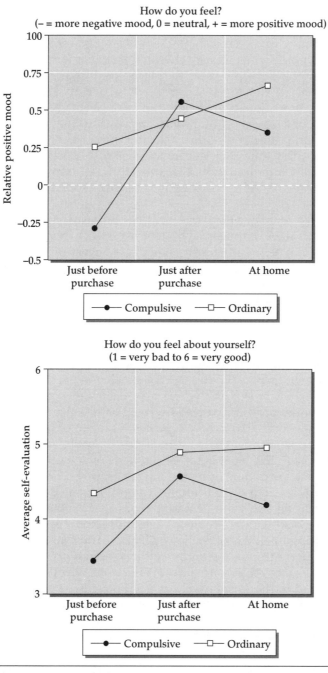

Figure 13.3 Compulsive and Ordinary Buyers' Changes in Mood and Self-Evaluation during Three Consumption Phases

drive their buying. However, there is a more radical possibility: Mood change may not be the main, or at least the only, driver, but may be interwoven with other psychological processes.

Retail therapy may not simply be about wanting to feel better but also wanting to feel better about ourselves. Mood and feelings may be interwoven with how we

see and evaluate ourselves at any given time. Global self-evaluation was also assessed in the diary study, and the bottom graph in Figure 13.3 shows how compulsive and ordinary women felt about themselves (on average) at all three stages
of buying. The similarity in pattern between self-evaluation and mood is striking.
Ordinary women have mainly positive effects from impulse buying, given that
they feel better about themselves after purchase and that this boost lasts until
they get home. For compulsive women, the initial boost seems greater. Feeling
much worse about themselves than ordinary women, they are almost on a par
with them just after an impulse buy. But, in contrast to ordinary women, their
boost reduces by the time they get home; therefore, it seems that compulsive
women experience improved self-evaluation through impulse buying but that
these perceived benefits related to identity are more short-lived than for ordinary
consumers.

Because the patterns for mood and identity are so strikingly similar, this suggests that mood is likely entwined with identity, rather than free-standing. Identity seeking can also help explain why compulsive buyers carry on despite adverse
consequences. Despite recognizing that the self-image boost may be short-lived,
the hope persists that all that is needed is just one more thing to achieve a better
self-image, leading to a vicious cycle of repetitive impulse buying (excerpt H in
Box 13.3).

Identity   The notion that consumerism is bound up with our sense of identity
was touched on at several points in this chapter, and moving closer to an ideal
identity was shown to be a buying motivation that is particularly important to
compulsive buyers. A broad, easily understandable definition of identity is the
subjective concept of oneself as a person. People buy consumer goods to express
who they are and would like to be, to construct a sense of being unique and different from others, and to acquire new identities. Symbolic self-completion theory
(Wicklund & Gollwitzer, 1982) is important here, which proposes that when we
perceive shortcomings in our concept of ourselves, we become motivated to compensate and that we often do so through symbols. Among diverse strategies, this
can involve acquiring and using material goods that symbolize those aspects of
identity that are lacking (e.g., Braun & Wicklund, 1989). For example, by wearing
a recognized masculine symbol, such as a black leather motorbike suit, a young
man can compensate for not feeling masculine enough by using clothing to tell
both himself and others that he is, indeed, masculine. Identity concerns are more
clearly articulated in the social psychological literature, and a focus on compulsive buyers as identity seekers is different in emphasis than the clinical views of
sufferers as repairing their mood or being dysfunctional in their impulse control.

As already mentioned, I developed this view of compulsive buyers as identity
seekers into a social-psychological, two-factor model: materialistic values and distance from ideal identity. According to this model, the first characteristic of compulsive buying is a value commitment to identity construction through material
goods, a belief in the materialistic values at the heart of consumer society. Individuals who are antimaterialistic are likely to choose avenues other than shopping
when they attempt to repair or improve their sense of who they are. Depending on
what they value, they might exercise excessively, work excessively, or eat excessively. Thus, value commitment identifies who is disproportionately more likely to
develop compulsive buying tendencies. The second characteristic taps into how

strong the tendency to buy is likely to be. This depends on how different a person feels from who they would like to be—the distance from their ideal identity or the perceived discrepancy between actual and ideal self. The further away you feel from who you would like to be, the more you are motivated to try and move closer to a better, more acceptable, and more ideal self.

Materialistic values are a "set of centrally held beliefs about the importance of [material] possessions in one's life" (Richins & Dawson, 1992, p. 308). They have been described as a dark side of consumer behavior because they can be associated with unrealistic expectations about benefits of consumer goods, negative emotions after purchasing, lower life satisfaction, and lower subjective well-being. For instance, a classic U.S. study found that those who value material success above all other domains, such as affiliation with others or community engagement, show less vitality, more anxiety and depression, and impaired social and personal functioning (Kasser & Ryan, 1993). Materialistic values may lead people to focus on goals that ultimately cannot fulfill their real needs for authenticity and connectedness to others (Ryan & Deci, 2000). Negative effects seem to occur for those individuals for whom they are primary, overriding other types of values (such as affiliation with others) and whose underlying motivations for desiring money and possessions are linked to concerns with power, status, and depleted self-esteem (Srivastava, Locke, & Bartol, 2001). In my U.K. project, I used a conceptualization of materialistic values, which focuses on identity concerns. Materialistic values mean a strong commitment to identity construction through material goods because they are characterized by three key themes: believing that acquiring material goods is a central life goal; that they are the main route to identity, success, and happiness; and that material goods are the yardstick by which to evaluate self and others. They can be measured through a questionnaire (Richins & Dawson, 1992), and examples of items that illustrate these three themes in turn are "Some of the most important achievements in life include acquiring material possessions," "The things I own say a lot about how well I'm doing in life," and "I admire people who own expensive homes, cars, and clothes." In terms of empirical evidence, we found that compulsive buyers scored in the upper half of the scale, while ordinary consumers (on average) scored below the scale midpoint. Thus, this form of materialistic values—a commitment to identity construction and evaluation through material goods—seems a significant factor in understanding compulsive buying because it channels individuals toward consumption as a strategy to deal with perceived discrepancies or shortcomings in their identity. Additional support for this viewpoint comes from two U.S. studies, one of which showed that young adults from disrupted families have both higher materialistic values *and* higher levels of compulsive consumption than their counterparts from intact families (Rindfleisch, Burroughs, & Denton, 1997), whereas the other demonstrated that materialism was a significant predictor of compulsive buying tendencies in some individuals (DeSarbo & Edwards, 1996).

In addition to materialistic values, the second factor in the social psychological model concerns identity directly. If materialistic people buy material goods to aspire to a better, more ideal, identity, then that drive should become stronger the further away they get from their ideal identity. They should engage in more buying as the discrepancy increases between how they see themselves now (actual identity) and how they would like to be (ideal identity). This idea of identity discrepancies as a significant factor in compulsive buying is certainly consistent with the common reports of low self-esteem because a greater distance from one's ideal identity is likely to lead to negative self-evaluation. The measure we used in the U.K. study was designed specifically for our research (Dittmar et al., 1996). We first ask respondents to list aspects of themselves that they would like to change to elicit directly those discrepancies between actual and ideal identity that are subjectively meaningful to them. They do this by completing "I am _____ , but I would like to be _____" a number of times. Next, we find out how strong, psychologically, these identity discrepancies are. For this, they rate each of their statements in turn, using magnitude (how far they feel they are away from their ideal) and importance (how much they are concerned about this discrepancy). Findings from the U.K. project confirmed that compulsive buyers' discrepancies between actual and ideal identity were more than 50% larger and psychologically salient than those of ordinary buyers.

In a series of studies, as further support of the two-factor model, I found that compulsive buying tendencies in women can be predicted meaningfully from a person's identity discrepancies—but only if they hold materialistic values (e.g., Dittmar, 2003). To make sense of this finding in nonstatistical terms, I will illustrate how the two-factor model works with respect to particular groups of women who took part in the U.K. research project. For the purpose of the illustration, I selected 40 women from the total sample of almost 300, to create four groups of 10 women each, that differed with respect to the two characteristics central to the theory. Two of these groups are nonmaterialistic (they do not attach much importance to money, material goods, and their supposed social and psychological benefits), whereas the other two groups hold strong materialistic values. Of the two materialistic groups of women, one group was selected because they felt quite close to how they would like to be. These 10 women are those for whom there is the least distance from her ideal identity. For each of these women her discrepancies between actual and ideal self are low. The other group, in contrast, are those 10 women who were highest in identity discrepancies: Each of them feels very different from how she would ideally like to be, and these differences are something she worries about frequently. The same extreme contrast selection was also used when choosing the two groups of nonmaterialistic women, so one group is the 10 women lowest in self-discrepancies, and the other group is the 10 women who were highest in self-discrepancies. These four groups of women can be represented in a four-square diagram, as shown in Table 13.3.

For each of these four extreme groups, the general prediction that the model makes for their compulsive buying tendencies is given. The model predicts that

Table 13.3
Materialistic Values and Self-Discrepancies as Predictors of Compulsive Buying (CB)

Materialistic Values	Self-Discrepancies (Distance from Ideal Identity)	
	Low	High
Low	Prediction: Low CB score 17.6	Prediction: Low CB score 25.6
High	Prediction: Low CB score 30.9	Prediction: **High** CB score **56.5**

Note: The cut-off point for classification as a compulsive buyer is a scale score of 43 or above.

only women who are *both* materialistic *and* high in self-discrepancies should have strong compulsive buying tendencies, while the other three groups should not. The numbers given underneath the prediction in each of the four squares is the actual average score on a validated compulsive buying-screener found in the project for each group of 10 women (d'Astous et al., 1990). Scores on this scale range from 11 to 66, with higher scores indicating stronger compulsive buying tendencies. A score of 43 or above means that an individual is classified as a compulsive buyer. Compulsive tendencies are lowest among those women who do not hold materialistic values and who are close to their ideal identity. Scores go up somewhat for women who are high in one of these factors, but low in the other (i.e., nonmaterialistic women high in self-discrepancies and materialistic women who are close to their ideal identity). However, they remain in the bottom half of the scale. It is only women who are both materialistic and far from their ideal identity who score high on this scale. Their mean score lies above the cut-off point for classification as a compulsive buyer. It is interesting to note that every one of these 10 women had a score higher than 43, and thus was classified as a compulsive buyer. These four groups of women were selected on the basis of their extreme scores on the two factors of materialism and identity, and the findings support the social psychological model very well.

STATE OF THE ART AND FUTURE TRENDS

The profiles of compulsive buyers that emerged in this chapter show some typical or frequent characteristics. Sufferers are hooked into an addictive cycle of repetitive buying, where they experience irresistible impulses to shop and loss of control over their behavior to some extent, and they carry on despite adverse personal, social, and financial consequences. Yet, there are similarities between compulsive and particular kinds of everyday shopping in terms of consumers' needs and rewards. Shopping has hedonic benefits and material goods offer instrumental gains, such as social status. Most important, it also fulfils central psychological functions of mood change and enhancement on the one hand and identity concerns on the other, such as expressing who we are or seeking a better, more ideal identity through consumption. In addition, we know that sufferers are predominantly women, at least at this time, and that compulsive buying appears to show a sudden and dramatic rise in incidence. In terms of understanding compulsive buying, an addiction framework is ideally suited because it can accommodate psychiatric approaches as well as social-psychological perspectives.

The strengths of the clinical models reviewed in this chapter lie in highlighting that some sufferers may have generalized psychiatric problems, with uncontrolled buying among an array of other symptoms, highlighting mood as an important psychological process, and offering guidance on drawing some diagnostic line between unhealthy and healthy shopping. The complimentary strengths of the social-psychological perspective emerge in its emphasis on understanding compulsive buying in the context of the transformation of consumer culture and behavior in many developed economies. It offers an account of compulsive buying that focuses on underlying motivations as an extreme form of identity seeking through buying material goods, which lies on a continuum with everyday impulsive buying. This kind of model is probably best applicable to cultures and to subpopulations within them, for whom there is a preexisting cultural link between identity construction and shopping, such as women in Western mass-consumer societies. The type of ideal-self buying described in the identity section of this chapter may only occur in such societies.

ARE THERE ONE OR TWO TYPICAL COMPULSIVE BUYERS?

It is possible that the clinical model offers a better explanation for some compulsive buyers and the social-psychological perspective for others. This raises the possibility that compulsive buyers are not a single, homogenous group of sufferers but may include different subpopulations with a different pathway into compulsive buying. Some people may have a general propensity to experience negative affect, which can then lead to a variety of psychiatric symptoms, while there may be a direct value precursor (materialism) for others that channels them toward buying behavior specifically. Thus, one subpopulation may be psychiatric compulsive buyers and another identity-seeking compulsive buyers, and future research should attempt to examine this possibility through studying both comorbidity between different addictions and underlying motivations, particularly in terms of mood and identity. At the level of the individual sufferer, it is clearly important to understand and assess possible comorbidity, if treatment is to be maximally helpful to that particular person. This issue is discussed in more detail in Chapter 14. Sufferers trying to find other behaviors to engage in so they will *not* to go on a shopping spree need to avoid doing things that could easily trigger other addictions (e.g., overeating).

FUTURE TRENDS

Compulsive buying was shown to be strongly gender linked, supporting the notion of a cultural link between women's gender identity and shopping. Male compulsive buyers tend to be both young and highly educated, suggesting that their gender identification is less traditionally male compared to other subpopulations of men. This finding implies a potential future increase in the prevalence of compulsive buying among young men as they become more interested in the form of self-image-related buying discussed earlier, given the recent and increasing emphasis on body image, fashion, and consumption of goods for men, which is reflected in advertising and marketing. Also worth considering in the context of gender is a different issue: While there is a cultural link between identity construction and *shopping* for women, there may be links between identity construction and other forms of aberrant consumer behavior for men who are materialistic and high in self-discrepancies, such as pathological collecting or excessive spending on cars.

A recent European Union research project in Spain, Italy, and the United Kingdom detected worrisome trends among adolescents (Garcés Prieto, 2001). In terms of being attracted to visiting shops and shopping, or spending money impulsively, young people exceeded adults, showing a much higher level of addiction to buying stimuli and a much lower level of financial self-control. The final report on the project, referred to in the chapter, concludes that the "current generation of young people may, in the future, become adults with serious problems of impulsive buying, over-indebtedness and consumer addiction." While not using an established measure of compulsive buying, the project identifies 46% of the adolescent samples studied as showing some addictive tendencies, which we can only hope is an overestimate. However, their estimate of 15% of adult addictive buyers is in line with several of the studies discussed earlier. Also interesting to note is their finding that the gender disparity in addictive tendencies is much less pronounced in adolescents compared to adults, which is consistent with the suggestion that more men may become affected by compulsive buying in younger generations.

The number of consumers who buy goods on the Internet has increased phenomenally, a majority of adults think that buying online is a serious alternative to conventional shopping, and almost half of young U.S. adults are now buying online. There is a widespread assumption that e-commerce encourages rational buying and empowers consumers because it offers better information search, price and product comparison, convenience, freedom from time pressure, and less distractions and emotional involvement. However, there are also good arguments that online consumer activities can encourage uncontrolled buying and overspending. Shopping access is no longer limited by opening times or physical location, but exists 24 hours a day every day. Having your credit card swiped at a cash register feels less like spending money than handing over hard cash, and buying transactions on the Internet are so remote that it feels even less like spending money. Once you have bought online and given your credit card details, some retail sites offer a one-click purchase option to returning customers. You can become so immersed in the virtual reality of the Internet that you enter a trance-like state. Many retail web sites bombard you not only with advertisements for sales and discounts but also with visual stimulation. One analysis identifies a number of web site features that encourage uncontrolled buying (LaRose, 2001), and the highly successful online auction site eBay already had its first addicts a few years ago (Greenfield, 1999). Given that the Internet may well become the consumer route of the new millennium, it is imperative to identify factors that may lead consumers to uncontrolled online buying, causing distress and debt, and, thus, potentially another avenue for compulsive buying.

With these possible future trends, there is need for more consumer education and advice to prevent uncontrolled buying and debt, as well as expanded support services and treatment for those who start experiencing problems. Chapter 14 focuses on these issues.

RECOMMENDED READING

Benson, A. (Ed.). (2000). *I shop therefore, I am: Compulsive buying and the search for self.* New York: Aronson. This is the first book on compulsive buying that brings together diverse contributions by psychologists, sociologists, consumer researchers, psychiatrists, and therapists on both understanding additive buying and treating it. Its multidimensional approach successfully bridges academic, practitioner, and self-help interests.

Dittmar, H. (2003). *Addictive buying behavior: A growing concern? A review and empirical exploration of the role of gender, age and materialism.* University of Sussex. Manuscript submitted for publication, available from the author. This article provides a complementary perspective to the mainstream clinical approach in two ways: A comprehensive review of previous research studies on compulsive buying and an exploration of gender, age, and materialistic value endorsement as predictors of addictive buying in a set of three empirical studies.

Faber, R. J., & O'Guinn, T. C. (1992). A clinical screener for compulsive buying. *Journal of Consumer Research, 19,* 459–469. This classic study was the first large-scale U.S. survey on additive buying, and the core aspects identified are used in a follow-up study to develop and validate a diagnostic questionnaire by comparing ordinary buyers with compulsive buyers who were identified either through the screener or self-identified.

Scherhorn, G. (1990). The addictive trait in buying behavior. *Journal of Consumer Policy, 13,* 33–51. This article offers a clear, accessible, and insightful analysis of the differences between conceptualizing excessive buying as a compulsion compared to an addiction, as well as an in-depth discussion of the individual and social causes of addictive buying.

REFERENCES

American Psychiatric Association. (2000). *Diagnostic and statistical manual of mental disorders* (4th ed., text rev.). Washington, DC: Author.

Babin, B. J., Darden, W. R., & Griffin, M. (1994). Work and/or fun: Measuring hedonic and utilitarian shopping value. *Journal of Consumer Research, 20,* 644–656.

Black, D. W. (1996). Compulsive buying: A review. *Journal of Clinical Psychiatry, 57,* 50–54.

Black, D. W. (1998). Recognition and treatment of obsessive-compulsive spectrum disorders. In R. P. Swinson et al. (Eds.), *Obsessive-compulsive disorder: Theory, research and treatment* (pp. 426–457). New York: Guilford Press.

Black, D. W., Repertinger, S., Gaffney, G. R., & Gabel, J. (1998). Family history and psychiatric comorbidity in person with compulsive buying. *American Journal of Psychiatry, 155,* 960–963.

Bloch, P. H., Ridgway, N. M., & Nelson, J. W. (1991). Leisure and the shopping mall. *Advances in Consumer Research, 18,* 445–452.

Braun, O. L., & Wicklund, R. A. (1989). Psychological antecedents of conspicuous consumption. *Journal of Economic Psychology, 10,* 161–187.

Campbell, C. (2000). Shopaholics, spendaholics, and the question of gender. In A. Benson (Ed.), *I shop, therefore, I am: Compulsive buying and the search for self* (pp. 57–75). New York: Aronson.

d'Astous, A. (1990). An inquiry into the compulsive side of "normal" consumers. *Journal of Consumer Policy, 13,* 15–31.

d'Astous, A., Maltais, J., & Roberge, C. (1990). Compulsive buying tendencies of adolescent consumers. *Advances in Consumer Research, 17,* 306–313.

DeSarbo, W. S., & Edwards, E. A. (1996). Typologies of compulsive buying behavior: A constrained clusterwise regression approach. *Journal of Consumer Psychology, 5,* 231–262.

Dittmar, H. (1992a). *The social psychology of material possessions: To have is to be.* London: Harvester Wheatsheaf.

Dittmar, H. (1992b). Perceived material wealth and first impressions. *British Journal of Social Psychology, 31,* 361–379.

Dittmar, H. (2001). Impulse buying in ordinary and "compulsive" consumers. In E. Wever, Y. Baron, & G. Loomes (Eds.), *Conflicts and tradeoffs in decision-making* (pp. 110–135). New York: Cambridge University Press.

Dittmar, H. (2003). *A new look at compulsive buying: Self-discrepancies and materialistic values as predictors of excessive buying behavior.* Manuscript submitted for publication.

Dittmar, H. (in press). Are you what you have? Consumer society and our sense of identity. *Psychologist, 16.*

Dittmar, H., Beattie, J., & Friese, S. (1996). Objects, decision considerations and self-image in men's and women's impulse purchases. *Acta Psychologica, 93,* 187–206.

Dittmar, H., & Drury, J. (2000). Self-image—is it in the bag? A qualitative comparison between "ordinary" and "excessive" consumers. *Journal of Economic Psychology, 21,* 109–142.

Dittmar, H., Long, K., & Meek, R. (in press). Buying on the Internet: Gender differences in online and conventional buying motivations. *Sex Roles.*

Edwards, E. A. (1993). Development of a new scale for measuring compulsive buying behavior. *Financial Counseling and Planning, 4,* 67–84.

Elliott, R. (1994). Addictive consumption: Function and fragmentation in postmodernity. *Journal of Consumer Policy, 17,* 159–179.

Faber, R. J., & Christenson, G. A. (1996). In the mood to buy: Differences in the mood states experienced by compulsive buyers and other consumers. *Psychology and Marketing, 13,* 803–820.

Faber, R. J., Christenson, G. A., de Zwaan, M., & Mitchell, J. (1995). Two forms of compulsive consumption: Comorbidity of compulsive buying and binge eating. *Journal of Consumer Research, 22,* 296–304.

Faber, R. J., & O'Guinn, T. C. (1992). A clinical screener for compulsive buying. *Journal of Consumer Research, 19,* 459–469.

Featherstone, M. (1991). *Consumer culture and postmodernism.* London: Sage.

Fischer, E., & Gainer, B. (1991). I shop therefore I am: The role of shopping in the social construction of women's identities. In G. A. Costa (Ed.), *Gender and consumer behavior* (pp. 350–357). Salt Lake City: University of Utah Press.

Franzen, G., & Bouwman, M. (2001). *The mental world of brands: Mind, memory and brand success.* Towbridge: Cromwell Press.

Fromm, E. (1976). *To have or to be?* Hammondsworth, England: Penguin.

Garcés Prieto, J. (2001). Experiencias de trabajo en la prevenciòn y tratamiento de la adicciòn al consumo. In I. García Ureta & E. Olibarri Fernández (Eds.), *El consumo y la adicciòn a las compras: Diferentes perspectivas* (pp. 199–222). University of the Basque Country Servicio Editorial.

Glatt, M. M., & Cook, C. C. H. (1987). Pathological spending as a form of psychological dependence. *British Journal of Addiction, 82,* 1257–1258.

Goodman, W. K., Price, L. H., Rasmussen, S. A., Mazure, C., Fleischmann, R. L., Hill, C. L., et al. (1989). The Yale-Brown Obsessive-Compulsive Scale: I. Development, use and reliability. *Archives of General Psychiatry, 46*(11), 1006–1011.

Greenfield, D. N. (1999). *Virtual addiction.* Oakland, CA: New Harbinger.

Hanley, A., & Wilhelm, M. S. (1992). Compulsive buying: An exploration into self-esteem and money attitudes. *Journal of Economic Psychology, 13,* 5–18.

Hassay, D. N., & Smith, M. C. (1996). Compulsive buying: An examination of the consumption motive. *Psychology and Marketing, 13,* 741–752.

Kasser, T., & Ryan, R. M. (1993). A dark side of the American dream: Correlates of financial success as a central life aspiration. *Journal of Personality and Social Psychology, 65,* 410–422.

LaRose, R. (2001). On the negative effects of e-commerce: A sociocognitive exploration of unregulated online buying. *Journal of Computer-Mediated Communication, 6*(3).

Lejoyeux, M., Adés, J., Tassian, V., & Solomon, J. (1996). Phenomenology and psychopathology of uncontrolled buying. *American Journal of Psychiatry, 153,* 1524–1529.

Lejoyeux, M., Haberman, N., Solomon, J., & Adés, J. (1999). Comparison of buying behavior in depressed patients presenting with and without compulsive buying. *Comprehensive Psychiatry, 40*(1), 51–56.

Lejoyeux, M., Tassian, V., Solomon, J., & Adés, J. (1997). Study of compulsive buying in depressed patients. *Journal of Clinical Psychiatry, 58*(4), 169–173.

Lunt, P. K., & Livingstone, S. M. (1992). *Mass consumption and personal identity.* Buckingham, England: Open University Press.

Magee, A. (1994). Compulsive buying tendency as a predictor of attitudes and perceptions. *Advances in Consumer Research, 21,* 590–594.

McCracken, G. (1990). *Culture and consumption.* Indianapolis: Indiana University Press.

McElroy, S. L., Keck, P. E., Pope, H. G., Smith, J. M., & Strakowski, S. M. (1994). Compulsive buying: A report of 20 cases. *Journal of Clinical Psychiatry, 55*(6), 242–248.

Nataraajan, R., & Goff, B. (1991). Compulsive buying: Toward a reconceptualization. *Journal of Social Behavior and Personality, 6,* 307–328.

O'Guinn, T. C., & Faber, R. J. (1989). Compulsive buying: A phenomenological exploration. *Journal of Consumer Research, 16,* 147–157.

Richins, M., & Dawson, S. (1992). Materialism as a consumer value: Measure development and validation. *Journal of Consumer Research, 19,* 303–316.

Rindfleisch, A., Burroughs, J. E., & Denton, F. (1997). Family structure, materialism, and compulsive consumption. *Journal of Consumer Research, 23,* 312–325.

Rook, D. W., & Fisher, R. J. (1995). Normative influence on impulsive buying behavior. *Journal of Consumer Research, 22,* 305–313.

Ryan, R. M., & Deci, E. L. (2000). Self-determination theory and the facilitation of intrinsic motivation, social development, and well-being. *American Psychologist, 55*(1), 68–78.

Scherhorn, G. (1990). The addictive trait in buying behavior. *Journal of Consumer Policy, 13,* 33–51.

Schlosser, S., Black, D. W., Repertinger, S., & Freet, D. (1994). Compulsive buying: Demography, phenomenology, and comorbidity in 46 subjects. *General Hospital Psychiatry, 16,* 205–212.

Srivastava, A., Locke, E. A., & Bartol, K. M. (2001). Money and subjective well-being: It's not the money, it's the motives. *Journal of Personality and Social Psychology, 80,* 959–971.

Travis, C. B. (1993). Women and health. In F. L. Denmark & M. A. Paludi (Eds.), *Psychology of women: A handbook of issues and theories* (pp. 283–323). Westport, CT: Greenwood.

Valence, G., d'Astous, A., & Fortier, L. (1988). Compulsive buying: Concept and measurement. *Journal of Consumer Policy, 11,* 419–433.

Verplanken, B., & Herabadi, A. (2001). Individual differences in impulsive buying tendency: Feeling and no thinking. *European Journal of Personality, 15,* 71–83.

Wapner, S., Demick, J., & Redondo, J. P. (1990). Cherished possessions and adaptation of older people to nursing homes. *International Journal on Aging and Human Development, 31*(3), 299–315.

Wicklund, R. A., & Gollwitzer, P. M. (1982). *Symbolic self-completion.* Hillsdale, NJ: Erlbaum.

CHAPTER 14

Treating Compulsive Buying

APRIL LANE BENSON and MARIE GENGLER

C OMPULSIVE BUYING IS finally coming out of the closet. First described by Kraepelin in 1915 and then Bleuler in 1924, it was largely ignored for the next 60 years. Only in the past 15 years have we seen specific and persistent inquiry into this disorder. There is more and more evidence, both research and anecdotal, that compulsive buying poses a serious and worsening problem, one with significant emotional, social, occupational, and financial consequences (Benson, 2000). In this handbook, compulsive buying is given equal billing with some of its psychological siblings. A forthcoming book, *Handbook of Impulse Control Disorders* (Hollander, in press) also includes a chapter on compulsive buying, written by Donald Black. Compulsive buying is now being accorded its rightful place in the consortium of addictive disorders of the twenty-first century.

Like other addictions, compulsive buying is complex and multidetermined. Many shopaholics try to counteract feelings of low self-esteem through the emotional relief and momentary euphoria provided by compulsive shopping. These shoppers, who also experience a higher than normal rate of associated disorders—depression, anxiety, substance abuse, eating disorders, and impulse-control disorders—may be using their symptoms to self-medicate. Others buy compulsively in a vain attempt to gain social status or move closer to what they believe is a better or ideal self. These compulsive buyers may have a lower rate of associated disorders than the first group, as discussed in Chapter 13.

COUNSELORS AND MONEY ISSUES

Counselors/therapists often have difficulty dealing with money issues that can pose a significant impediment when working with compulsive buying clients. "Three major surveys of psychotherapists revealed that money matters were the most difficult subject for the therapists themselves to discuss with their patients" (as stated by Stanny in McCall, 2000, pp. 458–459). Psychotherapists have chosen a humanitarian profession and are sometimes conflicted about feeling entitled to adequate payment for their services. Therapists and counselors, who often overwork and underearn, may have low self-esteem. These mental health professionals may resort to some of the same means of taking care of their unmet needs as do their clients, that is, by overbuying. Therapists and counselors may have had no better financial education in their own homes than their clients. Counselors/therapists may be just as susceptible as their clients to the advertising messages that suggest happiness is just the next purchase away and tout the "more is better" philosophy. If we are to be truly helpful to our clients as counselors and therapists, we need to look into our own buying habits and practices, our motivations for buying, and the consequences of our buying behavior. We need to educate ourselves about compulsive buying and develop some media literacy using some of the resources listed at the end of this chapter.

My (ALB) original interest in the subject of shopping focused on the actualizing possibilities of search—of shopping gone good, if you will, rather than bad. Over a number of years, I had become aware of the very important role that a particular store (and my relationships with the people who worked there) played in my life. Recognizing that shopping meant far more to me than its traditional associations with buying or having, I imagined this was true for others as well.

I knew that shopping, undertaken in the spirit of search, could be a constructive process, one that would promote self-definition, self-expression, creativity, even healing. I knew too that done to excess, it could pose a dangerous threat. I wanted to understand my own experience better. I also wanted to help people I worked with transform the relentless pursuit of material goods into a meaningful search for ideas and experiences. So I set out to learn, from an academic point of view, what shopping was really about. I also took workshops and attended conferences with people whose treatment specialty is money disorders, to gain a better clinical perspective. Three years of these activities resulted in the book *I Shop, Therefore, I Am: Compulsive Buying and the Search for Self* (Benson, 2000). I began to give workshops for other therapists and for compulsive buyers and did clinical work in my private practice with compulsive buyers. Bob Coombs learned of my work from my book and asked me to write this chapter on treatment. Initially, I hired Marie Gengler to assist in my research for it, but her organized and thoughtful approach to the material eventually led me to ask her to co-author the chapter. I am now in the process of developing a group treatment model for compulsive buyers and plan to speak at colleges and universities about the serious problem of compulsive buying in that population.

COMPULSIVE BUYING AND CULTURE

A significant challenge confronting the counselor/therapist is the normalization of "retail therapy" in our country. We live in a culture of "competitive consumption" (Schor, 1998), one that equates goods with happiness. We're told that if we just use the right hairspray, we'll be irresistible to the opposite sex; if we drive the right car, we will be seen as strong and successful. Consumption fuels our economy and we are taught that it is an act of citizenship to support that economy by spending. From the time we go to college, we are continually barraged by credit cards, offered discounts, promotions, and tempting interest rates. The effect of this easy credit and the ubiquitous equation of "more equals better" has been plummeting savings rates and a skyrocketing number of bankruptcies. In recent years, we have witnessed a nationwide outbreak of "affluenza," "luxury fever," and "aspendicitis," our modern American plagues of materialism and overconsumption. "... for every voice that echoes Thoreau's famous plea, 'Simplify, simplify,' a hundred others cry, 'Amplify, amplify'" (Sanders, 1998). In addition to traditional stores, other fertile grounds for the growth of compulsive purchase have sprung up: catalogues, dedicated television shopping channels, cybershopping, and online trading.

Keeping up with the Joneses is more of a challenge than ever before. The Joneses used to be the family next door, with a lifestyle not that different from our own; now the Joneses we want to keep up with are the people we see on television, rich or upper middle class (Schor, 1998). Thus, the gap between what we have and what we want keeps widening. This affects almost all of us, to varying degrees.

Sometimes called the "smiled upon addiction" (Catalano & Sonenberg, 1993), society conspires against our taking compulsive buying seriously. Shopping jokes and bumper stickers are everywhere. We've all seen the one that boasts "When the going gets tough, the tough go shopping" and the rah-rah message, "Shop 'til you drop!" Because compulsive buying has only recently entered the ranks of legitimate disorders requiring treatment, it is still not taken as seriously as drug abuse or alcoholism. As a result, it may be the source of more guilt and shame than those disorders. Although this is beginning to change, the other addictions profiled in this book, with the possible exception of workaholism, are thought of as diseases, or at least recognized as serious problems requiring treatment. Compulsive buyers worry that they will be considered materialistic and shallow rather than having a serious, treatable problem. Counselors and therapists need to assure their clients that they appreciate the gravity of the situation when compulsive buying is an active addiction.

COMPULSIVE BUYING AND OTHER ADDICTIONS

Compulsive buying counseling is different and in some ways more complicated than drug and/or alcohol counseling because, unlike those problems, it is impossible to abstain from the use of money, just as someone with an eating disorder can't abstain from the use of food. A big part of recovery involves learning to use money responsibly and healthfully. This is why we do not advocate the use of programs that relieve compulsive buyers of the responsibility of learning to handle their money. In some programs, clients turn over their paychecks to organizations that then pay all their bills, giving the client an allowance for day-to-day expenditures. This does not help compulsive buyers take the reins of their finances back into their own hands. If you are referring a client to an organization that claims to counsel people who buy compulsively, make sure that some of the cornerstones of compulsive buying counseling—for example, the requirement that the client incur no new unsecured debt and the creation and use of a spending plan—are included in the services that are being offered.

Compulsive buying is associated with a number of other addictions and psychiatric disorders. Studies have suggested that more than a quarter of compulsive buyers have histories of alcohol abuse, drug abuse, and/or eating disorders (Christenson et al., 1994; McElroy, Keck, Pope, Smith, & Strakowski, 1994). The greater the severity of compulsive buying symptoms, the more likely it is that the individual is also suffering from another addiction or from one of the following: anxiety disorder, most frequently obsessive compulsive disorder; affective disorder, most frequently depression; and/or impulse control disorder, most frequently pathological gambling. However, as Helga Dittmar notes in Chapter 13, most of the studies on which these statistics and conclusions are based have used psychiatric inpatients or outpatients for their samples. These people would be more likely than the general population to have other addictions. Self-identified compulsive buyers who are not psychiatric patients tend to report a much lower incidence of associated disorders.

If you are an addictions counselor specializing in another addiction, it's nevertheless important to know something about compulsive buying and its treatment. In the process of recovering from another active addiction, some clients lose control of their money and start buying compulsively. To adequately understand and treat the disorder, it is essential to determine the extent of coexisting addictions, mental illness, and/or posttraumatic stress disorder in someone who buys compulsively. When another active addiction threatens a client's health, that problem must be addressed either prior to or concurrently with the treatment for compulsive buying. Without having a full picture of the other difficulties a compulsive buyer may have, the therapist may not anticipate symptom substitution, a somewhat probable event. I (ALB) once worked with a compulsive buyer who had a history of bulimia. As she was gaining control over the compulsive buying behavior, for two weeks in a row she came into the office with a noticeably rounder face. She'd been eating with the same fervor that had fueled her compulsive buying. A common strategy for helping to curb an active addiction is to suggest competing behaviors that will substitute for the addictive one. While baking or going out to a restaurant could be useful to certain compulsive buyers, in those who also have an eating disorder, these things could trigger the concurrent addiction; in this case, other alternative behaviors need to be found.

Serious problems with debt exacerbate an individual's sense of helplessness and hopelessness, which can present a suicidal risk. In fact, a number of suicides among college students have been linked to debt (Mannix, 1999). "Feelings of hopelessness, despair and a general preoccupation with money matters may lead to 'emotional indebtedness'—manifested by high levels of stress and anxiety—and ultimately to thoughts of suicide" (Hayes, 1997, p. 3697).

Sometimes it is hard to know whether a client's buying behavior is truly compulsive and whether or not treatment geared specifically for this problem is in order. The counselor/therapist needs to determine whether the buying behavior is interfering with the client's life, and, if so, how and to what extent. You need to familiarize yourself with the most commonly accepted definition of compulsive buying. (See Table 13.2 in the previous chapter.) It might also be useful to familiarize yourself with the various assessment tools available, whether you decide to administer them to your client or use them simply as a source for questions to ask during a clinical interview. These can also be found in Chapter 13.

TREATMENT

Although there has been less study about compulsive buying and its treatment than other addictions in this handbook, the body of literature is growing. It has been suggested that we are at the same stage in the evolution and treatment of this disorder that alcoholism was in about 40 years ago. Counselors/therapists need to read some of the literature that exists to decide whether, when, and what kind of referral to make, or, if you decide to work with the client yourself, how best to do that. This chapter provides a comprehensive overview of the various forms of treatment and self-help currently in use for compulsive buying: drug treatment, individual therapy, group therapy, couples therapy, counseling for compulsive buying, Debtors Anonymous (DA), and Simplicity Circles. Becoming familiar with the available resources can make you more knowledgeable and confident in your treatment decisions, helping you to empower your clients.

DRUG TREATMENT

For the past dozen years, the use of psychotropic medication for the treatment of compulsive buying has been reported in the psychiatric literature. The particular type of psychotropic medication used has been related, to a certain extent, to how the compulsive buying is seen diagnostically. Some psychiatrists believe that compulsive buying is more indicative of an impulse control disorder; others think it more indicative of an obsessive-compulsive disorder; still others relate compulsive buying to depression or bipolar disorder.

In the first of these published reports, McElroy and her colleagues (McElroy, Satlin, Pope, Keck, & Hudson, 1991) reported a series of three consecutive patients who requested treatment for compulsive shopping. Each of these patients met the *DSM-III-R* (American Psychiatric Association [APA], 1987) criteria for an impulse control disorder not otherwise specified, which is the diagnostic category currently accorded to compulsive buying. Within 4 weeks of treatment with doses of medication typically reported effective for major depression, all three patients had significant decreases in both the urge to shop and actual shopping behavior. The three different antidepressants used were bupropion, fluoxetine, and nortriptyline. Though they differ in their mechanism of action, each was equally effective at lessening the shopping behavior and the associated, anxiety-provoking thoughts.

In a later study of 20 patients with compulsive buying (McElroy, Keck, Pope, Smith, & Strakowski, 1994), the majority was treated with one or more psychotropic medications. Because many of these patients were diagnosed with bipolar disorder, the researchers decided to use a number of different mood stabilizers (valproate, lithium, and antipsychotics). Several antidepressants (bupropion, nortriptyline, fluoxetine, trazodone, sertraline, and desipramine) were used alone or in conjunction with a mood stabilizer and 69% of the patients receiving treatment with psychotropic medications described a complete or partial reduction in buying impulses and behavior.

There is disagreement whether improvement in compulsive buying behavior has more to do with mood elevation or with control of buying thoughts and impulses. Lejoyeux asserts that depressed individuals with compulsive buying disorders are more likely to improve with antidepressants than those who are not depressed. Lejoyeux, Hourtane, and Adés (1995) describe two patients who stated that their compulsive buying behavior was like an antidepressant. Both of these patients also had major depressive disorder. The medical treatment of the mood disorder led to the disappearance of the compulsive buying. These researchers drew the conclusion that compulsive buying was thus directly induced by depression. In 1996, Lejoyeux, Adés, Tassian, and Solomon published a review of the phenomenology and psychopathology of uncontrolled buying; they found that "in most cases, uncontrolled buying can be understood as 'compensatory buying' that temporarily alleviates depressive symptoms . . ." (p. 1524). Their review of studies reporting treatment of compulsive buying with antidepressants suggested that antidepressant treatment was markedly successful when uncontrolled buying was associated with depression. They concluded that the treatment of depressed mood could lead to a significant decrease in the intensity and frequency of shopping urges.

This idea was refuted by Black, Monahan, and Gabel (1997), who treated 10 nondepressed compulsive buyers in an open-label trial using the SSRI fluvoxamine. Nine of the 10 noted substantial improvement in compulsive buying behavior. At the end of the 9-week protocol, when treatment was discontinued, there was a tendency for the patients to relapse. For this reason, 7 of the 10 asked to continue the drug treatment when the study was over. Black (personal communication, August 8, 2002) noted, to his surprise, that the symptoms and behaviors returned (albeit slowly and not to their pretreatment level) as the patients were tapered off fluvoxamine. Because the patients had adopted new behaviors, were spending more nonshopping time with family and friends, and had resumed old hobbies, Black had believed the results might persist.

Because these patients were not depressed, Black suggested that the benefit of the SSRIs in compulsive buying had little to do with mood elevation, but rather with the control of buying thoughts and impulses. Regardless of whether improvement occurred because an underlying depression was treated or whether it was related to control of buying thoughts and impulses, the results suggest that the use of psychotropic medications can be very useful in treating compulsive buying.

Compulsive buying, which is currently categorized in the *DSM-IV* (APA, 1994) as an impulse control disorder, not otherwise specified, has also been compared to obsessive compulsive disorder. The ritualized and repetitive nature of some buying sprees has led clinicians to use anti-obsessional medications to treat this behavior. The results of the open label trial cited above (Black et al., 1997) indicated a significant overall improvement in shopping-related obsessions and compulsions for 9 of the 10 compulsive buyers who received the SSRI fluvoxamine. These responders had a 50% or greater improvement in their shopping behavior as determined by both the Yale-Brown Obsessive-Compulsive Scale-Shopping Version (Goodman et al., 1989) and the Compulsive Buying Scale (Faber & O'Guinn, 1992).

Because of the success of the open-label study, Black developed a placebo-controlled, double-blind protocol to test the effectiveness of fluvoxamine (Black, Gabel, Hansen, & Schlosser, 2000), hypothesizing that nondepressed compulsive buyers treated with fluvoxamine would show greater improvement than similar subjects receiving placebo in a short-term trial. Instead, 70% of the patients in both the drug group *and* the placebo group showed improvement in their compulsive buying symptoms. There were 24 subjects in the study; 12 were randomly assigned to fluvoxamine treatment and the other 12 to the placebo. The participants in both groups were "much" or "very much" improved on the basis of clinical global impressions. Subjects in both groups showed improvement as early as the second week of the trial, and, for most, improvement continued during the 9-week study. Since subjects in both groups met on a regular basis with the study psychiatrist and research nurse to talk about many details of their shopping behavior and constructed shopping diaries that included daily recording of shopping behavior, the researchers hypothesized that this support and attention may have been the most significant factor in the patients' improvement. This is worth keeping in mind when trying to help a compulsive buyer find the best treatment options; drug treatment alone is probably not the best choice. Constructing a shopping diary and having the opportunity to review it with a professional may be just as effective, or even more so.

Another double-blind study of the use of fluvoxamine in compulsive buying was recently completed (Ninan et al., 2000). For the 37 participants in this study, compulsive buying was significantly reduced during the 12 weeks of active treatment—again, in both fluvoxamine *and* placebo groups, the drug and the placebo were equally effective. As in Black et al. (1997), the behavioral benefits of keeping a daily shopping diary may account for the high placebo-response rate. In any case, no definitive statement on the efficacy of treating compulsive buying with fluvoxamine can yet be made.

Stimulated by the result of Black et al. (1997) with fluvoxamine, Koran, Bullock, Hartston, Elliot, and D'Andrea (2002) tested the effectiveness of another SSSRI, citalopram, in an open label study. Citalopram produced marked improvement in 80% of the 24 subjects. Treatment in the 12-week open-label study was associated with rapid, marked, sustained improvement or with the complete remission of compulsive buying. Patients reported loss of interest in shopping, disposal of all catalogues, and "purchaseless" shopping expeditions. The authors initially hypothesized that improvement might have resulted from the behavioral intervention of keeping a shopping log, or from a placebo response, or from treatment of comorbid conditions, in particular the improvement of subclinical depressive symptoms. About three quarters of the subjects had at least mild mood symptoms, and these showed significant improvement by the end of the study. Most of the subjects who continued citalopram treatment for 3 months or more, however, have not relapsed, whereas those that discontinued the drug were much more likely to, suggesting to the authors of the study that a placebo response is not responsible for the symptomatic improvement. The authors suggest that acute and long-term, double-blind, placebo-controlled trials of citalopram and other SSRIs for the treatment of compulsive buying are indicated.

To this end, Koran, Chuoung, Bullock, and Smith (2003), tested the effectiveness of citalopram for compulsive buying in an open-label flexible-dose trial followed by a 9-week, double-blind, placebo-controlled trial in those whose symptoms had improved significantly in the open-label trial. Citalopram was associated with rapid, marked, sustained improvement or remission in most subjects. Responders got rid of catalogues, stopped browsing on the Internet or on TV shopping channels, were able to shop normally without purchasing impulsively, and were less interested in shopping altogether. Subjects in this study were not asked to keep a daily shopping log, nor was their shopping behavior reviewed. These factors, therefore—potentially significant in other studies—cannot explain the improvement here. Koran et al. note a significant correlation between an improvement in mood symptoms and an improvement in compulsive buying behavior. Their double-blind study is not yet completed, however, and so for the moment, they cannot determine whether the response associated with citalopram is a true drug effect or a placebo response.

One further prospect is worth noting here: A woman with a five-year history of compulsive buying showed improvement with the use of naltrexone, an opioid antagonist (Kim, 1998). Based on evidence that naltrexone has been effective in reducing the cravings associated with other urge-based impulse control disorders, such as pathological gambling (Kim, Grant, Adson, & Shin, 2001) and kleptomania

(Grant & Kim, 2002), three compulsive buyers reporting urges to shop were treated with high-dose naltrexone. In this yet unpublished series, Grant (2002) reports reduction in buying urges and complete cessation of compulsive buying in all three cases.

Referral for psychopharmacological treatment is a complicated issue, one that requires consultation with a psychopharmacologist, preferably one familiar with the research on drug treatment for compulsive buying. Whether or not the patient has other comorbid conditions and/or other addictions are important factors in deciding on the best course of drug treatment. If the compulsive buyer has a comorbid disorder with a known treatment, initiating treatment for that disorder may lead to improvement in the shopping behavior as well. Concurrent major depression, for example, would suggest initiating treatment with an antidepressant, and comorbid bipolar disorder or mild bipolar disorder, also known as psychlothymia, would suggest initial treatment with a mood stabilizer. If the compulsive buyer has obsessive-compulsive disorder, he or she might best be started on an SSRI.

Counselors need to encourage the compulsive buyer to weigh carefully, with a psychopharmacologist, the benefits of discontinuing an effective medication, since there appears to be a risk of relapse associated with cessation. Much more research is needed in this area. Clearly, it would be useful to know whether the combination of drug treatment with different forms of psychotherapy is more effective than drug treatment without the psychotherapy.

THERAPY

INDIVIDUAL THERAPY

Individual therapy for compulsive buying runs the gamut from traditional psychodynamic psychotherapy, with an almost exclusive focus on the underlying dynamics within a historical context, to a very strict focus on the here and now of the problem, with little attention to underlying dynamics. Dynamic psychotherapy may be the treatment of choice with a very high-functioning patient who does not have other addictive disorders, but those clients are very much in the minority. Most compulsive buyers need the addition of other specific tools for changing their behavior, including a shopping diary and a spending plan. Some people will need to participate in Debtors Anonymous, attend group therapy for compulsive buyers, and/or participate in counseling specifically geared for compulsive buying, especially if the individual therapist does not have experience with the tools of compulsive buying counseling.

It is still unusual, in my (ALB) clinical experience and that of most of my colleagues, for a compulsive buyer to refer him- or herself for treatment of this problem (although this is beginning to change). Much more frequently, a compulsive buying problem reveals itself in the course of ongoing psychotherapy. As treatment progresses, some clients begin to talk openly about it; with others, it emerges in the context of financial independence and responsibility issues, relationship problems, difficulties at work, or parenting problems. Compulsive buying may also present itself indirectly in therapy: a patient may wear something new or different to every session, or arrive with shopping bags week after week, or repeatedly give gifts to the therapist, or fall behind in paying the bill. Some patients will enact several of these behaviors simultaneously.

Even when these signs are evident, compulsive buying is easily missed by traditional therapists, who often have a great deal of difficulty talking about money issues with clients, particularly if the client is not talking about it in the therapy directly. Traditional therapists are less likely to have explored their own issues with money than counselors who specialize in money disorders. One therapist, Julia, was "unable to focus on her practice, she would see a client, then rush out to shop until it was time for her next session. There was no quality energy going into her work, which fed her already low self-esteem and contributed to the feeling, deep down, that she didn't deserve to have a successful practice" (McCall, 2000, p. 456). It goes without saying that a therapist's unresolved money issues will affect his or her counsel on that subject. As already suggested, therapists may deny or avoid dealing with clients' money problems, just as they do their own. Therapists may even join with the client and unconsciously reinforce his or her justifications for compulsive buying. Alternatively, therapists may be overly harsh once a client's money problems have been brought to light, in an unconscious effort to deny their own problems. For the therapist as well as the client, money is often the last taboo.

Traditional therapists trained in the treatment of addiction are generally more comfortable and more knowledgeable about treating patients who buy compulsively, even if they have relatively little direct experience with this problem. Addiction counselors know how important it is to help the client take control of the symptom as soon as possible, not only because the client can then begin to experience herself as competent and successful, but also because an active addiction to compulsive buying may threaten the continuation of the treatment; in the grip of his buying compulsion, a client may deem therapy expendable when finances stretch to the breaking point. And if someone else is paying the bill, the sponsor may decide to stop supporting treatment if he or she doesn't see enough progress being made.

When a compulsive buying problem comes to light, the first thing for a therapist untrained in money disorders and addiction treatment to do is to decide whether or not to be the person providing the structured help with it. A therapist interested enough in the problem to undertake the necessary reading, training, and supervision will likely serve the clients well. If you are unwilling to get immersed in the treatment of this money disorder should refer clients to someone specially qualified to treat compulsive buying and/or require that the client attend Debtors Anonymous meetings. This doesn't necessarily mean that therapist and client need to terminate; it simply means that the behavioral work needed to give the client mastery and control over compulsive buying will be taking place outside the individual psychotherapy. If the client agrees, it can be particularly useful for the traditional psychotherapist and the compulsive buying counselor to have an ongoing dialogue. This way, each can have a fuller perspective on the problem—and thereby render more help to the client.

We turn now to the work of individual psychotherapists who have written about their work with compulsive buyers. Here we can see what dynamic psychotherapy has to offer these patients that is not offered in the other forms of therapy included in this chapter. Traditional psychotherapy focuses on the emotional underpinnings and dynamic meaning of the compulsive buying. Compulsive buying both compensates for and defends against the phenomena that occur frequently in this population: narcissistic vulnerability, psychological dependency, affect intolerance, generalized compulsivity (often expressed through other addictions), a propensity to fantasize, a deep sense of emptiness and inadequacy, feelings of social undesirability, and negative affects like anger, fear, shame, and despair. The behavior "constitutes a flight from full awareness of these feelings, and from having them emerge undisguised for others to see" (Goldman, 2000, p. 246). Therapists need to convey to the patient their understanding that the symptom provides comfort, that there is a great deal of investment in holding onto the symptom because it is such a successful tension reducer and affect regulator. Therapists also need to convey their understanding of how difficult and anxiety-provoking it is for the patient even to consider relinquishing it. The therapist must listen empathically and with consistent therapeutic attention to the use of the symptoms: the motivation, the enactment, the experience of the symptomatic act itself, and the change in all of these over time.

Barth, who has written about her approach to treating these clients (2000), sees her function as helping the client to fill, in a healthy and permanent way, some of the gaps that the compulsive buying attempts to fill temporarily. Compulsive buyers are often *alexithymic*, a term that connotes someone's inability to use language to differentiate and explore emotions (or, if they can use language to describe their emotions, an inability to manage these emotions or to soothe and calm the self when they occur). For alexithymic patients who are compulsive buyers, the buying deadens, stimulates, and comforts simultaneously. Clients who use shopping in this way need to get in touch with their inner thought processes; they must develop the ability to conceptualize emotional cause and effect, to experience themselves as being at the helm of their actions. To build this kind of internal structure, the therapist needs to communicate genuine interest and curiosity about the most specific and concrete details of what is most important to the client. With compulsive buyers, this often means attending to every aspect of the actual shopping behavior. Not only is this a way of letting the client know that his or her compulsive buying is purposeful and meaningful; in addition, this very detailed and specific focus can also lead the client to pay focused, mindful attention to his or her own experience, to connect with self in an unprecedented way. Gradually, the client begins to develop and build an internal structure that includes "positive self-regard, trust in another, and an ability to both observe the self and tolerate a variety of affects" (p. 277). With this structure more firmly in place, therapist and client can together begin to sort out just what kinds of feelings trigger the compulsive buying. For those clients who suffer from more than one addiction, this same structure will allow them to explore the feelings that trigger other forms of compulsive behavior as well.

Krueger (2000) looks at compulsive buying as an example of the use of money as an *action symptom*. An action symptom is something that temporarily regulates feelings and tension states, creates the illusion of meeting a fundamental need, and also serves a symbolic self-object function. Krueger believes it important to understand all the facets of the story that the action symptom is telling. Most of his compulsive buyers have been women who buy clothes. Based on his experience, he concludes that compulsive buyers try very hard to please because their fragile sense of self and self-esteem depend on the responses of others. Compulsive buying can relate to the preoccupation that many women feel about the way they are viewed by others, not only physically, but also in regard to social skills and general competence. In her chapter, "Compulsive Buying as an Addiction," Goldman (2000) sums it up this way: "A well-chosen wardrobe that appears costly does much not only to enhance the wearer's appearance, but also to create an aura of someone in command of herself and her world" (p. 246). For these individuals, the compulsive acquisition of clothes often follows the disruption of an emotional bond with someone important. Such a disruption sets into motion a desperate need to appear attractive and desirable and a hope that new clothes will fulfill this need for affirmation. The same theory can be applied to compulsive buying of items other than clothing.

Psychodynamic therapists explore with each patient the particular family environment, as a way of understanding how the spending pattern develops and what its emotional significance is. Several familial scenarios can foster the development of compulsive buying in a child:

- Some parents of compulsive buyers were abused and/or neglected during their own childhoods—but were given compensatory gifts. They followed this pattern with their children, showering them with presents to offset perceived neglect, separation, divorce, or abuse. In such families, the children often feel inadequate, as though something vital were missing in themselves and their lives; they buy compulsively to fill this internal emptiness and to feel, at least temporarily, more complete, less alone.

- Some families reward good behavior and achievement with money and gifts rather than affection and affirmation. This behavior often passes to the next generation and may result in compulsive buying, compulsive gift giving, and/or compulsively picking up the tab. Having felt undervalued and essentially unwanted, such patients find the warmth and recognition of salespeople, or the gratitude expressed by the recipients of gifts or dinners, an important indication that he or she is, indeed, valuable.

- Researchers have described a disturbance of autonomy that results from being forced to deny genuine feelings to such an extent that they are no longer clearly grasped (Scherhorn, Reisch, & Raab, 1990). In these families, children don't get the time or energy from parents that would allow them to feel important; instead, the parents are attending to what they consider valuable, the acquisition and maintenance of their possessions. Because possessions have been given such value at a formative and critical time of development, the child's natural longings for personal acknowledgment and familial love become redirected into wishes for impersonal material objects. The resultant compulsive shopping is both an act of aggression and an attempt to confirm worth. It will require rescue by significant others, will force parents or spouses to make up for what the compulsive buyer has missed growing up.

- Sometimes a family that has suffered financial reversals fixates on lost luxury and deeply envies those that are more financially fortunate. Their concomitant reduction in power and status may lead to lowered self-esteem. If family members' view of themselves continues to be associated with the kind and quantity of possessions they can acquire, compulsive buying may become an unconscious solution to the problem. Recent economic conditions in the United States, including the burst of the Internet bubble, has led to significant financial reversals for many households. Whether or not we see an upsurge in compulsive buying in the next generation remains to be seen, but it's a distinct possibility.

- In other families where compulsive buying develops, a feeling of emotional and financial impoverishment has dominated the patient's childhood. The compulsive buyer wards off re-experiencing those painful feelings with orgies of purchase.

When we consider these different types of individual psychotherapy and the different family scenarios that give rise to this problem, it becomes clear that there are as many different psychodynamic explanations of compulsive buying behavior as there are compulsive buyers. We know that compulsive buying is a behavior designed to fill an internal void, enhance self-esteem, regulate negative affect, and provide stimulation. In addition, both research and clinical data suggest that the role of fantasy in compulsive buying is extremely important. For example, Winestine (1985) described a woman whose compulsive buying was eventually traced to a childhood seduction. In therapy, this woman recalled that as a child she had had erotic encounters with her maternal stepgrandfather. These had excited her, but also left her feeling ashamed, humiliated, and overwhelmed. During her shopping sprees, she fancied herself the wife of a famous multimillionaire with the power and the money to buy her anything. In succumbing to her irrepressible urges to shop for clothing, she satisfied some of the same urges that the sexual behavior in childhood had satisfied; but this time, instead of feeling helpless, humiliated, and worthless for being out of control, she felt strong, worthwhile, and powerful. The patient couldn't afford the clothes, but she enjoyed using credit cards that she then would not pay. She felt neither guilt nor responsibility for her behavior and the debts that resulted; instead, she held the banks that had extended her credit responsible: they had tempted her into an intensely conflictual state for which she had no suitable resolution. This was just what the stepgrandfather had done: she'd had either to succumb to the stepgrandfather's advances and feel ashamed, or resist and feel frightened and frustrated.

In another case, described by Richards (2000), compulsive buying demonstrated a wish to outmaneuver the intolerable reality of death. In still another case reported by Richards, a woman's compulsive buying was a way to protect valued ties to parents so as not to have to deal with her own conflicts about being an independent woman. In Boxes 14.1 and 14.2 detailed case reports illustrate how some of the issues discussed in this section occur and are worked with in actual therapy. While it is easy to be dazzled by some of the case reports in the literature, it is important to bear in mind that traditional individual psychotherapy without an adjunctive program for controlling symptoms and special considerations is of limited usefulness unless the compulsive buying problem is not too severe and there are no other addictive tendencies (see Table 14.1).

Symptom substitution takes place in all addictions treatment, and compulsive buying is no exception. As mentioned earlier, I (ALB) have seen patients successfully control their impulses to buy compulsively, only to come to therapy sessions noticeably heavier than they had been the week or two before. They had simply substituted eating for buying. Because of the everpresence of symptom substitution, treatment must seek to limit all harmful impulsivity and compulsivity, rather than merely to control compulsive buying.

Summary Traditional individual psychotherapy helps patients discover and tell their own story as a means to understanding and ultimately gaining control over

BOX 14.1
Detailed Case History

Faye was a married, 36-year-old clerical worker with a diagnosis of major depression and borderline personality disorder. She was a compulsive buyer of jewelry and clothing. Her buying sprees typically followed experiences of perceived rejection, after which she lost control and expressed strong negative emotion. She admitted to losing control during her shopping sprees and worried what her husband Harold would say. Harold was a passive, 45-year-old man whose social inhibitions and indifference to his appearance made him unappealing to his wife. He worked hard, earned modestly, and despaired over his wife's spending.

In one particular session, Faye explained her latest compulsive buying episode to me, which was prompted by her one-year anniversary at work. She had expected a gift from her supervisor, because he had given one to his personal assistant on her seventh anniversary, but she, Faye, did not receive one.

"You were hurt because he seemed not to appreciate you."

"Not only seemed! He said I wasn't fast enough. Now he wants me to learn the computer! I don't want to learn the computer. It makes me nervous! Why can't he appreciate me as I am?"

"Being asked to learn something new means . . ."

"I said, 'I've worked for you a whole year today and this is how you reward me.' And I started screaming, and everyone could hear me, and then I started to cry! I grabbed my coat and ran out the door and didn't go back! Oh, I must have lost my job. How can I tell Harold? How could I have done this again?"

"It seems we need to work more on your being angry and expressing your feelings without losing control."

"I wish I had gone right home, as I should have. I stopped at Lord & Taylor. Not to buy! Just to peek."

She smiled coquettishly and went on to tell me of several purchases, each a bargain. Then she paused, and added, "And also I bought a bracelet. It cost $375. But that's half-price! . . . And I just needed to do something . . . to buy something of value and have it for my own, no matter what!" She spoke with vigor, smiling, but now and then a look of alarm would cross her face and disappear.

This is the kind of affective split commonly seen in various addictions during times of relapse. The patient, though suffering from guilt and anxiety, had moments of exhilaration. Faye's ability to deny reality and to momentarily enjoy her purchases, despite upcoming trouble, is typical of compulsive buyers. Faye continued to explain that after each episode she tore a blank check from Harold's checkbook to pay the bill when it came. She had no concern that Harold would notice a check missing. Harold never even asked where the new things came from because he didn't notice them. He did little to stop this pattern, possibly even gaining an unconscious reward from the role of the morally superior, burdened spouse.

(continued)

Certain themes are prevalent in Faye's life: lack of experience of feeling valued, hence the exaggerated need to own valuables; a paranoid sense of not getting enough, with denial of the measured way in which she gave to others; a chronic state of underachievement and relative lack of skills due to an inability to focus on anything except her personal needs. Faye often chose to overlook certain realities. Her mother, now approaching 75, needed help with her business affairs. Her oldest daughter took on this responsibility. Faye could not see that this entitled her sister to their mother's generosity, just as she could not understand her supervisor's rewarding his assistant of seven years and leaving her out. This sense of entitlement permeated her thinking. As a result, she rarely got what she hoped for, and consistently felt deprived. She was often unaware of what others might expect from her. For example, she would complain of being left out of social events, but rarely extended an invitation to anyone. Having developed only the most modest skills, she expected rewards matching those of high achievers. Compounding all of this was the lack of boundaries in her emotional expression. She could not express strong negative feelings without losing control.

At the beginning of treatment, I was seen as a depriving figure—an expectable transference phenomenon. She was resistant to the ordinary demands of treatment—paying for missed sessions, not always being seen early if she arrived early, and the like. After each buying episode she would deride me for failing to cure her of her compulsion. When I suggested that her feelings of being uncared for by me were reminiscent of the deprivation of her childhood, she was pleased. She savored the word "deprivation," using it often to explain her behavior to herself. I saw that genetic interpretations were not helpful, as explaining her behavior made regressions seem acceptable. I changed my approach, and instead of interpreting her buying as a response to needs unfulfilled in childhood, I used an AA concept, that of *relapse triggers*. Without using these words, I helped her identify the events and feelings that preceded undue purchases and emotional eruptions. Few references were made to the origins of these reactions. Instead, she was encouraged to reflect, "When I feel this way, I *could* go shopping." Gradually the narrow focus on her most painful current feelings allowed her to use impulse control and delay gratification, and to increase her capacity for affect tolerance. She grew proud of her more mature behavior. When treatment ended, Faye's shopping sprees were far less frequent and less costly than at the beginning. When they did occur, she would usually tell Harold about them. At times, she was able to plan necessary purchases with him, before buying.

Source: "Compulsive Buying as an Addiction" (pp. 254–259), by R. Goldman, in *I Shop, Therefore, I Am: Compulsive Buying and the Search for Self*, A. L. Benson (Ed.), 2000, Northvale, NJ: Aronson. Reprinted with permission.

BOX 14.2
Detailed Case History

Linda, a 27-year-old unmarried woman, presented with significant depression that was the result of a turbulent relationship with her 40-year-old boyfriend, a wealthy, cocaine-abuser. He essentially kept Linda as his mistress even though he was unmarried.

Linda described her depression and discontent with her life. She complained of not having her own identity and of not being ready to break away from her boyfriend and be emotionally and financially independent. Lacking an identity and a structure for her life, she was understandably frightened.

She told of her frequent feelings of depletion and emptiness, and the resulting overwhelming urge to eat, drink, or shop. She spoke of her anger at those who had never done things for her and her compelling drive to spend money. What afforded Linda a temporary high was not so much the acquisition of clothes, but rather the power of possessing money and having the ability to spend it. An important component of her shopping was the devoted attention given by the salesperson, chosen to be someone who closely resembled Linda (a mirroring self-object) and who seemed most caring and attuned (empathic ability). The undivided attention, the attunement to her very specific needs and desires, formed a (pseudoemphatic) bond highly valued by Linda, one she wanted to prolong as far as possible. The actual purchase was, for her, anticlimactic, the end of the special, invigorating attention.

Linda described her shopping episodes as an intense urge to "go into a store and get something new—even some little thing like a silver bracelet or T-shirt—but just to buy something new." She indicated that she would then end up spending several hundred dollars—up to her charge card limit—and buy an entire outfit. She especially liked to go to a particular store she and her boyfriend had shopped in, indicating, "I wanted to go in [the store] and believe that I can still go and spend the money without him. At the moment I was purchasing those items, I felt powerful, confident at the same time when only a few moments before I was feeling empty and completely without power. When it hit me first—what I had done—was when they gave me the sales receipt. It was like reality hit me. I was nervous about it then and still when I came home."

She went on to recount how her boyfriend would think she looked fabulous in the outfit and how he would have to settle her bills. The shopping binge reestablished their bond. She stated, "I had to go back with him to get him to bail me out. If everything else fails, I would just have to go back to him." She would spend just enough to ensure that he would have to rescue her.

Linda recognized her shopping as an addiction and was afraid of it. At times, instead of going home she would try to think of things to buy, to gain temporary respite from being alone and feeling depressed. When she did not involve someone else in her spending addiction, Linda felt powerful in her ability to create a situation of risk or a financial disaster and to figure some way out of it. She felt sneaky and guilty, yet excited about the risk taking.

Source: "The Use of Money as an Action Symptom" (pp. 300–302), by D. Krueger, in *I Shop, Therefore, I Am: Compulsive Buying and the Search for Self,* A. L. Benson (Ed.), 2000, Northvale, NJ: Aronson. Reprinted with permission.

Table 14.1
Seven Essential Points for Treatment

---

1. Be directive in encouraging the patient to reduce or end excessive buying at the earliest point possible.
2. Recommend participation in Debtors Anonymous.
3. Consider referring the patient to a psychiatrist for consultation. Where depression is a factor, psychoactive medications may be nearly indispensable in helping the patient to progress.
4. Help patients examine those aspects of their history that make them susceptible to the buying addiction. This requires exploration of emotional states that occur before, during, and after excessive buying.
5. Use the above to identify relapse triggers. These should be clearly stated and referred to whenever appropriate, so that the patient has them firmly in mind.
6. Explore the use of fantasy in buying behavior. This can be difficult, as compulsive buyers are often reluctant to share their fantasies, which they know to be ridiculous. The fantasies predict extravagant rewards from the ownership of a desired item. In treatment, a growing sense of reality can reduce the power of such fantasies.
7. Express appreciation for the patient's strengths, especially those observed in current clinical work. Patients need to know that the therapist sees each of them as an adult fully capable of nonaddictive behavior.

Source: "Compulsive Buying as an Addiction" (p. 265), by R. Goldman, in *I Shop, Therefore, I Am: Compulsive Buying and the Search for Self*, A. L. Benson (Ed.), 2000, Northvale, NJ: Aronson. Reprinted with permission.

their symptom. "Some Jungians believe that money and material goods serve as a modern day 'talisman of the self' (Lockart, 1982, p. 21) onto which current psychic conflicts are projected and played out. If this is true, then psychotherapists need to pay close attention to the communications present in a client's financial beliefs, wishes, and patterns. Seizing the opportunity to help clients unveil and verbalize their spending and debt conflicts can be crucial in helping them create and build greater gratification in their lives. Just as the realms of work and love can be disabled by money disorders, so too can they be enhanced by financial recovery" (Boundy, 2000, p. 25).

GROUP THERAPY

Use of group therapy for compulsive buying has been reported since the late 1980s. At least five different forms of group therapy have been used with this population. There are certain obvious similarities among them, as well as significant differences. The first very detailed account of group therapy for compulsive shopping was described in Janet Damon's book, *Shopaholics: An 8-Week Program to Control Compulsive Spending* (1988), which was actually written as a self-help book, intended for the compulsive buyer. Several years later in 1993, James Mitchell, who had already done cognitive behavioral group treatment for bulimia, developed a similar program for compulsive buying at the University of Minnesota. He and his research coordinator, Melissa Burgard, described the program in a chapter of the book, *I Shop, Therefore, I Am: Compulsive Buying and the Search for Self* (Benson, 2000). Throughout the 1990s in New Jersey, Leonard Brazer led outpatient treatment groups for people with a variety of money disorders, including compulsive buying. This work is also described in detail in *I Shop, Therefore, I Am* (2000). In the late

1990s, David Parecki (2000), in fulfillment of his doctoral requirements at the California School of Professional Psychology, devised and ran, with a co-leader, a group treatment program for compulsive buyers. Parecki's doctoral dissertation described this group fully. And, most recently, psychologists at the University of Santiago de Compostela in Spain created and conducted a group treatment approach for compulsive buying, which they have outlined in their book *Adiciòn a la compra: Analysìs, evaluaciòn y tratamiento* [Buying Addiction: Analysis, Evaluation and Treatment] (Rodriguez-Villarino, Otero-Lopez, & Rodriguez-Casto, 2001). Doubtless there have been other unreported group treatments for compulsive buying in the United States and elsewhere. As compulsive buying is increasingly recognized as a very serious problem, there will certainly be more reports of group treatment for this population; the modality can be extremely important in the successful treatment of this disorder.

There are several reasons why group therapy assists the recovery from compulsive buying efficiently and effectively. "A powerful combination of peer support, encouragement, feedback, and confrontation, all delivered under the guidance of a trained clinician, group therapy provides an almost ideal forum for addressing core features . . ." (Washton, 2001, p. 240) of addictive problems like compulsive buying. One of the principal strengths of group therapy is that the group setting diminishes feelings of aloneness and increases feelings of being intuitively understood, because everyone present has the same problem. Group members feel a sense of belonging and community that allows and encourages open and honest sharing. The feedback that group members get from each other helps members correct distorted self-concepts, reframe dysfunctional thoughts, and engage in fewer of the maladaptive behaviors that stem from those distorted self-concepts and dysfunctional thoughts. The mere presence of others with the same addiction helps members to bear the overwhelming feelings of isolation, failure, guilt, pain, and humiliation that perpetuate compulsive buying behavior. Damon describes this as the opportunity to "meet others who have shared the experiences of addiction, from the euphoria to the shame" (1988, p. 167). Group therapy also helps to break through denial of the destructive behavior, which is typical of the compulsive buyer. Breaking through denial leads to confrontation rather than avoidance of the problem. Because group members know how compulsive buyers think, feel, and behave, they can help to identify the defenses that are used to rationalize the behavior, and minimize the tendency of compulsive buyers to disown personal responsibility and externalize blame. While encouraging others in the right direction, the group can grow together in hope and triumph. Individuals can see people at many different stages of recovery and know that others will be there to support them through the trials each will encounter along the way. A supportive peer atmosphere and group bonding encourages members to remain a part of the group. Finally, experiential learning and role modeling are additional tools for recovery. Although these tools are used in both individual and group therapy, in group therapy, members not only do their own experiential learning and role modeling, but also have the benefit of witnessing other people in the group doing that work. In combination, all of these features of group therapy provide a very powerful rationale for using this form of treatment for compulsive buying.

Although there are many differences among the reported forms of group therapy for compulsive buying, all groups share certain important characteristics, both in structure and content. The structural similarities include the selection process, frequency of meetings, and presence and role of the group therapist. Generally, group members respond to advertisements in newspapers, magazines, or fliers posted in local businesses like supermarkets, inviting people who believe they have this problem to join the group. Most therapists assess the appropriateness of the individual for the group through an individual interview. These meetings usually employ a formal assessment test such as the Edwards Compulsive Shopping Scale (Edwards, 1993) or the Compulsive Buying Scale (Faber & O'Guinn, 1992) and a set of questions about buying behavior, mental status, other addictions, and family history. Sometimes the assessments determine that therapy for compulsive buying is not suitable for an individual, often because of the presence of chemical dependency, eating disorders, extreme self-injurious behavior, or other addictions that need to be addressed first. A person with one or more of these problems, particularly if extreme, would have a hard time focusing simply on compulsive buying behavior and is therefore referred to more appropriate treatment programs. The size of the groups varies, but rarely exceeds 15 people; and trained professionals lead them. The short-term groups meet for between 6 and 14 weeks, one or two sessions per week, generally for 90 minutes. Although Damon's was the only open-ended long-term group, in some of the other groups, individuals continued to meet with the therapist in a group therapy setting, but without a structured plan for the weekly sessions. To promote an atmosphere of sharing and growth, confidentiality and a nonjudgmental attitude are emphasized. Since the group is specifically structured for the treatment of compulsive buying behavior, a restriction is placed on the extent to which personal histories and individual psychodynamics are discussed. The focus is on the here and now of the compulsion to buy.

In the content of the sessions, too, there are many similarities. The overarching goal of treatment groups is an awakening on the part of each group member about his or her buying behavior, the context in which it occurs (e.g., gift buying, Internet, collecting, catalog, television shopping), and an understanding of the relationship between the person's thoughts and emotions and the compulsive buying behavior. In each group, members learn about the internal and external triggers to their compulsive buying and begin learning how to gain control of this behavior. Strategies for controlling it are employed in every group; some of the more common ones are delaying for a period of time before buying, bringing only a certain amount of cash or a debit card without overdraft privileges, not using credit cards, or doing things incompatible with buying: bringing no money to the store or pursuing another fulfilling activity that has nothing to do with shopping and/or buying (Table 14.2). Credit card use is minimized or banned as a requirement of the group.

It is important to choose alternatives you enjoy. It is also important to have readily available alternatives. If, for instance, reading a book is an attractive alternative, make sure you have one that is interesting and even better, difficult to put down. There may be times when you find it necessary to try several alternatives before the urge to shop/buy diminishes. There also may be times when you try everything and yet the urge to shop/buy remains strong. On these occasions you may need to hold on to your chair or simply go to sleep. You will feel better the next day, especially after having made it through a difficult period.

The construction and use of a spending plan is another dominant feature in most groups. Many use a buddy system—either another group member or someone

Table 14.2
Alternatives to Problem Buying Behaviors

---

1. Call a group member or a friend. Keep calling until you reach someone.
2. Write the purchase down instead of actually buying it.
3. Take a bath or shower.
4. Take a walk.
5. Do a nonshopping-related activity outside shops. Stay out of the mall.
6. Write a letter.
7. Do a relaxation exercise or meditation.
8. Distract yourself with a craft project, book, or TV program.
9. Write out thoughts and feelings.
10. Go to a movie, museum, or play.
11. Read something inspirational.
12. Listen to music.
13. _____
14. _____
15. _____

Source: Buying Disorder Group Treatment Manual (p. 27), by J. Mitchell, 1993, Unpublished manuscript, Neuropsychiatric Research Institute, Fargo, ND. Reprinted with permission.

outside it—so that problem buyers can share their experiences as they develop control over their impulses; the compulsive buyer and the buddy are often in contact between sessions. All of the groups emphasize writing, either in the group or as homework, typically an articulation of feelings before, during, and after buying, or after successfully resisting it. Cognitive behavioral groups use standard cognitive behavioral methodology, in which the compulsive buyer learns to recognize and restructure his or her dysfunctional thoughts, using tools like the Restructuring Thoughts Worksheet (Box 14.3) and an active questioning method to subject dysfunctional thoughts to a reality test. Relaxation techniques, during which members are trained to relax particular muscle groups and then to evoke and remember that feeling of relaxation when confronted with buying anxiety, help group members begin to see that buying behavior can be under their personal control. Experiential exercises and visualizations are included within the sessions; these tools help compulsive buyers manage actual shopping experiences nondestructively. While the specific topics and skills presented vary somewhat, nearly all groups focus on knowledge, recovery skills, problem solving, assertiveness, troubleshooting, and relapse prevention. Some groups use the principles of Debtors Anonymous, reciting the Serenity Prayer as part of the overall structure and/or reading and discussing the 12-Step program. And some groups build in evaluation procedures, although the particular structure and frequency of the evaluation procedures differs. Thus far, little of this data has been published.

Each of the five forms of group therapy reported in the literature has a particular slant differentiating it from the others. Damon's method is a less structured group meeting that takes place in a private home and includes a relaxation exercise and guided visualization each week. These visualizations are processed and discussed along with members' recent shopping behavior. Inasmuch as there is less of a nuts-and-bolts approach in this type of group, it is more appropriate for people who have already mastered the ability to use a spending plan or who are

BOX 14.3
Restructuring Thoughts Worksheet

Cue	Responses		Consequences
	Thoughts	Behaviors	
Bad day at work	There is no way I can control myself once I have the urge to shop	Shopping at lunch	Guilt Shame Feel bad about self Hide purchases Lie to husband
	Feelings		
	Stressed Overwhelmed Upset		

Applying the Restructuring Thoughts Worksheet in a Group Setting

Once the Restructuring Thoughts Worksheet has been completed, the actual work to restructure the thoughts and feelings surrounding compulsive buying can begin. The worksheet helps the compulsive buyer to understand the cues, thoughts, feelings, behaviors, and consequences of compulsive buying episodes. The therapist can then introduce basic cognitive restructuring techniques to help participants begin to restructure thoughts linked to problem buying behaviors. The first step is to encourage members to evaluate whether their thoughts associated with compulsive buying, as documented on the worksheet, are realistic and reasonable. A straightforward way to challenge these thoughts is with four questions:

1. What is the evidence to support this thought?
2. What is the evidence to refute this thought?
3. What are the implications of this thought? In other words, what if this thought is really true?
4. What alternative explanations (thoughts) might explain the thought?

For example, "There is no way I can control myself once I have the urge to shop" can be challenged using the four questions. First, there may be some evidence to support this thought, such as past splurges; but there is also evidence to refute it. The fact that an individual *has* been able to control the urge at certain times in the past demonstrates that the statement it not unequivocally true. If someone is having a very hard time with the urge on a particular day and feels in danger of shopping, he or she can do something else, such as taking a walk or calling a friend. As far as alternative explanations, an individual can look into why he or she is thinking negatively; did she have a bad day at work or a fight with her spouse? Using this method, individuals can decide what thoughts about themselves are reasonable and draw rational conclusions about why they may have had negative thoughts to begin with. An individual will then be more able to understand whether these thoughts are even related to shopping. The method, in other words, helps get to the heart of the thoughts, determining what they are actually based on and whether or not they are truly reasonable.

Source: "Group Cognitive Behavioral Therapy for Buying Disorder" (pp. 380–382), by M. Burgard and J. Mitchell, in *I Shop, Therefore, I Am: Compulsive Buying and the Search for Self,* A. L. Benson (Ed.), 2000, Northvale, NJ: Aronson. Reprinted with permission.

learning to use this kind of tool outside of the group, as, for example, in Debtors Anonymous.

Damon cites an example of a guided visualization in which she asked the members to give themselves a gift. One woman, Claudia, described her gift as a statue of a woman bound around the chest. Damon (1988) explains:

> At this point, I intervened. First, I asked her if she was willing to work. When she said, "yes," I asked her to stand and "be" the statue—and to experience the rope around her chest. "Can you take it off and unbind yourself?" I asked. She did that easily, but then exclaimed, "There's another rope around my ankles. I can't stand on my own two feet!" For Claudia, this was an epiphany—a moment of revelation and sudden clarity. Every detail of her dependence rushed into her head: her dependence on men for validation; her dependence on those to whom she owed money; her dependence on shopping and on credit cards. (p. 170)

The epiphany motivated Claudia to cut up all but one of her credit cards at the following meeting.

Brazer, whose groups included people with a variety of money disorders, insisted that group members, in addition to participating in the group therapy, attend regular Debtors Anonymous meetings. Brazer's groups were made up of two 90-minute segments each week, the first one psychoeducational, focusing on a particular topic, and the second comprised of more standard group psychotherapy, related to the psychoeducational topic of the evening. Mitchell and Burgard's cognitive-behavioral group included homework assignments to facilitate active participation in the group. In the early phase of this group, members were required to bring their family and friends to one meeting and their buddies to a different meeting, as a way to build a wider support system. Parecki introduced another technique: Group members explore their weekly journals in small groups to focus on issues in a more intimate setting. The rationale is that in small dyads, an individual may feel more comfortable talking about very personal issues.

In a report of group treatment of compulsive buying that was conducted in Spain (Rodriguez-Villarino et al., 2001), there are still other distinctions. By presenting verbal and visual examples like movies, television commercials, and print ads, the Spanish group teaches media literacy to participants, so they become more attuned to the cues presented to them. Another feature that distinguishes Rodriguez-Villarino's form of group therapy is an in vivo desensitization technique to control buying impulses; the Spanish group refers to this as stimular exposition with buying response prevention. To achieve it, an individual, accompanied by a buddy, enters a buying situation in a store that causes him great stress. The buddy has to be a nonaddicted buyer with a nonjudgmental attitude toward the problem and must have made a commitment to helping the compulsive buyer. Buyer and buddy remain in the store until the compulsive buyer is calm and free of stress, however long that takes. Both record the compulsive buyer's stress level at 10-minute intervals. The buddy later provides information to the therapist about the specifics of the addicted partner's buying behavior and about emerging problems, so that the therapist can modify treatment. To recognize that we don't have to run away from things, that it's possible to see them, touch them, and even get bored with them, is a novelty for many compulsive buyers. While the compulsive buyer is developing sufficient knowledge, confidence, and control, it's very useful to be able to count on a buddy who can deal with buying triggers. Eventually, group members can use these techniques without a buddy in the store.

The buyer uses relaxation techniques, visualization of successful attempts to abstain from buying—whether real or fantasy—and cognitive restructuring to decrease anxiety, having performed a mental rehearsal of the situation in advance of entering the store. This mental rehearsal begins by specifically thinking about a situation that invokes the urge to shop. After visualizing the details of this situation, the individual decides how best to face it, what strategy to employ. Then, the buyer envisions using a specific technique to combat the urge to buy and resolve the situation. This image of successfully combating the urge to buy, whether an actual situation that has occurred or an imagined one, promotes a feeling of self-efficacy and self-control; it can be re-evoked whenever buying anxiety or impulses threaten. Box 14.4 is an example of one person's mental rehearsal.

The experience of leading these groups and the feedback the leaders have gotten have led to a number of thoughts and suggestions for the future. Burgard and Mitchell compiled a list of suggestions based on problems they encountered. For example, many participants in their group did not differentiate very well between compulsive and healthy buying behavior. Therefore, they suggest the therapist needs to clearly distinguish and stress the difference between the two (see Box 14.5). Further suggestions were the introduction of a financial counselor to speak to the group regarding savings and credit cards as well as a mandated exposure to a store. This exposure would involve the individual's visiting a store that provokes anxiety and not purchasing anything, a technique similar to the one already used by the group in Spain. Burgard and Mitchell were also concerned with the socioeconomic standings of the group members. They noticed that stark socioeconomic distinctions within the group minimized appreciation for each other's struggles and therefore impeded the sense of group unity. Separate groups for members of different financial status may have been more effective. An important final issue was the inclusion of a buddy and family members in the recovery process. Although group members continued to use buddies as part of their support system, sessions involving family, friends, and buddies were discontinued. Burgard and Mitchell believe that the inclusion of nongroup members could compromise the confidentiality that is central to the group.

Parecki also had recommendations for changes in subsequent groups. The group was run according to a very tight structure wherein group members were fined for being tardy or absent, unless they'd given 24-hours notice. This tended to demoralize some and led to a few dropouts. Parecki thinks that a more fluid structure might have avoided some of these problems. He also recommended shortening the group by combining lecture topics as well as introducing guest

---

BOX 14.4
Mental Rehearsal

"I get out of the office, I take the car and I go to the shopping mall. I arrive and as always, I try to park very close to the entrance door. I go to the floor where the jewelry section is—just to look, because I'm not going to buy anything. I don't need anything. I see watches and beautiful rings. The saleswoman asks me if I'd like to see something up close. Would I like her to take it out of the case? Certainly, everything is very beautiful, there's a particular watch and ring that I like, and I begin to feel like buying one of them. I know that if I leave at that moment, I'll be thinking the rest of the day about what I saw and I will almost surely go back at some other point and buy either the watch or the ring because I won't have been able to get them out of my mind. Then I think of the strategy that I've learned for dealing with the anxiety that leads to my buying impulse. That's how I come to decide to try the watch and the ring. I look at it. I try it on. I ask the saleswoman about what the case is made of, what kind of movement it is, how long a warranty it has, and then I try on the ring. I ask what kind of setting it is, how large the stones are, and I go on and on like that until the anxiety disappears completely. I realize that I can see, touch, and try on something I'm tempted to buy, and I can speak with people at the store, and I do not have to buy anything at all. I realize that I can talk to the salesperson, but I do not have to worry about her being angry with me if I don't buy something. It's her job to show me her merchandise and answer my questions so that I can determine if I really want it. Not everyone buys every time they go into a store. I felt great to have realized all this and I left the store very happy . . . with myself, knowing that I'm beginning to control myself"

Source: Adicion a la Compra: Analysis, Evaluaction y Tratamiento [Buying Addiction: Analysis, Evaluation, and Treatment] (p. 143), by R. Rodriguez-Villarino, J. L. Otero-Lopez, and R. Casto, 2001, Madrid: Piramide. Reprinted with permission.

---

speakers who have overcome financial difficulties in order to enhance motivation. A final suggestion was the addition of follow-up booster sessions for those who desire supplementary support.

Summary   These reports on the various forms of group therapy reflect the more serious focus on compulsive buying within the professional community and the increasing body of literature regarding compulsive buying. Research studies that demonstrate the effectiveness of each type of group, compare the effectiveness of the different forms of group treatment, and compare the effectiveness of group treatment with other forms of treatment still need to be done. This will ultimately lead to more individualized and better treatment results overall.

COUPLES THERAPY

There are times when overspending becomes such a threat to a relationship that a couple needs to work together in couples therapy to resolve the problem. Couples

---

BOX 14.5
What Is Healthy Spending?

Healthy spending is using money thoughtfully for past, present, and future purposes. Thoughtful spending means allocating money in ways that reflect priorities you establish to enable you to live the kind of life you want to live.

Thoughtful spending for past purposes means gradually paying off bills you've already accumulated. Thoughtful spending for present purposes means spending the right amount of money—neither too much nor too little—on life's necessities: shelter, clothing, food, taxes, and charity. Thoughtful spending for future purposes means setting aside the right amount of money—again, neither too much nor too little—for future needs: emergencies, retirement, educating children, helping elderly parents. "The right amount of money," of course, depends directly on your income and obligations as well as your values. But all of these—income, obligation, values—are influenced by what money means to you.

For some people, money means *success*. These people use money as a signal to themselves and others that they are successful, that they are competent, that they are up to the task, whatever it might be. For other people, money means *affection*. These people use money, and the things money can buy, to attract other people, to draw them closer and hold on to them. For still others, money means *expression*. These people use money to express themselves, to show that they are distinctive, special. And for still other people money means *security*. They hold on to it, save it eagerly, spend it cautiously, keep it under control at all times. Many of us use money for two or more of these purposes.

There is nothing wrong with using money for any or all of these purposes. It is good to be successful. It is good to attract people. It is good to express yourself. And it is good to have plans and be cautious.

What is not so good, though, is using money for these different purposes without recognizing that that is what you are doing—to buy more and more symbols of success, affection, expression, or security without recognizing the meaning of the behavior. The deeper our needs to tell other people and ourselves that we are successful or attractive or distinctive or cautious, the more desperately we may use money for those purposes, and the further we will be from thoughtful spending.

Source: J. Mitchell, *Buying Disorder Group Treatment Manual* (p. 32), 1993, Unpublished manuscript, Neuropsychiatric Research Institute, Fargo, ND. Reprinted with permission.

---

therapy for compulsive buying is an extremely important treatment modality, because couples act as a financial unit and generally blend income as well as spending. Money issues are an intrinsic part of marriage and are often a source of intense and pervasive friction, which can, in turn, seep into other aspects of the relationship. Regardless of which person in the couple has been identified as having the problem, it is critical for the therapist to keep in mind that both partners play roles in the couple's money-related drama.

Couples therapy is indicated when the compulsive spending problem cannot be dealt with adequately on an individual basis. Either the compulsive buyer is extremely ambivalent about dealing with the problem and needs the presence of the partner to stay with it, or the partner enables the habit. When this happens, any progress the spender might make in individual therapy is undermined by the partner's unconscious support of the problem.

Olivia Mellan, author of *Money Harmony* (1994) and *Overcoming Overspending* (1995) and an expert in the field of couples therapy for money disorders, has treated a great number of couples in which one of the partners is a compulsive buyer. She believes that the "duel personalities" (Mellan, 2000) of some couples can lead to a polarized state that often needs to be pursued in couples therapy. In addition to the couples therapy, Mellan often refers one or both members of a couple for individual therapy and strongly recommends attendance at Debtors Anonymous meetings. The couples therapist helps promote financial balance in the relationship by assisting each partner to explore his or her individual relationships with money and the way these relationships play out in the marriage. Couples need to improve their communication about money issues and must eventually recognize money as merely a tool for managing their lives together, rather than an emotionally loaded symbol for love, power, security, independence, control, freedom, or self-worth.

In couples where compulsive buying is a problem, one person is likely to be a spender and the other a hoarder. Spenders use money for pleasure and have trouble managing a spending plan and postponing pleasure for a long-term goal. Hoarders, at the opposite end of the spectrum, are excellent at saving and budgeting, but find it hard to spend money comfortably. In the course of their relationship, if one becomes more of a spender, the other often develops into more of a hoarder, an instinctive attempt at maintenance of the couple's financial equilibrium. This reaction may not necessarily be extreme. The strength of a partner's reaction to overspending depends on how risky he or she perceives it to be.

Individuals have different money personalities, shaped by their historical relationships with money, by what they learned about money growing up. We normally imitate our parents' way of dealing with money, or we reject the relationship to money we saw growing up and behave in just the opposite way as adults. If, for example, mom was a profligate spender, her son may turn into a serious hoarder. At home, he may have heard a lot of fighting about his mother's spending and he may resolve that minimal spending is the best way to avoid the problems he grew up with. Conversely, an individual whose parent hoarded may have felt deeply deprived and may resolve, as an adult, never to feel that way again. Perhaps because of her family's "depression mentality," a daughter never felt that her desire for new clothes was met. She may become an overspender and justify her purchases as necessary need fulfillment.

Gender socialization, too, plays a part in an individual's relationship with money. Men are expected to be knowledgeable and confidently autonomous regarding their finances. Despite the gains that women have made, they are still typically socialized to be more vulnerable and dependent regarding financial knowledge and skills. These socialized roles are plagued with differing burdens and fears that must be understood by each partner if a couple is to grow together. Men typically feel the provider role as a heavy burden, whether or not they are the chief wage-earner. Women often feel the burden of the "second shift," with its characteristic feeling of being "all things to all people": wife, mother, career woman, caretaker of aging parents, and so on. Men are afraid of getting laid off or injured or dying young—of not being able to provide their family with financial security. Women often fear that they will lose everything and be unable to support themselves.

This gender socialization also extends into the discussion of joint finances. For women, autonomy has traditionally been a more difficult state. They've often found it harder to manage their own money and not join all of the couple's money. Men, on the other hand, typically find merged finances to be the more difficult arrangement. A man's sense of independence may be challenged by a nontraditional situation in which his partner earns significantly more than he does, particularly if household responsibilities then fall to him rather than her. The complications of gender socialization and how they play out in a particular situation, with a particular couple, can aggravate any conflicts about sharing the financial burden. The specific division of finances, if any, and the responsibilities each member of a couple will bear, must be discussed openly for an effective decision to be reached.

Often couples wait so long to come to therapy and are in such a polarized state that it takes a while to neutralize the years of conflict and fighting over one partner's spending. It may be necessary for the therapist to hear a lot about what has gone on in the couple's past—as well as each individual's past—before the healing begins. Structured and focused communication helps to depolarize a couple's money stance. For them to address a compulsive buying problem successfully, each needs to listen to and appreciate the other's point of view. Mellan's techniques help couples develop empathy for each other and launch open communication, creating an atmosphere of warmth and caring. As is the case in most couples therapy, partners are encouraged to use "I" and not "you" statements to alleviate one partner feeling blamed. It's also important for each partner to see and verbalize the positive aspects of the overspending problem. These positive aspects can be difficult to tease out, especially when there's been great friction within the couple. However, contrary to the belief that showing any support for spending will encourage it, expressing positive feelings can be helpful in the treatment. If, for example, the spouse of an overspender can show support for the beneficial aspects of the partner's buying, as in "I can really see how much thought and creativity you put into buying things to beautify our home," the spender may say, "Thanks, but I feel like I'm just not able to stop." The overspender understands that the discussion will not consist entirely of critique and judgment and was able to feel more open to self-exploration. Once each person knows that the other is determined to work through their issues in a caring manner, communication is much more fruitful.

In addition to empathy and more open communication, successful therapy also requires both partners to face their own realities regarding the problem. The overspending partner must first acknowledge that he or she has this problem, and the other partner must learn to offer support and compassion without enabling or rescuing. Both members of the couple need to see compulsive buying as an addiction, the recovery from which is often slow and includes advances and retreats. The overspender's partner needs to confront his or her own conflicts related to money and share them, so that the buyer doesn't feel alone or judged and realizes that this problem is one that both partners create or maintain. An atmosphere of mutual respect is vital. Not until that atmosphere is established can discussion and negotiation be effective.

Once the partners gain greater empathy for each other's point of view and better face the realities of their individual contributions to the problem, more focused work on concrete solutions can begin. Mellan uses a sequence of activities within the couple's therapy to help them address overspending in a healthy manner; gradually integrating these activities into their lives gives the couple channels for growth outside of therapy. The first activity is a goal-setting exercise. Each member of the couple must independently come up with short-, medium-, and long-term goals, which they'll share with each other in the presence of the therapist. Each partner is asked to rewrite those goals over the course of a month to see which remain the same. Eventually the couple tries to combine their goals in a spirit of compromise and arrive at a list that is mutually satisfying.

The money dialogue, which couples begin at the same time that they're setting their goals, is another technique Mellan has developed to help overspending couples learn to talk about money. She begins by instructing one of the partners to "Imagine a conversation between yourself and money, as if money was a person with whom you had a relationship." It might sound like this:

MONEY: "Why do you treat me so poorly? You seem to like me when you work hard for me, but then you throw me away, as if you don't care at all."

OVERSPENDER: "I do respect you when I'm working to get you, but you are there just to spend on what I want. Why would I need to respect you anymore than it takes to get you?"

MONEY: "What about respecting my value for the future and not just your immediate gratification?"

Reflecting on your inner dialogue with money makes it much easier to understand your relationship with it. Once you have brought your dialogue with money to a conclusion, significant influences on your relationship with money can be examined. To do this, think of the comments your parents and other important people in your life would make if they had just witnessed the dialogue with money. The voices you are to imagine should be those of your parents, of some Higher Power or inner wisdom (this for a more balanced perspective), and of another prominent person, past or present, in your life, perhaps your spouse. The voices might say something like this:

MOTHER: "You have always been spoiled and now you're just trying to keep up that lifestyle."

FATHER: "You work hard and deserve to spend your money as you wish."

SPOUSE: "Your hard work isn't enough to support your spending and plan a future for us at the same time. Without savings, we won't be able to fulfill our dreams."

HIGHER POWER: "Is immediate gratification really all you want? Don't you want more? You can learn to be happy without the immediate gratification of buying."

These commentaries, with a little reflection, may suggest what has shaped your relationship with money.

Practicing the nonhabitual, which is the third piece of Mellan's money harmony approach, leads to greater empathy and encourages new behaviors. In this exercise, each member of the couple must choose one action a week that doesn't come naturally. For instance, if the husband buys electronics on a weekly basis, he can't purchase any electronics that week. If his wife rarely indulges in any purchases for herself, she must, in turn, splurge this week and buy herself something that she ordinarily would not have. An extension of this technique is something Mellan calls, "a walk in each other's shoes." This exercise involves an actual trip to a store in which each member of the couple acts as if he or she were the other partner. For example, the overspending wife must act like her hoarder husband, criticizing his purchases and talking about the need for savings. Her husband must act like his overspending wife would and exhibit an almost uncontrollable need to buy practically everything he sees, savings be damned. This exercise must be done thoughtfully and without mockery. Role playing permits the individuals to see themselves as the partner already does and also to understand the partner's perspective on spending or hoarding. One couple, Mark and Rosemary, found the experience particularly enlightening. Mark was awed: "No wonder she worries about money so much; I refuse to set any limits at all!" Rosemary commented: "No wonder he loves shopping so much. It's really seductive . . . like a chemical high! I was in a trance-state in the store!" (Mellan, 1995, p. 115).

Couples are encouraged to practice their new communication skills at home. To do this effectively, they need to pick a low-stress time for discussion and they need to agree not to use trustingly confided information against each other either now or in the future. This safety net allows them to tackle the nitty-gritty of their money issues and to make decisions together, respectfully and openly. So many different variables enter into a couple's money issues that there is no one right way for them to save, share, and spend. Some couples may merge all accounts, and others may be comfortable only merging some or keeping all funds separate. The solution depends on the couple's financial and emotional needs. While the couples therapist must provide clients the tools they need for successful money discussions, this street is two-way; it is the responsibility of the clients to be thoughtful, to listen patiently to each other, and to assume the best of each other's communication. Couples therapy for overspending focuses on the healing of both partners and on rebuilding those aspects of the relationship that the overspending has eroded. Understanding both oneself and the other person, and communicating this understanding openly—these are the tools that make healing possible.

COUNSELING FOR COMPULSIVE BUYING

Counseling for compulsive buying targets the specific problem and creates an action plan to stop the behavior. Targeted counseling for this problem alters the negative actions of the behavior and concurrently works toward healing the underlying emotions, although less emphasis is placed on exploring the emotional significance of the compulsive act than in traditional individual psychotherapy. Counselors who work with compulsive buyers often refer their clients to traditional psychotherapists when the severity of the related emotional issues goes beyond the expertise of the counselor. Another situation in which individual psychotherapy might be indicated is the client with few financial constraints because of a very large personal or family income. With such a client, compulsive buying may still seriously affect marital harmony, relationships with children, or employment. This client may not have the motivation or the necessity, at least initially, to do structured money work and may be better off exploring the relevant emotional issues and their relationship to the compulsive buying. In addition to, or sometimes in place of, individual therapy, compulsive buying counselors may make attendance at Debtors Anonymous meetings a requirement. With certain clients, the combination of counseling, psychotherapy, and/or Debtors Anonymous goes several steps beyond the work of any one of these methods alone.

Karen McCall of California and Ron Gallen of New York are two counselors with significant expertise in this area; both have written about it and both train counselors and therapists to do this type of work. McCall has published the *Money Minder: Financial Recovery Workbook* (2002), an approach for clients to achieve financial success; Gallen elucidates his method in *The Money Trap: A Practical Program to Stop Self-Defeating Financial Habits So You Can Reclaim Your Grip on Life* (2002). The major premise of counseling for compulsive buying is the idea that insight alone will not stop the behavior. All stages in the compulsive buying cycle must be identified—the triggers, the feelings, the dysfunctional thoughts, the behavior, the consequences of the behavior, and the meaning of the compulsive buying. The client needs to learn how to work with each stage in the cycle so that he or she gains more control of the problem. In this sense, counseling for compulsive buying is similar to counseling for alcohol and drug abuse. However, recovery from compulsive buying is different and, in some ways more complicated. With alcohol and drugs, abstinence is the treatment goal, but it is impossible to abstain from buying or using money.

Counseling for compulsive buying addresses the entire scope of the problem. It helps the client answer such questions as:

- How and when did the compulsive buying begin?
- What form does it take? Is it buying on the Internet, from catalogues, on TV, in stores? Is it done on holidays? When buying gifts? In the service of a "collection"?
- What emotions underlie the compulsive buying? (Boredom? Loneliness? Anger? Anxiety?)
- Is it a means to self-soothe?
- Is it done to try to enhance self-esteem or feel more socially desirable?
- Is it done to enliven the self because of an internal feeling of deadness?
- Is it a response to a change in another addictive behavior?

The possibilities are endless, because each person's story is different. The central question, however—and the one that compulsive buying counselors are in a unique position to address—is always the same: What can be done to end the compulsive buying? The counseling process has as its goal to break the cycle of compulsive buying and to create a workable financial structure, one that will enhance, rather than erode, a client's quality of life. To do this, some of the underlying emotional turmoil must be dealt with, from both historical and current perspectives. There are multiple stages in recovery from compulsive buying, and counseling also has to proceed in a stepwise fashion. Admitting where you stand is the key to recovery. Before any change can occur, the compulsive buyer must take a long, hard look at his current situation; as with any addiction, denial is almost endemic. What I've found useful (ALB) is to ask my clients to record all of their expenses for a one-month period, whether a 50-cent tip on a cab ride or a $500 insurance premium. This provides us with some baseline spending data. I gather somewhat different data from compulsive clothing buyers, who are mostly, though not exclusively, women. Each is asked to compile a list of everything in the clothes closet: every dress, every blouse, every belt, each pair of socks, stockings, and shoes. Just compiling this list—some people take weeks to complete it!—is sometimes sobering enough to have an impact on the behavior. Once people have a sense of where their money is going, the next step is to create a spending plan. Some clients have a good deal of difficulty with this. For those people, Ron Gallen (2002) has devised something that he calls the time plan. (An example of a time plan can be found in Box 14.6.) Once these clients have learned to allot their available time in a way that best reflects their priorities, they find it much easier to move on to the spending plan.

Clients who are ready to create a spending plan will likely need some help. Spending categories are not intuitive, and they'll want to think through their expenses category by category, in as much detail as possible. Listed should be the physical basics—food, shelter, and clothing—and the particular mix of other categories that is unique to each individual. Counselors should encourage clients to allocate some money for spiritual growth or greater sense of community, whatever form that might take.

Clients will need to assemble information on all of their debts, savings, investments, and earnings. Then we begin to estimate their expenses. Some of these remain the same, month after month—rent, mortgage and loan repayments, childcare, gym membership, for example—but in addition to these fixed expenses there are flexible ones, regular items that change each month: food, clothing, medications, automobile maintenance, entertainment, and such. Finally, we must also attend to periodic expenses, those that occur from time to time: physician's visits, insurance premiums, gifts, vacations, and the like. Keep in mind that the categorization of fixed, flexible, and periodic expenses changes from client to client, and rely on hard data—bills, receipts, tax records, and cancelled checks—to stay close to reality. An accurate record of expenses and income is the first step toward coming out of what McCall (2000, p. 463) has termed "financial fog" or "money coma." An individual must face the reality of these numbers, must genuinely recognize what it means to live within available means. "Breaking a compulsive money cycle," says Gallen, "means developing a way to take care of yourself in every respect" (2002, p. 11). Recovery is not about deprivation, but balance. A spending plan directs this process and prescribes a financially acceptable way to take care of needs and desires.

Another important part of creating and using a spending plan is the distinction between needs and wants. Both are personally determined, but the two occupy different ends of the budgeting continuum. Needs can be met in a myriad of ways, each with its own financial implications. A multimillion dollar mansion and a modest bungalow both fulfill the requirement for shelter. Yet a compulsive buyer may consider the impressiveness of her home before considering financial reality, while most others would reverse these priorities. "Finances before features" must be the mantra of fiscal responsibility; as long as that's maintained, there's no shame in owning a lavish home.

While some needs are universal, others are entirely individual. One person may, for example, need to join a house of worship to practice his or her religion; another might want nothing to do with organized religion. The former will allot some income to church or synagogue, while the latter can use this money for another purpose. Both counselor and client must watch for the possibility of one need masquerading as another. Gallen (2002) tells this story of a client: "Donna's

BOX 14.6
Time Plan

To help people become more comfortable with the idea of writing a spend-ing plan, Gallen suggests first creating a time plan. Though based on the same principles as a spending plan, it simply allots the hours available to you, rather than the dollars, in a way that best reflects your priorities. The time plan is more concrete: It's easier to fully grasp the finitude of the week's hours than the exact amount of money available for its needs. Com-pulsive buyers learn, in this process, to prioritize their needs. Gallen re-minds them that "the first order of business is to allot time for the things that mean something to you, and time for the things that feed your heart."

Here is an example of an individual's time plan:

Total hours in the week   168

SELF-CARE

Dinner out with spouse and children	4
Therapy	2
Concert, Theatre, Movies, or Museum	2
Meditation	2
Reading	5
Phone or e-mail with friends	7
Television	4
Floral Design Class	1
Lunch with friends	3
Exercise	3
Day spa/Massage	1
Sleeping	49
Eating	6
Shopping	4
Housekeeping	2
Errands	3
Travel/Getting around	10

FAMILY

Visiting sister	3
Talking to mother	2

OTHER VALUES

Volunteer work	3
Buffer time (time not planned for)	3
Time to do nothing (important)	4
Work	45

Source: The Money Trap: a Practical Program to Stop Self-Defeating Financial Habits so You Can Reclaim Your Grip on Life, by R. Gallen, 2002, New York: Harper Resource.

closets are filled with clothes she has never worn. . . . Those who run the hospital thrift shop to which she donates . . . are thrilled as they can be when she comes in; most of the tags are still hanging" (p. 37). When she went shopping, Donna had no "need" for clothing; it was her need to shop, actually to buy, that operated. McCall (2002) provides a quick test to help her clients determine the difference between a want and a need. She suggests that they "try framing each item as either a 'could' or 'should.' For example: 'I *could* go on a shopping trip if I cut down on another category' (desire) or 'I really *should* get my oil changed—the car is several thousand miles over the scheduled service date' (need)" (p. 161). Using this simple criterion can help your clients prioritize their purchases.

In a spending plan, needs must be attended to first. Ignoring them will lead to a sense of deprivation and provide apparent justification for more lavish spending. On the other hand, your clients are likely to be shocked at how much less needy they feel when all of their basic needs have been met. An individual with a weight problem, for example, may spend a lot of her income on clothing while scrimping on food. Long-term, this arrangement cannot work: eating macaroni and cheese several times a week—and avoiding the expense of fresh fruits and vegetables—inverts a more sensible prioritization. The same individual might be surprised to find that reallocating her expenses can address the weight problem more successfully. By applying the money previously spent on clothing to a better diet and a gym membership, she is likely to feel more satisfied, healthier. Once the problem is addressed on this more comprehensive level, a sense of wholeness and accomplishment, along with a decrease in compulsive shopping, can result.

Debt and savings are both needs and cannot be neglected in a spending plan. Your clients may be tempted to pay off as much debt as possible, at the cost of other needs, or perhaps to ignore savings altogether. This is not a balanced solution. To make sure that debt and savings are accounted for, both should be included in the spending plan; a balanced approach to financial recovery is the basis of compulsive buying counseling. Individuals may become frustrated that their debt will not be paid off immediately, but debt repayment is only one aspect of a new financial framework and a more balanced life. While there is an abundance—even an overabundance—of programs for credit counseling, debt consolidation, and repayment, these will not really help a compulsive buyer. Quick fix debt resolution may get your client out of an individual jam, but it doesn't address the whole person, the issues and patterns that got them indebted. Only a holistic approach can reduce the likelihood of recurrence.

McCall (2000) advises clients to begin with a month-long spending plan, based on the spending data they've collected—fixed, flexible, and periodic—and careful attention to needs and wants. She and the client evaluate this plan mid-month to account for any periodic expenses or others that may have not been included initially. They reevaluate it at the end of the month as they are creating the next month's spending plan. This biweekly development of an effective spending plan helps individuals gain a feel for the process. Once they are comfortable with a monthly spending plan, they can move on to a quarterly, semi-annual, or yearly one. As spending plans are created, worked with, evaluated, and refined, clients get an overview of their finances and regain control of this aspect of their lives.

As the compulsive buying cycle is being broken, the emotions underlying it must be addressed. Gallen puts it this way: "money disorders are a way to avoid feeling all out intense feelings. If you have a money disorder, it is probably a safe bet that you also have deep wells of fear, anger, and sadness that have remained off-limits"

(2002, p. 11). The underlying pain may result from a variety of conflicting emotions—loss, for example, or anger, jealousy, insecurity. Developmental issues in the family are often relevant. Everyone, after all, is influenced by the way his family handled money. Was it used to assert power? Was it taboo as a subject? Was it used to punish? McCall (2002) helps her clients explore these issues by having them write a money autobiography. Writing a money autobiography "walks you through the process of writing your own 'life story' in regard to money" (p. 37). Exploring the emotional side of the issue can be done within compulsive buying counseling or in traditional therapy. However it is accomplished, the integration of the emotional and behavioral sides is the comprehensive solution needed for lasting recovery.

We can expect many twists and turns on the journey that recovery is. It will require courage and perseverance and time, and even with these, good counseling as well. One important concern is relapse. Almost every compulsive buyer backslides at some point, some dramatically, some less so. Counselors must prepare their clients for the event, so they will not be unduly discouraged if it happens. While the time and extent of relapse may vary, the shame and self-criticism that accompany it are the pretty much the same. Box 14.7 lists some strategies for relapse prevention.

Recovery is ultimately in the hands of the compulsive buyer. If he participates fully, he can look forward to the continuity and fulfillment of a regained and expanded sense of control over his life.

Compulsive buying counseling is perhaps the most comprehensive approach to treatment, teaming specific behavior-changing techniques with careful attention to the precipitating emotions. It works best in combination with individual psychotherapy or couples or group therapy, as well as participation in Debtors Anonymous. Although not in large numbers, there are now practitioners throughout the country doing this type of work. The resources section of this chapter will direct you to a program that can best address the needs of your clients.

SELF-HELP

DEBTORS ANONYMOUS

Debtors Anonymous (DA) can be a powerful tool in recovery from compulsive buying, especially for those who have developed problems with debt. Some compulsive buyers will come to your attention already going to DA meetings; with others, you will need to encourage attendance. Some of your clients will accept the suggestion readily, and some will feel profoundly threatened. For these last, you'll need to decide how important DA attendance is likely to be in a particular individual's recovery. Whatever methods you've found successful with clients resistant to other 12-Step programs likely will work here as well. DA is a good modality for compulsive buyers, because it allows them to get started from whatever point they're at personally, without any pressure for immediate action. Joining DA, fighting the passivity and denial so characteristic of this disorder, is a step in itself. Once clients have settled into the process of DA, shame, indecisiveness, and self-criticism can be transformed into a focus on recovery.

Debtors Anonymous is a 12-Step program modeled after the Alcoholics Anonymous (AA) program that sees debting as a disease similar to alcoholism. It can be cured with solvency, which means abstinence from any new debt—the equivalent of sobriety for an alcoholic. Levine and Kellen (2000) note that "in 12-step programs, addiction is viewed as a misguided attempt to manage all issues and problems by

---

BOX 14.7
Relapse Prevention: Some Useful Strategies

- Follow purchasing plans.
- Avoid using credit cards.
- Practice stress management. It's essential to confront stressors, expected or unexpected, with increasing confidence and self-esteem.
- Practice controlled exposure to high-risk situations.

At the beginning of treatment, it was recommended that you avoid high-risk cues, hair triggers for excessive buying behavior. Now you can begin to incorporate these situations into your life. *Make a hierarchy of them,* with the least difficult first. Then *expose yourself to it.* (Example: Accompany a friend to a high-risk store). Be sure you *have structure and support* to ensure success. (Specify, for example, exactly where you'll go and what you'll purchase. You may need someone to go with you.) If you want, *schedule a pleasurable activity immediately afterward* to combat anxiety. *Take note of your feelings and thoughts after you have accomplished a new task.* You may choose to discuss these with a friend. If feelings or thoughts make exposure to a new situation particularly difficult, you might delay it until you have worked them through. Expose yourself to the high-risk situations until you can comfortably handle them. This may occur after one try, or may take numerous attempts. Do not move to the next difficult situation until you are comfortable with the item before it. Do not combine more than one high-risk situation at once.

Lapses—even relapse—happen, sometimes even after prolonged abstinence from excessive buying. Typically, the event is precipitated by emotional stress, or inadequate attention to high-risk situations, or anger, or anxiety. Preparing yourself for the possibility of relapse can help to make the process manageable if it happens. You might write your own scenario of an imagined relapse or design a step-by-step plan to carry out if relapse occurs, focusing not only on what you'll do, but also on how you'll change your thoughts.

Source: J. Mitchell, *Buying Disorder Group Treatment Manual* (pp. 81, 92), 1993, Unpublished manuscript, Neuropsychiatric Research Institute, Fargo, ND. Reprinted with permission.

oneself" (p. 433), and this perspective is echoed in the DA process of recovery. To help control lives addicted to debting, DA offers a program of surrender and recovery with a strong spiritual emphasis. Members work through their steps with a sponsor, a more experienced member of the group.

Central to DA are the 12 steps that an individual takes during the process of recovery. These begin with an admission of powerlessness over the situation and the addiction (Step 1) and the acknowledgment that a higher power is involved in directing the debtor's life. DA is very broad about the concept of a higher power—there are members who relate best to the acronym GOD, which stands for "Good Orderly Direction," or the collective wisdom of the group—but some debtors have great difficulty relating to it. Encourage these to keep an open mind and not let this one bit of static block their receptiveness to the rest of the program.

Once a member comes to terms with her personal understanding of a higher power, she writes what is called a "moral inventory." This includes both her personal characteristics—for example, "a generous giver of gifts"—and their effects: "my friends are grateful but I'm deeply in debt." The inventory also includes a personal financial history and a list of current outstanding debts. Reading this inventory to a sponsor, someone in the group, or a trusted friend is the next step. This "admission of wrongs"—to a higher power, to herself, and to another person—will help the debtor let go of shame over earlier actions and behaviors, and establish those actions as firmly in the past. Recovery is seen as a fresh start.

In the next steps, the debtor asks the help of her higher power to remove her defects of character. Once she has recognized them, understood their harm to others, and asked for help with their removal, she moves on to "making amends" to those previously harmed, working with her sponsor's supervision to issue verbal apologies or actual debt repayment. At this point, the slate is clean; the recovering debtor can begin anew. The next step is to make the examination of self a daily exercise, one that eventually becomes integrated with prayer and meditation as a way of maintaining spiritual contact. The final goal of the step process is to extend this recovery to all areas of life as well as to share individual recovery with others afflicted with the same issues, possibly as a sponsor.

The 12 steps are the backbone of DA but not the only aspects of the program. Several strategies facilitate the progression of members through the steps, smoothing and straightening the path to financial sobriety. The first one is an absolute commitment not to incur additional, unsecured debt (debt without collateral)—credit card debt, for example, or personal or family loans. (Debt repayment is the complement to this solvency, but DA maintains that a slow and steady route to debt repayment is best.) A second key strategy is a carefully kept record of all daily finances; this gives shape to debtor's financial reality, thereby setting the stage for a realistic spending plan. Before a realistic spending plan is created, however, the debtor imagines an ideal one. Such a plan "does not take into account income or debt"; it is instead "a structure for creating a vision for the future. In an ideal spending plan, the member outlines what he or she wants and needs, and adds up what that will cost. This helps conceptualize a future where the member's spending will be based on more and more money. It is a way of coping with the feelings of deprivation that may arise as he or she stops debting and faces the need to delay gratification. The ideal spending plan also provides concrete motivation to increase earnings" (Levine & Kellen, 2000, p. 437), particularly for the many members of DA who are underearners. The ideal plan is then tempered with reality to achieve an acceptable spending plan, one that reflects the best possible life under specific financial circumstances.

Other strategies involve using what the group can offer. The first principle, for example, is anonymity, which requires that neither the identity nor the stories be shared outside DA; this makes the group a haven, a place where truths can be faced safely. Another strategy is the pressure relief meeting, where members invite a male and female mentor whom they've chosen from the group, and together they discuss the individual's spending plan and set monthly goals. Still another strategy is the pooling of experience on handling creditors. Members advise fellow members on reasonable debt repayment, reinforcing this DA credo:

"The goal is not that recovering addicts do penance by living in deprivation, but that they make consistent, manageable financial restitution to their creditors" (Levine & Kellen, 2000, p. 440).

DA is an intense program. While its fixed structure and attendant strategies can benefit people at all levels of compulsive buying, some individuals may not be well suited to the program. Before recommending it, counselors must conclude that a client can tolerate this highly structured, somewhat emotionally confrontational process, a process that takes place without the safety net of professional support. Two classes of client for whom DA is not recommended are those with a strong, stated need for professional guidance—usually these are debtors with other significant impulse control disorders—and people who have extreme difficulty in groups. For some debtors, DA is best in conjunction with another modality, whether individual therapy, group therapy, or compulsive buying counseling; all are powerful recovery combinations.

SIMPLICITY CIRCLES

> Americans are denounced again and again as a shallow, materialistic, and status-seeking group of people. But the truth may be that we are instead a lonely people starved for affection and attention. Much of the research on compulsive or addictive shopping seems to indicate that it is not the stuff we want, but the sensation. It's not another blouse or a new sweater so much as a friendly smile and a compliment. It's not a new VCR we need, but another way to find self-esteem and a sense of belonging. To help people deal with their compulsive shopping, we need to help them find new ways to deal with the stresses and anxieties of our commercialized, competitive, consumerist society. (Andrews, 2000, p. 484)

Simplicity circles can help compulsive buyers, although specific elements of compulsive buying are not dealt with as directly here as they are in the various therapies—individual, group, or couples—or in DA. What simplicity circles do offer is a place to gather with others to discuss personal transformation and the satisfactions of a simpler life; as such, they are a healthy way to meet some of the principal needs that a compulsive buyer seeks to fill in shopping. As Cecile Andrews, the educator who brought the simplicity circle concept to the United States, has pointed out, compulsive buyers are not simply materialistic; rather, they are starved for interaction and satisfaction. Andrews believes that simplicity circles can help them in two ways, offering the positive sensations of meetings and generating outside activities that satisfy. Simplicity circles, in short, proffer the interaction and connection that compulsive buyers crave, and in a setting that isn't contrary or dangerous to their financial realities.

The weekly meetings are discussion groups that explore the notion of voluntary simplicity through a form of adult education called a *study circle*. Each meeting begins with a question relevant to the lives of the circle members, who then reflect aloud on it in the group. There is no specific leader and each person gets a chance to speak, a design that encourages everyone to see his viewpoint as valuable. Members respond to such questions as "When in your life did you experience real community?" and, assisted by the circle's nurturing atmosphere, they often do so with critical thinking and new breadth. Sharing experiences and wisdom, the circle members both teach and learn from each other.

For a compulsive buyer, the simplicity circle is fresh country air: Only people wishing to simplify their lives attend the meetings. More than a few circle members believe that they've become slaves to their possessions and want to learn how to live happier with less; and many compulsive buyers believe and want the same. Voluntary simplicity encourages "a turning away from activities that have failed to deliver satisfaction and contentment—activities such as shopping and scrambling up the career ladder—to activities that bring true joy and meaning—creativity, community, and the celebration of daily life" (Andrews, 2000, p. 485). The movement has grown as more and more people, unfulfilled by a life of relentless consumption, get out of the economic fast lane and begin satisfying their innermost needs. Though few sessions focus distinctly on consumerism, the circle's aims and credo and atmosphere work well with compulsive buyers, who are led to address the life issues that underlie their behavior.

It must be understood that the circle's drive toward simplicity is not at all a withdrawal from the world; it is instead a strategy for identity growth. Members speak thoughtfully and in a nonjudgmental atmosphere about their perspectives, and this promotes self-confidence and offers each individual a chance to find and embrace her real voice. For the compulsive shopper, the group is a particularly attractive alternative: Whereas shopping is usually escapist, simplicity circle encourage members to face personal situations and their connection with the world head on. This contemplative straightforwardness is a powerful antidote to compulsion.

CONCLUSION

Compulsive buying treatment is still very much in a formative stage. The resource lists that follow are designed to give you and your clients relevant places to turn.

Hwoschinsky (1992) notes that society, advertising, and the media all conspire against the cultivation of "true wealth," and few thoughtful observers of contemporary culture could disagree. Yet, we know at some level that self-esteem, family, friendships, good health, creativity, education, sense of community, communion with nature—all of these and others have value that money cannot match. Encouraging compulsive buyers to reencounter these elements of true wealth serves to counterweight their disorder. Boundy develops this point: "Because a sense of inner poverty, emotional and spiritual, is at the core of most compulsive spending, clients must build real gratification into their lives as part of recovery" (2000, p. 25).

No matter who the client is and what treatment options will be pursued, "we need to help clients embrace the self-actualizing possibilities of shopping as search by facilitating the transformation of their need for ever more meaningless goods and services into meaningful ideas and experiences" (Benson, 2000, p. 502). We sincerely hope that this chapter helps you to help them.

RECOMMENDED READING

SUGGESTED READINGS

Boundy, D. (1993). *When money is the drug: Understanding and changing self-defeating money patterns.* Woodstock, NY: Maverick Media Resources.

Catalano, E. M., & Sonenberg, N. (1993). *Consuming passions: Help for compulsive shoppers.* Oakland, CA: New Harbinger.

Damon, J. (1988). *Shopaholics: An 8-week program to control compulsive spending.* New York: Avon Books.

Debtors Anonymous. (1999). *A currency of hope.* Brainerd, MN: Bang Printing.

Wesson, C. (1990). *Women who shop too much.* New York: St. Martin's Press.

VIDEOS

Affluenza, 56 minutes. Bullfrog Films, Oley, PA, www.bullfrogfilms.com. This videotape takes both a lighthearted and a serious look at "affluenza," our modern-day plague of overconsumption and materialism and explores its personal, familial, societal, and environmental impact.

Escape from Affluenza, 56 minutes. Bullfrog Films, Oley, PA, www.bullfrogfilms.com. This sequel to *Affluenza* presents humorous and thought-provoking vignettes to show how people from many walks of life are escaping from affluenza, reducing their consumption, simplifying their lives, and feeling more satisfaction.

In the Prime: Couples and Money with Olivia Mellan, 45 minutes. WETA-TV, http://www.moneyharmony.com/form1.htm. Much of the information in the section on couples therapy in this chapter is expanded on in this videotape that features Olivia Mellan at work, helping couples who are learning to work on their money issues harmoniously.

INFORMATION RESOURCES

Debtors Anonymous (www.debtorsanonymous.org). In addition to providing a general overview, the DA web site offers a quiz and describes warning signs of compulsive debting to help someone decide if he or she has a serious problem with debting and overspending. The site also helps people to locate meetings in their communities and online, offer suggestions for starting meetings, and provides listings of DA-related books and tapes.

Financial Recovery Institute (www.financialrecovery.com). This site connects people interested in the ideas of financial recovery to the resources that can actually change their lives. The Money Minder system, featured and offered on the site, is a core resource. This plan emphasizes the money mind connection and helps an individual create and manage a spending plan. Individual counseling via telephone or in person is available through the Institute, which also trains financial recovery counselors. Monthly Teleclasses, which are offered as CDs and tapes, offer lecture-style conference calls that connect people all across the country.

MyVesta (www.myvesta.com). MyVesta, a Financial Recovery Center, offers recovery counseling for compulsive buyers, either in person or on the phone for help with self-defeating money behaviors.

National Endowment for Financial Education (www.nefe.org). NEFE is a nonprofit organization dedicated to helping individuals to gain the necessary skills to take control of their personal finances. NEFE attempts to increase financial literacy through a variety of publications and programs that they offer to individuals, schools, and organizations throughout the country.

Institute of Consumer Financial Education (www.financial-education-icfe.org). This organization's site has a large number of financial education resources aimed at helping people of all ages to manage their money. The resources are organized into categories such as mending spending, but they are primarily directed at people that have already overcome compulsive buying and are seeking tips to keep their spending on track.

Simplicity Circles (www.simplicitycircles.com). This site has detailed information on the voluntary simplicity movement. There are listings of and resources for simplicity circles and study groups and online discussion groups. On this site, you can also obtain the tools to start your own group.

Spenders Anonymous (www.spenders.org). Spenders Anonymous is a 12-Step fellowship for compulsive buyers based on the principles of Alcoholics Anonymous. The web site includes signposts of compulsive buying, steps toward healing, and a list of meetings. A meeting kit is also available for individuals to start SA fellowships in their own town or city.

Training Resources

April Benson, PhD (www.stoppingovershopping.com). Based in New York, Benson offers training workshops and supervision for counselors and therapists who want to do individual and/or group treatment with compulsive buyers. She also does individual work with compulsive buyers and has created a 10-session group treatment program.

Financial Recovery Institute (www.financialrecovery.com). With its extensive network, the Financial Recovery Institute trains counselors across the country. Individuals seeking help are referred by Financial Recovery Institute director, Karen McCall, to trained financial recovery counselors.

Ron Gallen (www.rongallen.com). Based in New York, Gallen offers training weekends for counselors and therapists who want to learn how to work with people with money disorders, including compulsive buying. Gallen also treats individuals and couples with money disorders.

Olivia Mellan (www.money harmony.com). Author of four books about money disorders and how to work with them, Washington-based Mellan offers consultation, supervision, and teleclasses for therapists. She also does individual and couples money therapy.

REFERENCES

American Psychiatric Association. (1987). *Diagnostic and statistical manual of mental disorders* (3rd ed., rev.). Washington, DC: Author.

American Psychiatric Association. (1994). *Diagnostic and statistical manual of mental disorders* (4th ed.). Washington, DC: Author.

Andrews, C. (2000). Simplicity circles and the compulsive shopper. In A. L. Benson (Ed.), *I shop, therefore, I am: Compulsive buying and the search for self* (pp. 484–496). Northvale, NJ: Aronson.

Barth, F. D. (2000). When eating and shopping are companion disorders. In A. L. Benson (Ed.), *I shop, therefore, I am: Compulsive buying and the search for self* (pp. 268–287). Northvale, NJ: Aronson.

Benson, A. L. (2000). Introduction. In A. L. Benson (Ed.), *I shop, therefore, I am: Compulsive buying and the search for self* (pp. xxi–xxxvii). Northvale, NJ: Aronson.

Black, D. W., Gabel, J., Hansen, J., & Schlosser, S. (2000). A double-blind comparison of fluvoxamine versus placebo in the treatment of compulsive buying disorder. *Annals of Clinical Psychiatry, 12*(4), 205–211.

Black, D. W., Monahan, P., & Gabel, J. (1997). Fluvoxamine in the treatment of compulsive buying. *Journal of Clinical Psychiatry, 58*(4), 159–163.

Bleuler, E. (1924). *Textbook of psychiatry.* New York: Macmillan.

Boundy, D. (2000). When money is the drug. In A. L. Benson (Ed.), *I shop, therefore, I am: Compulsive buying and the search for self* (pp. 3–26). Northvale, NJ: Aronson.

Brazer, L. (2000). Psychoeducational group therapy for money disorders. In A. L. Benson (Ed.), *I shop, therefore, I am: Compulsive buying and the search for self* (pp. 398–427). Northvale, NJ: Aronson.

Burgard, M., & Mitchell, J. (2000). Group cognitive behavioral therapy for buying disorder. In A. L. Benson (Ed.), *I shop, therefore, I am: Compulsive buying and the search for self* (pp. 367–397). Northvale, NJ: Aronson.

Catalano, E., & Sonenberg, N. (1993). *Consuming passions: Help for compulsive shoppers.* Oakland, CA: New Harbinger.

Christenson, G. A., Faber, R. J., de Zwaan, M., Raymond, N. C., Specker, S. M., Ekern, M. D., et al. (1994). Compulsive buying: Descriptive characteristics and psychiatric comorbidity. *Journal of Clinical Psychiatry, 55*(1), 5–11.

Damon, J. (1988). *Shopaholics: An 8-week program to control compulsive spending.* New York: Avon Books.

Edwards, E. A. (1993). Development of a new scale for measuring compulsive buying behavior. *Financial Counseling and Planning, 4,* 67–84.

Faber, R. J., & O'Guinn, T. C. (1992). A clinical screener for compulsive buying. *Journal of Consumer Research, 19,* 459–469.

Gallen, R. (2002). *The money trap: A practical program to stop self-defeating financial habits so you can reclaim your grip on life.* New York: Harper Resource.

Goldman, R. (2000). Compulsive buying as an addiction. In A. L. Benson (Ed.), *I shop, therefore, I am: Compulsive buying and the search for self* (pp. 245–267). Northvale, NJ: Aronson.

Goodman, W. K., Price, L. H., Rasmussen, S. A., Mazure, C., Fleischmann, R. L., Hill, C. L., et al. (1989). The Yale-Brown Obsessive-Compulsive Scale: I. Development, use and reliability. *Archives of General Psychiatry, 46*(11), 1006–1011.

Grant, J. E. (2002). *Three cases of compulsive shopping treated with Naltrexone.* Manuscript submitted for publication.

Grant, J. E., & Kim, S. W. (2002). An open label study of Naltrexone in the treatment of kleptomania. *Journal of Clinical Psychiatry, 63,* 349–356.

Hayes, T. A. (1997). Social and self-labeling processes in recognizing compulsive indebtedness: Findings from Debtors Anonymous (Doctoral dissertation, Vanderbilt University, 1997). *Dissertation Abstracts International, 57* (8A), 3697. Abstract retrieved January 27, 2003, from PsychINFO database: http://www.ucla.edu.

Hollander, E. (in press). *Handbook of impulsive control disorders.* Washington, DC: American Psychiatric Press.

Hwoschinsky, P. (1992). *True wealth.* Berkeley, CA: Ten Speed Press.

Kim, S. W. (1998). Opioid antagonists in the treatment of impulse-control. *Journal of Clinical Psychiatry, 59*(4), 1159–1162.

Kim, S. W., Grant, J. E., Adson, D., & Shin, Y. C. (2001). Double-blind Naltrexone and placebo comparison study in the treatment of pathological gambling. *Biological Psychiatry, 49,* 914–921.

Koran, L. M., Bullock, K. D., Hartston, H. J., Elliott, M. A., & D'Andrea, V. (2002). Citalopram treatment of compulsive shopping: An open-label study. *Journal of Clinical Psychiatry, 63*(8), 704–708.

Koran, L. M., Chuoung, H. W., Bullock, K. D., & Smith, S. C. (2003). Citalopram for compulsive shopping disorder: An open-label study followed by double-blind discontinuation. *Journal of Clinical Psychiatry, 64,* 793–798.

Kraepelin, E. (1915). *Psychiatrie* (8th ed.). Leipzig, Germany: Verlag Von Johann Ambrosius Barth.

Krueger, D. W. (2000). The use of money as an action symptom. In A. L. Benson (Ed.), *I shop, therefore, I am: Compulsive buying and the search for self* (pp. 288–310). Northvale, NJ: Aronson.

Lejoyeux, M., Adés, J., Tassian, V., & Solomon, J. (1996). Phenomenology and psychopathology of uncontrolled buying. *American Journal of Psychiatry, 153,* 1524–1529.

Lejoyeux, M., Hourtane, M., & Adés, J. (1995). Compulsive buying and depression [Letter]. *Journal of Clinical Psychiatry, 56*(1), 38.

Levine, B., & Kellen, B. (2000). Debtors Anonymous and psychotherapy. In A. L. Benson (Ed.), *I shop, therefore, I am: Compulsive buying and the search for self* (pp. 431–454). Northvale, NJ: Aronson.

Lockart, R. A. (1982). Coins and psychological change. In J. Hillman, A. Vasavada, J. W. Perry, & R. A. Lockhart (Eds.), *Soul and money* (p. 21). Dallas, TX: Spring.

Mannix, M. (1999, September 6). The credit card binge. *U.S. News & World Report, 127,* 89.

McCall, K. (1995). *Financial recovery workbook.* San Anselmo, CA: Financial Recovery Press.

McCall, K. (2000). Financial recovery counseling. In A. L. Benson (Ed.), *I shop, therefore, I am: Compulsive buying and the search for self* (pp. 455–483). Northvale, NJ: Aronson.

McCall, K. (2002). *Money minder: Financial recovery workbook.* San Anselmo, CA: Financial Recovery Press.

McElroy, S. L., Keck, P. E., Pope, H. G., Smith, J. M., & Strakowski, S. M. (1994). Compulsive buying: A report of 20 cases. *Journal of Clinical Psychiatry, 55*(6), 242–248.

McElroy, S. L., Satlin, A., Pope, H. G., Keck, P. E., & Hudson, J. I. (1991). Treatment of compulsive shopping with antidepressants: A report of three cases. *Annals of Clinical Psychiatry, 3,* 199–204.

Mellan, O. (1994). *Money harmony: Resolving money conflicts in your life and relationships.* New York: Walker.

Mellan, O. (1995). *Overcoming overspending: A winning plan for spenders and their partners.* New York: Walker.

Mellan, O. (2000). Overcoming overspending in couples. In A. L. Benson (Ed.), *I shop, therefore, I am: Compulsive buying and the search for self* (pp. 341–366). Northvale, NJ: Aronson.

Mitchell, J. (1993). *Buying disorder group treatment manual.* Unpublished manuscript, Neuropsychiatric Research Institute, Fargo, ND.

Ninan, P. T., McElroy, S. J., Kane, C. P., Knight, B. T., Casuto, L. S., Rose, S. E., et al. (2000). Placebo-controlled study of fluvoxamine in the treatment of patients with compulsive buying. *Journal of Clinical Psychopharmacology, 20*(3), 362–366.

Parecki, D. M. (2000). *Addressing compulsive buying behavior: A treatment program for self-identified compulsive buyers.* Unpublished doctoral dissertation, California School of Professional Psychology, Berkeley.

Richards, A. K. (2000). Clothes and the couch. In A. L. Benson (Ed.), *I shop, therefore, I am: Compulsive buying and the search for self* (pp. 311–337). Northvale, NJ: Aronson.

Rodriguez-Villarino, R., Otero-Lopez, J. L., & Rodriguez-Casto, R. (2001). *Adicion a la compra: Analysis, evaluaction y tratamiento* [Buying addiction: Analysis, evaluation and treatment]. Ediciones Piramide.

Sanders, S. (1998, November/December). The stuff of life. *Utne Reader,* 47–49.

Scherhorn, G., Reisch, L. A., & Raab, G. (1990). Addictive buying in West Germany: An empirical investigation. *Journal of Consumer Policy, 13,* 155–189.

Schlosser, S., Black, D. W., Repertinger, S., & Freet, D. (1994). Compulsive buying: Demography, phenomenology, and comorbidity in 46 subjects. *General Hospital Psychiatry, 16,* 205–212.

Schor, J. (1998). *The overspent American: Upscaling, downshifting, and the new consumer.* New York: Basic Books.

Washton, A. M. (2001). Group therapy: A clinician's guide to doing what works. In R. H. Coombs (Ed.), *Addiction recovery tools: A practical handbook* (pp. 239–256). Thousand Oaks, CA: Sage.

Winestine, M. (1985). Compulsive shopping as a derivative of childhood seduction. *Psychoanalytic Quarterly, 54,* 70–73.

PART VIII

PUBLIC POLICY AND PREVENTION

CHAPTER 15

Public Policy on Addictive Disorders

BEAU KILMER and ROBERT J. MacCOUN

T HERE ARE TWO reasons to care about addictive disorders: Those with disorders may be harming themselves and they may be harming others. Most agree that addictions are bad for society, but there is less agreement about how to mitigate the harms associated with addiction—especially when the government is involved.

Public policy on addictive disorders has been a subject of American debate for well over a century. Cigarettes and alcohol weren't always legal, and cocaine and heroin used to be readily prescribed (Musto, 1999; Troyer & Markle, 1983). Further, in one generation gambling went from being universally prohibited to universally accepted with state governments now promoting the activity (MacCoun & Reuter, 2001). Were these changes for the better? Should these policies be revised or reconsidered? We do not attempt to answer these grand questions here; rather, we hope to provide insight about how to best assess and compare various government policies on addictive disorders.

This chapter focuses on the policies associated with addictions to drugs, gambling, food, and sex. While this is not a complete list of disorders, it does include those that seem to do the most damage to the addicted and to society. We describe the epidemiology and dynamics of these disorders and review the strategies and tactical policies intended to affect them. These sections are infused with information from the fields of economics, psychology, public health, and criminal justice that is important to decision making about addictive disorders. We also offer frameworks for thinking about these policies and suggestions for new directions in addiction-related policy and research.

EPIDEMIOLOGY

Understanding the populations affected by addictive disorders and how they have changed is essential for comparing and creating useful public policies. But information about those affected by these four disorders ranges from abundant to

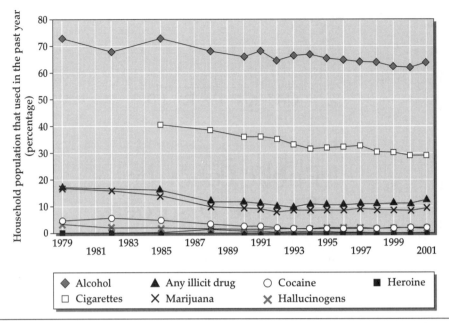

Figure 15.1   Share of Drug Users in the Household Population, 1979–2001. *Source:* SAMHSA, selected years.

scarce. When possible, we discuss the socioeconomic and demographic correlates of dependence and include trend data.

LICIT AND ILLICIT DRUGS

In 2001, approximately two-thirds of the country used alcohol, one-third used to-bacco, and one-eighth used illicit drugs—largely marijuana (Substance Abuse and Mental Health Services Administration [SAMHSA], 1994, 1995, 1996, 1997, 1998, 1999, 2000, 2001, 2002).[1] These rates are noticeably lower than they were in the late 1970s and early 1980s (Figure 15.1). Alcohol and cigarette use slightly de-creased during the 1990s while illicit drug use remained fairly stable for the household population. For high school seniors, annual surveys since the early 1990s suggest that past-year use of alcohol hovered around 73% while illicit drug use roughly increased from 30% to 40% (Johnston, O'Malley, & Bachman, 2002).

It is important to acknowledge those who may not be captured in the household and school-based surveys, especially the incarcerated. The Bureau of Justice Statis-tics (BJS; 1999, 2000) reports that 55% of jail and 57% of state prison inmates used illicit drugs in the month (not year) before their commitment offense. The rates are similarly high for those who were arrested and not necessarily convicted.[2] Whether or not this drug use contributed to their crime is a subject of much debate (see

---

[1] The National Household Survey on Drug Abuse (NHSDA) surveys those in the household popula-tion aged 12 years or older.
[2] The 2001 Arrestee Drug Abuse Monitoring Program (ADAM) drug-tested random samples of ar-restees in 33 counties (NIJ, 2002). The median county rate for male arrestees testing positive for any drug was 64%, cocaine 29%, opiates 5%, marijuana 43%, methamphetamines 3%, and PCP 1%.

MacCoun, Kilmer, & Reuter, 2003), but with two million prisoners (Harrison & Beck, 2002) and almost 14 million arrests in 2001 alone (Federal Bureau of Investigation [FBI], 2002), this population deserves special policy attention.

Most individuals who use licit and illicit drugs in any given year do so with few problems. It is the small portion of dependent users who seem to do a large amount of harm to themselves and others. That being said, occasional users can and do create significant harms, too (e.g., driving under the influence). Table 15.1 highlights the lifetime and past-year rates of clinical dependence as well as the statistically significant correlates from large, nationally representative surveys. Since there are no consistent longitudinal data on drug dependence, it is difficult to determine if addiction rates have changed over time.[3]

The results from these studies are more consistent for alcohol and tobacco than for illicit drugs. Lifetime and past-year dependence on cigarettes are 24% and 10%, respectively. Lifetime alcohol dependence is 14%, with past-year dependence in the 4% range. The most recent estimates for past-year alcohol dependence are closer to 2%, but this is likely attributable to changes in the screening tool (SAMHSA, 2001). While past-year dependence on cocaine remained stable at 0.3% throughout the 1990s, the number of individuals dependent on marijuana appears to have doubled from 0.7% to 1.4% of the household population. This increase may be attributable to measurement difference between the two studies, but it seems reasonable given the significant increase in marijuana use among adolescents and young adults during this period (Johnston et al., 2002).

There appears to be a discrepancy between the two studies that report lifetime rates of illicit drug dependence: Warner, Kessler, Hughes, Anthony, and Nelson (1995) estimate lifetime drug dependence at 7.5% while Grant (1996) estimates it at 2.9%. Grant suggests that there are differences "between the surveys in diagnostic criteria and the psychiatric interviews used to operationalize them" (p. 206) and that the studies looked at slightly different age groups. However, data from these surveys yielded similar results for lifetime alcohol dependence (about 14%). This is an important discrepancy but, for policy discussions, it is probably not as important as focusing on dependence rates for specific drugs.[4]

Based on Table 15.1, we cautiously generalize that males, individuals who did not complete high school, individuals with low-income levels, and individuals who live in the West are more likely to be addicted to illicit and licit drugs. Race and ethnicity were significant correlates of dependence in many of the studies, with Whites being more likely than African Americans to ever be dependent on tobacco and alcohol. Kandel, Chen, Warner, Kessler, and Grant (1997) found that African Americans were more than twice as likely to be dependent on cocaine in the *past year* than Whites, but this finding may be attributable to the fact that they used data from the end of the crack explosion, which disproportionately affected inner-city African Americans (Tonry, 1995). This is difficult to assess, however, since crack use is not separated from powder cocaine use in these dependency studies, and some crack users are not captured in the household population surveys.

---

[3] The closest measure is the NHSDA; it was changed in 1994 and 2000 and the U.S. Department of Health and Human Services warns against longitudinal comparisons.

[4] The transition from use to dependence for specific drugs has also been studied. Using the *DSM-III-R*, Anthony, Warner, and Kessler (1994) estimated that of those aged 15 to 54 years who had tried cocaine, approximately 17% became clinically dependent. The corresponding figures were 9% for marijuana, 15% for alcohol, 23% for heroin, and 32% for tobacco.

Table 15.1

Rates and Correlates of Drug Dependence by Drug Type

Source	Noninstitutionalized Sample	Measure of Dependence	Lifetime (L) or Past-Year (P)	Significant Correlates for Dependence, Holding Other Factors Constant[a]
Alcohol				
Anthony et al., 1994	15 to 54 1990 to 1992 $N = 8,098$	*DSM-III-R*	14% (L)	Males; those <45 years old; Whites are more likely than Blacks; those who work are more likely than those who are homemakers or students, but less likely than others; those with less than 16 years of education; those who make <$20K are more likely than those who make ≥$70K; those who live alone; Catholics and Protestants were less likely than those with no preference; those who did not live in the South.
Grant, 1996	18+ 1992 $N = 42,862$	*DSM-IV*	13.3% (L)	*Lifetime use subsample:* Whites more likely than Blacks; those with <12 years more likely than those ≥16 years of education; those who are not married; those who make <$72K; those who live in the S are less likely than W or MW, but more likely than NE.
			4.4% (P)	*Prior to the past year dependence sample:* Blacks and Hispanics; those with <16 years of education; those who are not married; those who make ≤$20K are more likely than those who make ≥$72K.
Kandel et al., 1997	12+ 1991 to 1993 $N = 87,915$	Proxy *DSM-IV*	3.4% (P)	*Among past year users:* males: <50; not graduating from high school; those with family incomes $9K to $75K are less likely than those who make <$9K; those who live in the West; those in the central city are more likely than those in rural areas.
SAMHSA, 1996, 1997, 1998, 1999, 2000, 2001, 2002[b]	12+ 1995, 1996, 1997, 1999 $N = 20–60,000$ annually	Proxy *DSM-IV*	3.7% to 4.7% (P)	
	12+ 2000, 2001 $N = \sim$70,000 annually	*DSM-IV*	2.3% and 2.4% (P)	
Tobacco				
Anthony et al., 1994	15 to 54 1990 to 1992 $N = 8,098$	*DSM-III-R*	24% (L)	45 to 54 more likely than 15 to 24; Whites more likely than Blacks and Hispanics; those who work are more likely than students, but less likely than homemakers and others; those with <16 years of education; those who make $20K to $34K are more likely than those who make ≥$70K; those who live with their parents are less likely than those who live alone; those who were never married are less likely; Catholics less likely than no preference.

Study	Sample	Instrument	Prevalence	Findings
Breslau et al., 2001	15 to 54 1990 to 1992 N = 4,414	DSM-III-R with WHO	24% (L)	*Predictors for daily smoking:* 45 to 54 more likely than 15 to 24; male; being White. *Nicotine dependence in daily smokers:*[c] Being <45; Blacks less likely than Whites.
Kandel et al., 1997	12+ 1991 to 1993 N = 87,915	Proxy *DSM-IV*	8.6% (P)	*Among past year users:* females; those >50 are more likely than those aged 12 to 17, but less likely than those 26 to 49; being White; not graduating from high school.
SAMHSA, 1996, 1997, 1998[b]	12+ 1995, 1996, 1997 N = ~20,000 annually	Proxy *DSM-IV*	9.8% to 10.8% (P)	
Drugs				
Anthony et al., 1994	15 to 54 1990 to 1992 N = 8,098	*DSM-III-R*	7.5% (L)	Males; those <45 years old; Whites are more likely than Blacks; workers are less likely than homemakers and others; those with ≤12 years of education are more likely than those ≥16 years; those who make <$20K are more likely than those who make ≥$70K; those who lived alone were more likely than those who lived with spouses or parents; Catholics and Protestants were less likely than those with no preference; those who live in the West are more likely than those in the South.
Warner et al., 1995	15 to 54 1990 to 1992 N = 8,098	*DSM-III-R*	7.5% (L) 1.8% (P)	*User subsample:* those with ≤12 years more likely than those ≥16 years of education; those who make <$20K are more likely than those who make ≥$70K; those who live in the West are more likely than those in the Midwest. *Lifetime dependent sample:* Blacks are more likely than Whites.
Grant, 1996	18+ 1992 N = 42,862	*DSM-IV*	2.9% (L) 0.8% (P)	Those with ≤12 years more likely than those ≥16 years of education; those that were separated, widowed, or divorced were more likely than married; those who make ≥$72K; those who live in the S are less likely than W, but more likely than NE. Blacks and Hispanics are more likely than Whites; those with <12 years more likely than Whites; those ≥16 years of education; those that were never married were more likely than those who were married.
SAMHSA, 1996, 1997, 1998[b]	12+ 1999, 2000, 2001 N = ~70,000 annually	*DSM-IV*	1.6%, 1.2%, 1.6% (P)	

(continued)

499

Table 15.1 *Continued*

Source	Noninstitution-alized Sample	Measure of Dependence	Lifetime (L) or Past-Year (P)	Significant Correlates for Dependence, Holding Other Factors Constant[a]
Marijuana				
Anthony et al., 1994	15 to 54 1990 to 1992 N = 8,098	DSM-III-R	4.2% (L)	
Kandel et al., 1997	12+ 1991 to 1993 N = 87,915	Proxy DSM-IV	0.7% (P)	*Among past year users:* male; those 12 to 17 are more likely than those ≥35; those with more than high school are less likely than those who did not complete high school; those who live in the W are more likely than those in the NE.
SAMHSA, 1996, 1997, 1998[b]	12+ 1995, 1996, 1997 N = ~20,000 annually	Proxy DSM-IV	1.3% to 1.5% (P)	
	12+ 2000, 2001 N = ~70,000 annually	DSM-IV	0.8% and 0.9% (P)	
Cocaine				
Anthony et al., 1994	15 to 54 1990 to 1992 N = 8,098	DSM-III-R	2.7% (L)	
Kandel et al., 1997	12+ 1991 to 1993 N = 87,915	Proxy DSM-IV	0.3% (P)	*Among past year users:* Blacks are more likely than Whites; college graduates are less likely than those who did not complete high school; those who make between $9K to $40K are less likely than those who make less than $9K; those live in urban, noncentral city areas are more likely that those in rural areas.
SAMHSA, 1996, 1997, 1998[b]	12+ 1995, 1996, 1997 N = ~20,000 annually	Proxy DSM-IV	0.3% to 0.4% (P)	

12+
2000, 2001
$N = \sim 70,000$ annually

DSM-IV

0.2% and
0.3% (P)

[a] Relationships are positive unless otherwise noted. Most models included gender, ethnicity, education, marital status, family income, region, and urbanicity, but the models are not identical.

[b] SAMHSA (2000) estimates pre-2000 are from the published report and the detailed tables on the Internet and are unavailable for some years. Post-1999 estimates are not comparable to pre-2000 figures because additional dependence criteria were added and the wording of some of the questions changed (http://www.samhsa.gov/oas/Dependence/appendixc.htm).

[c] The analysis of nicotine dependence was performed on persons with a history of daily smoking, excluding persons with onset of nicotine dependence before or in the year of onset of daily smoking and persons with onset of daily smoking in the year of the interview.

Gambling

Approximately 60% of the country gambles each year, including those who only participate in private betting such as perennial Super Bowl pools. Nationally representative surveys from 1975 and 1998 found that the number of past-year bettors was fairly stable at 61% and 63%, respectively, but the number of lifetime gamblers increased from 68% to 86% (Gerstein et al., 1999; Kallick, Suits, Dielman, & Hybels, 1976).[5] During this time, casinos proliferated in 27 states, and 37 states now actively promote lotteries (Volberg, 2002). Not surprisingly, the number of past-year bettors who visited casinos and played the lottery doubled during this period.

Interestingly, not only did lottery and casino gambling increase, but bingo playing and horse racing dropped off. There was both an increase in total gambling, and a shift from some forms to others. From a policy perspective, this raises the question of whether this was a shift toward greater versus lesser harms to self and to others and whether there were any redistributional consequences.

Table 15.2 shows that past-year prevalence rates are higher for males and have slightly increased for females from 1975 to 1998. Males are slightly more likely to play casinos and women are much more likely to play bingo. The increases are occurring in the older cohorts, with 117% increase in the number of past-year gamblers aged 65 and older. Gerstein et al. (1999) caution that this statistic should not sound the alarm of a senior gambling epidemic, but it should raise concerns about an increase in dependency for an age group that is fairly new to those who treat gambling addiction (see Petry, 2002a).

A meta-analysis of pathological gambling studies found an average past-year rate of 1.5% and a mean lifetime rate of 1.9% for adult community samples (Shaffer & Hall, 2001). The meta-analysis also suggests that youth, college students, prisoners, and those in treatment for drug or psychiatric disorders were at special risk for gambling disorders. Shaffer and colleagues (Shaffer & Hall, 2001; Shaffer, Hall, & Vanderbilt, 1999) found an increase in lifetime dependence from 1975 to 1999 and attribute it largely to a cohort effect and an increase in prevalence among adults in the general population.

Using *DSM-IV* criteria, Gerstein et al. (1999) estimate that there are currently 2.5 million pathological gamblers and 3 million problem gamblers in the United States. These estimates come from a study that surveyed the household population as well as patrons at casinos and other gambling venues. For this merged sample, significant correlates of pathological and problem gambling include being male, less than 65, African American, divorced, and those who live with minor children.

An important new development is Internet gambling, currently the eighth largest business on the Web (Sager, Elgin, Elstrom, Keenan, & Gogoi, 2002). One study of Internet gamblers found that 8% of patients at a university health center reported lifetime gambling and 4% reported online gambling in the past week (Ladd & Petry, 2002). Internet gamblers were significantly more likely to be young and non-Caucasian compared to those who had never gambled on the Web. The study also found that those who gambled online were much more likely to be problem and pathological gamblers. Patients at a university health center do not

---

[5] While these two surveys used different techniques (in-person versus telephone), Gerstein et al. (1999) claim "The 1975 survey and NORC's 1998 survey for the National Gambling Impact Study Commission were in many respects similar enough to permit ready comparison between their results" (p. 5).

Table 15.2
Past-Year Gambling Participation Rates, 1975 and 1998

	1975 (%) (N = 1,769)	1998 (%) (N = 2,417)	Change (%)
Game			
Casino	10	29	+190
Lottery	24	52	+117
Bingo	19	6	−68
Horse racing	14	7	−50
Gender			
Males	68	67	−2
Females	55	60	+10
Age			
18–24	73	64	−12
25–44	69	67	−3
45–64	60	66	+10
65+	23	50	+117

Sources: Gambling Impact and Behavior Study, D. Gerstein et al., 1999, Chicago: National Opinion Research Center; and *Survey of American Gambling Attitudes and Behaviors*, M. Kallick, D. Suits, T. Dielman, and J. Hybels, 1976, Washington, DC: U.S. Government Printing Office.

represent the general population, but these findings, if replicated, could indicate increased risk for gambling disorders among young adults.

EATING DISORDERS

Although there is a rich clinical literature on eating disorders, the epidemiological literature is far spottier. Studies of eating disorders usually focus on anorexia nervosa (AN), bulimia nervosa (BN), and sometimes, binge eating disorder (BED). Anorexia nervosa and BN affect about 3% of all women during their lifetime, primarily occurring during adolescence and young adulthood (Walsh & Devlin, 1998). These disorders are not unheard of among males, with Canadian community samples finding female-to-male ratios to be approximately 10 to 1 for BN and 4.2 to 1 for AN (Garfinkel et al., 1995; Woodside et al., 2001). BED appears to be more evenly distributed by age and gender and is believed to be at least as prevalent as BN (Walsh & Devlin, 1998).

It is estimated that subclinical forms of AN and BN are "two to five times more common than full diagnosis in adolescent girls, ranging from 4% to 16% of the general population" (Mussell, Binford, & Fulkerson, 2000, p. 766). These numbers, however, should be interpreted with caution, as a roundtable of experts recently noted, "It is assumed that eating disorders begin during adolescence, yet no nationally representative study has been conducted with adolescent participants" (Pearson, Goldklang, & Striegel-Moore, 2002, p. 234).[6]

---

[6] The authors do note: "The currently fielded National Comorbidity Survey-Replication and National Survey of African Americans will administer an eating disorders diagnostic module to the adolescent sample and to a proportion the adult sample" (p. 234).

Reviews suggest that the incidence of these disorders is increasing (Hsu, 1996), but their rarity and the lack of longitudinal epidemiological studies makes this difficult to assess. A recent study found an increase in male hospitalizations for eating disorders (Braun, Sunday, Huang, & Halmi, 1999), but it was noted that it is not clear whether this is a true increase or the manifestation of increased awareness of male eating disorders (Pearson et al., 2002).

Aside from gender, age, and race, there do not appear to be any other well-documented socioeconomic or demographic correlates of eating disorders within the United States. A female twin study classified respondents into seven eating disorder groups (AN, BN, BED, three subclinical groups, and no eating disorder) and found that "There were no significant differences across the six classes and the comparison group on education, parental education, financial status, or size of community in which the individual lived" (Bulik, Sullivan, & Kendler, 2000, p. 889). Hay and Bacaltchuk (2001) also suggest that there appears to be an even social class distribution for BN in community-based samples.

Little was known about the effect of race and ethnicity on eating disorders because early studies focused on affluent, White, clinical samples (Mussell et al., 2000 quoting Striegel-Moore, 1999). A review of the research as it pertains to other racial and ethnic groups found that these disorders do affect minority populations (Striegel-Moore & Smolak, 2000). Further, research finds that BED is not only clinically significant in African American and White women, but these groups differ significantly on all associated eating disorder features, such as binge frequency, history of other eating disorders, and treatment-seeking behavior (Pike, Dohm, Striegel-Moore, Wilfley, & Fairburn, 2001). This raises questions about the course of these disorders within different subgroups and how different groups may need different treatments.

SEXUAL ADDICTION

The concept of sexual addiction or sexual dependence is not included in the *DSM-IV* (Schneider & Irons, 1996) and considerable debate exists about its definition and whether it should be classified (see Gold & Heffner, 1998; Goodman, 1998, chap. 1). The research distinguishes between paraphilias and other sexual disorders in that the former include unconventional sexual behaviors, such as pedophilia, sadism, and frotteurism (Coleman, 1992). Some also focus on paraphilia-related disorders which can be defined as:

> [S]exually arousing fantasies, urges or activities that are culturally sanctioned aspects of normative sexual arousal and activity but which increase in frequency and intensity (for greater than 6 months duration) so as to preclude or significantly interfere with capacity for reciprocal affectionate activity. (Kafka & Hennen, 1999, p. 306)

A few clinicians estimate that about 5% of the population suffers from these disorders, with males accounting for most of the clients (Carnes, 1991; Coleman, 1992). There are, however, no epidemiological studies in the field and clinical samples may be biased because those with the most extreme disorders may be incarcerated or reluctant to seek treatment.

It is reasonable to think that more could be learned about this phenomenon by looking at those involved with prostitution. Data from the 1992 National Health and Social Life Survey suggests that 18% of men ages 18 to 59 have paid for sex with a woman and 2% of women received money for sex (Laumann, Gagnon, Michael, & Michael, 1994; Sullivan & Simon, 1998). Unfortunately, it is hard to get a clear picture about prostitutes and their clients since most studies focus on one segment of the prostitution population—street workers. A review article noted:

> [T]he literature about prostitution is still much more about sex, noticeably sexual victimization and risk, than it is about work. The groups most researched are the ones that are also more vulnerable and to whom a victim status most applies (i.e., groups who do not only work sex but for whom additional problems, such as economic hardship, victimization, homelessness, and drug abuse shape their daily realities). Many researchers still study or feature only street workers (Vanwesenbeeck, 2001, p. 279).

While it is impossible to determine how much of the prostitution business is concentrated on the street—as opposed to saunas, massage parlors, or via escort services—estimates suggest that street workers account for at most 20% of prostitution in large cities (see Kuo, 2002, chap. 5). This suggests a large segment of the prostitution industry is understudied.

However, data about johns are becoming increasingly available as jurisdictions mandate that those arrested for prostitution attend prostitution education classes. (Bringing this heterogeneous and elusive group of men together significantly reduces the cost of collecting data.) A study sponsored by the National Institute of Justice (2002) found that for over 1,300 men attending these classes in four Western cities, 12% had sexual relations with a prostitute on at least a monthly basis in the previous year (Monto, 2000).[7] While arrestees attending these classes may not be representative of all johns, this is clearly a group that should interest those wanting to learn more about sexual "addiction" and its related harms (including the harm associated with arrest).

Finally, the ubiquity of sex on the web has generated debate about whether there is such thing as Internet sex addiction (Griffiths, 2001). Some people seek free pornography, some frolic in chat rooms, and some pay to watch live sex shows that can be custom designed to satisfy consumer needs. A nonrandom survey of almost 10,000 individuals who use the Internet for sex purposes found that about 5% were "sexually compulsive" and of this group, 23% were classified as cybersex compulsive" (being sexually compulsive and spending more than 11 hours a week in online sexual pursuits; Cooper, Delmonico, & Burg, 2000). This cybersex compulsive group was more likely to be female, nonheterosexual, nonmarried, in school, and to use chat rooms for sexual pursuits than the other respondents. This does not sound like those in the aforementioned male-dominated clinical samples and may suggest a new or ignored population needing treatment.

DYNAMICS

Understanding the personal and public environments in which these behaviors occur is critical to effectively mitigate the harms associated with these addictive disorders. Large and important research literatures exist on the neuroscientific

---

[7] This figure is based on our analysis of the source data. Of the 1,342 observations, 288 were missing data for this question (v27) and 126 reported sexual relations with a prostitute on at least a monthly basis for the previous year. There was an 80% response rate.

and psychological etiology of these disorders, but many of the variables of interest to addiction theorists have little or no relevance for policy making (MacCoun, in press). Here, we focus instead on aggregate, population-level causal factors to which public policy interventions can be targeted: prices, links to related activities, and delivery mechanisms.

PRICE EFFECTS

There is an extensive literature on the economics of alcohol and tobacco use and an emerging literature on illicit drugs and other addictive behaviors. While many researchers used to assume that the consumption of addictive goods was beyond the realm of standard economic analysis, it is now abundantly clear that prices matter, even to those who are dependent. Sensitivity to prices is of interest for several reasons. From a scientific perspective, it teaches us something about the nature of addiction: Are addicts "enslaved" or do they have some ability to control their habits under changing circumstances? From a policy perspective, for licit goods and activities, price sensitivity informs decisions about taxation and other regulatory strategies. For illicit goods and activities, price sensitivity helps us forecast the likely effects of supply reduction, including the question of whether some addicts will commit income-generating crimes to compensate for price increases.

Economists measure a person's sensitivity to prices by calculating the price elasticity of demand—the percentage change in consumption for a 1% change in price (Table 15.3). The price elasticity is generally a negative number (because economists assume that when the price of a good increases, demand for it decreases), with values smaller than −1 said to be elastic and those greater than −1 said to be inelastic.

Tobacco and Alcohol   Recent literature reviews of the economics of substance use literature find licit drug users are sensitive to price (Chaloupka & Pacula, 2000;

Table 15.3
Price Elasticity of Demand by Good

Good	Price Elasticity of Demand
Cigarettes	−0.5 to −0.3
Alcohol	−0.7
Marijuana	−0.69 to −0.13
Cocaine	−2.5 to −0.41
Heroin	−1.0 to −0.2
Lotteries	−1.55 to −0.81
Betting	−2.5 to −1.19
Horse racing	−1.59
Food	−0.21*
Automobiles	−1.20*
Rental housing	−0.18*

Note: The smaller the number, the more sensitive consumers are.

*Source: *Microeconomic Theroy: Basic Principles and Extensions,* W. Nicholson, 1998, Fort Worth, TX: Dryden Press.

Grossman, Chaloupka, & Shim, 2002). Increasing the price of cigarettes not only decreases the number of cigarettes consumed by current smokers, it also causes more adults to quit and fewer adolescents to start. The consensus estimate for the price elasticity for cigarettes is –0.5 to –0.3, suggesting that a 10% increase in the price of cigarettes would reduce overall consumption by 3% to 5% (Chaloupka & Pacula, 2000; Manning, Keeler, Newhouse, Sloss, & Wasserman, 1991).

Prices matter for heavy drinkers as well as for recreational users. The estimates for alcohol seem to depend on consumption level and population, but they appear to cluster around –0.7 (Manning et al., 1991). It does appear, however, that consumers are more responsive to changes in the price of hard liquor that they are to beer and wine (Cook & Moore, 1999). Reviews also suggest that youths are more sensitive to the price of licit drugs than adults, but all age groups show price sensitivity (Chaloupka & Pacula, 2000).

Illicit Drugs Illicit drug use is inversely related to drug prices, and again, contrary to popular belief, even heavy and dependent users appear to reduce their consumption as prices increase. Estimates from several studies suggest that the price elasticity of demand for cocaine ranges between –1.00 and –0.41 for the household population (Grossman et al., 2002). Caulkins (1995, 2001) suggests that heavy cocaine users may be even more sensitive to prices than the general population. This may be a result of heavy users spending a disproportionate amount of their income on drugs relative to recreational users. Estimates for the price elasticity of heroin range from –1.0 (Van Ours, 1995) to –0.2 (Moore, 1991; also Becker, Grossman, & Murphy, 1992). We are unaware of any estimates for methamphetamines or designer drugs (e.g., ecstasy).

As for marijuana, Pacula and colleagues (2000) estimate the price elasticity for American youth to be between –0.69 to –0.30. Using data from the Australian household population, Cameron and Williams (2001) calculate the elasticity to be –0.13. The difference in estimates might indicate that youth are more price sensitive than adults, but it may also be attributable to cultural or measurement differences.

Gambling Gamblers can choose among different games and different forms of entertainment, and evidence suggests that they are sensitive to price. Price in this sense means more than just the cost of a lottery ticket—it also includes the expected value of winning money (Expected value = Probability of win × Jackpot × Expected share of jackpot if win; Cook & Clotfelter, 1993). Thus, the price elasticity of demand shows how the demand for the lottery varies with the expected value (Farrell & Walker, 1999). Paton, Siegel, and Vaughan Williams' (2001) review finds a price elasticity for lotteries ranging from –1.55 to –1.03 and an elasticity for horse racing at –1.59. The authors also find a price elasticity for National Lottery (United Kingdom) to be between –0.99 and –0.81 and elasticities ranging from –2.50 to –1.19 for betting.

SUBSTITUTION, COMPLEMENTARITY, AND GATEWAY EFFECTS

The acquisition and consumption of goods (e.g., substances, experiences, pictures) do not occur in a vacuum. These goods have prices, and there are other products from which to choose. Two goods are considered substitutes if an increase in the price of good A leads to an increase in the demand for good B. They are considered complements if an increase in the price of good A leads to a decrease in the demand for goods A and B. Some argue that these complementary relationships between substances help prove that there is gateway effect. But the gateway hypothesis goes beyond simple complementarity, requiring a fixed temporal sequence in which one risky activity at an earlier time increases the likelihood of another more hazardous activity at a later time. Thus, the use of soft drugs (like tobacco, alcohol, and marijuana) is purported to serve as a gateway to hard drug use (like heroin and cocaine), and perhaps addiction.

Alcohol, Tobacco, and Illicit Drugs   We know that price increases can reduce demand, but do users just turn to other substances? The small but growing number of econometric studies of polysubstance use and abuse have generally found that these substances are economic complements, not substitutes (Pacula & Chaloupka, 2001). But the debate is far from settled.

Studies of the alcohol-cigarette link are inconsistent (Cameron & Williams, 2001; Decker & Schwartz, 2000), but studies of the marijuana-cigarette link seem to suggest a complementary relationship (Cameron & Williams, 2001; Chaloupka, Pacula, Farrelly, Johnston, & O'Malley, 1999; Farrelly, Bray, Zarkin, Wendling, & Pacula, 1999; Pacula, 1998). More research has been done on the relationship between marijuana and alcohol. Chaloupka and Pacula (2000) conclude:

> The mixed evidence with respect to alcohol and marijuana can be attributed to differences in the level of aggregation of the data as well as to differences in the populations being studied. When individual-level data are employed, and demand equations for marijuana can also be estimated, the findings are generally supportive of the complementary relationship between alcohol and marijuana. (p. 105)

As for harder drugs, DeSimone (1998) predicts that prior use of marijuana increases the probability of using cocaine in the following four years by more than 29%. Saffer and Chaloupka's (1999) study of the relationships among alcohol, marijuana, cocaine, and heroin found that they are generally complementary except for the relationship between alcohol and marijuana (results were inconsistent). Some question the generalizability of Saffer and Chaloupka's study because they used a proxy for the price of marijuana (decriminalization status) instead of the observed price (Grossman et al., 2002). Only recently have studies been able to use drug price information from the Drug Enforcement Agency (DEA).

Another study using decriminalization status found different results. Using data from emergency-room records from 1975 to 1978, Model (1993) found that states that lowered the penalties for marijuana possession not only had more marijuana mentions, but they also had fewer mentions of drugs other than marijuana in the records. She interprets this as evidence that individuals used marijuana instead of harder drugs in the states with lower penalties.

There is also evidence from laboratory studies that give subjects imitation money and a menu of illegal drugs and ask how much they would purchase. One such experiment with heroin addicts suggests that increases in the price of heroin led to a strong increase in valium purchases (Petry & Bickel, 1998). Petry and Bickel found that cocaine was a heroin substitute for a minority of the sample and that there was "an independent or weak substitute relationship . . . between heroin price and purchase of marijuana and alcohol" (p. 332). The authors do note, however, that it is not clear that users would choose these same amounts in natural settings, especially since the experiment assumed that there was no fear of being arrested.

Not only is it difficult to establish a causal relationship between the use of different substances, but even if proven, it would be unclear about what policymakers should do since there are many competing interpretations of the gateway effect (MacCoun, 1998a, lists at least seven). While cannabis intoxication might entice users to experiment with other kinds of intoxication, it is also possible that the gateway association is due to contact with drug sellers or drug-using subcultures, or the correlation could be spurious due to some common risk factors (Morral, Mc-Caffrey, & Paddock, 2002). MacCoun and Reuter's (2001) review of the gateway literature led them to call for additional research about the causal mechanism (e.g., longitudinal and animal) because of its potential policy implications:

> Given the current state of knowledge, one can coherently argue that (a) the gateway is a myth—it doesn't exist; (b) the gateway is very real and it shows why we must sustain or strengthen our ban on marijuana; or (c) the gateway is very real and shows why we should depenalize or even legalize marijuana. It all comes down to which interpretation of the available evidence one favors. (p. 351)

Gambling   What about the interaction between the different kinds of games? Table 15.2 shows from 1975 to 1998, lottery and casino gambling increased dramatically in the United States while horse racing and bingo decreased, but it is not clear that they are substitutes. For Lotto, early evidence suggests that its introduction in the 1980s did not hurt the sales of existing games (numbers and tickets; Clotfelter & Cook, 1990; Cook & Clotfelter, 1993). A sophisticated analysis by Kearney (2002) also discredits substitution as well as suggests the introduction of state lotteries decreased household consumption on nonlottery products:

> A complementary analysis of participation in various forms of gambling finds that there is no substitution away from participation in other forms of gambling when a lottery is introduced. In fact, my analysis of household nongambling consumption suggests that household spending on lottery tickets is financed completely by a reduction in other forms of household consumption. The introduction of a state lottery is associated with a decline in household nongambling consumption of $115 per quarter. (p. 26)

But there is some evidence to the contrary. While researchers in the United Kingdom found that the introduction of a National Lottery did not affect the demand on other types of gambling, they did find a substitution effect between lotteries and betting (Paton et al., 2001). Further, an econometric study of Arizona found that the expansion of slot machines is associated with a reduction in lottery revenue, especially Lotto (Siegel & Anders, 2001). But the authors caution that this may not be applicable to other states, and the actual displacement effect is difficult to measure because of other factors that may have also offset lottery sales. In addition, these authors did not find a substitution effect between horse racing and lotteries.

As for trading off with other forms of entertainment, this is more difficult to assess without individual-level data. We do know that "Americans spend more on legal gambling than they spend on movie tickets, recorded music, theme parks, spectator sports, and video games combined" (Volberg, 2002, p. 176), but it is not clear how spending on gambling has affected spending on these other activities. Siegel and Anders (1999) found that the growth of riverboat gaming led to a decrease in revenue for other businesses in the entertainment and amusement sector, but more evidence is needed before a conclusion is drawn.

Could there be a gateway effect for gambling? Whether the concept generalizes to gambling depends on three issues: whether certain forms of gambling consistently precede others, whether the early forms increase the likelihood of the later forms, and whether the later types of gambling are more harmful. We do know that heavy gamblers tend to have experience with more than one form of gambling, but there is little research on developmental sequence or on relative harms associated with various forms of gambling. (Presumably, harms vary with frequency and stakes, but most modalities have both light and heavy gamblers.) We are just starting to learn about compulsive gamblers on the Internet, and there is a great need for incidence studies in the field (Shaffer et al., 1999).

Sexual Behaviors   When thinking about sex, it is useful to remember that just as there are drugs of choice, there are also sexual behaviors of choice. There are a variety of acts, from intercourse to masturbation, and a variety of tools, from regular partners to prostitutes to pornography to sexual aids. Are some of these acts and tools more addictive than others? This is difficult to ascertain without a clear definition of this disorder, but Cooper et al.'s Internet study raises the point that the:

> Anonymity, accessibility, and affordability (of cybersex) seem to increase the chances that the Internet will become problematic for those who either already have a problem with sexual compulsivity or those who have psychological vulnerabilities rendering them at risk for developing such compulsivity. (p. 7)

As for other pursuits, Kafka and Hennen's (1999) study of men with sexual impulsivity disorders examined the rates of six paraphilia-related disorders: compulsive masturbation, promiscuity, pornography dependence, telephone-sex dependence, severe desire incompatibility, and excessive use of sex accessories (e.g., dildos). They found that telephone-sex dependence was positively related with heterosexual promiscuity and pornography dependence. There was not a statistically significant relationship between pornography dependence and promiscuity, but these findings should be cautiously interpreted given the small, nonrandom sample. (The smaller the sample, the harder it is to detect significant differences.) It would be fruitful to further explore how these disorders are related to promiscuity, which may leave these individuals and their partners open to a host of risks.

Substitution or Complementarity across Behavioral Classes?   An important question for future research is whether addictive behaviors of different sorts (drug use, alcohol use, sexual behaviors, gambling) are substitutes or complements. There is considerable evidence for comorbidity of these behaviors; for example, heavy alcohol consumption and drug use are correlated with heavy gambling (Petry, 2002b; Vitaro, Ferland, Jacques, & Ladouceur, 1998) and unsafe sexual behavior (Donovan & McEwan, 1995; Fitterling, Matens, Scotti, & Allen, 1993; Scheidt & Windle, 1995).

One reason for comorbidity might be a common propensity due to personality and/or biological factors—the so-called "addictive personality." The existence of such a personality type has been controversial since the 1980s (see Eysenck, 1997; Kerr, 1996; Nathan, 1988; Sutker & Allain, 1988). Nathan's (1988) review of the evidence led him to suggest that researchers were simply relabeling the comorbidity without explaining it:

> [W]hat is most striking about this literature is the extent to which the [common] factors identified are overt, reactive, and shared. By contrast, our definition of personality portrays it as internal, causal, and unique. Thus, it is primarily behavior and not personality that those who have identified predictors of alcoholism and drug abuse have found. (p. 187)

A more promising individual-differences approach might be rooted in the behavioral economics of low self-control (Ainslie, 2001; Baumeister, Heatherton, & Tice, 1994; Elster & Skog, 1999; Gottfredson & Hirschi, 1990). For example, across many vices, addicts share a common tendency to discount delayed rewards steeply, and, in a fashion that promotes behaviors, the actor will later regret (hyperbolic discounting; e.g., Ainslie, 2001; Petry & Bickel, 1998). This suggests that personality factors interact with situational factors (salience and delay of competing rewards) to produce addictive behavior, and that susceptible individuals need training in self-control techniques and perhaps environmental contingency-management interventions. Focusing across risky behaviors is especially desirable because there is some evidence that efforts to control one vice deplete a person's ability to stave off other temptations (Muraven & Baumeister, 2000). The classic example is weight gain among those trying to quit cigarettes.

DELIVERY MECHANISMS

In thinking about addictive behaviors, it is useful to draw lessons from the evolution of thinking about criminal behaviors. Traditional debates in criminology revolved around whether criminal behavior was a property of criminogenic traits (genetics, personality, somatypes, etc.) versus criminogenic environments (poverty, racism, child abuse, etc.). Such debates were unresolvable; wisdom suggested that both are true but this answer itself provides little useful insight. But in the late 1980s, criminological theories became explicitly interactionist, focusing on how moderate to extreme levels of nearly universal human traits (momentary anger, the difficulty of resisting temptation) could combine with properties of the immediate situation (unprotected and/or highly salient targets, lack of supervision or surveillance) to increase the probability that crimes would take place (see Felson, 1998; Gottfredson & Hirschi, 1990). This interactionist perspective not only sidesteps an unproductive debate, but it also focuses attention on variables susceptible to policy influence. Policy makers cannot in any direct (and constitutionally tolerable) way bring about changes in citizens' personalities; nor can they simply eliminate poverty (or racism, or child abuse) as a means of solving addiction problems. But they can take steps to re-engineer local environments to discourage destructive behavior and promote constructive behavior.

There are many examples of such "local" environmental variables in the specialized literature on particular addictions. The alcohol literature is replete with studies of the effects of advertising restrictions, limits on tavern hours, the packaging of liquors, and so on (see Edwards et al., 1994; MacCoun, Reuter, & Schelling, 1996). The gambling literature has detailed studies of the behavioral consequences of games of chance versus skill, the effects of lottery ticket and slot machine design, and so on (see Griffiths, 1999, or almost any issue of the *Journal of Gambling Studies*). The illicit drug literature has analyses of the behavioral consequences of crack versus powder cocaine, smoked versus injected heroin, as well as the harm-producing consequences of sales locations—indoor sales versus outdoor sales, street markets versus cannabis coffeeshops (see MacCoun & Reuter, 2001; MacCoun et al., 2003). What's needed is a more systematic theory of *addictive situations* that would integrate these diverse literatures (see Heyman, 1996; Rachlin, 2000).

STRATEGIES AND TACTICS

Decision makers armed with the knowledge of the epidemiology and dynamics of addictive behaviors can make more informed decisions about the policies intended to affect them. But the policy debates surrounding these addictive behaviors often focus more on the polar extremes, especially in the case of drug policy. Based on frameworks developed for thinking about illicit drug policies (MacCoun & Reuter, 2001; MacCoun et al., 1996; also MacCoun, 1998a), this section extends these concepts to other addictive behaviors. This section largely focuses on alcohol, tobacco, illicit drugs, and gambling, but references are also made to sexual addiction and eating disorders.

Though we hesitate to perpetuate military metaphors for addressing addictive disorders, we think it is useful to distinguish broad strategies from specific tactics. As befits its largely clinical orientation, the addiction literature is rich with tactical research on specific treatment and prevention interventions. Much less attention is given to broader strategic questions about goals, the allocation of scarce resources across interventions, and the question of optimal targeting of those interventions.

STRATEGIC ISSUES

We discuss six strategic issues to consider when shaping addiction policy or considering an evaluation. These issues include: supply reduction versus demand reduction, use reduction versus harm reduction, targeting casual participants versus the hardest core, costs versus benefits of different policy regimes, harms to users versus harms to others, and costs versus benefits of delivery mechanisms. While these issues are framed as dichotomies or alternatives, the choices are not mutually exclusive, but are rather matters of emphasis and priority. We leave our discussion of tactics—the specific techniques of intervention—for the next section.

Supply Reduction versus Demand Reduction   This is a prominent debate in American drug policy and is also evident in discussions about the regulation of online gambling and prostitution. The argument for reducing demand suggests that where there is demand there will always be someone who will supply the good or service in order to make a profit; thus, reducing demand should be the priority. On the other hand, those touting supply reduction argue that price is inversely related to supply. An increase in supply results in a lower price, thus making the good or service more attractive to nonusers and increasing the demand among current users. Increased supply also has an additional effect in that it reduces the transaction time involved in obtaining the good.

Table 15.4
Strategies and Goals for Addressing Addictive Disorders

Strategy	Goal
Prevalence reduction	Reduce total number of users.
Quantity reduction	Reduce total quantity consumed.
Micro-harm reduction	Reduce average harm per incident of use.
Macro-harm reduction	Reduce aggregate use-related harm.

Source: Adapted from *Drug War Heresies: Learning from Other Places, Times, and Vices,* by R. J. MacCoun and P. Reuter, 2001, New York: Cambridge University Press.

It is estimated that at least 75% of the money spent to reduce drug use by the federal and state governments is focused on supply reduction efforts such as law enforcement and source-country control (MacCoun & Reuter, 2001, p. 33). The Drug Enforcement Agency argues that the massive decrease in drug use from the late 1970s to the present proves that our current strategy is effective (Hutchison, 2002),[8] but this is difficult to verify. Some data on drug price changes and perceived availability suggest that it is "highly implausible that enforcement was the principle cause" of this decline (p. 32).[9] Further, a committee of the National Research Council, including MacCoun, noted:

[L]ittle is known about the effectiveness of law enforcement operations against retail drug markets. In particular, the consequences of increasing or decreasing current levels of enforcement are not known. It is not known whether a significant decrease in law enforcement activity would lead to a significant increase in drug dealing and use. Nor is it known whether a significant increase in law enforcement would have the opposite effect. (Manski, Pepper, & Petrie, 2001, p. 177)[10]

Use Reduction versus Harm Reduction   The discussion about supply and demand reduction is largely a funding debate in which advocates generally agree on one thing: "The highest, if not exclusive, goal of drug policy is to reduce (and, if possible, to eliminate) psychoactive drug use" (MacCoun & Reuter, 2001, p. 385). This use-reduction paradigm is synonymous with reducing the prevalence of use, but this is not the only strategy for reducing total consumption. Further, there are other goals aside from just reducing use, such as reducing the harm associated with each act of consumption. Table 15.4 lists the various strategies that can be employed for addictive behaviors and the goal they intend to achieve.

---

[8] DEA Director Hutchison argued: "Maybe it's time Europeans looked to America's drug policy as their model. Our approach—tough drug laws coupled with effective education programs and compassionate treatment—is having success. It's a great myth that there's been no progress in our anti-drug effort. To the contrary, there's been remarkable success. Overall drug use in the United States is down by more than a third since the late 1970s. That's 9.5 million fewer people using illegal drugs. We have reduced cocaine use by an astounding 70% in the past 15 years."
[9] The authors did find that marijuana prices rose from 1981 to 1992, but then decreased back to their 1981-level.
[10] MacCoun was on the committee.

The harm associated with a behavior can surely be reduced by eliminating the behavior but, in the drug policy debate, it is argued that the use reduction paradigm has done little to alleviate harms and, in fact, use reduction policies actually create harms (Nadelmann, 1989). Harm reduction really is not a policy or program; it is a *goal* for policies and programs (Inciardi & Harrison, 2000). This distinction is often ignored and sometimes manipulated. For example, the concept of harm reduction and the legalization of drugs are sometimes erroneously viewed as synonymous. This is incorrect for at least three reasons:

1. The legalization of drugs is a policy; harm reduction is a goal;
2. Some policies with the goal of harm reduction are inconsistent with legalization (see Caulkins, 2002); and
3. The European nations that have pioneered policies that reduce harm are prohibitionist drug law regimes (MacCoun & Reuter, 2001).

A distinction can also be made between different kinds of harm reduction: micro and macro. Micro-harm reduction focuses on strategies that reduce average harm per each unit of drug used (e.g., policies that encourage intravenous drug users to bleach their needles). Macro-harm is the product of the number of users, the average units consumed per user, and the average harm per unit. In other words, Macro harm = Prevalence × Intensity × Micro harm (see MacCoun, 1998b; MacCoun & Caulkins, 1996; MacCoun & Reuter, 2001; Reuter & MacCoun, 1995).

Quantity reduction aims to reduce the total quantity consumed and could unite the use reduction and harm reduction camps. It has received relatively little attention compared to the other strategies in illicit drug policy. This is the rationale behind controlled drinking, the highly controversial notion that those dependent on alcohol do not necessarily need to achieve abstinence (see MacCoun 1998b). MacCoun notes that quantity reduction does not necessarily have to focus on those who drink the most. Getting moderate users to drink less would have a more desirable impact on alcohol-related harms than focusing on the heaviest users (see Edwards et al., 1994).

Targeting Issues: Hardest Core versus Casual Participant   Most individuals with addictive disorders do not become immediately dependent. But we know that of the users who become dependent on cocaine within 10 years after first use, about 33% become dependent in the first year (Wagner & Anthony, 2002). The comparable figure for marijuana and alcohol is closer to 10%. This leads to the obvious argument that prevention and early desistance strategies could reduce future dependence. However, casual participants are not innocuous; they create harms, too (e.g., driving under the influence, less condom use when intoxicated).

But it is the hardest core that creates a disproportionate amount of the harm associated with participating in potentially addictive behaviors. The classic example here is cocaine use in the 1980s and early 1990s. As the prevalence of cocaine use drastically decreased during this period, the harms associated with cocaine use actually increased. Those who continued to use, used a lot, and ended up in emergency rooms and in prisons at unprecedented rates. This example is not unique: It is those with chronic anorexia that are most likely to die from starvation and other complications; it is those who unsafely inject heroin more often that are more likely to contract HIV; and it is regular smokers who are more likely to die of lung cancer and heart disease.

Costs versus Benefits of Different Legal Regimes   None of the strategic issues mentioned so far has depended on the legal regime. There is a range of possible legal regimes for addictive behaviors, each with its own set of costs and benefits. Figure 15.2 modifies the spectrum originally developed by MacCoun et al. (1996) for illicit drug control that can be applied to other addictive behaviors. This spectrum classifies 10 policy options into four distinct regimes: prohibition, prescription, regulation, and promotion—each with unique costs and benefits.

Prohibition: Prohibition in general raises the monetary and nonmonetary costs of consumption (search time, expected cost of arrest) and its contribution to

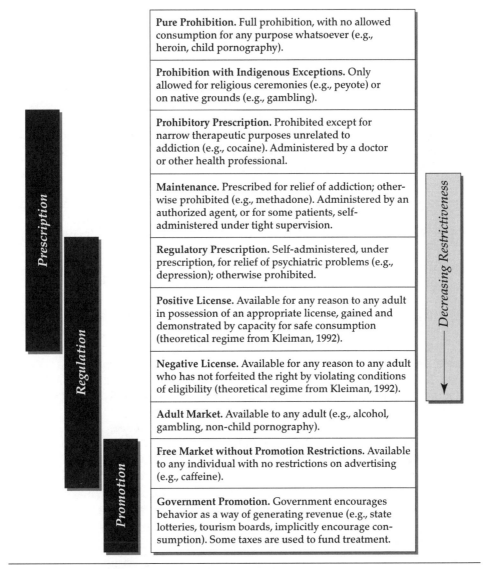

Figure 15.2   The Spectrum of Legal Regimes for Potentially Addictive Goods and Behaviors. *Source:* "Assessing Alternative Drug Control Regimes," R. J. MacCoun, P. Reuter, and T. Schelling, 1996, *Journal of Policy Analysis and Management, 15,* pp. 1–23.

corruption cannot be ignored. It does, however, send a strong signal that use is discouraged and it gives authorities tremendous power to eliminate the activity.

Prescription: Specific to illicit drugs, prescription allows the benefits of use to be realized by a select few. Benefits are also realized because the substance is without impurities normally found in street drugs. Aside from this, the costs and benefits are generally the same as prohibition.

Regulation: The largest costs of regulatory regimes are increased consumption and increased addiction. Savings would arise from eliminating enforcement and removing bans on policies with harm reduction goals (e.g., needle exchange, safe injection rooms, purity testing). Benefits to reducing the black market (including corruption) would also accrue.

Promotion: The benefits of this regime are increased revenue to the government and a decreased black market. We see this explicitly with state lotteries and implicitly with tourism boards that encourage visitors to gamble in their state or city.

Conspicuously missing is a discussion of the nonmedical benefits. Benefits are not taken seriously by policy makers and this is likely the reason why the government contracts out for cost analyses of the effects of illicit drugs and alcohol, but not cost-benefit analyses. However, simply equating the amount spent on drugs as the benefit it provides is complicated by the fact some of those addicted to these substances may prefer to stop using, but can't (Kleiman, 1992).

Harms to Users versus Harms to Others   A useful comparison of these legal regimes depends on a comprehensive list of the harms associated with the behaviors and the policies intended to affect these harms. MacCoun et al. (1996) developed a taxonomy of drug-related harms and, in this section, we adapt it to create a general model for other addictive behaviors. In addition to listing the harms, we also identify who bears the harm: consumers, intimates, employers, or society.

Table 15.5 includes four general cost categories (Health, social and economic functioning, safety and public order, and criminal justice) and more than 25 harms to be considered. Ideally, each harm would be assigned a monetary value so comparisons could be made between different regimes as well as between the costs of harms to users and harms to society. But MacCoun et al. (1996) argue that because monetarization is unlikely to be feasible or convincing for many of these harms, the list should instead serve a heuristic function of encouraging analysts and debaters to think broadly rather than narrowly about types of harm.

Ignoring the externalities associated with addictive behaviors, the question remains whether the behavior should be permitted if it does not cause harm to anyone (even the user). Libertarians would answer with a forceful "Yes," while those morally opposed to gambling, nonmarital sex, and intoxication would reply "No." It is not only important to keep these deontological arguments in mind when projecting the political ramifications of public policy, it is also crucial to recognize that these moral arguments are often mixed with consequentialist dialogue (MacCoun & Reuter, 2001, chap. 4).

Costs versus Benefits of Delivery Mechanisms   There are also trade-offs associated with the delivery mechanisms for these addictive goods or behaviors. It may be

Table 15.5
Abbreviated Taxonomy of Harms Related to Addictive Behaviors

Harms	Who Bears the Harm?[a]	Potentially Applicable to Which Addictions?[b]
Health		
Public health care costs.	E, S	All
Private health care costs.	C, I	All
Suffering due to physical illness.	C, I	A, T, D
Suffering due to mental illness.	C, I	A, D, G(?)
HIV/Disease transmission.	C, I, S	A, D, S
Social and Economic Functioning		
Reduced performance, school.	C, I, E, S	A, D
Reduced performance, workplace.	C, I, E, S	A, D, T(?), G(?)
Poor parenting, child abuse.	I, S	A, D, S(?)
Harms to self-esteem associated with consumption.	C	A, D
Harm to reputation associated with consumption.	C	D
Harm to employability associated with consumption.	C, I, E, S	A, D
Accruing criminal experience.	C	D, A (if underage)
Acquaintance with criminal networks.	C, I	D
Prevention/restriction on benefits of consumption.	S	D
Foregone taxes by not regulating.	S	D, G (some forms)
Safety and Public Order		
Accident victimization (work, road, etc.).	C, I, E, S	A, D
Property/acquisitive crime victimization.	C, I, E, S	A, D
Violence associated with use.	C, I, S	A, D
Reduced property values near market.	E	D, S (prostitution?)
Observably widespread violation of law.	S	D, A (if underage)
Criminal Justice		
Increased enforcement costs.	S	D
Increased incarceration costs.	S	D
Corruption of legal authorities.	S	D
Devaluation of arrests as a moral sanction.	S	D, S (prostitution?)
Fines.	C, I	A, D, S (prostitution)
Stigma of criminal record, prison record.	C, I	D, A (if underage)

Source: Based on "Assessing Alternative Drug Control Regimes," R. J. MacCoun, P. Reuter, and T. Schelling, 1996, *Journal of Policy Analysis and Management, 15*, pp. 1–23.
[a] C = Consumers, E = Employers, I = Intimates, S = Society.
[b] A = Alcohol, G = Gambling, I = Illegal Drugs, S = Sex, T = Tobacco.

the way that these goods are obtained and used that cause harm to users and society. Questions can range from "Should we ban tobacco machines so it is more difficult for youths to gain access?" to "Should we drive the crack market indoors since open-air markets are prone to violence?"

The Internet has drastically changed the face of addictive transactions. *Business-Week* (Sager et al., 2002) reported that black-market activity conducted online will reach an estimated $36.5 billion in 2002—about the same as the $39.3 billion U.S. consumers will spend on the legitimate Internet. Addictions to gambling, sex, and

---

BOX 15.1
Research Topics for Public Policy on Addictive Disorders
(In Order of Appearance)

Relationships between specific drugs and specific crimes.

Differences in the rates and consequences of addictions to crack cocaine and powder cocaine.

Approaches to treating pathological gambling for older cohorts.

Epidemiology of Internet gamblers.

Longitudinal epidemiological studies of adolescents that focus on eating disorders.

Characteristics of nonstreet-working prostitutes and their clients.

Harms imposed and suffered by those who use prostitutes.

Analysis of local prices for methamphetamines and designer drugs.

Economic relationships between alcohol and marijuana consumption for different populations.

Economic relationships for different types of gambling.

Are different classes of addictive disorders substitutes or complements?

Theories of addictive situations that would integrate the delivery mechanism literatures.

Ability of law enforcement to reduce addictive behaviors.

Systematically identifying the harms associated with the addictive disorders and who is affected.

What share of public assistance dollars are spent on alcohol, tobacco, illicit drugs, and gambling?

Effect of reductions in public assistance on drug use, drug overdoses, and crime.

Do online sexual pursuits increase or decrease the frequency or harmfulness offline sexual pursuits?

What is the magnitude of the online market for illegal drugs?

Costs and benefits of widespread implementation of contingency management techniques.

Does harm reduction send the wrong message?

Long-term effects for being convicted of a drug charge.

Implications of the United Kingdom's heroin prescription program for the United States.

How has Internet gambling affected government tax revenue?

Could online gambling truly be eliminated or made to be prohibitively expensive?

---

drugs can surely be exacerbated by "one-click" accessibility, but can the Internet create these addictions?

The privacy associated with web-based sexual pursuits (pictures, chat rooms, video cams) surely makes these activities more attractive to some individuals, but there is little evidence as to whether these virtual pursuits turn into real-world problems, especially any more than nonvirtual pursuits. Does online sexual compulsivity translate into or facilitate potentially damaging behavior offline? Are individuals who engage in online pedophilic pursuits more or less likely to ultimately engage in these behaviors offline (Cooper et al., 2000)? Longitudinal and cross-sectional analyses of crime statistics have failed to find any association between the availability of pornographic magazines and films and national rates of rape or sexual assault (Diamond & Uchiyama, 1999; Kutchinsky, 1991; Linz, Penrod, & Donnerstein, 1987). But various well-publicized cases suggest that the interactive nature of Internet chat rooms creates new opportunities for victimization; whether the technology actually increases the probability of such events is an open question. The hyperconnected nature of web links also raises new concerns about possible "gateway" effects, whereby access to soft-core web porn increases the likelihood of escalation to more extreme and/or illicit forms of pornography, like sadomasochism or child pornography.

A point should also be made about purchasing drugs on the Internet. Stories about purchasing prescription pills from foreign online pharmacies abound, but are illegal drugs like marijuana, ecstasy, and cocaine available online? Mail-order marijuana is hardly a new phenomenon, but the advent of the Internet drastically decreases the cost of entering the market and makes it easier to find a supplier. We are unaware of any formal study that has examined this issue, but a few clicks on the Internet leads us to places where marijuana seeds can be purchased as well as to a site that essentially serves as a *Consumer's Report* for purchasing marijuana seeds and drug paraphernalia online. While harder drugs are being purchased online,[11] it would take more than a Google search to really learn about this market and if it is having any effect on other forms of distribution.

Tactical Issues

This section covers the specific techniques of intervention used to address addictive disorders and related harms. Our intent is not to assess the effectiveness of these policies; rather, to provide a brief overview of these legal, financial, regulatory, prevention, treatment, and harm-reducing policies and practices. We focus on American public policy but use insights from other countries when appropriate.

Criminal Law   Some of these addictive behaviors are legal if individuals are above the minimum age, not prohibited from consumption as a condition of probation or parole, and not consuming in a prohibited area. Other behaviors are strictly prohibited for everyone. This section examines the implications of breaking the laws associated with these disorders, focusing on the less severe punishments first.

---

[11] The DEA recently completed Operation Webslinger that led to the arrest of 115 individuals in 84 cities who were e-trafficking drugs like GHB and GBL. Available from http://usinfo.state.gov/topical/global/ecom/02092001.htm.

Smoking is illegal for minors,[12] alcohol cannot be consumed until age 21, and age restrictions on gambling and strip clubs range from 18 to 21 years old. These restrictions are determined at the state (and sometimes local) level, but federal pressure can play an important role.[13] Penalties for underage consumption usually result in warnings or citations (even for tobacco; Tworek et al., 2002) and suppliers of these goods can be fined or lose their distribution licenses if they do business with a minor.

Prostitution is illegal everywhere except for rural counties of Nevada. As for the rest of the country, some cities are clearly more aggressive than others when it comes to enforcing prostitution laws. Some cities publish names and pictures of arrestees on the Internet, even if they have not been convicted (e.g., St. Paul, Minnesota) and others attempt to deter johns by seizing their vehicles in sting operations. Oakland, California, has made thousands of dollars selling seized vehicles from prostitution stings, but in most of these cases the suspects are convicted only of a misdemeanor (Lee, 2002).

While citations are also issued for marijuana possession in certain states, possession can either be a misdemeanor or felony depending on the state and type of drug. Drug selling is usually a felony, but prosecutors can push for a lower charge. Cases can be charged by either the federal or state governments, and interstate differences are significant. For example, the maximum statutory first offense sentence for possessing one gram of cocaine ranges from 6 months in Washington, DC, and West Virginia to 15 years in Georgia and South Carolina (McBride, Pacula, & Chriqui, 2002). While the federal government spends much of its resources targeting major traffickers, they do prosecute low-level dealers and even convict some on drug possession charges (BJS, 2002). As with prostitution, those suspected of drug activity can have their assets seized (and not just their cars). State and local governments have a strong incentive to bring these drug cases to federal jurisdiction since "federal laws allow generous payments (up to one-half) to state and local agencies involved in a federal seizure" (MacCoun & Reuter, 2001, p. 119).

Convicted drug offenders contributed to a massive increase in prisoners and probationers throughout the 1980s and 1990s and they now account for almost one-third of the 1,600 prisoners that are released each day (Travis, Solomon, & Waul, 2001). With most probationers and parolees subject to drug tests and random searches, many are being sent to prison for violating the condition of release that they abstain from illegal drugs or alcohol.

But the legal sanctions for drug offenders do not stop with prison or community corrections. Those convicted of any felony are often no longer allowed to vote, run for office, and may be deported if they are an immigrant (U.S. Department of Justice, 2000). In many states, felony drug offenders are ineligible for welfare and California has also excluded drug felons from food stamps and general assistance programs (Adams, Onek, & Riker, 1998). This not only makes survival difficult but it eliminates a funding stream that can be used to pay for drug treatment. Additionally, Iguchi et al. (2002) describe a host of services and privileges

---

[12] In most states, a minor is anyone under 18; in Alabama, Alaska, and Utah the threshold is 19 years old (American Lung Association, 2002).

[13] The federal government withheld highway funds from states that did not have 21-year-old drinking limits and the last state complied in 1988 (King, 1987; Toomey, Rosenfeld, & Wagenaar, 1996).

that may be denied to drug felons; including housing benefits, student aid, employment, and in some cases child custody.

Taxation and Other Regulatory Controls   Sin taxes on alcohol and tobacco generate tremendous revenues for federal and state governments as well as decrease consumption by raising the price. In 2000, state and federal government tax revenue was over $12 billion from alcohol and over $15 billion from tobacco (Tax Policy Center, 2002).[14] Most states have a licensing system for selling alcohol and some states sell the alcohol in state-run stores (Wagenaar, 2000). The process of obtaining a liquor license is neither easy nor automatic. We are unaware of restrictions on who can sell tobacco products, but states know who is selling tobacco because they must register and transmit tax revenue.

The Bureau of Alcohol, Tobacco, and Firearms is responsible for testing new alcohol products coming onto the market, and there are several federal and state agencies that regulate alcohol advertising (Nelson, 2001). Several agencies are involved in the regulation of tobacco advertising and data reporting, but an Institute of Medicine panel reports "No agency is responsible for ensuring that any standards are met in the manufacturing and composition of tobacco products" (Stratton, Shetty, Wallace, & Bondurant, 2001, p. 30). In contrast, the panel notes, there is a strict regulation of nicotine replacement products, and this disparity puts these treatments "at a serious marketing disadvantage" (p. 30). Further complicating the tobacco story is the fact that the federal government gives subsidies to tobacco farmers—in the ballpark of $300 million a year (Womach, 2001).

Government revenue from gambling is difficult to calculate because it includes the sale of lottery tickets and other government products, taxes on betting places and casinos, and income taxes on the winnings. Approximately $37 billion was spent on state lotteries in 1999 and, on average, the state collects $0.33 for every dollar spent (Kearny, 2002). States franchise casino operators with taxes ranging from 6% to 20% of gross revenues (MacCoun & Reuter, 2001, p. 138), but this does not apply to the Indian casinos that are, for the most part, exempt from taxation (National Gambling Impact Study Commission [NGISC], 1999).

Governments are getting creative about regulating illegal online gambling by focusing on the credit card companies. State attorneys general are pressuring the banks (Sager et al., 2002), and the results seem to be dramatic ("Credit cards seek," 2002):

> Numerous banks, including some of the nation's largest, now entirely prohibit the use of their cards for online gambling. The banks say that they are not sure that Internet gambling is legal, and that they do not know if they will be repaid for extending credit when some courts have ruled gambling debts are unenforceable.

The *Times* also reports that the credit card companies are beginning to take "anti-fraud" actions that directly affect online pornographers and cybersex outlets.

---

[14] State revenue from alcohol and tobacco in 2000 was $4,104,405,000 and $8,380,080,000 respectively. Federal excise taxes reported to or collected by the Internal Revenue Service for 2000 were $8,119,714,000 for alcohol and $7,019,968,000 for domestic tobacco sales (Tax Policy Center, 2002).

Public Assistance   The government has some control over income (especially for the poor) and this may affect the frequency and intensity of addictive disorders. We are unaware of estimates for the amount of public assistance spent on alcohol, tobacco, gambling, and illegal drugs, but back-of-the-envelope calculations based on arrestee surveys and Office of National Drug Control data put the figure for illegal drugs somewhere around $5 to $10 billion a year (Boyum & Reuter, 2001).

The Personal Responsibility and Work Opportunity Reconciliation Act of 1996 drastically changed public assistance policy for some drug users and dealers. This federal welfare reform included a provision that banned those convicted of a drug felony from receiving food stamps or welfare for the rest of their lives. Each state had the ability to opt out of this provision and 22 states neither eliminated nor modified the ban as of fall 2000 (Hirsch, 2001). We are unaware of any estimates of how many welfare recipients have been banned for life because of these provisions.

Prevention and Education: Health prevention and education campaigns primarily occur in schools as well as in primary care and public settings. We acknowledge that the deterrence generated by law enforcement is itself a form of prevention (Moore, 1991), and these strategies were addressed earlier.

Most drug prevention programs occur in schools, and a five-year study by the Research Triangle Institutes suggests they are far from uniform (Silvia & Thorne, 1997). Another analysis estimated that every student in the United States could have state-of-the-art substance abuse prevention for a meager $550 million annually, "but it would not dramatically affect the course of drug use and the benefits would take years to accrue" (Caulkins, Rydell, Everingham, Chiesa, & Bushway, 1999, p. xxxi). One obvious problem with school-based programs is that they do not include those who have dropped out of school. Additionally, the mean age of initiation for using cocaine and heroin is about 20 (SAMHSA, 1994, 1995, 1996, 1997, 1998, 1999, 2000, 2001, 2002), a few years beyond the age of graduation. Mass media campaigns to reduce substance use are funded by a host of organizations (e.g., private companies, Mothers Against Drunk Driving) and Congress has allocated almost $200 million annually for the Youth Anti-Drug Media Campaign since 1998 (Office of National Drug Control Policy [ONDCP], 2003).

Aside from funding treatment research and treatment programs, one of the few policy options available to combat eating orders is to focus on prevention. Most campaigns to prevent eating disorders occur in schools, but classroom instruction is not the only option (Levine & Piran, 2001). There are also targeted approaches for at-risk youth that tend to be psychoeducational, with newer initiatives using computer technologies like CD-ROMs, Internet-based homework, [and] guided chat rooms (Pearson et al., 2002, p. 238).

Finally, it appears that most prevention of gambling disorders occurs in clinical settings, with a recent assessment suggesting "enhanced prevention efforts in physical and mental health care settings appear warranted" (Potenza, 2002, p. 204). Potenza argues that primary care facilities are under-used sites for routine screening and also that substance abuse and mental health care settings may be target-rich environments given the high rates of comorbidity.

Treatment   This volume is full of excellent chapters about treating addiction and we defer to them for the state of the knowledge. Instead, we highlight some of the policy levers used to get individuals to enter and complete treatment.

An obvious lever is one of coercion via the criminal justice system. In addition to abstinence, courts have often made attending 12-Step programs a condition of probation. This is true for offenders with drug and alcohol problems as well as for offenders with gambling problems. In addition, some prisons force inmates to attend these programs.[15]

The criminal justice system also creates incentives for completing treatment with drug courts and special diversion programs for drunk drivers. As of November 2002, there were 946 drug courts for adults or juveniles nationwide and an additional 441 in the planning process (National Drug Court Institute, 2002). These programs offer treatment as an alternative to incarceration for offenders with judges often waiving the offenses upon successful completion. These collaborative courts often bring defenders, prosecutors, probation officers, judges, treatment providers, and defendants together to regularly monitor a defendant's progress. Defendants who relapse can face intermediate sanctions (ranging from writing an essay to going back to jail for a few weeks) and usually given multiple chances before being officially terminated from a program.

Voters in California and Arizona have taken the drug court concept a step further by passing initiatives allowing arrestees for simple drug possession to attend treatment in lieu of a normal criminal sentence. The proposition in California not only changed the drug possession laws, it also authorized the state to allocate hundreds of millions of dollars to pay for treatment programs. These initiatives raise a host of policy questions, such as whether treatment slots are being filled by those who do not need treatment or whether use increased because the expected sanction associated with use decreased. Evaluations of these programs are underway and we look forward to the results.

Another way to get individuals to remain in treatment and comply with the requirements is to simply bribe them. There is a growing literature on contingency management, which uses positive incentives (like movie passes, food vouchers—never cash) to reward negative drug tests in treatment settings. The available evidence suggests this is a useful technique for reducing cocaine and heroin use (see Farabee, Rawson, & McCann, 2002; Higgins et al., 1995; Rawson et al., 2002). This approach has also been successful at encouraging positive, non-drug-related behaviors among treatment participants such as attempting to find a job (Iguchi, Belding, Morral, Lamb, & Husband, 1997).

Should contingency management become part of the mainstream treatment practice and actively funded by the government? Such programs would clearly meet resistance since it is politically unpopular to reward lawbreakers for obeying the law (Kleiman, 2001), and people would worry about the message it would send to users and nonusers. But given its demonstrated effectiveness for certain populations and potential impact on problem drug use and other behaviors, contingency management clearly deserves additional empirical attention.

Policies Intended to Reduce Harm First   Harm reduction also manifests itself as a vector of interventions that focus on reducing harm first, with any goals of eliminating use being purely secondary. Harm reduction is not unique to discussions

---

[15] Given the religious tone of most 12-Step groups, there is debate about whether legal coercion violates the Establishment Clause (Congress shall make no law respecting an establishment of religion) as well as other parts of the Constitution (Apanovitch, 1998).

about illegal drugs or even addictions. For example, mandatory seat belt laws, provision of benefits to illegal immigrants, and school condom programs are all policies intended to mitigate the harms of risky behaviors (dangerous driving, illegal entry into the United States, and unprotected sex, respectively; MacCoun & Reuter, 2001, p. 389).

We predominantly hear about harm reduction in terms of drug policy, even though it permeates many addictive disorders. Table 15.6 defines and gives examples of four harm-reducing tactics: safe-use technologies, safe-use campaigns, maintenance regimes, and zones of tolerance. While these tactics could be classified as public health initiatives, the urge to juxtapose harm reduction and law enforcement should be resisted. There are a number of roles that criminal justice agencies can play in efforts intended to reduce harm. Caulkins (2002) lists a host of possibilities, a few of which are:

- Colocate treatment centers with police substations to discourage drug dealers from locating near the center and to decrease public resistance to having a treatment center located in their community.
- Redesign performance reviews and promotion criterion in the police department to focus on outcomes that are more closely tied to harm reduction (e.g., create a list of the most harmful drug dealers and reward those who arrest them).
- Focus on pushing all drug market activity inside.

A large criticism of harm reduction is that it may encourage use or participation in these activities by making them safer. Whether harm reduction sends the wrong message is an empirical question that depends on the addiction and tactic. But even if it is demonstrated that a tactic increases use, this does not mean that it should be rejected on face value.

Table 15.6
Tactics That Focus on Reducing Harm First

Tactics	Definition	Examples
Safe-use technologies	Goods intended to make use less harmful.	Syringe exchange, tobacco filters, Internet screening, condoms, and other forms of birth control, 3.2 beer.
Safe-use campaigns	Messages to convince users to use/participate in a less dangerous manner.	Designated drivers/anti-drunk driving, overdose prevention, heroin smoking, controlled drinking, safe sex.
Maintenance regimes	Shifts harmful addictions to safer addictions.	Tobacco patches, methadone, medical grade heroin.
Zones of tolerance	Places that reduce the harms of criminal sanctions and promote safe-use technologies.	Platzpitz, safe-injection rooms.

DIRECTIONS FOR POLICY RESEARCH

Approaching these addictive disorders from a harm-reduction framework greatly increases the questions that must be answered to create and evaluate different policy levers. Our discussions about the dynamics of these disorders, as well as our focus on strategies and tactics, will hopefully serve as launching points for future analyses. While many questions and issues have been raised for future research for public policy on addiction (see Table 15.6), three seem especially important and timely and warrant further discussion.

WHAT ARE THE LONG-TERM EFFECTS FOR BEING CONVICTED OF A DRUG CHARGE?

There is growing interest in policies that penalize felons with more than probation or prison and parole (Iguchi et al., 2002). One reason for the increased attention is that massive numbers of offenders imprisoned for drug offenses are now returning home and looking for work and services (Travis et al., 2001). What is life like for these drug felons and their families 5, 10, or 20 years postconviction? Do they have a more difficult time transitioning from prison because of the felonies associated with their drug conviction?

Special attention should be paid to those banned from welfare for life and those who are ineligible for federal student aid because of drug felonies. For the drug-dependent individuals banned from welfare, we wonder if they confront barriers to entering drug treatment since some long-term programs use clients' welfare dollars to pay for treatment. Some of this information can be teased from existing studies, but a significant investment in qualitative research is required to understand the interactions of the drug conviction, drug use, and social policy.

WHAT ARE THE IMPLICATIONS OF THE UNITED KINGDOM'S "NEW" HEROIN PRESCRIPTION PROGRAM FOR THE UNITED STATES?

Jurisdictions in at least seven developed countries are prescribing heroin to addicts, are conducting clinical trials, or are seriously considering trials.[16] The justification for these programs is that giving the drug to heroin abusers in a clean and safe environment will decrease many of the harms associated with use (e.g., crime, disease). Heroin maintenance targets those long-time users who have not been able to manage their addictions with other forms of treatment. The available research on the Swiss trials seem to be very positive in terms of reduced crime and improved social functioning and mental health, but methodological shortfalls and small samples in some cities severely limit the internal validity of such findings (see Reuter & MacCoun, 2002).

Special attention should be paid to the United Kingdom. General practitioners in the United Kingdom used to routinely prescribe heroin to those dependent on the drug. Reforms in the late 1960s heavily restricted this practice, but 300 to 480 patients currently receive heroin treatment for opiates (Home Office, 2002). The

---

[16] The United Kingdom has a small prescription program; Germany, the Netherlands, and Switzerland are conducting experiments; Canada, Denmark, and Spain are seriously considering experiments (Canadian Broadcasting Corporation, 2002; MacCoun & Reuter, 2002; Wodak, 2001).

Home Office's 2002 Drug Strategy boldly argues for prescribing heroin for all of those "who have a clinical need for it" (p. 56). Considering that there are between 150,000 and 250,000 heroin users in the United Kingdom and 35,000 receiving substitution treatment (EMCDDA, 2002, Online Table 11), it will be fascinating to see how a country fairly similar to the United States implements such a program—especially in terms of who will be eligible and how long they will receive free heroin. Further, understanding how the program is shaped by politics and public opinion will be as interesting as learning about the effectiveness of a large-scale prescription program.

SHOULD ONLINE GAMBLING BE ELIMINATED, TAXED, IGNORED, OR PROMOTED?

About 75% of adults disapprove of online gambling (Gallup, 1999)—about the same percentage of adults who are opposed to marijuana legalization (MacCoun & Reuter, 2001, chap. 3). Despite the strong disapproval rates, the laws surrounding this issue are not very clear and rarely enforced. Also complicating this issue is the debate about whether banning Internet gambling infringes on free speech (NGISC, 1999).

Federal attempts to explicitly prohibit the activity have failed, but some argue that existing laws and judicial interpretations may restrict the use of the Internet for these purposes (see Rodefer, 2002). There is great variation in state-level regulations that seem to be changing routinely (NGISC, 1999; Rose, 2002). Virtually no one is arrested for Internet gambling and the fact that online casinos are often located in other countries and outside of American jurisdiction makes enforcement difficult. The better question may be to ask whether online gambling could ever be taxed or eliminated.

Despite the billions of dollars spent on Internet gambling, we still know very little about how this phenomenon affects participation in other forms of gambling. Are states losing significant amounts of money because bettors prefer to game at foreign cybercasinos rather than purchase lottery tickets at the local convenience store? We also have to wonder whether states will eventually use the Internet to sell their own gambling products.

CONCLUSION

Addictive disorders can create tremendous harms for those who are addicted as well as for society. We hope our interpretation of the dynamics, strategies, and tactics associated with these disorders are useful for practitioners, policy makers, and researchers. Integrating this information with the spectrum of policy regimes and taxonomy of related harms should make it easier to think about different ways to create and evaluate public policy on addictive disorders.

Understanding the macro- and micro-harms associated with these addictions lead us to consider some controversial and counterintuitive policies. While treatments for these addictive disorders should be scientifically evaluated and made available if relatively cost-effective, we cannot restrict ourselves to the use-reduction paradigm. Doing so limits the critical debate about what are the most appropriate public policies on addictive disorders.

RECOMMENDED READING

MacCoun, R., & Reuter, P. (2001). *Drug war heresies: Learning from other places, times, and vices.* New York: Cambridge University Press. This book provides a comprehensive and nonpartisan analysis of illicit drug policy. The discussions of other places, times, and vices include detailed information about other addictive disorders.

Manski, C., Pepper, J., & Petrie, C. (2001). *Informing America's policy on illegal drugs: What we don't know keeps hurting us.* Washington, DC: National Academy of Sciences. This book highlights what we do and do not know about drug policy and drug use. Its focus on what information deserves priority is useful for researchers and practitioners looking to develop new agendas and/or fund pilot programs.

National Gambling Impact Study Commission. (1999). *National gambling impact study commission final report.* Available from http://govinfo.library.unt.edu/ngisc/reports /fullrpt.html. Based on hearings, expert studies, and surveys, this report includes a wealth of information about gambling, gambling addictions, and the public policies intended to affect these behaviors. The Commission's recommendations should be read and considered by those with an interest in gambling policy and dependence.

Stratton, K., Shetty, P., Wallace, R., & Bondurant, S. (2001). *Clearing the smoke: Assessing the science base for tobacco harm reduction.* Washington, DC: National Academy Press. Provides an extensive discussion of harm reduction in a non-illicit drug setting.

REFERENCES

Adams, R., Onek, D., & Riker, D. (1998). *Double jeopardy: An assessment of the felony drug provision of the welfare reform act.* Washington, DC: Justice Policy Institute.

Ainslie, G. (2001). *Breakdown of will.* Cambridge, MA: Cambridge University Press.

American Lung Association. (2002). *State legislated actions on tobacco.* Available from http://slati.lungusa.org/StateLegislateAction.asp.

Anthony, J., Warner, L., & Kessler, R. (1994). Comparative epidemiology of dependence on tobacco, alcohol, controlled substances, and inhalants: Basic findings from the National Comorbidity Study. *Experimental and Clinical Psychopharmacology, 2,* 244–268.

Apanovitch, D. (1998). Religion and rehabilitation: The requisition of God by the state. *Duke Law Journal, 47,* 785–852.

Baumeister, R. F., Heatherton, T. F., & Tice, D. M. (1994). *Losing control: How and why people fail at self-regulation.* San Diego, CA: Academic Press.

Becker, G., Grossman, M., & Murphy, K. (1992). Rational addiction and the effect of price on consumption. In G. Loewenstein & J. Elster (Eds.), *Choice over time* (pp. 361–370). New York: Russell Sage Foundation.

Boyum, D., & Reuter, P. (2001). Reflections on drug policy and social policy. In P. Heymann & W. Brownsberger (Eds.), *Drug addiction and drug policy: The struggle to control dependence* (pp. 239–264). Cambridge, MA: Harvard University Press.

Braun, D., Sunday, S., Huang, A., & Halmi, K. (1999). More males seek treatment for eating disorders. *International Journal of Eating Disorders, 25,* 415–424.

Breslau, N., Johnson, E., Hiripi, E., & Kessler, R. (2001). Nicotine dependence in the United States. *Archives of General Psychiatry, 58,* 810–816.

Bulik, C., Sullivan, P., & Kendler, K. (2000). An empirical study of the classification of eating disorders. *American Journal of Psychiatry, 157,* 886–895.

Bureau of Justice Statistics. (1999). *Substance use and treatment, state and federal prisoners, 1997.* Available from http://www.ojp.usdoj.gov/bjs/pub/pdf/satsfp97.pdf.

Bureau of Justice Statistics. (2000). *Drug use, testing, and treatment in jails.* Available from http://www.ojp.usdoj.gov/bjs/pub/pdf/duttj.pdf.

Bureau of Justice Statistics. (2002). *Compendium of federal justice statistics, 2000.* Available from http://www.ojp.usdoj.gov/bjs/pub/pdf/cfjs0005.pdf.

Cameron, L., & Williams, J. (2001). Cannabis, alcohol, and cigarettes: Substitutes or complements? *Economic Record, 77,* 19–34.

Canadian Broadcasting Corporation. (2002). *Prescription heroin pilot project proposed.* Available from http://vancouver.cbc.ca/template/servlet/View?filename=bc_heroin021106.

Carnes, P. J. (1991). *Don't call it love: Recovery from sexual addiction.* New York: Bantam Books.

Caulkins, J. (1995). Estimating elasticities of demand for cocaine and heroin with data from the Drug Use Forecasting System. *H. John Heinz III School of Public Policy and Management Working Paper 1995-13.* Pittsburgh, PA: Carnegie Mellon University.

Caulkins, J. (2001). Drug prices and emergency department mentions for cocaine and heroin. *American Journal of Public Health, 91,* 1446–1448.

Caulkins, J. (2002). *Law enforcement's role in a harm reduction regime.* Sydney, Australia: NSW Bureau of Crime Statistics and Research.

Caulkins, J., Rydell, C. P., Everingham, S., Chiesa, J., & Bushway, S. (1999). *An ounce of prevention, a pound of uncertainty: The cost-effectiveness of school-based drug prevention programs.* Santa Monica, CA: RAND.

Chaloupka, F., & Pacula, R. (2000). Economics and antihealth behavior: The economic analysis of substance use and misuse. In W. Bickel & R. Vuchinich (Eds.), *Reframing health behavior change with behavioral economics* (pp. 89–111). Mahwah, NJ: Erlbaum.

Chaloupka, F., Pacula, R., Farrelly, M., Johnston, L., & O'Malley, P. (1999). *Do higher cigarette prices encourage youth to use marijuana?* (Working Paper No. 6938). Cambridge, MA: National Bureau of Economic Research.

Clotfelter, C., & Cook, P. (1990). On the economics of state lotteries. *Journal of Economic Perspectives, 4,* 105–119.

Coleman, E. (1992). Is your patient suffering from compulsive sexual behavior? *Psychiatric Annals, 22,* 320–325.

Cook, P., & Clotfelter, C. (1993). The peculiar scale economies of lotto. *American Economic Review, 83,* 634–643.

Cook, P., & Moore, M. J. (1999). *Alcohol* (Working Paper No. 6905). Cambridge, MA: National Bureau of Economic Research.

Cooper, A. C., Delmonico, D. L., & Burg, R. (2000). Cybersex users, abusers, and compulsives: New findings and implications. In A. Cooper (Ed.), *Cybersex: The dark side of the force* (pp. 5–30). Philadelphia: Brunner-Routledge.

Credit cards seek new fees on web's demimonde. (2002, November 18). *New York Times,* p. C1.

Decker, S., & Schwartz, A. (2000). *Cigarettes and alcohol: Substitutes or complements?* (Working Paper No. 7535). Cambridge, MA: National Bureau of Economic Research.

DeSimone, J. (1998). Is marijuana a gateway drug? *Eastern Economics Journal, 24,* 149–164.

Diamond, M., & Uchiyama, A. (1999). Pornography, rape and sex crimes in Japan. *International Journal of Law and Psychiatry, 22,* 1–22.

Donovan, C., & McEwan, R. (1995). A review of the literature examining the relationship between alcohol use and HIV-related sexual risk-taking in young people. *Addiction, 90,* 319–328.

Edwards, G., Anderson, P., Babor, T. F., Casswell, S., Ferrence, R., Giesbrecht, N., et al. (1994). *Alcohol policy and the public good.* Oxford, England: Oxford University Press.

Elster, J., & Skog, O.-J. (Ed.). (1999). *Getting hooked: Rationality and addiction.* Cambridge, MA: Cambridge University Press.

European Monitoring Centre for Drugs and Drug Addiction. (2002). *2002 Annual report on the state of the drugs problem in the European Union and Norway.* Available from http://annualreport.emcdda.eu.int/en/home-en.html.

Eysenck, H. J. (1997). Addiction, personality and motivation. *Human Psychopharmacology Clinical and Experimental, 12,* S79–S87.

Farabee, D., Rawson, R. A., & McCann, M. J. (2002). Adoption of drug avoidance activities among patients in contingency management and cognitive-behavioral treatments. *Journal of Substance Abuse Treatment, 23,* 343–350.

Farrell, L., & Walker, I. (1999). The welfare effects of lotto: Evidence from the U.K. *Journal of Public Economics, 72,* 99–120.

Farrelly, M., Bray, J., Zarkin, G., Wendling, B., & Pacula, R. (1999). *The effects of prices and policies on the demand for marijuana: Evidence from the National Household Surveys on Drug Abuse* (Working Paper No. 6940). Cambridge, MA: National Bureau of Economic Research.

Federal Bureau of Investigation. (2002). *Crime in the United States.* Washington, DC: U.S. Department of Justice.

Felson, M. (1998). *Crime and everyday life* (2nd ed.). Thousand Oaks, CA: Pine Forge Press.

Fitterling, J. M., Matens, P. B., Scotti, J. R., & Allen, J. S. (1993). AIDS risk behaviors and knowledge among heterosexual alcoholics and noninjecting drug users. *Addiction, 88,* 1257–1265.

Gallup Poll. (1999). *Gambling in America.* Available from http://www.gallup.com/poll /specialreports/socialaudits/Gamblingrelease.asp.

Garfinkel, P., Lin, E., Goering, P., Spegg, C., Goldbloom, D., Kennedy, S., et al. (1995). Bulimia nervosa in a Canadian community sample: Prevalence and comparison of subgroups. *American Journal of Psychiatry, 152,* 1052–1058.

Gerstein, D., Hoffmann, J., Larison, C., Engelman, L., Murphy, S., Palmer, A., et al. (1999). *Gambling impact and behavior study.* Chicago: National Opinion Research Center.

Gold, S., & Heffner, C. (1998). Sexual addiction: Many conceptions, minimal data. *Clinical Psychology Review, 18,* 367–381.

Goodman, A. (1998). *Sexual addiction: An integrated approach.* Madison, CT: International Universities Press.

Gottfredson, M. R., & Hirschi, T. (1990). *A general theory of crime.* Stanford, CA: Stanford University Press.

Grant, B. (1996). Prevalence and correlates of drug use and *DSM-IV* drug dependence in the United States: Results of the National Longitudinal Alcohol Epidemiologic Survey. *Journal of Substance Abuse, 8,* 195–210.

Griffiths, M. (1999). Gambling technologies: Prospects for problem gambling. *Journal of Gambling Studies, 15,* 265–283.

Griffiths, M. (2001). Sex and the Internet: Observations and implications for Internet sex addiction. *Journal of Sex Research, 38,* 444–342.

Grossman, M., Chaloupka, F., & Shim, K. (2002). Illicit drug use and public policy. *Health Affairs, 21,* 134–145.

Harrison, P. M., & Beck, A. (2002). *Prisoners in 2001.* Washington, DC: U.S. Department of Justice, Bureau of Justice Statistics.

Hay, P., & Bacaltchuk, J. (2001). Bulimia nervosa. *British Medical Journal, 323,* 33–37.

Heyman, G. M. (1996). Resolving the contradictions of addiction. *Behavioral and Brain Sciences, 19,* 561–610.

Higgins, S., Budney, A., Bickel, W., Badger, G., Foerg, F., & Ogden, D. (1995). Outpatient behavioral treatment for cocaine dependence: One-year outcome. *Experimental and Clinical Psychopharmacology, 3,* 205–212.

Hirsch, A. (2001). The world was never a safe place for them: Abuse, welfare reform, and women with drug convictions. *Violence Against Women, 7,* 159–176.

Home Office. (2002). *Updated drug strategy 2002.* London: Author.

Hsu, L. (1996). Epidemiology of eating disorders. *Psychiatric Clinics of North America, 19,* 681–700.

Hutchison, A. (2002, October 9). Drug legalization doesn't work. *Washington Post,* p. A31.

Iguchi, M., Belding, M., Morral, A., Lamb, R., & Husband, S. (1997). Reinforcing operants rather than abstinence in drug abuse treatment: An effective alternative for reducing drug use. *Journal of Consulting and Clinical Psychology, 65,* 421–428.

Iguchi, M., London, J., Forge, N., Hickman, L., Fain, T., & Riehman, K. (2002). Elements of well-being affected by criminalizing the drug user. *Public Health Report, 117,* S146–S150.

Inciardi, J., & Harrison, L. (2000). Introduction: The concept of harm reduction. In J. Inciardi & L. Harrison (Eds.), *Harm reduction: National and international perspectives* (pp. 1–26). Thousand Oaks, CA: Sage.

Johnston, L., O'Malley, P., & Bachman, J. (2002). *National survey results on drug use from the Monitoring the Future study.* Rockville, MD: National Institute on Drug Abuse.

Kafka, M. P., & Hennen, J. (1999). The paraphilia-related disorders: An empirical investigation of nonparaphilic hypersexuality disorders in outpatient males. *Journal of Sex and Marital Therapy, 25,* 305–319.

Kallick, M., Suits, D., Dielman, T., & Hybels, J. (1976). *Survey of American gambling attitudes and behaviors.* Washington, DC: U.S. Government Printing Office.

Kandel, D., Chen, K., Warner, L., Kessler, R., & Grant, B. (1997). Prevalence and demographic correlates of last year dependence on alcohol, nicotine, marijuana and cocaine in the U.S. population. *Drug and Alcohol Dependence, 44,* 11–29.

Kearney, M. (2002). *State lotteries and consumer behavior* (Working Paper No. 9330). Cambridge, MA: National Bureau of Economic Research.

Kerr, J. S. (1996). Two myths of addiction: The addictive personality and the issue of free choice. *Human Psychopharmacology Clinical and Experimental, 11,* S9–S13.

King, R. (1987). The politics of denial: The use of funding penalties as an implementation device for social policy. *Policy Science, 20,* 307–337.

Kleiman, M. (1992). *Against excess: Drug policy for results.* New York: Basic Books.

Kleiman, M. (2001). Controlling drug use and crime with testing, sanctions, and treatment. In P. Heymann & W. Brownsberger (Eds.), *Drug addiction and drug policy: The struggle to control dependence* (pp. 168–192). Cambridge, MA: Harvard University Press.

Kuo, L. (2002). *Prostitution policy: Revolutionizing practice through a gendered perspective.* New York: New York University Press.

Kutchinsky, B. (1991). Pornography and rape: Evidence from crime data in four countries where pornography is easily available. *International Journal of Law and Psychiatry, 14,* 47–64.

Ladd, G., & Petry, N. (2002). Disordered gambling among university-based medical and dental patients: A focus on Internet gambling. *Psychology of Addictive Behaviors, 16,* 76–79.

Laumann, E., Gagnon, J., Michael, R., & Michael, S. (1994). *The social organization of sexuality: Sexual practices in the United States.* Chicago: University of Chicago Press.

Lee, H. (2002, September 19). Cops seize some two dozen cars in sting. *San Francisco Chronicle,* A17.

Levine, M. P., & Piran, N. (2001). The prevention of eating disorders: Towards a participatory ecology of knowledge, action, and advocacy. In R. Striegel-Moore & L. Smolak (Eds.), *Eating disorders: New directions for research and practice* (pp. 233–253). Washington, DC: American Psychological Association.

Linz, D., Penrod, S. D., & Donnerstein, E. (1987). The Attorney General's Commission: The gaps between findings and facts. *American Bar Foundation Research Journal, 4,* 713–736.

MacCoun, R. J. (1998a). In what sense (if any) is marijuana a gateway drug? *Drug Policy Analysis Bulletin, 4,* 5–8.

MacCoun, R. J. (1998b). Toward a psychology of harm reduction. *American Psychologist, 53,* 1199–1208.

MacCoun, R. J. (in press). Is the addiction concept useful for drug policy? In R. Vuchinich & N. Heather (Eds.), *Choice, behavioral economics and addiction.* Oxford, England: Elsevier Science.

MacCoun, R. J., & Caulkins, J. (1996). Examining the behavioral assumptions of the National drug control strategy. In W. K. Bickel & R. J. DeGrandpre (Eds.), *Drug policy and human nature: Psychological perspectives on the control, prevention, and treatment of illicit drug abuse* (pp. 177–197). New York: Plenum Press.

MacCoun, R. J., Kilmer, B., & Reuter, P. (2003). Research on drug-crime linkages: The next generation. In *Drugs and crime: A research agenda for the 21st century* (National Institute of Justice Special Report). Washington, DC: U.S. Department of Justice.

MacCoun, R. J., & Reuter, P. (2001). *Drug war heresies: Learning from other places, times, and vices.* New York: Cambridge University Press.

MacCoun, R. J., Reuter, P., & Schelling, T. (1996). Assessing alternative drug control regimes. *Journal of Policy Analysis and Management, 15,* 1–23.

Manning, W., Keeler, E., Newhouse, J., Sloss, E., & Wasserman, J. (1991). *The costs of poor health habits.* Cambridge, MA: Harvard University Press.

Manski, C., Pepper, J., & Petrie, C. (2001). *Informing America's policy on illegal drugs: What we don't know keeps hurting us.* Washington, DC: National Academy of Sciences.

McBride, D., Pacula, R., & Chriqui, J. (2002). *Illicit drug policies: Selected laws from the 50 states.* Available from http://www.andrews.edu/BHSC/impacteen-illicitdrugteam/chartbook.htm.

Model, K. (1993). The effect of marijuana decriminalization on hospital emergency room drug episodes: 1975–1978. *Journal of the American Statistical Association, 88,* 737–747.

Monto, M. (2000). *Clients of street prostitutes in Portland, Oregon, San Francisco and Santa Clara, California, and Las Vegas, Nevada, 1996–1999.* Ann Arbor, MI: Inter-University Consortium for Political and Social Research.

Moore, M. H. (1991). Drugs, the criminal law, and the administration of justice. *Milbank Quarterly, 69,* 529–560.

Morral, A., McCaffrey, D., & Paddock, S. (2002). Reassessing the marijuana gateway effect. *Addiction, 97,* 1493–1504.

Muraven, M. R., & Baumeister, R. F. (2000). Self-regulation and depletion of limited resources: Does self-control resemble a muscle? *Psychological Bulletin, 126,* 247–259.

Mussell, M., Binford, R., & Fulkerson, J. (2000). Eating disorders: Summary of risk factors, prevention programming, and prevention research. *Counseling Psychologist, 28,* 764–796.

Musto, D. F. (1999). *The American disease: Origins of narcotic control* (3rd ed.). New York: Oxford University Press.

Nadelmann, E. (1989). Drug prohibition in the United States: Costs, consequences, and alternatives. *Science, 245,* 939–947.

Nathan, P. E. (1988). The addictive personality is the behavior of the addict. *Journal of Consulting and Clinical Psychology, 56,* 183–188.

National Drug Court Institute. (2002). *Drug court facts.* Available from http://www.ndci.org/courtfacts.htm.

National Gambling Impact Study Commission. (1999). *National Gambling Impact Study Commission Final Report.* Available from http://govinfo.library.unt.edu/ngisc/reports/fullrpt.html.

National Institute of Justice. (2002). *Drug use and related matters among adult arrestees, 2001.* Washington, DC: U.S. Department of Justice.

Nelson, J. (2001). Alcohol advertising and advertising bans: A survey of research methods, results, and policy implications. In M. Baye & J. Nelson (Eds.), *Advertising and differentiated products: Advances in applied microeconomics* (pp. 239–295). New York: JAI Press.

Nicholson, W. (1998). *Microeconomic theory: Basic principles and extensions.* Fort Worth, TX: Dryden Press.

Office of National Drug Control Policy. (2003). *National drug control strategy.* Washington, DC: Author.

Pacula, R. (1998). *Adolescent alcohol and marijuana consumption: Is there really a gateway effect?* (Working Paper No. 6348). Cambridge, MA: National Bureau of Economic Research.

Pacula, R., & Chaloupka, F. (2001). The effect of macro-level interventions on addictive behavior. *Substance Use and Misuse, 36,* 1901–1922.

Pacula, R., Grossman, M., Chaloupka, F., O'Malley, P., Johnston, L., & Farrelly, M. (2000). *Marijuana and youth* (Working Paper No. 7703). Cambridge, MA: National Bureau of Economic Research.

Paton, D., Siegel, D., & Vaughan Williams, L. (2001). *A time series analysis of the demand for gambling in the United Kingdom* (NUBS Discussion Paper). Nottingham University Business School, United Kingdom.

Pearson, J., Goldklang, D., & Striegel-Moore, R. (2002). Prevention of eating disorders: Challenges and opportunities. *International Journal of Eating Disorders, 31,* 233–239.

Petry, N. M. (2002a). A comparison of young, middle-aged, and older adult treatment-seeking pathological gamblers. *Gerontologist, 42,* 92–99.

Petry, N. M. (2002b). How treatments for pathological gambling can be informed by treatments for substance use disorders. *Experimental and Clinical Psychopharmacology, 10,* 184–192.

Petry, N. M., & Bickel, W. K. (1998). Polydrug abuse in heroin addicts: A behavioral economic analysis. *Addiction, 93,* 321–335.

Pike, K., Dohm, F., Striegel-Moore, R., Wilfley, D., & Fairburn, C. (2001). A comparison of black and white women with binge eating disorder. *American Journal of Psychiatry, 158,* 1455–1460.

Potenza, M. N. (2002). A perspective on future directions in the prevention, treatment, and research of pathological gambling. *Psychiatric Annals, 32*(3), 203–207.

Rachlin, H. (2000). *The science of self-control.* Cambridge, MA: Harvard University Press.

Rawson, R. A., Huber, A., McCann, M. J., Shoptaw, S. J., Farabee, D., & Ling, W. (2002). A comparison of contingency management and cognitive-behavioral approaches for cocaine-dependent methadone-maintained individuals. *Archives of General Psychiatry, 59,* 817–824.

Reuter, P., & MacCoun, R. (1995). Drawing lessons from the absence of harm reduction in American drug policy. *Tobacco Control, 4,* S28–S32.

Reuter, P., & MacCoun, R. (2002). Heroin maintenance: Is a U.S. experiment needed? In D. Musto (Ed.), *One hundred years of heroin* (pp. 159–180). Westport, CT: Greenwood Press.

Rodefer, J. (2002). *Internet gambling in Nevada: Overview of federal law affecting Assembly Bill 466.* Carson City: Nevada Officer of the Attorney General. Available from http://ag .state.nv.us/hottopics/int_gamb_nv.pdf.

Rose, I. (2002). *Understanding the law of Internet gambling.* Encino, CA: Author. Available from http://www.gamblingandthelaw.com/Internet_gambling.html.

Saffer, H., & Chaloupka, F. (1999). The demand for illicit drugs. *Economic Inquiry, 37,* 401–411.

Sager, I., Elgin, B., Elstrom, P., Keenan, F., & Gogoi, P. (2002, September 2). The underground web. *BusinessWeek,* 66.

Scheidt, D. M., & Windle, M. (1995). The Alcoholics in Treatment HIV Risk (ATRISK) Study: Gender, ethnic, and geographic group comparisons. *Journal of Studies on Alcohol, 56,* 300–308.

Schneider, J. P., & Irons, R. R. (1996). Differential diagnosis of addictive sexual disorders using the *DSM-IV. Sexual Addiction & Compulsivity, 3,* 7–21.

Shaffer, H. J., & Hall, M. H. (2001). Updating and refining prevalence estimates of disordered gambling behavior in the Unites States and Canada. *Canadian Journal of Public Health, 92,* 168–172.

Shaffer, H. J., Hall, M. H., & Vanderbilt, J. (1999). Estimating the prevalence of disordered gambling behavior in the United States and Canada: A research synthesis. *American Journal of Public Health, 89,* 1369–1376.

Siegel, D., & Anders, G. (1999). Public policy and the displacement effects of casinos: A case study of riverboat gambling in Missouri. *Journal of Gambling Studies, 15,* 105–121.

Siegel, D., & Anders, G. (2001). The impact of Indian casinos on state lotteries: A case study of Arizona. *Public Finance Review, 29,* 139–147.

Silvia, S., & Thorne, J. (1997). *School-based drug prevention programs: A longitudinal study in selected school* (Executive Summary Report). Research Triangle Park, NC: Research Triangle Institute.

Stratton, K., Shetty, P., Wallace, R., & Bondurant, S. (2001). *Clearing the smoke: Assessing the science base for tobacco harm reduction.* Washington, DC: National Academy Press.

Striegel-Moore, R., & Smolak, L. (2000). *The influence of ethnicity on eating disorders health.* Mahwah, NJ: Erlbaum.

Substance Abuse and Mental Health Services Administration. (1994). *National household survey on drug abuse.* Rockville, MD: U.S. Department of Health and Human Services.

Substance Abuse and Mental Health Services Administration. (1995). *National household survey on drug abuse.* Rockville, MD: U.S. Department of Health and Human Services.

Substance Abuse and Mental Health Services Administration. (1996). *National household survey on drug abuse.* Rockville, MD: U.S. Department of Health and Human Services.

Substance Abuse and Mental Health Services Administration. (1997). *National household survey on drug abuse.* Rockville, MD: U.S. Department of Health and Human Services.

Substance Abuse and Mental Health Services Administration. (1998). *National household survey on drug abuse.* Rockville, MD: U.S. Department of Health and Human Services.

Substance Abuse and Mental Health Services Administration. (1999). *National household survey on drug abuse.* Rockville, MD: U.S. Department of Health and Human Services.

Substance Abuse and Mental Health Services Administration. (2000). *National household survey on drug abuse.* Rockville, MD: U.S. Department of Health and Human Services.

Substance Abuse and Mental Health Services Administration. (2001). *National household survey on drug abuse.* Rockville, MD: U.S. Department of Health and Human Services.

Substance Abuse and Mental Health Services Administration. (2002). *National household survey on drug abuse.* Rockville, MD: U.S. Department of Health and Human Services.

Sullivan, E., & Simon, W. (1998). The client: A social, psychological, and behavioral look at the unseen patron of prostitution. In J. Elias, V. Bullough, V. Elias, & G. Brewer (Eds.), *Prostitution: On whores, hustlers and johns* (pp. 134–154). Buffalo, NY: Prometheus Books.

Sutker, P. B., & Allain, A. N. (1988). Issues in personality conceptualizations of addictive behaviors. *Journal of Consulting and Clinical Psychology, 56,* 172–182.

Tax Policy Center. (2002). *Excise taxes.* Available from http://www.taxpolicycenter.org/taxfacts/excise/main.cfm.

Tonry, M. (1995). *Malign neglect.* New York: Oxford University Press.

Toomey, T., Rosenfeld, C., & Wagenaar, A. (1996). The minimum legal drinking age. *Alcohol Health and Research World, 20,* 213–218.

Travis, J., Solomon, A., & Waul, M. (2001). *From prison to home: The dimensions and consequences of prisoner reentry.* Washington, DC: Urban Institute.

Troyer, R. J., & Markle, G. (1983). *Cigarettes: The battle over smoking.* New Brunswick, NJ: Rutgers University Press.

Tworek, C., Giovino, G., Barker, D., Sasso, B., Molnar, E., Ruel, E., et al. (2002). *State and local enforcement of possession, use, and purchase laws among, U.S. states and local communities.* Presentation for the Society for Prevention Research, Seattle, WA. Available from http://www.impacteen.org/generalarea_PDFs/SPR2002_tworek.pdf.

U.S. Department of Justice. (2000). *Federal statutes imposing collateral consequences upon conviction.* Available from http://www.usdoj.gov/pardon/collateral_consequences.pdf.

Van Ours, J. (1995). The price elasticity of hard drugs: The case of opium in the Dutch East Indies. *Journal of Political Economy, 103,* 261–279.

Vitaro, F., Ferland, F., Jacques, C., & Ladouceur, R. (1998). Gambling, substance use, and impulsivity during adolescence. *Psychology of Addictive Behaviors, 12,* 185–194.

Volberg, R. (2002). The epidemiology of pathological gambling. *Psychiatric Annals, 32,* 171–178.

Wagenaar, A. (2000). *Alcohol policies in the United States: Highlights from the 50 states.* Minneapolis: University of Minnesota.

Wagner, F., & Anthony, J. (2002). From first drug use to drug dependence: Developmental periods of risk for dependence upon marijuana, cocaine, and alcohol. *Neuropsychopharmacology, 26,* 479–488.

Walsh, B., & Devlin, M. (1998). Eating disorders: Progress and problems. *Science, 280,* 1387–1390.

Warner, L., Kessler, R., Hughes, M., Anthony, J., & Nelson, C. (1995). Prevalence and correlates of drug use and dependence in the United States. *Archives of General Psychiatry, 52,* 219–229.

Williams, J., Pacula, R., Chaloupka, F., & Wechsler, H. (2001). *Alcohol and marijuana use among college students: Economic complements or substitutes* (Working Paper No. 8401). Cambridge, MA: National Bureau of Economic Research.

Wodak, A. (2001). Overseas heroin trials point the way ahead. *Sydney Morning Herald.* Available from http://old.smh.com.au/news/0108/10/opinion/opinion2.html.

Womach, A. (2001). *Tobacco price support: An overview of the program.* Washington, DC: Library of Congress, Congressional Research Service. Available from http://www.ers.usda.gov/briefing/tobacco/Data/crs1.pdf.

Woodside, D., Garfinkel, P., Lin, E., Goering, P., Kaplan, A., Goldbloom, D., et al. (2001). Comparisons of men with full or partial eating disorders, men without eating disorders, and women with eating disorders in the community. *American Journal of Psychiatry, 158,* 570–574.

CHAPTER 16

Preventing Addictive Disorders

KENNETH W. GRIFFIN and GILBERT J. BOTVIN

T HE FIELD OF prevention has grown tremendously in the past two to three decades. For addictive behaviors such as drug abuse, a large variety of prevention programs are currently available for use in schools, families, and communities. The most effective of these are based on psychosocial theories that incorporate what is known about the most important risk and protective factors in the etiology of substance abuse. Some of these interventions have been shown in rigorous evaluation studies to produce significant and lasting changes in drug behavior. The most substantial progress to date has been made in school-based drug abuse prevention, particularly with interventions aimed at early adolescents. A much smaller but growing literature is beginning to emerge relating to preventing other addictive behaviors such as problem gambling and eating disorders. There has also been a notable shift in public attitudes and social policies that promote prevention, as can be seen in the frequency of prevention-oriented public service announcements in the media and in new laws and regulations such as those restricting use of tobacco products in public places. However, for several of the addictive disorders reviewed in this book, such as compulsive buying, workaholism, and sex addiction, research is in its early stages and focuses largely on increasing our basic understanding of these disorders and on diagnostic and treatment issues. Hence, less progress has been made in preventing these disorders. Taken together, the good news is that much progress has been made in making prevention a public health priority, but more work is needed in developing programs for a broader range of addictive behaviors.

The goals of the present chapter are to provide an overview of what is effective in the prevention of addictive disorders and to discuss how what has been learned can guide future efforts to prevent those addictive behaviors that have received less attention. Many of the lessons learned in the more established field of drug abuse prevention are beginning to be applied to the development of prevention programs for problem gambling, eating disorders, and depression. These lessons can inform us about next steps in developing prevention programs for compulsive buying, workaholism, compulsive sex, and related behavioral disorders.

Notably, much of the existing research on preventing addictive disorders focuses on adolescents. This is because adolescence is a time of life when young people begin to make independent decisions about their own behaviors related to substance use, eating, gambling, sexuality, work habits, and buying habits. It is also a time during which young people strive for independence and self-definition and are increasingly focused on developing a sense of who they want to be as adults. A variety of societal messages, media portrayals, adult role models, and peer influences have a significant influence on youth in terms of decisions about their own behavior. Furthermore, adolescence is a time of learning adult skills that can help young people to succeed in the new academic, social, and vocational challenges that they face. As young people explore new roles during adolescence, they often experiment with behaviors that involve taking risks. Indeed, research suggests that some risk-taking behavior is normative among teenagers (Baumrind, 1987). For a small number of adolescents, however, risk taking occurs with greater frequency, is more extensive in nature, and presents a higher level of danger to the youth themselves and others. Although most youth successfully navigate the changes and challenges that come with adolescence, it is also a period when a variety of problematic behaviors first appear (Kazdin, 1993; Lerner & Galambos, 1998). Every adolescent is different, and some will negotiate developmental challenges more successfully than others. Negative outcomes are more likely to appear among youth who are less successful in conventional pursuits, those that struggle with developmental tasks, or those who are most vulnerable to negative social influences. These youth may begin to engage in behaviors that later develop into addictive disorders.

A common thread that appears across the different prevention literatures is that prevention programs should aim to increase levels of *psychosocial resilience* to keep young people away from the precursors and risk factors that lead to various addictive behaviors. Resilience generally refers to positive adaptation within the context of significant adversity or positive functioning in high-risk environments (Luthar, Cicchetti, & Becker, 2000). Resilient youth have been found to have good problem-solving skills (weighing options and implementing solutions), high social competence (e.g., communication skills, assertiveness), autonomy (e.g., self-efficacy and self-control), as well as a sense of purpose and future (e.g., success orientation, optimism). Since not all adolescents live in high-risk environments, a more general approach to enhance these skills among all youth termed *competence enhancement* is clearly relevant to prevention. Thus, there is a large and growing literature in youth prevention and psychosocial development interventions that can be drawn on in developing prevention programs that target new addictive and compulsive behaviors.

We begin by defining various terms commonly used when discussing prevention. Next, we review several key topics that have laid the groundwork for effective prevention. The development of effective preventive intervention programs stems for a comprehensive knowledge of the etiologic risk and protective factors and psychosocial theory regarding the onset and escalation of addictive behaviors, as can best be seen in the drug abuse prevention literature. The most rigorously designed evaluation studies of prevention programs have typically occurred in school and community settings. We review several approaches to prevention in these settings, from traditional information dissemination approaches that have been largely ineffective in changing behavior to more effective contemporary approaches that are based on psychosocial theory and target the relevant risk and protective factors for a particular behavior. Several addictive and compulsive behaviors share a common set of risk and protective factors, and each negative outcome typically has unique risk and protective factors specific to that behavior. We review an example of an effective school-based prevention approach to drug abuse prevention, a program called *Life Skills Training*. Then, in the following sections, we examine lessons learned in drug abuse prevention and how to apply them to preventing other addictive behaviors. Here, the existing literature on preventing problem gambling, eating disorders, and depression are reviewed and promising programs are highlighted.

Finally, the chapter addresses some key issues in moving the prevention of addictive disorders forward, including a review of the general characteristics of effective prevention programs delivered in school settings, which is generally the most common location where prevention programs are implemented. A key step in identifying new, effective prevention approaches for addictive disorders is to test new interventions using scientifically rigorous methods. Thus, key components of scientific methodology, research design, and data analysis for testing preventive interventions are discussed to guide future attempts at identifying prevention programs for addictive behaviors that have received less attention. Also, the importance of disseminating prevention programs is reviewed, since effective programs will have a significant public health impact only if they are widely used in real-world settings.

DEFINITIONS OF PREVENTION

Over the past several decades, prevention has been discussed in terms of primary, secondary, and tertiary prevention. These definitions were derived primarily from a public health perspective on the incidence and prevalence of disease. *Primary prevention* seeks to decrease the number of new cases or incidence of disease through activities aimed at preventing the onset of a condition. *Secondary prevention* aims to lower the prevalence of disease in terms of existing cases through activities aimed at early identification (screening) of persons who have already developed risk factors or show early stages of disorder, but for whom the condition is not currently apparent. *Tertiary prevention* has to do with reducing the amount of disability associated with an existing condition and the ongoing care of persons with an established condition, with a goal of restoring highest functioning and minimizing negative complications of the condition.

There are several difficulties with this classification system: It is difficult to distinguish the difference between tertiary prevention and treatment because both involve care for persons with an established disorder. Virtually any intervention can be pulled under the umbrella of prevention, making it difficult to demonstrate how prevention is unique and important. In a 1994 report on preventive intervention research, the Institute of Medicine (IOM, 1994) proposed a new framework for classifying intervention programs as part of a continuum of care that includes prevention, treatment, and maintenance. While originally proposed as a system to classify interventions for mental disorders, the framework has been widely adopted and the terminology is now applied to other types of interventions. In this framework, *prevention* is reserved only for interventions that occur prior to the initial onset of a disorder. The prevention section of this continuum

(Figure 16.1) is further divided into three types: universal, selective, and indicated preventive interventions. These categories define prevention according to the groups to whom interventions are directed.

Universal prevention programs focus on the general population and aim to deter or delay the onset of a condition. While the level of risk for developing a condition may vary among individuals, universal programs recognize that all members of a population share some level of risk and can benefit from prevention programs that provide information and skills to help them avoid the outcome or condition. *Selective* prevention programs target selected high-risk groups or subsets of the general population believed to be at high risk due to membership in a particular group. Risk groups for selective interventions may be based on biological, social, psychological, or other risk factors. For example, selective interventions for drug abuse prevention might focus on children of drug users, pregnant women, or residents of high-risk neighborhoods, where an individual's level of risk is presumed to be higher than average. *Indicated* prevention programs are designed for those already engaging in the behavior or those showing early danger signs or engaging in related high-risk behaviors. For example, indicated programs for drug abuse prevention would be appropriate for individuals who have initiated illicit drug use, and the goal would be to reduce their chances of developing a drug abuse problem. Thus, where recruitment and participation in a selective intervention is based on *subgroup membership,* recruitment and participation in an indicated intervention is based on early warning signs demonstrated by an *individual.*

Although the terms primary, secondary, and tertiary prevention are still commonly used, the newer classification system of universal, selective, and indicated prevention is preferred. The two sets of terms are *not* interchangeable. While universal prevention programs are a form of primary prevention, the terms *selected* and *indicated* are also meant to be used exclusively for interventions that occur

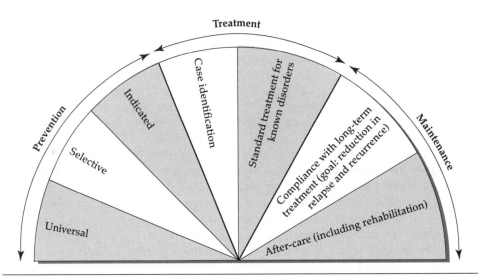

Figure 16.1 Intervention Continuum: Prevention, Treatment, and Maintenance. Reprinted with permission from *Reducing Risks for Mental Disorders: Frontiers for Preventive Intervention Research*, by the Institute of Medicine, 1994, Washington, DC: National Academies Press.

prior to the onset of a condition, while this is not necessarily the case for *secondary* and *tertiary* prevention. The IOM report (1994) points out that when the two sets of terms (primary, secondary, tertiary versus universal, selective, and indicated) are used interchangeably, it only serves to add to the confusion regarding boundaries and definitions of prevention.

PREVENTING DRUG ABUSE

By far, the largest body of research in the etiology and prevention of addictive disorders is in the area of drug abuse prevention. Effective preventive interventions and related initiatives to reduce substance abuse have been the focus of a great deal of research. A review of drug abuse prevention initiatives demonstrates that a wide variety of activities has been used to achieve the goal of reduced drug abuse, particularly among adolescents (Paglia & Room, 1999). These prevention activities range from educational and skills training activities that take place within schools, families, and communities, to mass media public service announcements, policy initiatives, such as required health warning labels on cigarettes and alcohol, changes in school rules (i.e., "zero-tolerance" policies), and laws and regulations, such as increased cigarette taxes and minimum purchasing age requirements. However, the bulk of the drug abuse prevention research has concentrated on universal school-based programs, and there has been remarkable progress in this area of prevention. This work is likely to hold important lessons for the development of effective prevention programs for other addictive behaviors.

The gains in drug abuse prevention over the past two to three decades have stemmed from advances in our knowledge regarding the patterns, etiologic risk and protective factors, and psychosocial theory relevant to drug use and abuse. In the next several sections, we review what has been learned from national trend data regarding drug use progression, the most salient risk and protective factors that contribute to the development of adolescent drug abuse, and how advances in psychosocial theory have been critical to the development of effective universal prevention programs.

PATTERNS OF ADOLESCENT DRUG ABUSE

Adolescents often begin to use alcohol, tobacco, marijuana, and other drugs during the middle school years, with a smaller number experimenting with substance use during elementary school. In the United States, national survey data (Johnston, O'Malley, & Bachman, 2001) show that most young people report engaging in the use of one or more substances by the time they are in secondary school. Alcohol and tobacco are the most commonly used substances among adolescents, with about one in three twelfth graders reporting drunkenness, binge drinking (i.e., five or more drinks in a row), or smoking cigarettes in the past month. Almost half of high school students report using marijuana in their lifetime and more than one in four report using marijuana in the past month. In fact, marijuana is the most commonly used illegal drug among American secondary school students.

There has been growing concern about the use of Ecstasy (MDMA), other "club drugs," and increasingly potent forms of certain illicit drugs among teenagers in recent years. Ecstasy, a synthetic compound with mildly hallucinogenic and stimulant effects, is now used by more American teenagers than cocaine. In fact, Ecstasy has shown the sharpest increase in use of any illicit drug over the past several years, from 6% of American teenagers having used Ecstasy in 1996 up to 11% in 2000. Other drugs, such as methamphetamines, cocaine (including crack cocaine), rohypnol, LSD, GHB, and heroin, have seen increased use among adolescents in the past decade. Some of these drugs are available in purer concentrations and can be obtained in a greater number of geographic locations (e.g., cities, suburbs, and rural areas) than in the past. Furthermore, the perceived risk of harm from substance use has been falling among teens in recent years (Johnston et al., 2001). Taken together, these data suggest that drug abuse and dependence is a serious threat among American youth. Although national data on prevalence of adolescent substance abuse disorder are not available, it appears to be a substantial problem. One large-scale study of over 75,000 youth found that 16% of high school seniors met criteria for substance use disorder and 7% had substance dependence (Harrison, Fulkerson, & Beebe, 1998).

ETIOLOGIC FACTORS IN ADOLESCENT DRUG ABUSE

A number of important etiological factors in the development of adolescent drug abuse have been identified, including the role of individual personality characteristics, family, peers, and community influences, as well as genetics and neurobiological factors. It is now clear that there is no single factor or pathway that serves as a necessary and sufficient condition leading to drug abuse. Instead, drug abuse is the result of a multivariate mix of factors some of which increase risk for drug involvement, and other (protective) factors decrease the potential for becoming involved with drugs (Hawkins, Catalano, & Miller, 1992). In Figure 16.2, we group the most significant risk and protective factors into three broad domains.

Background/Historical Factors   This broad domain includes biological factors (e.g., genetic factors, temperament), demographic factors (e.g., age, gender, social class), cultural factors (e.g., acculturation), and environmental influences (e.g., community disorganization, availability of drugs). Genetic factors, for example, are believed to be influential in some individuals who develop substance abuse problems. Research shows that children of parents with alcohol and drug problems are significantly more likely to develop substance abuse problems than children whose parents do not have alcohol or drug problems, even among identical twins reared apart. Research has demonstrated that certain addictive behaviors, such as eating and sexual behavior, stimulate the brain reward centers in ways similar to addictive drugs (DuPont, 1997), suggesting a common neurochemical pathway. On the other end of the spectrum, environmental influences, such as neighborhood disorganization, poverty, and criminal activity, increase adolescent substance abuse and other problem behaviors (e.g., Wills, Pierce, & Evans, 1996). For example, low socioeconomic status neighborhoods are often characterized by high adult unemployment, high rates of mobility, and a lack of informal social networks and controls, and these factors together may negatively affect adolescent development and contribute to drug abuse.

Social Factors   This domain includes school factors (e.g., school climate, school bonding), family factors (e.g., family management practices, discipline, parental drug use), peer influences (e.g., friends' drug use, friends' pro-drug attitudes), and

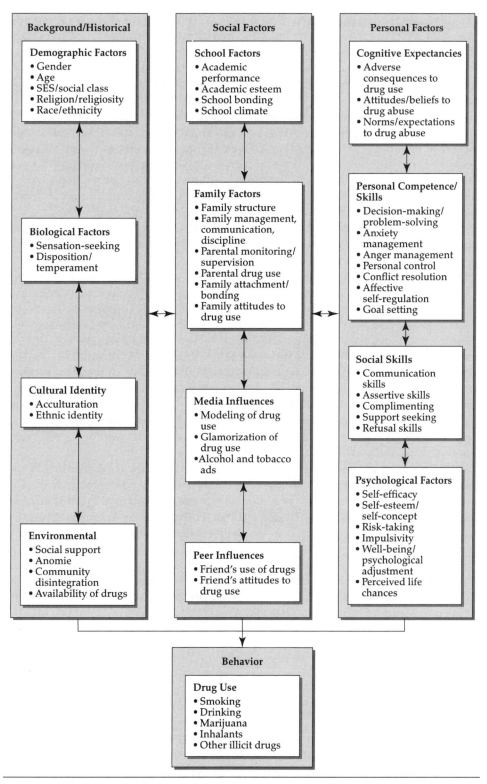

Figure 16.2   Etiologic Factors in Adolescent Drug Use and Abuse

media influences (e.g., television shows, movies, and advertisements that promote drug use). Family influences include the attitudes and behaviors of parents and siblings in regard to substance use, and research demonstrates that parents' use of alcohol, marijuana, and other illicit drugs and parental attitudes that are not explicitly against use often translate into higher levels of use among children and adolescents (e.g., Windle, 1996). Other family factors include the quantity and quality of parenting practices (monitoring, communication, and involvement) and family structure (e.g., two-parent versus single-parent families). Peer influences are one of the strongest social influence factors that contribute to youth substance abuse and dependence. Through social learning processes, associating with peers who engage in substance use is likely to foster attitudes and beliefs that promote drug abuse, establish drug use as normative behavior, and provide opportunities to learn and practice these new behaviors. In addition, media advertisements and television and movie portrayals that glamorize substance use, as well as the availability and cost of drugs, are central factors in the etiology of adolescent drug abuse.

Personal Factors   This domain includes cognitive expectancies (e.g., attitudes, beliefs, and normative expectations regarding drug use), personal competence skills (e.g., decision making, self-control), social skills (e.g., communication skills, assertiveness), and a set of relevant psychological factors (e.g., self-efficacy, self-esteem, psychological well-being). Individual-level factors associated with adolescent substance abuse include holding favorable attitudes or expectancies regarding substance use, believing that it is normative or highly prevalent, having a propensity for rebelliousness, sensation-seeking and risk-taking, and having poor social competence skills (e.g., the ability to use a variety of interpersonal negotiation strategies and to communicate clearly and assertively), and poor personal competence skills (e.g., cognitive and behavioral self-management strategies such as decision making and self-regulation).

The range and number of risk and protective factors for adolescent drug use and abuse is large. It is generally believed that the more risk factors and fewer protective factors that a young person has, the greater the likelihood that he or she will develop a problem with drug abuse. However, it is also acknowledged that the risk factors for drug use experimentation may differ from those for heavy or chronic drug abuse. Whereas peer and other social influences may largely be responsible for experimentation with drugs, it is likely that biological (e.g., genetic) and psychological factors (e.g., affect regulation, self-medication) are more salient for the development of drug abuse problems and chemical dependency disorders.

PSYCHOSOCIAL THEORIES OF ADOLESCENT DRUG ABUSE

A variety of theoretical models have been developed or applied to the phenomenon of adolescent drug abuse. These models attempt to integrate the large number of risk and protective factors that contribute to the etiology of substance use and abuse among youth. These theoretical models include social learning and social influence theories, social attachment and conventional commitment theories, personality and affective theories, cognitive and decision-making theories, and other more comprehensive theories (reviewed in Petraitis, Flay, & Miller, 1995).

Social learning and *social influence* theories describe the importance of substance-using role models, such as parents, siblings, relatives, and friends (e.g., Akers &

Cochran, 1985). In addition to the direct modeling of drug use behavior outlined in social learning models, various *social attachment* and *conventional commitment* theories such as the social development model (Hawkins & Weis, 1985) describe the processes by which youth withdraw from parents or school and begin to associate with peer groups that encourage drug use and other antisocial behavior. *Cognitively oriented* theories, such as the health belief model (Becker, 1974) and the theory of planned behavior (Ajzen, 1988), emphasize the importance of an individual's perception of risks, benefits, and norms, and personal vulnerability regarding substance use, and how these factors play a role in decision-making processes. *Personality and affective* theories, such as the self-medication hypothesis (Khantzian, 1997), highlight the roles of individual psychological vulnerabilities and affective characteristics that can lead to drug use and abuse. Broader *social psychological* theories, such as problem behavior theory (PBT; Jessor & Jessor, 1977), attempt to integrate multiple determinants of adolescent substance use. PBT proposes that drug use and other problem behaviors serve a functional purpose from the perspective of the adolescent because they believe engaging in the behavior can help them achieve social or personal goals they otherwise can't achieve. Peers are also believed to play a role in substance use in ways beyond mere social influences. For example, *self-derogation* theory (Kaplan, 1980) proposes that adolescents who are negatively evaluated by conventional others or feel deficient in socially desirable attributes will experience low self-esteem, which is in turn a central motivational factor leading to rebellious behavior against conventional standards, including drug use.

Working from the risk and protective factors domains shown in Figure 16.2, we present a general model of drug use initiation in Figure 16.3 that incorporates key elements from the most prominent theories of adolescent drug abuse. The

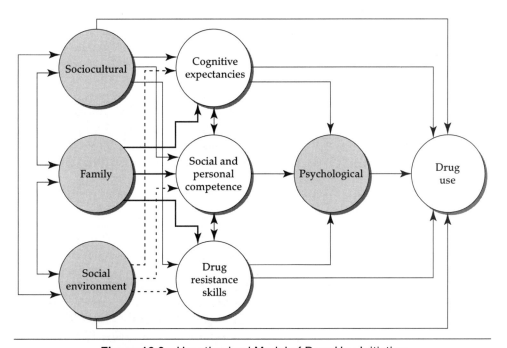

Figure 16.3 Hypothesized Model of Drug Use Initiation

psychosocial domains are conceptualized as superordinate constructs that comprise a causal framework of drug use initiation. The sociocultural domain consists of demographic factors (age, gender, social class), cultural factors (ethnic identity, acculturation), and drug availability. The social/environmental domain includes community factors (community resources and neighborhood organization), school factors (school bounding, school size, school climate), family factors (family management practices, communication, discipline, monitoring, parental drug use, and parental attitudes toward drug use), media influences promoting attitudes and norms conducive to drug use (TV shows, movies, rock videos, tobacco and alcohol advertising), and peer influences (friends' drug use and pro-drug attitudes). These factors both shape and interact with the adolescent's cognitive expectancies (attitudes, beliefs, normative expectations, drug-related health knowledge), general competencies (personal self-management skills, social skills), and a set of skills specific to resisting social influences from both the media and peers to use drugs. Vulnerability to these influences are in turn affected by psychological factors such as self-efficacy, self-esteem, personal control, psychological adjustment, and perceived life chances. These background, social, and personal factors can play an important role in the initiation and escalation of drug use among youth and act together to promote drug abuse. Specific factors play a larger or smaller role from individual to individual.

Although the model in Figure 16.3 is designed to organize key factors associated with the onset of drug involvement into a coherent framework, it is done from the perspective of how a preventive intervention may target these factors and prevent drug abuse. Interventions that target individual, family, and community determinants of drug abuse are likely to effectively prevent drug abuse to the extent that they have an impact on drug-related expectancies (knowledge, attitudes, and norms), drug-related resistance skills, and general competence (personal self-management skills and social skills). For example, the model indicates that psychological factors mediate the impact of general personal and social competence on drug abuse risk. This suggests that a preventive intervention that improves personal and social competence skills would reduce drug use by enhancing specific psychological protective factors (e.g., well-being or self-efficacy). However, this type of model also has some inherent limitations. First, it suggests a temporal flow of causality that is static and does not capture the dynamic and recursive nature of these mechanisms. Second, although reasonably comprehensive, this model does not contain an exhaustive list of etiologic factors, nor does it posit all possible interrelationships. However, it does provide a reasonably good organizing framework of the factors important in the etiology of drug use and suggests several targets in formulating an effective prevention strategy.

APPROACHES TO DRUG ABUSE PREVENTION

Based on what has been learned in the past few decades about the epidemiology, etiology, and psychosocial theory regarding adolescent drug abuse, many prevention programs for adolescent drug abuse aim to prevent early stage substance use or at least delay the initiation or onset of use among youth. Many of these programs are provided to middle school or junior high school students because this is when many youth begin to experiment with substances (Table 16.1). These programs typically target the use of tobacco, alcohol, and marijuana because these are the most widely used substances in our society and because preventing the

Table 16.1
Overview of School-Based Drug Abuse Prevention Approaches

Approach	Focus	Methods
Information dissemination	Increase knowledge of drugs, and the consequences of use; promote antidrug use attitudes.	Didactic instruction, discussion, audio/video presentations, displays of substances, posters, pamphlets school assembly programs.
Affective education	Increase self-esteem, responsible decision-making, interpersonal growth; generally includes little or no information about drugs.	Didactic instruction, discussion, experiential activities, group problem-solving exercises.
Social resistance	Increase awareness of social influence to smoke, drink, or use drugs; develop skills for resisting substance use influences; increase knowledge of immediate negative consequences; establish non-substance use norms.	Class discussion; resistance skills training; behavioral rehearsal; extended practice via behavioral homework; use of same-age or older peer leaders.
Competence enhancement	Increase decision making, personal behavior change, anxiety-reduction, communication, social and assertive skills; application of generic skills to resist substance use influences.	Class discussion; cognitive-behavioral skills training (instruction, demonstration, behavioral rehearsal, feedback, reinforcement).

use of these gateway substances may reduce the risk for later negative outcomes. In this section, we review the history of drug abuse prevention interventions, from the initial focus on knowledge-based interventions to today's theory-based and empirically supported comprehensive prevention approaches.

TRADITIONAL APPROACHES

Information Dissemination   The most commonly used approach to drug abuse prevention education involves providing factual information about drugs and alcohol to young people. Some information dissemination approaches attempt to dramatize the dangers of using drugs with the use of fear-arousal techniques designed to attract attention and frighten individuals into not using drugs with vivid portrayals of the severe adverse consequences of drug abuse.

Informational approaches may include classroom lectures about the dangers of abuse, as well as educational pamphlets and other printed materials and short films that impart information to students about different types of drugs and the negative consequences of use. Some programs have doctors or other health professionals come into the classroom and talk about the severe, often irreversible health effects of drug use. Other programs have police officers discuss law enforcement issues, including drug-related crime and penalties for buying or possessing illegal drugs.

Evaluation studies of informational approaches to drug prevention show that these programs may in some cases produce a short-term impact on knowledge and anti-drug attitudes. However, meta-analytic studies consistently fail to show any impact on drug use behavior or intentions to use drugs in the future (Tobler & Stratton, 1997). It has become clear that the etiology of drug and alcohol abuse is complex and prevention strategies that rely primarily on information dissemination are not effective in changing behavior.

Affective Education Another traditional prevention approach is *affective education*, which involves attempts to increase self-esteem, responsible decision making, and interpersonal growth through a variety of classroom activities such as discussion, experiential activities, and group problem-solving exercises. However, these programs typically include little or no information about drugs and therefore have not been effective in changing drug behavior.

CONTEMPORARY APPROACHES

Social Resistance Approaches Since the 1970s, there has been a growing recognition that social and psychological factors are key in promoting the onset of cigarette smoking, and later, drug and alcohol abuse. Drug prevention approaches have become increasingly more closely tied to psychological theories of human behavior. The social resistance approach to drug abuse prevention is based on the concept that adolescents engage in drug use and abuse due to exposure to pro-drug social influences from peers, adult role models who use drugs, and persuasive advertising appeals and media portrayals encouraging drug use. Therefore, social influence programs teach students how to recognize and deal with these social influences. These programs focus on skills training to increase students' resistance to negative social influences to engage in drug use, particularly peer pressure.

Resistance skills training approaches focus on teaching students new ways to avoid high-risk situations where they are likely to experience peer pressure to smoke, drink, or use drugs. These approaches also provide students with the knowledge, confidence, and skills needed to handle peer pressure in these and other situations. These programs frequently include a component that makes students aware of pro-drug influences from the media, with an emphasis on the techniques used by advertisers to influence consumer behavior. Also, because adolescents tend to overestimate the prevalence of tobacco, alcohol, and drug use, social resistance programs often attempt to correct normative expectations that nearly everybody smokes, drinks alcohol, or uses drugs.

Resistance skills programs have been shown to be largely effective in preventing adolescent drug involvement. A comprehensive review of resistance skills prevention studies published from 1980 to 1990 reported that the majority of studies (63%) had positive effects on drug use behavior, with fewer studies having neutral (26%) or negative effects on behavior (11%); with several in the neutral category having inadequate statistical power to detect program effects (Hansen, 1992). Furthermore, several follow-up studies of resistance skills interventions have reported positive behavioral effects lasting for up to three years, although longer term follow-up studies have shown that these effects gradually decay over time.

The most popular school-based drug education program based on the social influence model is Drug Abuse Resistance Education (DARE). The core DARE curriculum is typically provided to children in the fifth or sixth grades and contains elements of information dissemination and social influence approaches to drug abuse prevention. DARE uses trained, uniformed police officers in the classroom to teach the drug prevention curriculum. Despite the popularity and wide dissemination of DARE, evaluation studies of DARE using scientifically rigorous designs (i.e., large samples, random assignment, and longitudinal follow-up) have consistently shown that DARE has little or no impact on drug use behaviors, particularly beyond the initial posttest assessment (Rosenbaum & Hanson, 1998). Some of the possible reasons that DARE is ineffective may be that the program is targeting the wrong mediating processes (Hansen & McNeal, 1997), that the instructional methods are less interactive than more successful prevention programs, and/or that teenagers may simply "tune out" what may be perceived as an expected message from an ultimate authority figure.

Competence Enhancement Approaches   A limitation of the social influence approach is that it assumes that young people do not want to use drugs but lack the skills or confidence to refuse. For some youth, however, using drugs may not be a matter of yielding to peer pressure, but may have instrumental value; it may, for example, help them deal with anxiety, low self-esteem, or a lack of comfort in social situations. According to the competence enhancement approach, drug use behavior is learned through a process of modeling, imitation, and reinforcement and is influenced by an adolescent's pro-drug cognitions, attitudes, and beliefs (Botvin, 2000). These factors, in combination with poor personal and social skills, are believed to increase an adolescent's susceptibility to social influences in favor of drug use.

Although these approaches have several features that they share with resistance skills training approaches, a distinctive feature of competence enhancement approaches is an emphasis on the teaching of generic personal self-management skills and social coping skills (Botvin, 2000). Examples of the kind of generic personal and social skills typically included in this prevention approach are decision-making and problem-solving skills, cognitive skills for resisting interpersonal and media influences, skills for enhancing self-esteem (goal-setting and self-directed behavior change techniques), adaptive coping strategies for dealing with stress and anxiety, general social skills (complimenting, conversational skills, and skills for forming new friendships), and general assertiveness skills. These skills are best taught using proven cognitive-behavioral skills training methods: instruction and demonstration, behavioral rehearsal, feedback and social reinforcement, and extended practice through behavioral homework assignments (See Table 16.2).

Over the years, a number of evaluation studies have been conducted testing the efficacy of competence enhancement approaches to drug abuse prevention. These studies have consistently demonstrated behavioral effects as well as effects on hypothesized mediating variables. Long-term follow-up data indicate that the prevention effects of these approaches can last for several years (Botvin, Baker, Dusenbury, Botvin, & Diaz, 1995; Botvin et al., 2000). In summary, drug abuse prevention programs that emphasize resistance skills and general life skills (i.e., competence enhancement approaches) appear to show the most promise of all school-based prevention approaches.

A Focus on Life Skills Training   The Life Skills Training (LST) program is an example of an effective competence enhancement-based universal prevention program for adolescent drug abuse that targets risk and protective factors associated with the early stages of drug use.

Table 16.2
Classroom Skills Training Techniques

Cognitive/Behavioral Skills Training Steps	Example: Resisting peer pressure to smoke.
Instruction and Demonstration	
Explain a particular skill to students in a careful step-by-step fashion. Provide a clear explanation of when to use the skill. Demonstrate how to perform a particular skill.	Explain to students that when someone offers them a cigarette or pressures them to smoke, they can respond in a variety of ways, including saying no firmly and confidently, saying not now, changing the subject, leaving the situation, and so on.
Behavioral Rehearsal	
Provide an opportunity for students to practice the skill. Participate in brief behavioral rehearsal scenarios. Give each student a chance to participate. Observe students practicing.	Ask students to break up into small groups. Each student should take a turn in a behavioral rehearsal scenario in which a friend offers him or her a cigarette. If necessary, participate in some of the scenarios with selected students. Go from group to group and observe how individual students respond to the situation and what they say in response to the cigarette offer.
Feedback and Social Reinforcement	
Reinforce students for the most positive elements of his or her performance: –Discuss what elements need improvement. –Give specific recommendations concerning how to improve. –Provide all feedback in a constructive and supportive manner.	For one or two students in each group, review what they did well and what they could do better. For example, if a student was not convincing in assertively saying no to the cigarette offer, tell them in a constructive and supportive way that sometimes it is easier to simply make up an excuse and leave the situation.
Extended Practice	
Discuss ways to use the skill in everyday situations. Give behavioral homework assignments for practice of skill outside of classroom.	Ask students which responses to cigarette offers they think would work best in different everyday situations, such as at school, at a party, or with large groups of friends. Ask students to practice one of the techniques in a situation that comes up in their daily lives.

The LST prevention program consists of three major components. The first component is designed to teach students a set of general self-management skills, and the second focuses on general social skills. These two components are designed to enhance personal and social competence and to decrease motivations to use drugs and vulnerability to social influences that support drug use. The third component of LST focuses on information and skills that are specific to drug use in order to promote drug resistance skills, anti-drug attitudes, and anti-drug norms. A brief description of the major components of the LST program follows:

Personal self-management skills: The personal skills component of the LST program is designed to impact on a broad array of self-management skills. To accomplish this, the personal skills component contains material to foster the development of decision making and problem solving (e.g., identifying problems, defining goals, generating alternative solutions, considering consequences), teaches skills for identifying, analyzing, and resisting media influences, and provides students with self-control skills for coping with anxiety (e.g., relaxation training) and anger/frustration (e.g., inhibiting impulsive reactions, reframing, using self-statements).

Social skills: The social skills component is designed to impact on several important interpersonal skills in order to enhance general social competence. This social skills component contains material designed to help students improve general interpersonal skills such as how to overcome shyness, how to give and receive compliments, how to initiate social interactions, as well as skills related to dating relationships and assertiveness (verbal and nonverbal).

Drug-related information and skills: This component is designed to impact on knowledge and attitudes concerning drug use, normative expectations, and skills for resisting drug use influences from peers and the media. Included is a focus on the short-term consequences of drug use, knowledge about the actual levels of drug use among adolescents and adults in order to correct normative expectations about drug use, information about the declining social acceptability of cigarette smoking and other drug use, information and class exercises demonstrating the immediate physiological effects of cigarette smoking, and material concerning peer and media pressures to smoke, drink, or use drugs and ways to resist these pressures.

Program Materials and Methods Curriculum materials have been developed to standardize the implementation of the LST program and increase its exportability. These materials consist of a Teacher's Manual and Student Guide for each year of the program (more information is available at www.lifeskillstraining.com). The LST program is taught using cognitive-behavioral skills training techniques, facilitated group discussion, classroom demonstrations, and traditional didactic teaching methods. The material is most effectively taught through facilitated group discussion and skills training exercises, although conventional teaching methods are appropriate for some of the content. Because the major emphasis of the LST program is on the teaching of personal self-management skills, social skills, and drug resistance skills, the most important intervention method is skills training. The cognitive-behavioral skills in the LST program are taught using a combination of instruction, demonstration, behavioral rehearsal, feedback, social reinforcement, and extended practice in the form of behavioral homework assignments.

Effectiveness of the LST Program Since the early 1980s, a series of evaluation studies have demonstrated that the LST approach produces positive behavioral effects on alcohol, tobacco, and other drug use. The focus of the initial LST evaluation studies was on cigarette smoking and involved predominantly White middle-class populations. This research consisted largely of small-scale pilot studies testing the short-term effects of the intervention on cigarette smoking and related risk factors. Several early studies demonstrated that the LST approach effectively reduces cigarette smoking among youth receiving the program compared to a control group that does not (e.g., Botvin & Eng, 1982). Initial studies also demonstrated that the LST prevention program was made more effective by the inclusion of booster sessions after the initial year of intervention, that it is equally effective when taught by teachers, peer leaders, and health educators (Botvin, Renick, & Baker, 1983), and that the program was also effective in preventing alcohol and marijuana use (e.g., Botvin, Baker, Renick, Filazzola, & Botvin, 1984). These initial studies were among the first school-based prevention studies to show consistent behavioral effects on adolescent drug use.

More recent research on the LST program has focused on the intervention's long-term effects on drug use, effects on more serious levels of drug involvement, including illicit drug use, its impact on hypothesized mediating variables, and its effectiveness when used with inner-city minority populations. The evaluation designs have become increasingly sophisticated with time, including two large-scale multisite randomized prevention trials with long-term follow-up. The first of these prevention trials began in 1985 and focused on predominantly White, suburban youth. In this large, randomized controlled prevention trial, we examined the short- and long-term effects of the LST approach among close to 6,000 students from 56 junior high schools in New York State. Students in the LST condition received the intervention in the seventh grade and booster sessions during the eighth and ninth grades. Significant prevention effects were found among intervention participants at the end of the ninth grade in terms of cigarette smoking, marijuana use, and immoderate alcohol use (Botvin, Baker, Dusenbury, Tortu, & Botvin, 1990) as well as at the end of the twelfth grade (Botvin et al., 1995). In the latter follow-up study, there were significantly fewer smokers, heavy drinkers, marijuana users, and polydrug users among students who received the LST prevention program relative to controls. The strongest prevention effects were produced for the students who received the most complete implementation of the prevention program. A related study using data from a confidential and random subsample of these students ($N = 447$) found that there were lower levels of overall illicit drug use and significantly lower levels of use for hallucinogens, heroin, and other narcotics in the LST group relative to controls (Botvin et al., 2000).

More recently, a rigorous large-scale prevention trial of the LST program was conducted with a sample of predominantly African American (61%) and Hispanic (22%) sample of students ($N = 3,621$) in 29 urban schools. Results at the posttest and one-year follow-up indicated that those who received the LST program reported less smoking, drinking, drunkenness, inhalant use, and polydrug use relative to those in the control group who did not receive LST (Botvin, Griffin, Diaz, & Ifill-Williams, 2001a). Two additional studies using this data focused on prevention effects of the LST program in terms of cigarette smoking onset and binge drinking. The first of these examined prevention effects on the initiation and escalation of smoking in a subsample of girls from the larger study (Botvin, Griffin, Diaz, Miller, & Ifill-Williams, 1999). One-year follow-up data indicated that girls who participated in the LST program were significantly less likely to initiate smoking relative to controls, and 30% fewer LST participants escalated to monthly smoking relative to students in the control group. A second study showed that the LST program had protective effects in terms of binge drinking (five or more drinks per drinking occasion) among inner-city middle-school boys and girls (Botvin, Griffin,

Diaz, & Ifill-Williams, 2001b). In this study, the proportion of binge drinkers was over 50% lower in those who received the LST program relative to the control group at both the one-year and two-year follow-up assessments. In addition, a recent study of a subset of students from the larger sample examined the effectiveness of the prevention program among youth at high risk for substance use initiation. Findings indicated that those students in the prevention program who had poor grades in school and friends that engage in substance use were less likely to engage in smoking, drinking, inhalant use, or polydrug use compared to similarly matched controls that did not receive the intervention (Griffin, Botvin, Nichols, & Doyle, 2003).

While most evaluation research on LST has been conducted among suburban and inner-city youth, a recent study examined the effects of LST in a rural midwestern sample of 847 middle school students (Trudeau, Spoth, Lillehoj, Redmond, & Wickrama, 2003). This study used growth curve analysis to examine the effects of the LST prevention program on growth trajectories of substance initiation (alcohol, tobacco, and marijuana) and found that the intervention significantly slowed the rate of increase in substance initiation in intervention students compared to controls, and these effects were observed for both boys and girls. Taken together, the results from several large-scale randomized prevention trials provide strong evidence of the effectiveness of the LST program among students from different geographic regions (e.g., urban, suburban, rural), socioeconomic, and racial-ethnic backgrounds.

Generalizability of Prevention Effects Competence-enhancement based prevention programs such as LST teach young people ways to use cognitive and social skills to confront, struggle with, and master developmental tasks and also aim to increase resilience to the social, environmental, and intrapsychic forces that promote and maintain problem behaviors. Thus, this type of approach is likely to generalize to other risky behaviors. Indeed, skills-training programs that enhance social and personal competence have been found to be a useful prevention approach not only for drug abuse, but also for adolescent depression, delinquency, and aggression, and have been found to promote positive youth development and school success as well (Flay, 2002; Frey, Hirschstein, & Guzzo, 2000; Zins, Elias, Greenberg, & Weissberg, 2000).

As an example of the generalizability of effects, we recently examined the extent to which participation in the LST program during junior high school produced prevention effects on risky driving behavior among high school students (Griffin, Botvin, & Nichols, 2003). In this study, self-report data collected from students in the seventh and twelfth grades was matched by name to students' department of motor vehicles (DMV) records at the end of high school. The DMV data included the total number of violations on students' driving records as well as the number of "points" that indicate the frequency and severity of the violations. Controlling for gender and alcohol use, students who received the LST prevention program during junior high school engaged in less risky driving as seniors in high school (i.e., about 17% had violations/points on their driving records), relative to control group participants that did not receive the prevention program (about 26% of whom had violations/points). These results support the hypothesis that the behavioral effects of competence-enhancement prevention programs can extend to risk behaviors beyond the initial focus of intervention.

EXTENDING LESSONS LEARNED TO OTHER ADDICTIVE BEHAVIORS

Less research has examined the primary prevention of addictive disorders other than substance abuse. However, there are small but growing literatures in preventing problem gambling, eating disorders, and other compulsive behaviors. Also, because depression is a key risk factor for compulsive behaviors, prevention programs for depression may hold promise for preventing addictive behaviors, and several promising prevention approaches have been identified.

PREVENTING PROBLEM GAMBLING

The extent of problem gambling among youth in the United States is estimated to be between 4% to 8% of adolescents (Dickson, Derevensky, & Gupta, 2002). Many experts believe that problem gambling among youth and adults will become an increasingly important problem in years to come due to the rapid expansion of legalized gambling (including state lotteries) over the past 25 years. Furthermore, retrospective studies have found that the vast majority of adults with gambling problems began to gamble as adolescents, suggesting that it is important to intervene with adolescents. Several of the risk and protective factors for problem gambling among youth are similar to those for adolescent substance abuse. These *common* risk factors include low self-esteem, higher rates of depression and anxiety, and poor coping skills. Risk factors *unique* to problem gambling include paternal pathological gambling, access to gambling venues, and early onset of gambling experiences (Dickson et al., 2002). Gambling, like substance use, is often viewed by adolescents as a means of appearing grown-up, mature, and sophisticated. Little is known about specific protective factors for youth problem gambling.

There is currently a small number of prevention programs for youth problem gambling. The most common approach in gambling prevention is to apply concepts of mathematics to everyday life for young people in order to emphasize the mathematical odds against winning. For example, the National Center for Responsible Gaming (NCRG) and the Division on Addictions at Harvard Medical School have created a gambling prevention curriculum for middle-school students called *Facing the Odds: The Mathematics of Gambling and Other Risks* (see www.ncrg.org). The *Facing the Odds* curriculum is designed to increase students' interest and critical thinking abilities when it comes to the mathematics and probability so that they can develop rational views about gambling and make their own informed choices when confronted with the opportunity to gamble. Furthermore, in some areas of the United States, there are legislative efforts underway to introduce mandated gambling prevention messages into school curricula, and many educators have concluded that introducing this material in earlier grades (fifth through eighth grades) is most effective, before problem gambling begins (Kanigher, 2001).

However, it is somewhat unclear the extent to which existing gambling prevention approaches are based on psychosocial theory and address the relevant risk and protective factors for problem gambling. As in drug abuse prevention, we may find that simply providing information is an inadequate prevention approach for problem gambling and that more intensive approaches that promote impulse control and related self-management skills may be most effective. In fact, several studies of youth gambling have found a relationship between gambling

> "The sooner you can get preventive information into their brains, the more successful you can be at preventing chronic gambling problems later in life. We seem to be shifting a lot of social responsibilities to the schools, but that's because the students are not getting that information at home."
>
> ───────────
>
> Andrea Stillman, Connecticut Democratic Representative, who has cosponsored a bill that would target gambling prevention messages to students in fifth through eighth grades as quoted in "Gambling Prevention 101" by Steve Kanigher, *Las Vegas Sun*, February 17, 2001.

involvement and adolescent drug use. Vitaro, Ferland, Jacques, and Ladouceur (1998) found that those youth who were problem gamblers were more likely to engage in problematic levels of substance use and vice versa, compared to those without either problem. Furthermore, findings indicated that participants with both problems were more impulsive than those with only one of the problems. These findings suggest that problem gambling and substance abuse may develop simultaneously during adolescence and share a common origin related to deficits in impulse control. This suggests that a promising direction for prevention programs for problem gambling among youth is to incorporate the promotion of *resilience* as its main goal and to view problem gambling as part of a broad spectrum of problematic adolescent risk-taking behaviors (i.e., substance abuse, risky sexual activity, mental health problems) that can be prevented by reducing developmental risk factors and enhancing protective ones (Dickson et al., 2002).

PREVENTING EATING DISORDERS

Eating disorders are relatively rare, with estimates of lifetime prevalence of anorexia nervosa of less than 1%, and binge eating disorder estimated to occur in about 3% of American women. The ratio of eating disorder diagnoses among women and men is believed to be about 10:1. This, along with the complex etiology of eating disorders, has made it difficult to identify the most important risk and protective factors that prevention programs can focus on. Like problem gambling, eating disorders share a *common* set of risk and protective factors with substance abuse, including depression, anxiety, poor coping skills, negative life events, susceptibility to peer pressure, desire for social acceptance, and low self-esteem. Risk and protective factors *unique* to eating disorders include childhood obesity, body image dissatisfaction, weight concerns, drive for thinness, perfectionism, and inappropriate eating and weight loss behaviors, such as laxative use and fasting (McVey, Pepler, Davis, Flett, & Abdolell, 2002).

Reviews of the literature on preventing eating disorders have identified over 20 programs, most of which are universal prevention approaches designed for classroom settings (Austin, 2000; Levine & Smolak, 2001). Some experts caution against eating disorder education programs that simply focus on providing factual information about normal and disordered eating because such information alone may unintentionally reinforce the behaviors they intend to eliminate (Berel & Irving, 1988). Therefore, it is crucial that prevention programs are comprehensive and address the underlying societal influences promoting thinness as the ideal. The goals of such programs are to teach young people to refute the thinness ideal by critically evaluating unrealistic images of women in advertising and media, helping young people place less importance on physical appearance, emphasizing that diversity in physical body shape and size is natural and influenced in large part by genetics, and encourage healthy eating and exercise patterns. While some of the existing prevention programs have produced increases in knowledge and/or improvements in attitudes about body image, few have produced effects on eating behaviors, and none of the effects have been long-term. Some experts have argued that eating disorder prevention programs should also emphasize generic skills training, such as skills related to problem solving, decision making, assertiveness, communication, and other life skills that can help prevent negative affect, low self-esteem, social insecurity, and other potential contributors to negative body image and unhealthy eating behaviors (Levine & Smolak, 2001). However, such comprehensive programs for eating disorders have not been adequately tested to date.

There is considerable evidence that eating disorders aggregate in families, suggesting that genetics and/or social learning factors play an important etiologic role. This in turn suggests that targeted interventions for the children of parents with eating disorders may be appropriate, although such interventions have not yet been attempted (Pearson, Goldklang, & Striegel-Moore, 2002). Primary prevention programs for eating disorders in middle and junior school may be most helpful in identifying high-risk youth and referring these youth and their families into targeted or selected prevention programs or early treatment programs (Rosen & Neumark-Sztainer, 1988). Such programs should focus on parenting skills to increase the quality of communication between adolescents and their parents, preferably prior to the onset of puberty and the normative developmental challenges of this time of life.

There is some evidence that eating disorders prevention programs for older adolescents, such as intensive programs for high school and college students, can be effective. Several selective interventions have been tested with promising results. For example, one study tested an eating disorder prevention program among a high risk sample of junior and senior high school students attending a residential ballet school, and found significant reductions in disordered eating patterns and disturbed attitudes about eating and body shape, as well as significant increases in healthy eating patterns (Piran, 1999). Another preventive intervention designed as a college course titled "Eating Disorders" for female undergraduate students was tested in a controlled trial (Stice & Ragan, 2002). The intervention provided information about eating disorders, the risk factors and consequences of these behaviors, as well as information on healthy eating and weight control techniques. Findings indicated that students in the prevention program showed significant decreases in thin-ideal internalization, body dissatisfaction, dieting, eating disorder symptoms, and body mass over a 4-month period, while those in the control condition did not show any changes on these outcomes. The finding of a decrease in body mass in those who received the prevention program suggests that eating disorder prevention programs may also be effective in preventing overweight or obesity. The idea of combining eating disorders and obesity prevention is gaining currency, not only for practical reasons (e.g., reduced costs and increased efficiency and synergy of prevention programming) but also because obesity, eating disorders, and healthy weight loss practices may not be as conceptually distinct as previously thought (Irving & Neumark-Sztainer, 2002). This is an important area for future prevention research.

PREVENTING COMPULSIVE BUYING

Little research has examined the risk and protective factors for compulsive buying. However, in our consumer culture, it is widely recognized that many people value spending over saving, and many people purchase goods and services that they do not need for purposes such as status-enhancement, to provoke envy in others, and in the pursuit of pleasure. Social norms regarding buying and credit have changed for the worse in the United States where many young people view financial debt as normative and part of becoming an adult. Indeed, among young adults, obtaining one's first credit card may be viewed as a rite of passage into adulthood. Unfortunately, credit cards are widely available and aggressively marketed on college campuses, even to students with no jobs, income, or credit history (Fickenscher, 1994). Students often take advantage of this source of easy credit, with an estimated 60% of college students having their own credit cards. However, because college students are frequently inexperienced when it comes to credit, they may view the money involved in credit card transactions as unreal or abstract. This can precipitate patterns of overspending that can lead to compulsive buying. Compulsive buying has been referred to as "chronic, repetitive purchasing that becomes a primary response to negative events or feelings" and has been found to be widespread on college campuses (Roberts & Jones, 2001). Compulsive buying and the indiscriminate use of credit are believed to play a central role in the record number of personal bankruptcies in the United States, which peaked in 1998 (Adler, 2000).

Several programs are available to help young people make good decisions about spending and credit. Many financial experts recommend that parents teach their adolescent children about responsible spending and the pitfalls of credit card debt. Many initiatives aimed at preventing problem buying target high school students, a time when many young people get their first paying jobs, and college students, when young people are likely to have their first access to credit. For example, the National Endowment for Financial Education (NEFE)—a nonprofit organization that provides publications and programs to enhance financial literacy for individuals, schools, and organizations—offers a six-part program on financial planning for high school students called NEFE High School Financial Planning Program (HSFPP). HSFPP is a classroom-based program that provides young people with information and skills to help them manage their personal finances in the areas of goal setting, budgeting, and saving, as well as in other areas of effective money management. It is targeted to high school students so that it can affect young people as they are developing habits and attitudes about money that will influence them for years to come. This program is available at no cost to high schools throughout the country (see www.nefe.org). For college students, some universities are starting to counsel students who get into trouble with their credit cards, and some universities teach students how to handle debt even before classes start. For example, Boston University makes incoming freshmen attend a seminar on the use of credit cards (Schembari, 2000). A variety of other publications are available to help young people learn money management skills, including resources from the Nellie Mae Foundation, which offers a guide to borrowing and using credit for college-bound students called *Meet the Challenge* (see www.nelliemae.com); Master-Card offers *Money Talks,* a brochure for parents and their high-school and college-age children (see www.collegeparents.org) and, along with the federal Office of Consumer Affairs, MasterCard publishes a booklet called *Kids, Cash, Plastic and You* (available from MasterCard by calling 800-999-5136) that helps parents teach their kids about money, credit, budgeting, and financial responsibility.

PREVENTING DEPRESSION

As mentioned earlier, depression is a key risk factor for compulsive behaviors, so prevention programs for depression may hold promise for preventing addictive behaviors. Psychosocial risk factors for adolescent depression include a variety of factors including negative life events, relationship difficulties, interpersonal skills deficits, and a cognitive style characterized by pessimistic attributions and expectations, whereas protective factors for adolescent depression include family and peer support, coping skills, positive self-esteem, interpersonal problem-solving skills, and positive problem-solving skills. With the exception of pessimistic explanatory style, these are similar to the risk and protective factors for other negative outcomes during adolescence that contribute to later addictive and compulsive behaviors.

Many prevention programs for adolescent depression have been selective or targeted interventions, such as programs for young people whose parents are depressed or have recently divorced (Greenberg, Domitrovich, & Bumbarger, 2001). However, a number of universal school-based programs for preventing depression are beginning to appear in the research literature. For example, the Problem Solving for Life (PSFL) program provides middle school students with training in cognitive restructuring and problem-solving skills. The teacher-led program includes eight class sessions designed to be implemented once a week for 8 weeks, and intervention methods include the presentation of didactic material, group interactive exercises and activities, out-of-school practice, and diary keeping. A recent study found that the PSFL program was effective in preventing symptoms of depression and increasing problem-solving skills at the posttest assessment, particularly among high-risk youth with initially elevated depression scores (Spence, Sheffield, & Donovan, 2003). However, results were not maintained at the 12-month follow-up assessment.

Programs for college students have also shown promising results. A selective preventive intervention that targeted university students with pessimistic explanatory styles was recently tested among 231 first-year undergraduate students (Seligman, Schulman, DeRubeis, & Hollon, 1999). The program taught skills that are normally the focus of cognitive therapy, such as understanding the relationship between thoughts, feelings, and behaviors; identifying automatic negative thoughts, disputing them, and replacing them with more constructive interpretations; interpersonal skills; stress management; coping skills. Participants were randomized to either the cognitive-behavioral workshops (2-hour sessions that met weekly for 8 weeks) or a control group and were followed for 3 years. Participants were excluded if they were receiving psychotherapy or medication for psychological problems or if they met criteria for past or present major depression, substance abuse or dependence, panic disorder, and several other psychiatric diagnoses. Findings indicated that the workshop group had significantly fewer episodes of generalized anxiety disorder and showed a trend toward fewer major depressive episodes compared to the control group, and the workshop group had significantly fewer moderate depressive episodes but no fewer severe depressive episodes. Women benefited more from the workshop than men. In terms of symptoms, the workshop group had significantly fewer depressive symptoms and anxiety symptoms than the control group, as measured by self-report but not by clinicians' ratings. These promising results are important because they suggest that episodes of depression and anxiety can be prevented at an early stage of life by interventions in schools and colleges. This is particularly important because it is estimated that fewer than 20% of individuals with an affective disorder seek treatment.

MOVING PREVENTION FORWARD

Several lessons have been learned from the field of adolescent drug abuse that will help prevention research in other areas of addiction move forward. First, the scientific knowledge base describing the epidemiology and risk/protective factors for each addictive disorder will need to be broadened and expanded, particularly for some of the addictive disorders that have received less research attention. This will be a critical component in the development of relevant psychosocial theory regarding the etiology of each disorder, which in turn can be used as the basis for developing theory-driven preventive intervention programs. Furthermore, the short- and long-term harmful consequences of each addictive behavior will need to be documented, including the consequences of early onset of behaviors that may serve as precursors to later clinical disorder. By documenting these consequences, researchers and practitioners will be in a better position to call attention to the need for prevention and, in turn, obtain the funding needed for well-designed prevention research.

The latter issue—funding for prevention research—is an important one because the process of developing preventive interventions and adequately testing their efficacy and effectiveness is a complex and expensive task. In the history of drug abuse prevention research, a number of lessons have been learned regarding what the key components of effective prevention programs are and the characteristics of programs that work. Further, success in showing effectiveness of specific prevention programs has been linked to the ability to carry out increasingly sophisticated studies in terms of research design. The use of randomized controlled trials is the gold standard in drug abuse prevention research and will be so for other areas of prevention research. Fortunately, much has been learned regarding how best to design and carry out effectiveness studies in the field of prevention. We have learned much in terms of how to collect valid and reliable data, the importance of retaining participants in prevention trials over the follow-up period, and issues related to how to analyze prevention data, in particular when the unit of assignment is a school or other cluster and the unit of analysis is the individual. Another key factor in moving prevention forward (that is now at the forefront of drug abuse prevention research) is the issue of disseminating effective programs into real-world settings. No matter how effective evidence-based prevention programs may be, they will not have a significant benefit in terms of public health impact until they are widely disseminated and adopted. The next sections discuss these topics in depth: (1) the common characteristics of effective prevention programs, (2) how to design and carry out evaluation research to test the effectiveness of promising prevention programs, and (3) issues in disseminating effective prevention programs into real-world settings.

As mentioned earlier, most of the advances in the primary prevention of addictive disorders has been in the field of drug abuse prevention. Several effective prevention programs have been developed and tested in recent years. There are also a number of lists distributed by federal agencies that highlight promising and model prevention programs. To sort out what works and what doesn't work, a number of literature reviews and meta-analyses have sought to identify the factors that characterize effective prevention approaches (Cuijpers, 2002; Tobler & Stratton, 1997). Other researchers have conducted interviews with prevention experts to identify critical characteristics of programs that work (Dusenbury & Falco, 1995). Next, we present a list of essential characteristics of school-based prevention programs for adolescents, compiled from the existing literature.

Effective School-Based Prevention Programs

- *Based on a sound theoretical foundation.* Prevention programs should aim to reduce specific risk factors and promote specific protective factors, and these targeted factors for intervention should be guided by a comprehensive psychosocial theoretical framework that addresses key etiologic factors in the behavioral outcome derived from empirical evidence.
- *Provide developmentally appropriate information.* Information about the behavior that is the focus of the prevention program should be age-appropriate and match the level of intervention (i.e., universal, targeted, or indicated). Universal prevention programs should focus on initiation of the behavior rather than outright addiction. For example, universal drug prevention programs for early adolescents should focus on gateway substance use (alcohol,

---

Criteria for Effective School-Based Prevention Programs

Based on a sound theoretical foundation.

Provide developmentally appropriate information.

Include social resistance skills training.

Include normative education.

Include personal and social skills training.

Delivered using interactive methods.

Culturally sensitive to target population.

Include adequate dosage and booster sessions.

Target multiple behaviors.

Include the use of peer leaders.

Provide comprehensive training to teachers or other program providers.

Include family or community components in addition to school component.

Have demonstrated behavioral effects in a randomized controlled trial.

Have produced durable behavioral effects.

tobacco, and marijuana) rather than injection drug use; universal programs for preventing problem gambling should focus on the odds against winning rather than compulsive gambling.

- *Include social resistance skills training (i.e., peer refusal skills).* It is important to teach young people how to recognize and resist pressures to engage in unhealthy behaviors, be it experimenting with drug use, unhealthy eating, or gambling. Students should be taught ways to avoid high-risk situations in which they are likely to experience social pressure, as well as skills in ways to handle social pressure when it occurs.

- *Include normative education.* Adolescents often overestimate the prevalence of behavior problems. Thus, a key ingredient of prevention programs is to provide accurate information regarding actual rates of behavior in order to reduce the perception that a particular behavior is common and normative behavior. Adolescents should be given appropriate information demonstrating that in fact most young people do not use drugs, most gamblers lose money, and most women are not thin.

- *Include personal and social skills training.* Students should be taught a variety of general skills that will help them successfully maneuver through adolescence, such as assertiveness, decision-making, problem-solving, and communication skills.

- *Delivered using interactive methods.* School-based prevention programs that use interactive methods (e.g., classroom discussion, structured small group activities, role-playing scenarios, interactive games, other group processes and classroom dynamics) to deliver program content are much more effective than those using more didactic formats (e.g., lectures, films, videotapes). One meta-analysis concluded that the most effective drug abuse prevention programs use these types of interactive techniques to introduce program content, stimulate participation of students, and promote the acquisition of skills (Tobler & Stratton, 1997).

- *Culturally sensitive to target population.* Prevention programs should aim to foster cultural identity by including relevant language and audiovisual content that is familiar to the target audience. The type of content that would be appropriate for the target population can be obtained through focus group data.

- *Include adequate dosage and booster sessions.* School-based programs should ideally be delivered in many sessions across multiple years and should be most intensive during the years when youth first begin to experiment with the outcome behavior. Booster sessions in subsequent years should be used to reinforce and update what is learned.

- *Target multiple behaviors.* Programs that target more than one behavior will generally be more efficient because many risk factors for addictive behaviors are interrelated, and an individual's motivation for engaging in maladaptive behavior often extends to multiple behaviors. Programs that target multiple outcomes are likely to be more feasible in terms of time commitment and expense compared to several single topic prevention programs.

- *Include the use of peer leaders.* One way to facilitate interaction and discussion among peers is to use same-age or slightly older peer leaders as program providers or discussion leaders. Because adolescence is a time characterized by some degree of rebellion against adult authority figures peer providers often have greater credibility than adults when discussing decisions about behavior among school-age students. Peer providers may also serve as influential role models that can help to alter school norms regarding the social acceptability of various risk behaviors. However, because peer providers may lack the teaching, motivational, and classroom management skills that adult providers possess, they may function best as assistants to adult program providers who supervise them and give them well-defined responsibilities.

- *Provide comprehensive training to teachers or other program providers.* Teacher training is a key factor in generating teacher enthusiasm and support for an evidence-based prevention program. Training should use the type of interactive techniques commonly found in effective school-based programs (e.g., group discussion and other interactive, skill-based, cognitive-behavioral teaching techniques) so that teachers can learn and increase their confidence in being able to teach using these methods. Comprehensive training can also enhance program implementation fidelity by providing high-quality technical assistance resources to teachers—before, during, and after program implementation.

- *Include family or community components in addition to school component.* School-based programs combined with parent or community interventions can lead to greater behavioral effects than school-based programs by themselves. These additional components are likely to reinforce what is taught in the school-based program and provide opportunities for family discussions about the dangers of risk behaviors and setting family rules regarding these behaviors. In smoking prevention, for example, Flynn and colleagues (1994) reported that school-based smoking prevention programming led to less smoking over two years of follow-up when it was combined with community-wide radio and television announcements, and the school-plus-media intervention was more effective than the school-only intervention.

- *Have demonstrated behavioral effects in a randomized controlled trial.* Many evaluation reports have traditionally focused on knowledge and attitudes without reporting on behavior. Effects on knowledge and attitudes, even in a direction consistent with decreased risk behavior, is increasingly viewed as inadequate evidence of program effectiveness. The outcome measure that is most important is actual behavior.

- *Have produced durable behavioral effects.* A challenge for most areas of prevention is to demonstrate long-term behavioral effects. In drug abuse prevention, several programs show short-term prevention effects, and the next challenge is to demonstrate the durability of these effects. Several longer term follow-up studies (e.g., Ellickson, Bell, & McGuigan, 1993) have indicated that prevention effects produced during junior high school erode by the end of high school. There are several possible explanations for this pattern (Resnicow & Botvin, 1993). These include (1) the length of the intervention may have been inadequate, (2) booster sessions were either not included or were inadequate, (3) the intervention was not implemented with sufficient fidelity to the intervention model, and/or (4) the intervention model was based on faulty assumptions, was incomplete, or was otherwise deficient.

EFFECTIVELY EVALUATING PREVENTION PROGRAMS

In addition to important advances in understanding the etiology and prevention of adolescent problem behaviors, there have also been substantial methodological advances in terms of how to best design a study to evaluate the efficacy or effectiveness of a prevention program. Increasingly, decision makers responsible for selecting prevention programs are required to choose *evidence-based* or *research-based* programs that have been shown to be effective in an appropriately designed evaluation study.

A well-designed evaluation study of a preventive intervention includes the following features:

1. Inclusion of a control group that did not receive the intervention that is assessed simultaneously to the intervention group,
2. Random assignment of individuals (or more commonly, schools or communities) to intervention or control conditions,
3. Pretest data collected from both intervention and control groups prior to the intervention demonstrates pretest equivalence in demographic and behavioral characteristics between groups,
4. Relatively low attrition rates that are similar across the intervention and control groups, and
5. Adequate training and written protocols for those involved in providing the intervention and those who collect the data.

ELEMENTS OF AN APPROPRIATE PROGRAM EVALUATION

Data collection instruments have been tested and shown to be valid and reliable.

Data collection protocols and procedures emphasize the confidential nature of the data being collected to enhance the truthfulness of participant responses.

When possible, biochemical indicators are collected simultaneously with survey data to enhance the validity of the self-report data.

A control or comparison group of participants who did not receive the intervention is assessed simultaneously with the intervention group.

The demographic and behavioral characteristics are similar across the intervention and control group participants.

Units are randomly assigned to the intervention and control conditions.

Pretest data is collected from both intervention and control groups prior to the intervention.

Program implementation fidelity is monitored as part of a comprehensive process evaluation.

Follow-up data collected after the intervention includes a large percentage of the original sample.

Attrition of participants is examined and shown to be similar across intervention and control groups.

Attrition of high risk youth is examined and shown to be similar across intervention and control groups.

Appropriate statistical techniques that control for school-level clustering are used to analyze the data.

Issues in Study Design   A crucial design component is the inclusion of a control group of participants that did not receive the intervention. The evaluation study must document that participation in the prevention program reduced the incidence or prevalence of the outcome behavior in the intervention group relative to a control group that did not receive the preventive intervention. Because overall rates of problem behaviors frequently escalate during adolescence, some increase would be expected even among a group of students receiving a prevention program. A successful prevention program will reduce the rate of increase of the behavior in those who receive the program compared to a comparison group that does not. Accordingly, an examination of pretest to posttest differences among students receiving a program is not adequate and will be misleading unless one also examines naturally occurring rates of the initiation or escalation in the behavior in a comparable control group.

The best-designed evaluation studies are those that attempt to minimize pretest differences by using random assignment to intervention or control conditions. It is generally advisable to assign entire units (such as schools) to a particular condition in order to avoid contamination across conditions. Prior to random assignment, units should be grouped or "blocked" on relevant covariates. In school-based studies, for example, one might block schools in terms of reading levels; schools with the highest reading levels would be randomly assigned to condition, then schools with moderate reading scores would be assigned, and so on. Studies that use this type of randomized block design are more likely to have equivalent intervention and control groups at the pretest relative to studies that do not.

Issues in Data Collection   Data collection instruments should be tested and shown to be valid and reliable. Data collection protocols and procedures should emphasize the confidential nature of the data being collected to enhance the truthfulness of responses. Biological or biochemical indicators of behavior should be collected simultaneously with survey data to enhance the validity of the self-report data if possible, such as carbon monoxide breath samples in smoking prevention studies. Program implementation fidelity should be monitored as part of a comprehensive process evaluation.

Issues in Participant Retention   Follow-up data should be collected after the initial intervention and should include a large percentage of the original sample. Attrition of participants should be examined and shown to be similar across intervention and control groups. Attrition of high-risk youth should be examined and shown to be similar across intervention and control groups. Whether or not random assignment is used, the evaluation should demonstrate that the intervention and control groups were equivalent on the outcome measures, other risk behaviors, and relevant demographic characteristics at the pretest assessment. This helps to establish that any observed behavioral differences after the intervention were due to the prevention program and not pretest differences. If such pretest differences do exist, they must be controlled for in the statistical analyses.

A well-designed evaluation study will also demonstrate that there is no differential attrition between the intervention and control groups. Participants who drop out of interventions are often at higher risk than those that remain in. Thus, if participants in the intervention condition drop out at a higher rate than those in the control condition, the program will appear to be more effective than it really was, particularly if these dropouts were engaging in the outcome behavior at the pretest measurement. Finally, a cardinal rule of experimental research is the importance of standardization. Intervention and data collection procedures should be documented in written protocols, and individuals involved in providing the program or collecting data must be thoroughly trained to ensure standardization.

Issues in Data Analysis   The primary focus in determining the efficacy of prevention programs rests with measurement of change at the individual level. Participants should be assessed over a period of time in terms of the outcome behavior and relevant risk and protective factors that are the targeted causal agents of change. Despite the emphasis on assessing individual-level change, individual participants are often *not* the unit of assignment to treatment condition in prevention programs. Instead, entire units (e.g., schools or communities) are typically assigned to a treatment condition, which affords a researcher the greatest level of control against potential biases such as contamination across conditions and other threats to internal validity. However, random assignment of units to treatment and control conditions raises several issues related to how to handle nested or multilevel units. One issue is statistical power. When larger units of participants are assigned to condition and the individual is the unit of observation (i.e., program-related change is based on assessment of individual participants' behavior), there is a considerable loss of statistical power because usually there are fewer units than individuals for conducting statistical comparisons (and therefore only very large effects will be noted). Researchers conducting prevention trials may have access to a large number of students but a relatively small number of units that are available for random assignment to the experimental conditions.

A second concern is that participants within larger units tend to cluster together with respect to the behavioral outcomes of interest, as well as risk and protective factor profiles. For example, in school-based studies, the behaviors among students within schools may be more similar than behavior of students across schools. This can result from factors such as social contagion, peer selection, and other peer socialization processes. Friendship groups share similar activities and interests, and these groups occur naturally within schools boundaries and can facilitate social learning regarding a wide variety of behaviors and contribute to similarities in normative beliefs regarding behavior.

Given the clustering of participants within larger units of assignment, prevention researchers must consider how the magnitude of clustering affects power calculations and statistical analysis of outcome data. For example, failure to correct for the magnitude of clustering (i.e., intragroup dependence) by examining only individual-level data results in misspecification of the model and poses a threat to internal validity. The most serious threat is a violation of the independence-of-errors assumption that is critical for conducting inferential statistical tests to determine treatment effects. Discounting the variation due to the cluster biases standard errors of the treatment effect estimates and increases the Type I error rate (i.e., the probability that a researcher will reject a true null hypothesis). On the other hand, restricting the analyses to include only group-level effects discounts important individual-level variation that may reflect hypothesized processes of individual-level change. One effective solution to this problem is to compute the degree of relatedness of students within intact assignment units and adjust any further statistical comparisons conducted at the individual level by the magnitude of intragroup dependence. The intraclass correlation coefficient (ICC) measures the magnitude of the variation in the data that is attributed to the unit of assignment and can range from −1.00 to +1.00. The formula for computing this appears in several publications and is defined as the ratio of school-level variance to the total variance for the individual. Statistical techniques that control for school-level clustering can be used to analyze multilevel data, including mixed models and generalized estimating questions (e.g., Norton, Bieler, Ennett, & Zarkin, 1996).

IMPORTANCE OF PROGRAM DISSEMINATION

While the number of research-based prevention programs has increased in recent years, a gap remains in what we know about how to effectively translate these programs into practice. A theoretical model that is useful for conceptualizing the process of bringing effective prevention programs to scale is the diffusion of innovations model developed by Rogers (1995). Diffusion of innovation refers to the process by which new knowledge is "communicated through specific channels over time among members of a social system" (Rogers, 1995, p. 5). This model represents a useful starting point for developing strategies to promote the use of efficacious programs and practices. Rogers proposes that the process of diffusing innovative health behavior interventions involves four stages: dissemination, adoption, implementation, and maintenance. Dissemination refers to the process by which effective innovations are spread or distributed, adoption refers to the decision processes by which organizations decide to use an innovation, implementation refers to the degree to which the program is delivered with fidelity to its original design, and maintenance refers to how a program is institutionalized over time.

Research is needed on each stage of the diffusion process so that the public health benefits of evidence-based prevention programs can be realized. Now that more effective prevention programs have been developed and some have been widely disseminated and adopted, the challenges of program implementation and maintenance are of key interest. In terms of implementation, the challenge is to understand how and why implementation fidelity usually deteriorates when effective programs are taken from research to real world settings. Typically, the initial efficacy trials of prevention programs are under the control of the program designer and implementation occurs under optimal conditions with high levels of funding, motivation, and support. In effectiveness studies, programs are disseminated to naturalistic settings under less favorable conditions, and the chances for inconsistencies in program delivery and for key program components to be modified become more likely (Dane & Schneider, 1998). In the next and final stage of dissemination, when programs are packaged and provided to prevention practitioners (i.e., end-users) for use in real-world settings, implementation fidelity is most variable and, in many cases, fidelity is poor. For example, a study of research-based drug prevention programs in 104 school districts in 12 states found that only 19% of the schools were implementing the programs with fidelity (Hallfors & Godette, 2002). A growing concern is that as evidence-based programs are taken to scale, poor implementation fidelity may reduce effectiveness in real-world settings where program providers are not trained as well or monitored when delivering the program.

THE IMPORTANCE OF PROCESS EVALUATIONS

The study of implementation process has been limited to date, and only recently have evaluation studies started to measure program implementation. In the field of drug abuse prevention, a review of 181 school-based studies published from 1980 to 1990 in seven journals known for behaviorally based interventions found that only 15% measured implementation integrity (Gresham, Gansle, Noell, Cohen, & Rosenbaum, 1993). Moreover, among studies that do measure implementation, many do not examine the relationship between implementation fidelity and program outcomes (Scheirer & Rezmovic, 1983). In a review of 34 rigorously evaluated programs to prevent mental disorders in school-age children, only 11 studies (32%) used implementation information in the outcome analyses (Domitrovich & Greenberg, 2000). Despite this relative lack of attention to implementation fidelity, research has clearly shown that implementation quantity and quality play a central role in how effective prevention programs will be. Studies that have included an analysis of implementation fidelity (i.e., process evaluations) have consistently shown superior outcomes when programs are implemented with high fidelity (Dane & Schneider, 1998; Gottfredson, Gottfredson, & Hybl, 1993; Gresham et al., 1993). In one of the largest meta-analyses of school-based drug abuse prevention programs, Tobler and Stratton (1997) concluded that problems related to program implementation have the largest impact in decreasing the effectiveness of these programs.

Due to the demonstrated importance of implementation fidelity in program effectiveness, the field of prevention must identify the factors that impede high-quality implementation and take steps to break down these barriers. Program developers, implementers, and sponsors must work together to develop strategies to facilitate and enhance implementation. Research has identified a large number of barriers that can interfere with high-fidelity implementation and reduce overall program effectiveness. These barriers included a lack of provider training and program materials, inadequate provision of information regarding the program characteristics and efficacy to the target audience, concerns about the appropriateness of a generic innovation "not invented here," and a lack of trust of scientific findings; institutional factors include decentralized decision making and a lack of program guidance from management personnel, and a focus on daily management and organizational survival that takes precedence over strategic planning and innovation (Backer, 1991; Domitrovich & Greenberg, 2000; Hallfors & Godette, 2002; Rogers, 1995).

In school-based prevention research, factors that promote fidelity include provider factors such as knowledge, skills, training, enthusiasm, self-efficacy, and "ownership" of the intervention, along with environmental or institutional factors such as administrative support from principals and district administrators and experienced staff (Rohrbach, Graham, & Hansen, 1993; Smith, Steckler, McCormick, & McLeroy, 1995). Other factors found to contribute to successful program implementation include a linkage to stated goals or missions of the school or district and an overall balance of support from new and seasoned administrators (Gager & Elias, 1997). In our own work, we have found that implementation fidelity is improved by having teachers involved in the adoption decision and having a "critical mass" of teachers and other school personnel from each school trained to implement the prevention program.

CONCLUSION

The field of prevention has grown tremendously in the past two to three decades. The largest body of research and theory in preventing addictive disorders is in the etiology and prevention of drug abuse where much progress has been made in developing effective preventive intervention programs at the school, family, and community levels. This work is likely to hold important lessons for the development of effective prevention programs for other addictive behaviors. A large knowledge base of research findings on the epidemiology, etiologic risk and protective factors, and psychosocial theory of drug use have been central to the development of effective prevention programs. Prevention approaches have developed from information dissemination to skills-based programs that focus on the risk and protective factors for adolescent risk behaviors. There is a small but growing literature on preventing problem gambling and preventing eating disorders that can benefit from lessons learned in drug abuse prevention. Much of the research on preventing drug abuse, problem gambling, and eating disorders focuses on adolescents because it is during this time of life when young people begin to make independent decisions about their own behaviors and are influenced by societal messages regarding adult behavior. A common thread that appears across the different prevention literatures is that a certain level of *psychosocial resilience* plays a central role in keeping young people away from the precursors and risk factors that lead to various addictive behaviors and disorders.

To move prevention forward, the scientific knowledge base describing the epidemiology and risk/protective factors for each addictive disorder will need to be broadened and expanded, particularly for some of the addictive disorders that have received less research attention. Relevant psychosocial theory regarding the etiology of each disorder will need to be developed or expanded. Furthermore, the harmful consequences of each addictive behavior will need to be documented, including the consequences of early onset of behaviors that may serve as precursors to later clinical disorders, to call attention to the need for prevention. Theory-driven preventive intervention programs will need to be tested for efficacy and effectiveness using methodologically rigorous study design and evaluation techniques. In the history of drug abuse prevention research, a number of lessons have been learned regarding what the key components of effective prevention programs are and the characteristics of programs that work. Another key factor in moving prevention forward (that is now at the forefront of drug abuse prevention research) is the issue of disseminating effective programs into real-world settings.

RECOMMENDED READING

Hawkins, J. D., Catalano, R. F., & Miller, J. Y. (1992). Risk and protective factors for alcohol and other drug problems in adolescence and early adulthood: Implications for substance abuse prevention. *Psychological Bulletin, 112,* 64–105. This article comprehensively reviews the research on risk and protective factors for adolescent substance use, including broad societal and cultural factors and factors that lie within individuals and their social environments. Findings are reviewed and implications for prevention intervention are discussed.

Institute of Medicine. (1994). *Reducing risks for mental disorders: Frontiers for preventive intervention research.* In P. J. Mrazek & R. J. Haggerty (Eds.). Washington, DC: National Academy Press. This book reviews recent scientific advances regarding how to effectively reduce risk factors for mental disorders and provides a conceptual framework for the design, application, and evaluation of preventive interventions aimed at risk reduction. The book reviews risk and protective factors and effective intervention approaches for a variety of mental disorders, including Alzheimer's disease, schizophrenia, alcohol abuse and dependence, depressive disorders, and conduct disorders. Recommendations on how to develop effective intervention programs and methods for effectively translating knowledge about prevention into clinical practice are provided.

Petraitis, J., Flay, B. R., & Miller, T. Q. (1995). Reviewing theories of adolescent substance use: Organizing pieces in the puzzle. *Psychological Bulletin, 117,* 67–86. This article reviews the multitude of theories that have been developed to explain why adolescents initiate substance use. These include cognitive theories which describe the role of poor decision-making processes, social learning theories which emphasize the negative influence of substance use role models, personality theories which outline individual vulnerabilities or affective characteristics that lead to drug use, conventional commitment or social attachment theories which outline the processes by which youth withdraw from parents or school and turn to deviant peer groups, as well as several broader theories that attempt to integrate the determinants of adolescent drug use.

Preventing drug use among children and adolescents: A research-based guide for parents, educators, and community leaders (2nd ed.). National Institute on Drug Abuse, National Institute of Health, Washington, DC. This guide reviews research and theory on the origins and pathways of drug abuse and the application of research results to the prevention of drug use among young people. The guide reviews important concepts and findings in order to assist in the development and implementation of effective drug abuse prevention programs, and also reviews several research-based drug abuse prevention programs with proven effectiveness. Included are descriptions of several effective universal, selective, and indicated prevention programs. Available from the National Clearinghouse for Alcohol and Drug Information (CADI) by calling (800) 729-6686.

REFERENCES

Adler, J. (2000). Bankruptcy: Is the worst over? *Credit Card Management, 12,* 58–66.

Ajzen, I. (1988). *Attitudes, personality, and behavior.* Chicago: Dorsey Press.

Akers, R. L., & Cochran, J. K. (1985). Adolescent marijuana use: A test of three theories of deviant behavior. *Deviant Behavior, 6,* 323–346.

Austin, S. B. (2000). Prevention research in eating disorders: Theory and new directions. *Psychological Medicine, 30,* 1249–1262.

Backer, T. E. (1991). *Drug abuse technology transfer.* Rockville, MD: National Institute on Drug Abuse.

Baumrind, D. (1987). A developmental perspective on adolescent risk taking in contemporary America. *New Directions for Child Development, 37,* 93–125.

Becker, M. H. (1974). *The health belief model and personal health behavior.* Thorofare, NJ: Slack.

Berel, S., & Irving, L. M. (1988). Media and disturbed eating: An analysis of media influence and implications for prevention. *Journal of Primary Prevention, 18,* 415–430.

Botvin, G. J. (2000). Preventing drug abuse in schools: Social and competence enhancement approaches targeting individual-level etiological factors. *Addictive Behaviors, 25,* 887–897.

Botvin, G. J., Baker, E., Dusenbury, L., Botvin, E. M., & Diaz, T. (1995). Long-term follow-up results of a randomized drug abuse prevention trial in a white middle-class population. *Journal of the American Medical Association, 273,* 1106–1112.

Botvin, G. J., Baker, E., Dusenbury, L., Tortu, S., & Botvin, E. M. (1990). Preventing adolescent drug abuse through a multimodal cognitive-behavioral approach: Results of a three-year study. *Journal of Consulting and Clinical Psychology, 58,* 437–446.

Botvin, G. J., Baker, E., Renick, N. L., Filazzola, A. D., & Botvin, E. M. (1984). A cognitive-behavioral approach to substance abuse prevention. *Addictive Behaviors, 9*, 137–147.

Botvin, G. J., & Eng, A. (1982). The efficacy of a multicomponent approach to the prevention of cigarette smoking. *Preventive Medicine, 11*, 199–211.

Botvin, G. J., Griffin, K. W., Diaz, T., & Ifill-Williams, M. (2001a). Drug abuse prevention among minority adolescents: Posttest and one-year follow-up of a school-based preventive intervention. *Prevention Science, 2*, 1–13.

Botvin, G. J., Griffin, K. W., Diaz, T., & Ifill-Williams, M. (2001b). Preventing binge drinking during early adolescence: One- and two-year follow-up of a school-based preventive intervention. *Psychology of Addictive Behaviors, 15*, 360–365.

Botvin, G. J., Griffin, K. W., Diaz, T., Miller, N., & Ifill-Williams, M. (1999). Smoking initiation and escalation in early adolescent girls: One-year follow-up of a school-based prevention intervention for minority youth. *Journal of the American Medical Women's Association, 54*, 139–143.

Botvin, G. J., Griffin, K. W., Diaz, T., Scheier, L. M., Williams, C., & Epstein, J. A. (2000). Preventing illicit drug use in adolescents: Long-term follow-up data from a randomized control trial of a school population. *Addictive Behaviors, 5*, 769–774.

Botvin, G. J., Renick, N. L., & Baker, E. (1983). The effects of scheduling format and booster sessions on a broad-spectrum psychosocial smoking prevention program. *Journal of Behavioral Medicine, 6*, 359–379.

Cuijpers, P. (2002). Effective ingredients of school-based drug prevention programs: A systematic review. *Addictive Behaviors, 27*, 1009–1023.

Dane, A. V., & Schneider, B. H. (1998). Program integrity in primary and early secondary prevention: Are implementation effects out of control? *Clinical Psychology Review, 18*, 23–45.

Dickson, L. M., Derevensky, J. L., & Gupta, R. (2002). The prevention of gambling problems in youth: A conceptual framework. *Journal of Gambling Studies, 18*, 97–159.

Domitrovich, C. E., & Greenberg, M. T. (2000). The study of implementation: Current findings from effective programs that prevent mental disorder in school-aged children. *Journal of Educational and Psychological Consultation, 11*, 193–221.

DuPont, R. L. (1997). *The selfish brain: Learning from addiction.* Washington, DC: American Psychiatric Press.

Dusenbury, L., & Falco, M. (1995). Eleven components of effective drug abuse prevention curricula. *Journal of School Health, 65*, 420–425.

Ellickson, P. L., Bell, R. M., & McGuigan, K. (1993). Preventing adolescent drug use: Long term results of a junior high program. *American Journal of Public Health, 83*, 856–861.

Fickenscher, L. (1994). Lenders defend marketing cards to students. *American Banker, 159*, 16–17.

Flay, B. (2002). Positive youth development requires comprehensive health promotion programs. *American Journal of Health Behavior, 26*, 407–424.

Flynn, B. S., Worden, J. K., Secker-Walker, R. H., Pirie, P. L., Badger, G. J., Carpenter, J. H., et al. (1994). Mass media and school interventions for cigarette smoking prevention: Effects 2 years after completion. *American Journal of Public Health, 84*, 1148–1150.

Frey, K. A., Hirschstein, M. K., & Guzzo, B. A. (2000). Second step: Preventing aggression by promoting social competence. *Journal of Emotional and Behavioral Disorders, 8*, 102–112.

Gager, P. J., & Elias, M. J. (1997). Implementing prevention programs in high-risk environments: Application of the resiliency paradigm. *American Journal of Orthopsychiatry, 67*, 363–373.

Gottfredson, D. C., Gottfredson, G. D., & Hybl, L. G. (1993). Managing adolescent behavior: A multiyear, multischool study. *American Educational Research Journal, 30*, 179–215.

Greenberg, M. T., Domitrovich, C. E., & Bumbarger, B. (2001). The prevention of mental disorders in school-aged children: Current state of the field. *Prevention and Treatment, 4*, Article 1, posted March 30, 2001. Available from http://journals.apa.org/prevention/volume4/pre0040001a.html.

Gresham, F. M., Gansle, K. A., Noell, G. H., Cohen, S., & Rosenbaum, S. (1993). Treatment integrity of school-based behavioral intervention studies. *School Psychology Review, 22,* 254–272.

Griffin, K. W., Botvin, G. J., & Nichols, T. R. (2003). *Long-term follow-up effects of a school-based drug abuse prevention program on adolescent risky driving.* Manuscript under review.

Griffin, K. W., Botvin, G. J., Nichols, T. R., & Doyle, M. M. (2003). Effectiveness of a universal drug abuse prevention approach for youth at high risk for substance use initiation. *Preventive Medicine, 36,* 1–7.

Hallfors, D., & Godette, D. (2002). Will the "Principles of Effectiveness" improve prevention practice? Early findings from a diffusion study. *Health Education Research, 17,* 461–470.

Hansen, W. B. (1992). School-based substance abuse prevention: A review of the state-of-the-art in curriculum. *Health Education Research, 7,* 403–430.

Hansen, W. B., & McNeal, R. B. (1997). How D.A.R.E. works: An examination of program effects on mediating variables. *Health Education and Behavior, 24,* 165–176.

Harrison, P. A., Fulkerson, J. A., & Beebe, T. J. (1998). *DSM-IV* substance use disorder criteria for adolescents: A critical examination based on a statewide school survey. *American Journal of Psychiatry, 155,* 486–492.

Hawkins, J. D., Catalano, R. F., & Miller, J. Y. (1992). Risk and protective factors for alcohol and other drug problems in adolescence and early adulthood: Implications for substance abuse prevention. *Psychological Bulletin, 112,* 64–105.

Hawkins, J. D., & Weis, J. G. (1985). The social development model: An integrated approach to delinquency prevention. *Journal of Primary Prevention, 6,* 73–97.

Institute of Medicine. (1994). *Reducing risks for mental disorders: Frontiers for preventive intervention research.* In P. J. Mrazek & R. J. Haggerty (Eds.), Washington, DC: National Academy Press.

Irving, L. M., & Neumark-Sztainer, D. (2002). Integrating the prevention of eating disorders and obesity: Feasible or futile? *Preventive Medicine, 34,* 299–309.

Jessor, R., & Jessor, S. L. (1977). *Problem behavior and psychosocial development: A longitudinal study of youth.* San Diego, CA: Academic Press.

Johnston, L. D., O'Malley, P. M., & Bachman, J. G. (2001). *Monitoring the future national results on adolescent drug use: Overview of key findings* (NIH Publication No. 01–4923). Bethesda, MD: National Institute on Drug Abuse.

Kanigher, S. (2001, February 17). Gambling prevention, 101. *Las Vegas Sun.*

Kaplan, H. B. (1980). *Deviant behavior in defense of self.* New York: Academic Press.

Kazdin, A. E. (1993). Adolescent mental health. *American Psychologist, 48,* 127–141.

Khantzian, E. J. (1997). The self-medication hypothesis of substance use disorders: A reconsideration and recent applications. *Harvard Review of Psychiatry, 4,* 231–244.

Lerner, R. M., & Galambos, N. L. (1998). Adolescent development: Challenges and opportunities for research, programs, and policies. *Annual Review of Psychology, 49,* 413–446.

Levine, M. P., & Smolak, L. (2001). Primary prevention of body image disturbances and disordered eating in childhood and early adolescence. In J. K. Thompson & L. Smolak (Eds.), *Body image, eating disorders, and obesity in youth* (pp. 237–260). Washington, DC: American Psychological Association.

Luthar, S. S., Cicchetti, D., & Becker, B. (2000). The construct of resilience: A critical evaluation and guidelines for future work. *Child Development, 71,* 543–562.

McVey, G. L., Pepler, D., Davis, R., Flett, G. L., & Abdolell, M. (2002). Risk and protective factors associated with disordered eating during early adolescence. *Journal of Early Adolescence, 22,* 75–95.

Norton, E. C., Bieler, G. S., Ennett, S. T., & Zarkin, G. A. (1996). Analysis of prevention program effectiveness with clustered data using generalized estimating equations. *Journal of Consulting and Clinical Psychology, 64,* 919–926.

Paglia, A., & Room, R. (1999). Preventing substance use problems among youth: A literature review and recommendations. *Journal of Primary Prevention, 20,* 3–50.

Pearson, J., Goldklang, D., & Striegel-Moore, R. (2002). Prevention of eating disorders: Challenges and opportunities. *International Journal of Eating Disorders, 31,* 233–239.

Petraitis, J., Flay, B. R., & Miller, T. Q. (1995). Reviewing theories of adolescent substance use: Organizing pieces in the puzzle. *Psychological Bulletin, 117,* 67–86.

Piran, N. (1999). Eating disorders: A trial of prevention in a high risk school setting. *Journal of Primary Prevention, 20,* 75–90.

Resnicow, K., & Botvin, G. J. (1993). School based substance use prevention programs: Why do effects decay? *Preventive Medicine, 22,* 484–490.

Roberts, J. A., & Jones, E. (2001). Money attitudes, credit card use, and compulsive buying among American college students. *Journal of Consumer Affairs, 35,* 213–240.

Rogers, E. M. (1995). *Diffusion of innovations* (4th ed.). New York: Free Press.

Rohrbach, L. A., Graham, J. W., & Hansen, W. B. (1993). Diffusion of a school-based substance abuse prevention program: Predictors of program implementation. *Preventive Medicine, 22,* 237–260.

Rosen, D. S., & Neumark-Sztainer, D. (1988). Review of options for primary prevention of eating disturbances among adolescents. *Journal of Adolescent Health, 23,* 354–363.

Rosenbaum, D. P., & Hanson, G. S. (1998). Assessing the effects of school-based drug education: A six-year multilevel analysis of Project D.A.R.E. *Journal of Research in Crime and Delinquency, 35,* 381–412.

Scheirer, M. A., & Rezmovic, E. (1983). Measuring the implementation of innovations. *Evaluation Review, 7,* 599–633.

Schembari, J. (2000, February 27). New college sticker shock: Junior's credit card bill. *New York Times,* p. C12.

Seligman, M. E. P., Schulman, P., DeRubeis, R. J., & Hollon, S. D. (1999). The prevention of depression and anxiety. *Prevention and Treatment, 2,* Article, 8, posted December 21, 1999. Available from http://journals.apa.org/prevention/volume2/pre0020008a.html.

Smith, D. W., Steckler, A., McCormick, L. K., & McLeroy, K. R. (1995). Lessons learned about disseminating health curricula to schools. *Journal of Health Education, 26,* 37–43.

Spence, S. H., Sheffield, J. K., & Donovan, C. L. (2003). Preventing adolescent depression: An evaluation of the Problem Solving for Life Program. *Journal of Consulting and Clinical Psychology, 71,* 3–13.

Stice, E., & Ragan, J. (2002). A preliminary controlled evaluation of an eating disturbance psychoeducational intervention for college students. *International Journal of Eating Disorders, 31,* 159–171.

Tobler, N. S., & Stratton, H. H. (1997). Effectiveness of school-based drug prevention programs: A meta-analysis of the research. *Journal of Primary Prevention, 18,* 71–128.

Trudeau, L., Spoth, R., Lillehoj, C., Redmond, C., & Wickrama, K. (2003). Effects of a preventive intervention on adolescent substance use initiation, expectancies, and refusal intentions. *Prevention Science, 4,* 109–122.

Vitaro, F., Ferland, F., Jacques, C., & Ladouceur, R. (1998). Gambling, substance use, and impulsivity during adolescence. *Psychology of Addictive Behaviors, 12,* 185–194.

Wills, T. A., Pierce, J. P., & Evans, R. I. (1996). Large-scale environmental risk factors for substance use. *American Behavioral Scientist, 39,* 808–822.

Windle, M. (1996). Effect of parental drinking on adolescents. *Alcohol Health and Research World, 20,* 181–184.

Zins, J. E., Elias, M. J., Greenberg, M. T., & Weissberg, R. P. (2000). Promoting social and emotional competence in children. In K. Minke & G. Bear (Eds.), *Preventing school problems—promoting school success: Strategies and programs that work* (pp. 71–99). Bethesda, MD: National Association of School Psychologists.

Author Index

Subject Index